# Teacher's Book

Virginia Evans – Jenny Dooley

Express Publishing

# Contents

| Reading & Listening | Speaking & Functions | Writing | Culture Corner/Curricular |
| --- | --- | --- | --- |
| | • describe a room<br>• describe the weather<br>• describe appearance<br>• tell the time | | |
| • *Police, Camera, Action* (T/F statements)<br>• Hot Spots (multiple matching)<br>• *The Florida Everglades: Surviving the Swamp* (open-ended sentences)<br>• emails about different types of houses (R/W/DS statements & comprehension questions)<br>• Listening for specific information (T/F) | • buying a ticket<br>• compare places<br>• make requests in the home<br>• ask for/give advice<br>• Pronunciation: /s/, /ʃ/, /dʒ/, /tʃ/ | • describe something happening<br>• sentences about a journey in your country<br>• a list of survival tips in the jungle<br>• an informal email about your house<br>• an informal email of advice | • *Pacific Coast Highway 1* (T/F/DS)<br>• (Citizenship) *Are you a good citizen?* (quiz) |
| • *Lemon Art: French style* (open-ended sentences)<br>• buying things in a supermarket (dialogue)<br>• *Chillout* (multiple choice cloze)<br>• *Can unhealthy be healthy?* (matching headings to paragraphs)<br>• a recipe (reading for specific information)<br>• Listening for specific information (Yes/No) | • talk about your eating habits<br>• order food in a café<br>• make a restaurant booking<br>• give instructions on how to make a dish<br>• Pronunciation: /n/, /ŋ/ | • a description of a food festival in your country<br>• short texts about places to eat out in your country<br>• a description of your own strange restaurant<br>• an informal email about your favourite dish | • *Eating out in the UK* (reading for specific information)<br>• (Science) *Food for life!* (note taking & summarising) |
| • *Is this the most talented person who ever lived?* (T/F/DS statements)<br>• *Heroes of the Ancient World* (quiz)<br>• *Creatures of Legend* (open-ended sentences)<br>• *The Vanishing Smile* (multiple choice)<br>• Listening (gap filling) | • discuss past activities<br>• talk about past actions<br>• read dates<br>• ask for & give personal information<br>• Intonation: stressed syllables/weak vowels | • a quiz about famous historical figures<br>• a description of a traditional celebration in your country<br>• a story about a legendary creature<br>• write about a theft<br>• a biography of a famous person<br>• a text about an explorer | • *The Pilgrims – Sailing to a new life!* (T/F statements)<br>• (US History) *Christopher Columbus* (matching headings to paragraphs) |
| • *Adventure Tour South America* (multiple matching)<br>• *Sculptures Under the Sea* (multiple choice)<br>• *Six Reasons to see Sydney* (answer questions)<br>• Listening (matching speakers to problems) | • future plans & intentions<br>• ask for information<br>• talk about your holiday<br>• Pronunciation: *'ll/won't;* /h/ | • an itinerary for a tour in your country<br>• a pamphlet advertising a national park or area of natural beauty in your country<br>• a letter about your holiday<br>• how to be a responsible tourist | • *Yellowstone National Park* (multiple matching & comprehension questions)<br>• (Citizenship) *How to be a responsible tourist* (T/F) |
| • *Haiti earthquake* (T/F/DS statements)<br>• listening for specific information<br>• *From Climbing Mountains ... to Moving Mountains* (filling in sentences in a text)<br>• *Animal SOS* (multiple matching)<br>• *Lead the Way* (multiple choice cloze) | • talk about a disaster<br>• ask for and offer help<br>• make suggestions/express preferences<br>• Pronunciation: homophones | • a short diary entry about a hurricane<br>• an interview<br>• an email giving your news<br>• information about any of the five oceans | • *Red Nose Day* (gap filling)<br>• (Geography) *The World's Amazing Oceans* (matching headings to paragraphs) |
| • *The Terracotta Army* (multiple choice)<br>• *Roadside Attractions you really can't miss* (T/F/DS)<br>• *It's Venice ... but not as you know it!* (multiple choice)<br>• *Totally cool!* (missing sentences)<br>• Listening (matching speakers to different places) | • describe a process<br>• describe a building/monument<br>• post a parcel<br>• report people's words<br>• express preferences<br>• Pronunciation: assimilation | • describe an experience<br>• write about a monument<br>• create your own mall<br>• an email describing a visit to a place | • *The Garma Festival* (complete sentences)<br>• (Art & Design) Art styles (reading comprehension questions) |

Word Formation pp. WF1-WF3
Key Word Transformations pp. KWT1-KWT3
Word List pp. WL1-WL24

Answer Section pp. AS1-AS4
Student's Book Tapescripts pp. SBT1-SBT6
Evaluations pp. E1-E12

Workbook & Grammar Book Key pp. WGK1-WGK20
Workbook & Grammar Book Tapescripts pp. WGT1-WGT5
Irregular Verbs

# Introduction to the Teacher

*Prime Time (CEF level B1)* is a modular secondary-level course for learners studying British English at pre-intermediate level. It allows a flexibility of approach which makes it suitable for classes of all kinds, including large or mixed ability classes.

*Prime Time (CEF level B1)* consists of six modules. Each module consists of nine units plus Language Review, Revision and Skills Practice sections. The corresponding module in the Workbook provides the option of additional practice.

## COURSE COMPONENTS

### Student's Book & Workbook

The Student's Book is the main component of the course. Each module is based on a single theme and the topics covered are of general interest. All modules follow the same basic structure (see **Elements of the Coursebook**).

The Workbook is in full colour and contains units corresponding to those in the Student's Book containing practice on all four language skills. It also contains a Grammar Bank, Revision Practice for students to prepare for their tests and an Exam-Practice section. It can be used either in class or for homework upon completion of the relevant unit in the Student's Book.

### Teacher's Book and Tests

The Teacher's Book contains Teacher's Notes which provide step-by-step lesson plans and suggestions about how to present the material. This book also includes a complete Key to the exercises in the Student's Book & Workbook and the tapescripts of the listening material.

### Class Audio CDs & Tests

The Class Audio CDs contain all the recorded material which accompanies the course. This includes the dialogues and texts in the Listening and Reading sections, as well as model dialogues, Pronunciation/Intonation section, and the material for all listening tasks. There is also one CD which contains the Tests in word format. The Tests, one per module, are available for teachers to use as a formal means of checking their Ss' progress. There is also a full key to the Tests, listening tasks & tapescripts.

### Student's Audio CD

The S's Audio CD contains the main texts or model dialogues in the Reading sections of the Student's Book, Pronunciation/Intonation tasks as well as the Listening tasks of the Workbook for the purposes of homework and preparation.

## ELEMENTS OF THE COURSEBOOK

Each module begins with a modular spread that contains: a brief overview of what will be covered in the module, pictures and words/phrases related to the theme of the module, and exercises to practice the vocabulary presented.

***Each module contains the following sections:***

### Vocabulary

Pictures are employed to introduce Ss to the vocabulary of each module. Vocabulary is practiced through various types of exercises. A particular feature of the book is the teaching of collocations, which helps Ss remember vocabulary items as parts of set expressions. *(See Student's Book Ex. 3, p. 12)*

### Grammar

- The grammar items of each module are presented by means of clear and concise theory boxes.
- **Grammar exercises and activities** reinforce Ss' understanding of these items. There is also a Grammar Reference section at the back of the Student's Book that offers more details.

### Listening tasks and Speaking practice

- Ss can develop their **listening skills** through a variety of tasks. These tasks employ the vocabulary and grammar practiced in each module, in this way reinforcing understanding of the language taught in the module.
- **Controlled speaking activities** have been carefully designed to allow Ss guided practice before leading them to **freer speaking activities**.

### Pronunciation/Intonation

Pronunciation activities help Ss recognise sounds and reproduce them correctly. Intonation activities help Ss improve their intonation patterns.

### Everyday English

These sections provide practice in real-life communication. Standard expressions and language structures associated with realistic situations are extensively practiced.

### Study Skills

Brief tips, explanations, and reminders at various points throughout each module help Ss develop strategies which improve holistic learning skills and enable Ss to become autonomous learners of the English language.

## Writing Bank

This section provides preparation of the writing task types as they are presented in the Student's Book. It contains theory, plans, full-length model compositions and useful language to help Ss produce successful pieces of writing.

## Reading texts

These texts or situational dialogues practice specific reading skills such as skimming, scanning, intensive reading for specific purposes, understanding text structure, and so on. The texts are usually exploited in four stages:
- a warm-up activity to intrigue students
- top-down activities (scanning and reading for gist)
- bottom-up activities (reading for detailed understanding)
- oral reproduction (Ss outline the main points of the text)

## Writing

The writing sections have been carefully designed to ensure that Ss systematically develop their writing skills.
- A model text is presented and thoroughly analysed, and guided practice of the language to be used is provided.
- The final task is based on the model text and follows the detailed plan provided.
- All writing activities are based on realistic types and styles of writing such as letters, emails, descriptions, postcards and reviews.

## Culture Corner & Curricular sections

Each module contains a Culture Corner and a Curricular section.
- In each **Culture Corner**, Ss are provided with culture information and read about aspects of English speaking countries that are thematically linked to the module. Ss are given the chance to process the information they have learned and compare it to the culture of their own country.
- Each **Curricular** enables Ss to link the themes of the module to a subject from their school curriculum, thus helping them contextualise the language they have learned by relating it to their own personal frame of reference. Lively and creative tasks stimulate Ss and allow them to consolidate the language they have learned throughout the module.

## Module Language Review & Revision sections

These follow every module and reinforce Ss' understanding of the topics, vocabulary, and structures that have been presented. Games enable Ss to use the new language in an enjoyable way, using the format of a team competition, and promoting humanistic learning.

The material has been designed to help Ss learn new language in the context of what they have already mastered, rather than in isolation. In the Revision sections, a grading scheme allows Ss to evaluate their progress and identify their weaknesses. The objectives of the module and the Ss' achievements are clearly stated at the end of each *Revision* section.

## Grammar Reference section

This section offers full explanations and review of the grammar structures presented throughout the book. It can be used both in class and at home to reinforce the grammar being taught.

## Vocabulary Bank

This section contains presentation and practice of vocabulary items related to the theme of the module.

## American English – British English Guide

An **American English – British English Guide** outlines and highlights differences between the two main international varieties of English.

## Irregular Verbs

This provides students with a quick reference list for verb forms they might be unsure of at times.

## Word List

A complete **Word List** contains the new vocabulary presented in each unit, listed alphabetically, with a phonetic transcription of each word.

## SUGGESTED TEACHING TECHNIQUES

### A Presenting new vocabulary

Much of the new vocabulary in *Prime Time (CEF level B1)* is presented through pictures. Ss are asked to **match the pictures to listed words/phrases**. *(See Student's Book, Module 1, p. 8, Ex. 1a.)*

Further techniques that you may use to introduce new vocabulary include:
- **Miming.** Mime the word you want to introduce. For instance, to present the verb **sing**, pretend you are singing and ask Ss to guess the meaning of the word.
- **Synonyms, opposites, paraphrasing,** and **giving definitions.** Examples:
  - present the word **strong** by giving a synonym: "powerful."
  - present the word **strong** by giving its opposite: "weak."
  - present the word **weekend** by paraphrasing it: "Saturday and Sunday."
  - present the word **famous for** by giving its definition: "very well – known (person or thing)."

- **Example**. Examples place vocabulary into context and consequently make understanding easier. For instance, introduce the words **city** and **town** by referring to a city and a town in the Ss' country: "Rome is a city, but Parma is a town."
- **Sketching**. Draw a simple sketch of the word or words you want to explain on the board. For instance:

- **Flashcards**. Flashcards made out of magazine or newspaper pictures, photographs, ready-made drawings, and any other visual material may also serve as vocabulary teaching tools.
- **Use of L1**. In a monolingual class, you may explain vocabulary in the Ss' native language. This method, though, should be employed in moderation.
- **Use of Dictionary**. In a multilingual class, Ss may occasionally refer to a bilingual dictionary.

The choice of technique depends on the type of word or expression. For example, you may find it easier to describe an action verb through miming than through a synonym or definition.

> **Note: *Check these words*** sections can be treated as follows: Go through the list of words before Ss read the text and present the new words by giving examples, synonyms/opposites, or miming their meaning.
>
> Alternatively, go through the list of words after Ss have read the text and ask Ss to explain the words using the context they appear in. Ss can give examples, mime/draw the meaning, or look up the meaning in their dictionaries.

### B  Choral and individual repetition

Repetition will ensure that Ss are thoroughly familiar with the sound and pronunciation of the lexical items and structures being taught and confident in their ability to reproduce them.
Always ask Ss to repeat chorally before you ask them to repeat individually. Repeating chorally will help Ss feel confident enough to then perform the task on their own.

### C  Listening and Reading

You may ask Ss to read and listen for a variety of purposes:
- **Listening and reading for gist**. Ask Ss to read or listen to get the gist of the dialogue or text being dealt with. *(See Student's Book, Module 4, p. 30, Ex. 2a. Tell Ss that in order to complete this task successfully, they do not need to understand every single detail in the text that follows.)*
- **Listening and reading for detail**. Ask Ss to read or listen for specific information. *(See Student's Book, Module 2, p. 30, Ex. 2. Ss will have to read or listen to the text on page 30 for a second time in order to do the task. They are looking for specific details in the text and not for general information.)*

### D  Speaking

- Speaking activities are initially **controlled**, allowing for guided practice. *(See Student's Book, Module 4, p. 72, Ex. 3b where Ss use the same structures to talk about holiday problems.)*
- Ss are then led to **freer** speaking activities. *(See Student's Book, Module 4, p. 72, Ex. 4 where Ss are invited to write about a holiday they had, provided with the necessary lexical items and structures.)*

### E  Writing

All writing tasks in *Prime Time (CEF level B1)* have been carefully designed to closely guide Ss to produce a successful piece of writing.

- Always read the **model text** provided and deal with the tasks that follow in detail. Ss will then have acquired the necessary language to deal with the final writing task. *(See Student's Book, Module 4, p. 73.)*
- Make sure that Ss understand that they are writing for a **purpose**. Go through the writing task in detail so that Ss are fully aware of **why** they are writing and **who** they are writing to. *(See Student's Book, Module 4, p. 73, Ex. 1/4. Ss are asked to write an email giving news.)*
- Make sure Ss follow the detailed **plan** they are provided with. *(See Student's Book, Module 4, p. 73, Ex. 4.)*
- It would be well-advised to actually complete the task orally in class before assigning it as written homework. Ss will then feel more confident with producing a complete piece of writing on their own.

### F  Projects

- When dealing with project work, it is necessary to prepare Ss well in class before they attempt the writing task at home.

## G  Assigning homework

When assigning writing tasks, prepare Ss as well as possible in advance. This will help them avoid errors and get maximum benefit from the task.

Commonly assigned tasks include:
**Copy** – Ss copy an assigned extract;
**Dictation** – Ss learn the spelling of particular words without memorising the text in which they appear;
**Vocabulary** – Ss memorise the meaning of words and phrases or use the new words in sentences of their own;
**Reading Aloud** – Assisted by the S's CDs, Ss practice at home in preparation for reading aloud in class;
**Project** – After they have been prepared in class, Ss complete the writing task; and
**Writing** – After thorough preparation in class, Ss are asked to produce a complete piece of writing.

## H  Correcting students' work

All learners make errors - it is part of the learning process. The way you deal with errors depends on what the Ss are doing.

- **Oral accuracy work:**
  Correct Ss on the spot, either by providing the correct answer and allowing them to repeat, or by indicating the error but allowing Ss to correct it. Alternatively, indicate the error and ask other Ss to provide the answer.
- **Oral fluency work:**
  Allow Ss to finish the task without interrupting, but make a note of the errors made and correct them afterwards.
- **Written work:**
  Do not over-correct; focus on errors that are directly relevant to the point of the exercise. When giving feedback, you may write the most common errors on the board and get the class to attempt to correct them.

Remember that rewarding work and praising Ss is of great importance. Post good written work on a display board in your classroom or school, or give "reward" stickers. Praise effort as well as success.

## I  Class organisation

- **Open pairs**
  The class focuses its attention on two Ss doing the set task together. Use this technique when you want your Ss to offer an example of how a task is done. *(See Ex. 4 on p. 18 of the Student's Book.)*

- **Closed pairs**
  Pairs of Ss work together on a task or activity while you move around offering assistance and suggestions. Explain the task clearly before beginning closed pairwork. *(See Ex. 5 on p. 13 of the Student's Book)*

- **Stages of pairwork**
  - Put Ss in pairs.
  - Explain the task and set time limit.
  - Rehearse the task in open pairs.
  - In closed pairs, get Ss to do the task.
  - Go around the class and help Ss.
  - Open pairs report back to the class.

- **Group work**
  Groups of three or more Ss work together on a task or activity. Class projects or role play are most easily done in groups. Again, give Ss a solid understanding of the task in advance.

- **Rolling questions**
  Ss one after the other ask and answer questions assisted by prompts. *(See Ex. 6b on p. 47 of the Student's Book.)*

## J  Using the Student's Audio CD

Dialogues, texts and Pronunciation sections are recorded on the Student's Audio CD. Ss have the chance to listen to these recordings at home as many times as they want to improve their pronunciation and intonation.

- S listens to the recording and follows the lines.
- S listens to the recording with pauses after every sentence/exchange. S repeats as many times as needed, trying to imitate the speaker's pronunciation and intonation.
- S listens to the recording again. S reads aloud.
- All listening tasks in the Workbook are also included in the Student's CD.

## K  Using L1 in class

Use L1 in moderation and only when necessary.

## ABBREVIATIONS

Abbreviations used in the Student's Book and Teacher's

| T | Teacher | p(p). | Page(s) |
|---|---|---|---|
| S(s) | Student(s) | e.g. | For example |
| HW | Homework | i.e. | That is |
| L1 | Students' | etc. | Et cetera |
|  | native language | sb | Somebody |
| Ex(s). | Exercise(s) | sth | Something |

# 1 Home and away

Topic

In this module Ss will explore the topics of life in the city versus life in the country.

## Module page    7

**Lesson objectives:** Overview of the module
**Vocabulary:** Place related adjectives (*busy, quiet, exciting, boring, safe, dangerous, dirty, clean, ugly, beautiful, modern, historical, cheap, expensive*); Features and places (*place, streets, nightlife, beaches, parks, buildings, town, city, shops, hotels, restaurants*)

## 1a    In the streets    8-9

**Lesson objectives:** To listen and read for gist, to read for specific information, to learn prepositions of movement, to describe a police chase, to write a description of a police chase
**Vocabulary:** Features of a town/city (*traffic lights, zebra crossing, bridge, tunnel, bus lane, level crossing, cycle lane, bus stop, pavement, road sign*); Verbs (*feature, focus on, draw, speed*); Phrasal verb (*cut sb off*); Nouns (*documentary, reality show, video footage, police car, hand-held camera, road crime, catchy title, narrator, viewer, voice-over, suspect, pedestrian, U-turn, oncoming traffic*); Adjectives (*popular, real-life, injured, shocked*)

## 1b    Hot spots    10-11

**Lesson objectives:** To listen and read for gist, to read for specific information, to compare the present simple and the present continuous
**Vocabulary:** Places (*bowling alley, games arcade, water park, shopping centre, sports centre, ice rink, gym, amusement park*); Phrasal verbs (*check out, track down*); Nouns (*selection, trendy shop, food outlet, discount, fitness freak, entrance price, absolute beginner*); Phrase (*treat yourself to*); Preposition (*except*)

## 1c    Culture Corner    12

**Lesson objectives:** To listen and read for gist, to read for specific information, to write about an interesting journey for tourists in your country
**Vocabulary:** Verb (*miss*); Nouns (*road trip, coast, cable car, sight, cliff, sandy beach, skyscraper, elephant seal, breeding season, fairytale mansion, zebra*); Adjectives (*impressive, steep, spectacular*)

## 1d    Everyday English    13

**Lesson objectives:** Buying a ticket, to pronounce /s/, /ʃ/, /dʒ/, /tʃ/
**Vocabulary:** Modes of transport (*plane, coach, underground, ferry, train, bike, car, motorbike, taxi*); Sentences (*Can I help you?, I'd like two tickets to Redwood National Park for tomorrow morning, please.; Single or return?, What time would you like to leave?, That's £24, please., Here you are., Here are your tickets., Have a nice day.*)

## 1e    Survival    14-15

**Lesson objectives:** To listen and read for gist, to read for specific information, to learn *can/be able to – can't – could – have to – don't have to – must – mustn't*, to write a list of survival tips for the jungle

**Vocabulary:** Dangers in the countryside (*get stuck in mud, get stung by bugs, meet dangerous animals, get caught in a flash flood, get a snake bite, get lost*); Verbs (*survive, escape, swallow, panic, fall (into), pull (in), crawl (out), shake, hide*); Phrasal Verb (*run away*); Phrases (*get into trouble, lie flat*); Nouns (*swamp, mosquito, scorpion, insect repellent, ground, cliff, bubble, reptile*); Adjectives (*poisonous, fatal*)

## 1f    Places    16-17

**Lesson objectives:** To listen and read for gist, to read for specific information, to learn the comparative and superlative, to compare places, to write an email about your home
**Vocabulary:** Housing (*block of flats, cottage, bungalow, townhouse, semi-detached house, detached house, villa, penthouse*); Verbs (*imagine, own*); Nouns (*front garden, view, forest, skyscraper*); Phrase (*pretty sure*); Adjectives (*lucky, bright, messy, dark, comfortable, old-fashioned, modern, colourful*)

## 1g    Skills    18

**Lesson objectives:** To listen for specific information, to make requests in the home
**Vocabulary:** Chores (*do the washing-up, mop the floor, dust the furniture, make the bed, take out the rubbish, hoover the carpets, lay the table, iron the clothes*); Making requests (*Can/Could you please …?, Do you mind …?, Do you think you could…?*); Replying (*Yes, of course., Yes, that's fine., Sure, no problem!, I'm afraid I can't., I'm sorry, but …, I'd like to, but …*)

## 1h    Writing    19

**Lesson objectives:** To read for specific information, to learn *should/shouldn't*, to write an informal email of advice

## 1i    Curricular: *Citizenship*    20

**Lesson objectives:** To listen for gist, to do a quiz, to make a speech
**Vocabulary:** Public services and facilities (*deposit/ withdraw some money, take up a new hobby, borrow/return books, buy a stamp, take someone who is ill, report a crime, check your car tyres, buy a train ticket, petrol station, train station, library, community centre, hospital, post office, bank, police station*); Verbs (*respect, volunteer, care (for)*); Nouns (*citizen, community, queue, public transport, public place*); Phrases (*obey laws, (be) involved in, wait (for) my turn, in need, report crimes*)

## Language Review    21

**Lesson objectives:** To test/consolidate vocabulary and knowledge attained throughout the module, to play a game, to do a quiz, to write a quiz

## Skills Practice 1    22-23

**Lesson objectives:** To read for specific information, to make comparisons, to listen for specific information, to write a note

## Revision 1    24

# Food & Drinks 2

# 3   Great people & legends

<table>
<tr><td valign="top" width="50%">



</td><td valign="top" width="50%">



</td></tr>
</table>

# On holiday 4 

# 5 Helping hands

X(T)

# Starter unit

## Objectives

**Lesson Objectives:** To practise *to be, have got, there is/ there are*; to revise vocabulary for nationalities, jobs, appearance, rooms & furniture, daily routines, family members, the weather, places in a town; to practise telling the time and everyday English exchanges

**Vocabulary:** Nationalities *(American, English, Polish, Portuguese, Mexican, Slovakian, German, Spanish, Irish, Italian)*; Jobs *(artist, actress, nurse, author, waiter, astronaut)*; Appearance *(straight hair, wavy hair, curly hair, slim, moustache, arm, beard, chin, leg, feet, cheek, hand, chubby, well-built, thin, short, young, middle-aged, old, fair)*; Rooms & furniture *(living room, bedroom, kitchen)*; Daily routines *(get up, have breakfast, have lunch, have dinner, go to school, go to bed, do my homework, brush my teeth, play sport)*; Family *(father, dad, son, husband, granddad, nephew, cousin, uncle, brother, mother, mum, daughter, wife, grandma, niece, aunt, sister)*; The weather *(boiling hot, snowing, freezing cold, foggy, cloudy, sunny, windy, raining)*; Places in a town *(theatre, café, museum, greengrocer's, baker's, post office, restaurant, hospital)*

**1 a)** **Aim** To practise nationalities

- Give Ss time to read the countries and write the correct nationality next to each one.
- Check Ss' answers around the class.

**b)** **Aim** To give personal information

Give Ss time to complete the sentences then ask various Ss around the class to read their sentences aloud.

***Suggested Answer Key***

*I'm Pedro Martinez. I'm from Spain. I'm Spanish.*

**2** **Aim** To revise jobs

- Ask various Ss around the class to read the clues for the rest of the class to guess the job and write it in the crossword.
- Check Ss' answers and elicit the hidden job.

***Suggested Answer Key***

| | | | | | |
|---|---|---|---|---|---|
| 1 | artist | 3 | nurse | 5 | waiter |
| 2 | actress | 4 | author | | |

***Hidden word:*** *astronaut*

**3 a)** **Aim** To revise vocabulary for appearance

Read the list of words in each category aloud and elicit the odd words out from various Ss around the classroom.

**b)** **Aim** To practise vocabulary for appearance

Ask various Ss around the class to describe themselves.

***Suggested Answer Key***

*I'm tall and slim with long brown hair and brown eyes.*

**4 a)** **Aim** To brainstorm for vocabulary related to rooms and furniture

- Tell Ss to write the headings in their notebooks and ask them to write as many words as they can think of related to the vocabulary topic.
- Write the headings on the board and elicit answers from Ss around the class and write them under the headings on the board in the form of a spidergram. Ss may copy the spidergram into their notebooks.

***Suggested Answer Key***

**Living room:** *sofa, carpet, armchair, coffee table, curtains, cushions, etc*
**Bedroom:** *bed, wardrobe, bookcase, desk, chair, pillows, etc*
**Kitchen:** *cooker, fridge, table, chairs, cupboards, sink, etc*

**b)** **Aim** To practise vocabulary for furniture

Elicit sentences from Ss around the class saying what furniture is in the living room.

***Suggested Answer Key***

*There is a sofa in the living room.*
*There are two armchairs in the living room.*
*There is a carpet on the floor.*
*There is a cupboard in the living room.*
*There is a coffee table in the living room.*
*There is a window behind the sofa.*
*There are two small tables in the living room.*
*There are two lamps on the small tables.*
*There are some cushions on the sofa.*
*There are some books on the coffee table.*
*There is a picture on the wall.*
*There is a chair in the corner.*
*There are some curtains in the living room.*

**5 a)** **Aim** To match verbs to actions related to daily routines

Explain the task and give Ss time to complete it. Then check Ss' answers.

**b)** **Aim** To talk about your daily routine

- Elicit a variety of answers from Ss around the class.
- Remind Ss to use the phrases in Ex. 5a.

***Suggested Answer Key***

*On Saturdays, I get up, brush my teeth and have breakfast. Afterwards, I go to the park and play football with my friends. Then I have lunch in town. Later, I go to the cinema and I go to bed around 11 pm.*

## Nationalities

**1** **a)** Write the nationalities.

| | | | | |
|---|---|---|---|---|
| **1** | the USA American | **6** | Slovakia Slovakian |
| **2** | England English | **7** | Germany German |
| **3** | Poland Polish | **8** | Spain Spanish |
| **4** | Portugal Portuguese | **9** | Ireland Irish |
| **5** | Mexico Mexican | **10** | Italy Italian |

**b)** Complete the sentences.

I'm .......................... . I'm from ............................ .
      **(name)**          **(country)**
I'm ................................. .
      **(nationality)**

## Jobs

**2** **Do the crossword. Guess the job.**

1 Bob draws pictures.
2 Ann plays in films.
3 Laura looks after sick people.
4 James writes novels.
5 Bill serves customers at a café.

**Hidden job:** _ _ _ _ _ _ _ _ _ _

## Appearance

**3** **a)** Circle the odd word out.

1 **Hair:** straight – wavy – curly – slim
2 **Face:** moustache – arm – beard – chin
3 **Body:** leg – feet – cheek – hand
4 **Weight:** chubby – well-built – thin – short
5 **Age:** young – middle-aged – old – fair

**b)** Describe yourself. Tell the class.

## Rooms & Furniture

**4** **a)** Complete the spidergram.

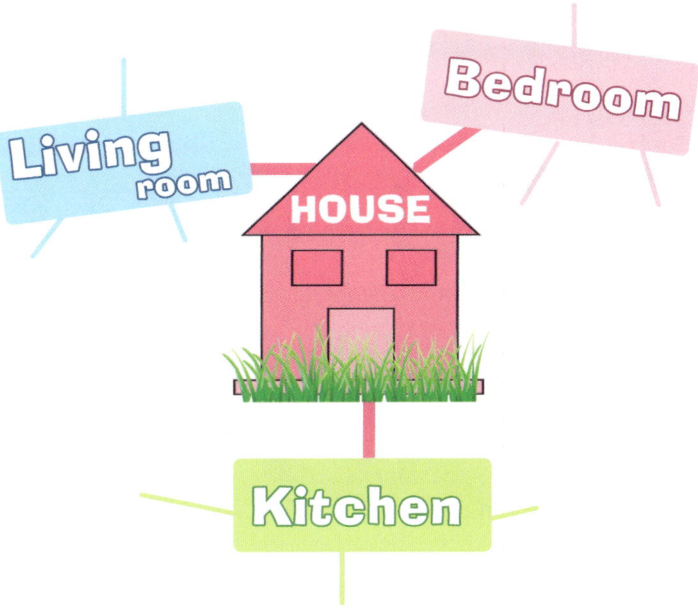


**b)** What is/are there in the living room?

## Daily routines

**5** **a)** Fill in: *have, do, get, brush, play, go*. **Use the phrases to describe a typical Monday.**

1 get up
2 have breakfast, lunch, dinner
3 go to school, to bed
4 do my homework
5 brush my teeth
6 play sport

**b)** What do you do on Saturdays?

## 6 What time is it?

**1** ........................     **2** ........................

**3** ........................     **4** ........................

**5** ........................     **6** ........................

### Family

**7**   **a)**   Complete the pairs.

**1** father (dad)  –  ........................................
**2** son           –  ........................................
**3** husband   –  ........................................
**4** granddad   –  ........................................
**5** nephew    –  ........................................
**6** cousin     –  ........................................
**7** uncle      –  ........................................
**8** brother    –  ........................................

**b)**   Present your family to the class.

### The weather

**8**   **a)**   Label the pictures.

**1** b...............    **2** s...............    **3** f...............
     h...............                        c...............

**4** f...............    **5** c...............    **6** s...............

**b)**   What's the weather like in your city in winter/spring/summer/autumn?

### Places in a town

**9**   Write the correct place.

**1** You can see performances at a t.................... .
**2** You can have coffee at a c.................... .
**3** You can see ancient statues at a m................. .
**4** You can buy vegetables at a g....................... .
**5** You can buy bread at a b.................... .
**6** You can post a letter at a p.................... .
**7** You can have dinner at a r.................... .
**8** You can visit a patient at a h.................... .

### *Everyday English*

**10**   Circle the correct response.

**1**   A: What was the film like?
     B:   **a**   Yes, sometimes I did.
            **b**   I quite liked it.

**2**   A: Let's go to the cinema.
     B:   **a**   Here you are.
            **b**   Great idea.

**3**   A: What can I get you?
     B:   **a**   I'd like a cola, please.
            **b**   Thank you.

**4**   A: What's your address, please?
     B:   **a**   21, Apple Street.
            **b**   It's on Apple Street.

**5**   A: How much is it?
     B:   **a**   It's £1,500 per month.
            **b**   It's 6 o'clock.

**6**   A: How's everything?
     B:   **a**   So-so.         **b**   Take care.

**7**   A: Goodbye.
     B:   **a**   Not bad.       **b**   See you later.

**7** w...............      **8** r...............

**6** **Aim** To practise telling the time

- Give Ss time to write the times.
- Check Ss' answers.
- As an extension, ask Ss to write the times in another way.

**Answer Key**

1  It's half past six./It's six thirty.
2  It's (a) quarter to eight./It's seven forty-five.
3  It's three o'clock.
4  It's nine o'clock.
5  It's twenty past four./It's four twenty.
6  It's ten to six./It's five fifty.

**7 a)** **Aim** To revise vocabulary for family members

- Explain the task. Allow Ss time to complete it.
- Check Ss' answers.

**Answer Key**

1  mother (mum)    4  grandma    7  aunt
2  daughter    5  niece    8  sister
3  wife    6  cousin

**b)** **Aim** To present your family

Ask various Ss around the class to present their family to the class.

**Suggested Answer Key**

*There are five people in my family. There is my mum, Sue, my dad, Bob, my older brother, Dan, and my sister, Jane.*

**8 a)** **Aim** To revise weather vocabulary

- Direct Ss' attention to the pictures and elicit what type of weather each one shows.
- Check Ss' answers around the class.

**Answer Key**

1  boiling hot    4  foggy    7  windy
2  snowy    5  cloudy    8  rainy
3  freezing cold    6  sunny

**b)** **Aim** To talk about seasonal weather

Ask various Ss around the classroom to describe what the weather is like in different seasons in their country.

**Suggested Answer Key**

*In winter it is freezing cold and snowy.*
*In spring it is sunny.*
*In summer it is boiling hot.*
*In autumn it is cloudy, windy and rainy.*

**9** **Aim** To revise vocabulary for places in a town.

- Explain the task and give Ss time to complete it.
- Check Ss' answers.

**Answer Key**

1  theatre    4  greengrocer's    7  restaurant
2  café    5  baker's    8  hospital
3  museum    6  post office

**10** **Aim** To identify appropriate responses to everyday English expressions

- Explain the task.
- Allow Ss some time to complete it.
- Check Ss' answers.
- As an extension ask pairs of Ss to act out the exchanges.

**Answer Key**

1  b    3  a    5  a    7  b
2  b    4  a    6  a

# Home and away



▶▶ **What's in this module?**

Read the title of the module *Home and away* and ask Ss to predict the content of the module *(the module is about features of towns/cities)*. Go through the contents list and stimulate a discussion about what Ss will learn in the module.

## Vocabulary

1 **Aim** **To present adjectives used to describe places**

- Go through the list of phrases with Ss. Point out that the adjectives are presented in opposites and can be collocated with the nouns that follow them *(e.g. busy place)*.
- Play the recording for Ss to hear the pronunciation of the words.
- Play the recording again with pauses for Ss to repeat individually or chorally.

2 **Aim** **To practise new vocabulary**

- Read the example aloud.
- Point out that Ss should use the vocabulary presented in Ex. 1 to describe the pictures 1-5.
- Give Ss time to think of sentences for each picture.
- Ask Ss to read out their sentences about each place.

*Suggested Answer Key*

1 *Mykonos is in Greece. I think Mykonos is a beautiful island/place. It has got quiet streets and beautiful buildings.*
2 *Acapulco is in Mexico. I think Acapulco is a modern city. It has got expensive hotels and exciting nightlife.*
3 *Montreal is in Canada. I think Montreal is a modern city. It has got crowded streets and expensive shops.*
4 *Edinburgh is in Scotland. I think Edinburgh is a historic city. It has got quiet streets and beautiful parks.*

## OVER TO YOU!

**Aim** **To practise talking about places**

- Ask various Ss to tell the class where they live and what their town/city has got *(e.g. clean streets, etc)*.
- Give Ss time to write down their answers. Check Ss' spelling.

*Suggested Answer Key*

*I live in Rome, Italy. It has beautiful buildings and busy streets.*

**Vocabulary:** adjectives describing places; features of a town/city; public transport; dangers in the countryside; homes; household chores; public services & facilities
**Grammar:** present simple, present continuous, stative verbs, prepositions of movement; comparative – superlative; modals *(can/can't/could/be able to – have to – must – must not; should/ought to)*
**Everyday English:** buying a ticket
**Pronunciation:** /s/, /ʃ/, /dʒ/, /tʃ/
**Writing:** a description of a scene; sentences about a journey in your country; a list of survival tips; an informal email about your home; an informal email of advice
**Culture Corner:** Pacific Coast Highway 1
**Curricular *(Citizenship)*:** Are you a good citizen?

# Module 1
## Home and away

## *Vocabulary*
### Adjectives

**1** Listen and say.

1  busy ≠ quiet (place, streets)
2  exciting ≠ boring (nightlife)
3  safe ≠ dangerous (place)
4  clean ≠ dirty (beaches/place)
5  ugly ≠ beautiful (city/town/hotels/parks/ buildings)
6  modern ≠ historic (city/town/buildings)
7  cheap ≠ expensive (shops/hotels/restaurants)

**2**  Use the adjectives above to describe the places 1-5.

*Rio de Janeiro is in Brazil. I think Rio de Janeiro is a modern city. It has got clean beaches and exciting nightlife.*

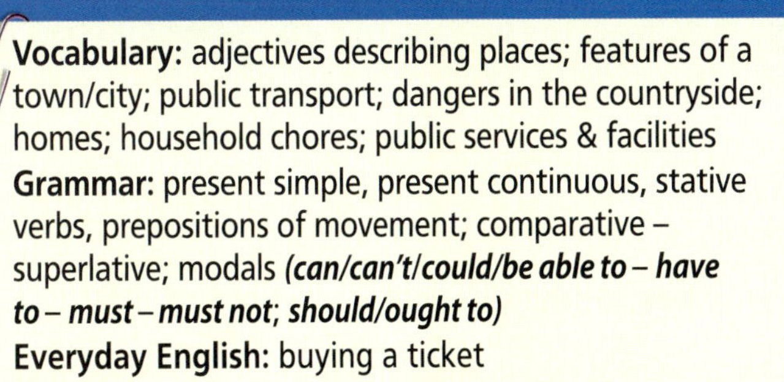


1  Mykonos, Greece

2  Acapulco, Mexico

3  Montreal, Canada

4  Edinburgh, Scotland

5  Rio de Janeiro, Brazil

# 1a In the streets

## *Vocabulary*
### Features of a town/city

**1** **a)** Match the words (1-10) to the items in the pictures (A-J). Listen and check.

| | | | | |
|---|---|---|---|---|
| **1** | traffic lights | **6** | level crossing |
| **2** | zebra crossing | **7** | cycle lane |
| **3** | bridge | **8** | bus stop |
| **4** | tunnel | **9** | pavement |
| **5** | bus lane | **10** | road sign |

**b)** Which of these features are there in your local area?

*In my local area there are traffic lights, but there isn't a zebra crossing.*

## Listening & Reading

**2** Read the title of the text and look at the pictures. What do you think is happening? Listen and read to find out.

**3** Read the text and mark the statements (1-6) as *T* (true) or *F* (false). Correct the false statements.

1 The programme features real police officers. ......
2 All the video footage is shot from helicopters. ......
3 *Police, Camera, Action!* shows lots of different crimes. ......
4 The suspect doesn't injure any pedestrians. ......
5 The suspect goes under a bridge. ......
6 The police car follows the suspect through a tunnel. ......

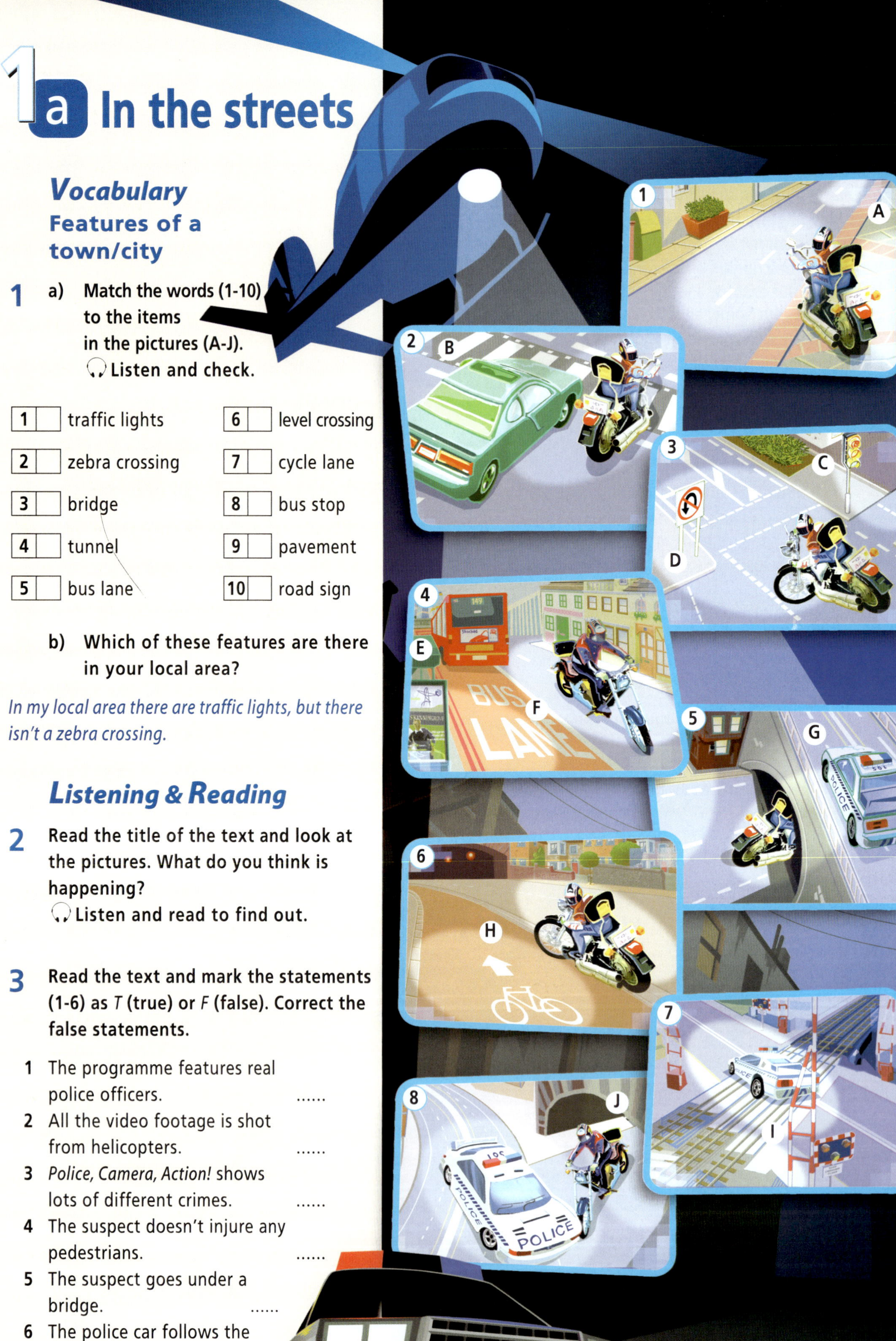

## Vocabulary

**1 a)** **Aim** To present vocabulary for features of a town or city

- Read the list of features and direct Ss' attention to the pictures on p. 8.
- Allow Ss time to complete the task in closed pairs.
- Play the recording for Ss to check their answers.
- Play the recording again with pauses for Ss to repeat individually or chorally.

**Answer Key**

| | | | |
|---|---|---|---|
| 1  C | 3  G | 5  F | 7  H | 9  A |
| 2  B | 4  J | 6  I | 8  E | 10  D |

**b)** **Aim** To practise new vocabulary

Read out the example, then ask various Ss to tell the class what features are/are not in their local area.

**Suggested Answer Key**

*In my local area there is a bridge, but there isn't a tunnel. There isn't a bus lane, but there is a level crossing. There isn't a cycle lane, but there are traffic lights. There is a bus stop, pavements and road signs.*

## Listening & Reading

**2** **Aim** To introduce and predict the content of a text; to listen and read for gist

- Ask Ss to look at the title of the text and the pictures. Ask Ss to say what they think the text is about *(police and road crime)*.
- Play the recording. Ss listen and follow the text in their books.

**Suggested Answer Key**

*The text is about a real life TV series that shows videos of the police and how they catch criminals on the road.*

- Explain/Elicit the meaning of words in the **Check these words** box.
- How to treat **Check these words** boxes.
  Ask Ss to find the words in the text and try to explain them in context giving a synonym, an antonym or an example. Make sure Ss identify what part of speech each word is *(e.g. noun, verb, etc)*. Ask Ss to have a vocabulary section in their notebooks and list all new words in alphabetical order together with a synonym or example sentence. Ss can look up any unknown words in their dictionaries.

**Suggested Answer Key**

*popular (adj):* liked by a lot of people
*real-life (adj):* not fictional
*documentary (n):* film/programme about a subject based on fact

*reality show (n):* TV show of real people/situations
*feature (v):* to show, present
*video footage (n):* film taken by a video camera
*police car (n):* vehicle that police use
*hand-held camera (n):* a small video camera that you hold in your hand
*focus on (v):* to concentrate on, deal with in depth
*road crime (n):* crime using a motor vehicle
*catchy title (n):* name that is easy to remember
*narrator (n):* person talking over a TV show/film
*draw (v):* to make sb interested in sth
*viewer (n):* sb who watches a TV programme
*voice-over (n):* words that are spoken by a narrator
*suspect (n):* person that the police think has committed a crime
*pedestrian (n):* person walking in a city/town
*injured (adj):* hurt
*U-turn (n):* the action of turning suddenly and moving in the opposite direction
*oncoming traffic (n):* line of cars etc that is coming towards sb
*shocked (adj):* surprised, stunned
*speed (v):* to drive fast
*cut (sb) off (phr v):* to stop sb from moving forward by placing yourself in their way
*channel hop (v):* to move from one channel on TV to another to find sth good to watch

**3** **Aim** To read for specific information

Give Ss time to read the text again and complete the task, then check Ss' answers.

**Answer Key**

1  T  *(l. 1-2)*
2  F  *(The video footage is from cameras in police cars, helicopters, and sometimes from hand-held cameras, too.)*
3  F  *(It shows road crime and bad driving.)*
4  T  *(l. 13-15)*
5  T  *(l. 20)*
6  F  *(The police go over the level crossing to cut him off at the end of the tunnel.)*

## Grammar

**4 a)** **Aim** **To present prepositions of movement**

- Read through the prepositions of movement.
- Go through the sketches. Demonstrate with a book (or similar object) the prepositions of movement. *(e.g. Hold the book and swing it in an arch over the desk to demonstrate **over**. Push it across the desk to present **across**.)* With each movement, ask Ss which preposition you are demonstrating.
- Ask Ss to use the prepositions of movement to comment on the pictures.

*Suggested Answer Key*

*In picture 2 the suspect is going **past** the car.*
*In picture 3 the suspect is turning **into** the street.*
*In picture 4 the suspect is going **along** the bus lane/driving down the street.*
*In picture 5 the suspect is going **under** the bridge.*
*In picture 6 the suspect is going **along** the cycle lane and **towards** the tunnel.*
*In picture 7 the police car is going **over** the level crossing.*
*In picture 8 the suspect is coming **out of** the tunnel.*

- **Extension:** Ask Ss to look at the pictures 1-8 and describe the event.

**b)** **Aim** **To practise prepositions of movement**

- Allow Ss time to do the task.
- Play the recording for Ss to check their answers.

*Answer Key*

| | | |
|---|---|---|
| *1 along* | *4 through* | *7 up* |
| *2 towards* | *5 into* | *8 down* |
| *3 past* | *6 across* | *9 over* |

## Speaking & Writing

**5** **Aim** **To practise new vocabulary**

- Explain the task to Ss and ask them to draw a scene with a speeding car and use the new vocabulary to describe what is happening.
- Allow Ss time to write a few sentences. Ask various Ss to read out what they have written.

*Suggested Answer Key*

*There he is! He's going along the cycle lane. Now he's driving on the pavement. The police are close behind, but the suspect is going through the traffic lights and they're red. That's very dangerous. Now the suspect is going up the bus lane. Oh no! There's a bus coming the other way. The suspect stops. The police are right behind him! They got him!*

*Police, Camera, Action!* is a popular TV series of real-life police videos. It is part-documentary and part-reality show. It features video footage from cameras in police cars, helicopters, and sometimes from hand-held cameras, too. It focuses on road crime and bad driving. Each episode has a catchy title and the narrator really draws the viewer into the action. A typical voice-over would go something like this:

*"As we join the scene from the air, the 'eye-in-the-sky' can see the suspect is driving his motorbike very fast through the town. He's driving on the pavement and on the road. There he's going across a zebra crossing. Luckily, there aren't many pedestrians around or else lots of people could be injured. Now he's going toward the traffic lights – no wait – he's doing a U-turn into oncoming traffic. That is so dangerous! Look at him now! He's going along the bus lane and up the hill. I hope no one is on the other side or they'll be shocked. Now where is he? There he is! I don't believe it! He's going under the bridge just as the police car is going over the bridge. They just missed him. He's going along the bike lane towards the tunnel. Now he's going into the tunnel. The officers on the ground are speeding over the level crossing to cut him off at the end of the tunnel. This is so exciting! Yes! It's all over. They got him!"*

*So next time you're channel hopping, make sure you catch an episode – you'll be glad you did!*



popular, real-life, documentary, reality show, feature, video footage, police car, hand-held camera, focus on, road crime, catchy title, narrator, draw, viewer, voice-over, suspect, pedestrian, injured, U-turn, oncoming traffic, shocked, speed, cut sb off, channel hop

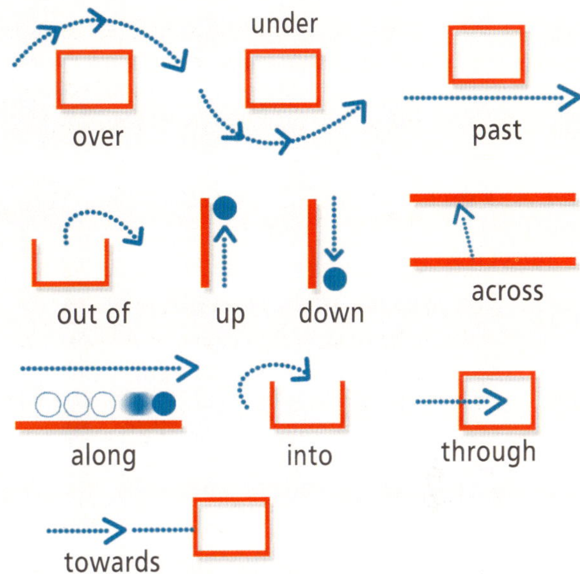

---

see p. GR1

### *Grammar*
### Prepositions of movement

**4 a)** Look at the sketches. Use them to describe what is happening in the pictures (1-8) in Ex. 1.

*In picture 1 the suspect is driving along the pavement.*

**b)** Linda wrote to her friend Kate to give her directions to her house. Choose the correct preposition.
Listen and check.

When you get off the bus, walk **1) along/through** Main Street **2) into/towards** the clock tower. Go **3) past/out of** some shops on your left and then turn right and go **4) through/along** some big gates **5) along/into** Stanley Park. Walk **6) into/across** the grass and then walk **7) up/under** the hill and **8) down/out of** the other side. Go **9) into/over** the bridge and you'll see a row of houses on the left. My house is number 22. Call me if you get lost!

### *Speaking & Writing*

**5** **THINK!** Imagine you are in a police helicopter chasing someone who is driving over the speed limit. Draw the driver and describe what is happening. Use prepositions of movement. In three minutes write a few sentences. Tell the class.

Vocabulary Bank 1 p. VB1

# 1b Hot spots

## *Vocabulary*

### Places & activities

**1** a) 🎧 Listen and say.

b) **What can you do in each place? Use the phrases to make sentences.**

- play sports • exercise • swim
- shop • skate • go on rides
- go bowling • play video games

*You can swim in a water park.*

c) **Which of the places in the photographs are there in your area? Which ones do you go to in your free time?**

## *Reading*

**2** a) 🎧 **Listen to and read the adverts. Which of the places in Ex. 1a does each one advertise?**

b) **Read again and match the adverts to the statements.**

1 An evening visit will be unforgettable. .....
2 You can buy something to eat there. .....
3 It is open until late on Saturdays. .....
4 You can find a large range of activities there. .....
5 You can go there six days a week. .....
6 You can work out there. .....
7 Some customers pay less there. .....
8 It is situated on different levels. .....

c) **Match the words in bold to their meanings:** *fashionable, find, not very expensive, feel like, a variety of, choice, reductions in prices, a set of clothes, people who are very enthusiastic about being in good shape, complete, supply and serve food.*

**A TEANLOWE CENTRE**

With a **selection** of **trendy** shops and food outlets, this is a popular place for anyone who loves shopping. Do you feel like treating yourself to a new **outfit**? Then come and check out the latest fashions and **track down** that must-have accessory. Open seven days a week.

**B THE CUBE**

With the latest video games, a coffee bar and a great atmosphere, The Cube is the place to be. You can meet your friends or have fun with your family. With three storeys, there's room for everyone. We offer **discounts** for students and **cater** to birthday parties.

**C THORNTON CENTRE**

Offering **a range of** classes and facilities, Thornton Centre has a wide selection of activities for all fitness levels and abilities. For **fitness freaks** there is a special weights room with a collection of machines as well as free weights. What are you waiting for?

**D DERBY PARK**

Popular with people of all ages Derby Park has a wide selection of rides and attractions. Entrance prices are **reasonable** and we stay open late every weekend. Ride the roller coasters at night for a thrilling new experience. It's a must!

**E CLEARWATER**

Do you **fancy** learning a new sport? Do you want to hang out with your friends in a fun and relaxed atmosphere? Then come to Clearwater. Everyone is welcome from experienced players to **absolute** beginners. Open every day except Monday. Join us today.

**Check these words**

selection, trendy shop, food outlet, treat yourself to, check out, track down, discount, fitness freak, entrance price, absolute beginner, except

d) **THINK!** Which place would you like to go? Why? Find someone in the class who agrees with your choice.

**THINK!** Choose three places from the text and compare them to places in your country.

## Vocabulary

**1 a) Aim To present vocabulary for places**

- Direct Ss' attention to the pictures.
- Play the recording. Ss listen and repeat chorally or individually.

**b) Aim To present and practise new vocabulary for places and free-time activities**

- Go through the list of activities, then read out the example.
- Ss make sentences in pairs.
- Ask various Ss around the class to read out their sentences.

### Answer Key

*You can play sports at a sports centre.*
*You can exercise at a gym.*
*You can shop in a shopping centre.*
*You can skate at an ice rink.*
*You can go on rides at an amusement park.*
*You can go bowling in a bowling alley.*
*You can play video games at a games arcade.*

**c) Aim To personalise the topic**

Elicit sentences from Ss around the class about which places there are in their area and which ones they go to in their free time.

### Suggested Answer Key

*There is a bowling alley, a shopping centre and a sports centre in my area. In my free time, I go to the shopping centre.*

## Reading

**2 a) Aim To listen for gist**

- Play the recording. Ss listen and match the adverts to the places in the pictures in Ex. 1a.
- Check Ss' answers. Explain/Elicit the meaning of words in the Check these words box.

### Suggested Answer Key

**selection (n):** *choice*
**trendy shop (n):** *modern shop*
**food outlet (n):** *shop that sells food*
**treat yourself to sth (phr):** *to do sth special for yourself*
**check out (phr v):** *to find out information*
**track down (phr v):** *to find*
**discount (n):** *reduction in price*
**fitness freak (n):** *person who loves exercising*
**entrance price (n):** *money one pays to enter a place*
**absolute beginner (n):** *complete beginner*
**except (prep):** *but, apart from*

### Answer Key

A   shopping centre   C   gym             E   sports centre
B   games arcade      D   amusement park

**b) Aim To read for specific information**

- Explain the task and give Ss time to read the adverts again.
- Ss match each statement to the adverts.
- Check Ss' answers.

### Answer Key

| 1 | D | 3 | D | 5 | E | 7 | B |
| 2 | A | 4 | C | 6 | C | 8 | B |

**c) Aim To expand vocabulary/To match words from a text to their meanings**

- Explain the task.
- Give Ss time to complete the task.
- Check Ss' answers.

### Answer Key

**fashionable:** *trendy*
**find:** *track down*
**not very expensive:** *reasonable*
**feel like:** *fancy*
**a variety of:** *a range of*
**choice:** *selection*
**reductions in prices:** *discounts*
**a set of clothes:** *outfit*
**people who are very enthusiastic about being in good shape:** *fitness freaks*
**complete:** *absolute*
**supply and serve food:** *cater*

**d) Aim To personalise the topic**

Elicit which Ss would like to visit which places with a show of hands and elicit Ss' reasons for their choices.

### Suggested Answer Key

*I'd like to go to the games arcade because I like playing video games. Also I can save some money as they offer discounts for students.*

**Aim To make comparisons with places in your country**

- Explain the task and give Ss time to prepare their answers.
- Ask various Ss around the class to share their answers with the rest of the class.

### Suggested Answer Key

*The Teanlowe Shopping Centre seems like the shopping centre in my city. It has got lots of shops and food outlets, too. The Thornton Centre seems similar to the gym in my town. It has got a free weights room and lots of facilities. It also offers a range of classes.*
*Derby Park amusement park seems similar to a park in my country. It is also open seven days a week and at night.*

## Grammar

**3 a)** **Aim** **To compare the present simple and the present continuous**

- Go through the table and explain the uses of the present simple *(habits and routines)* and the present continuous *(actions happening now or around the time of speaking)*.
- Point out that stative verbs do not have continuous forms.

*Answer Key*

*Refer Ss to the Grammar Reference Section.*

**b)** **Aim** **To identify the present simple, the present continuous and stative verbs**

Refer Ss back to the text on p. 10 and elicit examples from the adverts from various Ss around the class.

*Answer Key*

**Present simple:** *loves, Do you feel like, offer, cater (to), has, stay, Do you fancy, Do you want*
**Present continuous:** *What are you waiting for?*
**Stative verbs:** *loves, feel (like), fancy, has, want*

**4** **Aim** **To practise the present simple third-person singular**

- Ask Ss to copy the table into their notebooks, then give Ss time to complete it with the third-person singular of the verbs in the list.
- Play the recording to check Ss' answers.
- Play the recording again with pauses for Ss to listen and repeat chorally or individually. Check Ss' intonation and pronunciation.

*Answer Key*

| /s/ | looks, starts, talks, walks, wakes up |
| --- | --- |
| /z/ | drives, goes, has, listens, studies |
| /ɪz/ | catches, watches |

**5** **Aim** **To practise the spelling rules for the present continuous**

- Explain the task and elicit the correct spelling of the *-ing* forms from various Ss around the class.
- Elicit the spelling rules and write them on the board. Ss copy the rules into their notebooks.

*Answer Key*

| | | |
| --- | --- | --- |
| 1  making | 3  travelling | 5  swimming |
| 2  working | 4  playing | 6  coming |

*Verbs ending in -e, drop the -e and take -ing. Verbs ending in -ie, drop the -ie, add -y + -ing. Verbs ending in a stressed vowel between two consonants, double the last consonant and add -ing. Verbs ending in -l, double the -l and add -ing.*

**6** **Aim** **To practise the present simple and the present continuous**

- Explain the task and give Ss time to complete it.
- Check Ss' answers and elicit which verbs are stative.

*Answer Key*

1   *Do you walk, am not going, is raining*
2   *Is Dan doing, is watching*
3   *Do your parents work, visit, have*
4   *looks, Do you know, isn't sleeping*
5   *am waiting, Do you know, is studying*
6   *Do you want, am looking after*

**Stative verbs:** *have, look, know, want*

**7** **Aim** **To revise time words/expressions used with the present simple and the present continuous**

- Go through the time words/expressions in the list.
- Elicit which time words/expressions go with the present simple or the present continuous.
- Elicit which words are adverbs of frequency.
- Give Ss time to write sentences using the words and then ask various Ss around the class to read out the sentences.

*Answer Key*

**Present simple:** *usually, never, sometimes, often, always, once a week*
**Present continuous:** *now, this morning, these days, at the moment, this week*
**Adverbs of frequency:** *usually, never, sometimes, often, always*

*Suggested Answer Key*

*I never go to the gym on Tuesdays.*
*I am sitting at my desk now.*
*I am having lessons this morning.*
*I sometimes go to the ice rink at the weekend.*
*I often go to the water park in the summer.*
*I always get up early.*
*I am studying hard these days.*

## Grammar

*(see pp. GR1-GR2)*

### Present simple vs present continuous

**3** **a)** **Read the theory. How do we form the *present simple* and the *present continuous*?**

- We use the **present simple** for **habits** or **routines**.
  *I **get up** at 7 am every day. What time do you **get up**?* (routine)
  *He usually **watches** TV every night. He **doesn't go** out very often.* (habit)
- We use the **present continuous** for **actions happening now** or **around the time of speaking**.
  *We**'re listening** to the radio now.* (action happening now)
  *We **aren't watching** TV. What **are you doing** now?*
  *He**'s looking** for a job.* (action around the time of speaking)

**Stative verbs**

Some verbs (**believe**, **belong**, **hate**, **hear**, **know**, **like**, **love**, **need**, **own**, **seem**, **think**, **understand**, **want**, **wish**) do not have continuous forms. These verbs express a state or refer to our senses and emotions

*He **wants** to become an actor. (NOT: ~~He's wanting~~)*

**b)** **Find examples of the *present simple* and *present continuous* in the adverts. Then list all the stative verbs. Compare with a partner.**

**4** **Write the third-person singular of the verbs:** *catch, drive, go, have, listen, look, start, study, talk, walk, wake up, watch.*
🎧 **Listen and check. Listen again and say.**

| /s/ | |
|-----|-----|
| /z/ | |
| /ɪz/ | |

**5** **Write the *-ing* forms of these verbs. What are the spelling rules?**

1 make ......................
2 work ......................
3 travel ......................
4 play ......................
5 swim ......................
6 come ......................

**6** **Fill in the gaps with the *present simple* and the *present continuous* forms of the verbs in brackets. Which verbs are stative?**

1 A: ................................. **(you/walk)** round the lake every Sunday?
   B: Yes, but I ........................... **(not/go)** there now because it ................................ **(rain)**.
2 A: ................................................. **(Dan/do)** his homework at the moment?
   B: No, he's at the cinema. He ......................... **(watch)** a film with his friends.
3 A: ...................................................... **(your parents/work)** on Saturdays?
   B: No, we usually ............................................ **(visit)** my grandma and then ...................... **(have)** lunch.
4 A: Jenny ........................... **(look)** really tired. ...................................... **(you/know)** why?
   B: Yes, she ........................... **(not/sleep)** well these days.
5 A: I ........................................ **(wait)** for John. ........................... **(you/know)** where he is?
   B: Yes. He ...................... **(study)** in the library.
6 A: ................... **(you/want)** to go swimming?
   B: I'm afraid I can't. I ..................................... **(look after)** my little sister all day.

**7** **Which of the words below do we use with the *present simple/continuous*? Which are adverbs of frequency? Write 6-7 sentences using the words.**

- usually • never • now • this morning
- sometimes • often • always • these days
- at the moment • this week • once a week

*I usually go to the amusement park at the weekend.*

11

# Culture Corner

## Pacific Coast Highway 1

One of the best ways to see California is on a road trip.
One of the most impressive is along the Pacific coast on Highway 1!



road trip, impressive, coast, steep, cable car, miss, sight, spectacular, cliff, sandy beach, skyscraper, elephant seal, breeding season, fairytale mansion, zebra

**Ride up and down San Francisco's steep streets on a cable car. Don't miss a visit to see the most popular sight in the city, the Golden Gate Bridge.**

Drive along the 'Big Sur' coastline with its **spectacular** cliffs and sandy beaches. **Look out for** the ancient Redwood trees, the oldest trees in the world. Some of them are up to 2,000 years old and they are as tall as **skyscrapers**!

Stop and see the elephant seals at Piedras Blancas. Their **breeding season** is from December to February. Then the females go to Alaska to give birth to their pups and return in the autumn.

Last stop – Hearst Castle! This **fairytale mansion** has 165 rooms including 56 bedrooms and 61 bathrooms. There's also a cinema, two swimming pools and beautiful gardens. You can even see zebras there.

**1** Look at the map and the pictures. What can someone see along Pacific Coast Highway 1? 🎧 Listen, read and check.

**2** **a)** Read again and write *T* (true), *F* (false) or *DS* (doesn't say).

1 Cable cars are the most popular sight in San Francisco. F
2 There are skyscrapers along the Big Sur coastline. F
3 Elephant seal pups are born in Alaska. T
4 There are wild animals at Hearst Castle. T
5 Lots of tourists visit Hearst Castle. DS

**b)** Explain the words in bold. Look them up in the Word List.

**3** Fill in: *spectacular*, *breeding*, *steep*, *sandy*, *fairytale*, *cable*, and then use the phrases to make sentences about the places in the texts.

1 steep streets
2 cable car
3 spectacular cliffs
4 sandy beaches
5 breeding season
6 fairytale mansion

**4** **THINK!** Which do you think is the most interesting sight along Highway 1? Why? Tell your partner. Try to use words from the **Check these words** box.

## Writing

**5** Draw or find a map of your country. Write a few sentences about a journey in your country that is interesting for tourists. You can write about: *the places you can visit, what is special about each place.*



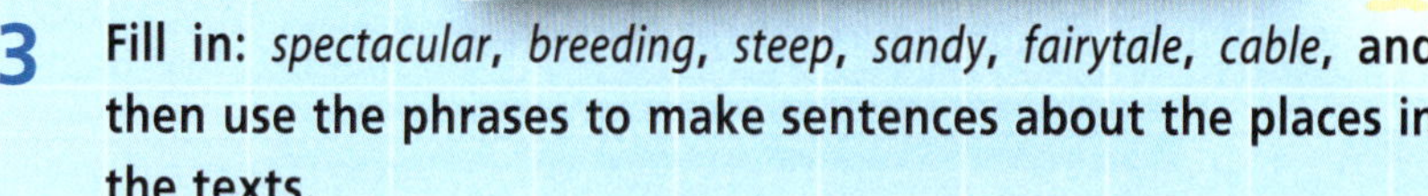

**1** **Aim** **To introduce the topic and predict the content of a text**

- Direct Ss' attention to the map and the pictures. Ask Ss if they know where they are from.
- Ask Ss what someone can see along Pacific Coast Highway 1 and direct Ss' attention to the names on the map.
- Play the recording. Ss listen and read and check.

***Suggested Answer Key***

*Someone can see San Francisco, Big Sur, Piedras Blancas and Hearst Castle along Pacific Coast Highway 1.*

- Explain/Elicit the meaning of words in the *Check these words* box.

***Suggested Answer Key***

*road trip (n): journey/holiday by car*
*impressive (adj): exciting, amazing*
*coast (n): area where the sea meets the land*
*steep (adj): rising at a sharp angle*
*cable car (n): means of transport like a tram*
*miss (v): to lose the opportunity to see or do sth*
*sight (n): interesting place that tourists often visit*
*spectacular (adj): stunning and attractive*
*cliff (n): a high face of rock at the coast*
*sandy beach (n): attractive area at the seaside with lots of sand*
*skyscraper (n): very tall building in a city*
*elephant seal (n): large sea-mammal*
*breeding season (n): time of the year when animals mate*
*fairytale mansion (n): large building like sth out of a fairy story*
*zebra (n): horse-like animal with black and white stripes*

**2** **a)** **Aim** **To read for specific information**

Allow Ss time to read the text again and complete the task, then check Ss' answers. Ask Ss to justify their answers.

**b)** **Aim** **To expand vocabulary**

- Explain the task.
- Give Ss time to complete the task.
- Check Ss' answers.

***Suggested Answer Key***

*steep: rising at a very sharp angle*
*spectacular: stunning and attractive*
*look out for: keep watching to see*
*skyscrapers: very tall buildings*
*breeding season: the time of year animals mate*
*mansion: a very big and impressive house*

**3** **Aim** **To consolidate new vocabulary**

- Explain the task and allow Ss time to complete the phrases. Check Ss' answers and ask Ss to write sentences about the places in the text using these phrases.
- Tell Ss not to copy sentences directly from the texts. Encourage them to rephrase the information as much as possible.
- Ask various Ss to read their sentences aloud.

***Suggested Answer Key***

*Filbert Street is one of the **steepest streets** in San Francisco.*
*The **cable cars** are a great way to see San Francisco.*
*We must explore the **spectacular cliffs** along the Big Sur coastline.*
*You can find **sandy beaches** along the bay.*
*Visitors come to see the seals during the winter **breeding season**.*
*Hearst Castle is a **fairytale** mansion located on the Central Coast of California.*

**4** **Aim** **To personalise the topic and practise new vocabulary**

- Ask Ss to look at the map and the information in the text and decide which place they think is the most interesting. Ask Ss to think of reasons why their chosen place is interesting. Encourage Ss to use words from the *Check these words* box.
- Ss discuss in pairs. Go round the classroom and check.
- Select various pairs to tell the class what they think.

***Suggested Answer Key***

*I think the most interesting sight along Highway 1 is Hearst Castle. It is an impressive fairytale mansion with lots to see including beautiful gardens and zebras.*

## Writing

**5** **Aim** **To personalise the topic of the text in relation to a place in the Ss' country**

- Explain the task.
- Remind Ss to think about an interesting journey through their country, the places you can visit and what is special about each place.
- Allow Ss time to complete the task.
- Ask various Ss to hold up their map and read their sentences aloud.

***Suggested Answer Key***

**Great Ocean Road**

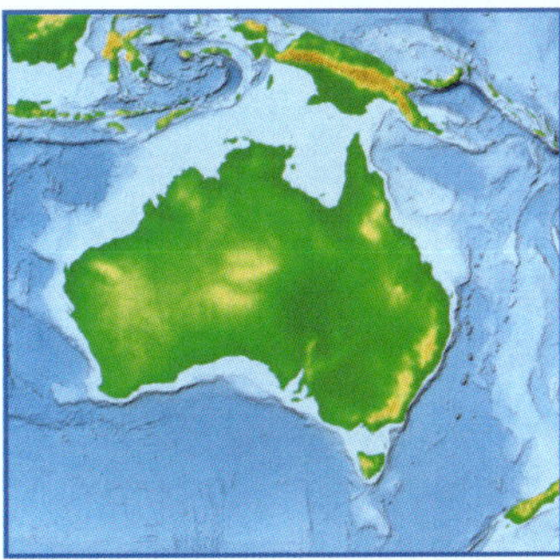

*Tourists in Victoria, Australia, can go on a road trip to experience this impressive area. The Great Ocean Road, Australia's most famous scenic road, stretches from Warrnambool to Torquay along the south-eastern coast. In Warrnambool, you can visit the Flagstaff Hill Maritime Village and find out about the history of this sea-going area. On the drive east, you can stop off to admire the wonder of nature at the world famous 12 Apostles. These rock stacks rise up to 45 metres out of the Southern Ocean. You can also explore the ancient rainforests and woodlands of Great Otway National Park. End the journey at Victoria's surfing capital, Torquay, home to the world famous Bells Beach.*

# 1d

**1 a)** **Aim** **To present vocabulary for transport**

- Play the recording.
- Ask Ss to look at the pictures and say the corresponding words aloud. Correct any mis-pronunciation.
- Write the following headings on the board: *the cheapest, the most expensive, the slowest, the fastest, the most comfortable* and *the safest*.
- Ask Ss which modes of transportation go under which heading. Have a vote and see how many Ss think that a train is the fastest means of transport, for example.

***Suggested Answer Key***

*I think that a bike is the cheapest means of transport.*
*I think that a plane is the most expensive means of transport.*
*I think that a bike is the slowest means of transport.*
*I think that a plane is the fastest means of transport.*
*I think that a car is the most comfortable means of transport.*
*I think that a train is the safest means of transport. etc*

**b)** **Aim** **To personalise the topic**

- Draw Ss' attention to the Note.
- Elicit answers from various Ss around the class as to how they prefer to travel.

***Suggested Answer Key***

*I prefer to travel by plane because it is fast and comfortable.*

**2 a)** **Aim** **To present situational language**

- Draw Ss' attention to the phrases.
- Play the recording with pauses for Ss to repeat individually or chorally.

**b)** **Aim** **To read for specific information**

- Play the recording and ask Ss to follow the dialogue in their books.
- Ask Ss the questions 1-3 and elicit answers from the class.

***Answer Key***

1   *Dan wants to go to Redwood National Park.*
2   *Dan wants to leave at 11 am.*
3   *The tickets cost £24.*

**3** **Aim** **To present synonymous phrases**

- Ask Ss to read the dialogue again and suggest which sentences match those in the dialogue.
- Explain that there are often two or more ways of saying the same thing.

***Answer Key***

*What would you like? – Can I help you?*
*When do you want to go? – What time would you like to leave?*
*Here's the money. – Here you are.*
*Enjoy yourselves. – Have a nice day.*

## Pronunciation

**4** **Aim** **To pronounce /s/, /ʃ/, /dʒ/,/tʃ/.**

- Draw Ss' attention to the box in Ex. 4.
- Play the recording with pauses so Ss have time to complete the boxes.
- Play the recording again with pauses so Ss can repeat each word.

***Suggested Answer Key***

|        | /s/ | /ʃ/ |       | /dʒ/ | /tʃ/ |
|--------|-----|-----|-------|------|------|
| short  |     | ✓   | jump  | ✓    |      |
| single | ✓   |     | cheap |      | ✓    |
| city   | ✓   |     | large | ✓    |      |
| shop   |     | ✓   | check |      | ✓    |

## Speaking

**5** **Aim** **To act out a dialogue**

- Explain the situation and divide the class into pairs.
- Ss take roles and act out their dialogues using the plan given and some of the sentences in Ex. 2a.
- Monitor the activity around the classroom. Ask some pairs to act out their dialogues in front of the class.

***Suggested Answer Key***

A:  *Can I help you?*
B:  *I'd like a ticket to the Isle of Man, please.*
A:  *Single or return?*
B:  *Return, please.*
A:  *What time would you like to leave?*
B:  *On the next ferry.*
A:  *OK. That's £24, please.*
B:  *Here you are.*
A:  *Thank you. Here is your ticket. Have a nice day.*
B:  *Thanks, you too.*

## Buying a ticket

**1** a) 🎧 **Listen and say. Which means of transport do you think is:** *the cheapest? the most expensive? the slowest? the fastest? the most comfortable? the safest?*

b) **How do you prefer to travel? Why? Tell the class.**

*I prefer to travel by ... because it's ... (cheap, the fastest etc.)*

**Note:**
We say: **by** car, plane, etc.
**BUT on** foot

**2** a) 🎧 **Listen and say.**

- Can I help you?
- I'd like two tickets to Redwood National Park for tomorrow morning, please.
- Single or return?
- What time would you like to leave?
- That's £24, please.
- Here you are.
- Here are your tickets.
- Have a nice day.

b) 🎧 **Listen and read to answer the questions.**

1 Where does Dan want to go?
2 What time does he want to leave?
3 How much do the tickets cost?

| Ticket seller: | Hello. Can I help you? |
|---|---|
| Dan: | I'd like two tickets to Redwood National Park, please. |
| Ticket seller: | Single or return? |
| Dan: | Return, please. |
| Ticket seller: | What time would you like to leave? |
| Dan: | We'd like to take the 11 am bus. |
| Ticket seller: | OK. That's £24, please. |
| Dan: | Here you are. |
| Ticket seller: | Thank you. Here are your tickets. Have a nice day. |
| Dan: | Thanks, you too. |

**3** **Find sentences in the dialogue which mean:** *– What would you like? – When do you want to go? – Here's the money. – Enjoy yourselves.*

## Pronunciation: /s/, /ʃ/, /dʒ/, /tʃ/

**4** 🎧 **Listen and check (✓) the correct boxes. Listen again and say.**

|  | /s/ | /ʃ/ |  | /dʒ/ | /tʃ/ |
|---|---|---|---|---|---|
| short |  |  | jump |  |  |
| single |  |  | cheap |  |  |
| city |  |  | large |  |  |
| shop |  |  | check |  |  |

## Speaking

**5** 👥 **You are in Liverpool and you want to go on a day trip to the Isle of Man by ferry. Your partner is the ticket seller. Act out your dialogue. Use the sentences in Ex. 2a. Follow the plan.**

| **A** | **B** |
|---|---|
| Ask how you can help. | Say how many tickets you'd like & where to. |
| Ask if customer wants single or return. | Say what you want. |
| Ask what time customer wants to leave. | Say what time. |
| Say cost. | Offer money. |
| Thank customer & wish them a good day. | Reply. |

# 1e Survival

## Vocabulary
### Dangers in the countryside

**1** 🎧 Listen and say. What are these phrases in your language?

1 get stuck in mud

2 get stung by bugs

3 meet dangerous animals

4 get caught in a flash flood

5 get a snake bite

6 get lost



### The Florida Everglades:
# SURVIVING THE SWAMP!

*The Florida Everglades is one of the USA's largest and most beautiful national parks and a great place to go to escape from the city. But every year, around 60 visitors get into trouble in its 6,000 square kilometres of swamps! So what are the dangers and what must you do to survive your trip there?*

**1 Mud bogs** The Everglades are full of dangerous mud bogs. They can swallow a car or a person in a few minutes. If you fall into one, you shouldn't panic! Moving a lot only pulls you in deeper! Pull each leg out slowly, then lie flat and crawl out carefully.

**2 Bugs and bites** There are hundreds of mosquitoes, scorpions, and poisonous spiders and snakes in the Everglade swamps. Their bites and stings can be very dangerous and sometimes fatal. Always look where you walk, wear long trousers, strong boots and lots of insect repellent.

**3 Flash floods** It can rain a lot in the Everglades and flash floods are a real danger. A flash flood is a wall of water that can travel at 96 kmph. Is the ground shaking? Can you hear a strange noise like an aeroplane engine? Climb up a cliff or a tree. You have to get to the highest place you can and quickly!

**4 Alligators** More than a million alligators live in the swamps and they hide without moving. So how can you see where they are? Well, bubbles on the water can be an alligator getting ready for lunch! These reptiles can run up to 48 kmph. They can't turn quickly, though, so if you see an alligator, you must run away as fast as you can.

## Reading & Speaking

**2 a)** Look at the title of the text, the introduction, and the headings. How can this place be dangerous? How can a visitor survive the dangers?
🎧 Listen and read to find out.

## Vocabulary

**1** **Aim** To present new vocabulary for dangers in the countryside

- Direct Ss' attention to the phrases and pictures.
- Play the recording for Ss to listen and repeat.
- Elicit the L1 equivalents.

*(Ss' own answers)*

## Reading & Speaking

**2 a)** **Aim** To introduce the topic and predict the content of a text

- Direct Ss' attention to the title and subheadings of the text. Ask Ss what they think some of the dangers of the Everglades are and how a visitor can be safe and avoid danger.
- Elicit answers from Ss and make two lists on the board: <u>Dangers</u> and <u>Staying</u> safe. Write Ss' answers under each heading.
- Play the recording and ask Ss to follow the text in their books.
- Refer back to the list on the board and elicit points from the text to add to the lists on the board. Check how many of the Ss' ideas were mentioned in the text.

*Answer Key*

| *Dangers* | *Staying safe* |
|---|---|
| • mud bogs can swallow a car or person | • pull each leg out slowly, lie flat and crawl out carefully |
| • mosquitoes, scorpions, poisonous spiders and snakes | • look where you walk, wear long trousers, boots and insect repellent |
| • flash floods | • climb up a cliff or tree at the highest point |
| • alligators | • run away very fast |

- Explain/Elicit the meaning of words in the **Check these words** box.

*Suggested Answer Key*

**survive (v):** *to manage not to die*
**swamp (n):** *large area of wet ground*
**escape (v):** *to get away*
**get into trouble (phr):** *find yourself in difficulties*
**swallow (v):** *to absorb as if to eat*
**fall (into) (v):** *to move down and into sth by accident*
**panic (v):** *to feel anxious or afraid*
**pull (in) (v):** *to use force to make sth move towards you*
**lie flat (phr):** *to be in a horizontal position against sth*
**crawl (out) (v):** *to move slowly out on hands and knees*
**mosquito (n):** *small flying insect that bites*
**scorpion (n):** *crawling insect with a tail that stings*

**poisonous (adj):** *having sth that can make a person very ill*
**fatal (adj):** *capable of causing death*
**insect repellent (n):** *chemical to protect against insects*
**ground (n):** *surface of the Earth*
**shake (v):** *to move repeatedly from side to side and/or up and down*
**cliff (n):** *large rock with a very steep side*
**hide (v):** *to stay somewhere where you cannot be seen or found*
**bubble (n):** *small ball of air in water*
**reptile (n):** *cold-blooded animal, such as a snake, a crocodile etc*
**run away (phr v):** *to move away from sth quickly*

### BACKGROUND INFORMATION

**The Everglades** is an area of wetlands in the southern portion of the US state of Florida. The Everglades, or the 10,000 Islands, as it is known, is a great place to visit. The Everglades is a massive ecosystem with over 600 species of birds and animals and thousands of plant varieties and is home to several of the world's endangered species. The Everglades experiences frequent flooding in the wet season and drought in the dry season.

**b)** **Aim** **To read for specific information**

- Direct Ss' attention to the unfinished sentences. Ask Ss to read the text again trying to locate what completes each sentence.
- Allow time for Ss to complete the task in pairs. Check Ss' answers as a class.

*Answer Key*

1 *largest and most beautiful national parks.*
2 *must pull each leg out slowly, then lie flat and crawl out carefully.*
3 *very dangerous and sometimes fatal.*
4 *look where you walk, wear long trousers, strong boots and lots of insect repellent.*
5 *96 kmph.*
6 *climb up a cliff or a tree /get to the highest place you can.*
7 *move.*
8 *turn quickly.*

**c)** **Aim** **To read for detailed comprehension (matching)**

- Explain the task and ask Ss to read the headings. Elicit any unknown words and explain their meanings.
- Give Ss time to read the text again and complete the task.
- Check Ss' answers. Ask Ss to justify their answers.

**3 a)** **Aim** **To introduce new vocabulary**

- Read out the *Study Skills* box.
- Ask Ss to look at the highlighted words in the text. Ask if any of the Ss are familiar with the words and if they can explain them.
- Ask Ss to try to explain each of the words by looking at the words around it.
- Ask Ss also to say what part of speech each word is i.e. verb, adjective, etc.

*Suggested Answer Key*

**escape (v):** *to get away*
**survive (v):** *to not die*
**fall (into) (v):** *to move down and into by accident*
**crawl (v):** *to move slowly, close to the ground*
**fatal (adj):** *capable of causing death*
**noise (n):** *a sound*
**run away (phr v):** *to escape, to move away*

**b)** **Aim** **To practise new vocabulary**

- Explain the task and allow time for Ss to complete it.
- Elicit answers for each sentence from various Ss and check the answers on the board.

**4** **Aim** **To personalise the topic of the text**

- Ask Ss to close their eyes and play the recording. Tell them to imagine they are lost in the Everglades. Ask them how they feel, what they can see and what is happening.
- Stop the recording and ask Ss to write a few lines about being lost in the Everglades. Encourage Ss to talk about what is happening, how they feel and what they can see and hear. Encourage Ss to use words from the *Check these words* box.

*Suggested Answer Key – see p. 16(T)*

## Grammar

**5** **Aim** **To present modals**

- Go through the table with Ss. Draw Ss' attention to what each modal means. Elicit/Explain that modals are the same in all persons and aren't followed by *"to-infinitive"*.
- Explain the task. Explain that the synonymous phrases in the theory table will help them do the task. Read item 1. Focus Ss' attention on "It's forbidden" and what modal is used in the new sentence *(can't/mustn't)*. Allow time for Ss to complete the task.
- Check Ss' answers inviting individual Ss to read out their sentences.

*Answer Key*

2 *Can/Could I use your insect repellent?*
3 *You can see alligators there.*
4 *We can put up our tent here.*
5 *Alligators can't move fast in circles.*
6 *You can get lost there.*

**6** **Aim** **To practise modals**

- Direct Ss' attention to the table. Read the first sentence out loud and ask Ss which modal verb is correct. Confirm that the correct answer is *must* because it is about a rule.
- Allow time for Ss to complete the task in pairs.
- Check Ss' answers and give a reason (from the table in the previous task) for the correct use of modal verbs.

## Writing

**7** **Aim** **To write a list of survival tips**

- Divide the class into groups and ask them to collect information on how to be safe in the jungle. Ask them to research on the Internet using the key words in the search bar and write a list of survival tips.
- Remind Ss to use modal verbs *can/can't/have to/must/mustn't* in their work.
- Ask Ss to read their jungle survival tips to the class.

*Suggested Answer Key – see p. 16(T)*

**b)  Read again and complete the sentences.**

1  The Everglades is one of the USA's ................. .
2  To get out of a mud bog you .......................... .
3  Bites from mosquitoes can be ....................... .
4  To keep spiders away you need to ................. .
5  A flash flood can go as fast as ....................... .
6  In case you get caught in a flash flood, .......... .
7  When alligators hide they don't .................... .
8  It's not easy for alligators to .......................... .

**c)  Match the headings to the paragraphs. There is one extra heading.**

| | | |
|---|---|---|
| A | Don't be a reptile's lunch. | 4 |
| B | Small creatures aren't always innocent. | 2 |
| C | Your life is in danger. | – |
| D | Sudden rush of water? Go high. | 3 |
| E | Very wet areas are dangerous. | 1 |

**Study skills**

**Guessing meaning**
Try to work out the meaning of a new word by looking at the words around it.

**3  a)**  Try to work out the meaning of the highlighted words in the text from their context. What part of speech is each?

*escape (v) = get away*

**b)  Fill in:** *shaking, swallow, fatal, escape, reptiles, poisonous.*

1  If you want to escape from the pressures of the big city, then go to the Florida Everglades.
2  Be careful while in the swamps as there are poisonous snakes whose bites can be fatal.
3  Suddenly, the ground started shaking. It was an earthquake.
4  Alligators and snakes are reptiles.
5  People say the bog can swallow anything.

**4  THINK!**  Listen to the sounds. Imagine you are lost in the Everglades and you are in trouble. What is happening? What can you see and hear? How do you feel? In three minutes write a few sentences. Tell your partner or the class. Try to use words from the **Check these words** box.

## Grammar

see p. GR2

***Can/Be able to – Can't – Could – (don't) have to – Must – Mustn't***

**5  Read the examples. Then rewrite the sentences using the correct modal verb.**

> You **can/can't** camp here. (It's allowed./It isn't allowed.)
> Snakes **can** be very dangerous. (It's possible.)
> Alligators **can/are able to** run very fast. (They are able to.)
> Sam **can't/isn't able to** swim very well. (He isn't able to.)
> **Can/Could** I borrow your boots? (Is it OK? Asking for permission – informal/formal)
> You **must** keep off the grass. (It's the rule.)
> You **mustn't** feed the alligators. (It isn't allowed. It's forbidden.)
> You **have to** be careful. (It's necessary.)
> You **don't have to** travel by ferry. (It isn't necessary.)

1  It's forbidden to swim in the lake.
   *You can't/mustn't swim in the lake.*
2  Is it OK to use your insect repellent?
3  It's possible to see alligators there.
4  We are allowed to put up our tent here.
5  Alligators aren't able to move fast in circles.
6  It's possible that you will get lost there.

**6  Choose the correct modal verb.**

## PARK RULES

1  You **must/can** drive slowly through the park.
2  You **mustn't/can't** litter. Take your garbage with you!
3  You **can/have to** keep your dog on a leash.
4  You **can/can't** fish everywhere – only in certain areas.
5  You **mustn't/don't have to** feed the animals. It's forbidden.

## Writing

**7  ICT**  In groups, collect information about how to be safe in the jungle. Write a list of survival tips. Use *can/can't/have to/must/ mustn't.* You can do Internet research using the key words: *jungle survival tips.* Read your tips to the class.

▶ Vocabulary Bank 1 p. VB2

# 1f Places

## Vocabulary
### Types of housing

**1** Match the words to the pictures.

1. [ ] block of flats
2. [ ] cottage
3. [ ] bungalow
4. [ ] townhouse
5. [ ] semi-detached house
6. [ ] detached house
7. [ ] villa
8. [ ] penthouse

🎧 Listen and check. Which types of housing are there in your country? Which one do you live in?

## Reading

**2 a)** Read the first two sentences in the emails. What are they about? Which type of house does each girl live in? 🎧 Listen and read to find out.

Dear Debbie,

Our new house is just great. I moved into a new house last week and I **couldn't wait** to tell you about it. The house is in one of the most beautiful places you can **imagine**. My parents call it 'our little paradise'. It's a bungalow with a front and back garden. From the front we have a **view** of the sea and behind the house there is a **forest**. It is much nicer than the blocks of flats in town and my bedroom is much bigger than my old one. I hope you can come and visit me one day. Write back soon and tell me about your house.

Jasmine

Dear Jasmine,

I'm glad to hear that you like your new home. It sounds much better than your old flat. As for me, I live in a townhouse in the city. Our house is larger than most townhouses; in fact we have three **storeys**. From our house you can see skyscrapers so the view is not as beautiful as it is from your house. I'm also **pretty sure** that it is noisier than where you live. We are very **lucky** though, because my parents also **own** a small cottage near the sea where we go on holiday. I think it would be a great idea for you to come with us next time. What do you think?

Debbie

> **Check these words**
>
> imagine, front garden, view, forest, skyscraper, pretty sure, lucky, own

**b)** Read the texts and mark the sentences *R* (right), *W* (wrong) or *DS* (doesn't say).

1. Jasmine likes her new house a lot. .........
2. Jasmine's house has got two floors. .........
3. They can see the sea from Jasmine's house. .........
4. Debbie lives in a small house. .........
5. Debbie's house is very expensive. .........
6. Debbie's parents own a small seaside house. .........

**c)** Read the emails again and answer the questions.

1. Why do Jasmine's parents call the house 'our little paradise'?
2. What type of house is it?
3. What is there behind her house?
4. What type of house does Debbie live in?
5. What is the view from Debbie's house?
6. Where does Debbie stay when she's on holiday?

## Vocabulary

**1** **Aim** **To present vocabulary for types of housing**

- Read the list of types of housing and direct Ss' attention to the pictures.
- Allow Ss time to complete the task.
- Play the recording for Ss to check their answers.
- Elicit what types of housing various Ss live in.

**Answer Key**

| | | | | | | | |
|---|---|---|---|---|---|---|---|
| 1 | D | 3 | C | 5 | G | 7 | B |
| 2 | F | 4 | A | 6 | E | 8 | H |

**Suggested Answer Key**

*In my town there are lots of blocks of flats and bungalows. I live in a blocks of flats.*

## Reading

**2 a)** **Aim** **To read for gist**

- Refer Ss to the emails and ask them to read the first two sentences in both emails.
- Play the recording. Ss listen and follow the texts in their books.
- Elicit answers to the questions in the rubric.

**Suggested Answer Key**

*The emails are about where two girls live and what their houses are like. Jasmine lives in a bungalow and Debbie lives in a townhouse.*

- Explain/Elicit the meaning of words in the **Check these words** box. Make sure Ss explain them as they are used in the text. Ask Ss to identify what part of speech each is.

**Suggested Answer Key**

*imagine (v): to think of*
*front garden (n): an area in front of a house, usually with grass and plants*

*view (n): the landscape or scene that you can see from a window or balcony*
*forest (n): an area of land with lots of trees*
*skyscraper (n): a very tall building usually found downtown*
*pretty sure (phr): almost certain*
*lucky (adj): fortunate*
*own (v): to have*

**b)** **Aim** **To read for specific information**

- Ask Ss to read the text again and mark the sentences.
- Check Ss' answers. Ss justify their answers.

**Answer Key**

1    T
2    F (bungalow with front and back garden)
3    T
4    F (three storeys)
5    DS
6    T

**c)** **Aim** **To read for detailed comprehension**

- Give Ss time to read the emails again and complete the task in pairs.
- Elicit answers from various students and check.

**Answer Key**

1    Jasmine's parents call the house 'our little paradise' because it is in a very beautiful place.
2    Jasmine's new house is a bungalow.
3    There is a forest behind her house.
4    Debbie lives in a townhouse.
5    The view from Debbie's house is of skyscrapers.
6    Debbie stays in a small cottage near the sea.

---

**Suggested Answers for Exs 4 & 7 on p. 15**

### Ex. 4

*I can't believe I'm lost, and it's getting late. I must try to find my friends. There are swamps all around me. I have to be careful not to fall into a mud bog. I will never escape if I do! I can see lots of trees and plants. What's that strange noise? Ahh, a snake! I hope it doesn't bite me! The snakes here in the Everglades are poisonous. I feel really scared here on my own. I can hear the mosquitoes. Hopefully they won't bite me and my friends find me soon!*

### Ex. 7

*You **can** follow a river because most rivers lead to a village.*
*You **have to** boil river water before you drink it.*
*You **can't** always eat fruit from the trees. Some **can** be poisonous.*
*You **have to** drink lots of water.*
*You **must** light a fire at night to frighten away any animals.*
*You **mustn't** make too much noise because it attracts animals.*

**d) Aim To expand vocabulary/To match words from a text to their meanings**

- Explain the task.
- Give Ss time to complete the task.
- Check Ss' answers.

*Answer Key*

**almost certain:** *pretty sure*
**think of:** *imagine*
**fortunate:** *lucky*
**an area you can see from a high place:** *view*
**an area with lots of trees:** *forest*
**was eager:** *couldn't wait*
**have:** *own*
**floors:** *storeys*

**3 Aim To practise new vocabulary**

- Give Ss time to think of which kind of house they would like to live in and why.
- Elicit answers from various Ss around the class.

*Suggested Answer Key*

*I would prefer to live in a bungalow in the countryside because it's quiet and very peaceful there. It would also have a nice view and big bedrooms./I would prefer to live in a townhouse in the city. These houses are large and close to the shops.*

## Grammar

**4 Aim To present the comparative and superlative form of adjectives**

- Give Ss time to study the table then explain the spelling rules.
- With one-syllable and two-syllable adjectives, we form the comparative by adding -er and the superlative by adding -est. *long – longer – longest*
- With one-syllable adjectives ending in -e, we add -r in the comparative and -st in the superlative. *simple – simpler – simplest*
- With one-syllable adjectives ending in a vowel + a consonant, we double the last consonant and add -er/-est. *big – bigger – biggest*
- With two-syllable adjectives ending in a consonant + y replace -y with -ier/-iest. *crazy – crazier – craziest*
- With adjectives of more than two-syllables, we form the comparative with *more* and the superlative with *the most. beautiful – more beautiful – the most beautiful*
- Elicit examples from the texts.

*Answer Key*

*the most beautiful, nicer, bigger, better, larger, noisier*

**5 Aim To practise the comparative**

- Read out the example and explain how the adjective *big* has been used in the comparative. Explain that Ss must make full comparative sentences using the prompts.

- Allow Ss time to complete the task.
- Elicit answers from various Ss.

*Answer Key*

2  *A block of flats is taller than a villa./A villa is not as tall as a block of flats.*
3  *The city centre is noisier than the suburbs./The suburbs are not as noisy as the city centre.*
4  *A cottage is smaller than a bungalow./A bungalow is not as small as a cottage.*
5  *Houses are more expensive than flats./Flats are not as expensive as houses.*
6  *Cities are more crowded than villages./Villages are not as crowded as cities.*
7  *The suburbs are more beautiful than the city centre./The city centre is not as beautful as the suburbs.*

**6 Aim To practise the comparative and superlative**

- Explain that in this task Ss will use both the comparative and superlative. Draw Ss' attention to the example and ask two Ss to read out the example.
- Allow Ss time to complete the task in pairs.
- Check Ss' answers on the board.

## Speaking

**7 Aim To practise using comparatives and superlatives**

- Ask Ss to think about places in their country and make sentences using the comparative and superlative. Direct Ss' attention to the example and ask them to use the same form in their answers.
- Elicit answers from various Ss. Correct any mistakes.

## Writing

**8 Aim To write an email describing your home**

- Explain the task. Write the headings on the board and elicit appropriate phrases under each heading. **Type** *(cottage, block of flats etc)*, **view** *(park, skyscrapers, etc)*, **location** *(near a park, opposite a school etc)*, **special features** *(garden, great view from balcony etc).*
- Remind Ss to use the emails in Ex. 2 as a model.
- Ss do the task. Ask various Ss to read their emails out to the class.

*Suggested Answer Key*

*Dear Sophie,*
*I live in a modern detached house. We have a great view of the city from the balcony. It is in a nice neighbourhood not far from the centre. It's very beautiful and my bedroom is very big. I hope you can come and visit me one day.*
*Love,*
*Lucy*

**d)** Match the words in bold to their meanings: *almost certain, think of, fortunate, an area you can see from a high place, an area with lots of trees, was eager, have, floors.*

**3** **THINK!** Which of the two girls' houses would you prefer to live in? Why? In three minutes write a few sentences. Tell the class.

## *Grammar*

see pp. GR2-GR3

### Comparative & Superlative

**4** Read the table. What are the spelling rules? Find examples in the texts.

| | ADJECTIVE | COMPARATIVE | SUPERLATIVE |
|---|---|---|---|
| **Short adjectives** | small<br>big<br>heavy | small**er** (than)<br>big**ger** (than)<br>heav**ier** (than) | the small**est** of/in<br>the big**gest** of/in<br>the heav**iest** of/in |
| **Long adjectives** | beautiful | **more** beautiful (than) | the **most** beautiful of/in |
| **Irregular** | good<br>bad<br>much/many | better (than)<br>worse (than)<br>more (than) | the best of/in<br>the worst of/in<br>the most of/in |

We use the **comparative form** to compare two people, things, places, etc. We use the **superlative form** to compare more than two people, things, places, etc. from the same group.

**Note:** We use **as ... as** to show that two things are the same. *Preston isn't **as** big **as** Manchester.*

**very + adjective:** *Canada is **very** big.*

**much + comparative:** *London is **much bigger than** York.*

**5** Write full sentences, as in the example.

1 Jasmine's new bedroom/big/her old bedroom
*Jasmine's new bedroom is bigger than her old bedroom. Jasmine's new bedroom isn't as big as her old bedroom.*

2 a block of flats/tall/a villa
3 the city centre/noisy/the suburbs
4 a cottage/small/a bungalow
5 houses/expensive/flats
6 cities/crowded/villages
7 the suburbs/beautiful/the city centre

**6** Make comparisons, as in the example.

1 Sue's bedroom is *smaller* (small) than Lisa's.
2 Lisa's bedroom is brighter (bright) than Sue's.
3 Lisa's house is bigger (big) than Sue's.
4 Sue's kitchen is the messiest (messy) of all.
5 Tom's bedroom is darker (dark) than the others.
6 Sue's bedroom is more comfortable (comfortable) than Tom's.
7 Tom's house is the biggest (big) of all.
8 Sue's living room is the smallest (small) of all.
9 Tom's bedroom is more old-fashioned (old-fashioned) than the others.
10 Lisa's room is the most comfortable (comfortable) of all.
11 Lisa's house is more modern (modern) than Tom's.
12 Sue's bedroom is more colourful (colourful) than Lisa's.

## *Speaking*

**7** Use these adjectives to make sentences comparing places in your country: *big, cold, small, quiet, noisy, modern, cheap, comfortable, sunny, beautiful, cosy, exciting, clean, boring, expensive, crowded.*     (Suggested Answer Key)

*... is bigger than ... . ... is the biggest city in my country.*
*... is as ... as ... . ... isn't as ... as ... .*
London is the biggest city in the country.
Inverness is colder than Bristol.
Glasgow is smaller than London.
Weymouth is sunnier than Manchester.
Leeds is more modern than York.
London is more expensive than Liverpool.
Birmingham isn't as beautiful as Edinburgh.
Cardiff is wetter than Cambridge.

## *Writing*

**8** Write an email to your English pen-friend about your home. Write about: *what type it is, what you can see from it, where it is, what makes it special.* Use the emails in Ex. 2 as models.

▶ Vocabulary Bank 1 p. VB3

# 1g Skills

## Vocabulary
### Home & Chores

**1 a)** In two minutes, write as many words as you can think of under the headings in the word map. Compare with your partner.



> **Study skills**
>
> **Using word maps**
> Organise words related to a topic into categories. This helps to build your vocabulary.

**b)** Use the words to describe your home to your partner.

*I live in a … . There are … rooms. It has a kitchen, a … . In the …, there is/are … . My neighbourhood is … .*

**2** Listen and say. Which chores do you have to/not have to do at home?

*I have to do the washing-up, but I don't have to … .*

## Listening

**3** You'll hear Tim and Sarah talking about their homes and home life. Listen and check (✓) *True* or *False*.

| | True | False |
|---|---|---|
| 1 Tim doesn't live alone. | | |
| 2 His favourite room is his bedroom. | | |
| 3 He has to do all the chores. | | |
| 4 Sarah lives in a noisy neighbourhood. | | |
| 5 Her home has three rooms upstairs. | | |
| 6 She doesn't do any chores. | | |

## Speaking
### Making requests

**4** You live in a dorm with your roommates. Use the language in the table and the chores in Ex. 2 to make requests, as in the examples.

| Requesting | Replying |
|---|---|
| • Can/Could you (please) …? | • Yes, of course. |
| • Do you mind (+ -ing) …? | • Yes, that's fine. |
| • Do you think you could …? | • Sure, no problem! |
| | • I'm afraid I can't. I … . |
| | • I'm sorry, but … . |
| | • I'd like to, but … . |

A: *Could you please take out the rubbish?*
B: *Sure, no problem!*

A: *Do you mind laying the table?*
B: *I can't. I have to mop the floor/finish my essay, etc.*

## Vocabulary

**1 a) Aim To brainstorm for vocabulary related to a topic**

- Direct Ss' attention to the headings in the diagram. Explain that they have to think of as many words as they can that fit those categories.
- Ask them to make a list under the appropriate headings and compare them with a partner.
- Allow Ss time to complete the task.

**Suggested Answer Key**

**neighbourhood:** *school, library, police station, shopping centre, cinema, etc*
**types of homes:** *cottage, house, bungalow, flat, etc*
**rooms:** *bedroom, kitchen, living room, bathroom, study, etc*
**furniture:** *bed, sofa, wardrobe, armchair, table, cupboards, bookcase, etc*
**other features:** *garden, balcony, swimming pool, garage, path, etc*
**equipment/appliances:** *fridge, cooker, TV, DVD player, kettle, toaster, etc*

**b) Aim To practise vocabulary**

- Ask Ss to use words from their list to describe their homes to their partners.
- Ask various Ss to describe their houses to the class.

**Suggested Answer Key**

*I live in a flat. There are four rooms. It has a kitchen, a bedroom, a bathroom and a living room. In the living room there is a fireplace and a TV. In the neighbourhood, there is a school and a library. My neighbourhood is quiet and friendly.*

**2 Aim To introduce new vocabulary**

- Direct Ss' attention to the pictures.
- Play the recording with pauses. Ask Ss to repeat the sentences after the recording.
- Do a class survey for the chores asking first which Ss have to do specific chores (*e.g. do the washing-up)* and which Ss don't have to do specific chores.
- Ask various Ss to tell the class which chores they have to do at home and which chores they don't have to do.

**Suggested Answer Key**

*I have to make my bed and take out the rubbish, but I don't have to dust the furniture.*

## Listening

**3 Aim To listen for specific information**

- Explain the task and direct Ss' attention to the sentences.
- Play the recording and allow time for Ss to complete the task.
- Play the recording again. Check Ss' answers.

**Answer Key**

1 T    2 F    3 F    4 F    5 T    6 F

## Speaking

**4 Aim To make requests**

- Ask Ss to imagine they live with other people.
- Direct Ss' attention to the Requesting/Replying table and ask them to read it carefully.
- In pairs, ask the Ss to make requests and reply about chores. Remind Ss to use the chores in Ex. 2 and direct them to the examples below.
- Ask various pairs to speak aloud.

**Suggested Answer Key**

A: *Do you think you could dust the furniture?*
B: *Yes, of course.*
A: *Can you hoover the carpets, please?*
B: *I'd like to, but I have to iron the clothes.*

**1** **Aim** To introduce a writing style

- Read the email extract aloud and ask Ss to follow in their books.
- Ask Ss to read it again themselves and elicit answers to the questions in the rubric.

***Answer Key***

*Jenny's flatmates don't help her with the housework.*

***Suggested Answer Key***

*I would tell Jenny to talk to her flatmates and ask them why they aren't helping.*

**2** **a)** **Aim** To read for specific information

- Ask Ss to read the reply alone.
- Elicit answers from Ss about what Anna's advice is.

***Answer Key***

*Anna's advice is to talk with her flatmates to explain how she feels. She also suggests that Jenny make a list of chores and share them with her flatmates.*

**b)** **Aim** To match paragraphs to headings

- Explain the task to Ss and ask them to match the paragraph numbers to the headings.
- Check Ss' answers.

***Answer Key***     *A   1      B   3      C   2*

**3** **a)** **Aim** To present *should/ought to*

Explain that *should/ought to* are used to give advice. Refer Ss to the box for examples. Read the examples and ask Ss to find another example in Anna's email.

***Answer Key***

*I think you **should** make a list of all the chores and together decide how to share them.*

**b)** **Aim** To practise *should/shouldn't*

- Explain the task and allow Ss time to complete it.
- Check Ss' answers.

***Answer Key***

*1  should      2  shouldn't      3  should      4  shouldn't*

**c)** **Aim** To identify functions of phrases

- Explain that Anna's email gives advice but also expresses an expected result *(what should happen if she takes the advice)*.
- Ask Ss to label the phrases according to the function and replace the phrases in bold from Anna's email with them.
- Check Ss' answers.

***Answer Key***

*Why don't you – give advice*
*If you do this – expected results*

*It's a good idea to – give advice*
*Then you can – expected results*
***Why don't you/It's a good idea** to talk about this with your flatmates. **Then you can** explain how you feel … **It's a good idea to/Why don't you** make a list … **If you do this,** everyone has responsibilities …*

**4** **Aim** To match advice to expected results

- Ask Ss to read the email extract and the advice and results boxes below.
- Allow Ss time to match the advice to the expected results.
- Check Ss' answers.
- Ask Ss to write a few lines including their advice for Matt's problem and what the expected results would be.
- Ask various Ss to read their advice aloud.

***Answer Key***     *1   b          2   a*

***Suggested Answer Key***

*Matt could move out of the flat. Then, he would have all the peace and quiet he needs.*

## Writing

**5** **Aim** To write an informal email of advice

- Explain the task and tell Ss that they can use ideas from Ex. 4. Write these phrases on the board for Ss to copy them in their notebooks and use them to write their emails.

| **Useful phrases for emails giving advice** | |
| --- | --- |
| **Opening remarks/ Reason for writing** | **Expected results** |
| *I'm sorry to hear that …* | *This way you can …* |
| **Giving advice** | *Then, …* |
| *The best thing you can do is …* | *If you do this, …* |
| *Why don't you …?* | *Then you can …* |
| *It's a good idea to …* | **Closing remarks** |
| *I think you should …* | *I really hope my advice helps.* |
|  | *I hope things work out well for you.* |

- Tell Ss to use the email in Ex. 2 as a model and to follow the plan in their books. Remind Ss that the email should be between 80-100 words in length.
- Allow Ss time to complete the task.
- Ask various Ss to read their emails aloud.

***Suggested Answer Key***

*Hi Matt,*
*I'm sorry to hear about your problem. I think I can help you. Why don't you talk to your flatmates and explain how you feel. This way, they will realise there is a problem and they can try to be quieter. You should also decide on a house rule like: no noise after 9 pm. Then, you know you can always study and sleep after this time.*
*I really hope my advice helps. Write and tell me what happens.*
*Dan*

19(T)

### An informal email of advice

**1** **Read the extract from Jenny's email. What problem does she have? What advice would you give her?**

> My house is OK, but I'm having some problems with my flatmates. The house is very dirty and untidy and I have to do all the housework! I can't invite my friends over because I feel embarrassed. What can I do?
> Jenny

**2** **a)** **Now read Anna's reply. What is her advice?**

**To:** Jenny
**From:** Anna
**Subject:** Your problem

Hi Jenny,

**1▶** I'm sorry to hear that you're having problems with your flatmates. I think I can help you!

**2▶** **The best thing you can do is** to talk about this with your flatmates. **This way, you can** explain how you feel and make them realise that you can't do all the housework yourself, as this is their house, too. Maybe they don't know that you're upset. **I think you should** make a list of all the chores and together decide how to share them. **Then,** everyone has responsibilities and they know what to do.

**3▶** I really hope my advice helps! Write back and tell me what happens.

Anna

**b)** **Match the paragraphs to the headings.**

| A | | greeting & opening comments |
| B | | closing comments |
| C | | advice & expected results |

### *Should/Ought to* see p. GR3

**3** **a)** **Read the examples. Find another example in Anna's email.**

> We use **should/shouldn't – ought/ought not to** to give advice.
> *We **should/ought to** share the household chores.* (It's a good idea.)
> *You **shouldn't/ought not to** walk alone at night.* (It isn't a good idea.)

**b)** **Fill in the gaps with** *should* **or** *shouldn't*.

1 Jenny ........................... talk to her flatmates.
2 She ........................ do all the chores herself!
3 They ........................... make a list of chores.
4 She ........................... be that upset.

**c)** **Which of the phrases in the list:** *give advice? express expected results?* **Use them to replace the phrases in bold in Anna's email.**

> • Why don't you • If you do this,
> • It's a good idea • Then you can

**4** **Read the extract from an email below. Then match the advice to the results. What is your advice? What can the expected results be?**

> My flatmates are so noisy! They invite their friends over and play loud music when I'm trying to study or sleep. It's awful! Any advice?
> Matt

| | Advice | | Results |
|---|---|---|---|
| 1 | Talk to your flatmates & explain how you feel. | a | You know you can always study & sleep after this time. |
| 2 | Decide on a house rule like 'no noise after 9 pm'. | b | If they realise there is a problem, they can try to be quieter. |

### *Writing (an informal email of advice)*

**5** **Use any of the ideas in Ex. 4 to write an email to Matt giving your advice (80-100 words). Follow the plan and use the email in Ex. 2 as a model.**

**Plan**

Hi .....................,
**Para 1:** opening remarks
*I'm sorry to hear ... . I think I can help you.*
**Para 2:** advice & expected results
*Why don't you ...? This way, ... .*
*You should also ... . Then, ... .*
**Para 3:** closing remarks
*I really hope ... . Write back and tell me ... .*
.....................

19

▶▶ Writing Bank p. WB1

# 1i Curricular: Citizenship

## Public services & facilities

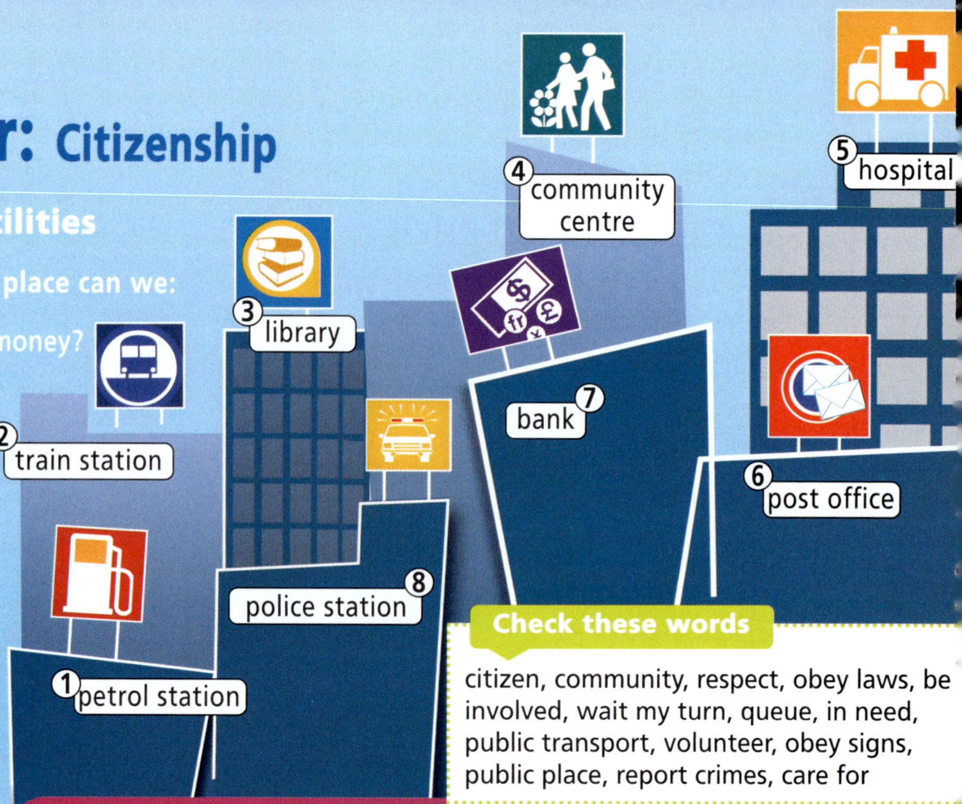

**1** 🎧 Listen and say. In which place can we:

- deposit or withdraw some money?
- take up a new hobby?
- borrow or return books?
- buy a stamp?
- take someone who is ill?
- report a crime?
- check our car tyres?
- buy a train ticket?

*We can deposit or withdraw some money at a bank.*

**2** 🎧 Listen to the short dialogues (1-4). In which of the places (1-8) in Ex. 1 does each take place?

1 ............... | 3 ...............
2 ............... | 4 ...............

**3** Read the dictionary entry. In your opinion, what makes a good/bad citizen? Do you think you are a good citizen? Do the quiz to find out.

**citizen** /ˈsɪtəzən/ (n)
person who lives in a particular city or town

**Check these words**

citizen, community, respect, obey laws, be involved, wait my turn, queue, in need, public transport, volunteer, obey signs, public place, report crimes, care for

# Are you a Good Citizen?

We can't have great communities without great citizens! To be a good citizen, you must respect and help others, obey rules and laws, and be involved in your community. So, is your community better because of you or worse?

| | | Always/ Nearly always | Sometimes | Rarely/ Never |
|---|---|---|---|---|
| | | A | B | C |
| 1 | I wait for my turn in queues at the bank or post office. | | | |
| 2 | I return my library books and pay my bills on time. | | | |
| 3 | I am polite to staff in shops, banks, libraries, etc. | | | |
| 4 | I help people in need e.g. I give my seat to senior citizens on public transport. | | | |
| 5 | I volunteer my time to help others e.g. helping at a community centre or kids' club. | | | |
| 6 | I follow rules and obey signs in public places. | | | |
| 7 | I take part in community activities & events e.g. festivals, sports events. | | | |
| 8 | I obey the law and report crimes. | | | |
| 9 | I care for the environment in my community e.g. I don't drop litter in the streets! | | | |

**Mostly A:** You're the perfect citizen! Keep it up!
**Mostly B:** Not bad, but think about how you can become a better citizen.
**Mostly C:** Oh no! You need to think about other people more!

**4** `ICT` Imagine you are giving a 3-minute speech about being a good citizen at a community centre. Collect more information and make notes under the headings:

- why it's important to be a good citizen
- ways to be a good citizen

You can do Internet research using the key phrase: *good citizens*. Give your presentation to the class.

▶▶ **Vocabulary Bank 1 p. VB4**

**1** **Aim** **To present vocabulary for public services and facilities**

- Read through the list and ask Ss to follow in their books.
- Play the recording. Ss listen and repeat the places 1-8.
- Elicit answers from various Ss where we can do each thing from the list.

***Answer Key***

*We can take up a new hobby at a community centre.*
*We can borrow or return books at a library.*
*We can buy a stamp at a post office.*
*We can take someone who is ill to a hospital.*
*We can report a crime at a police station.*
*We can check our car tyres at a petrol station.*
*We can buy a train ticket at a train station.*

**2** **Aim** **To listen for gist**

- Explain the task and tell Ss that they will hear four short conversations.
- Play the recording and allow Ss time to identify where each conversation takes place.
- Play the recording again.
- Check Ss' answers.

***Answer Key***

| | | | |
|---|---|---|---|
| 1 | post office | 3 | library |
| 2 | hospital | 4 | community centre |

**3** **Aim** **To discuss the topic/to do a quiz**

- Ask Ss to read the dictionary definition of *citizen*. As a class think of things that make someone a good citizen and write them on the board. Ask Ss to think of things that make someone a bad citizen and write this list on the board.
- Do a survey and ask how many Ss do things from the good citizen list and how many do things from the bad citizen list.
- Ask Ss to write a few lines about what makes someone a good citizen or a bad citizen using the answers from the board. Also ask them if they think they are good citizens.
- Allow Ss time to complete the quiz.

***Suggested Answer Key***

*A good citizen is someone who obeys laws and helps other people in his/her community.*
*A bad citizen is someone who does things that annoys others and causes problems in the community.*
*I think I am a good citizen because I like to help others in my community. I sometimes volunteer at the community centre and often visit elderly people in my neighbourhood.*

- Explain/Elicit the meaning of words in the **Check these words** box.

***Suggested Answer Key***

***citizen (n):*** *a person who lives in a particular city/town*
***community (n):*** *a group of people living in the same area*
***respect (v):*** *to be polite to and care for sb or sth*
***obey laws (phr):*** *to follow the rules made by the government*
***(be) involved in (phr):*** *to take part in sth*
***wait (for) my turn (phr):*** *to not go in line in front of others who were there first*
***queue (n):*** *a line of people waiting for sth*
***in need (phr):*** *wanting help*
***public transport (n):*** *vehicles that all people can use, like buses and trains*
***volunteer (v):*** *to do sth to help and give your time for free*
***obey signs (v):*** *to do what a sign tells you to do*
***public place (n):*** *an area that everyone can go to without having to pay entrance fee such as a square or a park*
***report crimes (phr):*** *to tell the police about sb breaking the law*
***care for (v):*** *to look after*

## BACKGROUND INFORMATION

### Being a Good Citizen

People who live in communities, whether they are small villages or large cities, have certain responsibilities to their community and surrounding area. The people who fulfill these responsibilities are known as good citizens. Some of the traits of being a good citizen are showing respect for other people in the community, taking care of the surrounding environment and living by the laws and rules of the area. A good citizen is someone who 'plays their part' in their community.

**4** **Aim** **To personalise the topic and practise new vocabulary**

- Explain the task and tell Ss to use ideas from the quiz and collect information from the Internet to prepare their talk.
- Allow Ss time to research and prepare.
- Ask various Ss to give their talk in class.

***Suggested Answer Key***

***Why it's important to be a good citizen***
*We all live and work in a community and there are rules and laws that help the community. When someone doesn't follow those rules and laws, it makes life unpleasant for some people. We must behave towards other people as though they were members of our family. Doing something good for others is doing something good for ourselves.*
***Ways to be a good citizen***
*You should think about and care for other people. You can help those who can't help themselves. You can give your time and volunteer. You should look after the area you live in and not litter or damage property. You can also encourage others to be good citizens.*

**1**   1  mop     3  make     5  take out     7  lay
      2  iron     4  dust     6  do         8  hoover

1   Don't forget to **mop the floor** after you sweep it.
2   I still have to **iron the clothes** and put them away.
3   Remember to **make the bed** before you leave.
4   You should **dust the furniture**, it's quite dirty.
5   Mark has to **take out the rubbish** every night.
6   I always **do the washing-up** when Sally cooks.
7   Could you **lay the table** for dinner, please?
8   Where is the vacuum cleaner, I want to **hoover the carpets**?

**2**   1  street     3  zebra crossing   5  pavement
      2  bad driving   4  traffic lights     6  cycle

**3**   1  G     3  E     5  A     7  F
      2  D     4  B     6  C

**4**   1  along     4  across     7  through     10  in
      2  down     5  on     8  by
      3  towards   6  in     9  in

**5**   1  road     4  petrol     7  be     10  community
      2  real-life   5  get into   8  insect
      3  snake     6  video     9  sandy

**Aim**   To consolidate vocabulary from the module

- Divide the class into 2 teams. Each team takes turns writing or saying a sentence with one of the words/phrases in the list.
- Each correct sentence earns one point. If the sentence is incorrect, the team misses a turn.
- The team with the most points after all the words have been used wins.

**Suggested Answer Key**

*The prime minister's speech **focuses on** the economy.*
*I like this song. It's got a **catchy tune**.*
***Pedestrians** should be careful when crossing busy city streets.*
*The **police car** picks up the suspect and takes him to the station.*
*The suspect is doing a U-turn into **oncoming traffic** which is really dangerous.*
*Let's go on a **road trip** to Scotland!*
*The Golden Gate Bridge is a **popular sight** in California.*
*Elephant seals' **breeding season** is from December to February.*
*Here are a few tips to **survive** your trip to the Everglades.*
*You have to wait in a queue at **public services** such as the post office.*

*A trip to the countryside is a great way to **escape from** the city for a day.*
*It's easy to **get into trouble** in the swamps.*
*A snake bite can be **fatal**.*
*We share the household **chores** at home.*
*If the **ground** is **shaking**, it could be a flash flood.*
*Good citizens must **obey rules**.*
*Good citizens should **report crimes**.*

## Quiz

**Answer Key**

1  F     3  F     5  T     7  F
2  T     4  F     6  T

Ss prepare their quiz in groups. Ask Ss to go through the pages of Module 1 and select information to compile their quiz. Ask groups to exchange quizzes. Ss do the quizzes, then check their answers.

**Suggested Answer key**

**Quiz**

1  F    *Police, Camera, Action! takes place in a police station. (on the streets)*
2  T    *Redwood trees can be up to 2,000 years old.*
3  T    *People ride cable cars in San Francisco.*
4  F    *You can see elephant seals at Hearst Castle. (zebras)*
5  F    *6,000 people get into trouble in the Everglades every year. (around 60)*
6  T    *Insect repellent is no good against alligators.*
7  F    *Alligators can move quicker than flash floods. (Alligators can travel up to 48 kmph whereas flash floods can travel at 96 kmph.)*

**1 Fill in:** *do, mop, dust, make, take out, hoover, lay, iron.* **Then make sentences.**

| | | | |
|---|---|---|---|
| 1 | ................ the floor | 5 | ............ the rubbish |
| 2 | ........... the clothes | 6 | ........................ the washing-up |
| 3 | ................. the bed | 7 | .............. the table |
| 4 | ...................... the furniture | 8 | ........... the carpets |

**2 Choose the correct words.**

## Road Safety

Most road accidents happen when people are crossing the **1) city/street** and are due to **2) street crime/bad driving**. We should always use a **3) zebra crossing/tunnel** or cross at the **4) road signs/traffic lights** for safety. Don't step off the **5) pavement/road** unless you're sure it's safe. If you're riding your bicycle, stay in the **6) bus/cycle** lane and take extra care.

**3 Match the words (1-7) to the sentences (A-G).**

| | |
|---|---|
| 1 ☐ police station | A You can borrow books there. |
| 2 ☐ community centre | B An area of very wet land. |
| 3 ☐ skyscraper | C This is where the sea meets the land. |
| 4 ☐ swamp | D People can meet and do things together there. |
| 5 ☐ library | E A very tall building. |
| 6 ☐ coast | F Someone walking in a city/town. |
| 7 ☐ pedestrian | G You report crimes there. |

## Prepositions

**4 Choose the correct preposition.**

1 Highway 1 runs **through/along** the coast.
2 Be careful! Don't fall **down/out of** the steps.
3 Keep walking **into/towards** me!
4 Never run **over/across** the road. Always walk.
5 Ben always goes to work **by/on** foot.
6 You can get stuck **to/in** mud in the Everglades.
7 Cars go under the river **past/through** the tunnel.
8 I prefer to travel around the city **by/on** bus.
9 There is a comfortable sofa **in/to** our living room.
10 Are you taking part **in/of** the football tournament?

## Collocations

**5 Fill in:** *insect, petrol, get into, road, real-life, snake, sandy, video, be, community.*

| | | | |
|---|---|---|---|
| 1 | .................... trip | 8 | .................... repellent |
| 2 | .................... videos | | |
| 3 | .................... bite | 9 | .................... beaches |
| 4 | .................... station | | |
| 5 | .................... trouble | 10 | .................... centre |
| 6 | .................... footage | | |
| 7 | .................... shocked | | |

In teams, make sentences. Use words/phrases from the list below. Each correct sentence gets one point. The team with the most points wins.

- focus on • catchy • pedestrians • police car
- oncoming traffic • road trip • popular sight
- breeding season • survive • public services
- escape from • get into trouble • fatal • chores
- ground shaking • obey rules • report crimes

## Quiz

Read through Module 1 and mark the sentences *T* (true) or *F* (false). Now write a quiz of your own. Give it to your partner. Check his/her answers.

1 Alligators can't run very fast. ......
2 Hearst Castle has 56 bedrooms. ......
3 Flash floods can travel up to 80 kmph. ......
4 The Golden Gate Bridge is in Australia. ......
5 The Florida Everglades area has 6,000 km² of swamps. ......
6 Alligators are reptiles. ......
7 You can see elephant seals in San Francisco. ......

### Reading

**Study skills**

**True/False statements**
Look out for absolute words like *all*, *none*, *always*, *every*, *never*, *only*, and *no*. They often indicate false answers. Qualifying words like *some*, *many*, *may*, *often*, *usually*, *most*, *sometimes* often indicate true answers.

**1  a)  Read the rubric. Then read sentences (1-6). Which sentences are absolute statements? Which are qualified statements? Underline the words which tell you this.**

> You are going to read a text about Rio de Janeiro. Read the text and mark the sentences (1-6) T (true) or F (false).

| | True | False |
|---|---|---|
| **1** Every rich person in Rio lives next to a poor person. | | |
| **2** Most people in Rio don't live in favelas. | | |
| **3** Favelas are often in unsafe places. | | |
| **4** Many people are happy living in favelas. | | |
| **5** You can only get into a favela if a guide is with you. | | |
| **6** Only rich people have the best views. | | |

**b)  Explain why each statement is true/false.**

Rio de Janeiro is a fascinating city. In many cities around the world, the rich and poor live in separate neighbourhoods. In Rio, though, extremely wealthy people often live side by side with the poor.

Walk around Rio and you can see luxurious apartment buildings, and expensive villas with beautiful gardens, directly across the road from crumbling shacks!

About 10 million people live in Rio. Roughly 2 million live in poor-quality housing. The worst areas in the city are slums known as favelas. Rio has about 750 favelas! Many have no electricity or running water. The streets are unpaved and there are no rubbish collections.

Life for the people who live in favelas is not easy. Accidents are common because they are usually built on steep hillsides so when it rains heavily there are mudslides. Disease is a problem because many favelas have no sanitation. In addition, the crime rate is very high.

Still, this is only part of the picture! Despite the difficulties, favelas are communities full of life. Most of the people who live in favelas are hard-working, honest people. In fact, a lot of favela residents are so proud of their community, they would not consider moving elsewhere.

The best way to understand a favela is by first-hand experience. Never walk into one on your own though! To be safe, you should only ever enter a favela on a professional tour with a guide.

When you are in Rio, make sure you visit one of the favelas along the steep hillsides of the city. The views are breathtaking. The favela of Vidigal, in south Rio, has a panoramic view of Rio de Janeiro's beautiful beaches and forested mountains. In fact, this is the unique thing about Rio – the wealthy people live on the flat, whereas the poor people live on the hillsides! In most other cities around the world, it is the rich who live in the areas with the best views, but not in Rio!

**1 a)** **Aim** To prepare for a reading task

- Read out the *Study Skills* box and point out that this tip will help Ss to complete the task successfully.
- Explain what an absolute statement is *(a definite statement of fact)* and what a qualified statement is *(a more general statement)*.
- Ask Ss to read the statements 1-6 and identify the absolute/qualified statements. Check Ss' answers and elicit the underlined words.

*Answer Key*

| | |
|---|---|
| 1 *absolute (every)* | 4 *qualified (many)* |
| 2 *qualified (most)* | 5 *absolute (only)* |
| 3 *qualified (often)* | 6 *absolute (only)* |

**b)** **Aim** To read for specific information and justify your answers

- Give Ss time to read the text and complete the task.
- Check Ss' answers and ask them to justify each one.

*Answer Key*

1  F  *(wealthy people often live side by side with the poor – i.e. NOT always)*
2  T  *(10 million people live in Rio ... 2 million in favelas)*
3  T  *(no electricity or running water ... disease ... crime rate is very high ...)*
4  T  *(vibrant communities ... favela residents ... proud ... not consider moving elsewhere)*
5  F  *(you should only ever enter with a guide)*
6  F  *(the favelas along the steep hillsides of the city ... favela of Vidigal ... and forested mountains – i.e. NOT only)*

## Speaking

**2** **Aim** To exchange information

- Explain the task and direct Ss' attention to the poster about Falcon gym and the prompts about it. Elicit what the poster shows. (information about Falcon gym – address, type of equipment, place to eat, membership fee, opening times, telephone number)
- Ask Ss to look at the prompts.
- Elicit an answer to the first prompt as an example *(What's the address? It's 36 Bramhall Lane)*.
- Ss then work in pairs and act out their dialogues. Monitor the activity around the class and then ask some pairs to act out their dialogues in front of the class.

**Suggested Answer Key**

*Has it got lots of equipment? Yes, it has.*
*What can you eat? A selection of healthy salads and sandwiches.*
*How much is the membership fee? It's £25 per month.*
*Is the gym open in the evenings? Yes, it is.*

## Listening

**3 a)** **Aim** To analyse a rubric and prepare for a listening task

- Ask Ss to read the rubric and elicit what they will listen to.
- Give Ss time to read the questions 1-5 and underline the key words.
- Check Ss' answers around the class.

**Suggested Answer Key**

*They are talking about (going to) a water park.*

**Key words**

*1  water park – high street, Station Road, Fulton Street*
*2  Holly doesn't want – take train, walk, get bus*
*3  entrance fee after first month – £4, £6, £10*
*4  bus ride to water park takes – ten, fifteen, twenty*
*5  water park sells – snacks, fast food, sandwiches*

**b)** **Aim** To listen for specific information

- Play the recording. Ss listen and complete the task.
- Check Ss' answers.

**Answer Key**

*1  C        2  B        3  C        4  C        5  A*

**Justifications**

*0  I can't. I work on Saturdays and Sundays.*
*1  It's in Fulton Street ...*
*2  Dylan: Don't worry. We don't have to walk there, ...*
*    Holly: ... I'm tired of walking everywhere.*
*3  It's usually £10 per person, ...*
*4  ... it's only twenty minutes to water park.*
*5  There's a café with snacks there, ...*

## Writing

**4 a)** **Aim** To prepare for a writing task

- Refer Ss to the Writing Bank and give them time to read through the relevant information there.
- Elicit the correct elements of a note from various Ss around the class.

**Answer Key**

*4, 5, 6*

**b)** **Aim** To analyse a rubric and prepare for a writing task

- Ask Ss to read the rubric and elicit what they are going to write (a note) and why *(they have to visit their aunt and they want to tell their flatmate sth).*
- Elicit which of the sentences 1-8 are appropriate for their notes.

**Answer Key**

*2, 3, 5, 6*

**c)** **Aim** To write a note

Give Ss time to complete the task and then check Ss' answers.

**Suggested Answer Key**

*Hi John,*
*I took out the rubbish and hoovered the carpets. Can you do the washing-up? Have to go see my aunt. Meet me at the Internet café at 8:00.*
*Paul*

## Speaking

**2** **Read the rubric, then do the task.**



Candidate A



Candidate B



## Listening

**3** **a)** **Read the rubric then the questions. What are the two speakers talking about?**

Listen to Dylan talking to Holly about a water park. For questions 1-5, tick (✓) A, B or C. You will hear the conversation twice.

**Example**

| | | | | |
|---|---|---|---|---|
| **0** | Holly can't go to the water park | **A** | on Thursday. | ☐ |
| | | **B** | on Friday. | ☐ |
| | | **C** | at the weekend. | ✓ |

| | | | | |
|---|---|---|---|---|
| **1** | The water park is | **A** | on the high street. | ☐ |
| | | **B** | in Station Road. | ☐ |
| | | **C** | in Fulton Street. | ☐ |
| **2** | Holly doesn't want to | **A** | take the train. | ☐ |
| | | **B** | walk there. | ☐ |
| | | **C** | get the bus. | ☐ |
| **3** | The entrance fee after the first month is | **A** | £4. | ☐ |
| | | **B** | £6. | ☐ |
| | | **C** | £10. | ☐ |
| **4** | The bus ride to the water park takes | **A** | ten minutes. | ☐ |
| | | **B** | fifteen minutes. | ☐ |
| | | **C** | twenty minutes. | ☐ |
| **5** | The water park sells | **A** | snacks. | ☐ |
| | | **B** | fast food. | ☐ |
| | | **C** | sandwiches. | ☐ |

**b)** Do the task. Give reasons for your answers.

## Writing (notes)

*(Writing Bank p. WB2)*

**4** **a)** **Decide which of the following are true when writing a note.**

1 begins with *Dear ...*
2 has paragraphs
3 ends with *Best wishes*
4 uses simple, short sentences
5 uses abbreviations
6 uses the imperative

**b)** **Read the rubric. Which of the sentences below can you use in the note?**

You got a phone call from your aunt and you have to go and see her. Leave your English flatmate a note. In your note:
• explain where you are going
• say what chores you've done
• ask your friend to do the washing-up
• ask your friend to meet you at the Internet café later

1 Call me if you need me.
2 Have to go see my aunt.
3 Can you please do the washing-up?
4 Be back at 9:00.
5 Meet me at the Internet café at 8:00.
6 I took out the rubbish and hoovered the carpets.
7 Call you later.
8 Let me know as soon as possible.

**c)** **Use the sentences from Ex. 4b to write your note.**

**1** Fill in: *poisonous, hand-held, breeding, signs, focus, police, cuts, fall into, fatal, borrow.*

1 Always obey the road ..................................... .
2 You mustn't panic if you .............................. a mud bog!
3 Do you ever ................. books from the library?
4 Some documentaries use video footage from ........................... cameras.
5 My dad hates it when another driver .............. him off.
6 December to February is ....................... season for elephant seals. They give birth to a single pup.
7 Try to ................. on what he is talking about.
8 The ............................... car was chasing the suspect through the streets.
9 Scorpion stings can be ..............................., so you should be very careful.
10 There are lots of ........................... spiders and snakes in a jungle. Their bites can be very dangerous.

*10x2=20 marks*

**2** Choose the correct word.

1 I **can't/don't have to** work tonight. Let's go to the cinema.
2 He **mustn't/doesn't have to** drive a car. He doesn't have a licence.
3 Cars **ought/must** stop when the traffic lights are red.
4 **Could/Should** you answer the phone, please?
5 You **can't/shouldn't** go into a forest without insect repellent.

*5x4=20 marks*

**3** Put the verbs in brackets into the *present simple* or the *present continuous*.

1 Ben always ................... (pay) his bills on time.
2 Tim ........................................ (stay) with his grandparents for the summer.
3 Sarah ............. (make) her bed every morning.
4 ...................................... (John/iron) the clothes at the moment.
5 My flatmate never ................... (tidy) the house and I feel embarrassed when I invite friends over.

*5x4=20 marks*

**4** Complete the sentences with the correct *comparative* or *superlative* form of the adjectives in brackets.

1 The Empire State Building is ........................... ................................................... (tall) Big Ben.
2 ...................................... (good) way to see San Francisco is on a cable car.
3 John thinks riding a bike is .............................. ...................................... (exciting) driving a car.
4 What's ............................................................. (busy) street in your town?
5 Big cities are usually ............................................ ...................... (dangerous) small towns.

*5x4=20 marks*

**5** Fill in: *Return, please. – Here you are. – I'd like two tickets to Manchester, please. – We'd like to take the 9:30 am bus.*

1 A: That's £36, please.
 B: ..................................................................
2 A: What time would you like to leave?
 B: ..................................................................
3 A: Hello. Can I help you?
 B: ..................................................................
4 A: Single or return?
 B: ..................................................................

*4x2=8 marks*

**6** Your friend has a problem with his/her neighbours. Their dog barks outside all night. Write a short email to your friend giving your advice (80-100 words).

*12 marks*

*Total: 100 marks*

## Check your Progress

- talk and write about city life and country life ____
- describe movement ____
- compare places ____
- buy a ticket ____
- talk and write about survival in the countryside ____
- make requests ____
- write an informal email giving advice ____

**GOOD ✓ VERY GOOD ✓✓ EXCELLENT ✓✓✓**

**1**  1  *signs*  5  *cuts*  9  *fatal*
2  *fall into*  6  *breeding*  10  *poisonous*
3  *borrow*  7  *focus*
4  *hand-held*  8  *police*

**2**  1  *don't have to*  3  *must*  5  *shouldn't*
2  *mustn't*  4  *Could*

**3**  1  *pays*  3  *makes*  5  *tidies*
2  *is staying*  4  *John is ironing*

**4**  1  *taller than*  4  *the busiest*
2  *The best*  5  *more dangerous than*
3  *more exciting than*

**5**  1  *Here you are.*
2  *We'd like to take the 9:30 am bus.*
3  *I'd like two tickets to Manchester, please.*
4  *Return, please.*

**6**  **Suggested Answer Key**

*Hi Jack,*

*Sorry to hear about your problem, but I think I can help!*

*Why don't you talk to your neighbours? Then, you can explain the problem. Maybe they don't think their dog is annoying anyone. I think you should ask them to keep their dog inside at night. Then, you could get a good night's sleep.*

*Hope my advice helps. Write back and tell me what happens.*

*Emma*

# Food & Drinks



Read the title of the module *Food & Drinks* and ask Ss to predict its content *(the module is about food and drinks, eating out and cooking)*. Go through the contents list and stimulate a discussion about what Ss will learn in the module.

## Vocabulary

**1** **Aim** **To present vocabulary related to food and drinks**

Draw Ss' attention to the pictures and the categories of food and drinks. Ask Ss to label the pictures A-E with the groups of food 1-5. Play the recording. Ss listen and check their answers. Then, Ss say the words chorally or individually.

*Answer Key*

*A 2        B 4        C 5        D 3        E 1*

**2** **Aim** **To listen for specific information**

Explain the task to Ss. Play the recording. Ss listen and complete the text. Check Ss' answers.

*Suggested Answer Key*

*Tim likes chicken and beef, but he doesn't like cheese, milk or cabbage.*
*Julie likes cherries, eggs and cheese, but she doesn't like tuna.*

## OVER TO YOU!

**Aim** **To personalise the topic**

- Ask Ss to look at the pictures of the food and drinks again and complete the sentences.
- Give Ss time to complete the task.
- Ask various Ss to read out their sentences to the class.

*Suggested Answer Key*

*I like orange juice.*
*I love yogurt.*
*I don't like trout.*
*I hate/can't stand cauliflower.*

**Vocabulary:** food & drinks, food groups, supermarket sections, containers/partitives, restaurants, food preparation, ingredients & measurements, adjectives describing food, healthy lifestyles

**Grammar:** countable/uncountable nouns, *a/an – some/any*, quantifiers *(how) many*, *(how) much*, *too many/much*, *a lot of*, *some*, *(a) few*, *(a) little*, *no/not any*, *too – enough*, *-ing form/(to) infinitive*

**Everyday English:** ordering food in a café

**Pronunciation:** /n/, /ŋ/

**Writing:** a description of a food festival; a text about places to eat out; a description of your own restaurant; an email about a favourite dish

**Culture Corner:** Eating out in the UK

**Curricular (Science):** Food for life

# Module 2
## Food & Drinks

## Vocabulary
### Food & Drinks

**1** **Label the groups.** 🎧 **Listen and check, then say.**

1 drinks
2 fruit & vegetables
3 meat, poultry, fish & seafood
4 dairy products
5 other

**OVER TO YOU!**

I like (♥) ........................
I love (♥♥) ....................
I don't like (✗) ...............
I hate/can't stand (✗✗)
........................

**2** 🎧 **Listen to Tim and Julie. Which foods/drinks do they like/not like?**

*Tim likes ..., but he doesn't like ...*
*Julie likes ..., but she doesn't like ...*

# 2a Food art

## Vocabulary
## Food

**1 a)** 🎧 **Listen and say.**

**b)** Which of these foods do you see in the pictures on pp. 26-27?

## Grammar  see p. GR3
## Countable/Uncountable nouns – A/An – Some/Any

**2 a)** Read the table. Which of the foods in Ex. 1 are: *countable*? *uncountable*?

---

**Countable nouns** (nouns we **can** count):

*a banana*           *an apple* 

*two/**some** bananas* 

**Uncountable nouns** (nouns we **can't** count):
***some** milk* (NOT: ~~a/one milk, two milks~~)

- We use **a/an** for singular countable nouns. *There's **an** apple.*
- We use **some** in the affirmative for uncountable nouns and for plural countable nouns. *There is **some** rice. We have **some** strawberries.*
- We use **any** in the negative and interrogative for uncountable nouns and for plural countable nouns. *There aren't **any** eggs./Do we have **any** pasta?*
- We can also use **some** in offers & requests. *Would you like **some** cake? Can I have **some** water, please?*

---

**b)** Fill in: *a/an*, *some* or *any*.

1 There is ......... tea, but there isn't ......... coffee.
2 Do you want ................... banana?
3 There are ............... cherries in the fridge.
4 Is there ................... milk left?
5 There are ............. strawberries and ............. apple in the bowl.
6 There aren't ................... carrots, but there are ................... potatoes.
7 "Can I have ................... orange juice, please?" "Sorry, but there isn't ................... ."
8 Would you like ................... coffee?

## Reading & Listening

**3 a)** Read the saying in the first sentence in the text. What do you think it means? Choose *A*, *B* or *C*.

A You must turn sour things into sweet things.
B You should make the most of everything.
C You should be grateful for what you have.

**b)** What do you think the text is about? 🎧 Listen and read to find out.

## Vocabulary

**1 a)** **Aim** **To present vocabulary for food**

Draw Ss' attention to the pictures and play the recording. Ss listen and repeat chorally or individually. Check Ss' pronunciation.

**b)** **Aim** **To recognise items of food and match them to the pictures**

Ask Ss to look at the photographs on pp. 26-27 and say which foods from Ex. 1 they see.

**Answer Key**

*Oranges and lemons.*

## Grammar

**2 a)** **Aim** **To present countable and uncountable nouns, *A/An – Some/Any***

- Go through the table with Ss.
- Explain that countable nouns are nouns that we can count *(a lemon, two lemons)* while uncountable nouns are nouns we cannot count *(broccoli – NOT: ~~two broccoli~~).*
- Explain that we use *a/an* with countable nouns, but we use *some* with uncountable nouns.
- Explain that we use *any* in the negative and interrogative for uncountable nouns and for plural countable nouns.
- Explain that we also use *some* with offers and requests. ***Would you like some juice? Can I have some apples?***
- Read out the examples and elicit further examples. Elicit which foods in Ex. 1 are countable/uncountable.

**Answer Key**

***Countable:*** *banana, lemon, carrot, strawberry, onion, cucumber, orange, potato*
***Uncountable:*** *broccoli, celery*

- As an extension elicit plural forms for countable nouns and elicit/revise plural noun endings.

Most nouns take **-s** to form their plural.
*book – books*
Nouns ending in -s, -ss, -ch, -x or -sh take **-es**.
*bus – buses, dress – dresses, church – churches, fox – foxes, brush – brushes*
Some nouns ending in *-f* or *-fe* drop the *-f* or *-fe* and take **-ves** to form their plural.
*wolf – wolves, wife – wives* **BUT** *roof – roofs*
Nouns ending in a consonant + *y* drop the *-y* and take *-ies. raspberry – raspberries, baby – babies*
Nouns ending in a vowel + *y* take **-s**.
*boy – boys, toy – toys*

Some nouns ending in *-o* take *-es. potato – potatoes* **BUT** *radio – radios, piano – pianos, photo – photos, video – videos, rhino – rhinos, hippo – hippos*

- Ask Ss to look at the foods on p. 25 and decide which are countable and which are uncountable then say the singular forms of the countable nouns.
**Countable nouns:** *tomato – tomatoes, pepper – peppers, cherry – cherries, pear – pears, cauliflower – cauliflowers, grape – grapes, bean – beans, egg – eggs, prawn - prawns (or prawn).*
**Uncountable nouns:** *cabbage, yogurt, cheese, butter, milk, bread, pasta, cereal, rice, beef, lamb, chicken, salmon, trout, cod, tuna, coffee, tea, lemonade, orange juice.*

**Answer Key**

| | | | | | |
|---|---|---|---|---|---|
| 1 | *some, any* | 4 | *any* | 7 | *some, any* |
| 2 | *a* | 5 | *some, an* | 8 | *some* |
| 3 | *some* | 6 | *any, some* | | |

**b)** **Aim** **To practise *a/an, some/any* with countable and uncountable nouns**

- Explain the task. Allow Ss time to complete it.
- Go around the class monitoring Ss and helping where necessary. Check Ss' answers.

## Reading & Listening

**3 a)** **Aim** **To understand the meaning of a saying**

- Ask Ss to look at the first sentence of the text and explain that it is a saying that people often use to give advice about life.
- Ask Ss what they think the saying might mean. Read out the options A, B, and C and ask Ss to choose.

**Answer Key**

*B*

**b)** **Aim** **To predict the content of a text/To listen and read for gist**

- Ask Ss to look at the title of the text and the pictures. Elicit/Explain that the pictures show statues made from oranges and lemons.
- Ss predict the content of the text.
- Play the recording. Ss listen to and confirm if their guesses were correct.

**Suggested Answer Key**

*I think that the text is about artists making statues from lemons and oranges.*

- Explain/Elicit the meanings of the words in the **Check these words** box or ask Ss to look them up in their dictionaries. Ss also say what part of speech is each.

**Suggested Answer Key**

**dessert (n):** *sweet dish people usually eat at the end of a meal*
**juice (n):** *the liquid of a fruit or vegetable*
**picturesque (adj):** *(of a place) beautiful and with nice scenery*
**resort (n):** *a place where lots of people spend their holidays*
**celebrate (v):** *to do sth enjoyable for a special reason*
**attract (v):** *to cause people to come to see*
**design (v):** *to make a detailed drawing of sth you plan to make*
**statue (n):** *a large model of sb or sth*
**measure (v):** *to be particular a size, length, etc*
**citrus (adj):** *relating to fruits with a sour taste, such as oranges, lemons and grapefruits*
**creation (n):** *sth that sb designs and makes*
**float (n):** *an open vehicle which carries people or things for people to see, usually in parades*
**fireworks (pl n):** *small rockets that light up the sky when they explode*
**theme (n):** *the main idea*
**(let your) imagination run wild (phr):** *to imagine or dream up anything you like*

**c)** **Aim** To read for specific information

- Allow Ss time to complete the sentences.
- Check Ss' answers.

**Suggested Answer Key**

1   *... a seaside resort town in the south of France.*
2   *... the Lemon Festival.*
3   *... over 145 tons of lemons and oranges.*
4   *... Citrus Exposition.*
5   *... fireworks.*

**d)** **Aim** To consolidate new vocabulary

Allow Ss two to three minutes to make their sentences, then check Ss' answers around the class.

**Suggested Answer Key**

*You can use lemons to make a lot of different **desserts**.*
*Artists use whole lemons and not their **juice** to make statues.*
*Menton is a **picturesque** town.*
*Menton is a seaside **resort** town.*
*The people of Menton **celebrate** the Lemon Festival every year.*
*The festival **attracts** over 200,000 visitors each year.*
*Artists **design** amazing, giant statues for the festival.*
*The artists use lemons and oranges to make huge **statues**.*
*Some statues **measure** over 10 metres tall.*
*Oranges and lemons are **citrus** fruit.*
*Their **creations** include giant dinosaurs and huge bananas.*

*There is a huge parade of **floats** that carry the statues.*
*In the evening people gather to watch colourful **fireworks** in the sky.*
*There is a different **theme** each year.*
*The artists can really let their **imaginations run wild** and create unusual statues.*

**e)** **Aim** To expand vocabulary/To match words from a text to their meanings

- Explain the task.
- Give Ss time to complete the task.
- Check Ss' answers.

**Answer Key**

**regional** = *local*
**attractive** = *picturesque*
**huge** = *giant*
**plan** = *design*
**come together in a group** = *gather*
**main idea** = *theme*
**have the size of** = *measure*

## Speaking & Writing

**4   a)** **Aim** To read for specific information/To make notes, to present a festival

Write the headings on the board. Elicit answers from Ss and write notes under the headings. Ask Ss to copy the notes into their notebooks, then prepare a presentation. Ask individual Ss to make their presentations in class.

**Suggested Answer Key – see p. 28(T)**

**b)** **Aim** To consolidate information in a text

- Ask Ss to think about reasons why someone should go to the lemon festival.
- Ask various Ss to present them in class.

**Suggested Answer Key**

*It's a great opportunity to buy local products made from citrus fruit. You also get to see some really interesting works of art. Some of the statues are over 10 metres tall, so they are really impressive. Also, there are parades with music and dancers.*

**5** **Aim** To write a text about a festival

- Ask Ss if there is a similar festival in their country.
- Ask Ss to make notes about a festival under the headings in Ex 4a and use them to write about the festival.
- Check Ss' answers by asking various Ss to read out their texts.
- Alternatively, this task can be assigned as HW and checked in the next lesson.

**Suggested Answer Key – see p. 28(T)**

# Lemon Art: French style

Lemons are a great fruit. You can make lemonade and desserts from them or even use their juice for cooking or in salads.

'When life gives you lemons make lemonade,' the saying goes. In the beautiful and **picturesque** seaside resort town of Menton in the south of France, people make a lot more than just lemonade with their lemons. Believe it or not, they make art, and have a lot of fun doing it!

Every February to March, the people of Menton celebrate their lemons and oranges with a three-week long lemon festival that attracts over 200,000 visitors. Artists **design** and create amazing giant statues for the festival using over 145 tons of lemons and oranges. The artists make everything from **giant** bananas to dinosaurs and some of the statues can **measure** more than 10 metres tall. There is a daily Citrus Exposition where people come to see the amazing creations and buy **local** products made from oranges and lemons. On Sundays, floats carrying the citrus statues go through the town in the Parade of Golden Fruit and on Thursdays, crowds **gather** to watch colourful night parades with music and dancers as well as fireworks. Each year, there is a different **theme** and the creators let their imaginations run wild. Whether you like food and art, or simply need some vitamin C, Menton is a pretty good place to be in February and March.

**If you want to experience the festival next year, visit www.fete-du-citron.com and book your tickets online as places for each event go fast.**

**Check these words**

dessert, juice, picturesque, resort, celebrate, attract, design, statue, measure, citrus, creation, float, fireworks, theme, imagination runs wild

**c)   Complete the sentences.**

1  Menton is .....................................
2  Every spring, over 200,000 people come to Menton for .....................
3  Artists make statues with .............
4  People come to see the artists' creations at the .............................
5  After the parades on Thursdays people watch ...............................

**d)   Use five words from the Check these words box to make sentences about the festival.**

*The people of Menton celebrate the Lemon Festival every year.*

**e)   Match the words in bold in the text with their meanings:**
*regional, attractive, huge, plan, come together in a group, main idea, have the size of.*

## Speaking & Writing

**4   a)   Read the text again and make notes under the headings. Use your notes to present the festival to the class.**

- name of festival • place
- date • reason • activities

**b)   THINK!** In three minutes write a few sentences giving reasons why someone should go to the Lemon Festival. Tell the class.

**5   Is there a similar food festival in your country? Make notes under the headings in Ex. 4a, then write a short  text about it.**

Vocabulary Bank 2  p. VB5

# 2b At the supermarket

## Vocabulary
### Containers/Partitives

**1** 🎧 Listen and say. In which supermarket section can we usually find these products (1-11)? Make sentences as in the example.

*We can usually find **a loaf** of bread in the bakery section.*

**Products**

1 a **loaf** of bread
2 a **jar** of jam
3 a **tin** of soup
4 a **carton** of juice
5 a **box** of cereal
6 a **pot** of yogurt
7 a **tub** of ice cream
8 a **bottle** of cola
9 a **kilo** of minced beef
10 a **bunch** of bananas
11 a **bar** of chocolate

**Supermarket Sections**

Fruit & vegetables

Dairy products

Meat & fish

Drinks

Bakery

Sweets & snacks

Breakfast food

Tinned food

Frozen food

## Reading

**2** Ann and Tony are shopping for a barbecue. What do they need?
🎧 Listen and read to find out. What is the problem?

**Ann:** Right, that's all the meat and bread! What else do we need?

**Tony:** Well, here's the drinks aisle. Let's get a few cartons of juice … and some bottles of cola and lemonade.

**Ann:** OK … Let's go to the bakery section. We need some cakes.

**Tony:** Yes, let's get two of these big chocolate ones! They look tasty.

**Ann:** Good idea. Do we have any ice cream?

**Tony:** Only a little. We can get another tub if you want to.

**Ann:** We have a lot of food here, Tony! Are you sure it isn't too much?

**Tony:** No! We are expecting thirty people, remember?

**Ann:** Yes, you're right! Let's go and pay … Oh, no!

**Tony:** What's wrong?

**Ann:** I'm afraid I left my purse on the kitchen table! How much money do you have?

**Tony:** Erm, not much … only £5 … .

**Ann:** Oh, no! Now what are we going to do?

> **Check these words**
>
> aisle, expect, remember, What's wrong?, purse

28

## Vocabulary

**1** **Aim** To present vocabulary for containers and partitives

- Draw Ss' attention to the pictures and play the recording. Ss listen and repeat chorally or individually.
- Ask Ss where they would find the products (1-11) choosing from the supermarket sections. Ss match the items and make sentences. Check Ss' answers. **Note:** The supermarket sections listed can vary from one supermarket to the other.

*Answer Key*

2   *We can usually find a jar of jam in the tinned food section.*
3   *We can usually find a tin of soup in the tinned food section.*
4   *We can usually find a carton of juice in the drinks section.*
5   *We can usually find a box of cereal in the breakfast food section.*
6   *We can usually find a pot of yogurt in the dairy products section.*
7   *We can usually find a tub of ice cream in the frozen food section.*
8   *We can usually find a bottle of cola in the drinks section.*
9   *We can usually find a kilo of minced beef in the meat and fish section.*
10  *We can usually find a bunch of bananas in the fruit and vegetables section.*
11  *We can usually find a bar of chocolate in the sweets and snacks section.*

## Reading

**2** **Aim** To read and listen for specific information

- Explain the situation.
- Play the recording.
- Elicit answers. Play the recording again if necessary.

*Answer Key*

*Ann and Tony need a few cartons of juice and some bottles of cola and lemonade. They also need two chocolate cakes and a tub of ice cream. The problem is that Ann left her purse at home and Tony has only got £5.*

- Explain/Elicit the meanings of the words in the **Check these words** box or ask Ss to look them up in their dictionaries.

*Suggested Answer Key*

**aisle (n):** *a long narrow gap between rows of shelves in a supermarket where customers can walk*
**expect (v):** *to wait for, to look forward to*
**remember (v):** *to recall, to bring to mind*
**What's wrong? (phr):** *What's the problem?*
**purse (n):** *a wallet for women*

---

**Suggested Answers for Exs 4a & 5 on p. 27**

### Ex. 4a

**Name of festival:** *Lemon Festival*
**Place:** *Menton, south of France*
**Date:** *every February to March*
**Reason:** *to celebrate their lemons and oranges*
**Activities:** *creating giant fruit statues, visit the Citrus Exposition and see statues, buy local products, watch the Parade of Golden Fruit, watch night parades with music and dancers and fireworks*

*A Lemon Festival takes place every year from February to March in the town of Menton in the south of France. People celebrate their lemons and oranges. It is a huge event with a different theme every year. You can see artists creating giant sculptures made from oranges and lemons, visit the Citrus Exposition and admire the statues, buy local products, and watch the Parade of Golden Fruit. There are also night parades with dancers and fantastic fireworks.*

### Ex. 5

**Name of festival:** *Shrimp Festival (Fête de la Crevette)*
**Place:** *Honfleur, France*
**Date:** *October*
**Reason:** *to celebrate the history of the port*
**Activities:** *2 day festival, the little grey shrimp (the queen of the festival), shrimp-peeling competition, all types of seafood, musical performances, gathering of old sea vessels in the port*

*Fête de la Crevette, the Shrimp Festival, takes place in Honfleur, France, in October. It's a popular event that attracts many visitors to this old style port. The 2 day festival celebrates the port's history with the sea. Visitors to the festival can see and do a lot of things. They can see the little grey shrimp, the queen of the festival, and a gathering of old sea vessels in the port. They can watch musical performances of sea shanties and try all types of seafood, but the highlight of the festival is the shrimp peeling competition. It's a great festival where everybody has a lot of fun.*

## Grammar

**3** **Aim** To present quantifiers

- Go through the table with Ss and explain the uses of the quantifiers. Elicit more examples or ask comprehension questions e.g. Which quantifier do we use in affirmative sentences with countable and uncountable nouns? *(a lot of)*. Can we use *few* with uncountable nouns? *(No. We can use little)*. Do we use *any* in questions with countable nouns? *(Yes, we do.)* etc
- Ask Ss to find examples of quantifiers in the dialogue in Ex 2.

*Answer Key*

*a few cartons of juice, some bottles of cola and lemonade, some cakes, any ice cream, only a little (ice cream), a lot of food, too much (food), How much money, not much*

**4** **Aim** To practise quantifiers

- Explain the task and allow Ss time to complete it.
- Check Ss' answers.

*Answer Key*

| | | | |
|---|---|---|---|
| 1 | *much, little* | 5 | *any, a few* |
| 2 | *any, a lot of, many* | 6 | *little, much* |
| 3 | *many, many* | 7 | *no, some* |
| 4 | *much, some* | 8 | *too much, a lot of* |

- Go through the **Study skills** box with Ss and explain the importance of noting one's mistakes. Ask Ss to go through their mistakes, if any, and list them in their notebooks together with the correct answers. Ask Ss to update their notebooks each time they make a mistake and revise regularly.

## Listening

**5** **a)** **Aim** To listen for specific information

- Go through the shopping list with Ss and elicit/explain any unknown words.
- Explain the task.
- Play the recording. Ss listen and mark the items.
- Check Ss' answers.

*Answer Key*

| | |
|---|---|
| 1 kilo of cheese (✓) | 1 bag of rice (✓) |
| 3 bags of crisps (✓) | 20 sausages (✓) |
| 2 bottles of cola (✓) | |
| 1 carton of apple juice (✗) | |

**b)** **Aim** To practise quantifiers

- Ask a pair of Ss to read out the example.
- Explain the task. Point out that Ss need to use appropriate quantifiers. Ss practise in pairs.
- Go around the class monitoring the activity.
- Ask a few pairs to act out their exchanges in class.

*Suggested Answer Key*

A: *How much cheese does she need?*
B: *She needs a lot – one kilo. How many bags of crisps does she need?*
A: *She needs a few – three bags. How much cola does she need?*
B: *She doesn't need much – two bottles. How much apple juice does she need?*
A: *She doesn't need any apple juice. How much rice does she need?*
B: *She doesn't need much – one bag. How many sausages does she need?*
A: *She needs a lot – 20!*

## Speaking & Writing

**6** **Aim** To talk about eating habits

- Go through the words in the table with Ss and elicit/explain any unknown words.
- Explain the task and ask a pair of Ss to read out the example.
- Ss work in closed pairs. Go around the class and monitor the activity.
- Ask a few pairs to act out their exchanges in class.

*Suggested Answer Key*

A: *How much fruit do you eat each week?*
B: *I eat a lot of fruit. How many eggs do you eat each week?*
A: *I eat a few. How much meat do you eat each week?*
B: *I eat little meat. Do you eat much chocolate?*
A: *I love chocolate, but I only eat a little. Do you eat much bread?*
B: *I eat very little bread. How many vegetables do you eat each week?*
A: *I eat a lot of vegetables. Do you drink many fizzy drinks each week?*
B: *No, not many. Do you drink much milk?*
A: *Yes, I drink a lot of milk. How much water do you drink?*
B: *I drink a lot. How much lemonade do you drink each week?*
A: *Not much. How much tea do you drink each week?*
B: *Too much, I'm afraid. Do you drink much orange juice?*
A: *I drink some, but not much. Do you drink much coffee?*
B: *No, I don't drink any coffee.*

**7** **Aim** To write about eating habits

- Ask Ss to use their answers in Ex. 6 to write a few sentences about their eating habits.
- Allow Ss time to complete the task.
- Check Ss' answers.
- Alternatively, this task can be assigned as HW and checked in the next lesson.

*Suggested Answer Key*

*I eat a lot of fruit, but I don't eat many eggs. I don't eat much meat and only a little chocolate. I eat very little bread. I really like vegetables, so I eat a lot. I drink a lot of milk and water. I drink some orange juice but I don't drink any coffee. I don't drink much lemonade but I do drink tea. Tea is my favourite and I drink too much of it.*

## *Grammar*
## Quantifiers

see pp. GR3-GR4

**3** Read the table. Find more examples in the dialogue in Ex. 2.

| COUNTABLE | UNCOUNTABLE |
|---|---|
| *How many sweets are there?* | *How much milk is there?* |
| *There are* **too many** *sweets.* | *There is* **too much** *milk.* |
| *There are* **a lot of** *sweets.* | *There is* **a lot of** *milk.* |
| *There are* **some/ a few** *sweets.* | *There is* **some/ a little** *milk.* |
| *There are (very)* **few** *sweets./ There aren't many sweets.* | *There's (very)* **little** *milk./ There isn't much milk.* |
| *Are there* **any** *sweets? There aren't* **any** *sweets./ There are* **no** *sweets.* | *Is there* **any** *milk? There isn't* **any** *milk./ There's* **no** *milk.* |

**4** Choose the correct word. Compare with your partner.

**1** A: How **many/much** butter have we got?
  B: Very **few/little**. Get some more.
**2** A: Is there **many/any** fruit?
  B: There are **much/a lot of** bananas and apples, but there aren't **some/many** oranges.
**3** A: How **much/many** eggs do we need for the omelette?
  B: Not **a lot/many**. Just three or four.
**4** A: There isn't **some/much** flour left in the cupboard. Only half a bag.
  B: OK. Get **some/few** more then.
**5** A: Do we need **some/any** tomatoes?
  B: Yes, there are only **a little/a few** left.
**6** A: There's very **few/little** cheese left.
  B: I'll get some. How **many/much** do you want?
**7** A: There's **many/no** bread left.
  B: Let's buy a loaf, then, and **some/any** biscuits.
**8** A: There's **too much/too many** sugar in my coffee. I can't drink it.
  B: Really? I always put **a lot of/much** sugar in my coffee.

### Study skills

**Learning grammar**
Make a note of your grammar mistakes and their corrections. This will help you to avoid making similar mistakes.

## *Listening*

**5** a) Julie is making a shopping list for a dinner party. Listen and put a tick (✓) next to the things she needs and a cross (✗) next to the things she doesn't need.

### Shopping List

| | |
|---|---|
| 2 kilos of chicken ✓ | 2 bottles of cola |
| 6 eggs ✗ | 1 carton of apple juice |
| 1 kilo of cheese | 1 bag of rice |
| 3 bags of crisps | 20 sausages |

b) Ask and answer questions, as in the example.

A: *How much chicken does she need?*
B: *She needs a lot – two kilos!*
  *How many eggs does she need?*
A: *She doesn't need any eggs.*

## *Speaking & Writing*

**6** Use the words below to ask and answer questions about your eating habits.

| EAT |
|---|
| • junk food • fruit • eggs • meat • chocolate • bread • vegetables |

| DRINK |
|---|
| • fizzy drinks • milk • water • lemonade • tea • orange juice • coffee |

• a lot of/lots • too much/many
• a few/a little • some
• very few/little

A: *How much junk food do you eat each week?/Do you eat much junk food?*
B: *I eat a little, but not too much.*

**7** Use your answers in Ex. 6 to write a few sentences about your eating habits. Read your sentences to the class.

Vocabulary Bank 2 p. VB6

29

# EATING OUT IN THE UK

There are many interesting places to eat a meal or grab a snack in the UK. Eating out in the UK offers much more than fast food restaurants, there's something to suit every taste.

## CHIPPIES

Fish 'n' chips is a popular and internationally famous English dish. It is deep fried fish in batter and fried, **chipped** potatoes with salt and vinegar. The restaurants and takeaway shops that sell it are traditionally called 'chippies'. You can also get a **range** of pies, sauces and side dishes with chips so you can choose your favourite combinations such as fish, chips and **mushy** peas or cheese and onion pie, chips and gravy.

## TRADITIONAL CAFÉS

Many Britons have lunch or a snack at a café. They serve delicious sandwiches, salads and hot snacks such as soup or jacket potatoes. There is also a wide range of cooked meals to choose from. You can also get tea, coffee and cold drinks as well as baked goods like cakes and biscuits.

### Did you know?

British people spend £42 billion on average per year on eating out.

## ETHNIC RESTAURANTS

Britain is a multi-cultural society and the cuisine shows this. The three most popular **ethnic** cuisines are Indian, Chinese and Italian. Indian restaurants serve chicken, prawns or meat with rice and a variety of curry sauces, such as chicken tikka masala. Chinese food is Cantonese with dishes like sweet and **sour** pork, chicken with cashew nuts and beef in black bean sauce. The most popular Italian dishes are pizza, spaghetti bolognese, and lasagna.

### Check these words

grab a snack, suit every taste, dish, deep fried, batter, chipped, vinegar, pie, sauce, side dish, mushy peas, gravy, ethnic cuisine, jacket potato, baked goods

**1** How often do you eat out? Where do you usually go?

**2**  a)  Look at the pictures and the headings in the text. What kind of food do you think you can get at each of these places? Listen and read to find out.

  b)  Read again and replace the words in bold with words from the text.

**1** **It** is England's most famous dish.
**2** **They** are Italian dishes most people like.
**3** The British often have a snack **there**.
**4** You can buy fish 'n' chips **there**.
**5** They serve **these** at cafés.
**6** You can usually eat **them** in an Indian restaurant.

  c)  Match the words in bold with their meanings: *variety, bitter, soft, cut into long thin pieces, from another country.*

**3** Use words from the Check these words box to complete the sentences.

**1** The British often grab a snack such as a sandwich for lunch.
**2** The restaurant serves a variety of dishes to suit every taste.
**3** Fish 'n' chips is a traditional British dish.
**4** Indian is one of the most popular ethnic cuisines in the UK.

**4** Tell your partner one thing you remember about each type of place to eat out.

**5** What kinds of places to eat out are there in your country? What kinds of food and drinks can you get there? Write short texts. Tell the class.

**1** **Aim** **To introduce the topic**

Ask Ss how often they eat out and where they like to go to eat. Elicit answers from Ss around the class and encourage a discussion.

*Suggested Answer Key*

*My family and I eat out once a week, usually at the weekend. We love Italian food so we often go to an Italian restaurant for pizza or spaghetti. I also like to go for a snack with my friends two or three times a week after school. We usually go to a local café.*

**2 a)** **Aim** **To predict the content of text, to read and listen for specific information**

- Draw Ss' attention to the pictures and the headings in the text. Explain/Elicit the meaning of any unknown words. Ask Ss to guess what kind of foods you can eat at each of the places. Help Ss if necessary. Say various foods for Ss to decide where each is served *(e.g. chippies – chips, café – sandwiches and cakes, ethnic restaurants – curry)*.
- Play the recording. Ss listen and read the text in their books.
- Elicit Ss' answers.

**Answer Key**

**Chippies:** *fish 'n' chips, pies, sauces, mushy peas, chips, gravy*
**Traditional cafés:** *sandwiches, salads, soup, jacket potatoes, cooked meals, tea, coffee, cold drinks, baked goods, cakes, biscuits*
**Ethnic restaurants:** *Indian food (chicken, prawns or meat with rice and a variety of curry sauces e.g. chicken tikka masala), Chinese food (sweet and sour pork, chicken with cashew nuts, beef in black bean sauce), Italian food (pizza, spaghetti bolognese, lasagna).*

**b)** **Aim** **To read for specific information**

- Explain the task.
- Allow Ss two minutes to complete the task.
- Check Ss' answers.

**Answer Key**

1   *Fish 'n' chips*
2   *Pizza, spaghetti bolognese and lasagna*
3   *(at a) café*
4   *(at) chippies*
5   *sandwiches, salads, hot snacks, soup, jacket potatoes, cooked meals, tea, coffee, cold drinks, baked goods, cakes, biscuits*
6   *chicken, prawns or meat with rice and a variety of curry sauces e.g. chicken tikka masala*

- Explain/Elicit the meaning of words in the *Check these words box* or ask Ss to look them up in their dictionaries.

*Suggested Answer Key*

***grab a snack (phr):*** *to get sth light to eat when in a hurry*
***suit every taste (phr):*** *to cater to everyone's preferences*
***dish (n):*** *food prepared in a certain way*
***deep fried (adj):*** *cooked in a large amount of oil*
***batter (n):*** *a mixture of milk, eggs and flour*
***chipped (pp):*** *cut into chip shapes*
***vinegar (n):*** *acetic acid used to flavour food*
***pie (n):*** *meat, vegetables or fruit baked in pastry*
***sauce (n):*** *a tasty liquid served with food*
***side dish (n):*** *a portion of food that accompanies a main meal*
***mushy peas (n):*** *a side dish of very soft peas*
***gravy (n):*** *a dark brown sauce served with meat dishes*
***ethnic cuisine (n):*** *cooking from another country that is very different from our own*
***jacket potato (n):*** *a potato baked in its skin in the oven*
***baked goods (pl n):*** *food that is baked in an oven e.g. bread, biscuits, etc*

**c)** **Aim** **To expand vocabulary/To match words from a text to their meanings**

- Explain the task.
- Give Ss time to complete the task.
- Check Ss' answers.

**Answer Key**

| | |
|---|---|
| **variety** = *range* | **cut into long thin pieces** = *chipped* |
| **bitter** = *sour* | **from another country** = *ethnic* |
| **soft** = *mushy* | |

**3** **Aim** **To consolidate new vocabulary**

- Ask Ss to look at the **Check these words** box again and use the words to complete the sentences.
- Ss complete the task.
- Check Ss' answers.

**4** **Aim** **To consolidate information in a text**

- Ask Ss to go through the text quickly, then close their books and try to tell their partner one thing about each place.
- Ask pairs to tell the class what they remember.

*Suggested Answer Key – see p. 32(T)*

**5** **Aim** **To personalise the topic/To describe places to eat out in your country**

- Ask Ss to think about the various places where people eat out in their country and what types of food and drinks people can order there.
- Ss, in groups, complete the task.
- Ask various Ss to read out their texts in class. Alternatively, assign the task as HW and Ss read their texts in the next lesson.

*Suggested Answer Key – see p. 32(T)*

**1** **Aim** **To introduce the topic**

Draw Ss' attention to the menu and explain/elicit any unknown words. Ask Ss what they usually have for breakfast, lunch and dinner. Ask them if any of the things they have are on the menu. Elicit answers from Ss around the class.

**Suggested Answer Key**

*For breakfast, I usually have orange juice and a bowl of cereal. For lunch, I have a sandwich. For dinner, my mum cooks soup and meat or fish with boiled potatoes and a salad.*
*Included in the menu: orange juice, sandwich, salad*

**2** **a)** **Aim** **To present situational language**

Play the recording. Ss listen and repeat chorally or individually. Check Ss' pronunciation.

**b)** **Aim** **To identify speakers in a situational dialogue**

- Draw Ss' attention to the phrases/sentences and ask them which ones a customer and a waiter would say.
- Draw Ss' attention to the dialogue. Play the recording. Ss listen and read the dialogue.
- Check Ss' answers.

**Answer Key**

**Waiter:**
*Are you ready to order or do you need a few more minutes?*
*Would you like any side orders?*
*And what would you like to drink?*
**Customer:**
*Not for me, thank you.*
*I'd like a glass of orange juice, please.*

**c)** **Aim** **To read for specific information**

Ask Ss to read the dialogue again then elicit what they order.

**Answer Key**

*Carl orders scrambled eggs on toast, chips and a glass of orange juice. Anna orders a cheese omelette and a cup of coffee.*

**3** **Aim** **To learn synonymous phrases**

- Draw Ss' attention to the sentences and elicit/explain any unknown words.
- Ask Ss to read the dialogue again and find the sentences which have the same meaning.
- Give Ss enough time to complete the task.
- Check Ss' answers.

**Answer Key**

*We can order now. – I think we're ready.*
*What about you? – And for you?*
*I don't want a side order, thanks. – Not for me, thank you.*
*That's correct. – That's right.*

## Pronunciation

**4** **Aim** **To pronounce /n/ and /ŋ/**

- Draw Ss' attention to the table and explain the task.
- Play the recording. Ss listen and check the sounds in the table.
- Check Ss' answers.
- Play the recording again for Ss to repeat chorally or individually. Check Ss' pronunciation.

**Suggested Answer Key**

|       | /n/ | /ŋ/ |        | /n/ | /ŋ/ |
|-------|-----|-----|--------|-----|-----|
| thin  | ✓   |     | tin    | ✓   |     |
| thing |     | ✓   | tongue |     | ✓   |
| king  |     | ✓   | ton    | ✓   |     |

## Speaking

**5** **Aim** **To role play ordering a meal at a café**

- Ask Ss to work in groups of three; one waiter and two customers.
- Go through the menu and the plan with Ss eliciting/explaining any words where necessary.
- In groups, Ss practise their dialogue. Go around the class monitoring Ss' work and helping where necessary.
- Ask groups to act out their dialogue in class.

**Suggested Answer Key**

A: *Hello. Are you ready to order or do you need a few more minutes?*
B: *I think we're ready. Can I have a full English breakfast, please?*
A: *Sure. What about you?*
C: *I'd like a burger and chips.*
A: *OK. Would you like any side orders?*
B: *Not for me, thank you.*
C: *A mixed salad for me, please.*
A: *And what would you like to drink?*
B: *I'd like a coffee, please.*
C: *A tea for me, please.*
A: *OK. So that's a full English breakfast, a burger and chips, a mixed salad, a coffee and a tea.*
B: *That's correct. Thank you.*

## Ordering food in a café

**1** What do you usually have for breakfast/lunch/dinner? Are any of these foods/drinks on Ruby's menu?

**2** a) 🎧 **Listen and say.**

- Are you ready to order or do you need a few more minutes?
- Would you like any side orders?
- Not for me, thank you.
- And what would you like to drink?
- I'd like a glass of orange juice, please.

b) **The sentences above appear in a dialogue at a café. Who says each: *a customer/the waiter*?**
🎧 **Listen, read and check.**

| | |
|---|---|
| Waiter: | Hello. Are you ready to order or do you need a few more minutes? |
| Carl: | I think we're ready … erm, can I have scrambled eggs on toast, please? |
| Waiter: | Sure. And for you, madam? |
| Anna: | I'd like a cheese omelette. |
| Waiter: | OK. Would you like any side orders? |
| Carl: | Erm … yes, chips, please. |
| Anna: | Not for me, thank you. |
| Waiter: | And what would you like to drink? |
| Carl: | I'd like a glass of orange juice, please. |
| Anna: | A cup of coffee for me, please. |
| Waiter: | OK. So that's scrambled eggs on toast, chips, a cheese omelette, a glass of orange juice and a cup of coffee. |
| Carl: | That's right. Thank you. |

c) **What do Carl and Anna order?**

**3** Find sentences in the dialogue which mean:
*We can order now. – What about you? – I don't want a side order, thanks. – That's correct.*

## Pronunciation: /n/, /ŋ/

**4** 🎧 **Listen and check (✓) the correct boxes. Listen again and say.**

| | /n/ | /ŋ/ | | /n/ | /ŋ/ |
|---|---|---|---|---|---|
| thin | | | tin | | |
| thing | | | tongue | | |
| king | | | ton | | |

## Speaking

**5** Work in groups of three. Take roles and act out a dialogue at Ruby's ordering lunch. Use the menu and the plan.

| A | B & C |
|---|---|
| Ask if customers are ready to order. | → B replies & orders food. |
| Ask what C wants. | ← C replies. |
| Ask if customers want side orders. | ← B&C reply. |
| Ask what customers want to drink. | ← B&C reply. |
| Repeat customer's order. | ← B confirms order. |

Outside it's boiling hot, but customers at **0)** ........ restaurant are **sipping** hot drinks and wearing thick coats! *Chillout* is in Dubai and it's a very unusual restaurant. Inside it's – 5˚C and nearly **1)** ........ there is made of ice. It has 40,000 tons of ice in it and it has ice walls, ice tables, ice chairs and ice curtains. The **customers** eat from ice plates and drink from ice glasses. **2)** ........ is even an 'ice gallery' of Dubai's **landmarks**.

Before the customers go into the restaurant, the **staff** give **3)** ........ coats, gloves and shoes so that they are warm enough to sit in the cold dining room. They wait in the Buffer zone for **4)** ........ minutes. This is a room that is cooler than outside, **5)** ........ warmer than the dining room. This way, their bodies can get used to the cold slowly. **6)** ........ the waiters show the customers to their table and serve them fruit juice or hot chocolate.

*Chillout* has a great **variety** of salads, cheese, sandwiches, ice cream, and healthy fruit drinks, as well as hot main dishes. Most of the customers only stay for about thirty to forty minutes, though. That's long **7)** ........ in the freezing cold! Those who work in the restaurant need to leave the place at **regular** intervals or else they **freeze**.

If you ever go to Dubai, why not cool down at this restaurant? But don't leave your food for too long! It gets cold **8)** ........ quickly.

| 0 | **(A)** this | B the | C that |
|---|---|---|---|
| 1 | A any | B everything | C each |
| 2 | A That | B It | C There |
| 3 | A they | B them | C their |
| 4 | A a few | B a little | C a lot |
| 5 | A but | B and | C so |
| 6 | A After | B When | C Then |
| 7 | A too | B enough | C much |
| 8 | A very | B much | C so |

**Check these words**

boiling hot, customer, sip, thick coat, ice, curtain, landmark, staff, get used to, waiter, serve, main dish, freezing cold, regular interval, cool down

### Reading & Listening

**1** What's your favourite restaurant? What do you like about it? What can you eat there? Tell the class.

**2** Look at the pictures of an unusual restaurant and read the first sentence of the text. Where do you think it is? What is unusual about it? Read to find out.

**3** Read again. Choose the best answer *A*, *B* or *C* for each space. Compare your answers with your partner.

## Reading & Listening

**1** **Aim** **To introduce the topic**

Ask Ss to say what their favourite restaurant is, what they like about it and what they can eat there.

### Suggested Answer Key

*My favourite restaurant is La Siesta. It has excellent food and it isn't expensive. You can eat tortillas, paella, various meat dishes and salads there.*

**2** **Aim** **To predict the content of a text and read for gist**

- Ask Ss to look at the pictures and read the first sentence of the text. Elicit answers to the questions from Ss around the class.
- Allow Ss time to read the text to check their answers.

### Suggested Answer Key

*The restaurant seems to have ice walls and furniture. It may be in Sweden or Russia. The customers are having drinks and wearing warm clothes. It must be very cold there.*

**3** **Aim** **To read for lexico-grammatical structure**

- Explain the task and ask Ss to check that the sentence after each gap follows on smoothly and makes sense. Check Ss' answers. Ask Ss to say which words helped them decide.
- Allow time for Ss to complete the task.
- Ss compare their answers with their partner.

### Answer Key

| | | | |
|---|---|---|---|
| 1  B | 3  C | 5  A | 7  B |
| 2  C | 4  A | 6  C | 8  A |

- Explain/Elicit the meaning of the words in the **Check these words** box.

### Suggested Answer Key

**boiling hot (adj):** *being at a very high temperature*
**customer (n):** *person who buys sth*
**sip (v):** *to drink in small mouthfuls*
**thick coat (n):** *a warm heavy garment worn outside over other clothes*
**ice (n):** *frozen water*
**curtain (n):** *a piece of material hung over windows*
**landmark (n):** *a building or feature which a place is famous for*
**staff (n):** *employees; people working e.g. in a shop*
**get used to (phr):** *to become accustomed to*
**waiter (n):** *a person who serves food in a restaurant*
**serve (v):** *to bring food and drink to sb*
**main dish (n):** *the main course in a meal*
**freezing cold (adj):** *being at a very low temperature*
**regular interval (n):** *an evenly spaced short break*
**cool down (phr v):** *to become less hot*

### BACKGROUND INFORMATION

**Dubai** is a large territory almost 4,000 km2 in size in the UAE. It is one of the seven emirates that make up the United Arab Emirates. It is in the Persian Gulf and has a population of 2.2 million people. It is a rich territory because of the oil industry and it is famous for its shopping malls and luxury hotels.

---

## Suggested Answers for Exs 4 & 5 on p. 30

### Ex. 4

*At a chippy you can get fish 'n' chips. At a café there's a wide variety of hot snacks and cooked meals. At an ethnic restaurant you can try ethnic cuisine.*

### Ex. 5

#### Traditional Restaurants

*Many Polish people eat at traditional restaurants. Here you can eat home-cooked dishes such as 'Kotlet schabowy' which is pork cutlet in breadcrumbs and different types of stew such as goulash with kasha.*

#### Seafood Restaurants

*They are very popular especially along the coast. You can try sole with prawns in a red pepper sauce or crispy goatfish. They are both delicious.*

**4 a)** **Aim** To practise new vocabulary

- Ask Ss to look at the *Check these words* box again and use some of the words to complete the sentences.
- Allow time for Ss to complete the task.
- Check Ss' answers.

**b)** **Aim** To expand vocabulary/To match words from a text to their meanings

- Explain the task.
- Give Ss time to complete the task.
- Check Ss' answers.

***Answer Key***

**employees** = staff
**even** = regular
**drinking slowly** = sipping
**famous buildings** = landmarks
**feel very cold** = freeze
**clients** = customers
**range** = variety

**5** **Aim** To present and practise new vocabulary

- Explain the task and ask a S to read out the example.
- Allow time for Ss to complete the task.
- Check Ss' answers by asking individual Ss to read out their sentences.

***Suggested Answer Key***

A friendly waiter always comes to **take your order**.
Waiters **show you to your table**.
Shall we **ask** the waiter **for the menu**? I'm hungry.
I'd like to leave now. Let's **pay the bill**.
When I get good service, I always **leave a tip**.
This restaurant is usually busy on Saturdays, so it's a good idea to **book a table**.

## Grammar

**6 a)** **Aim** To present *too* and *enough*

- Go through the theory box with Ss and explain the theory. Explain that we use *too* with an adjective or adverb to show that there is more of sth than is needed and that we use an adjective or adverb with *enough* or *enough* and a noun to show that there is as much of sth as needed.
- Ask Ss to find examples of *too* and *enough* in the text.

***Answer Key***

warm enough, long enough, too long

**b)** **Aim** To practise *too* and *enough*

- Explain the task.
- Allow time for Ss to complete the task.
- Check Ss' answers.

**7 a)** **Aim** To listen and read for general understanding

- Play the recording.

- Ss listen and read the dialogue.
- Elicit/Explain any unknown words.

**b)** **Aim** To act out dialogues making a booking

- Ask Ss to work in pairs and take the roles of a restaurant employee and a customer.
- Go through the prompts with Ss, and ask Ss to use them to act out dialogues using the one in Ex. 7a as a model.
- Go around the class monitoring the activity and helping where necessary.
- Ask some pairs to act out their dialogue in class.

***Suggested Answer Key***

A: Hello. Chillout Restaurant.
B: I'd like to book a table for four for Sunday lunch, please.
A: Certainly, madam. What time?
B: 1:30, please.
A: That's fine. Can I take your name, please?
B: Yes, it's Grimes. That's G-R-I-M-E-S.
A: OK. See you on Sunday.

A: Hello. Pete's Restaurant.
B: I'd like to book a table for two for next Friday, please.
A: Certainly, sir. What time?
B: Nine o'clock, please.
A: That's fine. Can I take your name, please?
B: Yes, it's Brentwood. That's B-R-E-N-T-W-O-O-D.
A: OK. See you on Friday.

## Speaking & Writing

**8 a)** **Aim** To personalise the topic

- Play the recording. Ss listen and follow the text in their books.
- Ask Ss if they would like to visit the restaurant in Dubai and to explain why (not).
- Encourage Ss to express their views and stimulate a discussion.

***Suggested Answer Key***

Yes, I would like to visit the ice restaurant in Dubai because it's an unusual place. I would enjoy eating there in my thick coat./No, I wouldn't like to visit Chillout because I don't think I would enjoy eating my food while I feel cold. Also, I like my food really hot and that seems difficult in Chillout!

**b)** **Aim** To write about a restaurant

- Ask Ss to think of an unusual restaurant and to write sentences about it. Ss can work in pairs.
- Allow Ss time to complete the task.
- Ask individual Ss to read out their sentences in class.

***Suggested Answer Key***

My restaurant is called "Underwater". It is a restaurant 5 metres underwater. It has glass walls and a glass roof so customers can see out. Outside, there are a lot of colourful fish. They come close to the walls and look at the people. I think it is a bit strange to eat there, but I'm sure everyone can have a great time.

**4  a)** Use words from the  box to complete the sentences.

1  It's **boiling hot** in Dubai in the summer.
2  A lot of the customers at *Chillout* **sip** hot chocolate to keep warm.
3  Customers at *Chillout* have to wear a **thick coat** to keep warm while they eat.
4  The Buffer zone helps customers to **get used to** the cold.
5  Most customers don't stay in the restaurant for long because it's **freezing cold**!

**b)** Match the words in bold with their meanings: *employees, even, drinking slowly, famous buildings, feel very cold, clients, range.*

**5**  Match the words.
🎧 Listen and check. Use each phrase to write a sentence of your own.

| | | | | | |
|---|---|---|---|---|---|
| 1 | b | serve | a | the bill |
| 2 | g | take | b | customers |
| 3 | f | show you | c | the menu |
| 4 | c | ask for | d | a tip |
| 5 | a | pay | e | a table |
| 6 | d | leave | f | to your table |
| 7 | e | book | g | your order |

*Waiters* **serve customers** *hot chocolate at* Chillout.

## Grammar
### Too – Enough
see p. GR4

**6  a)** Read the theory box. Find examples in the text.

- *too* + **adjective/adverb** (more than someone needs or wants) *His steak is* **too salty**. (He can't eat it.) *The waiter speaks* **too quickly** *for me to understand.* (I can't understand him.)
- **adjective/adverb** + *enough* / *enough* + **noun** (as much as someone wants or needs) *Is your soup* **hot enough?** (Is it OK?) *Don't worry. We've got* **enough money** *to pay the bill!* (We can pay it.)

**b)** Fill in *too* or *enough*.

1  The service is **too** slow in this restaurant.
2  Is your coffee sweet **enough**?
3  That new restaurant is **too** expensive for us to afford to eat there.
4  This chicken is **too** spicy. I don't like it.
5  There isn't **enough** oil in the salad.

## Making a restaurant booking

**7  a)** 🎧 Listen and read.

A:  Hello, Maddison's Restaurant.
B:  I'd like to book a table for six for Saturday night, please.
A:  Certainly, madam. What time?
B:  8:30, please.
A:  That's fine. Can I take your name, please?
B:  Yes, it's Walton. That's W – A – L – T – O – N.
A:  OK. See you on Saturday.

**b)** Use the words to act out similar dialogues.

*Chillout* – four – Sunday lunch – 1:30 – Grimes

*Pete's* – two – next Friday – 9:00 – Brentwood

## Speaking & Writing

**8  a)** **THINK!** 🎧 Listen to and read the text in Ex. 2. Would you like to visit the ice restaurant in Dubai? Why (not)? Tell the class.

**b)** Think of your own strange restaurant. In three minutes write a few sentences. Read them to the class.

▶ Vocabulary Bank 2 p. VB7  33

# 2f Healthy eating

People often say 'You are what you eat' and we all know that to be healthy we need to eat healthy food. What is really healthy, though?

**1** All fruit juices **contain** high amounts of sugar. Some juices have only very low **amounts** of fruit in them – and as much sugar as a glass of cola or a chocolate bar.

**2** It's true that salads are full of vitamins and minerals. Creamy mayonnaise-based salad dressings, however, can contain a lot of fat, sugar and salt. To enjoy a healthy, **tasty** salad at home, make a dressing by adding lemon juice or vinegar to a small amount of olive oil instead of using heavy mayonnaise.

**3** Food companies like using the words 'fat-free' or 'low-fat' on their labels. Unfortunately they often **replace** the fat in these 'healthier' products with salt and sugar to give them flavour. It's a good idea to read the whole label.

**4** People think chocolate is bad for them, but it has some **benefits**. Good quality dark chocolate helps protect your heart by **lowering** your cholesterol. Eating chocolate also has a positive effect on how we feel. All chocolate is high in fat, though, so you shouldn't eat it after every meal.

**5** Eggs are a good source of protein and vitamins. Frying an egg though, is less healthy than boiling them. A fried egg contains around 30% more fat than a boiled or poached egg. If you prefer fried eggs, try frying them in olive oil instead of butter.

**6** Red meat such as beef can be part of a healthy diet. Including red meat in a meal a couple of times a week helps your body to get enough iron and protein. Just make sure you **trim off** the fat and buy only **lean** meat.

> **Check these words**
>
> contain, vitamin, mineral, creamy, salad dressing, vinegar, olive oil, fat-free, low-fat, label, flavour, benefit, lower, cholesterol, source, iron, protein, lean

## Vocabulary
### Food/drinks

**1** Which of the foods/drinks (1-8) contain the following? Decide in pairs.

- sugar • fat • minerals • iron
- protein • vitamins • salt

🎧 Listen and read to find out.

**2 a)** Read the text and match headings A-G to paragraphs 1-6. There is one extra heading.

A  CHOOSE THE LIGHTER OPTION    B  REMOVE THE BAD BITS

C  ASK YOURSELF WHAT'S IN YOUR GLASS

D  ENJOY A SWEET SENSATION    E  SOME FAT IS GOOD FOR YOU

F  COOK WITH A HEALTHIER FAT

G  ALWAYS CHECK THE INGREDIENTS



▶ Vocabulary Bank 2  p. VB8

## Vocabulary

**1** **Aim** **To present new vocabulary**

- Go through the food/drinks 1-8 in the pictures and then read out the items in the list.
- Explain/Elicit the meanings of the words and then ask Ss to decide with their partner which food/drinks contain which of the items.
- Elicit answers from various pairs around the class and then play the recording for Ss to listen and check their answers. *sugar – fat – minerals – iron – protein – vitamins – salt*

### Answer Key

1   *red meat – iron and protein*
2   *fruit juice – sugar*
3   *poached egg – protein and vitamins*
4   *chocolate – sugar and fat*
5   *salad – vitamins and minerals*
6   *cola – sugar*
7   *fried egg – protein, vitamins, fat*
8   *mayonnaise – fat, sugar and salt*

### BACKGROUND INFORMATION

**sugar:** sweet substance which occurs naturally in food; when we eat it the body converts it into energy
**fat:** substance contained in meat, cheese, butter which forms an energy store in our body
**minerals:** substances such as salt found in food/drink
**iron:** element in our blood and in food
**protein:** substance in meat, eggs, milk
**vitamins:** substances we need to remain healthy found in food, needed as a nutrient in small amounts by an organism
**salt:** substance in the form of white powder or crystals; it occurs naturally in sea water

**2 a)** **Aim** **To read for general comprehension**

- Explain the task and ask Ss to read the headings and then give them time to read the text again.
- Ss complete the task. Check Ss' answers. Ask Ss to justify their answers.

### Answer Key

1   *C (fruit juices, glass of cola)*
2   *A (healthy salad, instead of using heavy ...)*
3   *G (read the whole label)*
4   *D (chocolate, positive effect)*
5   *F (try frying them in olive oil instead of butter)*
6   *B (trim off fat, lean meat)*

- Explain/Elicit the meanings of the words in the **Check these words** box or ask Ss to look them up in their dictionaries.

### Suggested Answer Key

*contain (v): to have inside*
*vitamin (n): a natural substance in food needed for good health (e.g. vitamin A, B, C, etc)*
*mineral (n): a substance in food needed for good health (e.g. iron)*
*creamy (adj): having a thick smooth texture*
*salad dressing (n): a sauce for salads*
*vinegar (n): acetic acid used to flavour food*
*olive oil (n): a liquid made from olives and used in cooking*
*fat-free (adj): having no fat*
*low-fat (adj): having little fat*
*label (n): the piece of paper on a product that gives information about it*
*flavour (n): taste*
*benefit (n): advantage*
*lower (v): to reduce*
*cholesterol (n): a substance found in your blood (having too much of it could cause heart disease)*
*source (n): the place where you get sth from*
*iron (n): an element essential for good health which occurs in blood and food*
*protein (n): a substance found in food such as meat, eggs, fish cheese, etc that we need to grow and be healthy*
*lean (adj): not having very much fat*

34(T)

b) **Aim** **To expand vocabulary/To match words from a text to their meanings**

- Explain the task.
- Give Ss time to complete the task.
- Check Ss' answers.

**Answer Key**

*cut away* = trim off  *without fat* = lean
*taste* = flavour  *have inside* = contain
*quantities* = amounts  *delicious* = tasty
*substitute* = replace  *advantages* = benefits
*reducing* = lowering

## Grammar

**3** **Aim** **To present *-ing*/*to*-infinitive**

- Go through the theory box.
- Explain/elicit that we use the *-ing form* as the subject of a sentence, after **like**, **hate**, **dislike**, etc, after prepositions, after certain verbs *e.g. avoid*, *continue*, *deny*, etc, and with certain phrases *e.g. it's worth, can't stand*, etc.
- Explain/Elicit that the infinitive is the base form of the verb and that there are two kinds of infinitive forms: the *to-infinitive* and the *infinitive* without *to*. Explain that we use the *to-*infinitive to express purpose, after *would like, would prefer, would love*, after *too/enough*, and after certain verbs *e.g. ask, want, hope, promise*, etc.
- Explain that we use the *infinitive without to* after modal verbs and after the verbs *make* and *let*.
- Elicit any similar structures in Ss' L1.

*(Ss' own answers)*

**4** **Aim** **To practise *-ing*/*to*-infinitive**

Give Ss time to complete the task and then check Ss' answers. Ss justify their answers.

**Answer Key**

| | | | |
|---|---|---|---|
| 1 | have, cook | 5 | to eat, go, to buy |
| 2 | to order, make | 6 | to go, join |
| 3 | to help, preparing | 7 | to take, worrying |
| 4 | eat | 8 | to ask, helping |

**5** **Aim** **To practise *to*-infinitive and *-ing* form**

Point out that this exercise practises the use of *to-infinitive* or *-ing form* after certain verbs with a change in meaning. Give Ss time to complete the task and then check Ss' answers. Ask Ss to check in the Grammar Reference section for differences in meaning.

**Answer Key**

| | | | |
|---|---|---|---|
| 1 | to bake | 5 | to eat | 9 | to tell |
| 2 | adding | 6 | eating | 10 | telling |
| 3 | to go | 7 | to turn | | |
| 4 | shopping | 8 | meeting | | |

## Speaking & Writing

**6** **Aim** **To practise *(to)* infinitive and *-ing* form using personal examples**

- Explain the task. Give Ss time to complete the task, referring back to the theory box as necessary.
- Check Ss' answers.

**Suggested Answer Key**

2 *I don't mind helping with the housework.*
3 *I'm tired of eating the same food all the time.*
4 *I can't stand cooking eggs.*
5 *I can bake well.*
6 *I'd rather not try sushi.*

**7** **Aim** **To consolidate information in a text**

- Read the rubric aloud and then give Ss a three-minute time limit to write some sentences.
- Ask various Ss around the class to read their sentences aloud.

**Suggested Answer Key**

*I knew that fruit juice has a lot of sugar. I also knew that salads and eggs are healthy. I didn't know that good quality dark chocolate can lower your cholesterol.*

**b)** Match the words in bold with their meanings: *cut away, taste, quantities, substitute, reducing, without fat, have inside, delicious, advantages.*

## Grammar *-ing/to-*infinitive
see p. GR4

**3** Read the theory. Are there similar structures in your language?

> We use the **-ing form**:
> * as the subject of a sentence. *Eating vegetables is good for you.*
> * after **like, have, enjoy, don't mind, dislike, hate**. *I **like drinking** milk.*
> * after **avoid, appreciate, be used to, consider, continue, deny, fancy, go** (+ activity), **imagine, miss, save, suggest, practise, prevent, spend/waste** (time/money) **on**. *Do you **fancy eating** out?*
> * after prepositions. *How **about making** a cake?*
> * with the phrases **it's worth, can't stand, have difficulty, look forward to, can't help**. *I **can't stand eating** spicy foods.*
>
> We use the *to-*infinitive:
> * to express purpose. *He went out **to buy** some milk.*
> * after **would like, would prefer, would love**. *I'd **like to have** a steak, please.*
> * after **too/enough**. *It was **too** difficult for her **to learn** how to cook.*
> * after **ask, decide, explain, want, hope, expect, promise, refuse**, etc. *He **decided to order** takeaway.*
> **BUT make, let** and **modal verbs** take infinitive without to.
> *I **can't go** to the supermarket today.*
>
> Certain verbs take *to-*infinitive or *-ing* form with a difference in meaning. Compare:
> *Oh, no! I **forgot to buy** some tea.* (not remember)
> *I'll never **forget trying** sushi. I really liked it.* (recall)

**4** Choose the correct item.

1 A: What will we **to have/have** for dinner tonight?
   B: I may **to cook/cook** some pasta.
2 A: Would you like **to order/order** a takeaway?
   B: No. Let's **to make/make** some sandwiches.
3 A: You promised **to help/help** me with the household chores.
   B: I know, but I was very busy **to prepare/preparing** the food.
4 A: You mustn't **to eat/eat** so much junk food.
   B: I guess you are right.
5 A: There's nothing **to eat/eat**.
   B: Let's **to go/go** to the supermarket **to buy/buying** some food.
6 A: The doctor advised me **going/to go** on a diet.
   B: That's a good idea. You should also **join/to join** a gym.
7 A: I promised **to take/taking** her shopping, but I can't.
   B: There's no point **to worry/worrying** about it. I'll go.
8 A: Have you seen Tom? I want **to ask/asking** him if he fancies **to help/helping** me with the cooking.
   B: No, sorry. I haven't.

**5** Put the verbs in brackets into the *to-*infinitive or *-ing* form.

1 I tried ..................................... **(bake)** a cake, but I burnt it.
2 Try ..................................... **(add)** some salt. It'll taste better.
3 Oh no! I forgot ..................................... **(go)** to the market.
4 I'll never forget ..................... **(shop)** at the floating market in Thailand.
5 Let's stop ........................... **(eat)** here. This café looks nice.
6 Lisa stopped ............................... **(eat)** meat five years ago.
7 Did you remember ............................... **(turn)** the oven off?
8 I remember ........................... **(meet)** John at Claire's party.
9 I'm sorry ..................... **(tell)** you this, but this cake is awful.
10 Paul was sorry for ....................... **(tell)** her that she was an awful cook.

## Speaking & Writing

**6** Complete the sentences about you. Tell the class.

1 I like *eating out.*
2 I don't mind ................................................................
3 I'm tired of ................................................................
4 I can't stand ................................................................
5 I can ................................................................
6 I'd rather not ................................................................

**7** **THINK!** How much of the information in the text did you know? What did you learn from the text? In three minutes write a few sentences. Tell the class or your partner.

## Vocabulary
### Food preparation

**1** 🎧 Listen and say. What are these verbs in your language?

**2** Fill in the gaps in the recipe with verbs from Ex. 1. 🎧 Listen and check.

**Note:**
tbs = tablespoon     tsp = teaspoon

## Apple-Cinnamon Blini

| | |
|---|---|
| 1 large apple | 1/2 tsp baking soda |
| 1 tbs sugar | 1/2 tsp salt |
| 1 tsp cinnamon | 1 egg |
| 2 tbs butter | 3/4 cup sour cream |
| 1 cup flour | 1/4 cup milk |

- **1)** ...................... the apple, then **2)** ...................... it.
- **3)** ...................... the butter in a frying pan, then cook the apple slices in the butter for 4 minutes.
  - **4)** ...................... the flour, salt, baking soda, sugar and cinnamon together in a large bowl.
  - **5)** ...................... the egg with ½ cup of the sour cream and the milk, then **6)** ...................... it to the flour mixture.
  - **7)** ...................... in the cooked apple.
- Put spoonfuls of the mixture into a hot frying pan. **8)** ...................... for a few minutes on each side.
  - Serve warm with a teaspoonful of sour cream on top.

## Listening

**3** 🎧 Listen to Frank talking about a TV programme and for questions 1 to 5 tick (✓) the correct box *Yes* or *No*.

| | Yes | No |
|---|---|---|
| **1** Frank really enjoyed watching *Chef Jeff* last night. | | |
| **2** Chef Jeff went to a restaurant that only serves steak. | | |
| **3** Maria never eats meat. | | |
| **4** Chef Jeff closed down the restaurant so they could clean it. | | |
| **5** Once, Chef Jeff showed a Spanish chef how to cook paella. | | |

## Speaking
### Giving instructions

**4** 👥 Tell your partner how to make apple-cinnamon blinis. Use *First, Next, Then, Finally*.

*First, peel and slice the apple. Then, melt … . Next, … . Finally, … .*

## Vocabulary

**1** **Aim** **To introduce new vocabulary**

- Draw Ss' attention to the pictures.
- Play the recording. Ss listen and repeat chorally or individually. Check Ss' pronunciation.
- Elicit what the verbs are in their own language.

*(Ss' own answers)*

**2** **Aim** **To practise new vocabulary**

- Ask Ss to use the vocabulary from Ex. 1 to complete the recipe.
- Allow time for Ss to complete the task.
- Play the recording. Ss listen and check their answers.

*Answer Key*

| | | | |
|---|---|---|---|
| *1 Peel* | *3 Melt* | *5 Beat* | *7 Stir* |
| *2 slice* | *4 Mix* | *6 add* | *8 Fry* |

## Listening

**3** **Aim** **To listen for specific information**

- Explain the task and allow Ss time to read the statements.
- Play the recording. Ss listen and choose A or B.
- Check Ss' answers.

*Answer Key*

*1 No    2 No    3 No    4 Yes    5 Yes*

## Speaking

**4** **Aim** **To practise giving instructions**

- Ask Ss to work in pairs and to tell their partner how to make apple-cinnamon blini.
- Encourage Ss to use the conjunctions first, next, then, etc.
- Go around the classroom monitoring the activity.
- Ask some Ss to give instructions to the class.

*Suggested Answer Key*

*First, peel and slice the apple. Then, melt the butter in a frying pan and cook the apple slices in the butter for 4 minutes. Next, mix the flour, salt, baking soda and cinnamon together in a large bowl. Beat the egg with half a cup of the sour cream and the milk, and then add it to the flour mixture. Finally, stir in the cooked apple. Put spoonfuls of the mixture into a hot frying pan and fry for a few minutes on each side. Serve the blini warm with a teaspoonful of sour cream on top.*

**1** **Aim** **To present informal writing style**

- Go through the *Writing Tip* with Ss and explain when and why we use the informal writing style.
- Ask Ss to find examples in the email. Check Ss' answers.

*Answer Key*

*Hi, Great to hear from you!, (informal greeting) So, you want to know …, (everyday expression) Well, it's a traditional dish …, it's very popular …, It's very easy …, (short forms) Hope you can try it one day!, (omitted pronoun) How about you?, Write soon! (informal closing remarks)*

**2** **Aim** **To read for gist**

- Explain the task.
- Allow time for Ss to complete the task.
- Check Ss' answers.

*Answer Key*

A   3      B   1      C   2

**3** **Aim** **To practise new vocabulary**

- Elicit/Explain the meanings of the words.
- Explain the task.
- Allow time for Ss to complete the task.
- Check Ss' answers.

*Answer Key*

| | | |
|---|---|---|
| *1 spicy* | *3 creamy* | *5 sweet* |
| *2 salty* | *4 delicious* | |

**4** **Aim** **To analyse a rubric**

- Go through the *Study Skills* box with Ss, explaining the importance of reading rubrics carefully.
- Draw Ss' attention to the rubric and the underlined words.
- Explain the task.
- Allow time for Ss to complete the task.
- Check Ss' answers.

*Answer Key*

*1   an email*
*2   my English pen-friend*
*3   information about my favourite dish from my country (ingredients, how to make it and what it tastes like)*
*4   80-100 words*

**Writing**

**5** **Aim** **To write an email about a favourite dish**

- Go through the plan and brainstorm in class and write Ss' ideas on the board. Write these phrases on the board. Ask Ss to copy them and use them in their email.



- Ask Ss to use their ideas and the plan provided to write their email.
- Check Ss' work.
- Alternatively, this task can be assigned as HW and checked in the next lesson.

*Suggested Answer Key*

*Hi Georgia,*
*How are you? So, you want to know about my favourite dish from my country? Well, it's a dish called smažený sýr and it's very popular here in the Czech Republic.*
*Smažený sýr is fried cheese and it is very easy to make. First, cut a thick, even slice of Edam cheese. Then cover it in flour, dip it in beaten egg and roll it in breadcrumbs. Fry the cheese slice in oil until it is golden brown and serve with chips and tartar sauce. This is a delicious dish. You should try it!*
*How about you? What is your favourite dish?*
*Write soon!*
*Anna*

37(T)

## An email about a favourite dish

**1** Read the writing tip. Find examples of informal style in Maria's email.

### Writing Tip

**Using informal style**

When we write emails to friends or relatives, we use informal style. This includes informal greetings/closing remarks (*How are you? That's all for now!*), short forms (*It's delicious!* NOT: ~~It is~~) and everyday vocabulary and expressions (*How are things? How about you?*). We may also omit pronouns (*Hope you are well!*).

Hi James,

**1►** Great to hear from you! So, you want to know about my favourite dish from my country. Well, it's a traditional dish called Moqueca and it's very popular here in Brazil.

**2►** Moqueca is a spicy seafood dish with fish, onions, tomatoes, peppers, chilies, garlic and herbs. It's very easy to make. First, we chop the vegetables and fry them with the garlic and herbs. Then, we add the fish and boil everything slowly for about five minutes. We usually serve this stew with rice. This is a very tasty dish! Hope you can try it one day!

**3►** How about you? Do you have a favourite dish from your country?

Write soon,
Maria

**2** Read again and match the paragraphs to the headings.

| A | | closing remarks |
| B | | opening remarks & reason for writing |
| C | | description of how to make the dish |

### Study skills

**Understanding rubrics**

Always read rubrics carefully. They give you important information e.g. *who you are writing to, what you have to write, what you should write about, how many words you should write*. Make sure you include everything in the rubric in your piece of writing.

**4** Read the rubric and look at the underlined words. Then answer the questions.

This is <u>part of an email</u> from your <u>English pen-friend</u>, Georgia. <u>Write an email</u> in reply (80-100 words).
*I'm doing a <u>school project</u> about <u>food around the world</u>. What's your <u>favourite dish</u> from <u>your country</u>? What are the <u>ingredients</u>? <u>How do you make it</u>? <u>What</u> does it <u>taste like</u>?*

**1** What are you writing?
**2** Who are you writing to?
**3** What must you include?
**4** How many words should you write?

**3** Complete the sentences with the words in the list.

**1** It's a very ......................... dish with a lot of chili peppers in it.
**2** This dish is usually quite ................................ . It has a lot of salt in it.
**3** You can add yogurt and milk to the sauce to make it ................. .
**4** You must try this. It's absolutely ..............................!
**5** There's a lot of sugar in this dessert so it's very ................... .

### Writing (an email about a favourite dish)

**5** Write your reply to Georgia's email. Follow the plan below.

### Plan

Hi ...................... ,

**Para 1:** opening remarks, reason for writing, name of dish (*How are you? So, you want to know … . Well, it's a dish called … .*)

**Para 2:** type of dish, ingredients, how to make it, how you serve it (*It's a … dish. It's got … . First, we … . Then, … . We usually serve it … .*)

**Para 3:** closing remarks (*How about you? …*)

......................

# Food for Life!

## The Brain

The brain **commands** our nervous system and controls our behaviour. It uses 20% of the energy from the food we eat! The brain needs green vegetables, healthy fats, such as those in **oily** fish, and carbohydrates like cereals, bread and pasta.

## Muscles

The human body has over 600 muscles! Without them, we couldn't move, breathe, pump blood around our body or **digest** our food. To build and **repair** muscles, we need protein. We can find this in foods like meat, fish and eggs.

## The Skin

Our skin is the natural covering of our body. It protects us and gives us our **sense** of touch. Foods that are very good for our skin include fruit and vegetables, nuts, cereals and oily fish.

## Bones

The human skeleton has over 200 bones which **support** and protect our body. Calcium in dairy products like milk, cheese and yogurt keeps our bones healthy.

### Check these words

command, nervous system, control, behaviour, energy, fat, oily, carbohydrate, breathe, pump blood, digest, repair, muscle, protein, bone, support, protect, calcium, sense of touch

**1** In a minute write as many parts of the body as possible. Compare with your partner.

**2** **a)** Look at the headings in the text. Which foods are important for keeping these organs/parts of the body healthy? Listen and read to find out.

**b)** Match the words in bold with their meanings: *break down, controls, mend, feeling, containing fat, hold together*.

**3** Read again and make notes under the headings. Use your notes to tell your partner about each organ/body part.

| Organ/Body part | What to eat to keep it healthy |
|---|---|
| *brain* | *green vegetables, healthy fats, oily fish, cereals, bread, pasta* |

*Our brain commands … . To keep it healthy we should eat … .*

**4** **ICT** Do some Internet research about other organs/parts of the body and the food we should eat to keep them healthy *e.g. the heart, the eyes, liver, etc.* Write a few sentences about it, then tell the class.

**1** **Aim** **To brainstorm for topic-related vocabulary**

- Ask Ss to write as many words as possible related to the body.
- Allow Ss time to write their words and compare with a partner.
- Ask various Ss for their words. Write them on the board and check Ss' understanding by saying a word and asking Ss to point to the relevant part of the body.

**Suggested Answer Key**

*head, arm, leg, hand, foot, nose, ear, eye, shoulder, back, elbow, knee, mouth, chin, hair, finger, toe, nail, stomach, eyebrow, forehead*

**2 a)** **Aim** **To introduce the topic**

- Ask Ss to look at the headings in the text and to think about what kind of food is good for the four parts of the body.
- Elicit ideas from around the class.
- Play the recording. Ss listen and read the text to find out.

**Suggested Answer Key**

***The Brain:*** *green vegetables, oily fish, cereals, bread, pasta*
***Muscles:*** *meat, fish, eggs*
***Bones:*** *milk, cheese, yogurt*
***The Skin:*** *fruit, vegetables, nuts, cereals, oily fish*

- Explain/Elicit the meanings of the words in the **Check these words** box or ask Ss to look them up in their dictionaries.

**Suggested Answer Key**

***command (v):*** *to direct, to control*
***nervous system (n):*** *the network of nerves that runs through the body*
***control (v):*** *to have power over sth*
***behaviour (n):*** *the way sb acts*
***energy (n):*** *the power to be physically and mentally active*
***fat (n):*** *oily or greasy substance found in plants and animals that is very high in energy*
***oily (adj):*** *containing a lot of oil or fat*
***carbohydrate (n):*** *substance found in foods like cereals and potatoes that provides a lot of energy*
***breathe (v):*** *to take air in and out of the lungs*
***pump blood (phr):*** *(of the heart) to send blood around the body*
***digest (v):*** *(of the body) to break down the food we eat*
***repair (v):*** *to mend*
***muscle (n):*** *a tissue in the body that helps us move*
***protein (n):*** *a substance found in foods like meat and eggs that builds muscles*
***bone (n):*** *a hard part inside your body that is part of your skeleton*
***support (v):*** *to hold sth together*
***protect (v):*** *to take care of*
***calcium (n):*** *a substance found in foods like milk and cheese that is good for teeth and bones*
***sense of touch (n):*** *the ability to feel things*

**b)** **Aim** **To expand vocabulary/To match words from a text to their meanings**

- Explain the task.
- Give Ss time to complete the task.
- Check Ss' answers.

**Answer Key**

| | |
|---|---|
| ***break down*** = *digest* | ***feeling*** = *sense* |
| ***controls*** = *commands* | ***containing fat*** = *oily* |
| ***mend*** = *repair* | ***hold together*** = *support* |

**3** **Aim** **To read for specific information, to make notes under headings**

- Draw Ss' attention to the table.
- Ask Ss to read the text again and to make notes under the headings in the table.
- Allow Ss time to make their notes.
- Ss then work in pairs to tell each other about each part of the body.
- Go around the class monitoring Ss' work.
- Ask various Ss to perform the task in class.

**Suggested Answer Key**

| Organ/Body part | What to eat to keep it healthy |
|---|---|
| muscles | meat, fish, eggs |
| bones | milk, cheese, yogurt |
| the skin | fruit and vegetables, nuts, cereals, oily fish |

**Note:** Point out to Ss that our skin only gives us our sense of touch from the inner layer, the dermis, which contains our nerve endings that are receptors for cold, heat, pain and pressure.

**Suggested Answer Key**

*Our brain commands our nervous system and the way we behave. To keep it healthy we should eat green vegetables, oily fish and carbohydrates like cereals, bread and pasta.*
*The muscles are very important because they control our movements. Muscles need food that is high in protein, like meat, fish and eggs.*
*Bones give our bodies the support they need. To keep them healthy we should eat dairy products, including milk, cheese and yogurt.*
*Our skin protects our bodies and gives us our sense of touch. To keep it healthy we should eat a lot of fruit and vegetables as well as nuts, cereals and oily fish.*

**4** **Aim** **To give a presentation on healthy eating and body parts**

Explain the task and assign it for HW. Ss work in groups and do their research on the Internet, in encyclopaedias or other reference books, and present their findings in the next lesson.

***Suggested Answer Key – see p. 39(T)***

**Aim** **To consolidate vocabulary from the module**

- Divide the class into 2 teams. Each team takes turns writing or saying a sentence with one of the words/phrases in the list.
- Each correct sentence earns one point. If the sentence is incorrect, the team misses a turn.
- The team with the most points after all the words have been used wins.

**Suggested Answer Key**

*Menton is a* **resort** *town.*
*The restaurant has a* **staff** *of ten people who work in two shifts.*
*Apple pie is my favourite* **dessert.**
*Chicken is* **poultry.**
*This soup is very* **creamy.**
*You can find cola in the* **drinks aisle.**
*Milk and cheese are* **dairy products.**
*You can get some ice cream from the* **frozen food** *section.*
*You* **grill** *steaks on a barbecue.*
*This soup is too* **salty.** *There's a lot of salt in it.*
*Let's buy a big* **tub of ice cream.**
*You can buy a* **loaf of bread** *at the bakery.*
*Meat and fish contain* **protein.**
*A diner* **looks like** *a train carriage.*
*Pretzels and bagels are* **baked goods.**
*Waiters* **serve** *customers in a restaurant.*
*My favourite* **dish** *is fish 'n' chips.*
*I eat* **scrambled eggs** *for breakfast.*
**Customers** *wear thick coats at Chillout.*
*There's fried chicken on the* **menu.**
*Can you* **chop** *the onions for me?*
*The food was great. Let's* **pay the bill** *and go home.*
*I don't like* **spicy** *food like chili peppers.*
*Waiters* **show you to your table** *at this restaurant and then take your order.*

## Quiz

**Answer Key**

1  145
2  *in the dairy products section*
3  *a fish 'n' chip shop or restaurant*
4  *dishes from a specific country or culture*
5  *-5°C*
6  *in Dubai*
7  *iron and protein*
8  *over 200*
9  *It covers our body, protects us and gives us our sense of touch.*
10  *dairy products like milk, cheese and yogurt*

Ss prepare their quiz in groups. Ask Ss to go through the pages of Module 2 and select information to compile their quiz. Ask groups to exchange quizzes, to do them, then to check their answers.

**Suggested Answer Key**

**Quiz**

1  *What are the most popular ethnic cuisines in the UK? (Indian, Chinese and Italian)*
2  *What are baked goods? (cakes and biscuits)*
3  *What are the tables and chairs in Chillout made of? (ice)*
4  *What do the letters 'tsp' stand for? (teaspoon)*
5  *What is the healthiest type of chocolate? (Good quality dark chocolate)*
6  *How many muscles are in the human body? (over 600)*
7  *When does the Lemon Festival in Menton take place? (every February to March)*
8  *What kinds of food are carbohydrates? (cereals, bread and pasta)*
9  *What do we need to build and repair muscles? (protein)*
10  *In which section can you usually find pears in a supermarket? (the fruit and vegetables section)*

---

**Suggested Answer for Ex. 4 on p. 38**

### Ex. 4

*The eyes are the body's camera (The light passes through the lens and the eye then 'records' a picture on the back part, called the retina. The retina sends a message to the brain and the brain tells you what you actually see.) For healthy eyes we should eat food with lots of vitamins, like carrots, spinach, oranges, kiwi fruit and tomatoes.*
*The heart pumps about 70 millilitres of blood around our bodies with each beat. That's about 1,900 gallons of blood per day! Green vegetables like spinach, olive oil and oily fish, nuts and oats are all good for the heart.*

*Healthy hair needs foods like beans, chicken, eggs and nuts. They provide proteins and minerals to keep our hair shiny and strong. It protects our head from extremes of heat and cold.*

### Activity for weaker classes

Read out the suggested answer. Ask Ss to keep notes, then write three sentences using their notes.

## 1 Put the words into the correct categories. Add one more word to each category.

- broccoli • beef • apple pie • lamb • milk
- banana • coffee • cabbage • chicken
- chocolate brownie • strawberries • cola
- tea • salmon • ice cream • waffles

broccoli banana, cabbage, strawberries (grapes)

beef, lamb, chicken, salmon (trout)

apple pie, chocolate brownie, ice cream, waffles (cherry pie)

milk, coffee, cola, tea (orange juice)

## 2 Choose the correct words.

The drive-through restaurant is one of the USA's great traditions. It's unusual because the **1) waiters/customers** don't usually go inside! They drive up to a speaker outside the restaurant, **2) grab/order** their food from a worker and get it from a window. Customers can go inside and eat at a **3) table/booth**, but taking your food to go is more **4) famous/popular**. Drive-throughs are very popular in the USA and sell a wide **5) variety/type** of **6) extra/fast** food, like burgers and fries.

## 3 Circle the odd word out.

1 tub – carton – jar – (jam)
2 (protein) – bones – muscles – skin
3 boil – fry – (order) – grill
4 pepper – onion – (prawn) – celery
5 salty – (fried) – sweet – creamy

### Collocations

## 4 Fill in: *side, fast, top, thick, scrambled, cherry, frying, French, freezing, cold.*

1 cold drinks
2 top chef
3 scrambled eggs
4 side order
5 frying pan
6 thick coat
7 fast food
8 cherry pie
9 French toast
10 freezing cold

### Prepositions

## 5 Choose the correct preposition.

1 Visitors buy local products made **of/from** oranges.
2 There's a great choice **of/from** snacks to choose **of/from**.
3 *Ann's* is famous **for/of** its delicious cherry pie.
4 Tables inside *Chillout* are made **of/from** ice.
5 Serve the stew **by/with** rice.

**In teams, make sentences. Use words/phrases from the list below. Each correct sentence gets one point. The team with the most points wins.**

- resort • staff • dessert • poultry • creamy
- drinks aisle • dairy products • frozen food • grill
- salty • tub of ice cream • loaf of bread • protein
- looks like • baked goods • serve • dish
- scrambled eggs • customers • menu • chop
- pay the bill • spicy • show you to your table

## Quiz

**Read through Module 2 and answer the questions. Now write a quiz of your own. Give it to your partner. Check his/her answers.**

1 How many tons of fruit do they use in the Menton Lemon Festival?
2 In which section can you find yogurt in a supermarket?
3 What is a chippy?
4 What can you eat in an ethnic restaurant ?
5 What is the temperature inside *Chillout*?
6 Where's *Chillout*?
7 What does red meat contain?
8 How many bones are there in the human body?
9 What does our skin do?
10 What foods have a lot of calcium in them?

# PIZZA

Pizza, as we know it today, (oven-baked flatbread covered with tomato sauce) originated in 18th century Naples, Italy. Food historians agree that oven-baked flatbread dishes were eaten in many Mediterranean countries long before the 18th century, but it was in Naples that people first began topping flatbread with tomatoes and modern pizza was born!

The story of how tomatoes came to be added to flatbread is an interesting one. Tomatoes are native to South America and were introduced to Europe sometime during the 16th century. For years, people believed that tomatoes were poisonous and so they only grew the plants for decoration. Sometime in the 1700s, though, the inventive (and most probably starving) poor citizens of Naples tried adding the 'deadly' fruit to their food. They didn't just discover that tomatoes weren't poisonous; they found out they tasted extremely good on flatbread!

Today, pizza is popular all around the globe. The people of Naples are very proud of their world-famous dish. They also take it extremely seriously! Many Neapolitans consider that there are two 'real' pizzas – the Marinara and the Margherita. In fact, many pizza restaurants in Naples serve only these two pizzas, and no other.

The Marinara is the older of the two. It has a topping of tomato, oregano, garlic and olive oil. It is named Marinara not because it has seafood on it (it doesn't), but because it was the food prepared by 'la marinara', the fisherman's wife, for her husband when he returned from fishing trips in the Bay of Naples.

Margherita pizza has a topping of tomato, basil and mozzarella cheese. It was invented in 1889 by Italian chef Raffaele Esposito to honour the visit of Queen Margherita of Savoy to Naples. Queen Margherita was visiting Naples to escape a cholera epidemic in the north of Italy. She asked Esposito to make her three different pizzas. Her favourite one had the colours of the Italian flag – green (basil leaves), white (mozzarella), and red (tomatoes) – on it. The Queen wrote a letter to Esposito telling him how much she liked his pizza, and Esposito decided to name it after her. Today, many Italians – not just those living in Naples – still prefer these two 'true' pizzas to all others!

## *Reading*

**1**   **a)**   **Read the rubric, then read the text quickly. What is the text about?**

> You are going to read a text about pizza. For questions 1-6 choose the best answer, A, B, C or D.

  **b)**   **Read the questions and possible answers. Underline the key words in each. Compare with a partner.**

  **c)**   **Do the reading task.**

**1**   Flatbread is a food that
  **A**   pre-dates pizza.
  **B**   was invented by the Italians.
  **C**   appeared in the 18th century.
  **D**   wasn't liked in Naples.

**2**   When tomatoes first arrived in Europe people
  **A**   did not like their flavour at all.
  **B**   believed they would die if they ate them.
  **C**   considered them a food for poor people only.
  **D**   thought they were a very ugly fruit.

**3**   Today, it is common in Naples to find
  **A**   people who don't like pizza at all.
  **B**   a lot of pizzas that aren't made anywhere else.
  **C**   restaurants that sell a very limited variety of pizzas.
  **D**   restaurants called Marinara and Margherita.

**4**   Marinara pizza
  **A**   used to be made with fish.
  **B**   gets its name from the Bay of Naples.
  **C**   was invented before pizza Margherita.
  **D**   was eaten by fishermen when they were at sea.

**5**   Margherita pizza was
  **A**   the idea of Queen Margherita.
  **B**   first made in northern Italy.
  **C**   invented to make a sick queen well.
  **D**   created so it looked like the Italian flag.

**6**   In the article, the author
  **A**   gives reasons for pizza's popularity.
  **B**   discusses the history of pizza.
  **C**   suggests that Italians make the best pizza.
  **D**   encourages tourists in Naples to try pizza.

**1 a)** **Aim** **To read for gist**

- Ask Ss to read the rubric and then skim the text to get the gist.
- Elicit answers.

*Answer Key*

*The text is about the history of pizza.*

**b)** **Aim** **To prepare for a reading task**

- Ask Ss to read the questions and possible answers and underline the words which they think are important in each option.
- Ask Ss to check their answers with their partners and compare.

*Suggested Answer Key*

1 *flatbread, pre-dates pizza, invented Italians, appeared 18th century, wasn't liked*
2 *tomatoes first arrived, not like flavour, die if ate, food for poor, ugly fruit*
3 *today common to find, people don't like pizza, pizzas that aren't made anywhere else, restaurants sell limited variety, restaurants called Marinara & Margherita*
4 *Marinara pizza, made with fish, name from Bay of Naples, invented before Margherita, eaten by fishermen when at sea*
5 *Margherita pizza, idea Queen Margherita, first made northern Italy, to make sick queen well, created to look like Italian flag*
6 *author, gives reasons for popularity, discusses history, suggests Italians best pizza, encourages tourists to try pizza*

**c)** **Aim** **To read for specific information**

- Give Ss time to read the text and complete the task using the key words they underlined in Ex. 1b to help them.
- Check Ss' answers. Ask Ss to justify their answers.

*Answer Key*

1 *A (long before the 19th century)*
2 *B (were poisonous)*
3 *C ( serve only two pizzas)*
4 *C (older of the two)*
5 *D (had colours of Italian flag)*
6 *B*

## Reading

**2** **Aim** **To read for lexico-grammatical structure**

- Draw Ss' attention to the rubric and the letters. Elicit Ss' guesses as to the context of the letters.
- Allow Ss time to read the text and check their guesses.

### Suggested Answer Key

*The first letter is about somebody who is asking their friend for ideas of what to cook for the meal they're making for their Dad's birthday. The second letter is a reply to the first one giving a recipe for a meal.*

- Explain the task and read the first sentence aloud as an example.
- Ask Ss to pay attention to the words before and after each gap as they will help them do the task. Ask Ss to read their completed text to see if it makes sense.
- Check Ss' answers.

### Answer Key

| | | | | | | | | |
|---|---|---|---|---|---|---|---|---|
| 1 | Can | 3 | are | 5 | of | 7 | to | 9 will |
| 2 | of | 4 | have | 6 | some | 8 | the | 10 any |

## Listening

**3 a)** **Aim** **To prepare for a listening task**

- Ask Ss to read the rubric and the food items A-H.
- Elicit what sort of language they should expect to hear *(e.g. (my) favourite, (he) likes, (she) prefers, etc).*

**b)** **Aim** **To listen for specific information**

- Play the recording. Ss listen and complete the task.
- Ask Ss to compare their answers for Ex. 3a with their partner.
- Play the recording again and ask Ss to say which words helped them decide.

### Answer Key

1  C  *(Sandra can't stop eating them.)*
2  H  *(Annie ... especially the strawberries.)*
3  A  *(... the tomatoes are her favourite.)*
4  B  *(... roast lamb is even better.)*
5  D  *(... he loves the homemade pasta though.)*

## Speaking

**4 a)** **Aim** **To describe a picture**

Explain the task and ask various Ss around the class to describe the picture to the rest of the class.

### Suggested Answer Key

*In the picture I can see a man in his mid-thirties with short brown hair. He is in a supermarket doing some shopping. He is holding a shopping basket and he is looking at the fresh vegetables.*

**b)** **Aim** **To compare your answer to a model answer**

- Play the recording. Ss listen and compare their answer to the model answer.
- Ask various Ss around the class to tell the rest of the class how (dis)similar the answers are.

### Suggested Answer Key

*The answers were quite similar because we both used the words given but the model answer was longer than my answer. It was also more detailed. For example, it described the man's clothing and the vegetables in the picture whereas I didn't.*

## Writing

**5** **Aim** **To analyse a rubric and write a notice**

- Explain the task and ask Ss to read the rubric.
- Give Ss time to read the statements 1-4 and mark them correctly.
- Check Ss' answers.

### Answer Key

| | | | |
|---|---|---|---|
| 1  F | 2  T | 3  F | 4  T |

- Give Ss time to complete the task. Remind Ss that their notice should answer *wh*-questions such as *What is the event about? Where will it take place? When will it take place? How long will it last? What else will there be?* Ask Ss to check that their piece of writing answers all the points in the rubric. Check Ss' answers.

### Suggested Answer Key

*All students are welcome to attend
an International Food Night
on 24th March
7-12 pm
in the school auditorium.
Please bring a typical dish from your country.
Refreshments will be provided.*

## Reading

**2** Read the rubric, then the letters. What are they about? Do the task.

> Complete these letters. Write ONE word for each space 1-10.

**Example**
0  *am*

Dear Luigi,
Help! I 0) ........... cooking dinner for my Dad's birthday tomorrow and I want to make a nice meal. 1) ...........
you think 2) ........... any ideas?
I hope you and the family 3) ........... well.
Thanks,
Philip

Hi Philip,
I think I have the perfect dinner. You 4) ........... to slice a kilo 5) ........... chicken and put 6) ........... cheese inside. Then, boil pasta in tomato soup and remember 7) ........... stir it all the time. Of all my recipes, this is 8) ........... easiest!
I'm sure this 9) ........... impress the family. Good luck and call me if you have 10) ........... problems.
Take care,
Luigi

## Listening

**3 a)** Read the rubric, then the list of food items.

> Listen to Tina talking to a friend about food at a party. Which food does each person prefer? For questions 1-5, write a letter (A-H) next to each person. You will hear the conversation twice.

**Example**
0  Tina  E

| People | | Food | |
|---|---|---|---|
| 1 | Sandra | A | tomatoes |
| 2 | Annie | B | lamb |
| 3 | Janet | C | chocolate brownie |
| 4 | Carl | D | pasta |
| 5 | Joe | E | apple pie |
| | | F | chicken |
| | | G | cheese |
| | | H | strawberries |

**b)** Do the task. Compare your answers with your partner's.

## Speaking

**4 a)** Look at the picture. Use these words to describe it.

- supermarket
- basket
- mid-thirties
- fresh vegetables

**b)** Listen to someone doing the task. How similar is his description to yours?

## Writing (notices)

*(Writing Bank p. WB3)*

**5** Read the rubric and mark the sentences *T* (true) or *F* (false). Write your notice.

> You are studying in England. Your school is organising an international food night. Write a notice. In your notice:
> - write where and when the event will be held
> - ask people to bring a typical dish from their country
> - explain what else there will be
> - write how long the event will last

1  The notice should be long and detailed.  .......
2  You need to use a lot of adjectives.  .......
3  You need to give contact details.  .......
4  You must write using formal style.  .......

# 2 Revision

## 1
**Fill in:** *tub, slices, order, fry, aisle, serve, spicy, attracts, run, dessert.*

1 The festival ........................... a lot of visitors every year.
2 Sam doesn't really like Indian food. He thinks it's too ........................................... .
3 We've got a ............................... of vanilla ice cream in the freezer.
4 Are you ready to ............................... , sir?
5 Chop the onions and ............................... them in olive oil.
6 Cut the cheese into thin ............................... .
7 The artist let his imagination ........................ wild and created statues from vegetables.
8 Harry's favourite ............................... is lemon cheesecake.
9 Do they ............................... breakfast 24 hours a day?
10 Here's the drinks ............................... . Let's get some cola.

*10x2=20 marks*

## 2
**Choose the correct word.**

1 Do you want **a/some** piece of cake?
2 How **much/many** eggs do we need?
3 There's only **a few/a little** pasta left.
4 You shouldn't eat **too many/too much** chocolate.
5 We have got **many/a lot of** food for the party.
6 Can I have **some/any** more coffee, please?
7 I only have **a little/a few** strawberries.
8 There aren't **many/much** cookies in the jar.
9 Is there **any/many** soup left?
10 I always eat **a/an** apple after lunch.

*10x1=10 marks*

## 3
**Fill in** *too* **or** *enough*.

1 Do we have ..................... cake for everyone?
2 This soup is ..................... salty for me!
3 Is your tea sweet .....................?
4 Oh no! I don't have ............. money for lunch!
5 My coffee is ..................... hot to drink.

*5x2=10 marks*

## 4
**Put the verbs in brackets into the** *-ing* **form or the** *(to) infinitive*.

1 Did you remember ................. **(buy)** tomatoes?
2 This dish is too salty for me ................. **(eat)**.
3 Do you fancy ................. **(go)** out for dinner?
4 Let me ................. **(help)** you with the dishes.
5 I forgot ................. **(put)** salt in the soup.
6 Can you ................. **(show)** me how to cook this dish?
7 I'd like ................. **(have)** a cheese omelette, please.
8 I can't stand ................. **(drink)** coffee.
9 He has difficulty ................. **(bake)** cakes.
10 He made me ................. **(wash)** the car.

*10x2=20 marks*

## 5
**Circle the correct response.**

1 A: Are you ready to order?
   B: **a** I think we are.    **b** Yes, that's fine.

2 A: What would you like to drink?
   B: **a** A cup of coffee, please.    **b** No, thanks.

3 A: Can I have scrambled eggs on toast?
   B: **a** That's great.    **b** Sure.

4 A: So that's eggs, pancakes and a coffee.
   B: **a** That's right.    **b** Sure.

5 A: Would you like any side orders?
   B: **a** Not for me, thank you.
      **b** No, I don't like them.

*5x4=20 marks*

## 6
**Write an email to your pen-friend about a traditional or popular dish in your country (80-100 words).**

*20 marks*

*Total: 100 marks*


### Check your Progress

- talk about food likes/dislikes ____
- talk and write about supermarket shopping ____
- write about places to eat in my country ____
- talk and write about restaurants ____
- order food in a restaurant ____
- write an informal email about a favourite dish ____

**GOOD ✓   VERY GOOD ✓✓   EXCELLENT ✓✓✓**

**1**
1  attracts
2  spicy
3  tub
4  order
5  fry
6  slices
7  run
8  dessert
9  serve
10  aisle

**2**
1  a
2  many
3  a little
4  too much
5  a lot of
6  some
7  a few
8  many
9  any
10  an

**3**
1  enough
2  too
3  enough
4  enough
5  too

**4**
1  to buy
2  to eat
3  going
4  help
5  to put
6  show
7  to have
8  drinking
9  baking
10  wash

**5**
1  a    2  a    3  b    4  a    5  a

**6**  *Suggested Answer Key*

*Hi Vanessa!*
*Thanks for your email. Here's my recipe for pierogi. Pierogi are traditional dumplings. First, make the dough with flour and water and roll it flat. Cut out circles. For the filling, boil and mash some potatoes and mix with fried onions and some cheese. Then, place the filling in the middle of the dough and fold it over to make half circles. Then, boil in a pan of hot water until they float. Serve with sour cream or with fried onions and garlic.*
*I hope you try them.*
*Write soon,*
*Peter*

# Great people and legends



**What's in this module?**

Read the title of the module *Great people and legends* and ask Ss to predict the content of the module *(the module is about famous people around the world and their achievements)*. Go through the contents list and stimulate a discussion about what Ss will learn in the module.

## Vocabulary

1 **Aim** **To present famous people and their achievements**

- Ask Ss if they recognise any of the people in the pictures.
- Allow Ss time to do the task individually and compare their answers with a partner.
- Play the recording for Ss to check their answers.
- Play the recording again with pauses for Ss to repeat individually or chorally.

*Answer Key*

*A 2     B 3     C 5     D 1     E 4     F 6*

## OVER TO YOU!

**Aim** **To practise talking about famous people and their achievements**

- Elicit what each person was and write on the board: Leonardo *Da Vinci – painter, George Washington – president, Neil Armstrong – astronaut, Christopher Columbus – explorer, Thomas Edison – inventor, Octavio Paz – writer*
- Ask different Ss to look at the pictures and say which famous person impresses them the most and why.
- Ask each S to name another famous person from history who impresses them. Allow Ss two or three minutes to think about their answers.

*Suggested Answer Key*

*Leonardo da Vinci impresses me the most because he was a great painter. He painted the Mona Lisa.*

*George Washington impresses me the most because he was a great president. He became the first president of the USA.*

*Neil Armstrong impresses me the most because he was a great astronaut. He was the first man who walked on the moon.*

*Christopher Columbus impresses me the most because he was a great explorer. He discovered America.*

*Thomas Edison impresses me the most because he was a great inventor. He invented the light bulb.*

*Octavio Paz impresses me the most because he was a great writer. He was the winner of the 1990 Nobel Prize in Literature.*

*Amelia Earhart really impresses me because she was a great pilot. She was the first female pilot to cross the Atlantic.*

*Queen Victoria really impresses me because she was a great queen. She ruled England for over 60 years and she was admired and respected by the people of her country.*

**Vocabulary:** great achievements, past activities, leaders, legendary creatures, jobs & nationalities of famous people, breaking the law
**Grammar:** past simple (regular & irregular verbs), *wh-* questions in the past simple, past continuous
**Everyday English:** discussing past activities
**Intonation:** word stress
**Writing:** a quiz; a description of a festival; a story; a biography of a famous person
**Culture Corner:** The Pilgrims – Sailing to a new life
**Curricular (*History*):** Christopher Columbus

# Module 3
# Great people and legends

## *Vocabulary*
## Great achievements

**1** **Match the sentences with the pictures.**
🎧 **Listen and check, then say.**

**A** ☐ Leonardo da Vinci **painted** the *Mona Lisa*.

**B** ☐ George Washington **became** the first president of the USA.

**C** ☐ Neil Armstrong was the first man who **walked** on the moon.

**D** ☐ Christopher Columbus **discovered** America.

**E** ☐ Thomas Edison **invented** the light bulb.

**F** ☐ Octavio Paz was the winner of the 1990 Nobel Prize in Literature.

### OVER TO YOU!

**Which of these people impresses you the most?**

*Leonardo da Vinci impresses me the most because he was a great painter.*

**Think of another famous person from history who impresses you. Complete the sentence.**

*… really impresses me because … .*

# 3a Special talents

## Vocabulary
### Past activities

**1** Label the pictures with the verbs.
🎧 Listen and check, then say.

- studied • designed • painted • invented
- sketched

**2** **invented** an early flying machine

**1** **painted** the *Mona Lisa*

**3** **designed** many machines

**4** **sketched** plants & animals

**5** **studied** the anatomy of the human body

## Reading

**2** **a)** Leonardo da Vinci did all the things in Ex. 1. What do you know about him? What else would you like to know? Write four questions.
🎧 Listen and read the text to see if you can answer your questions.

**b)** Read again and mark the sentences *T* (true), *F* (false) or *DS* (doesn't say).

| | | |
|---|---|---|
| **1** | Da Vinci learnt most things from others. | F |
| **2** | There are hundreds of da Vinci's paintings in museums all over the world. | F |
| **3** | He sketched maps of Europe. | DS |
| **4** | There is a bridge in Norway that da Vinci designed. | T |
| **5** | Da Vinci's flying machine looked like a modern aeroplane. | DS |
| **6** | His notes were easy to understand. | F |

**c)** Tell the class four things you learnt from the text.

**d)** Match the highlighted words to their meanings: *measurements, wanting to know more, smart, regard as, modelled after, thorough, succeeded in doing sth, exact.*

## Grammar
### Past simple (regular verbs)

see pp. GR4-GR5

**3** Read the table. How do we form the *past simple* of regular verbs? Find examples in the text on p. 45.

| AFFIRMATIVE | I/You/He, etc **painted** a picture. |
|---|---|
| NEGATIVE | I/You/He, etc **didn't paint** a picture. |
| INTERROGATIVE | **Did** I/you/he, etc **paint** a picture? |
| SHORT ANSWERS | **Yes**, I/you/he, etc **did**. <br> **No**, I/you/he, etc **didn't**. |

**Use**

We use the **past simple** for actions that happened at a certain time in the past or actions that happened one after the other.
*He **worked** late yesterday.*
*He **finished** his homework and then **watched** TV.*

**Time expressions used with the past simple:** yesterday, last week/month/year, a month/three days ago, etc.

## Vocabulary

**1** **Aim** **To present vocabulary related to past activities**

- Read the list of verbs and direct Ss' attention to the pictures.
- Allow Ss time to complete the task.
- Play the recording for Ss to check their answers.
- Play again with pauses for Ss to repeat individually or chorally.

## Reading

**2 a)** **Aim** **To introduce the topic of the text, to listen and read for specific information**

- Elicit from Ss what they know about Leonardo da Vinci to stimulate a discussion about the topic of the text.
- Ask Ss what else they would like to know about him and write four questions in their notebooks.
- Play the recording. Ss listen and follow the text and see if they can answer the questions.

***Suggested Answer Key – see p. 51(T)***

- Go through the **Check these words** box and explain/elicit the meaning of the words.

*talented (adj): having special natural abilities, like being creative or athletic*
*intelligent (adj): smart*
*curious (adj): wanting to learn more*
*lifetime (n): a period of time that one is alive for*
*achieve (v): to do sth with success*
*incredible (adj): amazing, astonishing*
*survive (v): to remain in existence*
*consider (v): to think of (sb) as (sth)*
*engineer (n): sb who designs machines and structures*
*industry (n): the people and companies involved in producing goods, like steel or cloth*
*accurate (adj): having no mistakes, exact*
*canal system (n): a waterway built by people for boats to travel through a city*
*construct (v): to build*
*based (on) (pp): modelled after or built according to*
*detailed (adj): very accurate, precise or thorough*
*a whole range (phr): a wide variety*
*ahead of their time (phr): very advanced for the time period*
*calculator (n): a small device used to make mathematical calculations*
*parachute (n): a piece of equipment made of thin cloth that people wear to safely jump from planes*
*material (n): element/thing you need to build, make sth or do an activity*
*mirror (n): a reflective glass ('mirror' writing means it was written backwards and could be read by reflecting it in a mirror)*
*perfect proportions (phr): accurate/balanced measurements*

*sculptor (n): sb who makes statues, usually out of clay or stone*
*philosopher (n): sb who seeks wisdom about or answers to the meaning of things such as life, truth, existence, etc*
*geologist (n): sb who studies the Earth's structure, surface and origins*

**b)** **Aim** **To read for specific information**

- Ask Ss to read the text again and complete the task.
- Elicit Ss' answers in class and check them.
- Ask Ss to correct the false statements.

***Answer Key***

1   *He learnt things by himself.*
2   *Only about 15 survived.*
6   *He used 'mirror' writing.*

**c)** **Aim** **To consolidate information in a text**

- Ask Ss to close their books and think of four things they learnt from the text.
- Ask various Ss to share their answers.

***Suggested Answer Key – see p. 51(T)***

**d)** **Aim** **To expand vocabulary/To match words from a text to their meanings**

- Explain the task.
- Give Ss time to complete the task.
- Check Ss' answers.

***Answer Key – see p. 51(T)***

## Grammar

**3** **Aim** **To present the past simple (regular verbs)**

- Ss close their books.
- Write on the board: *I/you/he/she/it/we/they* **worked** *late yesterday* and explain that this is the affirmative form of the past simple of regular verbs. Elicit/Explain that we use this tense for completed past actions, we know when they happened. Then write: *I/you/he/she/it/we/they* **did not work** and point out that this is the negative form. Then write: **Did** *I/you/he/she/it/we/they work? Yes, I/you/he/she/it/we/they* **did.***/No, I/you/he/she/it/we/they* **didn't.** to demonstrate how we form questions and short answers.
- Ss open their books and read the grammar table.
- Explain that most verbs form their past simple forms by adding **-ed**. Go through the spelling rules in the book and elicit/write further examples on the board.
- Ask Ss to find examples of the past simple in the text. Check their answers.

***Answer Key – see p. 51(T)***

**4** **Aim** To practise the past simple

- Allow Ss time to complete the task individually.
- Check Ss' answers.

## BACKGROUND INFORMATION

**Vincent van Gogh** (1853-1890) was a Dutch Impressionist painter. He saw little success during his lifetime and suffered from mental illness. He eventually shot himself at the age of 37. After his death he became known as one of the world's greatest painters and the founder of modern art. Some of his most famous works include: *Sunflowers* (1888), *The Starry Night* (1889) and *Portrait of Dr. Gachet* (1890).

**Claude Monet** (1840-1926) was a French Impressionist painter and a founder of the Impressionist Movement which is named after one of his paintings. His idea of creating series of paintings with a single theme or subject was unique. These are also among his best known works such as *The Haystacks* (1890-91), *Water Lilies* (1883-1926), *Houses of Parliament* (1900-1904), and *Poplar Trees* (1891-1900).

**Ludwig van Beethoven** (1770-1827) was a German composer and pianist. He is one of the most famous composers of all time and continued to compose, conduct and perform even after he went completely deaf. He wrote nine symphonies, seven concerti, 32 piano sonatas, 10 violin sonatas, 16 string quartet sonatas, an opera and much more.

**Diego Rodríguez de Silva y Velázquez** (1599-1660) was a Spanish painter and portrait artist at the court of King Philip IV. He painted many portraits of the Spanish royal family as well as important scenes from history. His works include: *Las Meninas* (1656), *Rokeby Venus* (1644-48) and *The Surrender of Breda* (1634-35).

**Alexander Graham Bell** (1847-1922) was a Scottish scientist, inventor and a founding member of the National Geographic Society. He invented the first working telephone in 1876. He also invented many other things including different aerial vehicles, hydro-airplanes, a metal jacket that helped breathing, an audiometer to identify hearing problems and a device to find icebergs.

**Isaac Newton** (1643-1727) was an English physicist, astronomer, mathematician and philosopher. His work *The Principia* (1687) which describes universal gravitation and the three laws of motion had a huge effect on science. He also helped develop calculus, made other important mathematical breakthroughs and invented the first reflecting telescope.

**Antoine Henri Becquerel** (1852-1908) was a French physicist. He discovered radioactivity with Marie and Pierre Curie and they won the 1903 Nobel Prize in Physics.

**5** **Aim** To practise the past simple interrogative

- Allow Ss time to complete the task in closed pairs.
- Check Ss' answers.

### Answer Key

2 *Did Leonardo da Vinci sketch plants and animals? Yes, he did.*
3 *Did Mozart invent an early flying machine? No, he didn't.*
4 *Did your parents visit a museum yesterday? Yes, they did./No, they didn't.*
5 *Did you study history last Monday? Yes, I did./No, I didn't.*

## Speaking & Writing

**6** **Aim** To consolidate information from a text

- Ask Ss to close their books and think of da Vinci's achievements.
- Ask Ss to write a few sentences about which of da Vinci's achievements impressed them the most.
- Ask various Ss to share their answers in class.

### Suggested Answer Key

*The achievement that impresses me the most is the Vitruvian Man sketch which presents the perfect proportions of the human body. It is probably the most popular drawing in the world.*

# Is this the most talented person who ever lived?

Leonardo da Vinci was born in a small village in Tuscany, Italy on 15th April 1452. He was very intelligent and curious and learnt lots of things by himself. In his lifetime, he achieved incredible things! So is this man the most talented person ever? Read this, then you decide!

Leonardo da Vinci, 1452-1519 (self-portrait)

## The Engineer

Da Vinci designed many working machines for war, industry, and transport. He sketched very accurate maps and he also designed a brilliant canal system for Florence, and a huge bridge. In 2001, architects constructed a bridge in Norway based on da Vinci's design. You can see it there today.

## The Inventor

Da Vinci's notebooks contain detailed sketches for a whole range of inventions which were centuries ahead of their time. These include a sort of helicopter, flying machines, a calculator, a parachute, and even robots. With today's technology and materials many of da Vinci's designs could work very well.

## The Scientist

Da Vinci studied plants, animals and the human body, and made detailed drawings and notes about them. He used 'mirror' writing, probably because he didn't want everyone to understand the notes! His sketch *Vitruvian Man* shows the perfect proportions of the human body. This is possibly the best-known drawing in the world.

## The Painter

As a young man, da Vinci studied painting in Florence. Two of his paintings, the *Mona Lisa* (or *La Gioconda*) and *The Last Supper*, are among the most famous paintings of all time! Today, only about 15 of his finished paintings survive (he often didn't finish them because he was busy with other things), but most people consider him to be one of the greatest painters who ever lived.

Da Vinci was also a sculptor, a musician, a mathematician, a philosopher, an architect, a writer, and a geologist. Five centuries after his death, he is still one of the most fascinating people in history.

### Check these words

talented, intelligent, curious, lifetime, achieve, incredible, survive, consider, engineer, industry, accurate, canal system, construct, based on, detailed, a whole range, ahead of their time, calculator, parachute, material, mirror, perfect proportions, sculptor, philosopher, geologist

---

**4** Use the *past simple* of the verbs in the list to complete the sentences.

- invent • not paint • die • start
- not discover

1 The artist van Gogh didn't paint *Wild Poppies*. Claude Monet did.
2 Beethoven started composing music at an early age.
3 The Spanish artist Diego Valazquez died in 1660.
4 Alexander Graham Bell invented the telephone in 1876.
5 Isaac Newton didn't discover radioactivity. Henri Becquerel did.

**5** Form questions, then answer them.

1 Picasso/paint the Mona Lisa?
   *Did Picasso paint the Mona Lisa? No, he didn't.*
2 Leonardo da Vinci/sketch plants and animals?
3 Mozart/invent an early flying machine?
4 your parents/visit a museum/yesterday?
5 you/study history/last Monday?

### Speaking & Writing

**6** **THINK!** Which of da Vinci's achievements impresses you the most? Why? In three minutes, write a few sentences. Read your sentences to the class.

# 3b Historical figures

## Vocabulary
### Leaders

**1** Look at the people in the pictures. Who was: *an Egyptian queen? an Asian warrior? an Italian explorer? a South American leader? a Roman ruler? an Egyptian king? a Macedonian king?*
🎧 Listen and check, then make sentences.

*Cleopatra was an Egyptian queen.*

## Listening & Reading

**2** **a)** Do the quiz to find out how much you know about these historical figures. 🎧 Listen and check.

**b)** Match the words in bold to their meanings: *having a substance that can kill sb, travelled around, pushed a knife into, battled, being successful in, cut into sth with teeth, took control by force.*

## Grammar  see p. GR5
### Past simple (irregular verbs)

**3** **a)** Read the theory box. How do we form the *past simple* of irregular verbs?

| AFFIRMATIVE | NEGATIVE |
|---|---|
| *I/You/He/She, etc* **went** to Italy. | *I/You/He/She, etc* **didn't go** to Egypt. |

| INTERROGATIVE | SHORT ANSWERS |
|---|---|
| **Did** *I/you/he/she, etc* **go** to China? | Yes, I/you, etc **did**. No, I/you, etc **didn't**. |

Irregular verbs have **irregular forms**.
*have – **had**, see – **saw**, take – **took**, buy - **bought** etc*

**b)** Fill in the *past simple* forms of the verbs from the quiz. Which are: *R* (regular)? *I* (irregular)?

| | | | |
|---|---|---|---|
| **1** | lead – *led* (I) | **10** | set out – set out (I) |
| **2** | fight – fought (I) | **11** | die – died (R) |
| **3** | explore – explored (R) | **12** | eat – ate (I) |
| **4** | do – did (I) | **13** | bite – bit (I) |
| **5** | win – won (I) | **14** | stab – stabbed (R) |
| **6** | start – started (R) | **15** | come – came (I) |
| **7** | discover – discovered (R) | **16** | see – saw (I) |
| **8** | build – built (I) | **17** | conquer – conquered (I) |
| **9** | travel – travelled (R) | **18** | be – was (I) |



# Heroes of the Ancient World

These people led their countries, **fought** against great armies, **explored** new lands and did amazing things. People didn't always like them, but they won a place in history forever. Do the quiz and test your knowledge about these amazing people!

**1** Which empire did Genghis Khan start?
- **A** the Ottoman Empire
- **B** the Persian Empire
- **C** the Mongol Empire

**2** According to legend, Manco Cápac was the man who ...
- **A** started the Inca Empire.
- **B** discovered South America.
- **C** built Mayan temples.

**3** Marco Polo travelled the 7,000-km-long Silk Road from Europe to China. He set out in 1271. When did he return home?
- **A** 5 years later
- **B** 12 years later
- **C** 24 years later

**4** According to many poets and historians, Cleopatra died after ...
- **A** she ate some **poisoned** food.
- **B** a poisonous snake **bit** her.
- **C** she **stabbed** herself.

**5** Who said "I came, I saw, I **conquered**." after **winning** a battle in Asia Minor?
- **A** Julius Caesar
- **B** Genghis Khan
- **C** Tutankhamun

**6** Alexander the Great conquered most of the known world. How old was he when he died?
- **A** 76
- **B** 49
- **C** 33

**Note:** c. = circa = about

**Check these words**

lead, fight against armies, explore, land, win a place in history, empire, according to legend, poisoned, bite, stab, conquer, win a battle

## Vocabulary

**1** **Aim** **To present vocabulary related to leaders**

- Direct Ss' attention to the pictures. Ask if Ss know any of these people.
- Allow Ss time to complete the task.
- Play the recording for Ss to check their answers.
- Give Ss time to make sentences, then check Ss' answers.

### Answer Key

- Genghis Khan was an Asian warrior.
- Marco Polo was an Italian explorer.
- Manco C'apac was a South American leader.
- Julius Caesar was a Roman ruler.
- Tutankhamun was an Egyptian king.
- Alexander the Great was a Macedonian king.

### BACKGROUND INFORMATION

**Tutankhamun** was an Egyptian king from the 18th dynasty. He was the son of Akhenaten. He spent his time as king building monuments and temples. The discovery of his tomb in 1922 created worldwide interest and today his burial mask is the iconic image of ancient Egypt.

**Genghis Khan** was a Mongol leader and warlord. He created the Mongolian empire by joining together lots of tribes in northeast Asia. People think of him as the founder of Mongolia.

**Marco Polo** was a Venetian merchant who travelled from Europe to China and all over Asia with his father and uncle. They returned to Italy after 24 years. Their journey helped to create new maps and inspired other explorers.

**Cleopatra** was an Egyptian queen and the last of the Pharaohs to rule Egypt. She famously joined forces with the Roman statesman, Caesar and then with his general, Mark Anthony. She struggled to keep Egypt independent, but when she was defeated she killed herself with a poisonous snake.

**Julius Caesar** was a Roman general and statesman. He helped create the Roman Empire. He started and won a civil war and reformed Roman society and government. A group of senators murdered him because they wanted to change things back. His adopted son Augustus established a permanent Roman Empire.

## Listening & Reading

**2** **a)** **Aim** **To do a quiz about ancient heroes**

- Explain the task.
- Ask Ss to read through the questions and discuss the answers with their partners.
- Allow Ss time to do the task.
- Play the recording for Ss to check their answers.

- Go through the **Check these words** box and explain/elicit the meanings of the words.

### Suggested Answer Key

**lead (v):** to be in charge of, to govern
**fight against armies (v):** to battle against groups of people in war
**explore (v):** to travel, for the purpose of discovery
**land (n):** territory, country or region
**win a place in history (phr):** to be widely remembered after many years
**empire (n):** a group of countries ruled over by a leader called an emperor
**according to legend (phr):** as shown/stated by an old and possibly true story
**poisoned (adj):** containing a harmful or deadly substance
**bite (v):** to grip or cut into with teeth
**stab (v):** to pierce into with a pointed weapon/object
**conquer (v):** to take by force, usually using armies
**win a battle (pl):** to succeed in defeating sb or an army in battle

**b)** **Aim** **To expand vocabulary/To match words from a text to their meanings**

- Explain the task.
- Give Ss time to complete the task.
- Check Ss' answers.

*Answer Key – see p. 49(T)*

## Grammar

**3** **a)** **Aim** **To present the past simple (irregular verbs)**

- Write on the board: *I played tennis. I went to Canada.* Elicit past simple regular verbs -*ed* ending. Explain that some verbs have their own irregular past simple forms which Ss have to learn.
- Go through the grammar table with Ss. Elicit that irregular verbs form their past simple negative, interrogative and short answers in the same way as regular verbs.
- Refer Ss to the list of irregular verb forms at the back of the Ss' Book.

*Answer Key – see p. 49(T)*

**b)** **Aim** **To practise the past simple of regular/ irregular verbs**

- Read the list of verbs and elicit which are regular and which are irregular.
- Allow Ss time to complete the task.
- Elicit answers around the classroom.

**4 a)** **Aim** **To practise the past simple of regular/irregular verbs**

- Explain the task.
- Allow Ss time to do the task.
- Elicit Ss' answers and write them on the board.

*Answer Key*

| | | | | | |
|---|---|---|---|---|---|
| 1 | became (I) | 5 | found (I) | 9 | ate (I) |
| 2 | ruled | 6 | had (I) | 10 | happened |
| 3 | died | 7 | opened | | |
| 4 | buried | 8 | got (I) | | |

**b)** **Aim** **To read for specific information**

- Explain the task. Choose one S to read the example aloud. Allow Ss time to do the task.
- Check Ss' answers.

*Answer Key*

2 Carter didn't find the tomb 2,000 years after Tut's death. He found it 3,000 years after Tut's death.
3 The tomb didn't have a beautiful silver mask inside. It had a beautiful gold mask inside it.
4 Carter didn't die soon after finding the tomb. One of Carter's men died soon after finding the tomb.
5 A cobra didn't eat Carter's pet dog. It ate Carter's pet bird.

**5** **Aim** **To practise the simple past interrogative**

- Give Ss time to complete the task.
- Ask Ss in pairs to read out their questions and answers in class.

*Answer Key*

2 Did Cleopatra speak Greek? Yes, she did.
3 Did Alexander the Great begin the war against Persia in 334 BC? Yes, he did.
4 Did Genghis Khan have two sons? No, he didn't.
5 Did Marco Polo grow up in Venice? Yes, he did.

**6 a)** **Aim** **To revise and practise *wh*-questions**

- Go through the example sentences with Ss.
- Play the recording for Ss to listen and repeat.
- Ask Ss to pay attention to the rising intonation in *wh*-questions.
- Ss find examples of *wh*-questions in the quiz in Ex. 2.

*Answer Key*

Which empire did Genghis Khan start? When did he return home? Who said "I came, I saw, I conquered."? How old was Alexander the Great when he died?

**b)** **Aim** **To practise asking and answering questions**

- Ss work in pairs asking and answering questions about King Tut. Check around the class and offer help if necessary.

- Invite some pairs to ask and answer in class.

*Suggested Answer Key*

B: How long did he rule Egypt?
A: Nine years. When did he die?
B: At the age of 18. Where did the people bury him?
A: In the Valley of the Kings in southern Egypt. When did Howard Carter find his tomb?
B: Over 3,000 years later, in 1922. What did the tomb have inside it?
A: It had a lot of treasures, including a beautiful gold mask. What happened after Carter opened the tomb?
B: One of his men died. What happened to Carter's pet bird?
A: A cobra ate it.
B: Why do people believe these things happened?
A: Because of a terrible ancient curse.

## Writing

**7** **Aim** **To write a quiz about famous historical figures**

- Ask Ss to work in pairs and collect information from the Internet using the key words in the search bar or from their school textbooks, encyclopaedias or other reference books.
- Allow Ss time to collect their information and write their quizzes. Alternatively, assign the task as HW.
- Ask Ss to swap their quizzes with another pair and try to complete it.

*Suggested Answer Key*

1 Who was Anne Boleyn married to?
  A  Philip II          C  Henry VIII
  B  Louis XIV          D  Richard III

2 Which island did Napoleon Bonaparte live in exile on from 1814 to 1815?
  A  Patmos             C  Sicily
  B  Corsica            D  Elba

3 Which American president abolished slavery?
  A  Abraham Lincoln    C  Andrew Jackson
  B  George Washington  D  Thomas Jefferson

4 What was James Cook famous for discovering?
  A  Australia          C  Africa
  B  America            D  Asia

5 What was William Shakespeare's job?
  A  a painter          C  an architect
  B  a scientist        D  a writer

6 Where was Mozart born?
  A  Germany            C  Belgium
  B  Austria            D  Russia

Alexander the Great, 356 – 323 BC

Manco Cápac, 12th century

Tutankhamun, 1341 – 1323 BC

Genghis Khan, c. 1162 – 1227

Marco Polo, c. 1254 – 1324

Julius Caesar, 100 – 44 BC

Cleopatra, 69 – 30 DC

**b)** Read the text again and correct the false statements.

1 Tutankhamun ruled Egypt for 18 years.
*He didn't rule Egypt for 18 years. He ruled it for 9 years.*
2 Carter found the tomb 2,000 years after Tut's death.
3 The tomb had a beautiful silver mask inside it.
4 Carter died soon after finding the tomb.
5 A cobra ate Carter's pet dog.

**5** Make questions, then answer them.

1 Julius Caesar/build Rome? (✗)
*Did Julius Caesar build Rome? No, he didn't.*
2 Cleopatra/speak Greek? (✓)
3 Alexander the Great/begin/the war against Persia in 334 BC? (✓)
4 Genghis Khan/have two sons? (✗)
5 Marco Polo/grow up in Venice? (✓)

*Wh-* **questions** see p. GR5

**6 a)** 🎧 Listen and say the examples. Find more examples in the quiz in Ex. 2.

| | |
|---|---|
| **Who** was he? | **What** did they do? |
| **Where** did she live? | **When** did they return? |
| **Why** did you leave? | **How** did he die? |
| **Which** war did he win? | **How long** did she live? |

**b)** Ask and answer *Wh-* questions about King Tut.

A: When did Tutankhamun become Pharaoh?
B: At a young age. How long did …?

## Writing

**7** ICT 👥 Collect information and write your own quiz about famous historical figures. Use the key words: *historical figures.*

**4 a)** Put the verbs in brackets into the *past simple*. Which are irregular past forms?

# King Tut's Tomb

Tutankhamun **1)** ..................... (become) Pharaoh of Egypt at a very young age. He **2)** ............... (rule) for only nine years because he **3)** ..................... (die) at the age of 18. The people **4)** ........................... (bury) him in the Valley of the Kings in southern Egypt.
Over 3,000 years later, in 1922 an archaeologist, Henry Carter, **5)** .................. (find) the forgotten tomb. It **6)** ................... (have) a lot of treasures inside it, including a beautiful gold mask. After Carter **7)** ............... (open) Tut's tomb, one of his men **8)** ................... (get) sick and died, a cobra **9)** ..................... (eat) Carter's pet bird and other strange things **10)** ..................... (happen). Some people believe this is because of a terrible ancient curse!

47

## The Pilgrims – Sailing to a new life!

**Check these words**

Pilgrims, sail, newly-discovered, land, ship, captain, voyage, ill, settle, survive, native, hunt, crops, corn, celebrate, feast, harvest, celebration, tradition

### Voyage to America

On September 6th 1620, 100 people sailed from England for a better life in North America, a newly-discovered land. They called this land 'the New World'. Their ship was called the *Mayflower* and its captain was Christopher Jones. Bad weather made the voyage very difficult and many people became ill. After 66 days, these first 'Pilgrims' finally saw land. They settled in an area where they started a new town, Plymouth.

### Life in the New World

At first, life wasn't easy for the Pilgrims, and only about half of them survived their first winter. The Native Americans who lived there taught them how to fish and hunt and grow crops, such as corn.

### Celebrating the First Harvest

In the fall of 1621, the Pilgrims had a big feast with all the foods from their first harvest. Every year after that, the people had a similar celebration, and this harvest feast soon became a very important American tradition called Thanksgiving.

**1** Who were the Pilgrims? Decide which sentences are *T* (true) and which are *F* (false).

1 The Pilgrims sailed to North America from Spain.
2 They sailed on the *Mayflower*.
3 The journey took one year.
4 Many Pilgrims died during their first winter.
5 The people they found were hunters and farmers.
6 The Pilgrims had a big celebration the next summer.
7 The local people were very unfriendly.

🎧 Listen and read to check. Correct the false sentences.

### Thanksgiving Today!

*Families get together and share a huge meal on the fourth Thursday in November. This usually includes roast turkey, sweet potato, corn, cranberry sauce and pumpkin pie. It's delicious!*

**2** Use words from the **Check these words** box in the correct form to complete the summary. Then, explain the highlighted words.

The **1)** ........................ were English people who **2)** ........................ to North America, a **3)** ........................ land. Their **4)** ........................ was difficult because of bad weather. They reached land two months later and **5)** ..................... in Plymouth. Half of the Pilgrims managed to **6)** ................................ the first winter. The natives helped them to **7)** ................................ and grow **8)** ................................ for food. The first **9)** ........................ was very good so they had a **10)** ................................ to celebrate it.

**3** **THINK!** Imagine you were one of the natives. In three minutes write sentences describing the Pilgrims' arrival and settling in, and your feelings about them.

**4** **ICT** Think of a traditional celebration in your country. Collect information, then write a few sentences about it. Write: *name, when & why you celebrate it, how you celebrate, how it started*. Tell the class.

## 1 Aim To read for specific information

- Ask Ss to read the title and look at the map. Elicit which continents *(Europe, North America)* and ocean *(the Atlantic)* they can see. Elicit the route shown on the map *(from England to North America)*.
- Ask Ss if they know who the Pilgrims were and what they know about them.
- Ask Ss to read through the sentences 1-7 then allow Ss time to read the text and decide which sentences are true and which are false.
- Play the recording. Ss listen and follow the text in their books and check their answers. Ask Ss to correct the false statements.

### Answer Key

*A group of people who left England to start a new life in North America.*

1  F  *(They sailed to North America from England.)*
2  T
3  F  *(It took 66 days.)*
4  T
5  T
6  F  *(They had a big celebration the next autumn.)*
7  F  *(They taught them how to fish, hunt and grow crops, such as corn.)*

- Explain/Elicit the meaning of the words in the **Check these words** box.

### Suggested Answer Key

**Pilgrims (n):** *a group of people who left England and settled in North America in 1620*
**sail (v):** *to travel by ship or boat*
**newly-discovered (adj):** *recently found out*
**land (n):** *a place/territory*
**ship (n):** *a very large boat*
**captain (n):** *the leader of the ship*
**voyage (n):** *a long journey on a ship*
**ill (adj):** *sick*
**settle (v):** *to set up/establish residence in a new place*
**survive (v):** *to stay alive*
**native (n):** *(of an American) sb that belongs to one of the groups that lived in North America before Europeans arrived*
**hunt (v):** *to search for animals to use for food*
**crop (n):** *a plant such as wheat and rice that people grow for food*
**corn (n):** *a type of crop that has yellow seeds called kernels, also called maize*
**celebrate (v):** *to do sth enjoyable because of a special event*
**feast (n):** *a large meal, usually shared by many people*
**harvest (n):** *the crops gathered in a season*
**celebration (n):** *a party or gathering*
**tradition (n):** *a custom that has existed for a long time*

## 2 Aim To practise new vocabulary

- Explain the task.
- Allow Ss time to complete the task.
- Check Ss' answers.

### Answer Key

1  *Pilgrims*              5  *settled*      9  *harvest*
2  *sailed*                6  *survive*     10  *feast*
3  *newly-discovered*      7  *hunt*
4  *voyage*                8  *crops*

- Explain the task.
- Give Ss time to complete the task.
- Check Ss' answers.

### Suggested Answer Key

**settled:** *started living in a place*
**survived:** *stayed alive*
**hunt:** *to chase animals for food*
**feast:** *a big meal often eaten as a celebration*
**harvest:** *crops gathered in a season*
**tradition:** *a custom from a long time ago*

## 3 Aim To consolidate information in a text

- Ask Ss to use their imagination and play the role of one of the natives.
- Allow Ss three minutes to write sentences describing the Pilgrims' arrival and settling in. Tell Ss to describe their feelings towards the Pilgrims.
- Ask various Ss to read their sentences in class.

### Suggested Answer Key

*About a year ago a ship arrived carrying a big group of people. They spoke a strange language and wore strange clothes. We were scared at first, but not anymore. We even helped them to plant crops and hunt on our land. They had a big feast to celebrate the harvest and they invited us.*

## 4 Aim To write about a traditional celebration

- Go through the short text about how Americans celebrate Thanksgiving nowadays. Ask if there's a similar celebration in Ss' country.
- Ask Ss to collect information from the Internet or from their school textbooks, encyclopaedias or other reference books, about a traditional celebration in their country.
- Allow Ss time to collect their information and write a few sentences about it. Alternatively, assign the task as HW.
- Ask various Ss to talk about the celebration.

### Suggested Answer Key

*A traditional celebration in my country is Canada Day. This celebrates the day that Canada became a nation. Every year on July 1st people celebrate with their friends and family with picnics, barbecues, fireworks, parades and more. It is a national holiday so schools and businesses close for the day.*

## 1 **Aim** To present new vocabulary

Refer Ss to the pictures and activities and play the recording with pauses for Ss to repeat. Check for correct pronunciation.

### BACKGROUND INFORMATION

**Colonial Williamsburg** is a living history museum in Williamsburg, Virginia, USA. The whole town is as it was in the 18th century with restored or rebuilt buildings and features. The people who work there re-enact all aspects of everyday life at that time and dress and talk as the people did then. It is a popular tourist destination and visitors can see famous historical figures, battle re-enactments, arts and crafts demonstrations and outdoor performances.

## 2 a) **Aim** To present situational language

- Ask Ss to read the sentences.
- Play the recording with pauses for Ss to repeat. Check for correct pronunciation.

## b) **Aim** To listen and read for specific information

- Play the recording and ask Ss to follow the text in their books.
- Elicit answers to the questions from around the class.

### Answer Key

*John went on a day trip to Colonial Williamsburg last weekend. He went on a tour of some historical buildings and gardens. He met actors playing famous people from the past, like George Washington. He also watched a re-enactment of the Battle of Williamsburg.*

## 3 **Aim** To present synonymous phrases

- Read out the phrases. Refer Ss back to the dialogue to find the synonymous ones.
- Check Ss' answers.

### Answer Key

*I want to visit that place. – I'd really like to go there!*
*Did you enjoy the visit? – Did you have a nice time?*

**Suggested Answers for Exs 2b & 3a on p. 46**

**Ex. 2b**
*having a substance that can kill sb: poisoned*
*travelled around: explored*
*pushed a knife into: stabbed*
*battled: fought*
*being successful in: winning*
*cut into sth with teeth: bit*
*took control by force: conquered*

*I think you had a nice time. – That sounds very interesting!*
*It was just a normal weekend. – I didn't do anything special.*

## Intonation

## 4 **Aim** To present and practise word stress

- Explain the meaning of a stressed syllable *(emphasis on a syllable to make it more pronounced than the rest of the word)* and weak vowel *(unstressed in pronunciation)*.
- Play the recording with pauses for Ss to repeat chorally and individually.
- Play the recording again for Ss to listen and mark the stressed syllables and the weak vowels in the words 1-6.

### Answer Key

| | | |
|---|---|---|
| 1 *battle* | 3 *garden* | 5 *invent* |
| 2 *include* | 4 *famous* | 6 *Saturday* |

## 5 **Aim** To act out a dialogue

- Refer Ss to the dialogue in Ex. 2b and tell them to read it again.
- Refer Ss to the sentences in Ex. 2a.
- In closed pairs, ask Ss to act out a similar dialogue using the sentences in Ex. 2a and the plan.
- Monitor the activity round the class. Help Ss if necessary.
- Ask some pairs to act out their dialogues in class.

### Suggested Answer Key

A: *Hi Jenny, how was your weekend?*
B: *It was great, thanks. I went to the cinema on Saturday and on Sunday I went to the beach.*
A: *Oh, really? Did you have a nice time?*
B: *Yes, it was great. We saw a great film and guess what! I met your cousin, too! He was there with Tom and Ann and then, we all went for a drink. What about you? Did you have a good weekend?*
A: *Oh, I didn't do anything special. I just read a book and then on Sunday I went to the cinema.*

**Ex. 3a**
*Irregular verbs have their own past simple forms. Each verb is different.*
*To form the negative of the past simple with irregular verbs, we use **didn't** + **the base form** of the verb. To form the interrogative, we use **did** + **subject** + **the base form** of the verb.*

## Discussing past activities

**1** These are some of the activities visitors can do at a popular 'living history' museum in the USA called Colonial Williamsburg.
🎧 Listen and say.

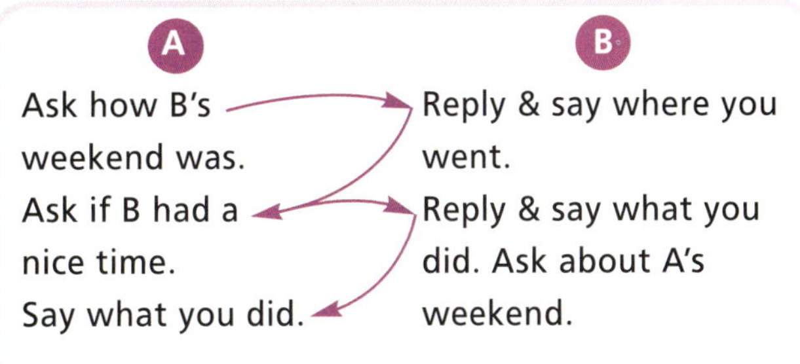


**2** a) 🎧 Listen and say.

- How was your weekend?
- It was great, thanks.
- Did you have a nice time?
- Yes, it was fantastic.
- That sounds interesting.
- Did you have a nice weekend?
- I didn't do anything special.

b) The sentences above are from a dialogue between two friends. Where did John go last weekend? What did he do there?
🎧 Listen and read to find out.

Sally: Oh, hi, John! How was your weekend?

John: It was great, thanks. I went on a day trip to Colonial Williamsburg on Saturday.

Sally: Oh, really? I'd really like to go there! Did you have a nice time?

John: Yes, it was fantastic. First of all, we went on a tour of some historical buildings and gardens. Then, we met actors playing famous people from the past, like George Washington, who told us about life in the 18th century.

Sally: That sounds very interesting!

John: It was! The best part of the day, though, was when we watched a re-enactment of the Battle of Williamsburg. How about you? Did you have a nice weekend?

Sally: Oh, I didn't do anything special. I just hung out with my friends and went to my grandmother's for Sunday lunch!

**3** Find sentences in the dialogue which mean: – *I want to visit that place.* – *Did you enjoy the visit?* – *I think you had a nice time.* – *It was just a normal weekend.*

## Intonation

**4** 🎧 Listen and say, then listen and mark the stressed syllable (•) and the weak vowel (·) in each word (1-6).

| | | |
|---|---|---|
| actors | special | village |
| around | survive | weekend |

1 battle    3 garden    5 invent
2 include    4 famous    6 Saturday

## Speaking

**5** 👥 Think of your last weekend. Use the sentences in Ex. 2a to act out your dialogue. Follow the plan.

| A | B |
|---|---|
| Ask how B's weekend was. | Reply & say where you went. |
| Ask if B had a nice time. | Reply & say what you did. Ask about A's weekend. |
| Say what you did. | |

49

## *Vocabulary*
### Legendary creatures

**1** 🎧 **Listen and say, then match each creature (A-F) with a description (1-6). Explain the words in bold.**

**1** D It **looks like** a snake with a **long neck**.

**2** E It's small, with **wings** and **magical powers**.

**3** A It looks like a **human** but it's **huge** and **terrifies** local people.

**4** C It looks like a horse with a single **horn**.

**5** B It can **breathe fire**.

**6** F It's **half** human and half fish.

**2** **THINK!** **Do you know any stories about any of the creatures A-F? Tell the class.**

## *Listening & Reading*

**3** **Look at the title of the text, the subheadings and the pictures. What is each myth about?** 🎧 **Listen, read and check.**

**4** **a)** **Read the text again and complete the sentences. Compare with your partner.**

**1** Because he was so big, Bolster could ........................................... .

**2** He lived in ................................. .

**3** He loved Agnes so he ................. .

**4** He died after he lost ................... .

**5** The mermaid Iara appeared to a man in ....................................... .

**6** She pulled the man .................... .

**7** Today, people sometimes hear ......
...................................... .

**b)** 👥 **Ask and answer questions based on the text.**

People all over the world love to tell stories of terrifying giants, magical unicorns and mysterious mermaids. Here are two of these magical tales!

## Bolster the Giant

Bolster was so big that with one step he could travel six miles from hilltop to hilltop! He lived in Cornwall on the tip of England and terrified the locals, stealing sheep and even eating people. One day, though, he fell in love with a young girl called Agnes and asked her to marry him. Agnes didn't want to, so she tried to think of a way to get rid of him for good. She asked him to do dangerous things to win her love but nothing worked, so she had one last idea. She asked him to fill up a hole in a nearby cliff with his blood. Bolster agreed. After all, how much giant's blood does it take to fill a small hole? The hole, though, led down into the sea. All his blood ran into the sea and that was the end of the evil giant. This is a very popular legend in Cornwall. Locals say you can still see a red stain on the cliffs at Chapel Porth!

## Vocabulary

**1** **Aim** **To present new vocabulary**

- Direct Ss' attention to the legendary creatures.
- Ask Ss if they know anything about them.
- Play the recording with pauses for Ss to repeat individually and chorally.
- Allow Ss time to do the task and compare their answers with a partner.
- Check Ss' answers and elicit synonyms/L1 equivalents for the words in bold.

**Suggested Answer Key**

*look like (v): to be similar to*
*long (adj): not short*
*neck (n): a body part that connects the head to the shoulders*
*wing (n): one of the parts of a bird/plane that helps it fly*
*magical powers (pl n): special, supernatural abilities*
*human (n): a person, a human being*
*huge (adj): very large*
*terrify (v): to scare sb a lot*
*horn (n): a hard, pointed body part attached to the head of an animal*
*breathe fire (phr): to make fire come out of the mouth*
*half (adj): one of two (nearly) equal parts*

**2** **Aim** **To talk about legendary creatures**

Ask various Ss to tell stories in class about any of the creatures in Ex. 1.

**Suggested Answer Key**

*Once there was a boy called Jack. Jack and his mother were very poor so Jack went to market to sell their last cow. He only got five beans for it and his mother was very angry. She threw the beans out of the window. The next morning, there was a huge beanstalk outside, reaching up into the clouds. Jack climbed to the top and found a giant's castle. The giant smelt the boy, but his wife hid the boy until he could escape. She also gave him some gold coins. The next time Jack went up the beanstalk, he stole a goose that laid golden eggs. On the last visit, Jack took a magic harp that could talk. It called out to the giant for help. The giant chased Jack down the beanstalk, but Jack cut down the beanstalk with an axe. The giant fell and died. After that, Jack was rich and he lived happily with his mother.*

## Listening & Reading

**3** **Aim** **To predict the content of the text**

- Refer Ss to the title and subheadings in the text and elicit what Ss know about these myths.
- Play the recording and ask Ss to follow the text in their books to see if they were correct.

**Suggested Answer Key**

*The first myth is about a giant called Bolster who terrified people. He fell in love with a girl and killed himself for her. The second myth is about a mermaid called Iara. A man went fishing with his father. She sang to him and pulled him under the water to be with her.*

- Explain/Elicit the meaning of the words in the **Check these words** box.

**Suggested Answer Key**

*legend (n): a story from the past that is not proven to be true*
*terrifying (adj): very scary*
*mysterious (adj): puzzling, strange*
*tale (n): story*
*step (n): a movement made by lifting up one foot and putting it down again or the distance covered by this movement*
*hilltop (n): the highest part of a small mountain*
*tip (n): the pointed end*
*terrify (v): to cause others to be scared or fearful*
*steal (v): to take sth from sb without their permission*
*fall in love (phr): to start having feelings of love for sb*
*get rid of (phr): to do sth to make sb leave because they are annoying or unwanted*
*for good (phr): finally and forever, permanently*
*win (v): to gain*
*fill up (phr v): to make sth become full*
*hole (n): an opening/cavity in sth solid*
*cliff (n): a high and steep face of rock*
*blood (n): a red liquid that the heart pumps through the body*
*lead (down) (v): to go in a particular direction*
*be the end of (phr): to not exist anymore, to not be a problem anymore*
*stain (n): a dirty or discoloured spot*
*hut (n): a small, simple shelter (usually with one or two rooms)*
*float (v): to stay on top of liquid without sinking*
*grab (v): to take or grasp sth suddenly*
*dive (v): to jump, headfirst, deep into water*
*to this day (phr): until now*
*deep (adj): being far beneath the top*
*lock (v): to secure sth using a key*
*far away (phr): at a great distance from*

**4** **a)** **Aim** **To read for detailed comprehension**

- Ask Ss to read the text again and allow Ss time to complete the task and compare with their partners.
- Check Ss' answers.

*Answer Key – see p. 52(T)*

**b)** **Aim** **To practise asking and answering questions**

- Ask Ss to form closed pairs and practise asking and answering questions based on the text.
- Monitor the activity around the class and then ask various pairs to ask and answer in class.

*Suggested Answer Key – see p. 52(T)*

**5 a)** **Aim** **To consolidate new vocabulary**

- Explain the task.
- Allow Ss time to complete it.
- Check Ss' answers.

**b)** **Aim** **To narrate a story**

- Ask Ss to look at the pictures.
- Invite various Ss to tell the legends in their own words.

### Suggested Answer Key

*Bolster the giant lived in Cornwall, England. He was huge and he could walk from one hilltop to the other. He terrified the local people and stole sheep. One day, he met a girl called Agnes and fell in love with her. He asked her to marry him. Agnes didn't want to. She made a plan to get rid of him. She told him to go to a cliff and fill up a hole with his blood. The giant lost all his blood in the sea and died. Agnes was then free.*

*A young man had a dream one night. He saw a beautiful young woman singing a sad song. The next day, he went out in a fishing boat with his father. He saw the woman from his dream singing to him. She was a mermaid and she grabbed him and pulled him into the water. His father never saw him again.*

**6** **Aim** **To recognise adjectives and their synonyms**

- Read the *Study Skills* box with Ss.
- Elicit that a synonym is a word with a similar meaning to another.
- Allow Ss time to do the task.
- Check Ss' answers.

**Suggested Answers for Exs 2a, 2c, 2d & 3 on p. 44**

---

### Ex. 2a

1 *When was he born? (In 1452)*
2 *Where was he from? (Italy)*
3 *What other paintings did he paint?* (The Last Supper)
4 *What sort of machines did he design? (a helicopter, a calculator, a parachute and even robots)*

### Ex. 2c

*Da Vinci studied painting in Florence. In 2001, architects in Norway constructed a bridge designed by Da Vinci. He had an idea for a robot. His famous drawing of the human body is called* Vitruvian Man.

### Ex. 2d

***measurements:*** *proportions*
***wanting to know more:*** *curious*
***smart:*** *intelligent*
***regard as:*** *consider*
***modelled after:*** *based on*
***thorough:*** *detailed*
***succeeded in doing:*** *achieved*
***exact:*** *accurate*

### Answer Key

| | |
|---|---|
| *unhappy – sad* | *gorgeous – beautiful* |
| *strange – mysterious* | *scary – terrifying* |
| *unsafe – dangerous* | *wicked – evil* |
| *tiny – small* | *well-known – popular* |

## Speaking & Writing

**7 a)** **Aim** **To consolidate information in a text**

- Give Ss three minutes to complete the task.
- Ask different Ss to read out their sentences in class.

### Suggested Answer Key

*I don't think that the stories are true. I think people made these stories up for fun. People in the past didn't have television or cinema, so they made up stories instead.*

**b)** **Aim** **To write a short story**

- Allow Ss time to write about a legendary creature from their country.
- Ask various Ss to read their stories in class.

### Suggested Answer Key

*The Wawle Dragon was a creature that lived under Wawle Hill in Krakow. It was a huge creature with sharp teeth that breathed fire. According to legend, it terrorised the people and liked eating young girls. The people sacrificed the girls to save themselves. Soon, the only girl left was the King's daughter. He promised that whoever killed the dragon could marry her. All the knights tried and died, then a poor boy called Skuba gave the dragon a sheep filled with sulphur. The dragon ate it and became very thirsty. He drank and drank, but he was still thirsty. He drank so much that he exploded. Skuba married the princess and they lived happily ever after.*

### Ex. 3

*We form the past simple of regular verbs using the main form of the verb and adding the ending -ed.*
*Text examples: designed, sketched, constructed, learnt, achieved.*
*When a verb ends in a consonant + e, we just add d.*
*Text examples: achieved, lived, used.*
*When a verb ends in a stressed vowel between two consonants, we double the last consonant and add -ed. Example: stop – stopped*
*When a verb ends in a vowel + l, we double the -l and add -ed. Example: travel – travelled, marvel – marvelled*
*When a verb ends in a consonant + y, the verb drops the y and takes -ied. Text example: studied.*
*To form the negative of the past simple, we use didn't + the base form of the verb.*
*Text examples: didn't finish, didn't want.*
*To form questions in the past simple, we use did + subject + the base form of the verb.*

# Iara the mermaid

In Brazil, the locals tell the myth of the mermaid Iara who lives in the Amazon River. One night, a young man dreamed of a *beautiful* woman singing a *sad* song. The next day, he went fishing with his father and saw the woman from his dream in a hut floating on the water. She sang to him and he went to her. Too late, the man's father saw that the woman had the long tail of a pink dolphin. She grabbed the young man and dived into the water with him. His father never saw him again. To this day, the locals still say that they sometimes see the mermaid swimming deep in the water. And when they hear the sad song of the mermaid Iara, they lock their doors and stay far away from the river!

**Check these words**

legend, terrifying, mysterious, tales, step, hilltop, tip, terrify, steal, fall in love, get rid of, for good, win, fill up, hole, cliff, blood, lead down, be the end of, stain, hut, float, grab, dive, to this day, deep, lock, far away

**5 a)** Use words/phrases from the **Check these words** box in the correct form to complete the sentences.

1 People say unicorns live in forests **far away** from humans.
2 The sea monster **grabbed** the boy and took him to the bottom of the ocean.
3 The dragon **terrified** the people of the village when it flew down from the sky!
4 The story of Bolster the giant is a very well-known **legend**.
5 Agnes thought of a plan to **get rid of** the giant forever.
6 People **lock** their doors and stay inside when the mermaid Iara sings!

**b)** Look at the pictures and narrate the tales to the class.

## Study skills

**Expanding vocabulary**
Learning adjectives together with their synonyms helps you enrich your vocabulary.

**6** Match the highlighted adjectives in the text with their synonyms below.

• unhappy • strange • unsafe • tiny
• gorgeous • scary • wicked • well-known

## Speaking & Writing

**7 a)** **THINK!** Do you think there is any truth in the legends in the text? In three minutes, write a few sentences, then read your sentences to the class.

**b)** Is there a story about a legendary creature in your country? Write a short text about it. Write *its name, place it lives, what it looks like, the story about it*. Read it to the class.

# 3f Events

## Vocabulary
### Breaking the law

1  a)  🎧 Listen and say.

   b)  Have you ever witnessed any of the above?

*Last Monday someone sprayed paint on the school walls. We were very upset.*

## Reading

2  Read the key words in the **Check these words** box and look at the picture. What do you think the text is about? 🎧 Listen, read and check.

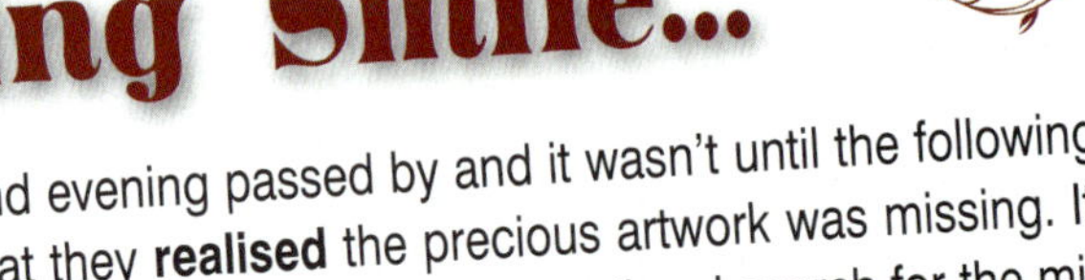

# The Vanishing Smile...

The *Mona Lisa* by Leonardo da Vinci is probably the most famous painting in the world. A star attraction at the Louvre Museum in Paris, her famous smile continues to inspire! However, did you know that a thief once stole the *Mona Lisa* from the museum and caused an international **scandal**?

### The Mystery:
7 am, 21st August, 1911 and just another Monday morning at the Louvre. Guards, cleaning staff, maintenance workers and curators were all working in the building before reopening its doors to the public on Tuesday. While they were working, though, at some time between 7 and 8:30 am, someone entered the empty Salon Carré, unhooked the *Mona Lisa* from the wall and carried it off down a stairwell. The stairs led to a door, locked from the outside, but somehow, the thief escaped through it. At first, museum workers **assumed** that the official photographer was shooting pictures of the painting in his **studio**. An afternoon

and evening passed by and it wasn't until the following day that they **realised** the precious artwork was missing. It was the beginning of a huge international search for the missing *Mona Lisa*. The only **clue** was the discovery of the painting's heavy frame **discarded** on the stairs. There were conflicting **rumours** in the newspapers; the *Mona Lisa* was now in Switzerland, South America, or in a small apartment in the Bronx, New York. No one knew who really **committed** the crime and how.

### The Solution:
On that fateful Monday morning, an Italian man called Vincenzo Peruggia was hiding in a small room within the museum. Peruggia, once a worker at the Louvre, knew the building very well. The guard **on duty** in the Salon Carré **admitted** leaving his post for a few minutes at around 8 am. While the guard was away, Peruggia lifted the *Mona Lisa* from her four iron pegs, entered the stairwell, **removed** the painting's frame and hurried down the steps. Then, he unlocked the door and escaped from the museum. Peruggia hid the painting in his small Paris flat where it remained, in a cupboard, for over two years. Later, Peruggia took the *Mona Lisa* to Florence, Italy, and **attempted** to sell it. It was there, back in the *Mona Lisa*'s hometown, that the police finally caught Peruggia.

Peruggia served a short prison sentence. He then went back to France and opened a paint shop in Haute-Savoie. And the *Mona Lisa*? After touring her Italian homeland, she returned to the Louvre museum, where she **resides** to this day, behind bulletproof glass, still smiling.



guard, reopen its doors, someone entered, unhooked from the wall, carried it off, thief escaped, precious artwork, huge international search, clue, discard, conflicting rumours, committed the crime, guard on duty, admitted leaving his post, unlocked the door, attempted to sell, police caught, served a sentence

52

## Vocabulary

**1 a)** **Aim** To present vocabulary related to breaking the law

Play the recording. Ss listen and repeat chorally or individually. Pay attention to Ss' intonation.

**b)** **Aim** To personalise the topic

Read the example sentence aloud and then elicit similar sentences from various Ss around the class.

### Suggested Answer Key

*Last month someone vandalised a statue in the town centre. We were angry.*

## Reading

**2** **Aim** To predict the content of a text

- Ask Ss to read through the **Check these words** box and then look at the picture.
- Elicit what Ss think the text is about.
- Play the recording. Ss listen and follow the text in their books and find out.

### Suggested Answer Key

*I think the text is about the theft of a precious artwork* (the Mona Lisa) *from a museum.*

- Explain/Elicit the meanings of the words in the **Check these words** box or ask Ss to look up the meanings of the words in their dictionaries.

### Suggested Answer Key

***guard (n):*** *a person who protects sb/sth*
***reopen its doors (phr):*** *to open to the public again after having been closed for some time*
***(someone) entered (v):*** *(someone) got into a room or a building*
***unhooked from the wall (phr):*** *removed from the wall (by undoing the hooks)*
***carried (it) off (phr v):*** *took it away*
***thief escaped (phr):*** *person who stole sth got away*
***precious artwork (n):*** *a valuable piece of art*
***huge international search (n):*** *an organised manhunt around the world*
***clue (n):*** *an object or piece of information that helps to solve a crime*
***committed the crime (phr):*** *did the illegal act*
***guard on duty (phr):*** *the person who was working to protect sb/sth at a certain time*
***admitted leaving his post (phr):*** *(of a guard, etc) confessed to going away from the place which they were supposed to guard*
***unlocked the door (phr):*** *opened the door with a key*
***attempted to sell (phr):*** *tried to get sb to buy sth*
***(police) caught (v):*** *police arrested*
***served a sentence (phr):*** *went to prison for a period of time*

---

## Suggested Answers for Exs 4a & 4b on p. 50

### Ex. 4a

1   travel from hilltop to hilltop/six miles in one step
2   Cornwall, England
3   asked her to marry him
4   all his blood
5   his dream
6   into the water
7   the sad song of Iara (the mermaid)

### Ex. 4b

A: *Where did Bolster the giant live?*
B: *In Cornwall on the southwestern tip of England. What did he steal?*
A: *He stole sheep. Who did he fall in love with?*
B: *A girl called Agnes. What did he ask her?*
A: *He asked her to marry him. Did Agnes want to?*
B: *No, she didn't. What did she do?*
A: *She asked him to fill a small hole with his blood. Did he do it?*
B: *Yes, he did. Where did the hole lead?*
A: *It led to the sea. What happened next?*

B: *He lost all his blood and died. Is this a popular legend?*
A: *Yes, it is. People say you can still see a red stain on the cliffs.*

A: *Where did Iara the mermaid come from?*
B: *Brazil. Where did she live?*
A: *In the Amazon River. What did the young man dream about?*
B: *A beautiful woman singing a sad song. Where did he go the next day?*
A: *He went fishing. What did he see?*
B: *He saw the woman from his dream. What did she do?*
A: *She sang to him. What did he do?*
B: *He went towards her. What happened?*
A: *She grabbed him and pulled him under the water. What happened after that?*
B: *His father never saw him again. What do people say today?*
A: *They say they can sometimes see a mermaid in the water. What do they do if they hear Iara's sad song?*
B: *They lock their doors and stay away from the river.*

**3** **Aim** To read for specific information

- Explain the task and ask Ss to read through the questions 1-5 and the 4 possible answers for each one.
- Give Ss time to read the text again and complete the task.
- Check Ss' answers.

**Answer Key**

1   B (before reopening its door to the public on Tuesday)
2   B (it wasn't until the following day)
3   A (was hiding ... within the museum)
4   C (in his small Paris flat)
5   C (Florence ... caught Perugia)

**4** a) **Aim** To consolidate new vocabulary

- Explain the task and give Ss time to complete the task, using their dictionaries to help them if necessary.
- Check Ss' answers.

b) **Aim** To expand vocabulary/To match words from a text to their meanings

- Explain the task.
- Give Ss time to complete the task.
- Check Ss' answers.

**Answer Key**

**tried to:** attempted
**evidence:** clue
**thought:** assumed
**a shocking event:** scandal
**became aware of:** realised
**a room where an artist works:** studio
**got rid of:** discarded
**at work:** on duty
**took sth away:** removed
**is in a particular place:** resides
**stories that may not be true:** rumours
**confessed to:** admitted
**carried out:** committed

## Grammar

**5** **Aim** To present the past continuous

- Direct Ss' attention to the theory box and ask various Ss to read sections of it aloud.
- Explain/Elicit that we form the past continuous affirmative with *personal pronoun + was/were + base form of the verb + -ing*; we form the negative form of the past continuous with *personal pronoun + wasn't/weren't + base form of the verb + -ing*; and we form the interrogative form of the past continuous with *was/were + personal pronoun + base form of the verb + -ing*.

- Explain that we use the past continuous for actions happening at a certain time in the past, two or more actions happening at the same time in the past and to give background information in a story.

**Answer Key**

*were working, was shooting, was missing, was hiding*

**6** **Aim** To practise the past continuous

Explain the task and give Ss time to complete it. Then check Ss' answers around the class.

**Answer Key**

1   was reading
2   were looking
3   was waving, (was) shouting
4   Were ... watching
5   was shining, was blowing

## Speaking & Writing

**7** **Aim** To practise the past simple and the past continuous using personal examples

- Explain the task and give Ss time to write their sentences.
- Check Ss' answers by asking various Ss to share their answers with the rest of the class.

**Suggested Answer Key**

*I visited a museum yesterday morning.*
*Last Wednesday afternoon, I was doing my homework.*
*The last time I travelled abroad was a week ago.*
*While I was playing computer games last night, the lights went out.*
*At 8 o'clock last night I was watching TV.*
*I was playing computer games when the ground started shaking*

**8** **Aim** To paraphrase information in a text as a first-person narrative

- Explain the task and give Ss time to read the text again and paraphrase the information and summarise the discovery of the theft of the painting as a first-person narrative.
- Ask various Ss to read their account to the class.
- Alternatively, assign the task as HW and check Ss' answers in the next lesson.

**Suggested Answer Key**

*On that Monday, I went to work as usual. I noticed the Mona Lisa wasn't on the wall, but I assumed, like everyone else, that the official photographer was taking photographs of it. It wasn't until Tuesday morning when the painting still wasn't back that I thought something was wrong. I asked the photographer if he had it. When he said no, I started to panic. I told the head of security and he called the police. Everyone was very worried and upset. We couldn't understand where the Mona Lisa was!*

⑤ spray paint on a wall | ⑥ escape out the back door | ⑦ arrest the thief

**3** **Read the text and for questions 1-5 choose the correct answer** *A, B, C* or *D*.

**1** On a Monday, 21st August, 1911, the Louvre
 **A** opened at 9 am.  **C** opened at 7 am.
 **B** was closed.  **D** closed at 8:30 am.

**2** Museum workers found out the painting was missing
 **A** later that morning.  **C** on Monday evening.
 **B** on Tuesday.  **D** during the afternoon.

**3** Peruggia
 **A** hid in the museum.  **C** was the guard on duty.
 **B** left his post.  **D** was working at the museum.

**4** For over two years, Peruggia kept the painting
 **A** at the museum.  **C** in his home.
 **B** flat.  **D** in Florence.

**5** The police arrested him
 **A** at his flat.  **C** in Florence.
 **B** in his hometown.  **D** in Paris.

**4** **a)** **Complete the sentences with:** *inspire, unhook, assume, admit, remove, hurry, attempt, reside, commit, catch* **in the correct form.**

**1** The thief **removed** the frame from the painting so it was easier to carry.
**2** The thief **admitted** stealing the painting.
**3** The police have no idea who **committed** the crime or why.
**4** Leonardo da Vinci continues to **inspire** artists even today.
**5** The police set a trap to **catch** the thief.
**6** The caretaker **unhooked** the painting from the wall for cleaning.
**7** People shouldn't **assume** things, they should find out the truth.
**8** We have to **hurry** or we'll miss the bus!
**9** The *Mona Lisa* **resides** in the Louvre Museum.
**10** Thieves are often caught when they **attempt** to sell stolen property.

**b)** **Match the words in bold to their meanings:** *tried to, evidence, thought, a shocking event, became aware of, a room where an artist works, got rid of, at work, took sth away, is in a particular place, stories that may not be true, confessed to, carried out.*

***Grammar*** see p. GR5
**Past continuous**

**5** **Read the theory box. How do we form the** *past continuous*? **Find examples in the text.**

We use the **past continuous**:
- for actions happening at a certain time in the past.
  *He **was working** at 12 o'clock yesterday.*
- for two or more actions happening at the same time in the past (simultaneous actions).
  *While he **was working**, she **was cleaning** the house.*
- to give background information in a story.
  *That morning Peter **was walking** down the street. The wind **was howling** and it **was raining**.*

**Time expressions used with the past continuous:** while, as, at … o'clock yesterday morning/evening etc.

**6** **Use the verbs in the list in the** *past continuous* **to complete the sentences.**

- blow • shout • watch • read • look • shine • wave

**1** While he ................................. a book, the lights went out.
**2** They ........................................ at the exhibits when the fire alarm went off.
**3** She ......................... her arms and ................... for help hoping someone would notice her.
**4** ................... you ............................... TV when he called you?
**5** The sun ........................................ and a light wind ..................................... .

## Speaking & Writing

**7** **Write sentences about yourself using the phrases below and the verbs in the** *past simple* **or the** *past continuous*.

- yesterday morning
- last Wednesday afternoon
- a week ago • while
- last night • when
- at 8 o'clock last night

- travel abroad
- play computer games
- visit a museum
- do my homework
- watch TV

**8** **THINK!** Imagine you were the person who found out that the *Mona Lisa* was missing. Describe the scene and how you felt.

Vocabulary Bank 3 p. VB9 53

# 3g Skills

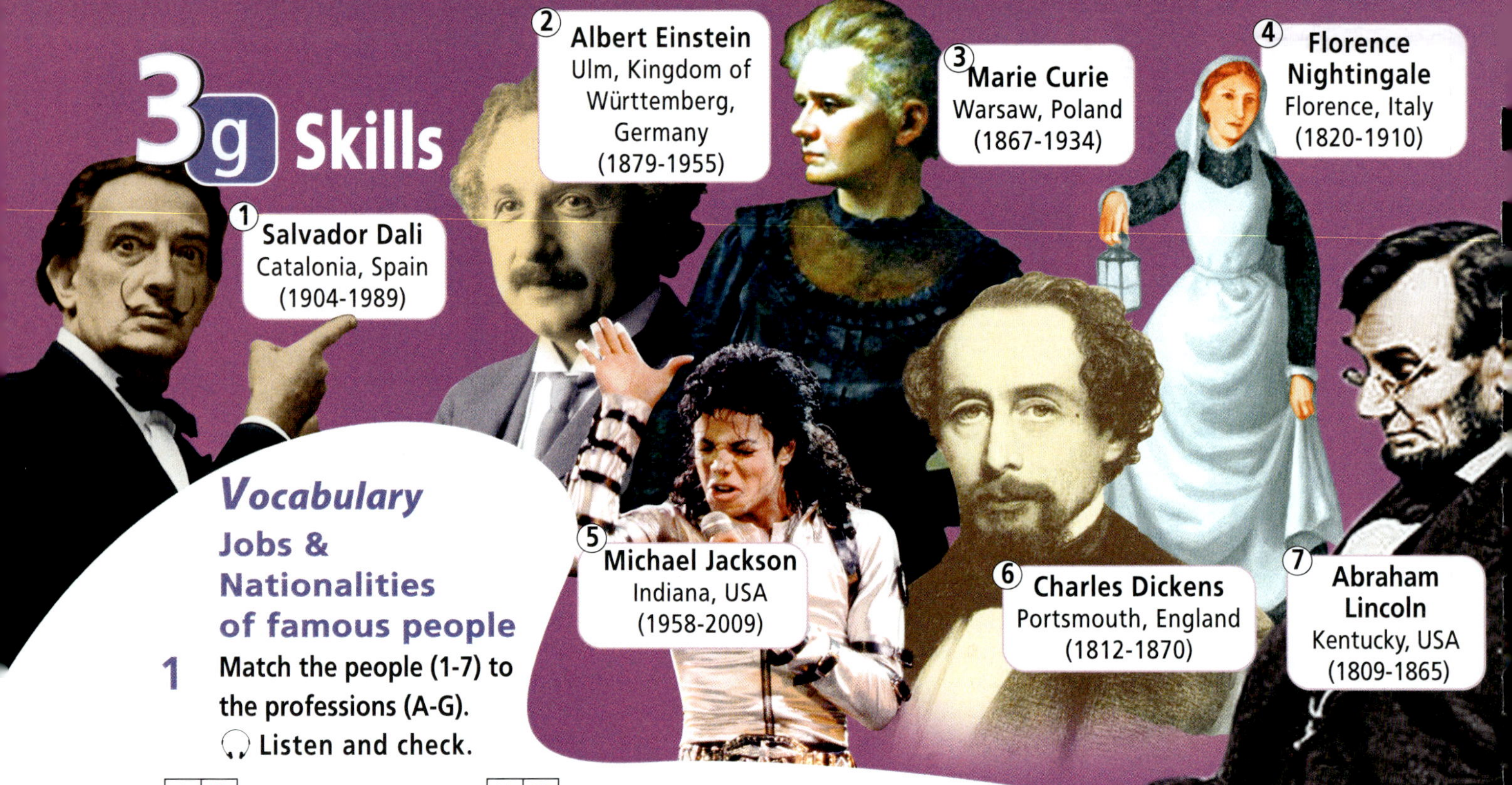

## Vocabulary

### Jobs & Nationalities of famous people

1 Match the people (1-7) to the professions (A-G). 🎧 Listen and check.

| | | |
|---|---|---|
| **A** | 1 | Spanish artist |
| **B** | 4 | British nurse |
| **C** | 6 | British writer |
| **D** | 5 | American pop singer |
| **E** | 7 | American president |
| **F** | 3 | Polish scientist |
| **G** | 2 | German physicist |

### Study skills

**Reading years**
In English, we read the years as two sets of two-digit numbers.
**1652** = sixteen fifty-two
**1804** = eighteen oh four
**1938** = nineteen thirty-eight
                BUT
**2006** = two thousand and six

## Speaking

### Asking for/Giving personal information

2 👥 Ask and answer questions about the people in Ex. 1, as in the example.

A: *Who was Salvador Dali?*
B: *He was a Spanish artist.*
A: *Where was he born?*
B: *In Catalonia, Spain.*

A: *When was he born?*
B: *In 1904.*
A: *When did he die?*
B: *In 1989.*

### Study skills

**Gap filling Listening**
Read the notice and try to work out what information (e.g. number, noun etc) is missing. This will help you do the listening task.

## Listening

3 🎧 You will hear some information about a museum. Listen and complete the gaps.

**Tickets:** Adult £5.80
Child **1)** £ 4.80
(included museum audio **2)** tour)

Exhibitions: 1st *The Gilded Cage*
2nd **3)** *The Calling*
3rd *Reform* **4)** *and Inspire*

Opening hours: 10 am – 5 pm **5)** daily



▶ **Vocabulary Bank 3  p. VB10**

## Vocabulary

**1** **Aim** **To present new vocabulary**

- Refer Ss to the pictures of famous people and elicit who these people are and what Ss know about them. Use the background information to stimulate a discussion.
- Allow Ss time to do the task.
- Play the recording for Ss to check their answers.

### BACKGROUND INFORMATION

**Salvador Dalí** was a Spanish surrealist artist who created unusual paintings, sculptures, drawings and photographs. His best-known works are *The Persistence of Memory* (1931) and *Swans Reflecting Elephants* (1937).

**Albert Einstein** was a physicist and philosopher. He was born in the Kingdom of Württemberg which is now part of Germany. He is most famous for his Theory of Relativity which contains the equation $E=MC^2$.

**Marie Curie** was a Polish chemist and physicist who lived and worked in France. She discovered polonium and radium, created a theory of radioactivity and won two Nobel Prizes.

**Florence Nightingale** was a British nurse and writer who pioneered modern nursing during the Crimean War. She was named after the Italian city she was born in, but her parents were English and she grew up in England. Many people came to know her as 'the lady of the lamp'.

**Michael Jackson** was a world-famous pop star from the USA. Guinness World Records call him the most successful entertainer of all time.

**Charles Dickens** was a famous English writer. His Victorian novels are classics of English literature. They are popular all over the world, and have never gone out of print. Some of his most famous novels are *Oliver Twist* (1837-39), *David Copperfield* (1849-50) and *Bleak House* (1853).

**Abraham Lincoln** was the 16th American president and is famous for his involvement in the American Civil War and the abolition of slavery.

## Speaking

**2** **Aim** **To practise asking and answering questions**

- Explain the task and read the *Study Skills* box aloud.
- Ask Ss to work in pairs and ask and answer questions about the famous people, as in the example.
- Monitor the activity around the classroom and then ask some pairs to ask and answer in class.

## Answer Key

**2** A: *Who was Albert Einstein?*
B: *He was a German physicist.*
A: *Where was he born?*
B: *In Ulm in the Kingdom of Württemberg, Germany.*
A: *When was he born?*
B: *In 1879.*
A: *When did he die?*
B: *In 1955.*

**3** A: *Who was Marie Curie?*
B: *She was a Polish scientist.*
A: *Where was she born?*
B: *In Warsaw, Poland.*
A: *When was she born?*
B: *In 1867.*
A: *When did she die?*
B: *In 1934.*

**4** A: *Who was Florence Nightingale?*
B: *She was a British nurse.*
A: *Where was she born?*
B: *In Florence, Italy.*
A: *When was she born?*
B: *In 1820.*
A: *When did she die?*
B: *In 1910.*

**5** A: *Who was Michael Jackson?*
B: *He was an American pop singer.*
A: *Where was he born?*
B: *In Indiana, USA.*
A: *When was he born?*
B: *In 1958.*
A: *When did he die?*
B: *In 2009.*

**6** A: *Who was Charles Dickens?*
B: *He was a British writer.*
A: *Where was he born?*
B: *In Portsmouth, England.*
A: *When was he born?*
B: *In 1812.*
A: *When did he die?*
B: *In 1870.*

**7** A: *Who was Abraham Lincoln?*
B: *He was an American president.*
A: *Where was he born?*
B: *In Kentucky, USA.*
A: *When was he born?*
B: *In 1809.*
A: *When did he die?*
B: *In 1865.*

## Listening

**3** **Aim** **To listen for specific information (gap fill)**

- Explain the task and explain/elicit what sort of information is missing from each gap.
- Play the recording. Ss listen and complete the task. Check Ss' answers.

**1** **Aim** To read for gist

- Allow Ss three minutes to read the text in their books.
- Elicit answers to the questions in the rubric.
- Read the *Writing Tip* box with Ss.

*Answer Key*

*Frida Kahlo was a Mexican artist. She was famous for a style that combined Mexican folk art with surrealism.*

**2** **a)** **Aim** To scan a text

- Ask Ss to scan the text and find examples of phrases showing the sequence of events.
- Check Ss' answers.

*Answer Key*

- on 6th July, 1907
- As a child
- in 1922
- at the age of 18
- It was then that
- When Frida was 21
- in 1929
- Nine years later
- on 13th July, 1954

**b)** **Aim** To give a summary from notes

- Write the headings on the board and give Ss time to prepare their answers. Elicit Ss' answers and write them under the headings.
- Tell Ss to give their partner a summary of Frida Kahlo's life using the notes.
- Monitor the activity. Then ask some Ss to give their summary in class.

*Suggested Answer Key*

*where and when born: Coyoacán, Mexico, 6th July, 1907*
*early years: dreamed of becoming a doctor, in 1922 began studying Medicine, bus accident at age of 18, taught herself to paint while recovering, developed her own style of Mexican folk art and surrealism*
*later years & achievements: met artist Diego Rivera at age of 21, married in 1929, first exhibition nine years later in New York City, Paris exhibitions*
*where and when died: in her hometown, 13th July, 1954*

*Frida Kahlo was born in Coyoacán, Mexico, on 6th July, 1907. As a child, she dreamed of becoming a doctor, so she began studying Medicine in 1922. She had to stop at the age of 18 because she had an accident. She had to stay in bed to recover and she felt bored, so she taught herself to paint, and developed her own style of Mexican folk art and surrealism. At the age of 21, she met the artist Diego Rivera, and they got married in 1929. Nine years later she had her first exhibition in New York City. She also exhibited work in Paris. She died in her hometown on 13th July, 1954.*

**3** **a)** **Aim** To read for specific information

- Read the *Study Skills* box with Ss.
- Ask Ss to read the biography of Frida Kahlo again and find examples of linking words.
- Check Ss' answers.

*Answer Key*

*and, so, also, but*

**b)** **Aim** To practise using linking words

- Give Ss time to complete the task.
- Check Ss' answers.

*Suggested Answer Key*

1 His concerts were always sold out **because** his music was very popular.
2 Frida had a mirror **so** she could paint herself.
3 He started writing when he was young **and** he wrote over 50 books.
4 She sang well. She danced well, **too**.
5 He was a genius, **but** people didn't recognise his talent.

## Writing

**4** **a)** **Aim** To prepare to write a biography of a famous person

Read through the plan of a biography with Ss. Play the recording and tell Ss to take notes about Albert Einstein.

*Suggested Answer Key*

**Albert Einstein:** *scientist, philosopher, physicist – born 14th March 1879 in Ulm – grew up in Munich, attended Luitpold Grammar School, interested in Maths and Science, played violin – at 15 left school, went to Milan, ambition to be Maths/Physics teacher – finished university in Zurich in 1900 – in 1901 got job in Swiss Patent Office- worked on maths problems in spare time – in 1905 published scientific theories including 'Special Theory of Relativity' – Nobel Prize in 1921 – published over 400 scientific works, gave lectures in Europe and America – died 18th April 1955 at 76*

**b)** **Aim** To write a biography

- Write these phrases/sentences on the board and ask Ss to copy them in their notebooks and use them to do the task.

<table>
<tr><td colspan="2" align="center">**Useful phrases for biographies**</td></tr>
<tr><td>… is a famous artist, scientist, etc.</td><td>When he/she was … years old.<br>He/She became …</td></tr>
<tr><td>… was born in (place), on (date).</td><td>He/She got married etc.<br>He/She died in (place), on</td></tr>
<tr><td>At the age of …</td><td>(date)</td></tr>
<tr><td>As a child …</td><td>He/She was a genius …</td></tr>
</table>

- Allow Ss time to write their biographies using their notes. Alternatively, assign the task as HW.
- Ask Ss to read out their biographies in class and check.

*Suggested Answer Key – see p. 57(T)*

## A biography of a famous person

**1** Who was Frida Kahlo? What was she famous for? Read to check.

# Frida Kahlo

Frida Kahlo is one of the most famous female artists in the world. She was born on 6th July 1907 in Coyoacán, Mexico.

As a child, Frida dreamed of becoming a doctor and in 1922 she began studying Medicine. Unfortunately, at the age of 18, Frida was in a bus accident and spent a long time recovering in bed. It was then that she taught herself to paint. She even had a mirror above her bed so she could paint herself. Frida's style combined Mexican folk art with surrealism.

When Frida was 21, she met the famous artist Diego Rivera. He recognised her talent and encouraged her to keep painting. Diego and Frida got married in 1929, but it was a difficult marriage. Nine years later, Frida had her first exhibition in New York City. She also exhibited her work in Paris.

Frida was weak throughout her life and she died in her hometown on 13th July, 1954. She was one of the most famous artists of the 20th century, not only in Mexico, but all around the world.

### Writing Tip

**Writing biographies**

When we write a biography, we always put the events of the person's life in chronological order. We also use phrases that show the sequence of events *e.g. In 1943, On 3rd July, 1840, At the age of 24, As a child, etc.* This helps the reader follow the biography better.

**2**

**a)** Find examples of phrases showing the sequence of events in the biography.

**b)** Make notes under the headings. Use your notes to tell the class a summary of Frida Kahlo's life.

| where & when born | early years |
|---|---|
| *Coyoacán, 6th July …* | |

| later years & achievements | where & when died |
|---|---|

*Frida Kahlo was born on 6th July 1907. As a child, she … . At the age of 15, …*

**3**

**a)** Read the *Study Skills* box and find examples of linking words in Kahlo's biography.

**b)** Rewrite the sentences using *so, because, too, and, but.*

**1** His concerts were always sold out. His music was very popular.
**2** Frida had a mirror. She could paint herself.
**3** He started writing when he was young. He wrote over 50 books.
**4** She sang well. She danced well.
**5** He was a genius. People didn't recognise his talent.

### *Writing (a biography of a famous person)*

**4**

**a)** Look at the plan below.
🎧 Listen to someone talking about Albert Einstein and take notes.

### Study skills

**Linking words**  see p. GR6

We use linking words to connect different parts of a sentence. We use **because** to show the reason for something. *He spent a long time in the hospital **because** he had an accident.* We use **so** to show the result of something. *She wanted to become a doctor **so** she studied Medicine.* We use **too, and** or **also** to show addition. *He organised concerts in Madrid, **too**.* We use **but** to show contrast. *He tried hard **but** he failed.*

### Plan

**Para 1:** name, who he was, where/when born *(… was … . He was born … . He was one of the most famous … .)*
**Para 2:** early years *(As a child … . At the age of … . When he was … .)*
**Para 3:** later years, achievements *(In … , … . years later… .)*
**Para 4:** where/when he died, your thoughts/feelings about the person *(… died on … in … . He was … .)*

**b)** Use your notes to write a short biography about Einstein (100-120 words). Use the biography in Ex. 1 as a model and follow the plan.

▶ Writing Bank p. WB4

# 3i Curricular: US History

**1**
a) Who was Christopher Columbus? What do you know about him?

b) Think of three questions you would like to ask about Columbus. Read to see if you can answer your questions.



**Matching headings**
Read the headings and underline the key words. Read the text and try to find words/phrases related to the key words.

**2** Read again and match the headings with the paragraphs. There is one extra heading.

A COLUMBUS' PLAN
B OTHER JOURNEYS & COLUMBUS' IMPORTANCE
C EARLY YEARS
D PROBLEMS AT SEA
E HIS FIRST VOYAGE

**3** Match the words in bold with their definitions: *expensive things, left by boat, love, journey by sea, laughed at, way, bring in.*

**4** **THINK!** Listen to the text. Imagine you are one of Christopher Columbus' men and you just returned home from one of his voyages. Tell the class: *what it was like at sea, what you saw in 'the New World', how you felt, what you think of Columbus.*

**5** ICT Collect information about another famous explorer. Use textbooks, encyclopaedias or the Internet. You can use these key words: *famous explorers.* Present your information to the class.

# Christopher Columbus
## (1451-1506)

**1**

Christopher Columbus was born in Genoa, Italy in 1451. He worked with his father as a weaver, but the sea was always his real **passion**.

**2**

In the 15th century, it was difficult and dangerous to travel to Asia around the southern tip of Africa. Columbus decided to try to sail west to find a new trade **route**. People **made fun of** him, but finally King Ferdinand and Queen Isabella of Spain gave him supplies, men and three sailing ships for his **voyage**. They wanted to find a way to **import** gold and spices from Asia.

**3**

Columbus **set sail** from Spain in August 1492 with his three ships the *Niña*, the *Pinta* and the *Santa María*. Ten weeks later, he reached an island in the Bahamas. As he thought he was in India, he called the people there Indians! On the voyage home, Columbus lost the *Santa María* in a terrible storm. He arrived safely back in Spain in March 1493, with plants, gold, cloth, ornaments, and other **riches**.

**4**

Columbus made three more voyages to 'the New World'. He explored the coasts of Cuba, Hispaniola (modern-day Haiti and the Dominican Republic), Venezuela and Central America. On each voyage, he believed he was in India! He died in 1506 without knowing the importance of what he found on his voyages. Columbus was a brilliant, brave sailor and we remember him as one of the most important explorers in history.



weaver, southern, tip, sail, trade route, supplies, sailing ship, import, gold, spice, cloth, ornament, explore, coast, importance, brilliant, brave, sailor

**1 a)** **Aim** **To present a famous person**

Ask various Ss to say what they know about Christopher Columbus and stimulate a discussion on what Ss will learn in the text.

***Suggested Answer Key***

*Christopher Columbus was an explorer. He lived in the 15th century and he is famous for discovering the New World.*

**b)** **Aim** **To read for specific information**

- Elicit various questions from Ss around the classroom. Write three on the board.
- Allow Ss time to read the text and answer the questions.
- Check Ss' answers.

***Suggested Answer Key***

*Where was Columbus from? (Genoa, Italy) How many voyages did he make? (5) What things did he bring back with him from his voyages? (plants, gold, cloth, ornaments and other riches)*

- Explain/Elicit the meaning of the words in the **Check these words** box.

**weaver (n):** *a person whose job is to make baskets or cloth out of threads or strips*
**southern (adj):** *located in the south*
**tip (n):** *the pointed end of sth*
**sail (v):** *to travel by boat or ship*
**trade route (n):** *a passage of travel used by merchants and traders*
**supplies (pl n):** *things, like food and materials, needed to do sth*
**sailing ship (n):** *large boat with sails*
**import (v):** *to bring in goods from a foreign land in order to sell them*
**gold (n):** *a type of yellow metal that is used to make jewellery or coins*
**spice (n):** *a type of powder/seed that comes from plants, used to give food flavour*
**cloth (n):** *a woven material, like cotton or silk, that people use to make clothing and blankets*
**ornament (n):** *an object people use to decorate*
**explore (v):** *to travel with the aim of discovering sth*
**coast (n):** *the part of land that is next to the sea*
**importance (n):** *significance*
**brilliant (adj):** *great, amazing*
**brave (adj):** *showing or feeling no fear, having courage*
**sailor (n):** *a person who works on a ship*

**2** **Aim** **To read for specific information**

- Read the **Study Skills** box with Ss. Do item 1 with Ss to help them understand how to do this type of exercise.
- Allow Ss time to complete the task.

- Check Ss' answers.

***Answer Key***

| | | | |
|---|---|---|---|
| *1 C* | *2 A* | *3 E* | *4 B* |

**3** **Aim** **To consolidate new vocabulary**

- Allow Ss three minutes to do the task.
- Check Ss' answers.

***Answer Key***

| | |
|---|---|
| *expensive things – riches* | *laughed at – made fun of* |
| *left by boat – set sail* | *way – route* |
| *love – passion* | *bring in – import* |
| *journey by sea – voyage* | |

**4** **Aim** **To listen for specific information and narrate an imaginary experience**

- Play the recording for Ss to listen to the text.
- Ask Ss to imagine they were on one of Christopher Columbus' voyages and have just returned home.
- Allow Ss two minutes to prepare their answers.
- Ask various Ss to talk about their experience.

***Suggested Answer Key***

*We had a long tiring **voyage** and sailed through a terrible **storm**. It took ten long **weeks** to get there, but the New World was an amazing place. We saw long sandy **beaches** and palm **trees**. We met the **natives** there and they seemed friendly. I saw some strange **plants**. I didn't know what they're called, but Columbus wanted to bring some back **home**. He was very happy when we **arrived** in India. He is a very **brave** man and loves exploring.*

### Activity for weaker classes

Photocopy the text in the Suggested Answer Key, make it a gapped text giving the missing words in a list. Ask Ss to fill in the words. For a suggested list of words use the words in bold in the Suggested Answer Key.

**5** **Aim** **To give a presentation on a famous explorer**

- Ask Ss to work in small groups and collect information from the Internet using the key words in the search bar or from their school textbooks, encyclopaedias or other reference books, about another famous explorer.
- Allow Ss time to collect their information and write their presentation. Alternatively, assign the task as HW.
- Invite Ss to present their information in class.

***Suggested Answer Key – see p. 60(T)***

**Aim** To consolidate vocabulary from the module

- Divide the class into 2 teams. Each team takes turns writing or saying a sentence with one of the words/phrases in the list.
- Each correct sentence earns one point. If the sentence is incorrect, the team misses a turn.
- The team with the most points after all the words have been used, wins.

***Suggested Answer Key***

*Christopher Columbus **discovered** the New World.*
*Thomas Edison **invented** the light bulb.*
*Frida Kahlo was a very **talented** artist.*
*Genghis Khan **fought against** huge armies.*
*The family became ill after eating **poisoned food**.*
*The Pilgrims **survived** their journey to the New World.*
*Families get together and have a **big feast** on Thanksgiving.*
*There wasn't enough food to **share** on the huge ship.*
*Genghis Khan started the Mongol **Empire**.*
*Alexander the Great **fought against** many **armies**.*
*Columbus was a **brave sailor**.*
*Columbus wanted to **explore** the world.*
*Sailors have a **real passion** for the sea.*
*At Colonial Williamsburg you can see a **re-enactment of a battle**.*
*Caesar **conquered** Asia Minor.*
*A sea monster **terrified the locals** for centuries.*
*Dragons can **breathe fire**.*
*Columbus sailed in many **sailing ships**.*
*The captain **set sail** from England and sailed to the New World.*
*During the celebration people wore **traditional clothing**.*
*A unicorn has a **single horn** on its head.*
*The statue was beautiful with **perfect proportions**.*

## Quiz

***Answer Key***

1   F   *(Florence)*
2   T
3   T
4   T
5   F   *(a dragon)*
6   F   *(Mayflower)*
7   F   *(she taught herself)*
8   F   *(1492)*

Ss prepare their quiz in groups. Ask Ss to go through the pages of Module 3 and select information to compile their quiz. Ask Ss to exchange quizzes, do them and then check their answers.

***Suggested Answer Key***

1   *George Washington was a sailor. (F – US president)*
2   *Thomas Edison was an inventor. (T)*
3   *Da Vinci sketched Vitruvian Man. (T)*
4   *The best known drawing in the world is by Van Gogh. (F – Da Vinci)*
5   *Julius Caesar was a Roman ruler. (T)*
6   *A snake killed Genghis Khan. (F – Cleopatra)*
7   *Tutankhamun died young. (T)*
8   *Thanksgiving is in October. (F – November)*

**Suggested Answer for Ex. 4b on p. 55**

---

### Ex. 4b

#### Albert Einstein

*Albert Einstein was a world-famous scientist and physicist. He was born on 14th March, 1879 in Ulm, which is now in Germany.*

*As a child, he grew up in Munich. He attended Luitpold Grammar School where he was a quiet student interested in science and mathematics. He also enjoyed playing his violin. At the age of 15, he left school and went to live with his family in Milan. He wanted to become a Maths or Physics teacher. He took his exams in Switzerland and finished his studies in 1900, in Zurich.*

*In 1901, Einstein got a job as a technical assistant in the Swiss Patent Office. In his spare time, he worked on maths problems and in 1905, he published some of his famous scientific theories, one of which was the well-known 'Special Theory of Relativity'. During the 1920s, he received many different honours. He got the Nobel Prize for Physics in 1921. Throughout his life, he published over 400 scientific works and gave lectures in Europe and America. Albert Einstein died on 18th April, 1955. He was 76 years old. He was a genius.*

**1** **Fill in:** *writer, composer, architect, painter, warrior, inventor, queen, philosopher, engineer, explorer.*

1 Van Gogh was a great painter, but he only sold one painting in his lifetime!
2 Beethoven was an amazing composer. His music is superb.
3 Genghis Kahn was a great warrior and fought many battles.
4 Socrates was a famous philosopher in Ancient Greece. He was one of the wisest people of all time.
5 Columbus was a(n) explorer who went on four voyages to 'the New World'.
6 Elizabeth I was a great English queen. She ruled England for about 45 years.
7 Alexander Graham Bell was the inventor of the telephone.
8 Antoni Gaudí was a famous Spanish architect. He designed lots of buildings.
9 A(n) engineer designs machines and buildings.
10 James Joyce was an Irish writer. His most famous novel is *Ulysses*.

**2** **Choose the correct word.**

In Greek mythology, Cecrops was the first 1) **explorer/king** of the city of Athens. He was half man and half snake and he 2) **invented/ discovered** writing, brought peace to the 3) **land/place**, and 4) **fixed/ built** a city for his people. 5) **According to/Because of** legend, both the god Poseidon and the goddess Athena wanted Cecrops to name the city after them. So, Cecrops 6) **held/conquered** a contest between the two. Poseidon 7) **did/made** water flow from a hole in the rock of the Acropolis, but Athena 8) **created/invented** a single olive tree. Cecrops preferred Athena's olive tree and named the city Athens. Poseidon didn't like this and sent a(n) 9) **evil/terrifying** flood. The city still has the name Athens 10) **far away/to this day**!

## Prepositions

**3** **Choose the correct preposition.**

1 Leonardo da Vinci was ahead **in/of** his time.
2 Bolster the giant fell **in/into** love with a human.
3 Alexander the Great fought **against/at** the Persians many times.
4 Agnes tried to get rid **of/from** Bolster the giant.
5 The architect designed the building based **at/ on** Mr Smith's design.

## Collocations

**4** **Fill in:** *win, trade, popular, human, flying, poisonous, harvest, known, grow, magical.*

1 human body
2 have magical powers
3 win a battle
4 known world
5 trade route
6 popular legend
7 flying machine
8 poisonous snake
9 harvest feast
10 grow crops

In teams, make sentences. Use words/phrases from the list below. Each correct sentence gets one point. The team with the most points wins.

- discovered • invented • talented
- fought against • poisoned food
- survived • big feast • share
- empire • fight against armies
- brave sailor • explore • real passion
- re-enactment of a battle • conquer
- terrified the locals • breathe fire
- sailing ships • set sail
- traditional clothing • single horn
- perfect proportions

## Quiz

Mark the sentences *T* (true) or *F* (false). Read through Module 3 and write a quiz of your own.

1 Leonardo da Vinci designed a canal system for Venice. ......
2 Tutankhamun's tomb is in the Valley of the Kings. ......
3 The voyage of the *Mayflower* lasted 66 days. ......
4 Alexander the Great was quite young when he died. ......
5 A giant is a creature who can breathe fire. ......
6 The Pilgrims' ship was called the *Santa María*. ......
7 Frida Kahlo's husband taught her how to paint. ......
8 Christopher Columbus made his first voyage in 1592. ......

## Listening

**1** 🎧 **Read the rubric, then do the task.**

> You will hear five short conversations. For questions 1-5 put a tick (✓) under the right answer.

**Example**

**0** How old is Craig?

A

B

C ✓

**1** When was the re-enactment?


A


B


C

**2** What did the thieves take?

A

B

C

**3** Where is da Vinci's bridge?

A

B

C

**4** What was the weather like?

A

B

C

**5** How many people were on board the boat?

A

B

C

## Reading

**2** **a)** **Read the notices. What is each about? Now read the sentences 1-5. Underline the key words. This will help you do the task.**

> Which notices (A-H) says this (1-5)?

**b)** **Do the task. Give reasons for your answers.**

**Example**

**0** *There are special prices at a particular time.*     G

1 You don't have to pay an entrance fee.    ........
2 You must not enter the area.    ........
3 You cannot attend this event.    ........
4 Using the Internet can help you save money.    ........
5 You mustn't take pictures.    ........

**A** Museum opening hours:
Mon-Fri: 10-6, Sat: 9-7, Sun: Closed

**B** Historic battle re-enactment **CANCELLED**

**C** Stay off the battlefield

**D** Free Admission

**E** No flash photography

**F** Please do not touch the exhibits

**G** Happy hour 09:00-10:00 COFFEE & CAKE £2

**H** Book online for ticket discount ▼

## Reading

**3** **a)** **Read the announcement and the letter. What are they about?**

> Read the information about a guest speaker. Complete Wayne's notes.

**Historical Heroes**

**Medicine through the Ages** With Dr Adrian Chiles

**Monday 28 September 3 pm Assembly Hall**

Wayne,
Dr Chiles is arriving Sunday night and staying at the Four Seasons Hotel. Can you call them to confirm his booking? Also can you meet him at the entrance to the building half an hour before his talk and show him the way to the hall?
Thanks
Amanda

### Wayne's notes

Person to meet: Dr Chiles
Arriving: **1)** ..............................
Call "Four Seasons" to: **2)** ..........................
Meeting place: **3)** ..............................
Meeting time: **4)** ..............................
Take him to: **5)** ..............................

# Listening

**1** **Aim** To listen for specific information

- Ask Ss to read the rubric and the questions.
- Play the recording for the first dialogue.
- Ask Ss what words made picture C the correct answer, and what words made pictures A and B incorrect.
- Now play the recording for dialogues 1-5.
- Give Ss time to decide which picture each dialogue matches then check answers around the classroom.

**Answer Key**

1  B    2  B    3  A    4  C    5  C

# Reading

**2** **a)** **Aim** To prepare for a reading task

- Ask Ss to read the notices and say what each is about. Then ask Ss to read the sentences 1-5 and underline the key words.
- Ask Ss to check their answers with their partners and compare.

**Suggested Answer Key**

*Notice A: the opening hours of a museum*
*Notice B: the cancellation of a historic battle re-enactment*
*Notice C: a warning not to get close to a battlefield*
*Notice D: a place where you can enter for free*
*Notice E: a place where you mustn't take photographs*
*Notice F: a place where you cannot touch the exhibits*
*Notice G: a place where you can buy something at a better price at a particular time*
*Notice H: a way to get a better price for something you buy*

**Key words**

0  *special, prices, particular, time*
1  *don't, pay, entrance, fee*
2  *must, not, enter, area*
3  *cannot, attend, event*
4  *Using, Internet, save, money*
5  *mustn't, take, pictures*

**b)** **Aim** To read for matching information

- Put Ss in pairs and give them time to find the matching notices using the key words they underlined in Ex. 2a.
- Check Ss' answers on the board. Ask Ss to justify their answers.

**Answer Key**

1  D    2  C    3  B    4  H    5  E

**Justifications**

0  *special prices particular time – happy hour 09:00-10:00*
1  *don't pay entrance fee – free admission*
2  *must not enter area – stay off the battlefield*
3  *cannot attend event – re-enactment cancelled*
4  *Using Internet ... save money – Book online ... discount*
5  *mustn't take pictures – No ... photography*

# Reading

**3** **a)** **Aim** To prepare for a reading task

Ask Ss to read the announcement and the letter and say what they are about *(the announcement is about a talk about Medicine through time by Dr Adrian Giles – the letter is about making arrangements for a guest speaker)*

**b)** **Aim** **To extract relevant information from a text**

- Give Ss enough time to read the announcement, the letter and Wayne's notes and find the information that corresponds to each gap.
- Check answers around the classroom.

*Answer Key*

1   *Sunday night (= is arriving Sunday night)*
2   *confirm his booking (= Can you call them to confirm his booking?)*
3   *the (building) entrance (= can you meet him at the entrance to the building)*
4   *2:30/half past two (= can you meet him … half an hour before his talk / announcement: talk 3 pm)*
5   *the hall (= show him the way to the hall)*

## Reading

**4 a)** **Aim** **To complete short exchanges**

- Read through the rubric with Ss and explain the task.
- Read the example question and ask Ss to suggest possible answers.

*Suggested Answer Key*

0   *It was great, thanks.*
1   *Yes, it was fantastic.*
2   *It was just a normal weekend.*
3   *Yes, it was.*
4   *Yes, it was great.*
5   *I'd really like to go there.*

**b)** **Aim** **To complete short exchanges**

- Give Ss enough time to complete the task.
- Ask Ss to compare their answers with their partners.
- Then check the answers on the board.

*Answer Key*

1   C          2   A          3   C          4   B          5   A

## Speaking

**5** **Aim** **To practise asking for/giving information**

- Ask Ss to read the rubric, then put them in pairs to do the task. Give Ss 3 minutes to complete the task.
- Monitor the activity around the classroom and give assistance where necessary.
- Ss switch roles.
- Elicit correct question forms and write them on the board.

*Suggested Answer Key*

A:   *Who organises the re-enactment?*
B:   *The 5th Cavalry Society.*
A:   *Which battle are they re-enacting?*
B:   *The Battle of Weston Bridge.*
A:   *Where does the re-enactment take place?*
B:   *In Smythe Field Park.*
A:   *When does it take place?*
B:   *On Saturday 15th July and Sunday 16th July between 10 am and 5 pm.*
A:   *What's the telephone number for information?*
B:   *2548796*

## Writing

**6 a)** **Aim** **To prepare for a writing task**

- Read the rubric aloud and then write the points on the board.
- Brainstorm with the class for ideas and write them under the points. Ss copy the points and the ideas into their notebooks.

*Suggested Answer Key*

**Where you went:** *Louvre, Paris*
**What you did there:** *Went round Greek & Roman antiquities, saw the Mona Lisa*
**Why you liked the visit:** *saw famous works of art, favourite was the Venus De Milo*

**b)** **Aim** **To write an email to a friend**

- Give Ss time to write their email using the notes they made in Ex. 6a.
- Check Ss' answers.

*Suggested Answer Key*

*Dear Jenny,*
*How are you? Last week I went to the Louvre in Paris. It's a brilliant museum in the centre of the city.*
*I went round the Greek and Roman antiquities and saw friezes from the Parthenon. I also walked round the gallery on the 1st floor where they hang all the amazing painting and you can see the world famous Mona Lisa.*
*I really enjoyed the visit because I saw so many famous works of art. I especially liked the statue of the Venus De Milo. I want to go back again soon.*
*You would love it there.*
*See you soon,*
*Amanda*

b)  Read the headings in Wayne's notes.
    Complete them with information from
    the texts. Compare with your partner.

## Reading

**4**  a)  Read the questions/statements 1-5.
        Think of a possible answer/response.

> Complete the five conversations. Choose
> the correct answer A, B or C.

**Example**

**0**  How was        A  That sounds interesting.
       your         (B) Great, thanks.
       weekend?      C  Yes, it was fantastic.

**1**  Did you enjoy  A  I just hung out with my friends.
       the visit?     B  I think you had a nice time.
                      C  Yes, it was great.

**2**  How about      A  I didn't do anything special.
       you?           B  That sounds interesting.
                      C  I want to visit that place.

**3**  That sounds    A  I went on a day trip.
       very           B  I'd really like to go there.
       interesting.   C  It was!

**4**  Did you have   A  Yes, that's nice.
       a nice time?   B  It was just a normal weekend.
                      C  That sounds good.

**5**  I went on      A  Oh, really?
       a tour of      B  It was!
       the gardens.   C  It was great!

b)  Do the task. Compare with your
    partner.

## Speaking

**5**  Read the rubric, then do the task.

> Candidate A: here's some information
>              about a re-enactment.
> Candidate B: you don't know anything
>              about the re-enactment
>              so ask A about it.

## Writing (an email to a friend)
### (Writing Bank p. WB1)

**6**  a)  Read the rubric. Brainstorm for ideas
        under the points you need to include.

> You went to a museum last week.
> Write an e-mail to your English friend.
> In your e-mail you should:
> • say where you went.
> • describe what you did there.
> • explain why you liked the visit.
> Write 80-100 words.

b)  Do the writing task.

# 3 Revision

## 1

**Fill in:** *incredible*, *locals*, *won*, *discovered*, *settled*, *lifetime*, *voyage*, *accurate*, *empire*, *legend*.

1  Alexander the Great created a huge empire and ................................................ a place in history.

2  Genghis Khan's Mongolian ............................... stretched from Hungary to Korea.

3  Mozart was a(n) ......................... musician and composed his first concerto at the age of five.

4  Da Vinci's maps are extremely ......................... and show every detail.

5  According to ......................., the city of Atlantis sank into the sea after a huge earthquake.

6  The Pilgrims ................................... in an area near the sea and built a town called Plymouth.

7  The early Pilgrims made a long ......................... on the *Mayflower* to reach America.

8  The giant terrified the ..................................., stealing their sheep and eating people.

9  Henry Carter ........................... the lost tomb of Tutankhamun.

10  Julius Caesar achieved many things in his ................................. .

*10x2=20 marks*

## 2

**Complete the sentences with the *past simple* or the *past continuous* forms of the verbs in brackets.**

1  A:  How .........................................................
    **(the Pilgrims/survive)** their first winter?
   B:  The natives ........................................
    **(teach)** them how to hunt and grow crops.

2  A:  Who ................... **(kill)** Alexander the Great?
   B:  Nobody. He ......................... **(die)** of a fever.

3  A:  .........................................................
    **(the children/watch)** TV when you called?
   B:  No. They ...........................................
    **(have)** lunch.

4  A:  Einstein .............................................. **(not/start)** to speak until he was three years old.
   B:  Really? I ........................... **(not/know)** that.

5  A:  How .........................................................
    **(you/burn)** the chips?
   B:  The phone ............................... **(ring)** when I ................................................ **(cook)** them.

*5x4=20 marks*

## 3  Match the exchanges.

| | | |
|---|---|---|
| **1** ☐ How was your weekend? | **A** | In 1934. |
| **2** ☐ That sounds like a lot of fun. | **B** | Yes, I did, thanks. |
| **3** ☐ Where did you go? | **C** | It was great, thanks. |
| **4** ☐ When did she die? | **D** | We went to the zoo. |
| **5** ☐ Did you have a nice time? | **E** | It was. |

*5x4=20 marks*

## 4  Read the text and answer the questions.

Mark Twain was a famous American writer. He was born on 30th November, 1835 in Missouri.

When he was just twelve years old, he left school. Six years later, he started travelling, working as a printer. Mark became a steamboat pilot in 1859 and travelled up and down the Mississippi River. He also worked as a journalist and he discovered that he loved to write. He wrote many books and short stories. People consider *The Adventures of Huckleberry Finn* one of the first great American novels. Mark Twain died on 21st April, 1910, but people all over the world still love to read his books.

1  Where was Mark Twain born? .........................
2  How old was he when he left school? ..............
3  What jobs did he have? .................................
4  What kinds of things did he write? ................
5  When did he die? .........................................

*5x4=20 marks*

## 5

**Write a short biography of a famous person from your country. Write: *who they were, when & where they were born, the main events/ achievements in their life, when they died* (80-100 words).**

*20 marks*

*Total: 100 marks*

**Check your Progress**

•  talk and write about famous peoples' achievements ____
•  talk and write about historical figures ____
•  discuss past activities ____
•  talk and write about legends & myths ____
•  write a biography ____

**GOOD ✓   VERY GOOD ✓✓   EXCELLENT ✓✓✓**

**1**
| | | | |
|---|---|---|---|
| 1 | won | 5 | legend |
| 2 | empire | 6 | settled |
| 3 | incredible | 7 | voyage |
| 4 | accurate | 8 | locals |

9 discovered
10 lifetime


## BACKGROUND INFORMATION

**Hungary** is a country in central Europe that shares borders with Austria, Slovakia, Ukraine, Romania, Serbia, Croatia and Slovenia. The capital city is Budapest and the people speak Hungarian. The population is around 10 million people.

**Korea** is a territory in east Asia which is made up of two separate states, North Korea and South Korea. It covers an area of over 219,000 km$^2$ and the people speak Korean. It split in 1948 because of political differences.

**Wolfgang Amadeus Mozart** (1756-1791) was a composer. He was born in Austria and, in his short life, he composed over 600 works. He is probably the most popular classical composer of all time. Some of his most famous works include the operas: *The Magic Flute and The Marriage of Figaro.*

**Atlantis** is a mythical island said, by the Greek philosopher Plato, to have existed 9,000 years before his time. According to legend, it was built by the Greek god Poseidon and there were great palaces and beautiful temples filled with gold and riches. Then it mysteriously sank to the bottom of the sea.


**2**
1 did the Pilgrims survive, taught
2 killed, died
3 Were the children watching, were having
4 didn't start, didn't know
5 did you burn, rang, was cooking

**3** 1 C   2 E   3 D   4 A   5 B

**4**
1 He was born in Missouri.
2 He was 12 years old when he left school.
3 He was a printer, a steamboat pilot, a journalist and a writer.
4 He wrote books and short stories.
5 He died on 21st April, 1910.

**5** *Suggested Answer Key*

*Marie Curie was a Polish physicist and chemist. She was born on 7th November, 1867 in Warsaw, Poland.*

*As a child, she went to boarding school and she was a good student. She became a governess when she left school to help pay for her sister's education. A few years later, she left for Paris and went to university. She got degrees in Physics and Maths. In 1895 she married Pierre Curie. Together they discovered Polonium and Radium and Marie developed a theory of radioactivity.*

*They won the Nobel Prize for Physics in 1903. Eight years later, Marie Curie won the Nobel Prize in Chemistry.*

*Marie Curie was the first person to win two Nobel Prizes and the first woman to become a professor at the University of Paris. She was a scientific pioneer. She died on 4th July 1934 from exposure to radiation.*

---

**Suggested Answer for Ex. 5 on p. 56**

---

### Ex. 5

*Francis Drake was born in Devon, England in 1544. He started his sea career when he was a young boy. He had his own ship at the age of 20.*

*In 1567, Drake made one of his first voyages with his cousin John Hawkins to San Juan de Ulua in Mexico. There, the Spanish defeated him. He decided to take revenge by attacking and stealing Spanish treasure.*

*In 1577, queen Elizabeth I, sent him on an expedition against Spanish colonies on the American Pacific coast. He successfully defeated Spanish ships and became the first Englishman to navigate the Straits of Magellan. Drake's most famous battle was the Battle of Gravelines in 1588, when he defeated the Spanish Armada.*

*Drake became a knight, a mayor and an MP (Member of Parliament). He was a hero to the English. In 1596, at the age of 55, he died of a disease on board his ship near Panama.*

# On holiday

> **What's in this module?**

Read the title of the module, *On holiday*, and ask Ss to predict the content of the module *(the module is about different kinds of holidays, holiday experiences and activities and problems that can occur while on holiday)*. Go through the contents list and stimulate a discussion about what Ss will learn in the module.

## Vocabulary

1 **Aim** To present different kinds of holidays

- Give Ss time to look at the pictures and words.
- Play the recording with pauses for Ss to repeat individually or chorally.

2 **Aim** To listen for specific information

- Draw Ss' attention to the sentences about Sarah. Explain that Ss must listen to the recording carefully and circle the correct answers.
- Play the recording.
- Ask Ss to complete the task and play the recording again to check Ss' answers in class.

*Answer Key*

*Sarah usually goes on a **camping holiday**. This summer, she wants to go on an **activity holiday**.*

## OVER TO YOU!

**Aim** To practise talking about different kinds of holidays

- Draw Ss' attention to the 'OVER TO YOU!' section and ask them to complete the sentences with their own answers. Point out that we use will to talk about the future. Explain that will is the same in all persons.
- Allow Ss time to complete the task.
- Ask various Ss to read out their answers.

*Suggested Answer Key*

*I usually go on a beach holiday. This summer, I'll probably go on a safari.*

# Module 4
## On holiday

### *Vocabulary*
### Types of holidays

**1** Look at the pictures. Listen and say.

**2** Listen to Sarah talking about her holiday and circle the correct answers.

Sarah usually goes on a **camping / beach** holiday.
This summer, she wants to go on **an activity holiday / a cruise**.





61

# 4a Activity holidays

**Check these words**

bored of, time of your life, surrounded by, stunning scenery, desert, enormous, canyon, set out, flight, top of, hill, view, snowy, volcano, lava lake, spend the night, lakeside resort, head back

## Vocabulary
### Holiday experiences

**1** **a)** **Match the phrases to the pictures. Listen and check then say.**

| | | |
|---|---|---|
| **1** G | go sandboarding | **5** C trek in the mountains |
| **2** F | climb a volcano | **6** B swim with piranha |
| **3** D | drive a dune buggy | **7** A mountain bike down a dangerous road |
| **4** E | explore ancient monuments | |

**b)** **THINK!** Which of these activities would you like/not like to do on holiday? Why? Tell your partner, using the adjectives in the list.

• interesting • exciting • boring • dangerous • scary
• difficult • fun

*I'd like to go sandboarding because I think it's fun!*

## Reading & Listening

**2** **a)** Look at the advert for an adventure tour. Which countries does the tour visit? How long does it last?

**b)** Which of the activities in Ex. 1 can you do in each country? Listen and read to find out.

**c)** Read again and write *Peru*, *Bolivia*, or *Chile*.

**Where will you ...**
1 see animals in danger? 2 sleep outside?
3 see parts of buildings built long ago?
4 see a city from a high place? 5 swim in dangerous waters?

**d)** Match the words in bold to their meanings: *opportunity, not far away, not wide, reserve, twisty, huge, breathtaking, going back to your starting point, not remember, travel around, rising at a very sharp angle.*

## Vocabulary

**1 a)** **Aim** **To present vocabulary for holiday activities/experiences**

- Draw Ss' attention to the pictures A-G. Read the activities listed in Ex. 1a and ask Ss to match the activities to the pictures.
- Allow Ss time to complete the task.
- Play the recording for Ss to check their answers.
- Play the recording again with pauses for Ss to repeat individually or chorally.

**b)** **Aim** **To practise new vocabulary and introduce related adjectives**

- Explain the task and read out the example. Go through the list of adjectives and explain/elicit their meaning.
- Divide Ss into pairs and allow Ss time to think of sentences about the activities using the adjectives. Monitor the activity around the class.
- Ask various pairs to tell the class some of their sentences.

***Suggested Answer Key***

*I'd like to go mountain biking down a dangerous road because I think it's exciting/fun. I'd like to explore ancient monuments because I think they're interesting. I'd like to trek in the mountains because I think it's fun. I wouldn't like to climb a volcano because I think it's difficult/ dangerous. I wouldn't like to drive a dune buggy because I think it's dangerous. I wouldn't like to swim with piranha because I think it's dangerous/scary.*

## Reading and Listening

**2 a)** **Aim** **To read for gist**

- Allow Ss a minute to read through the text.
- Point out that Ss should read carefully but skim the text in order to answer the questions in the rubric.
- Elicit answers from Ss around the class.

***Answer Key*** *The tour visits Peru, Bolivia and Chile. The tour lasts for 12 days.*

**b)** **Aim** **To listen/read for specific information**

- Ss in pairs, decide on the activities. Play the recording. Ss listen and read to answer the questions.

***Answer Key – see p. 64(T)***

- Explain/Elicit the meaning of words in the **Check these words** box. Ask Ss to identify what part of speech each is.

***Suggested Answer Key***

**bored of (adj):** *having no interest in sth*
**time of your life (phr):** *a really good experience*
**surrounded by (adj):** *in the middle of, and enclosed on all sides by sth else*

**stunning scenery (n):** *beautiful landscape*
**desert (n):** *a large sandy area of land with high temperatures and few plants*
**enormous (adj):** *very big, huge*
**canyon (n):** *a deep valley with high, steep sides*
**set out (phr v):** *to start a journey*
**flight (n):** *the time spent in the air when flying*
**top (of) (n):** *the highest point of sth*
**hill (n):** *a raised piece of land that slopes upwards to a peak, not as big as a mountain*
**view (n):** *a visual picture of the surroundings as seen from a certain point*
**snowy (adj):** *covered in snow*
**volcano (n):** *a gap on a mountain top which throws lava and ash*
**lava lake (n):** *an area of hot molten rock that is similar in form and shape to a lake*
**spend the night (phr):** *to stay somewhere for a night*
**lakeside resort (n):** *a place next to a lake that people visit for holidays or relaxation, often a hotel or guesthouse.*
**head (back) (v):** *to make a journey back to where you started from*

**c)** **Aim** **To read for detailed understanding**

Allow Ss time to read the text and write the correct country next to each question. Check Ss' answers.

***Answer Key – see p. 64(T)***

### BACKGROUND INFORMATION

**Peru** is a country on the west coast of South America. The capital city is Lima. It has a population of 29 million people. The people speak Spanish. Peru's neighbours are Ecuador, Colombia, Bolivia, Chile and Brazil. Some of the oldest civilisations in the world such as the Inca Empire started there.

**Bolivia** is a country in central South America. The capital city is La Paz and it has a population of almost 11 million people. The people speak Spanish, Quechua, Aymara and 34 other native languages. Bolivia's neighbours are Brazil, Paraguay, Argentina, Chile and Peru. Bolivia has a lot of natural minerals, especially tin.

**Chile** is a country that runs along the southwest coast of South America. The capital city is Santiago de Chile and it has a population of 17 million people. The people speak Spanish. Chile's neighbours are Peru, Bolivia and Argentina. Chile has a varied climate and has the world's driest desert the Atacama, as well as forests, volcanoes and lakes.

**d)** **Aim** **To expand vocabulary/To match words from a text to their meanings**

- Explain the task.
- Give Ss time to complete the task.
- Check Ss' answers.

***Answer Key – see p. 64(T)***

## Grammar

**3** **a)** **Aim** **To present the future simple** *(will)*

- Draw Ss' attention to the grammar box.
- Focus on the affirmative form and explain that *will* (and contracted form *'ll*) is used to discuss things happening in the future.
- Go through the table and point out the subject + *will* sentence structure.
- Do the same for the negative and interrogative forms.
- Ask Ss to look at the short answers and explain that they can be used instead of repeating information from the question. i.e. *Will he stay in a hotel? Yes, he will. (Yes, he will stay in a hotel).*
- Go through the uses and read out the examples.
- Allow Ss time to read the text again and write down any examples of *will*.
- Check Ss' answers.

**Answer Key**

**Information about the future:**
*we will travel …, we'll sandboard …, we will go on …, We will have the chance …, we will fly …, we will mountain bike …, we'll take a short flight …, we'll fly to …, we'll go on …, we'll get …, we'll travel south, we'll spend …*

**Prediction based on what we think/believe:**
*… you will never forget …, …you'll have the time of your life …*

## Pronunciation

**b)** **Aim** **To learn the correct pronunciation of contracted forms** *'ll* **and** *won't*

- Remind Ss that *'ll* is the contracted form of *will* and *won't* is the contracted form of *will not*.
- Play the recording with pauses for Ss to repeat individually or chorally.

**4** **Aim** **To practise the simple future tense** *(will)*

- Explain the task and ask Ss to complete the sentences using the correct form of the verb *will* and the given words.
- Allow Ss time to complete the task and then ask Ss to identify which sentences convey a prediction, an on-the-spot decision or information about the future.
- Elicit answers from various Ss around the class.

**Answer Key**

*1 will fly (information about the future)*
*2 will have (prediction)*
*3 will buy (on-the-spot decision)*
*4 will enjoy (prediction)*
*5 won't miss (prediction)*
*6 will come (on-the-spot decision)*

**5** **Aim** **To consolidate new vocabulary and grammar**

- Explain the task and divide Ss into pairs.
- Refer Ss back to the holiday activities in Ex. 1 and ask them to form questions using these activities.
- Remind Ss that they will use *will* to ask questions and short answers to reply.
- Read out the example.
- Ss ask and answer in pairs.
- Monitor the activity around the class.

**Suggested Answer Key**

*Will you climb a volcano? Yes, I will./No, I won't.*
*Will you drive a dune buggy? Yes, I will./No, I won't.*
*Will you go surfing? Yes, I will./No, I won't.*
*Will you try local food? Yes, I will./No, I won't., etc*

## Speaking and Writing

**6** **a)** **Aim** **To practise collocating words**

- Explain the task and allow Ss time to complete the collocations. Point out that Ss should learn and use collocations as this makes them sound natural.
- Refer Ss back to the text if necessary.
- Elicit answers from various Ss around the class.

**b)** **Aim** **To practise new vocabulary and narrate an experience**

- Explain the task and give Ss a three-minute time limit to write about the activity holiday in the first person.
- Allow Ss time to complete the task and tell their partners.
- Ask various Ss to read their sentences in class.

**Suggested Answer Key**

*… a dune buggy into the Huacachina Desert and sandboarded down the sand dunes. Then, we went on a three-day trek through the Andes. We saw the Colca Canyon, a giant condor and we camped out under the stars.*

- As an extension ask Ss to tell the class what they will do in Bolivia and Chile.

**Suggested Answer Key – see p. 70(T)**

**7** **Aim** **To write a tour itinerary**

- Divide Ss into groups of three.
- Assign the task as HW and remind Ss that each person should write one section. Tell Ss they can use the itinerary in Ex. 2 as a model. Ask Ss to draw a map showing the route.
- Ask various groups to present their itineraries to the class.

**Suggested Answer Key – see p. 70(T)**

**Peru: Days 1-5** After flying into Peru's capital, Lima, we will travel to Ica and drive a dune buggy into the Huacachina Desert, then we'll sandboard back down the **enormous** sand dunes! Next, we will go on a 3-day journey to trek through the Andes Mountains and see the beautiful Colca Canyon. We will have the **chance** to see endangered species here like the giant condor and camp out under the stars.

**Bolivia: Days 6-8** In the morning, we will fly to La Paz and then set out for Tiwanaku to **explore** the ancient ruins. The next day, we will mountain bike down the world's most dangerous road, *El Camino de la Muerte*. The road stretches for 67 km along the **steep** slopes of the Andes and is very **narrow** and **windy**. Afterwards, we'll take a short flight and a jeep ride to the Yacuma River in the Madidi National Park and swim with piranha! Fortunately, they're only small ones. They might even be on the breakfast menu the next morning!

**Chile: Days 9-12** We'll fly to the capital, Santiago, then we'll go on a bike ride to the top of San Cristobal Hill. From there, we'll get a **spectacular** view of the city. Then, we'll travel south to the Andes Mountains and climb the snowy volcano at Villarrica and see its lava lake! We'll spend the night in a **nearby** lakeside resort before **heading back** to Santiago for the flight home.

*Adventure Tour South America is a holiday you will never **forget**!*
***Book** your place on the tour now!*
*Visit our website @ www.starttrekking.com for further information.*

## Grammar
*see p. GR6*

### Will

**3** a) Read the table. Find examples in the text.

| AFFIRMATIVE | NEGATIVE |
|---|---|
| *I/You/He/She, etc **will/'ll go** on holiday this summer.* | *I/You/He/She, etc **will not/won't** go to the beach tomorrow.* |

| INTERROGATIVE | SHORT ANSWERS |
|---|---|
| ***Will** I/you/he/she, etc **stay** in a hotel?* | **Yes**, *I/you/he/she, etc **will**.* <br> **No**, *I/you/he/she, etc **won't**.* |

We use **will**:
- for predictions based on what we think or believe. *I think you**'ll have** a great time.*
- on-the-spot decisions. *It's raining. I**'ll take** my umbrella.*
- to give information about the future. *You**'ll stay** in a five-star hotel.*

## Pronunciation ('ll/won't)

b) 🎧 Listen and say.

- I'll have.  • He'll go.  • We won't buy.
- They'll camp.  • I won't swim.

**4** Complete the sentences with the correct form of *will* and the verbs in the list. Which sentence *is a prediction? is an on-the-spot decision? gives information about the future?*

• come • not miss • enjoy • have • fly • buy

1 We .......................................... into Lima when we visit Peru.
2 I'm sure you .......................... the time of your life on this trip.
3 These souvenirs are great. I ............................. some for my friends back home.
4 Why don't you go on an activity holiday? I think you ............................... it.
5 Don't worry, it's only 5 o'clock. He ................... his plane!
6 Are you going on a tour of the city today? I ............................... with you.

**5** Your partner is going on holiday. Use the activities in Ex. 1 and your own ideas to find out what he/she will/won't do.

A: *Will you go sandboarding?*
B: *Yes, I will./No, I won't.*

## Speaking & Writing

**6** a) Fill in: *spectacular, short, sand, ancient, steep, jeep, endangered, lakeside.*

| | | | |
|---|---|---|---|
| 1 | sand dunes | 5 | steep slopes |
| 2 | endangered species | 6 | spectacular view |
| 3 | ancient ruins | 7 | jeep ride |
| 4 | short flight | 8 | lakeside resort |

b) **THINK!** Imagine you are going to Peru. In three minutes write about your trip there. Tell your partner.

*We flew to Lima in Peru by plane. Then, we travelled to Ica. We drove … .*

**7** Draw a map and write an itinerary for a six-day tour in your country. Each person writes about one section of the tour (where you'll go, what you'll do). Then present your tour to the class.

▶ Vocabulary Bank 4 p. VB11

63

# 4b Having a great time

## Vocabulary
### Holiday activities

**1** Fill in: *go (x2), shop, sunbathe, enjoy, take, visit, stay, try.*

🎧 Listen and check, then say.

shop for souvenirs

sunbathe on the beach

stay in a hotel

take photographs

go sightseeing

try local food

enjoy nature

visit historical sites

9 go dog sledding

## Reading & Listening

**2** a) Look at the pictures and read the first and last exchange in the dialogue. Where is Linda? What activities do you think she'll do there? 🎧 Listen and read to find out.

**Linda:** Hi, John. It's Linda.

**John:** Oh, hi Linda! Are you enjoying yourself in Finland?

**Linda:** Yes, it's really cold and snowy, but I'm having a great time. Guess what! Tomorrow, we're going to go sledding with husky dogs through a pine forest!

**John:** Wow! So, what else are you going to do?

**Linda:** Well, this afternoon we're going to a restaurant to try some local food. Tim wants to try reindeer stew, but I'm not going to have that! No way! In the evening, we're going to go on a snowmobile tour to see the Northern Lights!

**John:** What are they?

**Linda:** A really beautiful display of natural colourful lights in the sky. They're common near the Arctic Circle. If we are lucky, we'll see them.

**John:** Promise me you'll take lots of photos.

**Linda:** Of course, John. See you next week! Bye!

**Check these words**

enjoy yourself, snowy, have a great time, guess what, sledding, husky dog, pine forest, reindeer stew, no way, Northern Lights, display, colourful lights, common, the Arctic Circle

b) Read again and complete the sentences.

1 The weather in Finland is ................................................. .
2 Linda and Tim are planning to go ..................... tomorrow.
3 Linda doesn't want to eat ............................................. .
4 Linda and Tim want to see ............................................. .
5 Linda is going back home in ........................................... .

**3** What do/don't you usually do on holiday? Use the phrases in Ex. 1 and your own ideas to tell your partner.

*I usually stay in a hotel on holiday. I sunbathe on the beach and … . I don't usually … .*

64

## Vocabulary

**1** **Aim** To present vocabulary for holiday activities

- Draw Ss' attention to the pictures 1-9 and the incomplete phrases.
- Ask Ss to look at the verbs in the list and explain that Ss must complete the phrases with these verbs.
- Allow Ss time to complete the task.
- Play the recording for Ss to check their answers.
- Play the recording again with pauses for Ss to repeat individually or chorally.

## Reading and Listening

**2 a)** **Aim** To listen and read for gist

- Ask Ss to read only the first and last exchanges from the dialogue and elicit answers to the questions from Ss around the classroom.
- Play the recording and ask Ss to follow the dialogue in their books and check.

### Answer Key

Linda is in Finland.
I think she will go dog sledding and see the Northern Lights.

- Explain/Elicit the meaning of words in the **Check these words** box.

### Suggested Answer Key

**enjoy yourself (phr):** to have a good time
**snowy (adj):** covered in snow (often the landscape)
**have a great time (phr):** to enjoy yourself or have a good time
**guess what (phr):** to predict
**sledding (n):** a sport where you ride on a sleigh (or sledge)
**husky dog (n):** a kind of dog with thick fur which is used for winter sports like sledding
**pine forest (n):** an area with lots of pine trees planted close together
**reindeer stew (n):** a hot dish made from the meat of reindeer

**no way (phr):** to say that the speaker will definitely not do sth that has been suggested
**Northern Lights (n):** a natural display of lights in the sky at night that come from the Arctic Circle
**display (n):** an event intended to entertain people when they see it
**colourful lights (n):** lights that are a range of different colours
**common (adj):** regular, normal
**the Arctic Circle (n):** a circle of latitude at the top of the globe that has a very cold climate

**b)** **Aim** To read for specific information

- Ask Ss to read the dialogue again and complete the sentences.
- Allow Ss time to complete the task.
- Elicit answers from various students around the class.
- Check Ss' answers.

### Answer Key

1. cold and snowy
2. sledding (with husky dogs through the pine forest)
3. reindeer stew
4. the Northern Lights
5. a week

**3** **Aim** To practise new vocabulary

- Allow Ss time to think of what they usually do/ don't do while on holiday.
- Divide Ss into pairs and remind Ss to use the holiday activities in Ex. 1
- Allow time for the pairs to talk and share their ideas.
- Elicit ideas from various pairs around the class.

### Suggested Answer Key

I usually try the local food while on holiday. I go sightseeing and visit museums and art galleries. I also try to visit historical sites.
I don't usually spend my time on the beach when I am on holiday. I don't stay in hotels. I don't go dog sledding on holiday. etc

---

**Suggested Answers for Exs 2b, 2c & 2d on p. 62**

---

### Ex. 2b

In Peru, you can go sandboarding, drive a dune buggy, and trek in the mountains.
In Bolivia, you can explore ancient monuments, mountain bike down a dangerous road and swim with piranha.
In Chile, you can climb a volcano.

### Ex. 2c

1. Peru
2. Peru
3. Bolivia
4. Chile
5. Bolivia

### Ex. 2d

**opportunity:** chance
**not far away:** nearby
**not wide:** narrow
**reserve:** book
**twisty:** windy
**huge:** enormous
**breathtaking:** spectacular
**going back to your starting point:** heading back
**not remember:** forget
**travel around:** explore
**rising at a very sharp angle:** steep

## Grammar

**4** **Aim** **To revise be *going to*, *will* and the present continuous (future meaning)**

- Explain the task and go through the uses 1-6 and explain elicit which tense we use in each instance.
- Give Ss time to read the sentences a-f and complete the task and then check Ss' answers.

### Answer Key

1  d    2  a    3  c    4  b    5  f    6  e

**5** **Aim** **To practise be *going to*, *will* and the present continuous (future meaning)**

- Explain the task.
- Give Ss time to complete it and then check Ss' answers. Ask Ss to justify their answers.

### Answer Key

1  *will call (on-the-spot decision)*
2  *is going to go (prediction based on what we see)*
3  *will visit (prediction based on what we think)*
4  *are travelling (fixed arrangement in the near future)*
5  *are taking (fixed arrangement in the near future)*
6  *is going to swim (prediction based on what we see)*

**6** **Aim** **To present and practise time clauses**

- Go through the theory box and write the examples on the board and elicit further examples from Ss around the class (*e.g. When I get home, I'll have a nap.*).
- Give Ss time to complete the task and then check Ss' answers.

### Answer Key

1  *is*          3  *go*          5  *finish*
2  *will show*   4  *will they be*

**7** **Aim** **To present and practise conditionals type 0, 1 & 2**

- Read through the theory and explain that we form the type 0 conditional with *if/when* + present simple → present simple and that we use it to talk about a law of nature or sth that is always true.
- Explain that we form the type 1 conditional with *if/when* + present simple → *will/can* + infinitive without *to* and that we use it to talk about a situation that is possible in the present or future.

- Explain that we form the type 2 conditional with *if* + past simple → *would/could* + *infinitive without to* and that we use it to talk about an unreal situation in the present or future and to give advice. Point out that when the if-clause precedes the main clause we separate them with a comma. Also point out that *unless = if not*.
- Give Ss time to complete the task and then check Ss' answers.

### Answer Key

1  *If you heat ice, it melts. (Type 0)*
2  *Unless she calls, we won't leave. (Type 1)*
3  *If I were you, I'd go on the adventure tour. (Type 2)*
4  *If you leave metal out in the rain, it rusts. (Type 0)*
5  *If she had more free time, she'd join a gym. (Type 2)*
6  *She would travel abroad if she had enough money. (Type 2)*
7  *If I were you, I wouldn't try this dish. (Type 2)*
8  *We'll go to the beach if it doesn't rain. (Type 1)*

**8** **Aim** **To practise conditionals**

- Give Ss time to complete the sentences.
- Check Ss' answers around the class.

### Suggested Answer Key

1  *you get four. (Type 0)*
2  *you'll love it. (Type 1)*
3  *I'd ask for their autograph. (Type 2)*
4  *we'll go to the beach. (Type 1)*

- As an extension ask Ss to continue the sentences using conditional Types 1, 2. *If you go to Finland, … . If I had more free time, … .*

### Suggested Answer Key

- **S1:** *If you go to Finland, you'll go on a snowmobile tour.*
  **S2:** *If you go on a snowmobile tour, you'll see the Northern Lights!*
  **S3:** *If you see the Northern Lights, you'll take great pictures of them.*
  **S4:** *If you take pictures of the Northern Lights, you'll show them to your friends.*
  **S5:** *If you show the pictures to your friends, they'll decide to go on holiday there, too.*
  **S6:** *If they go on holiday to Finland, they'll go sledding with husky dogs.*
  **S7:** *If they go sledding with husky dogs, they'll enjoy the view … etc.*

- **S1:** *If I had more free time, I'd join a gym.*
  **S2:** *If I joined a gym, I'd make new friends.*
  **S3:** *If I made new friends, we'd go out together.*
  **S4:** *If we went out together, we'd have a great time, etc*

## Grammar see p. GR6

### Going to – Will – Present continuous (future meaning)

**4** Match the sentences (a-f) to the uses (1-6).

a I think it**'ll be** sunny tomorrow.

b It's 3:00. We**'re going to miss** our plane!

c Accommodation **will be** in a five-star hotel!

d I**'ll come** with you to the pool.

e We**'re eating out** tonight.

f We**'re going to travel** the world next year.

1 ☐ an on-the-spot decision
2 ☐ a prediction based on what we think
3 ☐ a future event certain to happen
4 ☐ a prediction based on what we see
5 ☐ a future plan
6 ☐ a fixed arrangement in the near future

**5** Fill in the gaps with *be going to*, *will* or the *present continuous* and the verbs in brackets.

1 Do you need a taxi? The doorman ..................................... (call) one for you.

2 John's buying a ski jacket. He ....................................... (go) on a skiing holiday.

3 I think I ............................. (visit) Africa one day.

4 My parents ..................................... (travel) to Spain tomorrow. Here are their tickets.

5 They ................................. (take) a boat trip later today.

6 She's wearing her swimsuit. She ................................. (swim) in the sea.

## Time clauses see p. GR6

**6** Read the theory, then put the verbs in the correct tense.

> **Time clauses** tell us when something will happen.
> We use **when, before, after, by the time, until, as soon as**, etc to introduce **time clauses**. We don't use **will** after these time words. *I'll go out **after I have lunch** (NOT: after I will have) After I have lunch, I'll go out.*
> **Note:** *When he **comes**, we'll go out* (when: time word) **BUT** *When **will he come**?* (when: question word).

1 When she ................................... (be) ready, we will leave.
2 I ................... (show) you the photos as soon as I get them.
3 Before you ............................ (go) out, turn off the lights.
4 When ................................. (they/be) back from Gdansk?
5 By the time we ........................ (finish) dinner, it'll be dark.

## Conditionals 0, 1, 2 type see p. GR7

**7** Read the theory. Then, put the verbs in brackets into the correct tense. What type of conditional is each sentence? Put commas where necessary.

| Type 0 | **if/when + present simple → present simple** (to express sth that is always true) *If you **mix** red and white, you **get** pink.* |
|---|---|
| Type 1 | **if + present simple → will + infinitive without *to*** (to express a possible situation in the present/future) *If he **is** early, he **will** come with us.* |
| Type 2 | **if + past simple → would/could + infinitive without *to*** (to express an imaginary situation or give advice in the present/future) *If I **had** time, I'**d** visit the museum (but I haven't). If I **were** you, I'**d** go to Spain this summer (advice).* |

**Note: Unless = If not** *Unless he leaves now, he'll miss the bus* (= if he doesn't leave now, he'll miss the bus).
When the if-clause precedes the main clause we separate the two clauses with a comma. When the main clause precedes the if-clause no comma is used.

1 If you ................................... (heat) ice it melts.
2 Unless she .......................................... (call) we won't leave.
3 If I ........................... (be) you I'd go on the adventure tour.
4 If you leave metal out in the rain it ........................... (rust).
5 If she ................... (have) more free time she'd join a gym.
6 She ................... (travel) abroad if she had enough money.
7 If I were you I ....................................... (not/try) this dish.
8 We'll go to the beach if it ................................. (not/rain).

**8** Complete the sentences.

1 If you add two and two, ...............................................
2 If you come to my country, ...............................................
3 If I met a famous person, ...............................................
4 If the weather gets better, ...............................................

➡ Vocabulary Bank 4 p. VB12

# 4c Culture Corner

**1** Where is Yellowstone National Park? What can a tourist see and do there? 🎧 Listen, read and check your answers.

**2** **a)** Read again and match the sentences to the words: *Yellowstone Grand Canyon, Yellowstone supervolcano, Old Faithful.*

**1** Some people expect it to erupt. YS
**2** This is a beautiful place to go walking. YGC
**3** You may see animals here. YGC
**4** One day, this may cause a disaster in part of the US. YS
**5** You'll remember seeing this forever. OF

**b)** Match the words in bold to their meanings: *very big, people whose job is to study the physical world, astonishing, explodes, rough paths, a mountain with a hole at the top that sometimes bursts, ruin.*

**3** 👥 Take the roles of a tourist and a tour guide. Use the text to ask and answer questions.

A: *How big is the park?*
B: *It covers 8,980 square kilometres.*

**4** **a)** Fill in: *deep, grizzly, impressive, hot, erupts, thermal, hiking.*

1 thermal pools; 2 hot springs; 3 geyser erupts; 4 deep canyon; 5 hiking trails; 6 grizzly bears; 7 impressive waterfalls

**b)** **THINK!** In three minutes write two reasons why you want to visit this national park. Use the phrases in Ex. 4a. Tell your partner.

**5** ICT 👥 Find information about a national park or area of natural beauty in your country and write a short pamphlet to advertise it. Use the pamphlet in Ex. 1 as a model.



cover, state, on top of, thermal pool, geyser, hot spring, erupt, into the air, sight, canyon, deep, hiking trail, spectacular view, impressive, waterfall, watch out for, wildlife, wolf, elk, bison, grizzly bear, scientist, destroy

## Yellowstone National Park

A visit to Yellowstone National Park is a wonderful adventure! Yellowstone covers 8,980 km² in three states (Wyoming, Montana and Idaho). What makes this park really amazing though is that most of it is on top of a **huge volcano** 6 km below the park! This is why Yellowstone has more thermal pools, geysers and hot springs than anywhere else in the world!

### Old Faithful

Old Faithful is the most famous geyser in Yellowstone. It **erupts** every 90 minutes for up to 5 minutes, sending water 30 to 60 metres into the air! This is a sight you'll never forget!

### The Grand Canyon of Yellowstone

This is a huge, deep canyon full of beautiful hiking **trails** and with spectacular views of Yellowstone's most **impressive** waterfalls, Upper and Lower Falls. Also, watch out for wildlife in this area such as wolves, elk, bison and even grizzly bears!

### The Yellowstone supervolcano – will it erupt?

The last time this supervolcano erupted was 640,000 years ago. Some **scientists** think it is ready to erupt again, but they don't know exactly when. If it erupts, it could **destroy** the western US!

**1** **Aim** **To introduce the topic and predict content of a text**

- Ask Ss to look at the photographs in the text and try to answer the questions in the rubric. *(I think it's in the USA. Tourists can see waterfalls and a volcano there.)*
- Play the recording and ask Ss to follow in their books. Elicit answers from Ss around the class.
- Check Ss' answers.

*Answer Key*

*Yellowstone National Park covers three states, Wyoming, Montana and Idaho. A tourist can see thermal pools, geysers, hot springs, waterfalls and lots of amazing wildlife in Yellowstone National Park. A tourist can also go hiking there.*

- Explain/Elicit the meaning of words in the **Check these words** box. Ask Ss to identify what part of speech each word is.

*Suggested Answer Key*

*cover (v): to spread over the surface of sth*
*state (n): a part of a country that has been divided by borders*
*on top of (prep phr): to be at the highest point of sth*
*thermal pool (n): a pool of warm water that is heated naturally from the earth*
*geyser (n): a natural spring of hot water, geysers usually spurt water and steam into the air*
*hot spring (n): a spring of water which is warm due to the heat under the earth's surface*
*erupt (v): to force out of sth with a lot of pressure*
*into the air (prep phr): off the ground*
*sight (n): sth interesting that a lot of people want to see*
*canyon (n): a deep valley with high, steep sides*
*deep (adj): not shallow*
*hiking trail (n): a path that is suitable for walking or hiking*
*spectacular view (n): a beautiful sight from a certain point*
*impressive (adj): amazing*
*waterfall (n): a place where water falls off the edge of a steep cliff or mountain*
*watch out for (phr v): to be careful*
*wildlife (n): wild animals and rare plants*
*wolf (n): a wild dog-like animal*
*elk (n): a large moose-like animal with heavy bodies and antlers*
*bison (n): an animal like a bull or a buffalo with long hair*
*grizzly bear (n): a wild bear that is brown in colour*
*scientist (n): a person who works in the field of science*
*destroy (v): to ruin or spoil completely*

**2 a)** **Aim** **To read for specific information**

Allow Ss time to read the text again and complete the task. Elicit answers from various Ss. Check Ss' answers.

**b)** **Aim** **To expand vocabulary/To match words from a text to their meanings**

- Explain the task.
- Give Ss time to complete the task.
- Check Ss' answers.

*Answer Key*

*very big: huge*
*people whose job is to study the physical world: scientists*
*astonishing: impressive*
*explodes: erupts*
*rough paths: trails*
*a mountain with a hole at the top that sometimes bursts: volcano*
*ruin: destroy*

**3** **Aim** **To discuss information in a text**

- Explain the task and divide Ss into pairs.
- Ask Ss to think about what information tourists would ask tour guides. Write the phrases on the board (see Suggested Answer Key).
- Allow Ss time to ask and answer in pairs.
- Monitor the activity around the class.
- Ask various pairs to ask and answer in class.

*Suggested Answer Key – see p. 72(T)*

**4 a)** **Aim** **To practise new vocabulary**

Explain the task and allow Ss time to complete the collocations. Check Ss' answers.

**b)** **Aim** **To consolidate ideas and vocabulary from a text**

- Explain the task and allow time for Ss to write down their reasons. Encourage Ss to use phrases from Ex. 4a in their answers.
- Ask Ss to share their reasons with their partners.
- Ask various partners to say their reasons.

*Suggested Answer Key*

*I want to visit Yellowstone National Park because I can see grizzly bears there.*
*I want to visit Yellowstone National Park because there are hot springs there. etc.*

**5** **Aim** **To write a pamphlet about a national park**

- Explain the task and point out that they should use the text on this page as a model.
- Remind Ss to think about an interesting place of natural beauty in their country and what is special about it.
- Allow Ss time to complete the task.
- Ask various Ss to present their pamphlets.

*Suggested Answer Key – see p. 72(T)*

66(T)

**1** **Aim** **To read for gist**

- Draw Ss' attention to the two adverts and allow time for Ss to read them.
- Ask Ss what they think is being advertised in each of the adverts.

*Answer Key*

*1  A theme park*
*2  A museum*

**2  a)** **Aim** **To introduce situational language related to asking for information**

- Draw Ss' attention to the phrases.
- Play the recording with pauses for Ss to repeat individually and chorally.

**b)** **Aim** **To identify speakers in a situational dialogue**

- Explain that the dialogue in the task is between a tourist and an information desk employee.
- Read the sentences aloud and ask Ss to follow in their books.
- Ask Ss which of the speakers they think says each of the sentences.
- Draw two columns labelled *tourist* and *information desk employee* on the board. Elicit which sentences go in which column.
- Play the recording and ask Ss to follow in their books.
- Check Ss' answers and circle the phrases in the correct columns on the board. Rewrite incorrectly placed phrases in the right columns.

*Answer Key*

*Tourist: I'm calling for some information; What are the opening hours?; How much does it cost to get in?*
*Information desk employee: How can I help you?; What would you like to know?; Can I help you with anything else?; Enjoy your visit to the museum!*

**3** **Aim** **To present synonymous phrases**

- Write the phrases from the task on the board. Ask Ss to read the dialogue again and suggest which sentences match those on the board.
- Elicit answers for each sentence on the board.
- Explain that there are often two or more ways of saying the same thing.
- Check Ss' answers.

*Answer Key*

*What can I do for you? – How can I help you?*
*I'd like to ask you something else –Just one more thing.*
*How do I drive there? – What is the best way to get there by car?*

*I hope you have a nice time here – Enjoy your visit to the museum!*

## Pronunciation

**4** **Aim** **To pronounce /h/**

- Draw Ss' attention to the words in the box.
- Play the recording with pauses so Ss have time to tick the boxes. Explain that a silent /h/ means that the pronunciation of the word starts with the second letter *(e.g. hour, honest)*.
- Play the recording again so Ss can repeat each word individually or chorally.

*Answer Key*

|  | pronounced /h/ | silent /h/ |
|---|---|---|
| help | ✓ |  |
| hour |  | ✓ |
| hotel | ✓ |  |
| honest |  | ✓ |
| what |  | ✓ |

*Additional words:*
*hammer, helmet = pronounced /h/*
*rhino, where = silent /h/*

## Speaking

**5** **Aim** **To act out a dialogue**

- Divide Ss into pairs and explain the task. Tell Ss that the dialogue should be about ad 1 from Ex. 1.
- Go through the plan and ask Ss to follow it in their dialogue.
- If they need extra help, refer Ss back to Ex. 2 and tell them to use the same format for their dialogue.
- Ask various Ss to act out their dialogue in class.

*Suggested Answer Key*

*A:  Good afternoon, Silverwood Theme Park. How may I help you?*
*B:  Hello, I'm calling for some information.*
*A:  Sure. What would you like to know?*
*B:  Well, first of all, what are the opening hours?*
*A:  We're open from 11 am to 7 pm, seven days a week.*
*B:  Great. And how much does it cost to get in?*
*A:  It's $41.99 for adults and $21.99 for children aged 3-7 years old.*
*B:  OK. What is the best way to get there by car?*
*A:  Just take Highway 95 from Coeur D'Alene, Idaho and you'll find us.*
*B:  Highway 95?*
*A:  Yes. Can I help you with anything else?*
*B:  No. I think that's all. Thank you.*
*A:  You're welcome. Enjoy your visit to the park!*

## Asking for information

**1** **Read the adverts. What is each one advertising?**

**2** **a)** 🎧 **Listen and say.**

- How can I help you?
- I'm calling for some information.
- What would you like to know?
- What are the opening hours?
- How much does it cost to get in?
- Can I help you with anything else?
- Enjoy your visit to the museum!

**b)** **The sentences are from a dialogue between *a tourist* and an *information desk employee*. Who says each sentence?**
🎧 **Listen, read and check.**

A: Good morning, the Dinosaur Museum, Wyoming. How can I help you?

B: Oh, hi. I'm planning to visit the Dinosaur Museum tomorrow and I'm calling for some information.

A: Sure. What would you like to know?

B: Well, firstly, what are the opening hours?

A: The museum is open from 8 am to 6 pm seven days a week.

B: How much does it cost to get in?

A: It's $10 for adults and $5.50 for children.

B: OK. Just one more thing. What is the best way to get there by car?

A: Oh, it's easy. Just head for Thermopolis town centre on WY-120 and continue straight.

B: The WY-120, right?

A: Yes, that's it. Can I help you with anything else?

B: No, I think that's all, thank you.

A: You're welcome. Enjoy your visit to the museum!

**DINOSAUR MUSEUM, WYOMING**

- Over 20 dinosaur skeletons!
- Opening hours: 8 am - 6 pm, 7 days a week
- Admission: adults $10, children $5.50

Just a short drive from Yellowstone National Park. Head for Thermopolis town centre on WY-120 and continue straight.

Call 307- 864-2997  for more info

**3** **Find sentences in the dialogue which mean:** *What can I do for you? – I'd like to ask you something else. – How do I drive there? – I hope you have a nice time here.*

## Pronunciation: /h/

**4** 🎧 **Listen and tick (✓) the correct boxes. Listen again and say. Think of more words that include /h/.**

|  | pronounced /h/ | silent /h/ |
|---|---|---|
| help |  |  |
| hour |  |  |
| hotel |  |  |
| honest |  |  |
| what |  |  |

## Speaking

**5** **Act out a dialogue based on the advert for Silverwood Theme Park. Follow the plan.**

| A | B |
|---|---|
| Greet customer. Ask how you can help. | Say you're calling for information. |
| Ask what they'd like to know. | Ask about opening hours. |
| Reply. | Ask about cost. |
| Reply. | Ask how to get there. |
| Give directions. | Check directions. |
| Ask if you can help with anything else. | Say *no* & thank. |
| Wish customer a good visit. |  |

# Sculptures Under the Sea

*Tourists diving or snorkelling off the **beautiful** Yucatan Peninsula **near** Cancun, Mexico might not believe their eyes. That's because there are amazing sculptures of men, women and children up to 8 metres **below** the waves!*

Sea creatures will soon share the **bottom** of Mexico's Caribbean Sea with the world's **largest** underwater sculpture park! Eventually, there will be 400 life-size sculptures including people holding hands in a circle, cyclists, office workers and pets. The sculptor, Jason deCaires Taylor, casts his statues from local people, so divers might even see someone they recognise!

Jason hopes that his sculptures will **encourage** people to think about the environment. Pollution and hundreds of thousands of visitors per year are **damaging** Mexico's coral reefs. Jason wants people to swim to the underwater sculpture park instead of the **damaged** reefs. He creates the statues from cement that **attracts** sea creatures and encourages coral to grow on them.

So, if you ever visit Cancun, why not **put on** your flippers and snorkel and swim out to this amazing park? In time, you probably won't be able to see the sculptures, but you will see a stunning new coral reef!

## Vocabulary & Reading

**1 a)** 🎧 Match the words, then listen and check. Which of these things can you see in the pictures?

| | | | | |
|---|---|---|---|---|
| **1** | C | underwater | A | sculptures |
| **2** | D | coral | B | creatures |
| **3** | E | scuba | C | park |
| **4** | B | sea | D | reef |
| **5** | A | life-size | E | diver |

### Study skills

**Key words**
Key words help you predict the content of a text.

**b)** Read the title of the text and the key words in the **Check these words** box. What is the text about? 🎧 Listen, read and check.

**2** Now read the text again and for questions 1-4, choose the best answer *A, B, C* or *D*. **Find evidence in the text.**

**1** Visitors to the underwater sculpture park will be able to see ...
  **A** ancient treasures.
  **(B)** sculptures of people and animals. lines 6-7
  **C** sculptures of fish and wildlife.
  **D** divers making sculptures.

**2** Local people visiting the park may see ... lines 8-9
  **(A)** statues of themselves.　　**C** Jason at work.
  **B** a statue of Jason.　　**D** statues of famous people.

**3** Jason wants the park to ... lines 10-14
  **A** attract more divers to Mexico's coral reefs.
  **(B)** help protect Mexico's coral reefs.
  **C** keep sea creatures away from reefs.
  **D** attract more tourists to Mexico.

**4** In the future, it will be more difficult to see the sculptures because ... lines 17-19
  **A** they will become old and dirty.
  **(B)** a new coral reef will cover them.
  **C** the artist will move them somewhere else.
  **D** the area will be very polluted.

## Vocabulary and Reading

**1 a)** **Aim** To present vocabulary and topic specific collocations

- Read the two lists of words aloud and explain the task. Allow Ss time to match the words from each list.
- Play the recording for Ss to check their answers.
- Ask Ss which of the collocations they can see in the pictures.

*Answer Key*

*In the picture, I can see an underwater park, a coral reef, sea creatures and life-size sculptures.*

**b)** **Aim** To introduce the topic and predict the content of a text

- Explain that Ss should read only the title of the text and the words in the **Check these words** box.
- Allow Ss time to read.
- Elicit Ss' ideas about what they think the text is about.
- Play the recording and ask Ss to follow in their books.

*Answer Key*

*The text is about an underwater park with sculptures.*

- Explain/Elicit the meaning of words in the **Check these words** box.

*Suggested Answer Key*

*sculptures (n): statues*
*diving (part): swimming underwater*
*snorkelling (v): swimming with a snorkel*
*below the waves (phr): underneath the water*
*sea creatures (n): animals that live in the sea*
*share (v): to use the same space/object*
*underwater (adj): under the surface of the water*
*life-size sculptures (n): statues that are the same size and proportion as the real thing*
*cyclists (n): people who ride bikes*
*sculptor (n): a person who make sculptures*
*cast a statue (v): to make a statue*
*local people (n): people living in the local area*
*recognise (v): to be familiar with sth*
*encourage (v): to give support and persuade sb to do sth, or act in a certain way*
*think about (the environment) (v): to consider*
*pollution (n): poisoning of water (air or land)*
*damage (v): to harm*
*coral reefs (n): areas under the sea where coral grows*
*create statues (v): to make statues*
*cement (n): a hard material used to build houses, statues, etc.*
*attract (v): to draw close*
*grow (v): to live and increase in size and age*
*flippers (n): shoe-like footwear with long paddle extending from the toes which help with underwater swimming*
*stunning (adj): beautiful, amazing and visually attractive*



### BACKGROUND INFORMATION

**Cancun** is a city on the east coast of Mexico on the Yucatan Peninsula. It has a population of 705,000. It is a very popular tourist resort with lots of sandy beaches and beachfront hotels and is known as the Mexican Caribbean.

**The Yucatán Peninsula** is in the southeast of Mexico and it has the Caribbean Sea on one side and the Gulf of Mexico on the other. It contains the Mexican states of Yucatán, Campeche, Quintana Roo and part of Belize. It is in the Atlantic Hurricane Belt and often suffers as a result.

**Jason de Caires Taylor** is a sculptor who graduated from the London Institute of Arts in 1998. He has an English father and a Guyanese mother. He worked as a scuba diving instructor around the world before he started working on underwater sculpture projects. He created the world's first underwater sculpture park in Grenada, West Indies, in May 2006 and then went on to create the Museo Subacuático del Arte (MUSA) in Cancun, Mexico.

**Coral** is a living organism. It lives in a colony of large groups of polyps. Coral secretes calcium carbonate which makes a hard skeleton that we know as coral reef. Corals also have tentacles and stinging cells. They can use these to catch small fish and microscopic animals to eat, but for some corals their main food source is algae. Some, like those in the Great Barrier Reef in Australia, prefer sunlight and clear shallow water and develop in tropical waters. Other corals, like those in Alaska, live in deeper, colder water.



**2** **Aim** To read for specific information

- Explain the task to Ss and tell them that they should pick the most relevant answer depending on what is written in the text.
- Allow Ss plenty of time to read the text again carefully and complete the task.
- Elicit answers from various Ss in the class and ask them to give evidence from the text to reinforce their choice. Check Ss' answers.



### BACKGROUND INFORMATION

#### Coral Reefs

Coral reefs are structures of corals underwater. Most reefs are made up of stony corals which have a hard outer layer which protects them and gives them strength and structure.

Coral reefs are home to 25% of all sea creatures including fish and sea sponges and are an important part of our eco-system.

Coral reefs can be found in areas all over the world. The Pacific Ocean, with its shallow, warm and clear water, has the ideal conditions for coral reefs. Coral needs few nutrients to survive.

Today, coral reefs are under threat from pollution, fishing and climate change due to their sensitivity to water temperature.

**3** **Aim** To consolidate and practise new vocabulary in context

- Explain the task to Ss and tell them that they are to use only words from the **Check these words** box.
- Allow Ss time to complete the task.
- Elicit answers from Ss around the class.

**4** **Aim** To practise opposites

- Read the list of words aloud and explain that the words have opposites that can be found in bold in the text.
- Explain the term 'opposites', if necessary, using simple pairs *good/bad, happy/sad*.
- Allow Ss time to complete the task.
- Check Ss' answers.

### Grammar

**5** **Aim** To present *might – may – could – will probably – will definitely*

- Read out the grammar box.
- Explain *might* as meaning there is a slight possibility and that it is just possible. Use the example from the box to demonstrate its use in a sentence structure.
- Explain that *may* is about possibility and that it is used to say that something has a possibility of happening. Use the example to demonstrate. Explain that both *may* and *might* are modals we use when we are uncertain of what will happen.
- Explain that *could* also relates to possibility (*e.g. I could go to the park if I finish my homework.*)
- Explain that *probably* means that something is likely, or that there's a good chance of something happening. Tell Ss that it expresses more certainty than *may*, *might* and *could*.
- Explain that *definitely* means that something is sure to happen.
- Ask Ss to find examples in the text.

*Answer Key*

**might:** *… might not believe their eyes, … so divers might even see someone …,*
**(will) probably:** *… you probably won't be able …*

**6** **Aim** To practise *might – may – could – will probably – will definitely*

- Explain the task and read out the example.
- Allow Ss time to complete the task.
- Elicit answers from Ss around the class.
- Check Ss' answers.

*Answer Key*

2  *The underwater park could attract 750,000 visitors per year.*
3  *We may go snorkelling this afternoon.*

4  *Coral will probably grow on the sculptures in the underwater park soon.*
5  *We might swim to the park today.*
6  *We'll definitely go to Cancun next weekend.*

### Speaking & Writing

**7  a)** **Aim** To summarise points from a text

- Ask Ss to think of two reasons why someone should visit the underwater park.
- Allow Ss time to re-read the text.
- Elicit answers from Ss around the class and write their suggestions on the board.
- Ask Ss to vote on which two reasons are the best.

*Suggested Answer Key*

**Reason 1:** *You should visit this park because it is the largest underwater sculpture park in the world.*
**Reason 2:** *You should visit this park because you will get to see a very clever way in which people are trying to conserve coral reefs.*

**b)** **Aim** To consolidate information from the text

- Ask Ss why the park is important.
- Ask them to write a few sentences
- Allow Ss time to complete the task.
- Ask individual Ss to tell the class.

*Suggested Answer Key*

*The park is important because it protects sea life. It attracts sea creatures and encourages coral to grow on the statues. It also encourages people to think about the environment.*

**8** **Aim** To write an email to a friend about a holiday

- Explain the task. Elicit that Ss should write in informal style.
- Remind Ss to write about the underwater park and to include where they are going, how they are going to get there and what they will probably see there.
- Allow Ss time to complete the task.
- Ask Ss to read their emails to their partners.

*Suggested Answer Key*

*Dear Alex,*
*Guess what! I am in Cancun, Mexico. It's amazing here. Tomorrow, I am going to visit the world's largest underwater sculpture park! I'll put on some snorkelling gear and swim out to an underwater park full of life-size statues. There are hundreds of sculptures of people and animals. The sculptor made the statues to attract sea creatures and encourage coral to grow on them. I'll definitely have a great time. I can't wait!*
*See you,*
*Sam*

**Check these words**

sculptures, diving, snorkelling, below the waves, sea creatures, share, underwater, life-size sculptures, cyclists, sculptor, cast a statue, local people, recognise, encourage, (think about) the environment, pollution, damage, coral reefs, create statues, cement, attract, grow, flippers, stunning

**3** Use words from the **Check these words** box to complete the sentences.

1 Jason deCaires Taylor is a fantastic artist – he makes beautiful **sculptures** out of cement.
2 When snorkelling, you need to put **flippers** on your feet to help you swim.
3 Jason uses **local people** as models for his statues.
4 It's very easy to **damage** coral reefs if you touch them.
5 Jason hopes the park will **attract** lots of visitors.
6 There are thousands of colourful, exotic **sea creatures** in the Caribbean Sea.
7 Over time, coral will **grow** on the sculptures.
8 **Pollution** from factories and cars causes a lot of damage to the **environment**.

**4** Complete the opposites. Use the words in bold in the text. Check with your partner.

1 discourage ≠ **encourage**
2 ugly ≠ **beautiful**
3 repels ≠ **attracts**
4 top ≠ **bottom**
5 above ≠ **below**
6 far from ≠ **near**
7 protecting ≠ **damaging**
8 smallest ≠ **largest**
9 take off ≠ **put on**
10 repaired ≠ **damaged**

## Grammar <sup>see</sup> p. GR7
### Might – May – Could – Will probably – Will definitely

**5** Read the theory. Find examples in the text.

*We **may** visit the underwater park when we go to Cancun.* (It's possible; Perhaps)
*I **might** go to Chile for my summer holiday this year.* (It's just possible, There is a slight possibility)
*The park **could** help to protect Mexico's damaged coral reefs.* (It's possible)
*We'll **probably** go snorkelling tomorrow.* (It's likely/ There's a very good chance)
*I'll **definitely** be back home by Thursday.* (It's certain)

**6** Use the words in brackets to rewrite the sentences.

1 There's a very good chance that it will rain tomorrow. **(probably)**
   *It will **probably** rain tomorrow.*
2 It's possible that the underwater park will attract 750,000 visitors per year. **(could)**
3 It's possible that we'll go snorkelling this afternoon. **(may)**
4 It's likely that coral will soon grow on the sculptures in the underwater park. **(probably)**
5 It's just possible that we'll swim to the park today. **(might)**
6 It's certain that we'll go to Cancun next weekend. **(definitely)**

## Speaking & Writing

**7** a) **THINK!** Tell the class two reasons why someone should visit the Cancun underwater park.

b) Why is the park important? In three minutes write a few sentences. Tell the class.

**8** Imagine you are on holiday in Cancun and you are going to visit the underwater park. Write a short email to your friend telling them all about it. Write: *where you are, what you are going to visit, what you will do/see there.* Read your email to your partner.

69

# 

wide harbour

huge market

peaceful gardens

long bridge

large zoo

traditional houses

cosy restaurant

tall skyscrapers

## Vocabulary
### Places in a city

**1** 🎧 **Listen and say. Which of these features are there in your city?**

*In my city there are traditional houses but there isn't a long bridge.*

## Reading & Listening

**2** **a)** **What do you know about Sydney? What else would you like to know about it? Write three questions. Read the text and see if you can answer them.**

### Check these words

climate, exterior, interior, auditorium, acoustics, diverse, contemporary, fresh, produce, flea market, hectare, roar, pavilion

## Six reasons to see Sydney!

Sydney is the largest city in Australia and one of the most **0)** ......... cities in the world. It has one of the best climates in Australia, with long warm summers and **mild** winters.

Sydney has one of the most beautiful city **harbours** in the world. **1)** ......... a ferry across the **bay** and **experience** the **2)** ......... possible panorama of the city. The stunning views of the famous Sydney Harbour Bridge and the Opera House will blow you away.

Sydney Opera House is one of the most famous buildings in the world. Constructed **3)** ......... the 1960's, the Opera House is now a UNESCO world **heritage** site. Its spectacular exterior is **stunning** to look at, and tours of the interior are **4)** ......... . The Opera House auditorium has crystal clear acoustics and features a diverse programme of opera, classical concerts as well as **contemporary** pop, jazz and comedy **performances**.

There are two huge old markets in Sydney, Paddy's Flemington and Paddy's Haymarket. Flemington is the place to go for fresh produce and flowers, **5)** ......... Haymarket is more of a flea market selling clothes, giftware and souvenirs. You can **6)** ......... just about anything.

One of the largest zoos in the world, and just 12 minutes **7)** ......... ferry from central Sydney, Taronga homes 2,600 animals on 21 hectares of land. The zoo enjoys stunning views **overlooking** Sydney harbour. The animals have a lot of space in beautiful natural settings and visitors can enjoy **8)** ......... giraffes, elephants and, of course native kangaroos and koala bears! There is even the **option** to stay overnight at the zoo in one of their safari tents. Just imagine waking to the sound of a lion's roar!

The Chinese Garden of Friendship is a beautiful, peaceful place in the heart of the city. The garden celebrates the friendship between Australia and China and **9)** ......... like a traditional garden of the Ming Dynasty. It **features** a water pavilion and a bamboo forest.

What better way to end your day than at one of Sydney's many seafood restaurants **10)** ......... you can find all around the harbour and beyond. Top chefs serve all kinds of seafood dishes.

| | | | | | | | |
|---|---|---|---|---|---|---|---|
| 0 | Ⓐ | famous | B | favourite | C | best | C | excellent |
| 1 | A | Take | B | Bring | C | Hold | C | Keep |
| 2 | A | good | B | better | C | great | C | best |
| 3 | A | in | B | on | C | at | C | of |
| 4 | A | open | B | hand | C | available | C | there |
| 5 | A | when | B | while | C | so | C | and |
| 6 | A | find | B | come | C | meet | C | spot |
| 7 | A | at | B | on | C | by | C | with |
| 8 | A | noticing | B | seeing | C | looking | C | viewing |
| 9 | A | watches | B | appears | C | seems | C | looks |
| 10 | A | where | B | which | C | who | C | what |

**b)** **Read and choose the correct word.**

## Vocabulary

**1** **Aim** To present vocabulary for places in a city

- Direct Ss' attention to the pictures and play the recording.
- Ss listen and repeat chorally or individually. Pay attention to Ss' intonation.
- Read out the example and then ask various Ss around the class to say similar sentences about which features are in their town/city.

**Suggested Answer Key**

*In my city there is a large zoo and a huge market. There are peaceful gardens and cosy restaurants. There are traditional houses but there aren't any tall skyscrapers. There isn't a long bridge either.*

## Reading & Listening

**2 a)** **Aim** To introduce the topic, predict the content of a text and read for specific information

- Elicit what, if anything, Ss know about Sydney.
- Then elicit a variety of questions from Ss around the class and write the three best ones on the board. Ss copy the questions into their notebooks.
- Ask Ss to read the text and see if they can answer them.

**Suggested Answer Key**

1 *What can you do in Sydney?*
*You can take a ferry across the harbour, visit the Sydney Opera House, go shopping, visit the zoo and the Chinese Garden.*
2 *What can you see in Sydney?*
*You can see the Harbour Bridge and the Sydney Opera House.*

3 *Where can you eat in Sydney?*
*You can eat at one of Sydney's many seafood restaurants.*

**b)** **Aim** To read for lexico-grammatical structure

- Ask Ss to read the text again carefully and choose the correct words for each gap by looking at the words before and after each gap.
- Check Ss' answers.

**Answer Key**

| | | | | |
|---|---|---|---|---|
| 1  A | 3  A | 5  B | 7  C | 9  C |
| 2  C | 4  C | 6  A | 8  B | 10  B |

- Explain/Elicit the meanings of the words in the **Check these words** box or ask Ss to look up their meanings in their dictionaries.

**Suggested Answer Key**

*climate (n):* the weather, temperature, etc in a place
*exterior (n):* the outside part of a building
*interior (n):* the inside part of a building
*auditorium (n):* the part of a theatre where the audience sits
*acoustics (n):* the structural features which affect how well sound is heard in a place
*diverse (adj):* varied
*contemporary (adj):* up-to-date, modern
*fresh (adj):* recently produced
*produce (n):* fruit and vegetables
*flea market (n):* a market selling second-hand items and antiques
*hectare (n):* an area of land = 10,000 m2
*roar (n):* the sound a lion, tiger or other large wild animal makes
*pavilion (n):* an ornamental building in a garden or park

---

**Suggested Answers for Exs 6b & 7 on p. 63**

---

### Ex. 6b

*Tomorrow we are flying to La Paz in Bolivia. Then, we're setting out for Tiwanaku where we will explore the ancient ruins. Then, we will mountain bike down El Camino de la Muerte. Then, we'll take a short flight to the Yacuma River, where we will swim with piranha. After that, we're flying to Santiago in Chile. There, we'll bike ride to the top of San Cristobal Hill. Then, we'll travel to the Andes Mountains. I will climb a snowy volcano and stay at a lakeside resort before heading back home.*

### Ex. 7

*6 day Tour of Italy*
**Rome: Days 1-2**
*You will visit the Roman Forum and the Coliseum on a sightseeing tour of the city. In the evening, you will have a*
*delicious meal at a traditional Italian Restaurant. The next day, you will go on the Vatican Museums and Sistine Chapel tour.*
**Florence: Days 3-4**
*You will travel to Florence by train from Rome. In the morning, you will visit the Florence Accademia where you can see Michelangelo's famous statue of David. In the afternoon, you will visit the Uffizi Gallery. On the second day, you will have a Florentine Cooking Lesson and shop at the local market.*
**Venice: Days 5-6**
*Here you will go on a one day combined walking and boat tour of the city. Highlights include Marco Polo's house, the Rialto Bridge and, of course, St Mark's Square. On the last day, you will enjoy a ride in one of Venice's famous gondolas. Your gondolier will play music and sing to you as you glide along the canals. The perfect way to end your holiday.*

**3 a)** **Aim** To consolidate new vocabulary

Give Ss time to complete the collocations and then check Ss' answers around the class.

*Answer Key*

| | | | | | |
|---|---|---|---|---|---|
| 1 | warm | 4 | acoustics | 7 | roar |
| 2 | city | 5 | produce | 8 | seafood |
| 3 | heritage | 6 | settings | | |

**b)** **Aim** To expand vocabulary/To match words from a text to their meanings

- Explain the task.
- Give Ss time to complete the task.
- Check Ss' answers.

*Answer Key*

*gulf: bay*
*see and enjoy: experience*
*not cold: mild*
*impressive: stunning*
*modern: contemporary*
*productions such as a play or a concert: performances*
*includes: features*
*ports: harbours*
*having a view of: overlooking*
*choice: option*
*all the traditions, beliefs, customs, etc of a country: heritage*

**4** **Aim** To consolidate information in a text

- Explain the task.
- Play the recording. Ss listen and follow the text in their books.
- Give Ss a three-minute time limit to write their sentences then tell their partners.
- Check Ss' answers around the class.

*Suggested Answer Key*

*You should visit Sydney because it has lots to offer. You can visit the famous Sydney Opera House. You can go shopping and find just about anything in Paddy's markets. You can also visit Taronga Zoo which is one of the largest zoos in the world.*

## Grammar

**5** **Aim** To revise *a/an – the*

- Ask Ss to read the theory and elicit further examples from Ss around the class. Ask Ss to look at the *Grammar Reference section* for more details.
- Give Ss time to complete the sentences, then check Ss' answers.

*Answer Key*

| | | | | | |
|---|---|---|---|---|---|
| 1 | a, – | 4 | a, –, the | 7 | –, –, – |
| 2 | the, – | 5 | The, an, the | | |
| 3 | a, –, – | 6 | A, the | | |

**6** **Aim** To practise *a/an – the*

Give Ss time to complete the text and then check Ss' answers around the class.

*Answer Key*

| | | | | | | | |
|---|---|---|---|---|---|---|---|
| 1 | a | 4 | the | 7 | a | 10 | the |
| 2 | – | 5 | the | 8 | the | | |
| 3 | The | 6 | the | 9 | a | | |

**7** **Aim** To present relatives

- Ask Ss to read the theory and draw their attention to the relatives in bold and elicit what we use each one to refer to *(who/that – people, which/that – things, where – places, whose – possession)*.
- Give Ss time to complete the rules and then check Ss' answers around the class.

*Answer Key*

| | | | |
|---|---|---|---|
| 1 | who/that | 3 | which/that |
| 2 | where | 4 | whose |

**8** **Aim** To practise relatives

- Give Ss time to complete the task referring back to the theory box if necessary.
- Check Ss' answers.

*Answer Key*

| | | | | | |
|---|---|---|---|---|---|
| 1 | which | 4 | who | 7 | where |
| 2 | whose | 5 | which | 8 | which |
| 3 | where | 6 | who | | |

**9** **Aim** To practise relatives using personal examples

- Give Ss time to complete the task using personal examples.
- Ask various Ss around the class to read out their answers.

*Suggested Answer Key*

1 *I like people who are honest.*
2 *I prefer restaurants which serve seafood.*
3 *I like watching documentaries which are about nature.*
4 *I can't stand people who are rude.*
5 *I love reading books which are about magic.*

**3** **a)** **Fill in:** *heritage*, *produce*, *roar*, *warm*, *acoustics*, *seafood*, *city*, *settings*.

1 ............ summer; **2** ............ harbour; **3** world .................. site; **4** crystal clear .................; **5** fresh ............; **6** natural ................; **7** lion's ............; **8** .............. restaurant

**b)** **Match the words in bold to their meanings:** *gulf, see and enjoy, not cold, impressive, modern, productions such as a play or a concert, includes, ports, having a view of, choice, all the traditions, beliefs, customs etc of a country.*

**4** **THINK!** 🎧 **Listen and read the text. In three minutes write four reasons why someone should visit Sydney. Tell your partner.**

## *Grammar*
### *A/An – The*  see p. GR7

**5** **Complete the sentences with** *a*, *an* **or** *the* **where necessary.**

- We use **a/an** to refer to something in general. *There's **a man** over there.*
- We use **the** to refer to something specific or with a singular countable noun to refer to all the members of that certain group. ***The man** is waving.* ***The dolphin** is an intelligent animal.* (all the dolphins).

1 I saw .......... strange man outside .......... school yesterday.
2 Tom has gone to .......... Costa del Sol in .......... Spain on holiday.
3 Jane is going to see .......... doctor on .......... Harley Street in .......... London next week.
4 I saw ....... documentary about ...... Mount Everest in ........ Himalayas.
5 .......... tiger is .......... endangered animal, especially ...... Siberian tiger.
6 .......... group of celebrities walked across part of ......... Sahara Desert for charity.
7 Is ...... Lake Baikal in ........ Russia?

**6** **Fill in** *a*, *an* **or** *the* **where necessary.**

Dear Sam,
Hi! I'm having **1)** ................. great time here in **2)** ................. Rome. **3)** ................. weather is nice and **4)** ................. people are friendly. So far I've been to **5)** ................. Coliseum and **6)** ................. Roman Forum and I've taken **7)** ................. million photos! Tomorrow I'm going to see **8)** ................. Vatican and I want to eat **9)** ................. real Italian pizza! How are things in **10)** ................. UK?
Bye for now,
Sara

## Relatives  see p. GR7

**7** **Read the theory. Complete the rules with the words in bold in the examples.**

*Tom shouted at a driver **whose** car was blocking the street. I like meeting people **who/that** are friendly and nice. Hazel comes from Doncaster **which/that** is in the north of England. I can't remember the name of the hotel **where** we stayed in Paris.*

We use **1)** .......... with people. We use **2)** .......... with places. We use **3)** .......... with things or ideas. We use **4)** .......... to show possession.

**8** **Fill in** *who*, *which*, *where* **or** *whose*.

1 A: I like your bag. It's very stylish.
   B: This is the one ......... was on special offer. I got it for £5.
2 A: Isn't that Jo over there .............. brother works with us?
   B: Yes, I think you're right.
3 A: Taronga Zoo is a great place ...................... you can see a lot of animals.
   B: We're going there tomorrow.
4 A: Do you remember Sara .............. used to live next door?
   B: Yes, and I heard she's moved to Sydney.
5 A: What is the name of that restaurant ..... serves seafood?
   B: Rico's.
6 A: I met a nice girl today ................... showed me around.
   B: Lucky you!
7 A: Was it Paris ..................... you went on holiday?
   B: No, it was Prague.
8 A: Did you watch the film ..... was on Channel 4 last night?
   B: Yes, it was fantastic.

**9** **Complete the sentences about you.**

1 I like people ............ are ...................................................... .
2 I prefer restaurants ............ serve ...................................... .
3 I like watching documentaries ............ are ........................ .
4 I can't stand people ............ are ...................................... .
5 I love reading books ........ are about .................................. .

# 4g Skills

## *Vocabulary*
### Holiday problems

**1** Match the problems to the pictures. 🎧 Listen and check. Listen again and say. Pay attention to the intonation.

| | |
|---|---|
| 1 | The weather was awful. |
| 2 | We missed our flight. |
| 3 | The airline lost our luggage. |
| 4 | I got badly sunburnt. |
| 5 | Someone stole my passport. |
| 6 | Our hotel room was too small. |
| 7 | The beach was dirty and crowded. |
| 8 | I got food poisoning. |

**Listening for specific information**
Before you listen, read the answer choices carefully and think about synonymous words/phrases. This will help you do the task.

## *Listening*

**2** 🎧 Listen to Nancy talking to a friend about her holiday experience. Match the problems (A-H) to the names (1-5). There are 2 problems that do not match.

| | | | |
|---|---|---|---|
| 0 | G | Tristan | **A** no reservation |
| 1 | | Carly | **B** wallet stolen |
| 2 | | Janice | **C** missed flight |
| 3 | | Monica | **D** bad weather |
| 4 | | Roger | **E** lost luggage |
| 5 | | Douglas | **F** got sunburnt |
| | | | **G** forgot passport |
| | | | **H** food poisoning |

## *Speaking*
### Talking about your holiday

**3** a) Anna is calling her brother Steve from the UK. What problem does she have?
🎧 Listen and read to find out.

| | |
|---|---|
| Anna: | Hi, Steve, it's Anna! |
| Steve: | Hi, Anna! Are you having a nice time in the UK? |
| Anna: | Yes, but you'll never guess what happened! |
| Steve: | What? Tell me! |
| Anna: | Well, someone stole all my money! |
| Steve: | Oh, you poor thing! I'm so sorry! |

b) Imagine you are on holiday and you are on the phone with your friend back home. Use the language in the table below and ideas from Ex. 1 to act out a dialogue similar to the one in Ex. 3a.

| Asking | Saying what happened | Reacting |
|---|---|---|
| • Are you having a nice time in … ?<br>• Are you enjoying yourself in … ? | • You'll never guess what happened!<br>• Guess what!<br>• You won't believe what happened!<br>• Listen to this! | • Really? Oh dear!<br>• Oh, you poor thing!<br>• I'm so sorry!<br>• That's such bad luck!<br>• That's terrible/awful! |

**4** **THINK!** Think about a holiday you had where something went wrong. In three minutes, write a few sentences. Tell the class what happened.



➡ **Vocabulary Bank 4 p. VB13**

## Vocabulary

**1** **Aim** **To present vocabulary about holiday problems**

- Read through the list of holiday problems aloud and ask Ss to follow in their books.
- Explain the matching task and allow Ss time to complete it.
- Elicit answers from Ss around the class.
- Play the recording for Ss to check their answers.
- Play the recording again with pauses for Ss to repeat individually or chorally.

***Answer Key***

| | | | |
|---|---|---|---|
| 1 B | 3 G | 5 E | 7 H |
| 2 F | 4 A | 6 C | 8 D |

## Listening

**2** **Aim** **To listen for specific information**

- Read the *Study Skills* box aloud.
- Direct Ss' attention to the list of problems (A-H).
- Explain that thinking about synonymous word and phrases can help them when doing listening exercises.
- Explain the task to Ss.
- Play the recording and allow Ss time to match the problems to the names.
- Check Ss' answers.

***Answer Key***

| | | | | |
|---|---|---|---|---|
| 1 H | 2 E | 3 A | 4 F | 5 B |

## Speaking

**3 a)** **Aim** **To listen for specific information**

- Explain the task and draw Ss' attention to the dialogue.
- Play the recording and ask Ss to follow in their books.

- Ask various Ss what they think the problem is.
- Play the recording again. Check Ss' answers.

***Answer Key***

*Anna's problem is that someone stole all her money.*

**b)** **Aim** **To act out a dialogue**

- Explain the task. Remind Ss to use the problems from Ex. 1 and sentences from the table.
- Divide Ss into pairs and allow Ss time to prepare a dialogue. Monitor the activity and provide help if necessary.
- Ask various pairs to act out their dialogues in class.

***Suggested Answer Key***

A: *Hi Elaine, it's Samantha!*
B: *Hi Sam! How are you? Are you enjoying yourself in New York?*
A: *Yes, but listen to this! The airline lost our luggage.*
B: *Really? Oh dear!*
A: *We had to spend two whole days without any of our things!*
B: *Oh, that's terrible!*

**4** **Aim** **To write about a holiday problem**

- Explain the task and allow Ss time to think about a problem they had on holiday and write a few sentences about it.
- Ask various Ss to read their sentences aloud in class.

***Suggested Answer Key***

*When I went on holiday to Spain last year, I got really badly sunburnt on my second day. I had to spend an afternoon in hospital and I wasn't allowed to go out in the sun for the rest of my holiday!*

**Suggested Answers for Exs 3 & 5 on p. 66**

---

### Ex. 3

A: *What makes Yellowstone National Park so special?*
B: *What makes it so special is that a large part of it is on top of a huge volcano!*
A: *Are there any geysers in Yellowstone National Park?*
B: *Yes, there are. The most famous one is called Old Faithful and it erupts every 90 minutes.*
A: *What can you see in the Grand Canyon of Yellowstone?*
B: *You can see some incredible waterfalls and lots of amazing wildlife.*
A: *Is the Yellowstone supervolcano going to erupt soon?*
B: *No one knows. Some scientists think that an eruption will happen soon.*

### Ex. 5

***The Lake District***

*The Lake District National Park is England's largest national park. It is 2292 km$^2$ and has got some of the most beautiful scenery in the country. It consists of mountains, lakes and forests. Over 42,000 people live inside the park and almost 16 million visitors enjoy its sights and activities throughout the year.*

***Lake Windermere***

*The Lake District is famous for its lakes. It has got over 16 of them. Lake Windermere is the largest lake in the park. At 10.5 miles long is also the largest lake in England. You can enjoy rowing, sailing, windsurfing and fishing on the lake. Also, be on the look out for toads, birds, deer and other wildlife that make this National Park their home.*

## 4h

**1** **Aim** **To understand the structure of a letter**

- Explain the task and allow Ss time to match the paragraphs with the descriptions.
- Elicit answers from Ss around the class.
- Check Ss' answers.

*Answer Key*

A 2          B 1          C 4          D 3

**2 a)** **Aim** **To learn the use of adjectives**

- Read out the *Writing Tip*.
- Point out that adjectives like *good*, *bad* and *nice* are not very interesting in writing texts whereas words like *awful*, *delicious* and *great* can make a text more interesting.
- Allow Ss time to complete the task.
- Check Ss' answers.

*Answer Key*

**hotel:** *luxurious*          **fish:** *colourful*
**weather:** *cloudy*          **villages:** *lovely quiet fishing*

**b)** **Aim** **To practice using adjectives**

- Explain the task and give Ss time to complete it.
- Check Ss' answers on the board.

*Answer Key*

A   *bad* – **awful**, *nice* – **brilliant**, *good* – **exciting**,
    *nice* – **delicious**
B   *nice* – **beautiful**, *bad* – **crowded**, *good* – **interesting**

**3** **Aim** **To identify opening/closing remarks**

- Draw Ss' attention to the sentences and ask Ss to comment on whether each sentence is an opening or closing remark.
- Allow time for Ss to complete the task alone.

*Answer Key*

1 O     2 C     3 C     4 O     5 O     6 C

### BACKGROUND INFORMATION

**St Lucia** is an island in the Caribbean. It is also a country and the capital city is Castries. It is 616 km$^2$ in size and 173,000 people live there. It is a very exclusive tourist resort and the people speak English.

## Writing

**4** **Aim** **To write a letter about your holiday**

- Explain the task and tell Ss that they should imagine they are on holiday and they should write a letter to a friend about it.
- Ask Ss to write 80-100 words and include a bad experience.
- Draw Ss' attention to the plan and ask them to use the same layout in their letters.
- Remind Ss that they can use Steven's letter as a model.
- Elicit various ideas as to activities and bad experiences one can have while on holiday.
- Write these phrases/sentences on the board for Ss to use in their letters. Ask Ss to copy them in their notebooks.

### Useful phrases for informal letters about holidays

*I'm having a great time.*
*Greetings from …*
*The weather is perfect/great/awful, etc.*
*We're staying in a hotel/cottage/on a yacht, etc.*
*We swam/went sightseeing/went trekking/went surfing, etc.*
*Today we are going to the museum/aquarium/gallery/ on a tour round the island, etc.*
*The only bad thing is I got sunburnt/hotel is crowded/ someone stole my camera, etc.*
*See you soon/next week.*

- Allow Ss time to complete the task.
- Ask various Ss to read their letters in class.

***Suggested Answer Key***

*Dear Charlotte,*

*How are you? I'm having a great time here in Paris! We're staying in the city centre. The hotel room is very small but the weather is amazing!*

*Yesterday, we walked along the River Seine and visited Notre Dame. Unfortunately, it was very sunny outside and I got sunburnt on my shoulders. Today, we're going to climb the Eiffel Tower. Later, we are going to the Champs Elysees to do some shopping.*

*Tomorrow, we're going to visit the Louvre. It's full of paintings and statues and I'm really looking forward to seeing the Mona Lisa.*

*Well, I must go now. We're meeting some friends for lunch. See you next week.*

*Love,*
*Elena*

**1** Read the letter and match the paragraphs (1-4) with the descriptions (A-D).

- A ☐ activities so far and plans for today
- B ☐ greeting and opening remarks
- C ☐ closing remarks
- D ☐ plans for tomorrow

**2** **a)** **Read the tip. What adjectives does Steven use to describe the following?**

- hotel • weather • fish
- villages

## Writing Tip

**Using adjectives in descriptions**
Use a variety of adjectives instead of *good*, *nice*, *bad,* etc to make your descriptive writing more interesting.
*The weather was **awful**. (instead of bad)*

**b)** **Replace the words in bold with the adjectives in the lists.**

- delicious • exciting
- brilliant • awful

**A** The weather here is **bad**, but we're still having a **nice** time. Yesterday, we went on a speedboat tour of the island – it was really **good**! We're going to my favourite restaurant now. The food there is **nice**!

- interesting • crowded
- beautiful

**B** This is a really **nice** place. The beach is quite **bad** but there are a lot of **good** historical sights to see.

Dear Mark,

**1** How are you? I'm having a fantastic time here in St Lucia in the Caribbean. We're staying in a luxurious hotel right on the beach. The weather is a bit cloudy and yesterday there was a huge storm, but we're still having a lot of fun!

**2** Yesterday, we swam and sunbathed on the beach all morning. I went snorkelling in the sea around a coral reef and I saw lots of colourful fish. This afternoon, we are going trekking in the rainforest! My sister Zoe thinks it'll be scary, but I can't wait!

**3** Tomorrow, we're going to take a jeep tour of the island. We're going to visit a banana plantation and some lovely quiet fishing villages.

**4** Well, that's all for now. We're going for lunch at a fish restaurant now. See you in a week's time!

Best wishes,
Steven

**3** Mark the sentences (1-6) *O* for opening or *C* for closing remarks.

1 I'm really enjoying myself here in Brazil.       ........
2 I'd better go now. I'll tell you more when I see you.       ........
3 See you next week.       ........
4 It's wonderful here and the weather is fantastic.       ........
5 I'm on holiday in Portugal and it's great!       ........
6 Anyway, I must go now.       ........

## Writing (a letter about your holiday)

**4** **You have received a letter from your English pen friend, Peter.**

> *I hope you are having a great holiday. Where are you staying? What is the weather like? What did you do yesterday and what are your plans for today?*

**Write Peter a letter and answer his questions. Write 80-100 words. Follow the plan.**

### Plan

*Dear ... ,*
**Para 1:** opening remarks, where you are, where you are staying, the weather, how you like it *(How are you? I'm having ... . We're staying ... . The weather is ... .)*
**Para 2:** activities you did yesterday (include a bad experience you had), what you are planning to do today *(Yesterday ... ./ Unfortunately, .... . Today we are going to ... .)*
**Para 3:** plans for the next day *(Tomorrow we're going to ... .)*
**Para 4:** closing remarks, you are coming back, when *(Well, I must go now. We're ... . See you ... .)*

..............................

▶ **Writing Bank p. WB1**

**1 a)** Read the dictionary entry. What do you think a responsible tourist is? Read the introduction of the text to find out.

responsible /rɪˈspɒnsəbəl/ (adj) able to choose between right and wrong and make good decisions

## How to be a
# Responsible Tourist

*Responsible tourism has to do with **caring about** the place where you go on holiday and **treating** the people there with respect. Next time you travel abroad, remember to follow these simple **rules**.*

### SUPPORT THE LOCALS
- Buy **local** brands in supermarkets and handmade souvenirs like traditional arts and crafts. This way, you'll **support** local businesses.
- Walk around and get to know people. The locals will be very happy that you're interested in their country.

### RESPECT LOCAL CUSTOMS
- Learn a few words or phrases from the local language. This will show locals that you **respect** their culture. You'll probably get a smile from them too!
- Respect any local dress or behaviour codes. Ask before taking a picture of a monument or a person, for example.

### THINK GREEN!
- Don't leave the air-conditioning or the lights on all day in your hotel and clean up after yourself at the beach or the campsite, just like at home!
- Never buy souvenirs made from coral or endangered plants or animals and never take anything from a historical site. Take home nothing but your good **memories**!
- Book your holiday with an environmentally-responsible company.

*Above all, remember … when you're abroad, you're a **guest** in someone else's country. You're also a **representative** of your country - so make a good **impression**!*

**b)** What does the term 'responsible tourism' mean to you?
🎧 Listen and read the text to check.

**2 a)** Read the text and mark the sentences *T* (true) or *F* (false).

1 Tourists should buy local products. **T**
2 It's not a good idea to mix with the locals. **F**
3 Always learn the local language before you travel abroad. **F**
4 It's OK to photograph local people. **F**
5 Don't leave rubbish on a campsite. **T**
6 It's a good idea to buy things made of coral. **F**

**b)** Match the words in bold to their meanings: *behaving towards, feeling you have about sb or sth, instructions, being concerned about, things you remember from the past, visitor, honour, sb typical of the group they belong to, regional, help.*

**3** Use words from the Check these words box to complete the gaps.

### Responsible Tourists
- **1)** Treat locals with respect.
- Buy local products to **2)** support the local businesses.
- **3)** Show respect for the culture of the country they are visiting.
- **4)** Clean up after themselves and do not leave their rubbish behind.

**4** **THINK!** Do you consider yourself to be a responsible tourist? In three minutes write a few sentences on this. Read them to the class.

**5** ICT Use the Internet to research and suggest more ways to be a responsible tourist. You can use the key phrase: *responsible tourism*. Present your ideas to the class.

**Check these words**

care, treat, respect, abroad, support, local brand, handmade, arts and crafts, custom, show respect, behaviour code, clean up, memory, environmentally-responsible, guest, representative

**1 a)** **Aim** **To introduce the topic**

- Ask Ss to read the dictionary definition.
- Ask Ss what they think a responsible tourist is. Allow Ss time to read the introduction and check.

**Suggested Answer Key**

*I think a responsible tourist is someone who cares about the place he is visiting, and treats everyone he meets with respect.*

## BACKGROUND INFORMATION

### Responsible Tourism

Responsible tourism is tourism that respects, supports and maintains the culture and communities that people visit. The aims of responsible tourism are to minimise the negative effects of tourists and holidaymakers, to support local communities, groups and businesses and to improve awareness of cultural and national codes, traditions and sensitivities. Responsible tourism aims to involve local people in decisions about their area as well as improve working conditions and opportunities in their country. Responsible tourism protects the wildlife and sights of the host country, while improving and protecting its culture and heritage.

**b)** **Aim** **To predict the topic of a text**

- Ask Ss to think about what 'responsible tourism' means. Ask Ss what they think responsible tourists do and don't do.
- Write *Do* and *Don't* do in two columns on the board and put Ss' answers in the relevant column. *Do: buy local products, respect the environment, respect new culture, etc. Don't: buy souvenirs made from e.g. coral, throw rubbish on the floor, take things from historical sites, etc.*
- Play the recording and ask Ss to follow in their books.

**Suggested Answer Key**

*Responsible tourism includes trying to buy locally-made goods when abroad, learning some words of the local language to communicate with the people and showing respect for local dress and behaviour codes. A responsible tourist doesn't buy anything made from endangered animals or plants or take things from historical sites.*

**2 a)** **Aim** **To read for specific information**

- Explain the task. Allow Ss time to read the text again and complete the task.
- Elicit answers from Ss around the class and correct any mistakes.
- Explain/Elicit the meaning of words in the **Check these words** box. Ask Ss to identify what part of speech each is.

**Suggested Answer Key**

***care (v):*** *to have feelings for sth, to want to look after sth*
***treat (v):*** *to behave in a certain way towards sb or sth*
***respect (v):*** *to have high regard for sb or sth*
***abroad (adv):*** *in a different country*
***support (v):*** *to help, maintain*
***local brand (n):*** *a product that has a certain label or name that people make in the surrounding area or region*
***handmade (adj):*** *made by people and not machines*
***arts and crafts (n):*** *paintings and other objects that are handmade by people*
***custom (n):*** *tradition*
***show respect (phr):*** *to behave in a way that shows you have a good opinion of sb or sth*
***behaviour code (n):*** *the way that we act and react*
***clean up (v):*** *to tidy things away*
***memory (n):*** *a recollection we have of a past event*
***environmentally-responsible (adj):*** *caring about the environment*
***guest (n):*** *visitor*
***representative (n):*** *a person acting on behalf of another*

**b)** **Aim** **To expand vocabulary/To match words from a text to their meanings**

- Explain the task.
- Give Ss time to complete the task.
- Check Ss' answers.

**Answer Key – see p. 75(T)**

**3** **Aim** **To practise new vocabulary in context**

- Explain the task and tell Ss to use words only from the **Check these words** box.
- Allow Ss time to complete the task.
- Check Ss' answers.

**4** **Aim** **To personalise the topic**

- Ask Ss to think about whether they are responsible tourists. Remind them of some of the key points of responsible tourism. Ss can use the *Do/Don't* table.
- Allow Ss time to write a few sentences.
- Ask various Ss to read their sentences to the class.

**Suggested Answer Key – see p. 75(T)**

**5** **Aim** **To research and present further ideas about the topic**

- Explain that there is more to learn about responsible tourism and tell Ss that they should use the Internet to gather more information and type the key phrase in the search bar.
- Allow Ss time to research the topic and make notes about what they find.
- Ask Ss to present their ideas in class.

**Suggested Answer Key – see p. 75(T)**

**Aim** **To consolidate vocabulary from the module**

- Divide the class into 2 teams. Each team takes turns writing or saying a sentence with one of the words/phrases in the list.
- Each correct sentence earns one point. If the sentence is incorrect, the team misses a turn.
- The team with the most points after all the words have been used wins.

*Suggested Answer Key*

*He spent the whole morning **lying on the beach**; he didn't want to swim.*
*They decided to **go on a safari** to Africa to see the wildlife there.*
*The **road stretches** for 67 km along the steep slopes of the Andes.*
*We'll **drive a dune buggy** into the desert.*
*The Andean condor is an **endangered species**; we should protect it.*
*He prefers **adventure tours**; they are exciting as you can do lots of activities.*
*After a week in the desert they **headed back** to the capital.*
*We saw **stunning scenery** as we flew over the forest.*
*We **spent the night** in a small hotel and left early in the morning.*
*There are **hot springs** in Yellowstone National Park.*
*Scientists think the Yellowstone volcano will **erupt** again destroying the western US.*
*The **opening hours** are 8 am to 6 pm, 7 days a week.*
*He tried to **make a good impression** in front of his friend's parents.*
*Go to Venezuela and you'll have **the time of your life**; you won't regret it.*
*I got stuck in traffic and **missed my flight** to Paris.*

*We **went sightseeing** around the area and got some great photographs.*
*We'll volunteer to clean the **dirty beach**.*
*I can't afford to stay in a **luxury hotel**.*
*We'll **take a tour** of the city to see the sights.*
*When you travel to another country, you should **respect their culture**.*
*The Acropolis in Athens, Greece is a **historical site**.*
*We went back home with **good memories** of our holiday.*

## Quiz

*Answer Key*

1   *Bolivia.*
2   *They can sandboard on sand dunes.*
3   *Near the Arctic Circle./In Finland.*
4   *Every 90 minutes.*
5   *In Mexico, on the Yucatan Peninsula.*
6   *Wyoming, Montana and Idaho.*
7   *Piranha.*
8   *About 640,000 years ago.*

Ss prepare their quiz in groups. Ask Ss to go through the pages of Module 4 and select information to compile their quiz. Ask groups to exchange quizzes, do them, then check their answers.

*Suggested Answer key*

*Quiz*

1   *What is the capital of Peru? (Lima)*
2   *Where is the Madidi National Park? (In Bolivia)*
3   *What is a traditional dish in Finland? (Reindeer stew)*
4   *What's the name of the geyser in Yellowstone National Park? (Old Faithful)*
5   *Where is the Dinosaur Museum? (Wyoming)*
6   *What is Jason de Caires Taylor's job? (He's a sculptor.)*
7   *Where is Caires Taylor's underwater sculpture park? (In Cancun, Mexico)*
8   *Where is St Lucia? (In the Caribbean)*

**Suggested Answers for Exs 2b, 4 & 5 on p. 74**

**Ex. 2b**

***behaving towards:*** *treating*
***feeling you have about sb or sth:*** *impression*
***instructions:*** *rules*
***being concerned about:*** *caring about*
***things you remember about the past:*** *memories*
***visitor:*** *guest*
***honour:*** *respect*
***sb typical of the group they belong to:*** *representative*
***regional:*** *local*
***help:*** *support*

**Ex. 4**

*I think that I'm a responsible tourist because I try to buy local brands while I'm shopping on holiday. I love looking around and taking photos, but I always ask local people if I'm allowed to take their photos. Before I go abroad, I learn a few words of the language, even if it's just 'please' and 'thank you'. Local people love it when I speak their language. I also take care of the environment. I don't leave my rubbish behind and I always turn the air-conditioning off when I leave my hotel room.*

**Ex. 5**

*Other ways in which people can be responsible tourists:*
–   *using water sparingly*
–   *hiring a local guide – this provides employment in the local community*
–   *using public transport – this reduces pollution*
–   *donating money to a local project*

## Collocations

**1** **Match the phrases.**

| | | | | | |
|---|---|---|---|---|---|
| 1 | D | camp out | A | food poisoning |
| 2 | F | lose | B | a great time |
| 3 | G | visit | C | for souvenirs |
| 4 | B | have | D | under the stars |
| 5 | A | get | E | local food |
| 6 | I | put on | F | your luggage |
| 7 | J | go | G | historical sites |
| 8 | H | trek | H | in the mountains |
| 9 | E | try | I | your flippers |
| 10 | C | shop | J | on a cruise |

**2** **Fill in:** *behaviour, coral, endangered, spectacular, sea, ancient, dangerous, local, scuba, lava.*

1 **spectacular** view
2 **sea** creatures
3 **behaviour** code
4 **ancient** monuments
5 **coral** reef
6 **dangerous** road
7 **local** food
8 **endangered** species
9 **lava** lake
10 **scuba** diver

## Prepositions

**3** **Choose the correct preposition.**

1 He's interested **to/in** visiting the underwater park in Cancun.
2 Where are you going **on/for** holiday this year?
3 We are bored **of/from** beach holidays.
4 Jason deCaires Taylor creates his sculptures **of/from** cement.
5 There is an amazing view **of/to** the city from the top of the hill.
6 You should treat people **in/with** respect.
7 We climbed **through/to** the top of Mount Vesuvius when we visited Italy last year.

**4** **Choose the correct word.**

1 Hurry up! We don't want to **miss/lose** our flight.
2 From the hotel, we had a fantastic **sight/view** of the city.
3 I **lost/missed** my passport last year on holiday.
4 We are going on a **trip/journey** to China this summer.
5 My dad always **takes/makes** lots of photos on holiday.
6 We are going on a sightseeing **trip/tour** of the city tomorrow.
7 We usually **stay/live** in a tent on holiday.

**In teams, make sentences. Use words/phrases from the list below. Each correct sentence gets one point. The team with the most points wins.**

- lie on the beach • go on a safari • road stretches
- drive a dune buggy • endangered species • adventure tour
- head back • stunning scenery • spend the night
- hot springs • erupt • opening hours • make a good impression
- time of your life • miss my flight • go sightseeing
- dirty beach • luxury hotel • take a tour
- respect their culture • historical site • good memories

## Quiz

Read through Module 4 and answer the questions. Now write a quiz of your own. Give it to your partner. Check his/her answers.

1 Which country is *El Camino de la Muerte* in?
2 What can travellers do in the Huacachina Desert?
3 Where can you usually see the Northern Lights?
4 How often does Old Faithful erupt?
5 Where's Cancun?
6 Which three states is Yellowstone National Park in?
7 What fish are there in the Yacuma River?
8 When did the Yellowstone supervolcano last erupt?

## Reading

### Study skills

**Matching question stems to the text**
Read the text quickly to see what it is about. Read it again sentence by sentence. Pay attention to the words before and after each gap as they will help you decide on your choice. Read the completed text again to see if it makes sense.

**1 a)** **Look at the sentences and the possible answers. Which sentence:** *asks for a grammar structure*? *a lexical item*?

**1** Peter .......... to travel to France but he <u>went</u> to Poland instead.
   **A** has planned   **B** was planning
   **C** will travel

**2** The place offers a variety of activities to .......... <u>from</u>.
   **A** decide        **B** try
   **C** choose

**b)** **Choose the correct answers. The underlined words will help you.**

**2 a)** **Read the rubric. Then read through the text to get the gist.**

> You are going to read a text about a city. For gaps 1-8 choose the word A, B or C that best completes each gap.

**b)** **Do the task. Compare your answers with your partner's.**

Cape Town, the capital of South Africa, is the **0)** ........ popular tourist destination in Africa. With great weather and amazing natural landscapes, it's a wonderful place **1)** ........ visit. Located on the shore of Table Bay, it is one of the most multicultural cities in the world. Home to a variety of vegetation types, some of **2)** ........ exist nowhere else, the city attracts millions of visitors for **3)** ........ natural features. **4)** ........ best known is Table Mountain. You can reach the top either by hiking up or by taking the Table Mountain Cableway. The views from there are dramatic. A lot of tourists also visit the Two Oceans Aquarium where you can see life from **5)** ........ Indian and Atlantic Oceans.

The Victoria and Alfred Waterfront is a great place to go shopping. With hundreds of shops it promises something for everyone. The 'V & A', as locals call **6)** ........, is part of the port which continues to operate so it is possible to take a ferry and visit nearby islands. Cape Town's beaches are very popular **7)** ........ tourists and locals alike. The most visited one is Boulders Beach which has a colony of African penguins living in one of the inlets.

Cape Town has a lot to offer and can satisfy the most demanding visitor. You **8)** ........ not be disappointed.

| | | | | | | | |
|---|---|---|---|---|---|---|---|
| **0** | **A** | more | **(B)** | most | **C** | very |
| **1** | **A** | for | **B** | to | **C** | of |
| **2** | **A** | which | **B** | who | **C** | that |
| **3** | **A** | the | **B** | these | **C** | its |
| **4** | **A** | An | **B** | The | **C** | A |
| **5** | **A** | the | **B** | these | **C** | them |
| **6** | **A** | this | **B** | it | **C** | that |
| **7** | **A** | with | **B** | of | **C** | for |
| **8** | **A** | will | **B** | must | **C** | could |

## Speaking

### Study skills

**Communication repair**
If you don't know the English word for a key object in the photo, you can still find ways to describe it. You can talk about, for example, why and how people use it.

**3 a)** **Read the description. How does the writer describe the key object without using its name?**

A man on a ship is looking at something quite far away from him. I can't remember the English word, but he is using something people use to see things at a distance, at a sporting event, for example. It's like a big pair of glasses that you hold in front of your eyes.

**1 a)** **Aim** To introduce a type of reading task

- Read out the *Study Skills* box and explain that this tip will help Ss to complete the task successfully.
- Ask Ss to look at the questions and elicit what each one asks for.

***Answer Key***

*1 grammar structure*     *2 lexical item*

**b)** **Aim** To practise answering multiple choice cloze questions

- Elicit the answers for each question from various Ss around the class.
- Tell Ss the underlined words will help them choose the answer.

***Answer Key***

*1 B*                    *2 C*

**2 a)** **Aim** To prepare for a reading task

Read the rubric aloud and then give Ss time to read the text quickly for gist.

**b)** **Aim** To read for lexico-grammatical structure

- Give Ss time to read the text again sentence by sentence and complete the task.
- Check Ss' answers.

***Answer Key***

| | | | |
|---|---|---|---|
| *1 B* | *3 C* | *5 A* | *7 A* |
| *2 A* | *4 B* | *6 B* | *8 A* |



**3 a)** **Aim** To learn about communication repair

- Read out the *Study Skills* box and explain that they can use this tip to help them complete a speaking task successfully.
- Ask Ss to read the description and elicit how the writer has described the key object.

***Suggested Answer Key***

*The writer has described how and why people use the object and attempted to describe it.*

b) **Aim** **To describe a picture and answer questions about it**

- Read the rubric aloud and then ask Ss to describe the picture to their partners.
- Monitor the activity around the class and then elicit answers to the questions from various Ss around the class.

*Suggested Answer Key*

*In the picture, I can see five young children around eight years old sitting on the ground at a campsite. There are three girls and two boys. They are holding metal camping cups and banging them together as if they are making a toast. They are smiling and happy and they look like they are having fun. I think it's late afternoon.*

*Suggested Answer Key*

*1   I think they are having a good time camping. They may be on a school trip or an activity holiday.*
*2   Yes, I do. I love nature and fresh air./No, I don't. I prefer to be indoors.*
*3   The best holiday I ever had was when I went to Wales with my family as a child. We stayed in a caravan and we went to the beach every day and made sandcastles and swam in the sea. It was fantastic.*

## Listening

4  a) **Aim** **To familiarise Ss with the task**

Ask Ss to read the rubric and the list of holidays.

b) **Aim** **To listen for specific information**

- Ask Ss to re-read the rubric.
- Play the recording. Ss listen and match the people to the holidays.
- Check Ss' answers.

*Answer Key*

1  C          2  G          3  A          4  F          5  B

## Writing

5  **Aim** **To prepare for a writing task**

- Read out the **Study Skills** box and explain that this tip will help Ss to complete the task successfully.
- Ask Ss to read the rubric and then elicit what sort of language it asks for (*e.g. Would you like to come …?*).

- Give Ss time to think of a few phrases and then compare with their partner.
- Check Ss' answers around the class.

*Suggested Answer Key*

*We are going … Would you like to come …? My family …*
*We could go skiing/snowboarding, etc.*
*You should bring … You will need …*

6  **Aim** **To write a letter of invitation**

- Go through the rubric with Ss. Elicit phrases related to *inviting*, *making suggestions* and write them on the board.

### Useful phrases for inviting/making suggestions

| Inviting | Making suggestions |
| --- | --- |
| *I'd really like you to come.* | *We can/could go …* |
| *Why don't you come?* | *Let's go …* |
| *It would be great if you could come.* | *What about …?* |
| | *How about …?* |

- Elicit ideas for each bullet point and write them on the board under these headings.
  **DATE:** next month, next weekend, etc.
  **LENGTH OF STAY:** a week, four days, etc.
  **OUTDOOR ACTIVITIES:** skiing, snowboarding, sledging, etc.
  **CLOTHES:** ski jacket, heavy clothes, gloves, waterproof trousers, etc.
- Check Ss' answers.
- Give Ss time to complete the task using their answers and the plan provided.
- Remind Ss to include each of the bulleted points.
- Check Ss' answers.

*Suggested Answer Key*

*Dear Lisa,*
*How are you? I'm excited right now because my family and I are planning a winter holiday in our mountain chalet from 1st-15th December. It's near a really nice ski resort and I'd really like you to come.*
*There will be me, my parents and my brother, Hans, staying in the chalet, but there is plenty of room for you. We can go skiing, snowboarding and sledging. It'll be great fun!*
*You'll need to bring warm clothes, a ski jacket, waterproof trousers, a hat and gloves. The flight costs around £250 with Swiss Air lines. I really hope you'll come. Write back soon and let me know.*
*Love,*
*Heidi*

**b)** Read the rubric, then do the task.

> Describe the picture. Then answer the questions.

1 Why do you think these children look happy?
2 Do you like spending time outdoors? Why/why not?
3 What was the best holiday you ever had?

## Listening

**4** **a)** **Read the rubric, then the list of holidays.**

> Listen to Chris talking to a friend about summer holidays. What type of holiday is each person going on? For questions 1-5, write a letter A-H next to each person. You will hear the conversation twice.

**Example**

**0** Chris *E*

| People | | Holidays | |
|---|---|---|---|
| 1 Lauren | ☐ | **A** | cruise |
| 2 Anna | ☐ | **B** | activity holiday |
| 3 Ben | ☐ | **C** | beach holiday |
| 4 Sophie | ☐ | **D** | safari |
| 5 Tom | ☐ | **E** | camping holiday |
| | | **F** | backpacking holiday |
| | | **G** | historical holiday |
| | | **H** | walking holiday |

**b)** 🎧 **Do the task. Compare your answers with your partner's.**

## Writing (informal letters)
*(Writing Bank p. WB1)*



**Identifying useful language**
Read the rubric and identify what useful language is needed. e.g **suggest** means that *you can use phrases such as: How about …?, Let's …, Why don't you?*, etc. This will help you do the task.

**5** Read the rubric. What language does it ask for? Think of phrases related to: *inviting, making suggestions*. Compare with your partner.

> You are planning a winter holiday in your mountain chalet near a ski resort. You want your English pen-friend to come with you. Write a letter (80-100 words), where you:
> - say when you are going & how long you will stay
> - invite your friend to come & mention who else will be at the chalet
> - suggest what outdoor activities you will do together & what clothes your friend will need to bring
> - tell them how much the flight will cost and suggest an airline

**6** Do the writing task. Follow the plan.



*Dear … ,*
**Para 1:** opening remarks, tell friend about your holiday, when you are going to go and invite them to come
**Para 2:** say who will be at the chalet with you and what outdoor activities you will do together
**Para 3:** suggest what clothes your friend will need and airline details, closing remarks
*… (Name)*

# 4 Revision

**1** **Fill in:** *encourage, experience, crowded, stunning, clean up, make, spend, erupts, respect, attracts.*

1 Acapulco is a popular tourist destination, so the beaches there are very ............................. in the summer.
2 Driving the dune buggy was a really exciting .............................!
3 When you go camping, you should always ................................. after yourself.
4 Japan is famous for its ......................... scenery.
5 We need to ............................... people to care for the environment.
6 Tourists should always ......................... the local customs of a country.
7 Cancun ......................... lots of visitors every year.
8 They decided to ......................... the night at a campsite.
9 If the volcano ........................., it will cause a lot of damage.
10 When you are abroad, try to ......................... a good impression on the locals. *10x2=20 marks*

**2** **Complete the sentences with** *will* **or** *be going to* **and the verbs in brackets.**

1 I think you ............................. **(have)** a great time in St Lucia. It's an amazing place!
2 I ............................. **(not/swim)** with piranha. It's too scary!
3 She ............................. **(be)** 20 this year.
4 Oh no! It's 6 o'clock. We ............................. **(miss)** our flight.
5 Oh, you're going shopping. I ............................. **(come)** with you. *5x2=10 marks*

**3** **Complete with the** *present continuous* **forms of the verbs:** *visit, not climb, travel, eat, swim.*

1 Sally ............................. with dolphins this afternoon.
2 We ............................. in a fish restaurant this evening.
3 I ............................. abroad next month.
4 Tom and Lucy ............................. the museum this weekend.
5 I ............................. the volcano this afternoon. *5x2=10 marks*

**4** **Match the exchanges.**

| 1 | | Can I help you with anything else? | **A** | I'm calling for some information. |
| 2 | | How can I help you? | **B** | What are the opening hours? |
| 3 | | Sure, what would you like to know? | **C** | No, I think that's all. |
| 4 | | Someone stole my passport. | **D** | Thank you very much. |
| 5 | | Enjoy your visit! | **E** | Really? Oh dear! |

*5x4=20 marks*

**5** **Fill in:** *who, whose, which* **or** *where.*

1 That's the man ......................... lives next door.
2 Ann, ......................... father is our Art teacher, is my best friend.
3 Sydney is the place ................... we want to go this summer.
4 Sydney Opera House, ......................... is very impressive, is a UNESCO World Heritage Site.
5 Anthony, ......................... brother works at the zoo, has left Australia. *5x2=10 marks*

**6** **Fill in:** *a, an,* **or** *the* **where necessary.**

1 ............... Thames is ............... river in London.
2 ........... Lake Victoria is in ........... Africa.
3 There's ........... car outside our house. ........... car is a Mercedes.
4 ............... cheetah is ............. fastest animal on Earth.
5 ........... Pyrenees is a range of mountains in ........... southwest Europe. *5x2=10 marks*

**7** **You are on holiday in a city in your country. Write a letter to your pen-friend telling him/her all about your holiday. Write:** *where you are, what the weather is like, what you did yesterday, what you're doing this afternoon & what you're going to do tomorrow* **(80-100 words).** *20 marks*

*Total: 100 marks*


## Check your Progress

* talk and write about holiday experiences & activities ____
* ask for information about a tourist attraction ____
* talk about eco-tourism & responsible tourism ____
* talk about holiday problems ____
* write a letter about your holiday ____

**GOOD ✓   VERY GOOD ✓✓   EXCELLENT ✓✓✓**

**1**  1  *crowded*  5  *encourage*  9  *erupts*
   2  *experience*  6  *respect*  10  *make*
   3  *clean up*  7  *attracts*
   4  *stunning*  8  *spend*

**2**  1  *will have*  4  *are going to miss*
   2  *am not going to swim*  5  *will come*
   3  *will be*

**3**  1  *is swimming*  4  *are visiting*
   2  *are eating*  5  *am not climbing*
   3  *am travelling*

**4**  1  C  2  A  3  B  4  E  5  D

**5**  1  *who*  3  *where*  5  *whose*
   2  *whose*  4  *which*

**6**  1  *The, a*  3  *a, The*  5  *The, –*
   2  *–, –*  4  *The, the*

**7**  *Suggested Answer Key*

*Dear George,*

*Hi, how are you? I'm in Cancun. We're staying in a beautiful hotel right on the beach. The weather is amazing!*

*Yesterday, we went scuba diving. We spent three hours in the water. The fish we saw there were fantastic! This afternoon, we're playing volleyball on the beach.*

*Tomorrow, we're going to visit an underwater sculpture museum. We are going to see statues of people and animals about 790 metres below the waves. I can't wait!*

*Well, I must go now. We're meeting some friends for lunch. See you when I get back!*

*Best wishes,*
*Alex*

# Helping hands



Read the title of the module *Helping hands* and ask Ss to predict the content of the module *(the module is about social and environmental problems and what we can do to help those in need)*. Go through the contents list and stimulate a discussion about what Ss will learn in the module.

## Vocabulary

1 **Aim** To present new vocabulary

- Draw Ss' attention to the pictures (1-7).
- Play the recording. Ss listen and repeat.
- Explain/Elicit what *social* and *environmental* mean *(relating to society/the environment)*.
- Elicit which category each problem fits.

*Social problems: unemployment, racism, homelessness*
*Environmental problems: pollution, global warming, endangered animals, deforestation*

2 **Aim** To listen for gist

- Explain the task.
- Play the recording. Ss listen and decide which problem the speakers are talking about.
- Check Ss' answers around the class.

**Answer Key**

*Speaker 1: endangered animals*
*Speaker 2: global warming*
*Speaker 3: homelessness*

## OVER TO YOU!

**Aim** To express an opinion about world problems

Ask various Ss to say what they think the two most serious problems in their country are.

**Suggested Answer Key**

*I think global warming and pollution are the two most serious problems in my country.*

## Helping hands

**Vocabulary:** world problems, natural disasters, humanitarian problems, activities for a charity event, ways animals are endangered, activities at an eco-camp

**Grammar:** present perfect, present perfect continuous, *already/yet/for/since/never/ever/just*, present perfect vs simple past, -ing/-ed adjectives, past perfect, conditional type 3, wishes, *have been/have gone*

**Everyday English:** asking for & offering help

**Pronunciation:** homophones

**Writing:** a diary entry; an interview; a description of a charity event; an email giving news

**Culture Corner:** Comic Relief (a charity event)

**Curricular (*Geography*):** The world's oceans

## *Vocabulary*
### World problems

**1** Listen and say. Which problems are: *social? environmental?*

**2** Listen to three people talking. Which problem is each talking about?

**OVER TO YOU!**

Complete the sentence.

I think ........................ and ........................ are the two most serious problems in my country.

# 5a Disaster!

## Vocabulary
### Natural disasters

**1** a) Match the disasters (A-G) to the pictures (1-7). 🎧 Listen and check, then say.

| | | |
|---|---|---|
| A | 3 | drought |
| B | 2 | flood |
| C | 1 | earthquake |
| D | 6 | forest fire |
| E | 5 | tornado |
| F | 7 | tsunami |
| G | 4 | hurricane |

b) Which of these are common in your country?

*Forest fires are common in my country.*

## Reading & Speaking

**2** a) Read the first sentence of each entry (1-3) in Suzy's diary. Where is she? What do you think she is doing there? 🎧 Listen and read to find out.

b) Now read the diary entries and mark the sentences *T* (true), *F* (false) or *DS* (doesn't say).

1 Suzy is volunteering in Haiti with friends. **DS**
2 3 million people are now homeless. **F**
3 Natural disasters happen often in Haiti. **T**
4 The rescue team took five days to rescue the boy. **F**
5 The earthquake only hit Port-au-Prince. **F**
6 Suzy's team is helping to give out food. **DS**
7 Suzy thinks rebuilding will take a long time. **DS**

c) Match the words in bold to their meanings: *a difficult job, wounds, ruined, not dead, terrible, died, cleaned away, harmed.*

**3** Use the words from the **Check these words** box to complete the sentences.

1 He joined a volunteer team to help homeless people.
2 It was awful to see so many suffering people.
3 They managed to pull a boy alive from the rubble ten days after the earthquake.
4 We hope medical supplies will arrive shortly because people are suffering from disease and injuries.
5 A rescue team is working hard to get the trapped people out.

**4** **THINK!** Imagine you're in Haiti just after the earthquake. What can you hear, see and smell? How do you feel? In three minutes, write a few sentences. Tell the class.

## Vocabulary

**1 a) Aim To present new vocabulary**

- Read the list of natural disasters and direct Ss' attention to the pictures (1-7).
- Allow Ss time to complete the task.
- Play the recording for Ss to check their answers.
- Play the recording again with pauses for Ss to repeat individually or chorally.

**b) Aim To practise new vocabulary**

Ask various Ss to say what natural disasters are common in their country. Elicit the plural form of each disaster and write them on the board.

**Suggested Answer Key**

*Droughts are common in my country.*
*Floods are common in my country.*
*Earthquakes are common in my country.*
*Tornadoes are common in my country.*
*Tsunamis are common in my country.*
*Hurricanes are common in my country.*

## Reading & Speaking

**2 a) Aim To introduce and predict the content of a text**

- Ask Ss to read the first sentence in each diary entry and elicit answers to the questions in the rubric.
- Play the recording. Ss listen and follow the text in their books to find out if their guesses were correct.

**Answer Key**

*Suzy is in Port-au-Prince in Haiti. I think she is a volunteer working as part of a team to rebuild Haiti after the earthquake.*

**b) Aim To read for specific information**

- Allow Ss time to read the diary entries and mark the sentences.
- Check Ss' answers. As an extension, Ss can correct the false statements.

**Answer Key**

2 *(the earthquake has affected 3 million people)*
4 *(seven days)*
5 *(it affected all of Haiti)*

### BACKGROUND INFORMATION

On 12th January 2010, there was a terrible earthquake in Haiti. It measured 7.0 on the Richter scale and it affected over 3 million people. 230,000 died, 300,000 people were injured and 1 million people became homeless.
**Note:** The text is extracts from the diary of a fictional volunteer called Suzy, but the information is based on true facts as described by people who visited Haiti at that time.

**c) Aim To expand vocabulary/To match words from a text to their meanings**

- Explain the task.
- Give Ss time to complete the task.
- Check Ss' answers.

**Answer Key**

*a difficult job: challenge*   *terrible: awful*
*wounds: injuries*   *died: lost their lives*
*ruined: destroyed*   *cleaned away: cleared*
*not dead: alive*   *harmed: damaged*

**3 Aim To practise new vocabulary**

- Go through the **Check these words** box and explain/elicit the meanings of the words. Ask Ss to identify what part of speech each word is.

**Suggested Answer Key**

*volunteer team (n): a group of people who offer to do sth*
*destroy (v): to ruin*
*affect (v): to influence, cause to change*
*injury (n): damage done to the body*
*suffer (v): to feel mental/physical pain*
*challenge (n): sth difficult that requires determination to do*
*clear (v): to clean away*
*rubble (n): pieces of a destroyed building*
*rescue team (n): a group of people that work together to find and help victims*
*wage (n): money paid for work done*
*conditions (n): things which affect comfort, safety, etc*
*running water (n): water that comes from a tap*
*medical supplies (n): medicine, bandages, etc*
*awful (adj): terrible*

- Allow Ss time to complete the task.
- Check Ss' answers.

**4 Aim To describe a scene**

- Allow Ss time to think about what they could hear, see and smell after an earthquake, and how they might feel. Ss prepare their answers. Point out that Ss should use the present simple/present continuous.
- Elicit answers from Ss around the class.

**Suggested Answer Key**

*I can hear alarms and people crying. Someone nearby is screaming and other people are calling out the names of people in their families.*
*I can see fires in buildings and rubble all over the streets. Some people are lying injured on the ground and rescue teams are trying to help. Families are standing around looking at the damage to their homes. There is dust everywhere. I can smell burning plastic and smoke from the fires. I feel sad.*

## Grammar

**5** **Aim** To present the present perfect

- Ss close their books. Present the present perfect. Say: *I have walked the dog today.* Write it on the board. Underline *I have walked* and explain that this verb is in the present perfect. Explain that we use the present simple of the verb *have* and the past participle of the main verb to form the affirmative. Explain that we use this tense to talk about actions which started in the past and continue to the present. Refer Ss to the example sentence and point out that the action (have walked) has happened at a period of time that hasn't finished yet (it is still today). Point out that the past participle of regular verbs is formed adding *-ed* to the base form of the main verb. Refer Ss to the list of irregular verbs at the back of their books for irregular forms.
- Say, then write on the board: *I haven't walked the dog today.* Explain that this is the negative form of the present perfect. Elicit how it is formed.
- Say: *Have I walked the dog today?* Write it on the board. Underline *Have I walked* and explain that this is the interrogative form of the present perfect. Elicit/Explain that we answer using *Yes/No, + subject + have/has/haven't/hasn't*.
- Ss open their books. Go through the table then Ss complete the task.
- Elicit examples from the text.

**Answer Key**

1 Have  2 Has  3 haven't  4 has  5 hasn't

**Suggested Answer Key**

has destroyed, has affected, have lost, has offered, has caused, have damaged (and even) swept, have come, have cleared, have just arrived

**6** **Aim** To practise the present perfect

- Explain the task and give Ss some time to complete it, then check Ss' answers.
- Elicit more past participles from the text.

**Answer Key**

eat – eaten   have – had   give – given   buy – bought
go – gone      be – been     find – found   lose – lost
tell – told      say – said     see – seen

**Suggested Answer Key**

arrived, destroyed, affected, offered, caused, damaged, swept, come, cleared

**7** **Aim** To practise the present perfect

- Explain the task and allow Ss some time to complete it.
- Check Ss' answers on the board.

**Answer Key**

| | |
|---|---|
| 2 have worked | 5 have saved |
| 3 Has the tornado destroyed | 6 haven't arrived |
| 4 have lost | |

## Listening & Writing

**8 a)** **Aim** To listen for specific information

- Explain the situation. Ask Ss to read phrases 1-5.
- Play the recording. Ss listen and tick the boxes.
- Check Ss' answers around the class. Ask Ss to form complete sentences using the present perfect.

**Answer Key**

(ticked boxes) 1, 2, 5
They have cleared roads.
They have brought supplies.
They have taken photos.

**b)** **Aim** To write a diary entry

- Explain the task and tell Ss that they can use the ideas from Ex. 8a.
- Play the recording again.
- Remind Ss to use the diary entries in Ex. 2a as a model.
- Allow Ss three minutes to do the task. Alternatively assign it as HW.
- Ask various Ss to read out their diary entries in class.

**Suggested Answer Key**

*Well, here I am in the Caribbean and I can't believe my eyes! The hurricane has destroyed many buildings and the conditions are terrible. The strong winds and rain have pulled trees down and swept them across the roads. There is glass and rubble everywhere. Our team has started to clear the roads and medical supplies have arrived. Hopefully we can help rebuild the village after this awful disaster!*

### BACKGROUND INFORMATION

**The Caribbean** is an area between North and South America to the east of Central America. It includes the Caribbean Sea, the West Indies, the Bahamas and other island groups and the surrounding coastlines. It is a popular tourist destination due to the tropical weather, white sandy beaches, clear blue sea and plentiful wildlife.

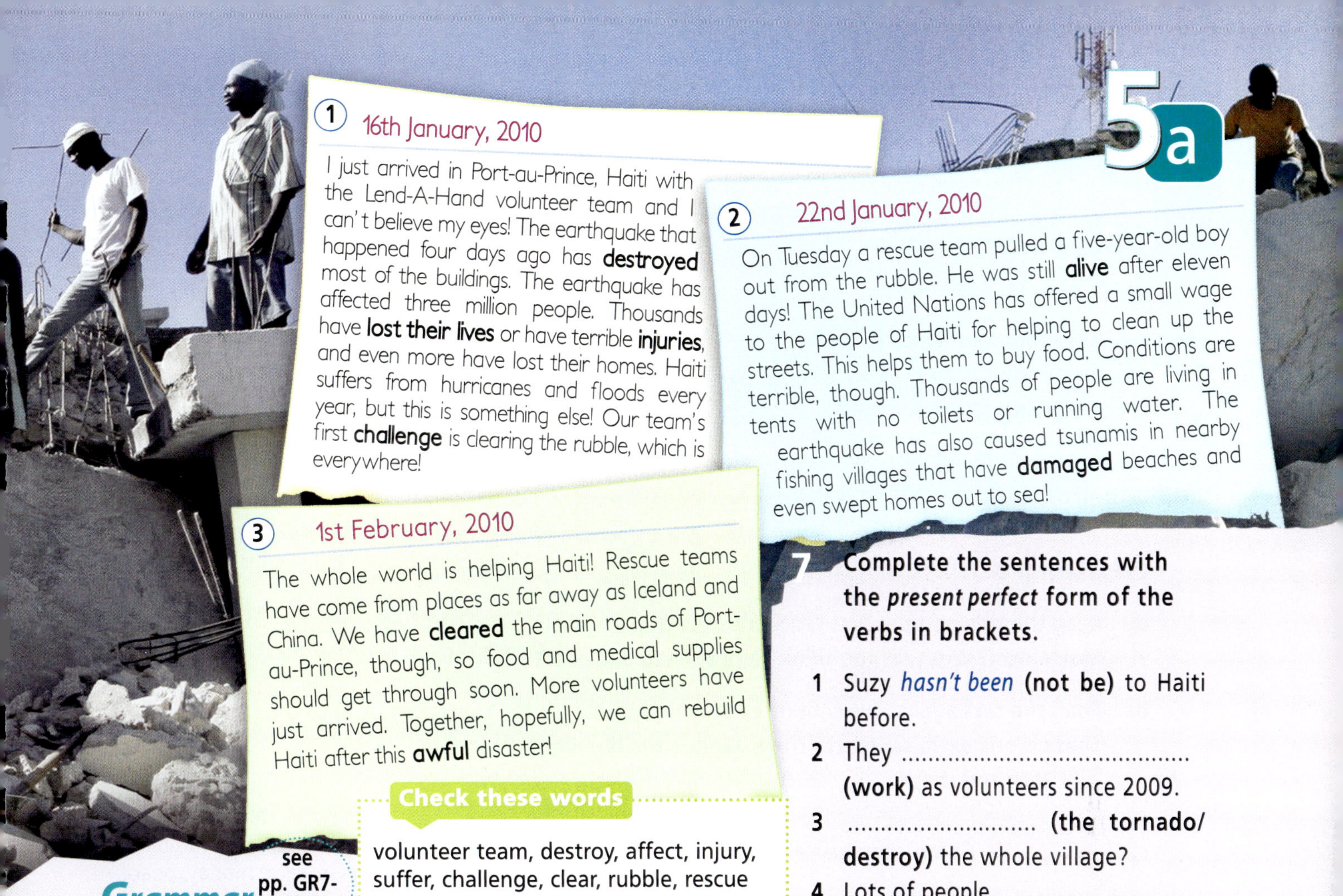

**① 16th January, 2010**

I just arrived in Port-au-Prince, Haiti with the Lend-A-Hand volunteer team and I can't believe my eyes! The earthquake that happened four days ago has **destroyed** most of the buildings. The earthquake has affected three million people. Thousands have **lost their lives** or have terrible **injuries**, and even more have lost their homes. Haiti suffers from hurricanes and floods every year, but this is something else! Our team's first **challenge** is clearing the rubble, which is everywhere!

**② 22nd January, 2010**

On Tuesday a rescue team pulled a five-year-old boy out from the rubble. He was still **alive** after eleven days! The United Nations has offered a small wage to the people of Haiti for helping to clean up the streets. This helps them to buy food. Conditions are terrible, though. Thousands of people are living in tents with no toilets or running water. The earthquake has also caused tsunamis in nearby fishing villages that have **damaged** beaches and even swept homes out to sea!

**③ 1st February, 2010**

The whole world is helping Haiti! Rescue teams have come from places as far away as Iceland and China. We have **cleared** the main roads of Port-au-Prince, though, so food and medical supplies should get through soon. More volunteers have just arrived. Together, hopefully, we can rebuild Haiti after this **awful** disaster!

> **Check these words**
>
> volunteer team, destroy, affect, injury, suffer, challenge, clear, rubble, rescue team, wage, conditions, running water, medical supplies, awful

*Grammar* see pp. GR7-GR8
**Present perfect**

**5** Read and complete the table. Find examples in the text.

Form: *has/have* + past participle

| AFFIRMATIVE | NEGATIVE |
|---|---|
| *I/We/You/They* **have arrived** in Haiti. *He/She/It* **has arrived** in Haiti. | *I/We/You/They* **haven't felt** an earthquake before. *He/She/It* **hasn't felt** an earthquake before. |

| INTERROGATIVE | SHORT ANSWERS |
|---|---|
| **1)** ............ I/you/we/they (ever) **climbed** a mountain? | **Yes**, I/you/we/they **have**. **No**, I/you/we/they **3)** ......... . |
| **2)** ................. he/she/it (ever) **climbed** a mountain? | **Yes**, he/she/it **4)** ............... . **No**, he/she/it **5)** ............... . |

We use the **present perfect** for:
- actions which started in the past and continue into the present. *She's worked here since last January.* (She still works here.)
- life experiences. *I've visited Haiti.* (We don't know when.)
- actions that happened in the past and we can see the result now. *They've cleared the snow from the road.* (We can see the road is clear.)

**Time expressions used with the present perfect:** so far, this morning, since, for, never, ever, already, yet, this week/month/year, etc.

**6** Match the infinitives to the *past participles*. Find more *past participles* in the text.

- eat • go • tell • have • be • say • give • find • see • buy • lose

- given • seen • said • bought • told • gone • had
- been • found • eaten • lost

**7** Complete the sentences with the *present perfect* form of the verbs in brackets.

1 Suzy *hasn't been* (not be) to Haiti before.
2 They ..................................... (work) as volunteers since 2009.
3 ........................... (the tornado/ **destroy**) the whole village?
4 Lots of people ........................... ............... (lose) their lives so far.
5 The rescue workers ................... ............. (save) ten people so far.
6 The food supplies ....................... (not arrive) yet.

## Listening & Writing

**8** a) Peter is in a volunteer team after a hurricane hit the Caribbean.
🎧 Listen and put a tick (✓) next to the things his team has done.

1 clear roads ☐
2 bring supplies ☐
3 help injured people ☐
4 collect money ☐
5 take photos ☐

b) Imagine you are Peter. Write a short diary entry. You can use the ideas in Ex. 8a and your own ideas. Read your entry to the class.

*Well, here I am in … and I can't believe my eyes! The hurricane has … . Our team has … etc*

▶ Vocabulary Bank 5 p. VB14

81

# 5b Going to help

## Vocabulary
### Social problems

**1** 🎧 Listen and say. Which is the most important to you. Tell your partner giving reasons.

*To me, war is the most important problem because a lot of people lose their lives.*

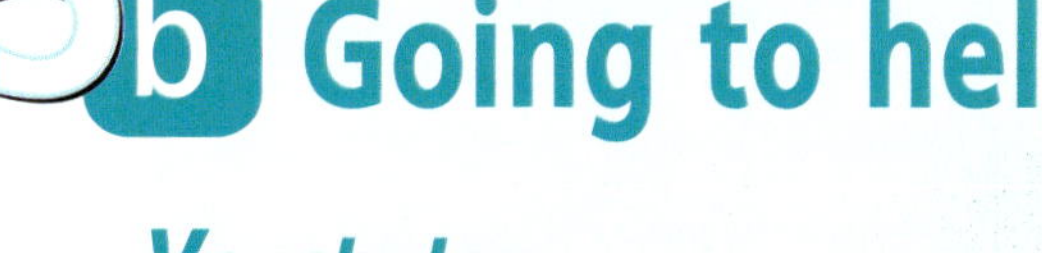


## Reading & Listening

**2** **a)** Read the title and the first sentence of each paragraph in the text. Who is Greg Mortenson? What do you think he did? Read and check.

**b)** Read the text again. Five sentences are missing. Match the sentences (A-F) to the gaps (1-5). There is one extra sentence. Then, explain the highlighted words.
🎧 Listen and check.

**c)** **THINK!** Complete the sentence.

I admire Greg because ...............................

### Check these words
achieve, end up, failure, set out, make it, top, stumble, injured, poor, hunger, ground, stick, promise, raise money, peace award, thrilling, proof, courage, best-selling, ignorance, cause, campaign, issue, look after

## From Climbing Mountains ... to Moving Mountains

Have you ever wanted to **achieve** something really amazing in life? Well, Greg Mortenson wanted to climb a mountain, but he **ended up** helping thousands of people to have a better life!

Greg Mortenson's story began with failure. In 1993, he **set out** to climb K2, the world's second highest mountain. But Greg never made it to the top. After five days, he stumbled into the village of Korphe in northern Pakistan, injured and hungry. **1 ▢**

Greg saw that the villagers were very poor and there was a lot of disease and hunger. Also, the village school didn't have a roof and the children wrote on the ground with sticks. **2 ▢** "I'll build you a school," he told the villagers. "I **promise.**"

Greg went back home to the USA to raise money for the school. He even lived in his car to save money! **3 ▢** But this was just the beginning of something much bigger! Since then, Greg's organisation has built around 80 schools and runs many others in Pakistan, Afghanistan and other countries, too.

Greg hasn't finished yet. **4 ▢** He has won many humanitarian and peace awards, but it's the smiles of the children he has helped that makes him happy!

**5 ▢** It's a thrilling read and **proof** of what ordinary people can do with **courage** and determination!

A Greg has just written a best-selling book about his story called *Three Cups of Tea*.
B He believes that poverty, illiteracy and **ignorance** cause many wars and other problems in the world, so he also organises many campaigns to fight these **issues**.
C Greg knew he wanted to do something to help.
D Greg has made a real difference to people's lives.
E The kind villagers there looked after him for several days.
F Finally, he went back to Korphe and built the school.

## Vocabulary

**1** **Aim** **To present new vocabulary**

- Draw Ss' attention to the pictures (1-6).
- Play the recording. Ss listen and repeat chorally or individually.
- Elicit answers to the question in the rubric.

### Suggested Answer Key

*To me, poverty is the most important problem because it can lead to hunger and other problems.*

## Reading & Listening

**2 a)** **Aim** **To introduce and predict the content of a text**

- Ask Ss to read the first sentence of each paragraph and elicit their answers to the questions in the rubric.
- Ss read the text in their books to find out if their guesses were correct.

### Suggested Answer Key

*Greg Mortenson is someone who saw poor villagers when he was climbing a mountain and wanted to help them. He raised money in the USA for a school for them and continues to help them.*

**b)** **Aim** **To read for cohesion and coherence/ To expand vocabulary**

- Allow Ss time to read the text again and match the sentences to the gaps. Point out that the words before and after each gap will help Ss complete the task.
- Play the recording.
- Ss listen and check their answers.

### Answer Key

| 1 E | 2 C | 3 F | 4 B | 5 A |
|-----|-----|-----|-----|-----|

*D is not used*

- Draw Ss' attention to the highlighted words.
- Give Ss time to find their meanings.
- Check Ss' answers.

### Suggested Answer Key

***achieve:*** *succeed in doing sth*
***ended up:*** *eventually did sth*
***set out:*** *started a journey*
***promise:*** *give my word*
***ignorance:*** *lack of knowledge*
***issues:*** *problems*
***proof:*** *evidence*
***courage:*** *bravery*

- Go through the ***Check these words*** box and explain/elicit the meanings of the words. Ss identify what part of speech each is.

### Suggested Answer Key

***achieve (v):*** *to accomplish*
***end up (phr v):*** *to eventually get somewhere/do sth, usually by accident*
***failure (n):*** *a lack of success*
***set out (phr v):*** *to begin a journey*
***make it (phr):*** *to succeed in sth*
***top (n):*** *peak*
***stumble (v):*** *to walk awkwardly almost falling*
***injured (adj):*** *hurt*
***poor (adj):*** *having no money*
***hunger (n):*** *shortage of food*
***ground (n):*** *earth*
***stick (n):*** *a piece of wood*
***promise (v):*** *to tell sb you will do sth*
***raise money (v):*** *to collect money for a specific purpose*
***peace award (n):*** *a prize for promoting non-violence*
***thrilling (adj):*** *exciting*
***proof (n):*** *evidence*
***courage (n):*** *bravery*
***best-selling (adj):*** *very popular (books, DVDs)*
***ignorance (n):*** *a lack of knowledge*
***cause (v):*** *to result in*
***campaign (n):*** *movement*
***issue (n):*** *problem*
***look after (phr v):*** *to protect, care for*

**c)** **Aim** **To practise new vocabulary**

- Explain/Elicit what **admire** means *(to like/ respect sb).*
- Allow Ss time to complete the task. Check Ss' answers.

### Suggested Answer Key

***I admire Greg because*** *he has made a difference in poor people's lives around the world.*

### BACKGROUND INFORMATION

**Pakistan** is a country in South Asia. It shares borders with India, Afghanistan, Iran and China. The capital city is Islamabad and it has a population of over 180 million. The people speak Urdu and English. It used to be part of India and became an Islamic republic in 1956. Poverty and illiteracy are problems there.

**Afghanistan** is a country in South Asia. It shares borders with Pakistan, Uzbekistan, Tajikistan, Turkmenistan and China. The capital city is Kabul and it has a population of 29 million. The people speak Persian and Pashto. Since the 1970s it has been in a state of civil war.

## Grammar

**3 a)** **Aim** **To present time expressions used with the present perfect**

- Ask various Ss to read out the examples.
- Allow Ss time to find examples in the text.
- Check Ss' answers.

*Answer Key*

*Have you **ever** wanted to ..., **Since** then, Greg's organisation has built... Greg hasn't finished **yet**. Greg has **just** written a best-selling book about his story called* Three Cups of Tea.

**b)** **Aim** **To practise time expressions used with the present perfect**

- Explain the task.
- Ss complete the task. Check Ss' answers around the class.

**4 a)** **Aim** **To compare the present perfect and the past simple**

- Read the table aloud. Draw on the board and write:

2007                                            Now

——×——————————————●——
        past simple

|————————————————————→
        present perfect

*John came here in 2007*
*He has lived here since 2007*

- Point out that we use the past simple for actions which happened in the past, whereas we use the present perfect for actions which started in the past and continue to the present.

- Elicit examples from the text on p. 82 from Ss round the class.

*Suggested Answer Key*

**Present Perfect:** *Have wanted, has built, hasn't finished, has won, has helped, has just written*
**Past Simple:** *wanted, ended up, began, set out, made, stumbled, looked after, saw, were, didn't have, wrote, knew, wanted, told, went, lived, built*

**b)** **Aim** **To practise the present perfect and past simple**

- Explain the task.
- Ss then fill in the gaps. Check Ss' answers.

**5** **Aim** **To present the present perfect continuous**

- Ss close their books. Present the present perfect continuous. Say: *I have been working all morning.* Write it on the board. Underline: **have been working** and explain that this verb is in the present perfect continuous. Explain that we use the present perfect continuous to emphasise the duration of an action that started in the past and continues to the present.
- Explain that we form the present perfect continuous with the auxiliary verb **have/has**, the past participle of the verb **to be (been)** and the main verb with the **-ing** ending.
- Ss open their books. Read the table. Explain that we form the negative by putting **not** between *have/has* and *been*. Explain that we form the interrogative by putting *have/has* before the subject. Elicit any similar structures in their L1.

*(Ss' own answers)*

**6** **Aim** **To practise the present perfect and the present perfect continuous**

Give Ss time to complete the task and then check Ss' answers.

## Speaking & Writing

**7** **Aim** **To write and act out an interview**

- Explain the task and ask Ss to work in pairs. Ss prepare and then ask and answer questions. (With weaker classes write the questions in the Suggested Answer Key on the board. Allow Ss time to do the task.)
- Monitor the activity around the class and then ask some pairs to act out their interview in class.

*Suggested Answer Key*

*Interviewer: Hello and welcome to the programme, Greg. Now, how did your story begin?*
*Greg: Well, it all started when I set out to climb K2. I never made it to the top, but I ended up in the village of Korphe. I was injured, hungry, and quite tired.*
*Interviewer: What happened to you there?*
*Greg: The villagers looked after me and they were very kind. I noticed everyone was very poor. People were sick and the children didn't have a proper school.*
*Interviewer: What did you do?*
*Greg: I returned home and raised money to help them. They helped me and I wanted to do something for them.*
*Interviewer: What did you do exactly?*
*Greg: I returned with the money and built them a school.*
*Interviewer: What have you done since then?*
*Greg: Since then I've built around 80 schools in other poor countries. I also organise campaigns to fight poverty and illiteracy.*
*Interviewer: You have won many peace awards. How does this make you feel?*
*Greg: What makes me happy and proud is the smiles of the children we have helped.*

## Grammar see p. GR8
### Yet – Already – Since – For – Never – Ever – Just

**3** a) **Read the theory. Find examples in the text in Ex. 2.**

> **Yet – Already – Since – For – Never – Ever – Just**
>
> *Jill hasn't arrived **yet**.* (We expect her to arrive soon.)
> *They've **already** booked their plane tickets.* (It's done. They don't have to do it any more.)
> *He's lived in Brazil **since** 2007.* (starting point)
> *We've been friends **for** 5 years.* (duration)
> *He has **never** travelled abroad.* (He hasn't travelled abroad.)
> *Have you **ever** thought about writing a book?* (thought about it at all)
> *He has **just** left.* (a few minutes ago)

b) **Choose the correct word.**

1 I haven't booked my plane ticket to Thailand **just/yet**. I'll do it tomorrow.
2 I haven't seen Danny **since/for** last week.
3 He taught in a village in India **since/for** 2 years.
4 She's **already/since** left for Haiti.
5 He's **yet/just** sent the email and is waiting for an answer.

## Present perfect vs Past simple see p. GR8

**4** a) **Read the theory. Find examples in the text.**

> **Present perfect vs Past simple**
>
> We use the **present perfect** for:
> * actions that started in the past and continue up to the present. *Max **has lived** here for three years.*
> * experiences. *Fran **has run** a marathon.* (When? We don't know.)
> * We use the **past simple** for actions that started and finished in the past. *I **went** to Argentina last year.* (When? Last year.)

b) **Put the verbs in brackets into the *past simple* or the *present perfect*.**

Hi Kathy,
I'm writing to you from India where I'm helping to build a village school! I 1) have been (be) here for 2 weeks now with my team and we 2) have already done (already/do) so many things!
The first day, we 3) went (go) into a nearby forest and 4) helped (help) to chop up wood. I 5) felt (feel) very tired afterwards, but I soon got used to it. 6) Have you ever done (you/ever/do) any volunteer work? It's amazing!
See you in a month.
Sam

## Present perfect continuous see p. GR8

**5** **Read the theory. Are there similar structures in your language?**

> **Form: *have/has been + verb -ing***
>
> | AFFIRMATIVE | NEGATIVE |
> | --- | --- |
> | *I/We/You/They **have been** sleeping.*<br>*He/She/It **has been** sleeping.* | *I/We/You/They **haven't been** sleeping.*<br>*He/She/It **hasn't been** sleeping.* |
> | INTERROGATIVE | SHORT ANSWERS |
> | ***Have** I/We/You/They **been** sleeping?*<br>***Has** he/she/it **been** sleeping?* | *Yes, I/we/you/they **have**.*<br>*No, I/we/you/they **haven't**.*<br>*Yes, he/she/it **has**.*<br>*No, he/she/it **hasn't**.* |

We use the **present perfect continuous**:
* to put emphasis on the duration of an action that started in the past and continues up to the present. *He **has been working** here for seven years.*
* for an action that started in the past and lasted for some time. It may be continuing or has finished but its results are visible in the present. *He **has been working** in the garden since morning. He's very tired.*

**6** **Put the verbs in brackets into the *present perfect* or the *present perfect continuous*.**

1 We haven't seen (not/see) Peter for a week. He's on holiday.
2 Their clothes are dirty. Have they been playing (they/play) in the garden?
3 They are very happy. They have won (win) the competition.
4 She's very angry. She has been waiting (wait) since 7 o'clock for Pete to call.
5 He has been living (live) in Rome for two years and he still can't speak Italian.
6 She has collected (collect) £5,000 for the charity so far.

## Speaking & Writing

**7** **Read the text again. Imagine you are interviewing Greg Mortenson for a radio programme. Prepare questions and answers. Read your interview to the class.**

*Interviewer: Hello and welcome to the programme, Greg. Now, how did your story begin? etc*

▶▶ Vocabulary Bank 5 p. VB15

# 5c Culture Corner

charity event, sort of, laughter, raise money, famine, take place, support, cause, get an education, viewer, make a donation, record a song, appear, celebrity, get involved, silly outfit

### So what's it all about?

'Red Nose Day' is part of Comic Relief, a big charity **event** in the UK that has become a **1)** sort of holiday of laughter! In 1985, a famous British comedy writer Richard Curtis organised the first Comic Relief to raise money for the terrible **famine** in Ethiopia. Since **2)** then, Comic Relief has taken **3)** place every two years and **supports** many different causes to help poor people in the UK and **4)** around the world, like helping kids in Africa to get an education.

### What happens on Red Nose Day?

On Red Nose Day, there are lots of special comedy shows on television and viewers can call in to **5)** make donations. Many famous people have recorded songs or appeared in comedy sketches to help. In 2009, a group of **celebrities**, including the pop singer Cheryl Cole, **6)** even climbed Mount Kilimanjaro to raise money! Everything **aims** to make people laugh and raise money for charity.

### How do people get involved?

Anyone can do **7)** something funny to raise money for Comic Relief, like wearing a silly **outfit** to work and collecting donations for it! Also, supermarkets sell red clown noses to wear **8)** on Red Nose Day to help raise money. Some people even put red clown noses on their cars!

**1** Look at the title and the pictures. What happens on 'Red Nose Day'? Read to find out.

**2** **a)** Read again and complete the gaps with the correct word.
🎧 Listen and check.

**b)** Match the words in bold to their meanings: *a situation in which people have little or no food, a set of clothes, occasion, plans to achieve, helps, famous people.*

**3** Use words from the Check these words box in the correct form to complete the sentences.

**1** We are organising a 10-km run to raise money for the animal shelter.
**2** Millions of viewers watch Comic Relief on TV.
**3** There was a terrible famine in Sudan in 1998. Over 70,000 people died of hunger.
**4** You can make a donation to the charity in cash or by cheque.

**4** You are a TV reporter covering this year's Red Nose Day. Use the text to present it to the TV viewers.

*It's Mike Smith live from London. Today we're celebrating Red Nose Day ...*

**5** ICT Is there a similar charity event in your country? Collect information, then make notes under the headings: *name, when it is, what happens.* Compare it to Red Nose Day. Tell the class.

**1** **Aim** **To introduce the topic and predict the content of the text**

- Direct Ss' attention to the title and the pictures. Ask what is unusual in them. *(people are wearing red noses.)*
- Elicit answers to the questions in the rubric.
- Ss read the text to find out if their guesses were correct.

*Suggested Answer Key*

*On Red Nose Day, people wear red clown noses and do funny things to help raise money for different causes.*

**2** **a)** **Aim** **To read for cohesion and coherence**

- Explain the task.
- Give Ss time to re-read the text and fill in the gaps with the appropriate words.
- Play the recording.
- Ss listen and check their answers.

**b)** **Aim** **To expand vocabulary/To match words from a text to their meanings**

- Explain the task.
- Give Ss time to re-read the text and fill in the gaps with the appropriate words.
- Check Ss' answers.

*Answer Key*

*event: occasion*
*famine: a situation in which people have little or no food*
*supports: helps*
*celebrities: famous people*
*aims: plans to achieve*
*outfit: a set of clothes*

**3** **Aim** **To practise vocabulary**

- Go through the **Check these words** box and explain/elicit the meanings of the words. Ask Ss to identify what part of speech each word is.

*Suggested Answer Key*

*charity event (n): an occasion to raise money*
*sort (of) (n): kind (of)*
*laughter (n): a sound made when people are happy*
*raise money (v): to collect money for*
*famine (n): a great hunger*
*take place (phr): happen*
*support (v): to back up*
*cause (n): an aim people fight for*
*get an education (phr): go to school and be educated*
*viewer (n): sb that watches sth*
*make a donation (phr): to give money*
*record a song (phr): to perform and put on tape, CD, etc*
*appear (v): to take part in*
*celebrity (n): a star, famous person*
*get involved (phr): participate (in)*

*silly outfit (n): a funny costume*

- Allow Ss time to complete the task in closed pairs.
- Check Ss' answers.

**4** **Aim** **To consolidate Ss' understanding of the topic**

- Explain the task. Point out that Ss need to use the present continuous in their presentation as they will be reporting an event live.
- Allow Ss time to write their presentation.
- Invite various Ss to present the event to the class.

*Suggested Answer Key*

*It's Mike Smith live from London. Today, we're celebrating Red Nose Day and as you can see lots of people all across the country are organising charity events to help poor people around the world. Live bands are performing in Hyde Park right now. Don't forget to buy a red nose to show you are helping, too. For those of you at home, stay tuned for some of the best comedy programmes on TV! Remember, every donation can make a difference!*

**5** **Aim** **To write about a charity event**

- Explain the task and brainstorm with Ss for various charity events in their country.
- Write the headings on the board and elicit ideas for some charity events under the headings below.
- Allow Ss time to complete the task using the notes.
- Ask various Ss to talk about the event they have chosen. Elicit how it compares to Red Nose Day.

*Suggested Answer Key* *– see p. 85(T)*

## BACKGROUND INFORMATION

**Cheryl Cole** is a British pop star. She was born in 1983 in Newcastle in the northeast of England. She is part of the girl band Girls Aloud and is a recording artist in her own right. She is a judge on the TV program X-Factor and is also the face of L'Oreal beauty products.

**Mount Kilimanjaro** is the highest mountain in Tanzania in Africa. It is also an inactive volcano. It is 5,893 metres or 19,334 feet high.

**Richard Curtis** is an English screenwriter and film director. He is best-known for romantic comedy films such as Notting Hill and Love Actually and comedy TV programmes such as *Blackadder* and *The Vicar of Dibley*.

**Ethiopia** is a country in east Africa. It shares borders with Eritrea, Sudan, Djibouti, Somalia and Kenya. The capital city is Addis Ababa and the country has a population of around 90 million people. The people speak Amharic. In the 1980s, a series of famines affected millions of people and caused the death of a million people.

**1** **Aim** **To present new vocabulary**

- Direct Ss' attention to the pictures. Play the recording. Ss listen and repeat individually or chorally.
- Elicit answers to the question in the rubric from various Ss around the class.

*Suggested Answer Key*

*I **put up posters** for our school's environmental day last year.*

*My friends and I **sold tickets** for our school party last week.*

*My mum **made banners** for the village charity event last weekend.*

*I **collected donations** with my sister for our local animal shelter last spring.*

*My friends and I have just **decorated the venue** for this year's concert.*

**2 a)** **Aim** **To present situational language**

Play the recording. Ss listen and repeat chorally or individually. Ask Ss to pay attention to their pronunciation. Play the recording again if necessary.

**b)** **Aim** **To introduce and predict the content of a text**

- Give Ss one minute to read the first exchange in the dialogue and elicit guesses to the questions in the rubric.
- Play the recording. Ss listen and follow the dialogue in their books to find out if their guesses were correct.

*Answer Key*

*Carol is making some banners for the Red Nose Day concert.*
*Darren offers to help her make the banners.*
*Carol asks Darren to help Jim and her to put up the posters and to sell tickets at the door.*

**3** **Aim** **To learn synonymous phrases**

Explain the task and read out the sentences. Refer Ss back to the dialogue and then elicit synonymous sentences from various Ss around the classroom.

**Suggested Answer for Ex. 5 on p. 84**

*Answer Key*

*I don't have anything to do this afternoon. – I'm free this afternoon.*
*Do you want me to help you? – Can I give you a hand?*
*There's something else you can do. – There's one more thing.*
*Sure I can. – Yes, that's no problem*

## Pronunciation

**4** **Aim** **To pronounce homophones**

- Explain the task and play the recording. Ss listen, identify and circle the word that doesn't sound the same.
- Play the recording again with pauses for Ss to listen and repeat chorally or individually. Pay special attention to Ss' pronunciation and intonation and correct as necessary.

## Speaking

**5** **Aim** **To practise role-playing and act out a dialogue**

- Explain the situation and the task.
- Remind Ss they can use the sentences in Ex. 2a and the dialogue in Ex. 2b as a model as well as their own ideas to complete the task. Ss can also use the phrases in Ex. 1.
- Draw Ss' attention to the plan. Ss can refer to it while doing the task.
- Monitor the activity around the class and ask some pairs to act out their dialogue in class.

*Suggested Answer Key*

*A:  Hi, Rachel! What are you doing?*
*B:  Oh, hi, Steve. I'm just making banners for the clean-up day at the local park tomorrow.*
*A:  Oh, really? Well, I'm free this afternoon. Can I give you a hand?*
*B:  Actually, I've nearly finished. Would you mind helping us with something else?*
*A:  Of course not.*
*B:  Thanks. Can you put up some posters later?*
*A:  Yes. That's no problem. What time?*
*B:  Around 7 would be great.*
*A:  OK, see you at 7!*
*B:  Thanks!*

---

**Ex. 5**
***Name:*** *MDA Labor Day Telethon*
***When it is:*** *Sunday of Labor day weekend*
***What happens:*** *6 hours of entertainment to raise money for the Muscular Dystrophy Association (MDA), live TV broadcast, celebrity performances, viewer's call in to donate money, online behind the scenes clips, backstage interviews and additional performances*

*The MDA Telethon is a live TV broadcast on the Sunday of Labor Day weekend in America to raise money for the Muscular Dystrophy Association (MDA) through viewer's donations. The broadcast features 6 hours of celebrity performances and online behind the scenes clips, backstage interviews and additional performances. Both the MDA Telethon and Red Nose Day raise money for people in need but Red Nose Day happens every 2 years whereas the MDA Telethon is an annual event.*

## Asking for and offering help

**1** 🎧 Listen and say. Have you or your friends/family members ever done any of these things for a charity event?

**2** a) 🎧 Listen and say. Pay attention to the pronunciation.

- What are you doing?
- Well, I'm free this afternoon.
- Can I give you a hand?
- Would you mind helping us with that?
- Yes, that's not a problem.
- Around 6 pm would be great.
- OK, see you at 6 tomorrow.

b) **Read the first exchange in the dialogue. What is Carol doing? What does Darren offer to do? What does Carol ask him to do?**
🎧 Listen and read to find out.

Darren: Hi, Carol! What are you doing?

Carol: Oh, hi, Darren. I'm just making some banners for the Red Nose Day concert tomorrow.

Darren: Oh, really? Well, I'm free this afternoon. Can I give you a hand?

Carol: Actually, I've nearly finished. Jim and I are going to put up some posters afterwards, though. Would you mind helping us with that?

Darren: Of course not!

Carol: That's wonderful! Oh, there's one more thing. Is there any chance you could come early tomorrow to help sell tickets at the door?

Darren: Yes, that's no problem. What time?

Carol: Around six would be great.

Darren: OK, see you at 6 tomorrow!

Carol: Great. Thanks, Darren!

**3** **Find sentences in the dialogue which mean:**
*I don't have anything to do this afternoon. – Do you want me to help you? – There's something else you can do. – Sure I can.*

## Pronunciation – Homophones

**4** 🎧 Listen and circle the word that does not sound the same as the others. Listen again and say.

1. wait – (white) – weight
2. (were) – where – wear
3. poor – pour – (pear)

## Speaking

**5** 👥 Imagine your class is helping to organise a clean-up day for the local park. Use the sentences in Ex. 2a and your own ideas to act out your dialogue. Follow the plan.

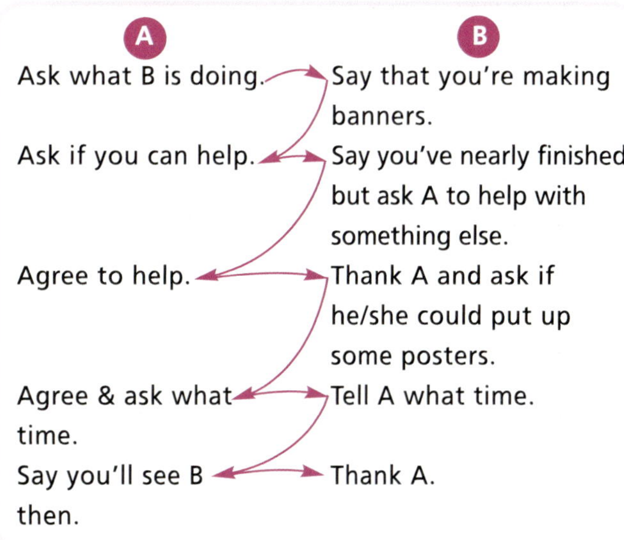

| A | B |
|---|---|
| Ask what B is doing. | Say that you're making banners. |
| Ask if you can help. | Say you've nearly finished but ask A to help with something else. |
| Agree to help. | Thank A and ask if he/she could put up some posters. |
| Agree & ask what time. | Tell A what time. |
| Say you'll see B then. | Thank A. |

# 5e Endangered Species

## Vocabulary
### Threats to animal species

**1** The sentences (A-E) describe ways animals are in danger. Match the sentences to the pictures (1-5).
🎧 Listen and check.

- **A** ☐ Tourists disturb their habitats.
- **B** ☐ They get caught in rubbish or fishermen's nets.
- **C** ☐ Deforestation destroys their habitats.
- **D** ☐ Poachers hunt them for their meat or fur.
- **E** ☐ Pollution poisons the sea or land where they live.

## Reading & Listening

**2** Look at the animals (A-C) in the text. Where do you think we can find these animals? Why is each species endangered?
🎧 Listen and read to find out.

# Animal SOS!

**Holidays that have made a difference …**

Did you know that there are more than 5,000 endangered animal species in the world today and at least one species **dies out** every year? Well, these three people decided to do something about it! They've all recently been on a working holiday to help an endangered species. They told us all about their experiences …

### Pink River Dolphin

**A**

Hayley has just spent three months on a floating house boat in the Amazon Rainforest in Brazil. "I was part of an observation team doing research, and it was amazing!" she says. "Every year, we lose about 10% of these clever creatures. They swim in polluted waters and sometimes get caught in fishermen's nets. There are more than 300 dolphins here and we had to **record** new births and monitor the babies. In the evenings, we sat on the porch and listened to the sounds of the jungle. Then, we went to sleep in hammocks! It was so relaxing!"

**Check these words**

species, floating, rainforest, observation team, monitor, porch, hammock, track, hunting, steep slope, record, location, cut down, farming, challenging, conservation project, lay their eggs, mistake for, dawn, survey, nest, spectacular, patrol

**3** Read the text again and write the name of the animal, *dolphin*, *gorilla* **or** *turtle*.

Which animal …

1. faces problems which visitors cause?
2. tries to survive in a dirty place?
3. is losing its habitat?
4. do people sometimes eat?
5. eats something dangerous by mistake?
6. goes back to a place it has been before?

**4** **a)** Match the words in bold to their meanings: *by mistake, disappears forever, demanding, write down, other possibilities.*

## Vocabulary

**1** **Aim** **To present new vocabulary**

- Read the list of threats to animal species (A-E) and direct Ss' attention to the pictures (1-5).
- Allow Ss time to complete the task.
- Play the recording for Ss to check their answers.

**Answer Key**

A 1     B 3     C 2     D 5     E 4

## Reading & Listening

**2** **Aim** **To predict the content of the text**

- Direct Ss' attention to the pictures and elicit answers to the questions in the rubric.
- Play the recording. Ss listen and follow the text in their books to find out if their answers were correct.

**Suggested Answer Key**

*1  I think we can find pink river dolphins in the Amazon River. They are in danger because of water pollution and they get caught in fishermen's nets.*

*2  I think we can find Cross River gorillas in Cameroon. They are in danger because of hunters who kill them for their meat and because deforestation destroys their natural habitat.*

*3  I think we can find loggerhead sea turtles in the Mediterranean Sea. They are in danger because people damage their nests and because they mistake rubbish for food.*

**3** **Aim** **To read for specific information**

- Allow Ss some time to read the text again and answer the questions.

**Answer Key**

*1  loggerhead sea turtle*     *4  Cross River gorilla*
*2  pink river dolphin*     *5  loggerhead sea turtle*
*3  Cross River gorilla*     *6  loggerhead sea turtle*

- Go through the **Check these words** box and explain/elicit the meanings of the words. Ask Ss to identify what part of speech each is.
- Check Ss' answers.

**Suggested Answer Key**

**species (n):** *a class of plants or animals*
**floating (adj):** *sitting on top of a liquid, without sinking*
**rainforest (n):** *a thick forest found in tropical areas*
**observation team (n):** *a group that studies sth*
**monitor (v):** *to observe*
**porch (n):** *a sheltered area at the front of a building*
**hammock (n):** *a swinging bed made of rope or cloth*
**track (v):** *to follow*
**hunting (n):** *killing sth for food or sport*
**steep slope (n):** *a side of a hill rising at a sharp angle*
**record (v):** *to write down*

**location (n):** *site*
**cut down (phr v):** *to cut through sth so it falls down*
**farming (n):** *raising plants or livestock*
**challenging (adj):** *difficult but enjoyable*
**conservation project (n):** *a scheme to save sth*
**lay their eggs (phr):** *produce eggs*
**mistake for (phr):** *wrongly think sth is sth else*
**dawn (n):** *the time when the sun first rises in the morning*
**survey (n):** *the measuring and recording of details*
**nest (n):** *a type of bird/animal home*
**spectacular (adj):** *amazing*
**patrol (v):** *to move around in an area to make sure there is no trouble there*

### BACKGROUND INFORMATION

**The Amazon Rainforest** is an area of tropical forest in South America in the region surrounding the Amazon River in the Amazon Basin. The area belongs to nine different countries: Brazil, Peru, Colombia, Venezuela, Ecuador, Bolivia, Suriname, French Guiana and Guyana. Sixty percent of the rainforest, though, is in Brazil. It is home to 2.5 million types of insects, almost 5,000 types of birds and animals and at least 225,000 types of plants and trees.

**Cameroon** is a country in central and western Africa. It shares borders with Nigeria, Chad, Central African Republic, Equatorial Guinea, Gabon and the Republic of the Congo. The capital city is Yaoundé, and the country has a population of around 19 million people. The people speak French and English. It has a diverse climate and it is famous for its football team.

**Zakynthos** is a Greek island in the Ionian Sea to the west of Greece. It is 157 square miles in size and around 41,500 people live there. It is a popular tourist resort with a rich history. Some of its beaches are protected as they are where the loggerhead turtles come to nest and lay their eggs every year.

**4  a)** **Aim** **To consolidate new vocabulary**

- Explain the task.
- Allow Ss time to  complete it.
- Check Ss' answers.

**Answer Key**

*by mistake – by accident*
*disappears forever – dies out*
*demanding – challenging*
*write down – record*
*other possibilities – alternatives*

**b)** **Aim** To practise new vocabulary

- Allow Ss time to complete the task. Ss can look up any words they are unsure of in their dictionaries.
- Check Ss' answers.
- Allow Ss time to write their sentences.
- Check Ss' answers by asking various Ss to tell their sentences in class.

*Answer Key*

| | | | |
|---|---|---|---|
| 1 *endangered* | 3 *spectacular* | 5 *working* |
| 2 *polluted* | 4 *conservation* | 6 *steep* |

*Suggested Answer Key*

2 Pink river dolphins swim in **polluted waters**.
3 Mary saw some **spectacular sunrises** on Zakynthos.*
4 Mary helped out with a turtle **conservation project**.
5 Hayley, Ryan and Mary each went on a **working holiday**.
6 Ryan walked for miles up **steep slopes** in the rainforest.

*We use *on* an island NOT *in* an island.

## Grammar

**5 a)** **Aim** To present *-ing/-ed* adjectives

- Go through the theory box with Ss.
- Allow Ss time to find examples in the text.
- Check Ss' answers.

*Answer Key*

endangered, working (holiday), floating, amazing, polluted, relaxing, shocked, excited, interesting, challenging, tiring

**b)** **Aim** To practise *-ing/-ed* adjectives

Give Ss time to complete the task, and then check Ss' answers.

*Answer Key*

| | | |
|---|---|---|
| 1 *shocked* | 3 *boring* | 5 *interested* |
| 2 *frightening* | 4 *tired* | |

## Listening

**6** **Aim** To listen for specific information

Explain the task and play the recording. Ss listen and match the speakers to how they felt. Check Ss' answers around the classroom. Elicit reasoning.

*Answer Key*

Mark felt frightened because he heard and saw a tiger near him.
Holly felt shocked because she saw a dead sea bird caught in a fishing net.
Jess felt excited because she saw many colourful fish and swam with sea lions.

## Speaking & Writing

**7 a)** **Aim** To make notes and summarise a text

- Ask Ss to read the text again and make notes about each person.
- Choose various Ss to share their notes in class.

*Suggested Answer Key*

Hayley was part of an observation team carrying out research on dolphins. She recorded new births and checked the babies.

Ryan tracked gorillas in the rainforests, so that he could learn more about their behaviour and living conditions. He also educated the locals about deforestation and suggested alternatives to cutting down forests for farming.

Mary helped out with a turtle conservation project. She worked with a team and did a survey of nests and eggs. She also patrolled the beach and told tourists about the turtles.

**b)** **Aim** To personalise the topic

- Give Ss three minutes to prepare their answers and write sentences.
- Invite Ss to read their sentences to the class.

*Suggested Answer Key*

I would choose a working holiday helping animal conservation. I think it would be a great opportunity to do something good for endangered animals. I would like to make a difference to the world we live in as I am concerned about worldwide problems.

## Cross River Gorilla

Ryan has just spent 6 months in a tent tracking these gorillas in the rainforests of Cameroon after he saw a documentary about them. He says, "I was very shocked when I heard there are only 300 of these gorillas left because of hunting and deforestation that has destroyed their habitat. Every day, we walked for miles up steep slopes in the rainforest. Our guide was a poacher in the past who hunted the gorillas for their meat! I was so excited when we saw our first gorilla. We recorded lots of information about its location and activities. We also talked to locals and suggested **alternatives** to cutting down forests for farming. This was the most interesting – and **challenging** – experience of my life!"

## Loggerhead Sea Turtle

Mary has just come back from the Greek island of Zakynthos after helping with a turtle conservation project there. She says, "Every summer, thousands of females return to lay their eggs in the sand on the beach. The problem is that tourists often damage their nests **by accident**. They also leave rubbish like plastic bags that the turtles mistake for food. Every day at dawn, our team did a survey of nests and eggs. It was tiring but we saw some spectacular sunrises! During the day, we patrolled the beach and told tourists all about the turtles. I've already told my friends that I'm going back next year – and that they're coming with me!"

**b)** Fill in: *steep, conservation, spectacular, endangered, working, polluted,* **then use the phrases to write sentences based on the text.**

1 ........................ animal species
2 ..................................... waters
3 ..................................... sunrises
4 ..................................... project
5 ..................................... holiday
6 ..................................... slopes

*Pink river dolphins and Cross River gorillas are endangered animal species.*

## Grammar

see p. GR9

### -ing/-ed adjectives

**5** **a)** Study the theory. Find examples in the text.

> **-ing/-ed adjectives**
> - We use **-ing adjectives** to express **what something is like.** *The holiday was* **exciting.** (What was it like? Exciting.)
> - We use **-ed adjectives** to express **how we feel about something.** *I was* **excited.** (How did I feel? Excited.)

**b)** Circle the correct adjectives.

1 We felt very **shocked / shocking** after watching the documentary about endangered species.
2 I once saw a bear while camping. It was such a **frightened / frightening** experience.
3 He nearly fell asleep during the film. It was so **bored / boring**!
4 We were so **tired / tiring** after the jungle trek!
5 Sally's very **interested / interesting** in helping to save endangered animals.

## Listening

**6**  Listen to three people talking about conservation holidays they went on. Who felt: *frightened? excited? shocked?* Why?

| Mark | Holly | Jess |
|---|---|---|

## Speaking & Writing

**7** **a)** Read the text again. How has each person helped these animals? Make notes, then tell the class.

**b)** **THINK!** Would you go on a working holiday like these people? Why? In three minutes write a few sentences. Read them to the class.

# 5f Determination

## Vocabulary
### Injuries

**1** 🎧 Listen and say. Have you ever had any of these injuries? How did it happen? Tell the class.

get sore feet

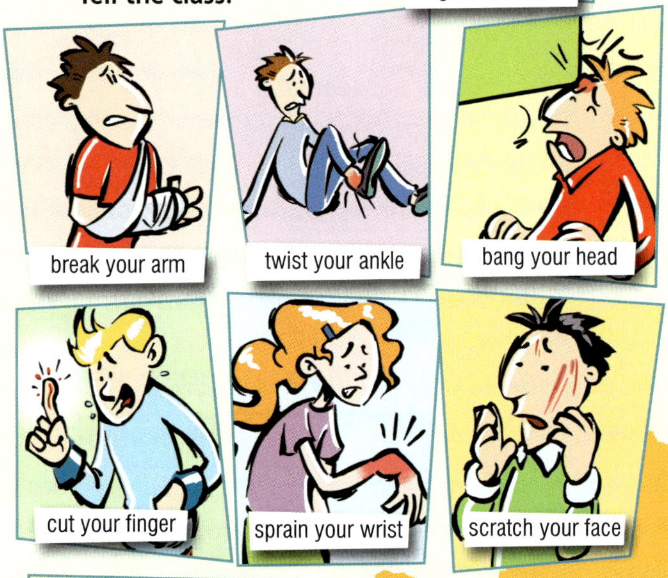

break your arm

twist your ankle

bang your head

cut your finger

sprain your wrist

scratch your face

get a swollen knee

## Reading

**2** **a)** Look at the picture and read the title and the first sentence of the text. What is the story about? Read through to find out.

**b)** Read again and complete the gaps 1-6 with the correct word A, B, C or D. Compare with a partner.

| | A | | B | | C | | D | |
|---|---|---|---|---|---|---|---|---|
| 1 | put | | made | | set | | fixed | |
| 2 | travel | | journey | | flight | | crossing | |
| 3 | There | | It | | These | | They | |
| 4 | suffer | | hurt | | ache | | pain | |
| 5 | Since | | As | | If | | Because | |
| 6 | draw | | happen | | reach | | come | |
| 7 | then | | after | | before | | so | |
| 8 | enough | | plenty | | lot | | much | |
| 9 | which | | whose | | what | | where | |
| 10 | raising | | raise | | raised | | raises | |

On 22nd January, 2007, Dave Cornthwaite from Wales became the first person to skateboard across Australia. He **1)** ...... a new world record, by skating a total of 5,823 kilometres. Jack Smith, the **previous** champ, had skated a total of 4,830 kilometres across the US in 2003. Dave's **2)** ...... started in Perth and ended in Brisbane travelling **on average** 60 kilometres per day. **3)** ...... took him five months, 13 pairs of shoes and over **a dozen** tubes of sunscreen. He went through great physical **4)** ...... and he got extremely **sore** feet.

**5)** ...... Dave hadn't believed in making his dreams **6)** ...... true, none of this would have happened. Dave quit his job two weeks after he had bought a skateboard and decided to go on a journey. He wanted this journey to be about something more than him **7)** ...... he created BoardFree an association that would raise money for **charities**. "If people follow my journey and make **donations**, then I'm doing a lot of people a lot of good," said Dave. This journey had **8)** ...... of challenges. He travelled across the Australian desert **9)** ...... temperatures reached 48°C in the day and 0° at night. He had a serious accident in Adelaide when he jumped on a piece of metal that cut through his heel. He also had a **nasty** fall down a hill where he banged his head hard on the pavement and **twisted** his ankle.

Dave helped **10)** ...... more than £50,000 (€74,000) for children's charities, wrote a book and **motivated** others to follow in his footsteps. I wish we had more people like him leading the way!

### Check these words

set a world record, champ, sunscreen, physical pain, dream come true, quit, association, raise money, make a donation, challenge, desert, nasty fall, motivate

Perth

Adelaide

## Vocabulary

**1** **Aim** **To present new vocabulary for injuries**

- Play the recording with pauses for Ss to repeat chorally or individually. Check Ss' intonation and pronunciation.
- Elicit who has had any of these injuries and how it happened. Ask various Ss to tell the class.

***Suggested Answer Key***

*I got sore feet once. I missed the bus and walked home in uncomfortable shoes.*

## Reading

**2 a)** **Aim** **To predict the content of a text and read for gist**

- Direct Ss' attention to the picture, title and first sentence in the text and elicit Ss' guesses as to what the text is about.
- Give Ss time to read through the text and find out.

***Answer Key***

*The text is about how Dave Cornthwaite from Wales skateboarded across Australia.*

**b)** **Aim** **To read for lexico-grammatical structure**

- Explain the task and ask Ss to read the text again and choose the correct lexical item or grammar structure for each gap.
- Ask Ss to compare their answers with their partner.
- Check Ss' answers.

***Answer Key***

| | | | | |
|---|---|---|---|---|
| *1 C* | *3 B* | *5 C* | *7 D* | *9 D* |
| *2 B* | *4 D* | *6 D* | *8 B* | *10 D* |

**3 a)** **Aim** **To expand vocabulary/To match words from a text to their meanings**

- Explain the task.
- Give Ss time to complete the task.
- Check Ss' answers.

*Answer Key*

*normally: on average*
*the one before: previous*
*inspired: motivated*
*twelve: a dozen*
*bad: nasty*
*injured a part of the body by bending it awkwardly: twisted*
*organisations that help good causes: charities*
*painful: sore*
*gifts to help good causes: donations*

**b)** **Aim** **To consolidate new vocabulary from a text**

- Explain/Elicit the meanings of the words in the **Check these words** box or ask Ss to use their dictionaries and look them up.
- Give Ss time to write their sentences and then ask various Ss to tell their sentences to the class.

*Suggested Answer Key*

*set a world record (phr): to achieve the best result in sth globally*
*champ (n): a champion, winner*
*sunscreen (n): a lotion to protect the skin against sunburn*
*physical pain (n): discomfort/hurt in the body*
*dream come true (phr): when sth you wish for becomes a reality*
*quit (v): to stop doing sth*
*association (n): an official group of people with a shared goal*
*raise money (phr): to collect cash*
*make a donation (phr): to give money to charity*
*challenge (n): a difficult situation*
*desert (n): a dry area of land covered in sand*
*nasty fall (n): hitting the ground badly and injuring yourself*
*motivate (v): to make sb want to do sth*

1 Dave set a **new world record** when he beat the previous **champ.**
2 Dave used over a dozen tubes of **sunscreen** to avoid getting sunburnt.
3 His journey caused him **physical pain.**
4 He quit his job and created the BoardFree **association** to **raise money** for charities.
5 His **challenge** took him across the Australian **desert.**
6 He has **motivated** other people to follow in his footsteps.

**c)** **Aim** **To imagine the topic from the author's point of view**

- Read the rubric aloud and set Ss a three-minute time limit to write some sentences and then tell their partner.

- Ask various Ss around the class to read their sentences to the class.

*Suggested Answer Key – see p. 90(T)*

### Grammar

**4** **Aim** **To present and practise the past perfect**

- Ss close their books. Present the past perfect. Say: *I had finished before they arrived.* Write it on the board. Underline: *had finished* and explain that this verb is in the past perfect. Explain that we use the past perfect to talk about a past action which happened before another past action or before a stated time in the past.
- Explain/Elicit that we form the past perfect with **had** and the past participle of the main verb.
- Ss open their books. Give them time to read through the theory box.
- Explain/Elicit that we form the negative with **hadn't** and the interrogative by putting **Had** before the subject.
- Remind Ss that we use the past simple for actions that happened in the past at a certain time.
- Allow Ss time to complete the task.
- Check Ss' answers.

**5** **Aim** **To present and practise the conditional type 3**

- Read the theory box aloud.
- Explain that we use the past perfect + *would/could have* + past participle to form the conditional type 3. Explain that we use the conditional type 3 to talk about an unreal past situation.
- Give Ss time to complete the task and then check Ss' answers.

*Answer Key – see p. 90(T)*

**6** **Aim** **To present and practise wishes**

- Read the theory box aloud and write the examples on the board.
- Explain that we use *wish/if only* + past simple to express a wish about something we would like to be different in the present and *wish/if only* + past perfect to express a regret about something we would like to be different in the past.
- Give Ss time to complete the task and then check Ss' answers.

*Answer Key – see p. 90(T)*

**7** **Aim** **To practise wishes and type 3 conditionals using personal examples**

- Give Ss time to complete the sentences, then ask Ss to compare their answers with their partner.
- Ask various Ss to read their answers out to the class.

**3** **a)** Match the words in bold to their meanings:
*normally, the one before, inspired, twelve, bad, injured a part of the body by bending it awkwardly, organisations that help good causes, painful, gifts to help good causes.*

**b)** 🎧 Listen to and read the text. Use six words from the **Check these words** box to make sentences about Dave.

**c)** **THINK!** Imagine you are David. In three minutes, write four things about your experience. Tell your partner.

## *Grammar*
## Past perfect
see p. GR8

**4** Read the theory. Then put the verbs in brackets into the *past perfect* or the *past simple*.

| Form: *had* + past participle | |
|---|---|
| **AFFIRMATIVE** | *I/you/he, etc* **had left**. |
| **NEGATIVE** | *I/you/he, etc* **hadn't left**. |
| **INTERROGATIVE** | **Had** *I/you/he, etc* **left**? |
| **SHORT ANSWERS** | Yes, *I/you/he, etc* **had**. <br> No, *I/you/he, etc* **hadn't**. |

We use the **past perfect** for:
- an action which happened before another past action or before a stated time in the past. *He had already left when we arrived.*
- an action which finished in the past and whose result was visible in the past. *He couldn't walk because he had broken his leg.*

**Time expressions:** before, after, already, just, for, since.

The past perfect is the past equivalent of the present perfect.
*He was happy because he had won the race.*
*He is happy because he has won the race.*

**1** He looked tired. He had spent **(spend)** the whole morning working in the garden.

**2** They had already booked **(already/book)** the tickets before they went to the theatre.

**3** It hadn't finished **(start)** to rain while we were at the beach.

**4** She hadn't finished **(not/finish)** typing the letters when he arrived.

**5** He won first prize for the story he had written/ wrote **(write)**.

**6** When did he decide **(he/decide)** to join the club?

## Conditional Type 3
see pp. GR8-GR9

**5** Read the theory. Rewrite the sentences as Conditional Type 3.

| Conditional Type 3 |
|---|
| *if* + past perfect → *would/could have* + past participle (to express an imaginary situation in the past) <br> *If he* **had left** *on time, he* **wouldn't have missed** *the bus.* (but he didn't leave on time) |

**1** He didn't play tennis because he had sprained his wrist.
*If he hadn't sprained his wrist, he would have played tennis.*

**2** I had a terrible headache so I didn't finish my homework.

**3** It rained hard so we didn't go out.

**4** They lost the match because they didn't play well.

**5** They worked hard and managed to raise £10,000 for charity.

## Wishes
see p. GR9

**6** Read the theory. Write wishes for the following situations.

- *wish/if only* + **past simple** (wish for something we would like to be different in the present)
  *I* **wish** *I* **had** *a flat of my own.* (but I don't)
- *wish/if only* + **past perfect** (regret that something happened/didn't happen in the past)
  *If only I* **hadn't twisted** *my ankle.* (but I did)

**1** I don't know how to drive a car.
*I wish I knew how to drive a car.*

**2** I want to go to Tom's party, but I can't.

**3** He didn't study so he failed his exam.

**4** She lost her gold earrings; she's very sad.

**5** He feels lonely because he doesn't know anyone in the neighbourhood.

**7** **THINK!** Complete the sentences. Compare with your partner.

**1** I wish I were rich.

**2** If only people cared more the the environment.

**3** If I had tried harder, I would've passed the test.

**4** I wish I hadn't lost my keys.

**5** If only I were more patient.

▶ Vocabulary Bank 5 p. VB16

# 5g Skills

## Vocabulary
### Activities at an eco-camp

**1** 🎧 Listen and say the activities that someone can do at a summer eco-camp.

1 plant trees

2 sit around a campfire

3 cook on a barbecue

4 sleep in wooden huts

5 grow vegetables

6 clean out a pond

7 go on a nature hike

8 collect rubbish for recycling

**2** 👥 Have you ever done any of the activities in Ex. 1? Ask and answer in pairs.

*A: Have you ever planted a tree?*
*B: Yes, I have. I planted one last year on the school's 'Plant a Tree' day. Have you ever … ? etc*



---

**Study skills**

**Real-life situations – filling out forms**
When you fill out a form, look for any special instructions. Make sure you fill out all the required information. Then carefully check for any errors.

## Listening

**3** 🎧 Listen to Judy helping Karl to fill in the form below. Fill in the missing information.

**Green Pines ECO-CAMP**

Application form for camp counsellors
* PLEASE USE CAPITAL LETTERS

Full name: KARL 1) ………………………………………… .
Age: 2) ………………………… . Nationality: MEXICAN
Email address: KARL@ZMAIL.COM
Tel: 213 - 3) ………………………………
Preferred camp (please tick (✓))
4) 16th – 31st July ☐  2nd – 16th August ☐
Previous experience: please tick (✓) I've …
- organised activities for children ☑
- taught sports ☑ If yes, which? 5) …………………
- completed a first-aid course ☐

## Speaking
### Making suggestions/Expressing preferences

**4** 👥 You are at Green Pines Eco-camp. Act out exchanges, as in the example.

**Green Pines Summer Camp - activities**
- go canoeing • cook on a barbecue • plant vegetables
- go fishing • play volleyball • go swimming in the lake

| Suggesting | Replying/Expressing your preference |
| --- | --- |
| • Would you like to … ? <br> • Why don't we … ? <br> • Do you want to …? | • OK. That would be fun! <br> • I'd love to. <br> • Sure. Why not? |
| | • I'd rather not. I'd prefer to … . <br> • I don't really feel like doing that. Why don't we … instead? |

*A: Would you like to go canoeing?*
*B: OK. That would be fun!*

## Vocabulary

**1** **Aim** **To present new vocabulary**

- Direct Ss' attention to the pictures.
- Play the recording with pauses for Ss to repeat individually or chorally.

**2** **Aim** **To personalise the topic and practise vocabulary**

- Explain the task and ask a pair of Ss to read out the example exchange.
- Ss work in pairs and ask and answer questions as in the example to complete the task.
- Monitor the activity around the class and then ask some pairs to ask and answer in front of the class.

***Suggested Answer Key***

A: *Have you ever sat around a campfire?*
B: *Yes, I have. I sat around one with my friends when we went camping last summer./No, I haven't. Have you ever cooked on a barbecue?*
A: *Yes, I have. I cooked on one on the last day of summer camp./No, I haven't. Have you ever slept in a wooden hut?*
B: *Yes, I have. I slept in one last year./No, I haven't. Have you ever grown vegetables?*
A: *Yes, I have. I grew some when I was at a camp last year./No, I haven't. Have you ever cleaned out a pond?*
B: *Yes, I have. I cleaned one out in my village last summer./ No, I haven't. Have you ever been on a nature hike?*
A: *Yes, I have. I went on one last weekend with my dad./No, I haven't. Have you ever collected rubbish for recycling?*
B: *Yes, I have. I collected a lot from the beach yesterday./ No, I haven't.*

## Listening

**3** **Aim** **To listen for specific information (gap-fill)**

- Explain the task and go through the *Study Skills* box. Go through the form with Ss and predict the content of the recording. Elicit what type of information is missing in each gap *(noun, number, etc)*.

- Play the recording. Ss listen and complete the gaps.
- Check Ss' answers on the board.

***Answer Key***

| | | | |
|---|---|---|---|
| 1 | *MARTINEZ* | 3 | *746–2254* | 5 | *VOLLEYBALL* |
| 2 | *17* | 4 | *2nd -16th August* | | |

## Speaking

**4** **Aim** **To practise making suggestions/ expressing preferences**

- Explain the task and ask two Ss to model the example exchange.
- Ss work in closed pairs and make suggestions/ express preferences. Remind Ss to use expressions from the boxes and vocabulary from the list.
- Monitor the activity around the class and then ask some pairs to make suggestions/express preferences in class.

***Suggested Answer Key***

A: *Would you like to cook on a barbecue?*
B: *Sure. Why not?*

A: *Why don't we plant vegetables?*
B: *I'd rather not. I'd prefer to go fishing.*

A: *Do you want to go fishing?*
B: *I don't really feel like doing that. Why don't we go canoeing instead?*

A: *Why don't we play volleyball?*
B: *I'd love to.*

A: *Do you want to go swimming in the lake?*
B: *OK. That would be fun! etc*

**Suggested Answers for Exs 3c, 5 & 6 on p. 89**

### Ex. 3c

*I was careful to use sunscreen every day to avoid sunburn. Some days my feet were so sore I almost gave up. It was really cold at night in the Australian desert. I got a few scars but I have some amazing memories from my journey.*

### Ex. 5

2 *If I hadn't had a terrible headache, I would have finished my homework.*
3 *If it hadn't rained hard, we would have gone out.*
4 *If they had played well, they wouldn't have lost the match.*
5 *If they hadn't worked hard, they wouldn't have managed to raise £10,000 for charity.*

### Ex. 6

2 *I wish/If only I could go to Tom's party.*
3 *He wishes/If only he had studied.*
4 *She wishes/If only she hadn't lost her gold earrings.*
5 *He wishes/If only he knew someone in the neighbourhood.*

**1** **Aim** **To skim a text for key information**

Ask Ss to skim the text quickly and identify the author and recipient of the email.

**Answer Key**

*Meg sends the email to Ryan.*

**2** **Aim** **To read for gist**

Explain the task and allow Ss some time to read the text and match the paragraphs to the headings.

**Answer Key**

*A   3        B   1        C   4        D   2*

## Grammar

**3** **Aim** **To compare *have been/have gone***

- Read out the examples and explain/elicit when we use **have gone/have been** *(have gone = still there, have been = come back)*
- Give Ss time to complete the task, then check Ss' answers.

**Answer Key**

*1   has gone to        3   have gone to*
*2   has gone           4   have been to*

**4** **Aim** **To learn synonymous phrases**

Explain the task and read out the sentences/ questions. Refer Ss back to the email and elicit synonymous ones from Ss around the class.

**Answer Key**

*1   How are things?*
*2   it isn't like that at all!*
*3   The best part about this camp, is that we help the environment…*
*4   … generally they are great kids!*
*5   Write back when you get a chance.*

**5** **Aim** **To write an email to a friend**

- Explain the task and go through the paragraph plan. Draw Ss' attention to the **Study Skills** box and tell Ss to proofread their work once it is completed.
- Allow Ss time to complete the task in class. Ask various Ss to read out their emails.
- Alternatively, assign as HW and check Ss' answers in the next lesson.

**Suggested Answer Key**

*Dear Angela,*
*How are things? I've been on the island of Zakynthos in Greece for a week now. I'm working with the loggerhead sea turtle conservation project as a volunteer, and I really love it!*

*Every day at dawn we do a survey of nests and eggs. Yesterday, we patrolled the beach and told tourists all about the turtles. We've seen some spectacular sunrises. The best part about being here is that we are helping endangered animals and still having fun.*
*I hope you're having a great summer. Write back when you have time.*
*Love,*
*Fiona*

## An email giving your news

**1** Look at the email. Who is it from? Who is it to?

**2** Read the email and match the paragraphs to the headings.

- **A** ☐ thoughts and feelings about the experience
- **B** ☐ where she is & opening remarks
- **C** ☐ closing remarks & request to write back
- **D** ☐ description of camp life/activities

### Grammar see p. GR8

### Have been/Have gone

**3** Read the examples. Then complete the sentences. Use *have/has been (to) – have/has gone (to)*.

> Meg **has gone to** Camp Greenfoot. (She's still there.)
> Peter **has been to** Chile twice. (He went to Chile, but he isn't there any more.)

**1** Jane isn't here at the moment. She ..................................... the lake.

**2** Ryan ............................................. on a trip to Cameroon. He'll be back next Monday.

**3** They ....................... the park and they won't be back until 6 o'clock.

**4** Ann and Bill ....................... Brazil three times and are planning to go again.

**4** Find the informal phrases/ sentences in Meg's email that mean:

**1** How are you doing?

**2** That isn't the truth.

**3** What I like best about the experience is that we have the opportunity to help the environment …

**4** … I don't have any problems with the children.

**5** Please write me a letter when you have time.

Dear Ryan,

▶ **1** How are things? I've been at Camp Greenfoot for a week now, where I'm working this summer as a camp counsellor and I really love it here!

▶ **2** Camp Greenfoot is an eco-camp. You probably think that all we do here is learn about recycling, but it isn't like that at all! Yesterday we went on a nature hike with the kids, and last night we all sat around a campfire and sang songs. We also organise lots of fun eco-projects with the kids. We've already planted trees to replace the ones that burnt down in a forest fire.

▶ **3** The best part about this camp is that we help the environment and still have fun. I'm responsible for a small group of kids, and that can be tough (like when I have to wake everyone up in the morning!) but generally they are great kids!

▶ **4** I hope you're having a great summer, too. Write back when you get a chance.

All the best,
Meg

### Study skills

**Proofreading**

Always proofread your work to check for mistakes. Make sure you have:

- included all the necessary information.
- checked for spelling/grammar mistakes.
- used an appropriate greeting/beginning/ending.
- used correct style: formal or informal.

**5** Imagine you are working to help the sea turtles on p. 87. Send an email to your English pen-friend describing the experience (100-150 words). Use the plan below. Proofread your work.

### Plan

*Dear (your friend's first name),*
**Para 1:** greeting, opening remarks (*How are things? I'm here at … .*)
**Para 2:** what the job is like & activities you did/have done (*We … . Yesterday, we … . We've also … .*)
**Para 3:** your thoughts & feelings (*The best part about … .*)
**Para 4:** closing remarks (*I hope you're … . Write back … .*)

....................

▶ **Writing Bank p. WB1**

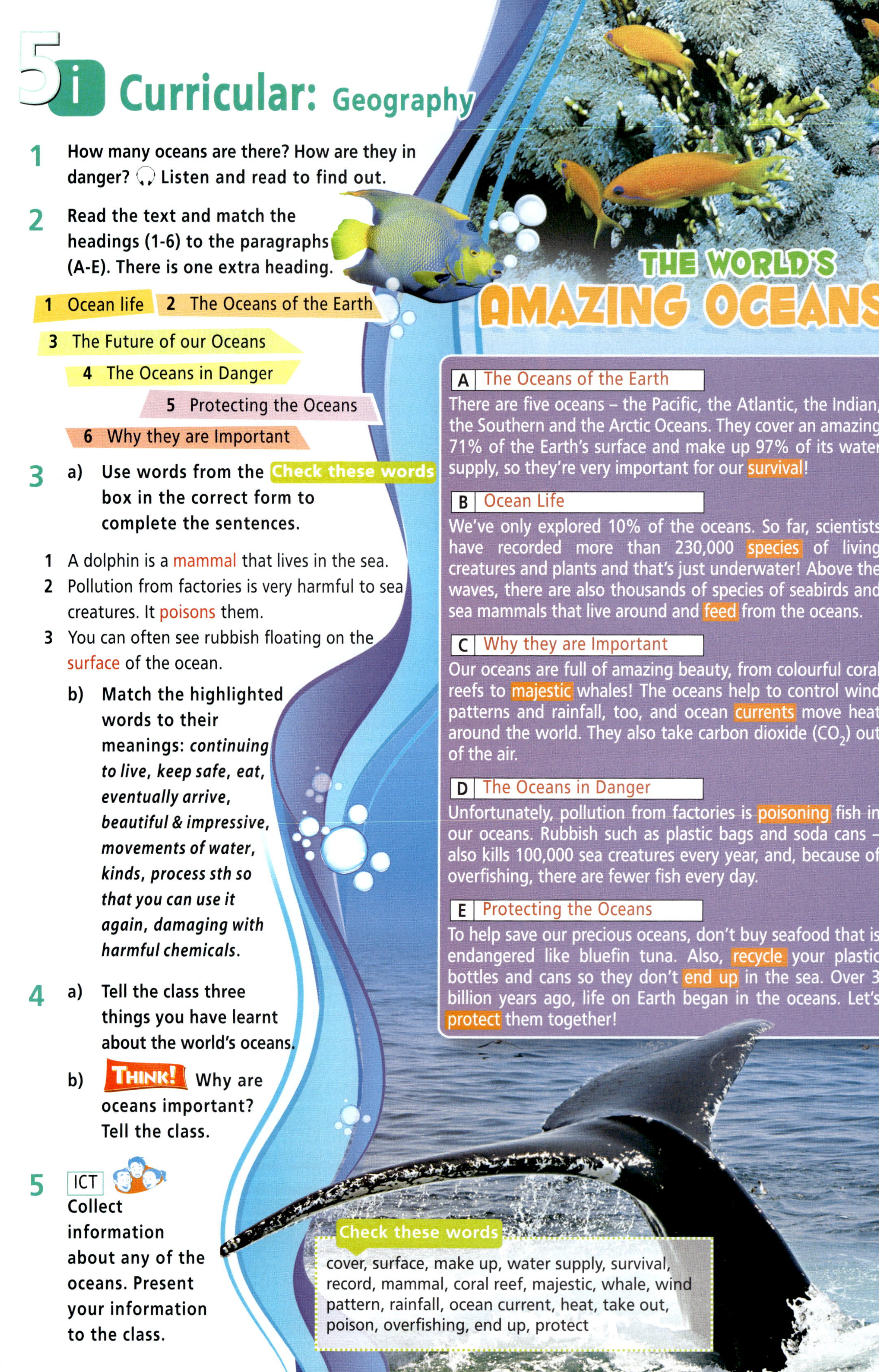

# 5 i Curricular: Geography

**1** How many oceans are there? How are they in danger? Listen and read to find out.

**2** Read the text and match the headings (1-6) to the paragraphs (A-E). There is one extra heading.

1 Ocean life    2 The Oceans of the Earth

3 The Future of our Oceans

4 The Oceans in Danger

5 Protecting the Oceans

6 Why they are Important

**3** **a)** Use words from the **Check these words** box in the correct form to complete the sentences.

1 A dolphin is a mammal that lives in the sea.
2 Pollution from factories is very harmful to sea creatures. It poisons them.
3 You can often see rubbish floating on the surface of the ocean.

**b)** Match the highlighted words to their meanings: *continuing to live, keep safe, eat, eventually arrive, beautiful & impressive, movements of water, kinds, process sth so that you can use it again, damaging with harmful chemicals.*

**4** **a)** Tell the class three things you have learnt about the world's oceans.

**b)** **THINK!** Why are oceans important? Tell the class.

**5** ICT Collect information about any of the oceans. Present your information to the class.

92

**1** **Aim** **To introduce the topic and predict the content of the text**

- Elicit answers from Ss to the questions in the rubric.
- Play the recording. Ss listen and follow the text in their books and check if their answers were correct.

*Suggested Answer Key*

*There are five oceans: the Pacific, the Atlantic, the Indian, the Southern and the Arctic oceans.*
*They are in danger because of pollution and overfishing.*

**2** **Aim** **To read for gist**

Explain the task and allow Ss some time to read the text and match the headings to the paragraphs.

**3** **a)** **Aim** **To practise new vocabulary**

- Go through the **Check these words** box and explain/elicit the meanings of the words.

*Suggested Answer Key*

*cover (v): to form a layer over the top of sth*
*surface (n): the outer layer of sth*
*make up (phr v): to form*
*water supply (n): a source of water*
*survival (n): managing to stay alive*
*record (v): to make notes on*
*mammal (n): an animal that produces milk to feed its young*
*coral reef (n): a long quantity of connected small sea animals that make a wall just below the surface of the water*
*majestic (adj): impressive*
*whale (n): a large mammal that lives in the sea*
*wind pattern (n): a specific path taken by moving air*
*rainfall (n): an amount of rain that comes to earth*
*ocean current (n): a movement of water in the ocean*
*heat (n): high temperatures*
*take out (phr v): to remove*
*poison (v): to kill with deadly substance*
*overfishing (n): catching too many fish*
*end up (phr v): to eventually arrive at*
*protect (v): to care for, look after*

- Allow Ss time to complete the task.
- Check Ss' answers.

**b)** **Aim** **To expand vocabulary/To match words from a text to their meanings**

- Explain the task.
- Give Ss time to complete the task.
- Check Ss' answers.

*Answer Key*

*continuing to live: survival*
*keep safe: protect*
*eat: feed*
*eventually arrive: end up*

*beautiful & impressive: majestic*
*movements of water: currents*
*kinds: species*
*process sth so that you can use it again: recycle*
*damaging with harmful chemicals: poisoning*

**4** **a)** **Aim** **To consolidate information in a text**

Read the rubric and elicit answers from various Ss around the class.

*Suggested Answer Key*

*I learned that the oceans cover 71% of the Earth's surface. They take carbon dioxide out of the air and we've only explored 10% of the oceans so far.*

**b)** **Aim** **To summarise information in a text**

- Read the rubric aloud.
- Allow Ss time to write their reasons.
- Choose various Ss to give their reasons to the class.

*Suggested Answer Key*

*The oceans are important because they provide 97% of the Earth's water supply. They are home to hundreds of thousands of creatures. They also help to control wind patterns, rainfall, temperature and carbon dioxide levels.*

**5** **Aim** **To give a presentation on one of the oceans**

- Ask Ss to work in groups and look up information on the Internet using the key word in the search bar, or in encyclopedias/other reference books.
- Ask various Ss to read out their presentations on one of the oceans in class.
- Alternatively, assign the task as HW and Ss give their presentations in the next lesson.

*Suggested Answer Key*

*The Pacific Ocean covers an area of 165.2 million km², It is the largest of the five oceans. There are more than 25,000 islands in the Pacific Ocean.*

*The Atlantic Ocean is the second largest of the Earth's oceans. It has an area of about 106.4 million km², and looks like an S shape.*

*The Indian Ocean is the warmest ocean in the world and it contains about 20% of the water on the Earth's surface.*

*The Southern Ocean is the fourth largest ocean in the world and is the coldest ocean on the planet with temperatures between -2°C and 10°C. Sailors believe it is the most dangerous ocean. It is also known as the Great Southern Ocean, the Antarctic Ocean and the South Polar Ocean.*

*The Arctic Ocean is the world's smallest ocean and the only place where polar bears live. More fish live along the edges of this ocean than anywhere else on Earth. The floating ice on the Arctic is four times bigger than the state of Texas.*

**1**
1 C   3 G   5 B   7 A
2 E   4 F   6 H   8 D

**2**
1 dawn   4 poor, conditions   7 issues
2 rubble   5 supplies   8 running
3 donation, raised   6 charity

**3**
1 rescue   5 medical   9 ocean
2 fishing   6 clear   10 put up
3 damage   7 cut down
4 conservation   8 endangered

**4**
1 by   3 for   5 of
2 for   4 for   6 from

**Aim** **To consolidate vocabulary from the module**

- Divide the class into 2 teams. Each team takes turns writing or saying a sentence with one of the words/phrases in the list.
- Each correct sentence earns one point. If the sentence is incorrect, the team misses a turn.
- The team with the most points after all the words have been used, wins.

***Suggested Answer Key***

*We can all **make a difference** by helping charities.*
***Deforestation** has already destroyed many forests and woodlands.*
*Loggerhead sea turtles **lay eggs** on the beach.*
*The huge tsunami **swept homes out to sea** and left hundreds homeless.*
*Volunteers **collected donations** to help the earthquake victims.*
*The fruit trees grow on these **steep slopes**.*
*Anyone can join the **volunteer team** and get involved in the eco–project.*
*This **organisation** has built over 80 schools around the world.*
*Rescue teams cleared roads and managed to bring in **medical supplies**.*
*The earthquake **affected** thousands of people.*
*People went without **running water** for three days.*
*Patrick O'Brian's **best-selling book** was about the Indian Ocean islands.*
*Volunteering in Brazil was a very **challenging experience**.*
*Too many sea creatures such as turtles **get caught in fishermen's nets**.*
***Overfishing** is a huge threat to wildlife.*
*I have seen **spectacular sunrises** early in the morning.*
*The **ocean currents** affect world temperatures.*
*Dolphins can die if they swim in **polluted waters**.*

## Quiz

**Answer Key**

1 T   5 F (2009)
2 F (K2)   6 F (Camaroon)
3 F (He lived in his car.)   7 F (100,000)
4 T

Ss prepare their quiz in groups. Ask Ss to go through the pages of Module 5 and select information to compile their quiz. Ask Ss to exchange quizzes, do them, and then check their answers.

**Suggested Answer Key**

**Quiz**
1 Port-au-Prince is in Haiti. T
2 K2 is in Pakistan. T
3 Comic Relief started in 1995. F (1985)
4 Richard Curtis is a singer. F (comedy writer)
5 10% of the pink river dolphins die every year. T
6 Cross River Gorillas live in Cameroon. T
7 The Bluefin tuna is endangered. T
8 The oceans cover 97% of the planet. F (71%)

## 1 Match the problems to the definitions.

| 1 | ☐ | drought | 5 | ☐ | disease |
|---|---|---------|---|---|---------|
| 2 | ☐ | homelessness | 6 | ☐ | war |
| 3 | ☐ | global warming | 7 | ☐ | flood |
| 4 | ☐ | illiteracy | 8 | ☐ | child labour |

A  a large amount of water that causes damage
B  illness that affects large numbers of people
C  a period when there is no rainfall
D  when children work in badly-paid or dangerous jobs
E  when people don't have anywhere to live
F  when people can't read or write
G  the rise in the Earth's temperature
H  fighting between countries and people

## 2 Fill in: *poor, supplies, running, dawn, rubble, issues, donation, raised, charity, conditions.*

1 Molly got up at .................. to see the sunrise.
2 They managed to pull a man out from the ......................... .
3 Thousands of people made a ....................... on Red Nose Day. They ........................... millions of pounds.
4 There are about 3 billion ..................... people in the world. Many live in terrible ................... and don't have enough to eat.
5 During the week, medical ................... arrived for the earthquake survivors.
6 Comic Relief is a well known ................. event in the UK.
7 Poverty is just one of the ........................ that affects the world.
8 After the Haiti earthquake, a lot of people didn't have .............................. water.

## Collocations

## 3 Fill in: *conservation, put up, damage, cut down, rescue, fishing, endangered, medical, clear, ocean.*

1 ................. team
2 ............. villages
3 ....... their habitats
4 .............. project
5 ............ supplies
6 ........... the rubble
7 ........................... forests
8 ............... species
9 ............ currents
10 .............. posters

## Prepositions

## 4 Choose the correct preposition.

1 They ate some poisonous mushrooms **in/by** mistake.
2 Loggerhead turtles mistake the bags **to/for** food.
3 He's responsible **for/in** patrolling the beach.
4 They worked hard to raise money **for/of** charity.
5 Greg's schools are proof **of/for** what people can really do.
6 Haiti suffers **of/from** hurricanes.

In teams, make sentences. Use words/phrases from the list below. Each correct sentence gets one point. The team with the most points wins.

- make a difference • deforestation • lay eggs
- swept homes out to sea • collect donations
- steep slopes • volunteer team • organisation
- medical supplies • affected • running water
- best-selling book • challenging experience
- get caught in fishermen's nets • overfishing
- spectacular sunrises • ocean currents
- polluted waters

## Quiz

**Mark the sentences *T* (true) of *F* (false). Read through Module 5 and write a quiz of your own.**

1 The Haiti earthquake happened on 12th January, 2010 ..........
2 Greg Mortenson tried to climb Mount Everest in 1993. ..........
3 Greg sold his car to save money to build a school. ..........
4 Comic Relief takes place every two years in the UK. ..........
5 Cheryl Cole climbed Mount Kilimanjaro in 2007. ..........
6 The Cross River Gorilla lives in the Amazon Rainforest. ..........
7 Rubbish in the ocean kills 230,000 sea creatures every year. ..........

## Listening

**1 a) Read the rubric, then the statements and possible answers. What is the dialogue about?**

> Listen to Jane talking to Robert about an eco-camp. For questions 1-5, tick (✓) A, B or C. You will hear the conversation twice.

**Example**

**0** Jane took part in
A a nature walk. ☐
B planting trees. ☐
C collecting rubbish. ✓

**1** Most of the rubbish on motorways comes from
A cars. ☐
B lorries. ☐
C tourists. ☐

**2** The clean-up ended at
A 4. ☐
B 5. ☐
C 10. ☐

**3** The number of bags they did not use was
A 16. ☐
B 50. ☐
C 60. ☐

**4** Jane does not want to eat
A a burger. ☐
B vegetables. ☐
C crisps. ☐

**5** Counsellors must sign up by
A June. ☐
B July. ☐
C August. ☐

**b)** 🎧 **Do the task. Give reasons for your answers.**

## Reading

### Study skills

**Missing sentences**

Pay attention to the words before and after each gap. They will help you decide on the sentence that best fits each gap.

**2 a) Read the rubric, then read through the text. What is the text about?**

> You are going to read a text about an unusual group of people. For gaps 1-4 choose the sentence A-E that best fits each gap. One sentence is extra.

**B**ig muscles, lots of tattoos and loud motorcycles are what these men like. Soon after they met, they realised they had something else in common. **1 E** Together they started helping animals that were not cared for properly. One day, when they read about a dog in their neighbourhood that was mistreated and killed, they decided to get really serious about saving animals so they formed Rescue Ink. These tough guys have dedicated themselves to the difficult but rewarding task of animal rescue. According to member 'Big Ant', who stands 1.83 m tall and weighs 145 kg, Rescue Ink investigates cases that other animal rescue organisations won't help or don't have the time for and they care about the owners, too. **2 A**

They never give up and will go back again and again until the problem is solved. Their tough appearance certainly makes people pay attention when they show up at someone's door. However, Rescue Ink members are careful never to break the law and work closely with the police. Rescue Ink receives over 250 calls and thousands of emails a day. The members meet at their clubhouse to plan each day. **3 D** They ride around on their motorcycles and in the Rescue Ink van investigating animals in neglected situations, rescuing dogs used for dog fighting and finding stolen animals. Sometimes they just help out. **4 B**

One dog, in particular, has become a symbol for Rescue Ink. Rebel, a red-nosed pit bull, was found wandering around after a dog-fighting group had been caught. He had cuts and wounds all over his body. Rescue Ink had his injuries treated and he quickly recovered. Despite all that Rebel has suffered, he still loves life, people and other dogs. For the men at Rescue Ink, he represents that a fresh start is possible for anyone and as these men have shown us, you can be tough and cool and still do the right thing!

**1 a)** **Aim** **To predict the topic of a text**

- Ask Ss to read the rubric and the statements/ possible answers.
- Elicit answers to the question from various Ss around the class.

***Suggested Answer Key***

*The dialogue is about the things two people have done at an eco-camp.*

**b)** **Aim** **To listen for specific information**

- Explain the task. Play the recording.
- Ss listen and mark the statements accordingly.
- Check Ss' answers. Elicit reasoning from Ss.

***Answer Key***

*1  C  (... the wind blows most of it off lorries.)*
*2  A  (... we worked from 10 to 4.)*
*3  A  (... we had 16 at the end of the day ...)*
*4  C  (... feel like having a big burger, crisps and a cola. The burger and cola are fine but I'd rather have fresh vegetables ...)*
*5  A  (... deadline isn't until the end of August ...)*

## Reading

**2 a)** **Aim** **To read for gist**

- Read out the **Study Skills** box and point out that this tip will help Ss complete the task successfully.
- Ask Ss to read the rubric and then the text to get the gist of what it is about.
- Elicit answers from around the class.

***Answer Key***

*The text is about a group of bikers with tattoos who rescue animals.*

b) **Aim** **To read for cohesion and coherence**

- Ask Ss to read the missing sentences A-E and then give them time to read the text again and complete the task.
- Check Ss' answers.

## Reading

3 a) **Aim** **To identify key words**

- Ask Ss to read the rubric and then look at the statements.
- Allow Ss time to underline the key words.
- Check Ss' answers.

***Suggested Answer Key***

1   This helps _reduce rubbish_.
2   You must _wash_ this _after cooking_.
3   If it had not _rained so much_, it wouldn't have _caused a problem_.
4   If there is _danger_, people will _go out here_.
5   You will _not get paid_ for _work_.

b) **Aim** **To read for gist**

- Direct Ss' attention to the notices.
- Elicit from Ss what each notice is about.

***Suggested Answer Key***

| | |
|---|---|
| A   A flood. | E   A cancelled event. |
| B   A job. | F   Giving time or money |
| C   Instructions | to charity. |
| at a campsite. | G   Recycling. |
| D   Where to go | H   A charity event. |
| in an emergency. | |

c) **Aim** **To read for comprehension**

- Allow Ss time to match the notices to the statements.
- Check Ss' answers. Elicit reasoning.

***Answer Key***

1   G   (If you recycle things, you don't throw away as much rubbish.)
2   C   (You have to clean the barbecue after you use it to cook on.)
3   A   (The road closed because of a flood.)
4   D   (In an emergency, such as fire, this is the exit people should use.)
5   F   (This job is for volunteers.)

## Speaking

4   **Aim** **To describe a photograph**

- Explain the task.
- Divide Ss into pairs.
- Ss read the rubric then look at their photo.
- Ss A describes picture one for one minute then the pairs swap roles and Ss B describes picture two.



- Monitor the activity and give assistance where necessary.
- Ask various Ss to describe their photo to the class.

***Suggested Answer Key***

**Student A**

*The girl in the photograph is recycling some glass bottles. It is very important to recycle as much as we can. You can recycle a lot of things including plastic, paper, glass, tins and cans. You can even recycle your old appliances. Our landfill sites are filling up fast and soon there will be no space left in them. Recycling reduces the amount of rubbish that goes to landfill and also the strain on natural resources used to produce materials such as glass, plastic and metal. It can also save energy and reduce pollution that the factories that make these materials cause. I think this girl is being very responsible and more young people should get involved in recycling.*

**Student B**

*This is a photograph of four teenagers. There are two girls and two boys. They are cleaning up an area in their neighbourhood. It looks like an allotment and they are collecting the rubbish that people have left there. It is very important to take care of the place that you live in and make sure that it is clean and safe. If a lot of people get together to do it, it can also be fun. You could make a day of it and get all your friends to help. If everyone does their bit, then the job will be done quicker. Doing something good like this can make you feel great because you are helping your community.*

## Writing

5 a) **Aim** **To prepare for a writing task**

- Ask Ss to read the rubric and the sentences 1-4 and then mark them accordingly.
- Check Ss' answers.

b) **Aim** **To write a memo**

- Read the rubric aloud. Refer Ss to the **Writing Bank** and revise layout of notes.
- Give Ss time to write their notes.
- Remind Ss to include all the information in the rubric and use their answers to Ex. 6a to help them.
- Check Ss' answers.

***Suggested Answer Key***

| | |
|---|---|
| To: | All members |
| From: | Club Secretary |
| Date: | 4th May |
| Subject: | Charity musical |

*All members are invited to attend a charity theatre performance to help the local animal shelter.*
*The performance will be a musical version of 'The Wind in the Willows' and the event will take place at the village hall on Hayes Road at 8 pm on Saturday 15th May.*
*Tickets will be £5 and all members are encouraged to attend.*
*Anna Campbell*

**b)  Do the task.**

A  They don't just try to take the mistreated animal from its owner, they often try to educate the owner.

B  For example, if the men go to a house and see a dog or dogs outside in the cold, they will build them a doghouse!

C  Rescue Ink has rescued dogs, horses and even chickens!

D  All the members are volunteers and often use their own money to help the animals they rescue.

E  They found out they all loved animals and wanted to help them.

## Reading

**3  a)  Read the rubric, then underline the key words in statements 1-5.**

> Which notices (A-H) says this (1-5)?

**b)  Read the notices. What is each about?**

**Example**

| | | |
|---|---|---|
| **0** | It is cheaper for kids. | *H* |

1  This helps reduce rubbish.
2  You must wash this after cooking.
3  If it had not rained so much, it wouldn't have caused a problem.
4  If there is danger, people will go out here.
5  You will not get paid for work.

**c)  Do the task. Give reasons for your answers.**

## Speaking

**4  Read the rubric, then look at the photos. Do the task.**

> Work in pairs. Each of you will talk on your own about something. You will each have a photograph to talk about. Student A: show your photograph to Student B and then tell him/her what you can see in your picture. (Approximately one minute.) Now, Student B: show your photograph to Student A and then tell him/her what you can see in your picture. (Approximately one minute.)

## Writing (memos) *(Writing Bank p. WB6)*

**5  a)  Read the rubric. Then mark the sentences below *T* (true) or *F* (false).**

> You are the secretary of the school English club. The club has decided to organise a theatre performance to raise money for the local animal shelter. Write a memo to all members to inform them of the event. In your memo:
> - give the reason for the event
> - explain what the performance is about
> - say where and when it will happen
> - ask members to be there

1  Memos start the same as letters *(Dear friends, …)*.  F
2  A memo should be clear and concise.  T
3  We sign off using our full name.  F
4  Long chatty sentences should be avoided.  T

**b)  Write your memo.**

**1** **Fill in:** *save, hunting, swept, suffers, poverty, raise, habitat, polluted, lay, affect.*

**1** Heavy floods in the area ................................ people's lives every year.
**2** Police caught two poachers ............................ in the forest.
**3** The tsunami ............................. many houses out to sea.
**4** The area ................................. from hurricanes and floods every year.
**5** Organising a concert is a good way for a charity to .................................... money.
**6** We can all help to fight ................ and hunger.
**7** The river is so ............................ that you can't swim in it.
**8** Rescue teams worked through the night to .................................... the earthquake victims.
**9** We watched the turtles ........................... their eggs in the sand.
**10** Deforestation has destroyed the gorillas' ................................. .

*10x2=20 marks*

**2** **Put the verbs in brackets into the** *present perfect, past perfect* **or the** *past simple*.

**1** A: .......................................................... **(you ever/do)** anything for charity?
 B: Yes, I .......................................................... **(run)** a marathon two years ago.
**2** A: I hear there ......................................... **(be)** a terrible hurricane in your country last week.
 B: Yes, but fortunately lots of rescue teams ...... .................................. **(arrive)** to help now.
**3** A: Why ............................................. **(he/lose)** the game last Monday?
 B: He .................................... **(sprain)** his ankle so he couldn't play well.
**4** A: Jack ............................... **(look)** very pleased when I saw him.
 B: Yes. They told him he ................................. **(pass)** his exam.
**5** A: ................................... **(she/arrive)** on time?
 B: No, we ............................ **(wait)** for her for an hour before she came.

*10x1=10 marks*

**3** **Choose the correct word.**

**1** They haven't finished building the new school **already/yet**.
**2** We've **already/since** cleaned the graffiti off the walls.
**3** Comic Relief has raised over £600 million **for/since** it started in the 1980s.
**4** Claire has **yet/already** filled out her application form. She sent it by post today.
**5** Peter had gone **before/ago** we arrived.

*5x2=10 marks*

**4** **Put the verbs in brackets into the correct tense.**

**1** I wish he .................... **(not/be)** late last night.
**2** If I ......................................... **(take)** your advice, I wouldn't have failed.
**3** If only I ............................. **(not/miss)** the bus. I got to work late.
**4** I wish he ...................................... **(not/lie)** to his parents. They are very upset.
**5** If I hadn't parked my car there, I ...................... **(not/get)** a fine.

*5x4=20 marks*

**5** **Match the exchanges.**

| | | |
|---|---|---|
| **1** ☐ What are you doing? | **A** | I'd love to. |
| **2** ☐ Can I give you a hand? | **B** | I'm putting up posters. |
| **3** ☐ What time? | **C** | Actually, I've nearly finished. |
| **4** ☐ Would you like to go fishing? | **D** | Great. |
| **5** ☐ What was your holiday like? | **E** | Around six. |

*5x4=20 marks*

**6** **You are spending the summer doing some volunteer work for your city. Write an email to your friend telling him/her about it (80-100 words).**

*20 marks*

*Total: 100 marks*

**Check your Progress**

• talk and write about natural disasters ____
• talk about social problems ____
• ask for and offer help ____
• speak and write about endangered animals ____
• make suggestions and express preferences ____
• write a letter giving news ____

**GOOD** ✓ **VERY GOOD** ✓✓ **EXCELLENT** ✓✓✓

**1**
| | | |
|---|---|---|
| 1 *affect* | 5 *raise* | 9 *lay* |
| 2 *hunting* | 6 *poverty* | 10 *habitat* |
| 3 *swept* | 7 *polluted* | |
| 4 *suffers* | 8 *save* | |

**2**

1 A: *Have you ever done*  
   B: *ran*

2 A: *was*  
   B: *have arrived*

3 A: *did he lose*  
   B: *had sprained/sprained*

4 A: *looked*  
   B: *had passed*

5 A: *Did she arrive*  
   B: *had waited*

**3**
| | | |
|---|---|---|
| 1 *yet* | 3 *since* | 5 *before* |
| 2 *already* | 4 *already* | |

**4**
| | |
|---|---|
| 1 *hadn't been* | 4 *hadn't lied* |
| 2 *had taken* | 5 *wouldn't have got* |
| 3 *hadn't missed* | |

**5**  1 B  2 C  3 E  4 A  5 D

**6**  *Suggested Answer Key*

*Hi Andrew,*

*How are you? I've just joined a volunteer team and I wanted to tell you all about it.*

*The project helps the homeless people here and we've already done so many things. We've collected food donations, winter clothes and shoes. We've also delivered them to shelters around the city. Last night, we gave out hot soup outside the library.*

*Tomorrow, the team is meeting early to make sandwiches. Then, we're going to give them to people sleeping outside the train station. It's hard work, but homeless people are really grateful to receive help.*

*Write back soon.*

*David*

# Art & Culture



Read the title of the module *Art & Culture* and ask Ss to suggest what they think this module will be about *(this module is about types of art and music, places of cultural interest, shopping and art styles)*. Go through the topic list and stimulate a discussion about what Ss will learn in the module.

## Vocabulary

**1**  **Aim**  To introduce new vocabulary

- Direct Ss' attention to the pictures and elicit what each one shows.
- Play the recording. Ss listen and check their answers.

*Answer Key*

1  *Picture 1 shows a statue*
2  *Picture 2 shows a historic building*
3  *Picture 3 shows a building that looks like a sailing ship*
4  *Picture 4 shows an oil painting*

**2**  **Aim**  To expand the topic

- Explain the task and read out the example.
- Elicit sentences from Ss around the class.

*Answer Key*

2  *Wawel Castle was built by King David I.*
3  *Sydney Opera House was designed by Jørn Utzon.*
4  *Swans Reflecting Elephants was painted by Salvador Dalí in 1937.*

## OVER TO YOU!

**Aim**  To personalise the topic

Elicit answers to the questions in the rubric from various Ss around the class and ask them to complete the sentences.

*Suggested Answer Key*

*The Eiffel Tower is located in Paris. It was originally built in the 19th century. It was built for the 1889 Exposition Universelle and was only supposed to last 20 years.*

# Module 6
## Art & Culture

## *Vocabulary*
### Art

**1** Look at the pictures. Which shows: *a statue? an oil painting? a historic building? a building that looks like a sailing ship?*

🎧 Listen and check.

**2** Use the information under each picture to make sentences as in the example.

*Moses was sculpted by Michelangelo.*



Moses (sculpted by Michelangelo)

*Swans Reflecting Elephants*
(painted by Salvadore Dalí in 1937)

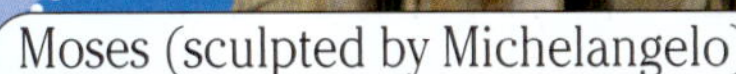
Wawel Castle (built by David I)

Sydney Opera House (designed by Jorn Utzon)

# Archaeological discoveries

## Vocabulary
### Materials

1 🎧 Listen and say. Make sentences as in the example.

*The vase was made of clay.*

## Reading & Listening

2 a) Look at the Terracotta Army. Where is it? What is special about it?
🎧 Listen and read to find out.

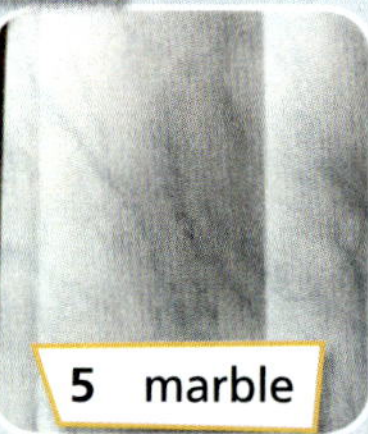

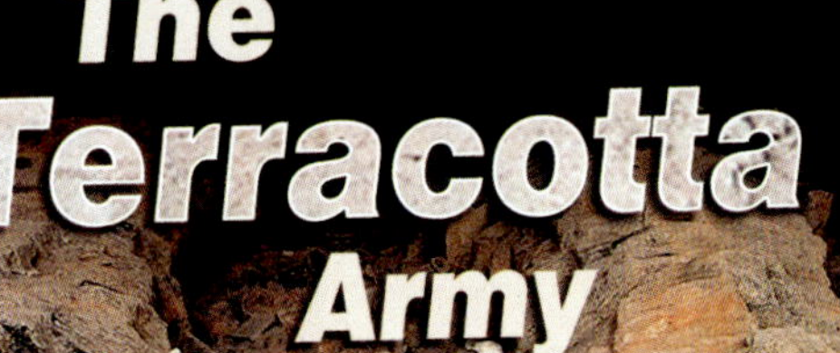

# The Terracotta Army

In 1974, a group of farmers in China were digging a well when they uncovered something strange: a life-sized statue of a soldier standing ready for battle. When the area was **excavated** later by archaeologists, one of the most incredible archaeological finds in history was **revealed**; a whole army of terracotta soldiers that have been **undisturbed** for over 2,000 years.

These statues were made to **guard** the tomb of Qin Shi Huang, the First Emperor of China. In ancient China, the dead were buried with their **possessions** because people believed that they could be taken into the afterlife with them. Qin Shi Huang wanted to be sure that he took all his belongings with him including his army, so he ordered his men to start working on it when he was just 13 years old. Around 700,000 men worked on building the **elaborate** treasure-filled tomb surrounded by an army of clay soldiers until the emperor's death.

Each one of the statues is unique. They each have their own **individual** facial expressions and **features**. Some have moustaches, others have beards and they are all different heights and builds. Some people believe that each one was modelled on the real soldiers of the First Emperor's personal army. In total, there are around 8,000 soldiers all lined up for battle in different pits alongside bronze horses and chariots and an armoury of weapons spread over 50 square kilometres.

The **splendour** of the burial site shows just how powerful Emperor Qin Shi Huang was. During his reign he brought the different states of China together to form the first Chinese Empire and he made the written language, the money and the laws the same for everyone. The first great fortresses that would become part of the Great Wall of China were also built during his **reign**. Strangely though, **despite** his importance and power, after his death, the emperor's tomb was forgotten and remained untouched for 2,000 years.

Today, the First Emperor's Tomb is a protected UNESCO World Cultural Heritage site. Archaeologists may never uncover all the riches of the tomb, but what has been found so far is a fantastic gift to the world. Any visitor to China will be amazed by the **spectacular** terracotta army. It is a sight not to be missed.

## Check these words

dig, life-sized, battle, excavate, reveal, guard, tomb, emperor, bury, elaborate, treasure-filled, unique, facial expressions, features, model, pit, chariot, armoury, splendour, burial site, reign, law, fortress, remain, untouched

## Vocabulary

**1** **Aim** **To introduce vocabulary for materials**

- Direct Ss' attention to the pictures and play the recording. Ss listen and repeat chorally or individually.
- Pay attention to Ss' intonation and pronunciation.
- Read out the example and then elicit further examples for the remaining materials from Ss around the class.
- Point out that we use *made of* to talk about the materials from which sth is constructed.

***Suggested Answer Key***

*2   The statues were made of wood.*
*3   The statue is made of terracotta.*
*4   The house is made of stone.*
*5   The columns are made of marble.*
*6   The helmet is made of metal.*

## Reading & Listening

**2** **a)** **Aim** **To introduce the topic and listen and read for gist**

- Direct Ss' attention to the picture and the title of the text.
- Elicit where it might be and what might be special about it.
- Play the recording. Ss listen and follow the text in their books to find out.

***Answer Key***

*The Terracotta Army is in China. It is special because it was made to guard the tomb of the First Emperor and it was undisturbed for 2,000 years.*

**b)** **Aim** **To read for specific information**

- Ask Ss to read the questions 1-5 and give them time to read the text again and choose the correct answers.
- Check Ss' answers around the class.

*Answer Key*

| | | | |
|---|---|---|---|
| 1 B | 2 C | 3 A | 4 D |

- Refer Ss to the **Check these words** box and explain/elicit the meanings of the words or ask Ss to use their dictionaries and look them up.

*Suggested Answer Key*

*dig (v): to make a hole in the ground*
*life-sized (adj): the same size as what it represents*
*battle (n): an armed fight between soldiers of opposing sides*
*excavate (v): to carefully remove earth from an area and look for artefacts*
*reveal (v): to uncover*
*guard (v): to protect from harm*
*tomb (n): a large grave*
*emperor (n): a man who rules an empire*
*bury (v): to put sth under the ground and cover it with earth*
*elaborate (adj): detailed*
*treasure-filled (adj): full of gold, jewels and valuables*
*unique (adj): one of a kind*
*facial expressions (n): the way a face shows feelings or emotions*
*features (n): eyes, nose, mouth, etc*
*model (v): to be made to look like sth*
*pit (n): a deep hole in the ground*
*chariot (n): an old-fashioned open mode of transport that was pulled by horses*
*armoury (n): weapons & military equipment*
*splendour (n): magnificence*
*burial site (n): the place where sb/sth is buried*
*reign (n): the length of time a monarch/ruler is in power*
*law (n): one of the rules in a country*
*fortress (n): a very strong building built to keep enemies out*
*remain (v): to stay*
*untouched (adj): not affected by anyone else*

**3** **Aim** **To consolidate information from a text**

- Ss work in closed pairs and ask and answer questions based on the text.
- Monitor the activity around the class and then ask some pairs to ask and answer in front of the class.

*Suggested Answer Key*

A: *When was the terracotta army discovered?*
B: *In 1974.*
A: *How was it discovered?*
B: *Some farmers were digging a well.*
A: *Why was the terracotta army made?*
B: *It was made to guard the tomb of Emperor Qin Shi Huang. … etc*

**4** **Aim** **To expand vocabulary/To match words from a text to their meanings**

- Explain the task.

- Give Ss time to complete the task.
- Check Ss' answers.

*Answer Key*

| | |
|---|---|
| **protect:** *guard* | **magnificence:** *splendour* |
| **dug up:** *excavated* | **rule:** *reign* |
| **detailed:** *elaborate* | **discovered:** *revealed* |
| **personal:** *individual* | **very impressive:** *spectacular* |
| **belongings:** *possessions* | **in spite of:** *despite* |
| **characteristics:** *features* | **untouched:** *undisturbed* |

**5** **Aim** **To present the passive**

Ss' books closed. Write on the board. *The museum **holds** exhibitions.* Ask Ss to identify the **S** (subject), **V** (verb) and **O** (object) in the sentence. Write: *exhibitions are held by the museum.* Explain that this is a sentence in the passive. Focus Ss' attention on the verb form *are held*. Elicit form (the *verb to be + past participle*). Ask Ss to identify the **S** (subject) in this sentence (*exhibition*) and compare it to the active (*exhibition* was the object in the active sentence). Explain that *by the museum* is the agent in the passive sentence. Point out that this was the subject (*the museum*) in the active sentence. Explain that we use the passive to emphasise the action, not the person who does it. Ss open their books.

- Direct Ss' attention to the table. Elicit the passive forms of verbs in the tenses mentioned.
- Explain that we use the passive to talk about actions when the person who carries out the action is unknown, unimportant or obvious from the context. We also use the passive in formal writing.
- Ask Ss to find examples in the text on p. 98, and identify the tenses.

*Answer Key – see p. 100(T)*

**6** **Aim** **To practise the passive**

- Explain the task and give Ss time to complete it.
- Check Ss' answers.

**7** **Aim** **To further practise the passive**

- Explain the task. Do the first heading with the class. Explain that headings don't include articles or full verb forms but Ss' sentences should contain them. Give Ss time to complete the task.
- Check Ss' answers.

*Answer Key – see p. 100(T)*

## Speaking & Writing

**8** **Aim** **To talk and write about an archaeological discovery**

Explain the task. Give Ss some time to prepare their answers and then ask various Ss to tell the class.

*Suggested Answer Key – see p. 100(T)*

**b)  Read the text and choose the best answer** *A, B, C or D.*

**1**  What is the writer's main purpose in writing the text?
- **A**  to say how some farmers discovered the tomb
- **B**  to explain why Qin Shi Huang's men built the tomb
- **C**  to encourage tourists to visit the First Emperor's Tomb
- **D**  to explain how UNESCO chooses its sites

**2**  What does the reader learn about Qin Shi Huang?
- **A**  He built the tomb to honour his army.
- **B**  He wanted to be taken to the afterlife with his father.
- **C**  He started the construction for the tomb when he was young.
- **D**  He ordered his army to continue guarding the tomb after his death.

**3**  During Huang's lifetime, he
- **A**  established a single currency.
- **B**  completed the Great Wall of China.
- **C**  increased his army to 8,000.
- **D**  uncovered very old treasures.

**4**  Which of the following might the writer say about the site?
- **A**  The site is in danger of closing so people should visit it soon.
- **B**  The site is especially great for students studying archaeology because it has more to reveal.
- **C**  The site should be visited only after everything has been uncovered.
- **D**  The site is amazing but my favourite part is the red clay soldiers.

**3**  In pairs ask and answer questions based on the text.

**4**  Match the highlighted words to their meanings: *protect, dug up, detailed, personal, belongings, characteristics, magnificence, rule, discovered, very impressive, in spite of, untouched.*

## *Grammar:* The passive

see p. GR9

**5**  Read the theory. Find examples in the text.

| Form: *be + past participle* of main verb | |
|---|---|
| **ACTIVE** | **PASSIVE** |
| **PRESENT SIMPLE** | |
| The museum **holds** exhibitions. | Exhibitions **are held** by the museum. |
| **PAST SIMPLE** | |
| They **found** a statue. | A statue **was found**. |
| **PRESENT PERFECT** | |
| A lot of people **have visited** it. | It **has been visited** by a lot of people. |
| **WILL** | |
| It **will impress** you. | You **will be impressed**. |
| **MODALS** | |
| Visitors **can take** photos. | Photos **can be taken**. |

We use the **passive**:
- when the person who carries out the action is unknown, unimportant or obvious from the context. *The Terracotta Army **is located** in China.*
- to make statements more formal or polite. *Taking photos in the museum **is prohibited**.*

**6**  Fill in: *is, was, were, will be, have.*

1  *Romeo and Juliet* **was** written by Shakespeare.
2  The museum **will be** opened by the mayor next week.
3  Two buried statues **were** found last Monday.
4  The site **is** visited by thousands every year.
5  The invitations **have** already been posted.

**7**  Rewrite the headings using passive forms.

1  TOMB OF FIRST EMPEROR LOCATED NEAR XIANG
2  OVER 8,000 SOLDIERS ESTIMATED TO EXIST
3  ARMY BURIED OVER 2,000 YEARS AGO
4  ARCHAEOLOGISTS AMAZED BY DISCOVERY IN 1974
5  SITE PROTECTED BY UNESCO FOR FUTURE GENERATIONS

## Speaking & Writing

**8**  **THINK!** Imagine you were one of the Chinese farmers who discovered the Terracotta Army. Describe what you found and how you felt. Tell the class.

*I was working with some other farmers. We were digging a well … . Suddenly, I struck something hard … . I was surprised … .*

Vocabulary Bank 6 p. VB17

## Vocabulary & Reading

**1** Work in pairs. Check the words in the Check these words box. Use them to write a short description of the three roadside attractions. Tell your partner.

**2** a) Read and mark the sentences as *T* (true), *F* (false) or *DS* (Doesn't say).

1  The dinosaur gives visitors the chance to admire the view. .....
2  The dinosaur is also a kind of art gallery and museum.    .....
3  You can stay in the Big Pineapple.    .....
4  The Big Pineapple is also a kind of amusement park and zoo. .....
5  The lion's head is considered to be an essential tourist stop.  .....
6  The lion's head is fibreglass.    .....

b)  ☐ Listen and read, then ask and answer questions.

**Check these words**

roadside attraction, transform, element, steel, fibreglass, dinosaur bone, fossil, on display, line, mural, plantation, wildlife reserve, dazzled, carve, limestone, pose, mighty beast

# Roadside attractions you really can't miss!

**A**  Our towns, cities and motorways can be **transformed** by unusual buildings, statues and ... huge roadside attractions! They bring an element of surprise and humour to everyday places and come in many shapes and sizes. Here are some of the largest roadside **attractions** in the world...

How would you like to stand in the mouth of the world's biggest dinosaur? It might sound scary, but this is no ordinary dinosaur. This creature is made out of steel and fibreglass, stands 26 metres tall and weighs an **astonishing** 65,770 kg. Since it was first opened, it has been toured by thousands of visitors to Drumheller in Alberta, Canada. You may think the climb up the 106 steps inside is scary, but visitors are entertained all the way up. Dinosaur bones and fossils have been put **on display** in cases **lining** the stairway. Also, the walls have been painted with beautiful murals by a local artist, and the fantastic view from the mouth of the beast makes the whole climb worthwhile.

**B**  If you are ever in Queensland, Australia, why not stop at Woombye to visit the Big Pineapple? This 16-metre-high fruit is made out of fibreglass and has been a popular tourist attraction since 1971. This huge creation was built at a pineapple plantation and wildlife reserve. Australian animals, like koalas, kangaroos, and emus can be seen there and people can take a ride around the plantation on the Nutmobile or on a small train. There's also a restaurant and anyone who has a sweet tooth will be **dazzled** by the selection of sweet treats made from pineapple and other tropical fruit.

**C**  People driving along Kennon Road to Baguio City in the Philippines have all **noticed** the same thing: a giant lion's head! The head is 12 metres high and has been **carved** out of limestone. Snacks and drinks can be bought from nearby stalls and miniature souvenir lion heads may be found there, too. A trip to Baguio wouldn't be complete without **posing** for a photo next to the **mighty** beast. So if you are ever driving down Kennon Road, don't forget to stop off for a nice **break**.

## Vocabulary & Reading

1 **Aim** **To introduce the topic and related vocabulary through pictures**

- Divide the class into pairs.
- Direct Ss' attention to the pictures and explain/ elicit the meanings of the words in the **Check these words** box or ask Ss to look them up in their dictionaries or in the **Word List**.

***Suggested Answer Key***

*roadside attraction (n): an interesting feature for tourists at the side of a road*
*transform (v): to change*
*element (n): an important quality/feature that sth has*
*steel (n): a hard metal*
*fibreglass (n): a manmade plastic and glass building material*
*dinosaur bone (n): a bone from a prehistoric creature*
*fossil (n): the remains of a prehistoric animal/plant found inside a rock*
*on display (phr): put in a place for everyone to see*
*line (v): to form rows along the sides of sth*
*mural (n): a large picture painted on a wall*
*plantation (n): a large piece of land where a certain crop is grown*
*wildlife reserve (n): an area where wild animals live in safety*
*dazzled (pp): amazed*
*carve (v): to cut out of wood or stone*
*limestone (n): a type of stone*
*pose (v): to stand in a position ready for a photo/picture*
*mighty beast (phr): a huge animal*

- Give Ss time to write a short description of each attraction in the pictures A-C and tell their partners.

***Suggested Answer Key***

A *This **roadside attraction** is a huge green and yellow dinosaur. It might be made of **steel** and **fibreglass**. I think there may be **dinosaur bones** and **fossils on display** there.*
B *This **roadside attraction** is a huge pineapple. It may be made of **steel**. It may be at the site of a pineapple **plantation**.*
C *This **roadside attraction** is a huge lion's head. It may be **carved** from **limestone**. It could mark the entrance to a **wildlife reserve**. It looks like a **mighty beast**.*

2 a) **Aim** **To read for specific information**

- Explain the task.
- Give Ss time to read the text and mark the statements accordingly.
- Check Ss' answers around the class.

***Answer Key***

| 1 T | 2 T | 3 F | 4 F | 5 T | 6 F |

b) **Aim** **To consolidate information in a text.**

- Play the recording. Ss follow the text in their books.
- Ss ask and answer questions in pairs.
- Monitor the activity around the class and then ask some pairs to ask and answer questions in front of the rest of the class.

***Suggested Answer Key***

A: *Where is the big dinosaur?*
B: *It's in Drumheller, Albert, Canada, How big is it?*
A: *It's 26 metres tall. How much does it weigh?*
B: *It weighs 65,770 kg. What can you see there?*
A: *Dinosaur bones, fossils, beautiful murals and a fantastic view. etc*

---

## Suggested Answers for Exs 5, 7 & 8 on p. 99

### Ex. 5

*was excavated (**past simple**), was revealed (**past simple**), have been undisturbed (**present perfect**), were made (**past simple**), were buried (**past simple**), could be taken (**modal**), was modelled (**past simple**), were also built (**past simple**), was forgotten (**past simple**), has been found (**present perfect**), will be amazed (**future**), to be missed (**infinitive**)*

### Ex. 7

1 *The tomb of the First Emperor was located near Xiang.*
2 *Over 8,000 soldiers are estimated to exist.*
3 *The army was buried over 2,000 years ago.*
4 *Archaeologists were amazed by the discovery in 1974.*
5 *The site will be protected by UNESCO for future generations.*

### Ex. 8

*I was working with some other farmers. We were digging a well in the fields. Suddenly, I struck something hard with my shovel. I was surprised when I saw the head of a soldier in the ground. It turned out to be a life-sized statue. I was amazed. We stopped digging and informed the authorities. A group of archaeologists came to excavate properly. What we had discovered was the tomb of the First Emperor and there were at least 8,000 more statues and other finds that hadn't been touched for at least 2,000 years. We were astonished.*

**3 a) `Aim` To consolidate new vocabulary**

- Explain the task.
- Give Ss time to complete it.
- Check Ss' answers.

**b) `Aim` To expand vocabulary**

- Explain the task.
- Give Ss time to complete the task.
- Check Ss' answers.

***Suggested Answer Key***

***transformed:*** *changed*
***attractions:*** *things that are interesting to see or do*
***astonishing:*** *surprising*
***on display:*** *put in a place for everyone to see*
***lining:*** *forming rows along the sides of sth*
***dazzled:*** *amazed*
***noticed:*** *become aware of*
***carved:*** *cut out of wood or stone*
***posing:*** *getting into position next to sth (for a photograph)*
***mighty:*** *huge*
***break:*** *a short rest*

**c) `Aim` To consolidate new vocabulary and personalise the topic**

Give Ss time to prepare their answers and then ask various Ss around the class to share their answers with the rest of the class.

***Suggested Answer Key***

***Roadside attractions*** *can transform our towns, cities and motorways.*
*Roadside attractions can **come in all shapes and sizes.***
*Some of them can **bring an element of humour** to a boring journey.*
*In Drumheller, Alberta, there is a huge dinosaur where dinosaur bones and fossils have been **put on display.***
*There are also murals painted by a **local artist.***
*Drumheller is a **popular tourist attraction.***
*In Woombye, Australia at the Big Pineapple, people can visit a **wildlife reserve.***
*It's a great place for people who **have a sweet tooth** because they have a large selection of sweets.*
*The sweets they serve are made of **tropical fruit.***
*Just outside Baguio City in the Philippines, there is a giant lion's head that many tourists stop at and **pose for a photo** next to.*

*I would like to visit the big dinosaur in Drumheller in Canada. I think it would be fun to climb to the top and look out of its mouth./I would like to visit the Big Pineapple in Australia. I think it would be fun to see all the wildlife there and try the sweets made from tropical fruit./ I would like to visit the giant lion's head in the Philippines. I think it would be fun to pose for a photo with it.*

**d) `Aim` To develop creative thinking skills**

- Explain the task and divide the class into pairs or small groups.
- Give Ss time to think of a roadside attraction and draw a picture of it.



- Ask various pairs/groups to describe their attraction to the class and give reasons for their choice.

***Suggested Answer Key – see p. 104(T)***

## Grammar

**4 `Aim` To present the passive**

- Read out the table and copy the diagram onto the board. Point out that when changing an active sentence to a passive sentence, the subject in the active sentence becomes the agent in the passive sentence. Explain that the verb changes to a passive form and the object in the active sentence becomes the subject in the passive sentence.
- Elicit examples of passive sentences from the text on p.100. Ask Ss to identify the verb tense forms.

***Answer Key – see p. 104(T)***

**5 `Aim` To practise the passive**

- Explain the task. Do the first sentence with Ss.
- Give Ss time to complete the task.
- Check Ss' answers.

***Answer Key – see p. 104(T)***

**6 `Aim` To further practise the passive**

- Explain the task and read out the example.
- Give Ss time to complete the task and then check Ss' answers around the class.

***Answer Key – see p. 104(T)***

## Speaking & Writing

**7 `Aim` To practise the passive**

- Explain the task, read out the example and go through the list of verbs. Explain/Elicit their meanings.
- Give Ss time to complete the task and then elicit sentences from Ss' around the class.

***Suggested Answer Key – see p. 104(T)***

**8 `Aim` To write about a monument from your country**

- Divide the class into pairs or small groups and ask them to use the Internet, encyclopaedias or other sources of reference to look up information about an interesting building or monument in their country.
- Give Ss time to collect their information and then ask various pairs/groups to present their building/monument to the class. Remind Ss to use the passive.
- Alternatively, assign the task as HW and check Ss' answers in the next lesson.

***Suggested Answer Key – see p. 104(T)***

**3** **a)** Fill in with: *local, tropical, roadside, attraction, wildlife, pose, shapes, sweet, humour, display.*

1 **roadside** attractions
2 to come in all **shapes** and sizes
3 to bring an element of **humour**
4 put on **display**
5 **local** artist
6 popular tourist **attraction**
7 **wildlife** reserve
8 to have a **sweet** tooth
9 **tropical** fruit
10 **pose** for a photo

**b)** Explain the words in bold.

**c)** **THINK!** Use the completed phrases to make sentences about each attraction. Which attraction would you like to visit? Why? Tell the class.

**d)** **THINK!** Draw a roadside attraction for your city/town/village. Present it to the class. Explain why you have decided on this.

## Grammar
### The passive

*see p. GR9*

**4** Read the table. Find examples in the text.

To change a sentence from the active into the passive:
- the object of the active sentence becomes the subject in the passive sentence.
- the active verb remains in the same tense, but it changes into a passive form.
- the subject of the active sentence becomes the agent.

| | Subject | Verb | Object |
|---|---|---|---|
| **Active** | *Mr Harris* | *sculpts* | *statues.* |
| **Passive** | *Statues* | *are sculpted* | *by Mr Harris.* |
| | **Subject** | **Verb** | **Agent** |

**Note: by + agent** (to say who carries out the action)
*Hamlet was written **by Shakespeare**.*

**with + agent** (to say what the agent used to carry out the action) *The field was covered **with snow**.*

**5** Rewrite the sentences in the passive.

1 Visitors can't use cameras in the museum.
2 Lots of people have visited the gallery today.
3 People can buy souvenirs in the gift shop.
4 A local artist will sculpt the new statue.
5 The museum displays dinosaur bones.
6 Paul invited Emma to the wildlife reserve.

**6** Rewrite the newspaper headlines as complete sentences.

> 1 NEW MUSEUM TO BE OPENED BY PRINCESS ANNE TOMORROW

> 2 ART GALLERY OPENING CALLED OFF YESTERDAY

> 3 ROCK CONCERT TO BE HELD TONIGHT AT BAGUIO

> 4 MUSEUM RENOVATION NOT COMPLETED YET

> 5 ART MUSEUM CLOSED FOR REPAIRS LAST MONDAY

1 *The museum will be opened by Princess Anne tomorrow.*

## Speaking & Writing

**7** Use the information to make complete sentences in the passive about the Statue of Liberty. Use these verbs: *locate, sculpt, start/complete, make of, give, visit, miss.*

**Name:** Statue of Liberty
**Location:** Liberty Island, New York
**Sculptor:** Frédéric Auguste Bartholdi
**Start/Complete:** 1876/1884
**Material:** copper
**Reason:** gift from France
**Visitors:** 3 million per year
**Recommendation:** don't miss it

*The Statue of Liberty is located on Liberty Island in New York.*

**8** ICT Collect information about a building/monument in your country and present it to the class. Use Ex. 7 as a model.

# The Garma Festival

The sound of the didgeridoo, the **traditional** musical instrument of Aboriginal Australians, **announces** the beginning of the Garma Festival. This **annual** celebration of Aboriginal culture is a call to all people to come together in unity. During the festival, visitors enjoy the traditional art, dance, music and song of the Yolngu tribe, but Garma is not just about the ways that the Yolngu did things in the past. The Garma Festival is also about their future.

Aboriginal Australians like the Yolngu have lived on the continent for over 40,000 years. There were many different tribes each with their own language. When European settlers arrived in the eighteenth century, though, the Aboriginals lost their land and many of them died. Luckily, their culture **survived** and is now an important part of Australian life.

Aboriginal Australians believe that everything has a soul or a **spirit**, including the landscape and the weather. This creates a unique bond between the people and the land. They tell stories and paint pictures about The Dreaming, the time when the world began. Aboriginal Australian art is famous not just for the **handmade** boomerangs or decorated didgeridoos for tourists, but for valuable bark paintings and carefully **constructed** dot paintings that now hang in art galleries around the world.

In the Yolngu language Garma is something that takes place when people from different backgrounds meet to share **knowledge**. The festival is held on **holy** ground in the forest as a way to highlight the past and raise awareness about the future of Aboriginal Australians. There are traditional dances and didgeridoo performances, but there are also **gatherings** to discuss ways of investing in the **native** people and their land.

Not everyone can attend the festival. This special event that brings together the past, present and future is so popular that **attendance** is by invitation only. People can **apply** through the Garma Festival website.

If you are interested, visit www.yyf.com.au

**Check these words**

didgeridoo, Aboriginal, announce, come together in unity, continent, tribes, settlers, soul, spirit, bond, handmade boomerang, bark, constructed, hang, background, holy ground, highlight, gatherings, discuss, invest, attendance

**1** 🎧 Listen to the music and look at the pictures. Imagine you are there. What is happening? How do you feel?

**2** a) Read the text and complete the sentences.

1 A didgeridoo is ................................................. .
2 The Aboriginals have lived in Australia for ........ .
3 The Aboriginal Australian land was taken ...... .
4 According to Aboriginal belief, all things have .... .
5 Aboriginal Australians make ......................... .
6 During the Garma Festival in ........................... .

b) Match the words in bold to their meanings:
*makes known, having been part of a culture for a long time, presence, continued to exist, made without using a machine, created, ask formally for sth, sacred, yearly, local, information you have about a subject, meetings, the non-physical part of sb or sth.*

**3** 🎧 Listen to and read the text. In pairs ask and answer questions based on it.

**4** a) 👥 Use your answers from Ex. 1 and words from the **Check these words** box to tell your partner about the Garma Festival and Aboriginal Australians.

b) **THINK!** Would you like to go to the Garma Festival? Why/Why not? Tell your partner.

**5** ICT Find out information about a cultural festival in your country. What/Who does it celebrate? What happens during the festival? Present the cultural festival to the class.

**1** **Aim** To introduce the topic

- Play the recording and direct Ss' attention to the pictures.
- Ask various Ss around the class to describe an imaginary scene based on the music and the pictures and elicit how they may feel.

**Suggested Answer Key**

*I am at a festival. There are people in traditional costumes. I think they are Aboriginal Australians. They are dancing and playing music around me. I feel very honoured to be here to visit and experience their tribal customs.*

**2 a)** **Aim** To read for specific information

- Give Ss time to read the text and answer the questions, then check Ss' answers.

**Suggested Answer Key – see p. 103(T)**

- Refer Ss to the **Check these words** box and explain/elicit the meanings of the words or ask Ss to use their dictionaries and look them up. Elicit what part of speech each is.

**Suggested Answer Key**

*didgeridoo (n):* an Aboriginal musical instrument
*Aboriginal (adj):* relating to the original inhabitants of a country
*announce (v):* to declare
*come together in unity (phr):* to meet and cooperate to help people
*continent (n):* one of the major land masses (e.g. Asia, Africa, Europe)
*tribes (n):* groups of people who share the same race, language and culture
*settlers (n):* people who arrive in a new country and make it their home
*soul (n):* part of a person that consists of a person's character, thoughts and feelings; spirit
*spirit (n):* soul
*bond (n):* a strong feeling of love or friendship that exists between people
*handmade boomerang (n):* an Aboriginal weapon that is flat and curved and comes back when you throw it, made by hand
*bark (n):* the outer layer of the trunk of a tree
*constructed (adj):* built
*hang (v):* to suspend on a wall
*background (n):* a person's family, culture, education, etc
*holy ground (n):* a piece of land that is important to a religion
*highlight (v):* to draw attention to
*gatherings (n):* get-togethers
*discuss (v):* to talk about sth
*invest (v):* to put money into sth to make it better
*attendance (n):* the number of people present at an event

**b)** **Aim** To expand vocabulary/To match words from a text to their meanings

- Explain the task.
- Give Ss time to complete the task.
- Check Ss' answers.

**Answer Key**

*makes known:* announces

*having been part of a culture for a long time:* traditional
*presence:* attendance
*continued to exist:* survived
*made without using a machine:* handmade
*created:* constructed
*ask formally for sth:* apply
*sacred:* holy
*yearly:* annual
*local:* native
*information you have about a subject:* knowledge
*meetings:* gatherings
*the non-physical part of sb or sth:* spirit

**3** **Aim** To consolidate information in a text

- Play the recording. Ss listen and follow the text in their books and ask and answer questions based on it.
- Monitor the activity around the class.

**Suggested Answer Key**

A: *What is the Garma Festival?*
B: *It's a celebration of Aboriginal culture. How long have Aboriginals lived in Australia?*
A: *Over 40,000 years. What do Aboriginals believe?*
B: *That everything has a soul. What is the Dreaming?*
A: *When the world began according to Aboriginal beliefs. What sort of art do Aboriginals make?*
B: *They make bark paintings and carefully constructed dot paintings. Where is the Garma Festival held?*
A: *It is held on holy ground in the forest. What is the aim of the festival?*
B: *It is to highlight the past and raise awareness about the future of Aboriginals. How can someone attend?*
A: *It is by invitation only. You can apply through the website.*

**4 a)** **Aim** To consolidate information in a text and new vocabulary

- Explain the task. Ss work in pairs.
- Give Ss time to complete the task, referring back to the text and using words from the **Check these words** box. Ss tell their partners.
- Check Ss' answers by asking various pairs to share their answers with the class.

**Suggested Answer Key – see p. 103(T)**

**b)** **Aim** To personalise the topic

- Read the rubric aloud and give Ss time to prepare their answers and tell their partners.
- Ask various Ss around the class to share their answers with the rest of the class.

**Suggested Answer Key – see p. 103(T)**

**5** **Aim** To present a cultural festival from your country

- Give Ss time to collect information about a local cultural festival and then ask various Ss to present it to the class. Remind Ss to include the reason for the festival and what happens during the festival.
- Alternatively, assign the task as HW and ask Ss to give their presentations in the next lesson.

**Suggested Answer Key see p. 103(T)**

## Vocabulary

**1** **Aim** **To present new vocabulary relating to posting a parcel**

- Direct Ss' attention to the pictures.
- Play the recording. Ss listen and repeat chorally or individually.
- Check Ss' intonation and pronunciation.

**2 a)** **Aim** **To present situational language and to identify the speakers**

- Play the recording with pauses for Ss to listen and repeat chorally or individually.
- Pay attention to Ss' intonation and pronunciation.
- Elicit which speaker would say which sentences.

***Answer Key***

***post office worker:*** *Hello, how can I help you? Could you put it on the scales, please? How would you like to send it? So, that's £2.29 then, please.*
***customer:*** *I'd like to post this parcel to Poland. I'll send it by airmail, please.*

**b)** **Aim** **To listen for specific information**

Play the recording for Ss to listen and check their answers.

**3** **Aim** **To read for specific information**

Give Ss time to read the dialogue and then elicit answers to the questions in the rubric from Ss around the class.

***Answer Key***

*Becky wants to send a boomerang painted with Aboriginal art to Poland.*
*It weighs 200 grammes.*
*She will pay £2.29.*

## Pronunciation

**4** **Aim** **To present assimilation**

- Read out the theory box and play the recording. Ss repeat chorally and individually.
- Point out how the sounds are assimilated and repeat if necessary.

**5** **Aim** **To practise role playing**

- Explain the situation and ask Ss to work in pairs and act out a dialogue using the diagram as a guide.
- Remind Ss to use phrases from the dialogue to help them complete the task.
- Monitor the activity around the class and then ask various pairs to act out their dialogues in front of the class.

***Suggested Answer Key***

A: *Hello. How can I help you?*
B: *Good morning. I'd like to post this parcel to Italy.*
A: *Could you put it on the scales, please?*
B: *Sure.*
A: *That's 500 grammes. How would you like to send it?*
B: *What are the choices?*
A: *Surface mail is £2.95, airmail is £4.50 and registered post is £7.95.*
B: *OK. I'll send it registered, please.*
A: *Can you fill in your name and address and a description of what's in the parcel on this form, please?*
B: *Shall I just write that it's a gift?*
A: *Actually, the description has to be more detailed than that.*
B: *Oh, right. It's a handbag.*
A: *That's fine if you just write that. So that is £7.95 then, please.*
B: *Here you are.*
A: *Thank you very much.*
B: *You're welcome.*

---

**Suggested Answers for Exs 2a, 4a, 4b & 5 on p. 102**

### Ex. 2a

1 *... the traditional musical instrument of Aboriginals*
2 *... over 40,000 years*
3 *... from them by European settlers*
4 *... a soul or a spirit*
5 *... handmade boomerangs, decorated didgeridoos, bark paintings and dot paintings*
6 *... the forest, there are traditional dances and didgeridoo performances*

### Ex. 4a

*The Garma Festival is an annual celebration of **Aboriginal** culture. It involves traditional music from **didgeridoos**, dance and art and allows people from different **backgrounds** to **come together in unity**. The Aboriginal people believe that everything has a **soul** or a **spirit**. They use the festival to **highlight** the past and **discuss** ways of **investing** in the future.*

### Ex. 4b

*Yes, I would like to go to the festival because I think it would be an interesting cultural experience. I don't know very much about Aboriginal Australians and it would be a great opportunity to learn more.*

### Ex. 5

*Las Fallas is a traditional festival in Valencia, Spain. It takes place in spring and celebrates the end of the dark winter. This celebration comes from the middle ages when carpenters used to hang pieces of wood in their workshops to hold their candles. At the end of winter, they would display these pieces of wood outside their shops dressed in human form and call them ninots. These ninots would then be burnt to welcome in spring. Nowadays, people spend months preparing and building their ninots. On the night of 15 March, the people put up their statues in the streets and squares where they stand until, on the 19th, they are all burnt on a massive bonfire on a night of light, music and fireworks.*

## Vocabulary
### Posting a parcel

**1** 🎧 Listen and say.

**2** a) 🎧 Listen and say. The phrases below appear in a dialogue between a post office worker and a customer. Who says each sentence?

- Hello, how can I help you?
- I'd like to post this parcel to Poland.
- Could you put it on the scales, please?
- How would you like to send it?
- I'll send it by airmail, please.
- So, that's £2.29 then, please.

b) 🎧 Listen to the dialogue and check.

**3** Read the dialogue and answer the questions. What does Becky want to send? How much does it weigh? How much will she pay?

A: Hello, how can I help you?

B: Oh, good morning. I'd like to post this parcel to Poland.

A: Certainly. Could you put it on the scales, please?

B: Sure.

A: That's 200 grammes. How would you like to send it?

B: What are the choices?

A: Surface mail is £1.89, airmail is £2.29 and registered post is £7.15.

B: Erm … I'll send it by airmail, please.

A: OK. Can you fill in your name and address and a description of what's in the parcel on this form, please?

B: OK … shall I just write that it's a gift?

A: Actually, the description has to be more detailed than that.

B: Oh, right. It's a boomerang painted with Aboriginal art.

A: That's fine if you just write that. So, that's £2.29 then, please.

B: Here you are.

A: Thank you very much.

B: You're welcome.

## Pronunciation
### Assimilation

**4** Read the theory.
🎧 Listen and repeat. Notice how sounds are assimilated.

> In assimilation, a sound takes the characteristics of another sound, either before or after it.

- His son is seventeen.
- Don't be silly!
- That's fine grandpa.
- That's my handbag.

**5** 👥 Imagine you are on holiday in an English-speaking country. You want to send a parcel to your friend. Use the diagram to act out your dialogue.

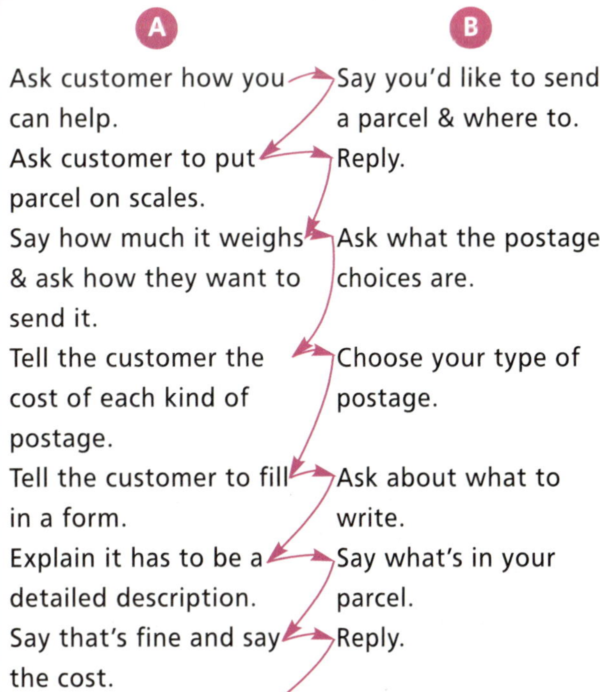

# 6e Shopping experiences

## Vocabulary
### Shops & products

**1** Which of the following can you buy in these shops?

- pens • eye drops • notebook
- gold ring • designer clothes
- pencils • sweets • shoes
- cakes • chocolates • contact lenses • high quality cheeses
- sunglasses • bread rolls
- cold meats • aspirin

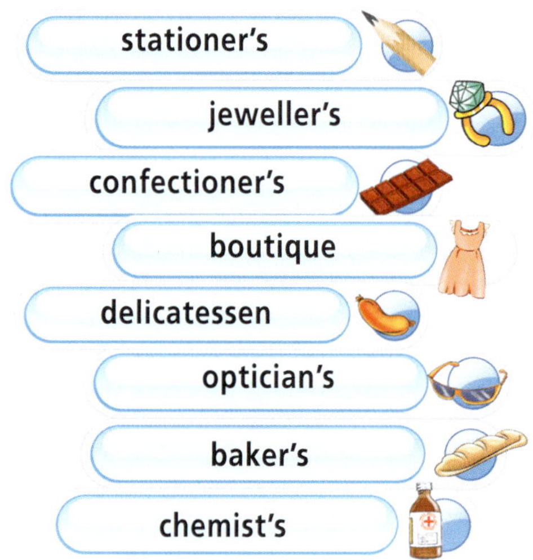

- stationer's
- jeweller's
- confectioner's
- boutique
- delicatessen
- optician's
- baker's
- chemist's

*You can buy pens, pencils and notebooks at a stationer's.*

**2** 🎧 Listen to four short exchanges. Where does each take place? Which words help you decide?

## Reading

**3** Look at the picture and the title of the article. What do you know about Venice? Where is it located? What is it famous for?

**4** Read the introduction to the text. How does Venice in Italy differ from Venice in Las Vegas? 🎧 Listen and read to find out.

*It's the perfect picture postcard: the sun shimmers on the blue-green water of a canal as gondoliers steer their boats along the water. Along both sides are elegant townhouses. There are no cars to disturb the charm of the scene. If you think this describes the Grand Canal, Venice, you'd be right, but this isn't Venice, Italy, it's Venice, Las Vegas!*

Las Vegas is full of extraordinary places. There's a hotel that is built like an ancient Egyptian Pyramid, a casino complete with an Eiffel Tower, and the Grand Canal Shops – an enormous 46,000 m² shopping mall. It was opened in 1999 and its inspiration is taken from Venice, the city built on water. It's one of the most popular indoor malls in the world, with 20 million visitors arriving every year for an authentic Venetian shopping experience!

As you enter the mall, look up and you'll see some amazing ceiling art inspired by Michelangelo, only remember to watch where you're going! Once inside, you'll be amazed at the attention to detail. Everything in the mall mirrors the floating city, even the streetlights and bridges crossing over the canals. Then of course, there's the fantastic atmosphere: as you stroll past the shops, or stop for a cappuccino, you'll be serenaded by the sweet violins of street musicians. There's also a juggler, an opera trio and a collection of marble statues: but, look twice and you'll see they're actually human!

The living statues line the sides of the canal and pose by the doors of exclusive fashion boutiques selling the finest clothes, including, some of the best Italian designers. Keep walking alongside any of the canals and you'll find they all lead to the mall's star attraction: a replica of St Mark's Square at twilight under a painted Italian sky! Here there are more performances of singers, actors and musicians and a marketplace selling souvenirs of Venice including carnival masks and costumes and pretty Venetian glass from Murano.

Before you leave the square, there's one thing you really must do to complete your day: experience a true tradition of Venice and take a ride on a gondola! The gondolas glide from St Mark's Square for half a mile along the canals, giving you a tour of the mall by water. All of this should inspire you to take a trip to the real Venice one day … I know it's definitely inspired me!

**Review by Sarah Myers. My shopping mall rating: **** (Excellent!)**

**Check these words**

shimmer, canal, gondolier, steer, elegant, disturb, charm, inspiration, authentic, inspire, attention to detail, stroll past, serenade, juggler, living statue, line, pose, exclusive, fashion boutique, replica, twilight, carnival mask, glide

## Vocabulary

**1** **Aim** **To present vocabulary for shops and products**

- Go through the list of products and explain/elicit the meanings of any unknown words or ask Ss to look them up in their dictionaries.
- Go through the list of shops and elicit what type of shop each one is and what type of products it sells.
- Read out the example and elicit similar sentences for the remaining shops and products from Ss around the class.
- Point out that we only use the plural forms of cheeses and meats in special circumstances when we are referring to a variety of different types of cheese and meat (*e.g. cheeses: feta, stilton, cheddar, camembert, etc or cold meats: pastrami, salami, pepperoni, etc*).

*Answer Key*

*You can buy a gold ring at a jeweller's.*
*You can buy sweets and chocolates at a confectioner's.*
*You can buy designer clothes and shoes at a boutique.*
*You can buy high quality cheeses and cold meats at a delicatessen.*
*You can buy contact lenses and sunglasses at an optician's.*
*You can buy cakes and bread rolls at a baker's.*
*You can buy eye drops and aspirin at a chemist's.*

**2** **Aim** **To listen for gist**

- Explain the task and play the recording. Ss listen and say in which of the shops in Ex. 1 each conversation takes place.

**Suggested Answers for Exs 3c, 4, 5, 6, 7 & 8 on p. 101**

### Ex. 3c

*We chose a huge statue of a dragon. Dragons are a big part of our folklore so we thought it would be a good idea. Our dragon is made of steel and fibreglass like the big dinosaur in Alberta, Canada. Tourists climb up to its mouth to get a fantastic view of the surrounding countryside.*

### Ex. 4

*can be transformed (**modal**), is made out of (**present simple**), was first opened (**past simple**), has been toured (**present perfect**), are entertained (**present simple**), have been put (**present perfect**), have been painted (**present perfect**), is made out of (**present simple**), was built (**past simple**), can be seen (**modal**), will be dazzled (**future**), has been carved (**present perfect**), can be bought (**modal**), may be found (**modal**)*

### Ex. 5

1 *Cameras can't be used in the museum.*
2 *The gallery has been visited by lots of people today.*
3 *Souvenirs can be bought in the gift shop.*
4 *The new statue will be sculpted by a local artist.*
5 *Dinosaur bones are displayed by the museum.*
6 *Emma was invited to the wildlife reserve by Paul.*

### Ex. 6

2 *The art gallery opening was called off yesterday.*

- Check Ss' answers and elicit which words helped them decide on their answers.

*Answer Key*

1 *confectioner's (box of chocolate truffles)*
2 *chemist's (sore throat, syrup, lozenges)*
3 *delicatessen (salami, stilton)*
4 *jeweller's (silver earrings)*

## Reading

**3** **Aim** **To introduce the topic and predict the content of the text**

Direct Ss' attention to the picture and the title of the article and elicit what, if anything, Ss know about Venice.

*Suggested Answer Key*

*Venice is a city in Italy. It is famous for its canals and bridges and the gondoliers that take people up and down the canals.*

**4** **Aim** **To listen and read for specific information**

- Ask Ss to read the introduction of the text only and elicit how Venice in Italy is different from Venice in Las Vegas.
- Play the recording. Ss listen and follow the text in their books and find out.

*Suggested Answer Key*

*Venice is a city in Italy. Venice in Las Vegas is a representation of the Italian City.*

3 *A rock concert will be held tonight at Baguio.*
4 *The museum renovation has not been completed yet.*
5 *The art museum was closed for repairs last Monday.*

### Ex. 7

*It was sculpted by Frédéric Auguste Bartholdi.*
*It was started in 1876 and it was completed in 1884.*
*It is made of copper.*
*It was given (to the USA) as a gift from France.*
*It is visited by 3 million people per year.*
*It is a sight not to be missed.*

### Ex. 8

*Wilanów Palace is located in Warsaw, Poland. It was designed by Augustyn Wincenty Locci. It is built in the Baroque style. It was started in 1677 and it was completed in 1696. It was built for the Polish King John III Sobieski but today it is owned by the Wilanów Palace Museum.*

**5** **Aim** **To read for specific information**

- Ask Ss to read the five questions and the possible answers.
- Give Ss time to read the text again and complete the task. Ss, in closed pairs, compare their answers.
- Check Ss' answers.
- Refer Ss to the **Check these words** box and explain/elicit the meanings of the words or ask Ss to use their dictionaries and look them up.

*Suggested Answer Key*

*shimmer (v): to shine with a light that moves*
*canal (n): a long narrow stretch of water*
*gondolier (n): a man who controls a gondola (a long narrow boat steered with a pole)*
*steer (v): to control the direction of a vehicle*
*elegant (adj): beautiful and refined*
*disturb (v): to interrupt or bother sb/sth*
*charm (n): the quaint beauty of sth*
*inspiration (n): a feeling of enthusiasm that gives you new ideas*
*authentic (adj): relating to the real thing*
*inspire (v): to stimulate*
*attention to detail (phr): making sure all the aspects of sth are correct*
*stroll past (phr): to walk slowly and in a relaxed way past sth*
*serenade (v): to sing or play music for another person*
*juggler (n): an entertainer who throws things into the air and catches them again*
*living statue (n): an entertainer who pretends to be a real statue*
*line (v): to form rows along the sides of sth*
*pose (v): to get in a particular position for sb to see or photograph you*
*exclusive (adj): only accessible to a few people*
*fashion boutique (n): a small shop that sells trendy clothes (usually designer labels)*
*replica (n): a copy of sth else*
*twilight (n): the time of day just before nightfall*
*carnival mask (n): a face covering that people wear during a festival*
*glide (v): to move smoothly along*

**6 a)** **Aim** **To expand vocabulary/To match words from a text to their meanings**

- Explain the task.
- Give Ss time to complete the task.
- Check Ss' answers.

*Answer Key*

*interrupt: disturb*
*influence: inspiration*
*attractiveness: charm*
*shines: shimmers*
*remaining on the surface of water: floating*
*not widely available: exclusive*
*copy: replica*

*move gracefully: glide*
*played music to: seranaded*
*try: experience*

**b)** **Aim** **To consolidate new vocabulary/ distinguish between words with similar meanings**

- Explain the task. Give Ss time to complete it, using their dictionaries if necessary.
- Check Ss' answers.

**7** **Aim** **To practise changing the passive to the active**

- Ask Ss to look back through the text and elicit all the passive forms. Check Ss' answers on the board.

*Answer Key – see p. 114(T)*

- Give Ss time to change the passive forms to active forms. Check Ss' answers.

*Suggested Answer Key – see p. 114(T)*

## Speaking & Writing

**8 a)** **Aim** **To make notes on a text**

- Ask Ss to copy the headings into their notebooks.
- Give Ss time to read the text again and make notes under each heading.
- Check Ss' answers on the board.

*Suggested Answer Key – see p. 114(T)*

**b)** **Aim** **To personalise the topic**

Ss work in pairs to write their phone conversation. Monitor the activity round the class. Ask some pairs to act out their dialogues in front of the class.

*Suggested Answer Key – see p. 114(T)*

**9** **Aim** **To express a personal opinion**

- Explain the task and give Ss three minutes to prepare their answers.
- Ask various Ss around the class to share their answers with the class.

*Suggested Answer Key – see p. 114(T)*

**10** **Aim** **To develop creative thinking skills**

- Divide the class into small groups and give Ss time to prepare their answers.
- Ask Ss to be as creative as possible and think of as many attractions as possible.
- Ask various groups to present their imaginary malls to the class.

*Suggested Answer Key – see p. 114(T)*

**5** **Read the text and choose the best answer** *A*, *B*, *C* **or** *D*.

**1** In the text, Sarah Myers is describing
A her trip to Italy.   C the elegance of Venice.
B an authentic Italian city. **D** an amazing shopping experience.

**2** What does the writer say about Las Vegas?
A It is full of foreigners.   **C** It is a weird and wonderful city.
B It has strange houses.   D It is an ancient city.

**3** What does the reader learn about the mall?
**A** The architect took great care to match the actual city in every way.
B The architect loves the city of Venice.
C The people who built it were Italian.
D The architect's only interest was creating a pleasant place to shop.

**4** How has the experience at the mall influenced Sarah?
A She now appreciates the Venetian traditions.
B She can't wait to go again.
C She wants to learn more about Venice.
**D** It has made her want to visit its inspiration.

**5** What is the overall message of the text?

**A** The people who built the mall have gone to great lengths to recreate the city and it is better than the original.

**B** This amazing shopping extravaganza gives you a real taste of Italy with an atmosphere not to be missed.

**C** The mall is so authentic that you don't have to travel all the way to Italy to experience the real thing.

**D** The city of Venice has beautiful examples of Italian architecture with the atmosphere to match.

**6** **a)** Match the highlighted words to their meanings: *interrupt, influence, attractiveness, shines, remaining on the surface of water, not widely available, copy, move gracefully, played music to, try.*

**b)** Choose the correct word.

**1** The gondoliers were **driving/steering** their boats down the canal.
**2** The mall allows you to experience a **true/real** tradition of Venice.
**3** The shopping mall is **authentic/enormous**. You get lost easily in there.
**4** The mall resembles Venice, they have **paid/given** great attention to detail.
**5** Trees **border/line** the sides of the road.
**6** You must **experience/taste** a ride on a gondola.
**7** The film will **inspire/influence** you to travel to Italy.

**7** Find all passive forms in the text. Rewrite the sentences in the active voice.

## Speaking & Writing

**8** **a)** Read the text and make notes under the headings.
Name   Place   What to see   What to do

**b)** Imagine you are in this mall. Call your English pen-friend and tell them about your visit there. Use your notes in Ex. 8a to write your telephone conversation.

**9** **THINK!** In three minutes write a few sentences giving reasons why you would like to visit Venice. Tell the class.

**10** **THINK!** In groups create your own mall. Try to make it as unusual as possible. Present your mall to the class.

▶ Vocabulary Bank 6 p. VB18   105

## Vocabulary
### Music

**1** **a)** In a minute list as many types of music as possible. What's your favourite type of music?

**b)** 🎧 Listen to three music extracts. What type is each?

| 1 | | heavy metal |
| 2 | | grunge |
| 3 | | hip house |

**2** **a)** Write two musical instruments for each category.

| String | Wind | Brass | Percussion |
|--------|------|-------|------------|
| *violin* | *flute* | *trumpet* | *drum* |

**b)** Do you play a musical instrument? If not, which one would you like to learn to play? Why?

## Reading

**3** Look at the musician in the picture. Why is he called the 'ice musician'? Read through to find out.

**4** Read the text again. Four sentences are missing. Match the sentences (A-E) to the gaps (1-4). There is one extra sentence.

**A** Even though he only used the horn 50 times, it was worth it.

**B** He experimented by making percussion instruments from icicles.

**C** Have they tuned in to his music?

**D** If the success of his music so far is anything to go on, then it looks like it is.

**E** Terje also says that the temperature inside the concert hall affects the sound of the music.

*Terje Isungset, is a Norwegian-born musician, who has developed a unique way of using ice to make music. He thinks it is the music of the future and he could be right!*

Isungset had been a percussionist playing drums in different bands for many years when his music suddenly took a whole new direction. He said that his interest in ice music began when he played at a concert held behind a frozen waterfall. As he played his music he **wondered** what kind of sounds he could get out of ice. **1** ☐ He soon moved on to making other instruments from ice, including horns, harps and trumpets. He has even made ice guitars, ice harps and an ice didgeridoo. Isungset is the world's only ice musician, **composing** music just for ice instruments, he makes. Terje calls his ice music chill-out music.

His instruments aren't just made out of any old ice, either. He gets blocks from glaciers and some of the ice he uses is hundreds of years old. According to Isungset, the quality of the ice **affects** the quality of the sound the ice instrument produces. Another problem with ice instruments is that they only last for one or two concerts before they melt. He has a crew who bring freezers to the concerts and as soon as he's finished playing an instrument the crew puts it straight into the deep freeze. **2** ☐ Although, as far as he is concerned, it is up to nature what kind of music he makes during a performance. Terje said that he wanted to raise people's **awareness** of nature through his instruments and ice music.

So why does Terje want to play music that is so different? He said that the only way he could escape normal musical traditions was to change the instruments he used as well as the way he **approached** music. But what about music fans? **3** ☐ Isungset has recently been busy with a concert tour across Europe. He has also recorded six albums of ice music, which have received good reviews from music critics and are **in demand** by his fans. Even though he's very busy with all his projects, he still finds time to run the Ice Music Festival in Geilo, Norway, which he started in 2006.

So what does the future hold for Isungset? Is ice music here to stay? **4** ☐ The music he creates is beautiful and the sounds from his instruments are ones that you would never expect to hear. Isungset is a very talented musician who, with the help of Mother Nature, makes very beautiful music.

## Vocabulary

**1 a) Aim** **To brainstorm for topic-related vocabulary (music)**

- Set a one-minute time limit and ask Ss to write down as many types of music as they can think of.
- Check Ss' answers.
- Elicit Ss' favourite types of music from around the class.

*Suggested Answer Key*

*pop, rock, rap, heavy metal, folk, soul, hip hop, jazz, electronic, classical, blues, house, etc*

**b) Aim** **To identify musical genres**

- Go through the three music genres and then play the recording.
- Ss listen and match the extracts to the genres.
- Check Ss' answers.

*Answer Key*

1  *Extract 2*     2  *Extract 3*     3  *Extract 1*

**2 a) Aim** **To brainstorm for topic-related vocabulary (musical instruments)**

- Ask Ss to write the categories into their notebooks and explain/elicit what they are.
- Give Ss some time to think of two more instruments for each category.
- Check Ss' answers on the board.

*Suggested Answer Key*

**String:** *cello, guitar*
**Wind:** *oboe, clarinet*
**Brass:** *trombone, French horn*
**Percussion:** *xylophone, cymbals*

**b) Aim** **To personalise the topic**

Read the rubric aloud and elicit a variety of answers from Ss around the class.

*Suggested Answer Key*

*Yes, I play the violin./No, I don't, but I would like to play the piano because I like the sound of it a lot.*

## Reading

**3 Aim** **To predict the content of the text**

- Direct Ss' attention to the man in the picture and elicit why he is called 'the ice musician'.
- Give Ss time to read the text and find out.

*Answer Key*

*He is called 'the ice musician' because he makes musical instruments out of ice and plays them in ice music concerts.*

**4 Aim** **To read for cohesion and coherence**

- Explain the task. Give Ss time to read the text again and complete it.
- Check Ss' answers. Ask Ss to say which words helped them decide.

*Answer Key*

1  B  *(he wondered what kind of sounds … – he experimented, percussion instruments – he soon moved on to making other instruments.*
2  E  *(he played at a concert held behind a frozen waterfall)*
3  C  *(… music fans? – they tuned in … – concert tour around Europe)*
4  D  *(Is ice music here to stay? – … the success of his music …, it looks like it is)*

- Refer Ss to the **Check these words** box and explain/elicit the meanings of the words or ask Ss to use their dictionaries and look them up.

*Suggested Answer Key*

**percussionist (n):** *a person who plays percussion instruments*
**frozen (adj):** *solid because of the cold temperature*
**waterfall (n):** *a place where water flows off the edge of a steep cliff*
**icicles (n):** *long piece of ice hanging from an edge formed by dripping water freezing*
**horn (n):** *a brass musical instrument*
**harp (n):** *a large string musical instrument*
**didgeridoo (n):** *Aboriginal Australian wooden wind instrument*
**compose (v):** *to write music*
**chill-out (adj):** *relaxing*
**glacier (n):** *a large area of ice that moves slowly*
**freezer (n):** *an appliance that allows you to freeze and store frozen food*
**deep freeze (n):** *a freezer*
**escape (v):** *to get away from a place or thing*
**approach (v):** *to deal with or think about sth in a certain way*
**music critic (n):** *a person who writes his opinion on music in newspapers, magazines, etc*
**Mother Nature (n):** *nature*

**5 a)** **Aim** **To consolidate new vocabulary**

- Explain the task and give Ss time to complete it.
- Check Ss' answers.
- Give Ss time to use the phrases in sentences about Isungset.
- Check Ss' answers around the class.

*Suggested Answer Key*

*Isungset was a percussionist whose music **took a new direction**.*
*He was playing in a concert behind a **frozen waterfall** when he became interested in ice music.*
*Now he **composes music** for ice instruments.*
*He calls his music **chill-out music**.*
*He puts the instruments in the **deep freeze** after each performance to prevent them from melting.*
*He says that the quality of the ice can **affect the quality of the sound**.*
*He uses his music **to raise** people's **awareness** of nature.*
*These days he is **in demand** and has recorded six albums so far.*
*He is a very **talented musician**.*

**b)** **Aim** **To expand vocabulary**

- Explain the task.
- Give Ss time to complete the task.
- Check Ss' answers.

*Suggested Answer Key*

***wondered:*** *questioned*
***composing:*** *writing and producing*
***affects:*** *changes*
***awareness:*** *knowledge and understanding*
***approached:*** *dealt with*
***in demand:*** *popular*

**6** **Aim** **To consolidate information in a text**

- Play the recording. Give Ss three minutes to prepare their answers.
- Ask various Ss around the class to share their answers with the rest of the class.

*Suggested Answer Key*

*The message of his music is about the beauty of nature. I think he tries to show people that nature can provide us with everything we need, even music.*

## Grammar

**7 a)** **Aim** **To present reported speech**

- Direct Ss' attention to the table and explain that we use reported speech to say the meaning of what someone said but not their actual words.
- Explain that the tenses change in reported speech and ask Ss to study these in the table. Point out that we don't use inverted commas in reported speech.

- Refer Ss back to the text and elicit examples of reported speech.

*Answer Key – see p. 114(T)*

**b)** **Aim** **To practise say/tell**

- Explain that we use say + that without an object pronoun (he **said that** he liked rock), say + to + object pronoun (he **said to us that** he liked rock) and tell + object pronoun (he **told us** he liked rock).
- Ask Ss to fill in say or tell in the correct form in the sentences.
- Check Ss' answers on the board and elicit the reported sentences from Ss around the class.

*Answer Key – see p. 114(T)*

**8 a)** **Aim** **To present reported questions/orders**

- Read each direct question and the corresponding reported question and elicit how each one is different.
- Explain/Elicit that with question words, we use the same question word in the reported question and with *yes/no* questions we use *if/whether* in the reported questions. Point out that the verb in the reported question is in the affirmative.
- Explain/Elicit that we report orders using *(not)* + *to*-infinitive.

*Suggested Answer Key see p. 114(T)*

**b)** **Aim** **To practise reported questions/orders**

- Explain the task and give Ss time to complete it.
- Then check Ss' answers.

*Answer Key – see p. 114(T)*

**9** **Aim** **To practise reflexive pronouns**

- Write on the board *I made this cake **myself**.* Elicit that *myself* is a reflexive pronoun. Elicit that we use reflexive pronouns to emphasise the subject of the sentence *(I)*. Revise all forms. Refer Ss to the Grammar Reference for more details.
- Read out sentence 1.
- Give Ss time to complete the task.
- Check Ss' answers.

## Speaking

**10** **Aim** **To practise reporting information**

- Divide the class into small groups and explain the task.
- Give Ss time to talk about what they have heard in the news this week and then ask various Ss from each group to tell the rest of the class.

*Suggested Answer Key – see p. 114(T)*

**Check these words**

percussionist, frozen, waterfall, icicles, horn, harp, didgeridoo, compose, chill-out, glacier, freezer, deep freeze, escape, approach, music critic, Mother Nature

**5** a) Fill in: *compose, deep, take, chill-out, demand, talented, raise, affect, frozen.* **Make sentences about Isungset using the completed phrases.**

1 to **take** a new direction
2 **frozen** waterfall
3 to **compose** music
4 **chill-out** music
5 **deep** freeze
6 to **affect** the quality of the sound
7 to **raise** awareness
8 to be in **demand**
9 **talented** musician

b) **Explain the words in bold.**

**6** **THINK!** Listen and read the test. **What message does Isungset's music carry? In three minutes write a few sentences. Tell the class.**

## *Grammar*
### Reported speech
see pp. GR9-GR10

**7** a) **Read the theory. Find examples in the text.**

Direct speech is a person's actual words.
Reported speech is the meaning of what someone said, but not the actual words.

| DIRECT SPEECH | REPORTED SPEECH |
| --- | --- |
| *"I **love** rock," he said.* (present simple) | *He said that he **loved** rock.* (past simple) |
| *"I **am playing** the piano," he said to me.* (present continuous) | *He said to me that he **was playing** the piano.* (past continuous) |
| *"We **will** go out," he said.* (will) | *He said that they **would go** out.* (would) |
| *"I **saw** Terje live," he told me.* (past simple) | *He told me that he **had seen** Terje live.* (past perfect) |
| *"I'**ve met** Terje," he said.* (present perfect) | *He said that he **had met** Terje.* (past perfect) |

Time expressions and some words change as follows:
now → **then**, today → **that day**, tomorrow → **the next day**, yesterday → **the day before**, next week → **the following week**, ago → **before**, this/these → **that/those**, come → **go**, etc

**Note:** *say (without an object pronoun) + that*
*say + to +object pronoun*
*tell + object pronoun*

b) **Fill in *said* or *told*, then report the sentences.**

1 "This song is great," he **said** to us.
2 "We went to a concert last night," she **said**.
3 "We're seeing U2 tonight," she **told** me.
4 "He's played the banjo once," she **said** to me.
5 "I'll buy you Gaga's new CD," he **said**.
6 "He can play the piano," she **said**.
7 "She bought tickets," he **said** to me.
8 "I went to the opera yesterday," she **told** me.

### Reported questions/orders
see p. GR10

**8** a) **Read the examples. How do we report questions? orders?**

| DIRECT SPEECH | REPORTED SPEECH |
| --- | --- |
| *"Where's the music hall?" he asked.* | *He asked **where** the music hall **was**.* |
| *"Is he here?" she asked.* | *She asked **if/whether** he was there.* |
| *"Come," he said to me.* | *He told me **to go**.* |
| *"Don't sing," he said to me.* | *He told me **not to sing**.* |

b) **Report the following.**

1 "How much did the ticket cost?" he asked.
2 "Can we come with you?" they asked.
3 "Are you going to the concert?" he asked.
4 "Don't take photographs," he said to us.
5 "Show me the way," he said to me.
6 "Follow me, please," he said to us.
7 "Turn the radio down," he said to me.
8 "Don't play music that loud, please," he said.

### Reflexive pronouns
see p. GR10

**9** **Read the first sentence. What does a reflexive pronoun express? Complete the sentences.**

1 Terje makes the musical instrument *himself*.
2 We did it **ourselves**.
3 She fixed the door **herself**.
4 Can you help **yourself**?
5 Don't worry. I'll do it **myself**.

## *Speaking*

**10** **Work in groups. Tell the class two things you have heard in the news this week.**

*I heard that Lady Gaga was about to …*

Vocabulary Bank 6 p. VB19

107

# 6g Skills

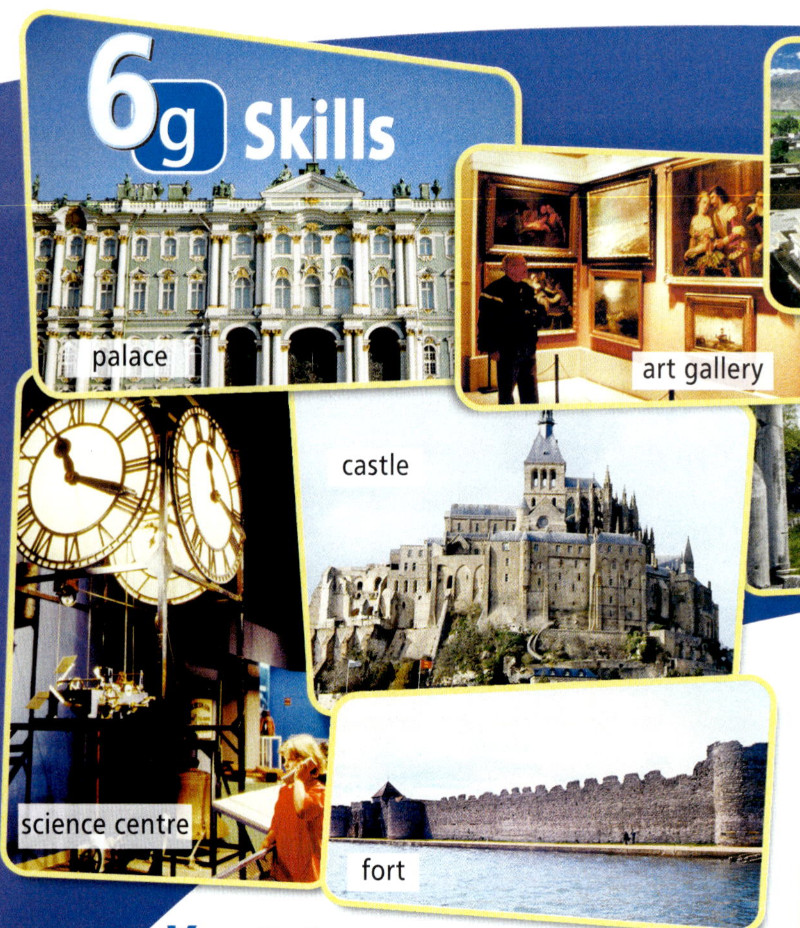


## Vocabulary
### Places of cultural interest

**1 a)** 🎧 Listen and say. Which of these places of cultural interest are there in your town?

**b)** Choose a picture and describe it to your partner.

## Listening

**2 a)** 🎧 Listen to five people talking about visiting different places. Match each speaker 1-5 to the correct sentence A-F. One sentence is extra.

**A** The view from the top was spectacular.

**B** I had the feeling I had travelled back in time.

**C** It was so crowded we had to wait for two hours to get in.

**D** We needed almost a week to see everything.

**E** It was so huge I almost got lost.

**F** There was so much to see we spent the whole day there.

| Speaker 1 | B |
|---|---|
| Speaker 2 | D |
| Speaker 3 | A |
| Speaker 4 | F |
| Speaker 5 | E |

**b)** Compare your answers with your partner. Which words helped you decide?

## Question Tags

see pp. GR10-GR11

**3 a)** Read the theory, then complete the gaps with question tags.

Question tags are short questions at the end of statements formed with an auxiliary verb and a subject pronoun.
Negative sentences take an affirmative question tag. *He isn't here, **is he**?*
Affirmative sentences take a negative question tag. *She is here, **isn't she**?*
We use rising intonation (↗) when we aren't sure of the answer, but we use falling intonation (↘) when we are sure of the answer.

**b)** 🎧 Listen and tick (✓) the correct box to show the intonation.

|  | ↗ | ↘ |
|---|---|---|
| 1 The statue is beautiful, *isn't it*? |  | ✓ |
| 2 He likes painting, *doesn't he*? |  | ✓ |
| 3 You won't go out, *will you*? | ✓ |  |
| 4 He hasn't come yet, *has he*? |  | ✓ |
| 5 Peter left yesterday, *didn't he*? | ✓ |  |
| 6 They are taking photos, *aren't they*? | ✓ |  |

## Speaking
### Expressing preferences

**4** Read the table. Use the language and the places in Ex. 1 to act out exchanges, as in the example.

| ASKING | RESPONDING |
|---|---|
| Do you fancy + -ing form ...? | I'd quite like + to infinitive |
| Would you rather (+ infinitive without to) ...? | Sure – Why not? |
| Would you prefer to ... or (infinitive without to) ...? | Sounds perfect to me. |
| Do you want to ...? | I'd rather not. I don't really ... |
| I'm thinking of going to ... Do you like ...? | I don't like ... much. |
|  | I'm not very keen on ... |

A: *Would you prefer to visit the national history museum?*
B: *I'd quite like to go to the science centre.*



➡ **Vocabulary Bank 6 p. VB20**

## Vocabulary

**1 a)** **Aim** **To present new vocabulary for places of cultural interest**

- Direct Ss' attention to the pictures. Play the recording. Ss listen and repeat chorally or individually.
- Check Ss' intonation and pronunciation.
- Elicit which places are in Ss' town.

*Suggested Answer Key*

*In my town there is an art gallery and a natural history museum.*

**b)** **Aim** **To describe a picture**

- Ss work in closed pairs and describe one of the pictures to their partner.
- Monitor the activity around the room and ask various Ss to describe their picture to the class.

*Suggested Answer Key*

- *I can see a large palace with blue walls and white columns. There are statues on the roof and gold decorations above every window.*
- *I can see a man looking at paintings. He is in an art gallery. I think they are oil paintings.*
- *I can see a huge temple. It has got several floors. It's white and gold. Behind it there are fields.*
- *I can see an ancient round stone theatre. There are rows of seats round a stage. It's an open theatre. I think it is in Greece.*
- *I can see a boy looking at a huge clock. He is in a science museum. The boy has got fair hair and is wearing a red sweater.*
- *I can see a huge castle. It has got lots of rooms and it's very big. I think it's medieval.*
- *I can see ancient ruins in an open space. There are some white marble columns. They look like they are from ancient Greece.*
- *I can see the skeleton of a dinosaur in a natural history museum. The bones are huge.*
- *I can see an ancient fort. The walls are grey. The fort is by the sea.*

## Listening

**2 a)** **Aim** **To listen for specific information**

- Explain the task and ask Ss to read the sentences 1-6 and underline the key words in each sentence.
- Play the recording. Ss listen and complete the task.

**b)** **Aim** **To compare and analyse your answers**

- Ask Ss to compare their answers for Ex. 2a with their partner.

- Play the recording again and ask Ss to say which words helped them decide.

*Suggested Answer Key*

*Speaker 1 – I could image, through history*
*Speaker 2 – seven days in a row to see*
*Speaker 3 – 300 steps to the top, panorama*
*Speaker 4 – engrossed, didn't notice time passing, very late*
*Speaker 5 – long queues*

**3 a)** **Aim** **To present and practise question tags**

- Write on the board: *He is Spanish, **isn't he**? He doesn't drive, **does he**?* Explain that the underlined phrases are question tags. Explain/ Elicit that we use question tags to confirm information and we use a positive question tag with a negative statement and a negative tag with a positive statement.
- Read out the theory box and elicit further examples from Ss around the class.
- Explain that we use rising intonation when we aren't sure of the answer and falling intonation when we are sure of the answer.
- Give Ss time to complete the question tags for items 1-6.
- Check Ss' answers.

**b)** **Aim** **To listen and mark intonation**

- Explain the task.
- Play the recording. Ss listen and mark the intonation.
- Check Ss' answers.

## Speaking

**4** **Aim** **To express preferences**

- Explain the task and go through the useful language box.
- Read out the example and then ask Ss in pairs to use the places in Ex. 1 and make similar exchanges.
- Monitor the activity around the class and then ask some pairs to express preferences in front of the class.

*Suggested Answer Key*

- A: *Do you fancy visiting the art gallery?*
  B: *Sure – why not?*

- A: *Would you rather visit the castle or the temple?*
  B: *I'd quite like to go to the castle.*

- A: *Do you want to go to the fort?*
  B: *Sounds perfect to me.*

- A: *I'm thinking of going to the palace. Do you like palaces?*
  B: *I don't like palaces much. etc*

1 **Aim** **To read and identify the contents of an email**

- Read the *Writing Tip* aloud and introduce the type of writing.
- Give Ss time to read the email and elicit what each paragraph is about.

*Answer Key*

Para 1:     *opening remarks, reason for writing*
Paras 2-3: *description of the museum and what he saw/did there*
Para 4:     *closing remarks*

2 **Aim** **To improve writing skills using adjectives**

- Explain the task and explain/elicit the meanings of the adjectives in the list.
- Give Ss time to read the sentences (1-5) and replace the adjectives in bold with the ones in the list.
- Check Ss' answers.

*Answer Key*

1  *nice – spectacular*     4  *nice – simple*
2  *best – most famous*     5  *nice – thick, nice – beautiful*
3  *good – impressive*

3 **Aim** **To prepare for a writing task**

- Read the rubric aloud and give Ss time to prepare their answers.
- Check Ss' answers around the class.

*Suggested Answer Key*

1  *Edinburgh Castle*
2  *Edinburgh, Scotland*
3  *It was built in 1130.*
4  *It is a castle with various exhibitions and museums.*
5  *It looks impressive from the outside. It is built on an extinct volcano and its stone walls tower over the city.*
6  *You can go on a free guided tour and see the Great Hall and State rooms. You can also see the Scottish crown jewels there.*

4 **Aim** **To write an email describing a visit to a place**

- Read the rubric aloud and underline the key words. Go through the plan and elicit answers for each bullet point.
- Give Ss time to write their email using their answers from Ex. 3, the useful language in the box and the plan.
- Check Ss' answers.
- Alternatively, assign the task as HW and check Ss' answers in the next lesson.

*Suggested Answer Key*

*Dear Simon,*
*I hope you're well. Thank you for your letter. It will be great to see you. There are a lot of interesting things to see in Edinburgh, but the best is the castle.*
*It was build in 1130 and is the most popular tourist attraction in the city. Visitors can explore museums and exhibitions and go on a free guided tour.*
*I went on the guided tour and saw some amazing things. We walked through the Great Hall which was completed in 1511. It still has its original medieval wooden ceiling. We also saw the Royal Palace. But the highlight was definitely seeing the Scottish crown jewels.*
*I had a wonderful time and learnt so much about the history of the Royal Scots. I think you would love it too.*
*See you soon,*
*Margaret*

## An email describing a visit to a place



### Writing Tip

A descriptive email consists of:
- an **introduction** in which we write our opening remarks and reason for writing.
- a **main body** in which we describe the place (location, sights, facilities, specific details), then, we write what we did and saw there.
- a **conclusion** in which we write our impression, feelings, thoughts about it.

We use a variety of adjectives (huge, ideal, etc) to make our description more interesting to the reader. We use present tenses to describe the place and past tenses to describe what we did and saw there.

**1** **Read the email. What is each paragraph about?**

**2** **Replace the adjectives in bold with** *impressive, simple, thick, spectacular, beautiful, most famous.*

1 The view from the top is **nice**.
2 The palace is the **best** attraction.
3 From the outside the gallery is certainly **good** with its red brick walls.
4 The rooms are furnished with **nice** wooden furniture.
5 There are **nice** carpets on the floor and **nice** paintings on the walls.

**3** **Think of a place in your country that you have recently visited and has impressed you. Answer the questions.**

1 What is the name of the place?
2 Where is it?
3 When was it built?
4 What kind of place/building is it?
5 What does it look like from the outside?
6 What can you do/see inside?

Hi Jane!

**1** I hope you're well! I've just returned from my trip to Krakow. I had a great time and we visited many interesting places. The highlight for me was the Krakow Underground Museum below the city's main market square.

**2** The museum opened in September 2010 and includes medieval artefacts that archaeologists found in the city. Visitors can walk along underground paths and see the ruins of medieval buildings and monuments as well as exhibits of everyday objects such as coins and jewellery.

**3** The entrance to the museum was really amazing. We walked through a smokescreen and as soon as we came out the other side, we all felt like we had gone through a time machine! The first thing I saw was a 3D hologram of a scene from a medieval market, and I could hear sound effects of the hustle and bustle of buyers and sellers. In fact, there were all kinds of high-tech exhibits in the museum. There were even 3D projections of objects that we could 'touch' and 'turn' any way we liked!

**4** I had a wonderful time and got an excellent idea of what life was like in the Middle Ages. I think you would love it too!

See you soon,
Michael

**4** **Read the rubric. Use your answers in Ex. 3, the plan below and the phrases in the Useful language box to write your email.**

> Your English pen-friend, Peter, is coming to your town on a trip. He wants to know which place to visit while there. Write him an email in which: *you suggest a place and give a reason for visiting it, you state where the place is and what it is famous for, you describe the place from the outside and inside, you describe a visit of yours there and how you liked it.* (100-120 words)

### Plan

Dear ...,
**Para 1:** opening remarks, place & reason to visit it
**Paras 2 & 3:** describe the place; describe a visit of yours
**Para 4:** feelings/thoughts about it, closing remarks
Yours,

### Useful language

... is situated/is located ..., It is made of ..., It was built ..., It is an amazing ..., It includes ..., There was/were ..., I had a wonderful time ..., I think you would love it ...

Writing Bank p. WB1 109

*Café Terrace at Night* (Vincent Van Gogh) (1888)

*Stage Rehearsal* (Edgar Degas) (1878-9)

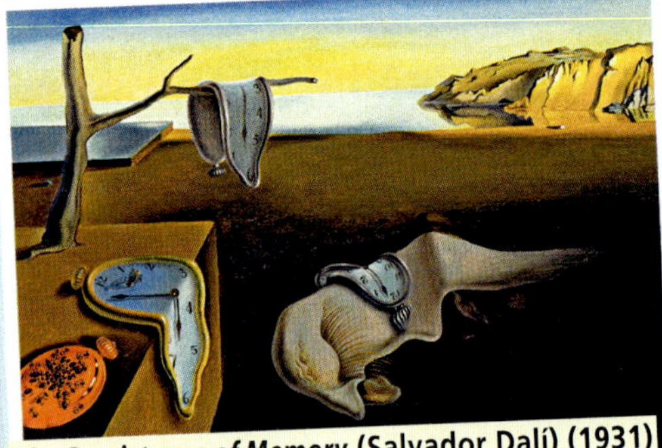

*The Persistence of Memory* (Salvador Dalí) (1931)

# Art Styles

## Surrealism

Surrealism was **founded** by a young group of European artists led by the French poet André Breton in 1924. It was partly created as a **reaction** to the horror of World War I. The group wanted to show that our dreams and thoughts were just as important as the world we can see and touch. They hoped to shock people and make them look at things in new ways. Therefore, their paintings **combined** the world of fantasy with **reality** in **odd** ways, just like in a dream. Salvador Dalí, René Magritte and Marcel Duchamp were some of the most famous surrealists.

## Impressionism

Impressionism was **developed** in France during the last **decade** of the 19th century. The movement was born when a group of French artists, including Paul Cézanne and Edouard Manet, began to paint in a style that broke the strict **conventions** set by the academies. Critics were **outraged**, nevertheless, the movement continued to grow. The Impressionists tried to **capture** moments and sensations, using small touches of paint. Many of them painted outdoors and focused on how the time of day and the season could **affect** a landscape. Other famous Impressionists were Edgar Degas and Pierre-Auguste Renoir.

## Expressionism

Expressionism emerged in the early 1900s and was most concentrated in Germany. The **aim** of the artists was to paint an image that would reflect their **emotions**. Expressionist artists used bright colours mixed with dark brushstrokes and images were often **distorted** to portray anxiety and horror. They were **influenced** by Munch and Vincent Van Gogh. The most famous artists of this movement were Max Beckmann, Jacques Rouault, Wassily Kandinsky and Otto Dix.

> **Check these words**
>
> found, reaction, combine, fantasy, odd ways, develop, strict convention, set, academy, outrage, capture, touches of paint, focus, affect, emerge, concentrate, reflect, brushstroke, distort, portray, influence

**1** Use the phrases to describe the paintings. How do they make you feel? *anxious, confused, excited, shocked*?

- melting watches • seaside and rocks in the background
- ballet dancers rehearsing • people sitting outside a café
- some people walking down a cobbled street

**2** Which art style: *Surrealism, Expressionism* or *Impressionism* does each painting represent? 🎧 Listen and read the texts to find out.

**3** Read the texts and answer the questions. Then, explain the words in bold.

1 How did Surrealism start?
2 What did surrealists want to show people?
3 Who are some famous surrealists?
4 Where and when did Impressionism start?
5 What is Impressionism characterised by?
6 Who are some impressionist artists?
7 What do expressionists aim to do?
8 Why do Expressionist paintings look distorted?

**4** a) **THINK!** Say four things you've learnt from the text. Use the words from the **Check these words** box.

b) **THINK!** Which style of art do you like the most? Why? In three minutes write a few sentences. Tell the class.

**5** **ICT** In groups collect information about another style of art. Present it to the class. Talk about:

- style • when/where started
- famous artists & their works of art • what shows

**1** **Aim** **To describe paintings using key vocabulary**

- Go through the phrases and the adjectives in the rubric and elicit the meanings of any unknown words.
- Ask various Ss to choose a picture and describe it to the rest of the class using the phrases.
- Elicit how each painting makes them feel or which adjectives they associate with each picture.

***Suggested Answer Key – see p. 111(T)***

**2** **Aim** **To listen and read for gist**

- Explain the task. Play the recording. Ss listen and follow the text in their books and match the paintings with the art styles.
- Check Ss' answers.

***Answer Key***

Café Terrace at Night – *Expressionism*
Stage Rehearsal – *Impressionism*
The Persistence of Memory – *Surrealism*

**3** **Aim** **To read for specific information/To expand vocabulary**

- Ask Ss to read the questions 1-8.
- Then give Ss time to read the texts again and answer the questions.
- Check Ss' answers around the class.

***Answer Key***

*1  It started as a reaction to the horror of World War I by a group of young European artists.*
*2  They wanted to show people that dreams and thoughts are important.*
*3  Salvadore Dalí, Rene Magritte, Marcel Duchamp.*
*4  In France In the 1890s.*
*5  It is characterised by small touches of paint.*
*6  Edgar Degas, Pierre-Auguste Renoir, Paul Cézanne and Edouard Manet.*
*7  They aim to paint images that reflect their emotions.*
*8  Because the artists use this technique to portray anxiety and horror.*

- Draw Ss' attention to the highlighted words.
- Give Ss time to find their meanings.
- Check Ss' answers.

***Suggested Answer Key***

***founded:*** *established*
***reaction:*** *response*
***combined:*** *joined together*
***reality:*** *truth*
***odd:*** *unusual*
***developed:*** *formed*
***decade:*** *a period of ten years*
***conventions:*** *styles*
***outraged:*** *extremely angry*
***capture:*** *record a representation of*
***affect:*** *influence*
***aim:*** *goal*
***emotions:*** *feelings*

***distorted:*** *changed from what sth usually looks like*
***influenced:*** *affected*

**4 a)** **Aim** **To consolidate information in a text**

- Refer Ss to the **Check these words** box and explain/elicit the meanings of the words or ask Ss to use their dictionaries and look them up.
- Ask Ss to use these words to say four things they have learnt from the text.

***Suggested Answer Key***

***found (v):*** *to start, set up*
***reaction (n):*** *an action or behaviour that is a result of sth else*
***combine (v):*** *to mix two or more things*
***fantasy (n):*** *a dream or imagined scene*
***odd ways (phr):*** *unusual ways*
***develop (v):*** *to grow and change*
***strict convention (phr):*** *correct way of behaving*
***set (v):*** *to fix, put sth in place*
***academy (n):*** *a society that maintains the standard in a certain field*
***outrage (v):*** *to shock*
***capture (v):*** *to express what sth or sb is really like*
***touches of paint (phr):*** *small dots/marks of paint*
***focus (v):*** *to concentrate on*
***affect (v):*** *to influence sb to change in some way*
***emerge (v):*** *to come out from being hidden*
***concentrate(v):*** *to be all in one area*
***reflect (v):*** *to mirror*
***brushstroke (n):*** *the marks made by a painter's brush on a canvas*
***distort (v):*** *to change sth so it seems unclear*
***portray (v):*** *to show*
***influence (v):*** *to use a power to change others' opinions*

*1  Surrealism was founded in 1924.*
*2  Surrealism combines fantasy with reality.*
*3  Impressionism was developed in France.*
*4  Expressionist paintings reflect emotions.*

**b)** **Aim** **To express a personal opinion, to develop critical thinking skills**

Explain the task and allow Ss time to write their sentences. Then ask various Ss to tell the rest of the class which style of art they like the most and why.

***Suggested Answer Key – see p. 111(T)***

**5** **Aim** **To give a presentation on a style of art**

- Divide the class into small groups.
- Explain the task and direct Ss to the Internet, encyclopaedias or other reference sources to collect information on another style of art.
- Ask various groups of Ss to present their information to the class.
- Alternatively, assign the task as HW and ask Ss to give their presentations in the next lesson.

***Suggested Answer Key – see p. 111(T)***

**Aim** To consolidate vocabulary from the module

- Divide the class into two teams. Each team takes turns writing or saying a sentence with one of the words/phrases in the list.
- Each correct sentence earns one point. If the sentence is incorrect, the team misses a turn.
- The team with the most points, after all the words have been used, wins.

***Suggested Answer Key***

*Archaeologists were amazed when they discovered the **treasure-filled** tomb.*
*Valuable artefacts **remain untouched** in the depths of the tomb.*
*I'd love to see the **terracotta** army.*
*This is a great museum **you really can't miss.***
*Have you ever seen a **dinosaur bone?***
*The lion's head on Kennon Road in the Philippines looks like a **mighty beast.***
*People **come together in unity** at the Garma Festival.*
*A **boomerang** is an Aboriginal weapon.*
*At the Grand Canal Shops in Venice, Las Vegas, the designers have paid great **attention to detail.***
*There are lots of shops and **fashion boutiques** in the mall.*
*You can buy a souvenir **carnival mask** in Venice, Las Vegas.*

*Terje Isungset is a **percussionist**.*
*Terje played at a concert behind a **frozen waterfall**.*
*Terje calls his ice music **chill-out music**.*
*Terje puts his instruments in the **deep freeze** after the concert to preserve them.*
*Impressionism went against the strict conventions set by the academies.*

## Quiz

***Answer Key***

| | | | | |
|---|---|---|---|---|
| 1 | T | | 5 | T |
| 2 | F | (Michelangelo) | 6 | F (Norway) |
| 3 | F | (red clay) | 7 | T |
| 4 | F | (copper) | 8 | F (2010) |

Ss prepare their quiz in groups. Ask Ss to go through the pages of Module 6 and select information to compile their quiz. Ask groups to exchange quizzes, do them, then check their answers.

***Suggested Answer Key***
**Quiz**
1 *The Terracotta Army was found in Japan. (F – China)*
2 *The Big Dinosaur is a roadside attraction in Australia. (F – Canada)*
3 *The Statue of Liberty was completed in 1884. (T)*
4 *The Yolngu tribe is from Australia. (T)*
5 *The Grand Canal Shops is 46,000 m². (T)*
6 *Rene Magritte was an Impressionist painter. (F – Surrealist)*
7 *Wassily Kandinsky was a Surrealist artist. (F – Expressionist)*
8 *The Persistence of Memory was painted in 1931. (T)*

**Suggested Answers for Exs 1, 4b & 5 on p. 110**

### Ex. 1

*In Café Terrace at Night by Van Gogh, I can see a café with chairs and tables outside. There are people sitting outside a café. There is a waiter serving customers at the café. Some people are walking down a cobbled street. It is night-time but the street is well-lit because of the lights from the café. The painting makes me feel excited because the place seems quiet and people look relaxed. I'd love to be there.*
*In Stage Rehearsal by Degas, I can see ballet dancers rehearsing on stage. The director/composer is directing the dancers. Some of the girls have their hands at the back of their necks. The painting makes me feel anxious because the rehearsal seems to be very tough.*
*In The Persistence of Memory by Dalí, I can see melting watches. There is a seaside and rocks in the background. It is a barren landscape. The painting makes me feel confused as it is an unusual landscape.*

### Ex. 4b

- *I like Surrealism the most because the images make you think and look at things in a new way. I like the way the pictures look like images from a dream.*
- *I like Impressionism the most because I like the way the paintings capture moments and sensations. My favourite artist is Renoir.*
- *I like Expressionism the most because I like paintings that have bright colours and that reflect emotions. My favourite artist is Van Gogh.*

### Ex. 5

> **Style:** *Realism*
> **When/where started:** *France 1850s*
> **Famous artists and their works of art:** *Gustave Courbet: Bonjour, Monsieur Courbet, Jules Breton: The Song of the Lark*
> **What shows:** *Bonjour, Monsieur Courbet shows an almost photographic image of three men talking on the road, The Song of the Lark shows a field worker stood listening to birdsong*

*Realism emerged in France in the 1850s as a reaction against Romanticism. They wanted to portray subjects so that they looked objectively real. Artists of this movement include Gustave Courbet and Jules Breton. Bonjour, Monsieur Courbet by Gustave Courbet shows an almost photographic image of three men talking on the road. The Song of the Lark by Jules Breton shows a field worker stood listening to a birdsong.*

## 1 Match the products to the shops.

| | | | | | |
|---|---|---|---|---|---|
| 1 | B | aspirin | A | baker's |
| 2 | E | sunglasses | B | chemist's |
| 3 | F | blouse | C | stationer's |
| 4 | G | cold meats | D | jeweller's |
| 5 | C | pencil | E | optician's |
| 6 | A | white loaf | F | boutique |
| 7 | D | earrings | G | delicatessen |
| 8 | H | cream cake | H | confectioner's |

## 2 Fill in: *excavated, elaborate, armoury, plantation, mural, Aboriginal, brushstroke, authentic, stroll, compose.*

1 Terje Isungset loves to compose music for his ice instruments.
2 The guards had a huge armoury of weapons.
3 Most of the local people pick fruit in the summer at the plantation.
4 A local artist painted a beautiful mural on the wall in the school auditorium.
5 Qin Shi Huang was buried in an elaborate tomb guarded by an army of soliders.
6 You don't have to go to Italy for authentic Italian food.
7 When John was in Australia, he bought a piece of Aboriginal art.
8 I love to stroll along the beach at sunset.
9 When archaeologists excavated the area they found the ancient ruins of a fort.
10 In some Impressionist paintings, you can see every brushstroke.

## Collocations

## 3 Fill in: *statue, burial, roadside, wildlife, holy, attention, living, Mother, odd, natural history*

1 living statue
2 Mother Nature
3 natural history museum
4 wildlife reserve
5 holy ground
6 life-sized statue
7 roadside attraction
8 burial site
9 attention to detail
10 odd way

## Prepositions

## 4 Choose the correct preposition.

1 Wawel Castle is located **at/in** Poland.
2 The soldiers looked ready **for/of** the battle.
3 It was one of the most important archaeological finds **of/in** history.
4 The tomb was surrounded **with/by** terracotta soldiers.
5 The dinosaur is made **up/of** fibreglass.
6 A large selection of dinosaur bones are **in/on** display in the museum.
7 Admittance to the event is **from/by** invitation only.
8 I'd like to send this parcel **with/by** airmail, please.

In teams make sentences. Use words from the list. Each correct sentence gets one point. The team with the most points wins.

- treasure-filled • remain untouched
- terracotta • you really can't miss
- dinosaur bone • mighty beast
- come together in unity • boomerang
- attention to detail • fashion boutique
- carnival mask • percussionist
- frozen waterfall • chill-out music
- deep freeze • strict convention

Mark the sentences *T* (true) or *F* (false). Read through Module 6 and write a quiz of your own.

1 Jorn Utzon designed the Sydney Opera House. ......
2 Moses was sculpted by da Vinci. ......
3 Terracotta is red wood. ......
4 The Statue of Liberty is made of steel. ......
5 Aboriginal Australians have lived there for 40 thousand years. ......
6 Terje Isungset is from Finland. ......
7 The Ice Music Festival started in 2006. ......
8 The Krakow underground Museum opened in 2007. ......

111

## Reading

**1**  **a)**  **Read the rubric, then read the descriptions of people and underline the key words.**

> The people below are looking for a book to read. Read the descriptions of eight new books (A-H). Decide which book would be the most suitable for the following people. For questions 1-5, mark the correct letter A-H.

**1** **Kerry** enjoys going to concerts and wants to know what it is like to play on stage. She also wants to find out more about the way music is made.

**Adam** likes books with a sense of humour. He loves travelling but often hires a car when he goes on holiday because he doesn't like crowds of holiday-makers.

**2**

**Felicia** has recently started an Archaeology degree. She wants to read something for her studies, but prefers books about people's lives.

**3**

**Justin** likes reading about different cultures around the world. He also enjoys travelling to festivals abroad and learning something about the locals and their history.

**4**

**Konrad** has just finished a History degree at university. He likes trips into the countryside at the weekend, but he doesn't have a job yet so can't spend a lot of money.

**5**

**b)**  **Do the task. Read the descriptions of the books and try to find synonymous phrases to the underlined words in the people's descriptions.**

**c)**  **Compare your answers with your partner's.**

## New Books

**A** **On Site** is a book about the men and women behind all the major excavations as well as their amazing finds. In a series of interviews, the writer finds out what got them interested in history and how they got started. It is not an easy read, though, and is perhaps best for university students.

**B** **Speaking Volumes** is for people who want to talk about all the great books, but don't have time to read them. Learn about the characters and plots of 101 of the world's most famous novels. This wonderful book also includes short biographies of the writers. You'll never be lost for words again.

**C** **Are We There Yet?** is an amusing look at a very different kind of road trip. Instead of the historical and cultural sights around the country, this writer introduces us to the roadside attractions that only a few tourists take the time to enjoy. It's a book that tells us that the journey is definitely more important than the destination.

**D** **Living Art** is about Expressionism, Impressionism and Surrealism. As well as discussing the lives of the artists and their art, the writer looks at the historical events behind the different movements. Complete with full-colour photographs, this is a must for any art lover.

**E** **On the Road** is the story of a year in the life of one of the most popular bands in the world, *Drop in the Ocean*. The book follows them as they record a new CD, tour Europe and win top awards. The book has interviews with all the band members as well as the people behind the scenes.

**F** **King of the Castle** is a guidebook for people who want a special holiday far from the city – why stay in a hotel, when you can stay in a castle? This book has a list of all the castle accommodation in the country as well as prices. Even if you're just looking for a short break, there's something here for everyone's budget so buy this book and live like a king!

**G** **A Beautiful Noise** is a history of musical instruments and how they have changed through technology. The writer looks at the past, present and future of a wide variety of musical instruments as well as some of the strange ways that people have made music over the years.

**H** **Getting Together** is a book about different kinds of tribal gatherings worldwide. There's a short description that explains how these celebrations started and why they are important to the tribes. It's a fascinating look at the music, dance and art in distant countries.

**1 a)** **Aim** To identify key information

- Ask Ss to read the rubric and then the five descriptions.
- Explain to Ss that to help them match the people to the books they should work out the key words and phrases in each description.
- Check Ss' answers.

*Suggested Answer Key*

1    ... to *know what it is like to play on stage*./... the *way music is made*.
2    ... *with a sense of humour*./... often *hires a car* when ...
3    ... an *Archaeology degree*./... prefers *books about people's lives*.
4    ... about *different cultures around the world*./... enjoys *travelling to festivals* aboard .../... and *learning something about the locals and their history*.
5    ... the *countryside* at .../... so *can't spend a lot of money*.

**b)** **Aim** To read for specific information

- Ask Ss to read the text and match the books (A-H) to the people (1-5), point out that there are 3 books that do not match.
- Remind Ss that they should look for words or phrases in the book descriptions that say the same as the words and phrases they underlined.
- Allow Ss time to complete the task.

*Answer Key*

1    E    (... *record a new CD* .../... *tour Europe*...)
2    C    (... *amusing* .../... *road trip* .../... *journey* ...)
3    A    (... *men and women behind all the major excavations* .../... *university students*.)
4    H    (... *different kinds of tribal gatherings worldwide*./ ... *how these celebrations started and why* ...)
5    F    (... *in the country* .../... *something here for everyone's budget* ...)

**c)** **Aim** To make a comparison with a partner

- Ask Ss to compare their answers from Ex. 1b with their partner.
- Check Ss' answers and elicit reasoning.

**2 a)** **Aim** **To introduce the topic**

- Ask Ss to read the rubric and then direct their attention to the pictures.
- Elicit what places Ss can see in the pictures.

*Answer Key*

*I can see a park, an archaeological site, an art gallery, a castle, a market and a museum.*

**b)** **Aim** **To practise useful language for making decisions**

- Divide the class into pairs and explain the task.
- Go through the *Useful language* box.
- Ss work in closed pairs.
- Monitor the activity around the class.
- Ask various pairs to act out their dialogue in front of the class.

*Suggested Answer Key*

A: *I think we could visit the park because it's good for us to get some fresh air and exercise.*
B: *I'd rather not go to the park because there's not much to see there. I think it would be a good idea to visit an archaeological site so we can learn about history.*
A: *I couldn't agree more but some people might not be very interested in that. Maybe we could visit an art gallery.*
B: *I'd prefer to go to a museum that an art gallery because it has so much more than just art.*
A: *A museum might be better than an art gallery but it could be fun to go to a market instead.*
B: *I think you're right; it would be fun but not very educational. I think we should visit a castle because we can learn about the history of the place and see beautiful pictures and furniture and maybe even hear a ghost story.*
A: *I couldn't agree more. I think a visit to a castle would be fun and interesting.*

## Listening

**3 a)** **Aim** **To read for specific information**

- Ask Ss to read the rubric then the advert and decide what information is missing in each gap.
- Allow Ss time to complete the exercise then check Ss' answers.

*Answer Key*

| 1 | *number* | 3 | *number* | 5 | *name* |
|---|---|---|---|---|---|
| 2 | *name* | 4 | *name* | 6 | *name* |

**b)** **Aim** **Listening for specific information**

- Play the recording. Ss listen and complete the advert with the correct information.
- Ss check their answers with their partners.
- Check Ss' answer around the class.

*Answer Key*

| 1 | *90 minutes* | 4 | *its pop concerts in* |
|---|---|---|---|
| 2 | *Station Road* | 5 | *the sea* |
| 3 | *3 hours* | 6 | *(lively) nightlife* |

## Writing

**5** **Aim** **To write a postcard**

- Read the rubric aloud and explain the task.
- Give Ss time to write their postcard and remind them to include all the bullet points. Refer them to the Writing Bank for more details.
- Ask various Ss to read their postcard to the class.

*Suggested Answer Key*

*Dear Peter,*
*Greetings from Rome! I'm having a wonderful time and the weather is great. I've visited the Vatican, St Peter's Square and the Basilica. I've also seen the Sistine Chapel. It was really beautiful.*
*Tomorrow, we're going to the Colosseum and the Roman Forum. After that, we're going souvenir shopping.*
*See you when I get back.*
*Brian*

**2** a) **Read the rubric. What places can you see in the pictures?**

> Your class is going on a school trip and your teacher has allowed you to choose from the local places of interest. Look at the pictures and discuss what there is to see and do. Then choose the places that you think most suitable for a school trip.

b) **Do the task in pairs. Use phrases from the Useful language box.**

## Useful language

**Suggesting:** I think we could visit... because (there's lots to do/see.); It would be a good idea to ... because...
**Agreeing:** I think you're right. Then we could ... ; I couldn't agree more.
**Disagreeing:** I don't think it's a good idea ... because...; I'd rather not go... because...

*Listening*

**3** a) **Read the rubric, then look at the advert. What word is each gap asking for i.e. name, date, number, etc.**

> You will hear some information about a city tour. For each question, fill in the missing information in the numbered space.

## CITY TOUR

Tour lasts **1)** ......................

**SHOPPING:** Best place to get souvenirs is **2)** ......................

**SIGHTS AND ATTRACTIONS:** Guided tours at the Roman fort every **3)** ......................
Old Town Hall now known for **4)** ......................
The top of City Road has a view of **5)** ......................

**ENTERTAINMENT:** Woodland Park area famous for **6)** ......................

b) 🎧 **Do the task. Check your answers with your partner's.**

*Writing* (postcards)
*(Writing Bank p. WB7)*

**4** **Read the rubric and do the task.**

> You have received this from your English pen-friend, Peter.
>
> *Are you enjoying your holiday? What's the weather like? What have you done so far? What are you going to do next?*
>
> Write your penfriend a postcard answering the questions (60-80 words).

# 6 Revision

## 1

**Fill in:** *glide, chariot, reign, fossil, pose, highlight, shimmers, steer, icicles, approached.*

1 In some cities there are living statues that **pose** in doorways and on the streets.
2 The **highlight** of our trip was visiting the national museum.
3 In the past people travelled in a **chariot** pulled by a horse.
4 At first, he made musical instruments from **icicles**.
5 I love the way the sun **shimmers** on the blue water.
6 Gondolas **glide** along the canals for half a mile.
7 He changed the way he **approached** music and did something new.
8 The emperor built his tomb during his **reign**.
9 Gondoliers **steer** their boats along the narrow canals with skill.
10 The archaeologist found an interesting **fossil** while he was digging.

*10x2=20 marks*

## 2 Put the verbs in brackets into the correct passive form.

1 A: Let's go to the art exhibition.
   B: I can't. My car **is being serviced** (service) today.
2 A: Has the new museum opened yet?
   B: Yes. It **was opened** (open) by the mayor yesterday.
3 A: **Was this cake made** (this cake/make) by your mum?
   B: No, actually I made it.
4 A: When **will the competition winners be announced** (competition winners/announce)?
   B: Today, I think.
5 A: This art gallery **has been visited** (visit) by millions of people this year.
   B: Really?

*5x2=10 marks*

## 3 Rewrite the sentences in the passive.

1 Visitors mustn't eat food in the museum.
   Food mustn't be eaten (by visitors) in the museum.
2 Shakespeare wrote *Romeo & Juliet*.
   *Romeo & Juliet* was written by Shakespeare.
3 James will paint Sue's portrait.
   Sue's portrait will be painted by James.
4 People can buy tickets online.
   Tickets can be bought online.
5 Photographers have photographed her many times.
   She has been photographed many times (by photographers).

*5x4=20 marks*

## 4 Write the sentences in reported speech.

1 "I live in Warsaw," she said.
   She said that she lived in Warsaw.
2 "We've been to the zoo today," they said.
   They said that they had been to the zoo that day.
3 "He'll meet us here," he said.
   He said that he would meet us there.
4 "I'm thinking of going shopping tomorrow," he said.
   He said that he was thinking of going shopping the next day.
5 "They went to Krakow yesterday," he said.
   He said that they had gone to Krakow the day before.

*5x3=15 marks*

## 5 Match the exchanges.

| | | | | |
|---|---|---|---|---|
| 1 | C | I'd like to post this parcel. | A | What are the choices? |
| 2 | A | How would you like to send it? | B | £3.56, please. |
| 3 | B | I'll send it by airmail, please. | C | Put it on the scales, please. |
| 4 | E | What's in the parcel, please? | D | Thank you. |
| 5 | D | Here you are. | E | It's a gift. |

*5x3=15 marks*

## 6

You went on a trip to an important place in your country. Write an email to your English pen-friend. In your email write:

• when you went  • what you saw

*20 marks*

*Total: 100 marks*


## Check your Progress

• talk and write about an archaeological discovery ____
• write about a building/monument ____
• talk and write about a cultural festival ____
• express preferences ____
• write an email describing a visit to a place ____

**GOOD ✓   VERY GOOD ✓✓   EXCELLENT ✓✓✓**

**6** *Suggested Answer Key*

*Dear Steve,*

*Sorry, I didn't write earlier but I was on a trip to York, one of the most beautiful places in England.*

*We went there last Monday and stayed for a week. I did a lot of sightseeing. What really impressed me was the Jorvik Viking Centre. The museum opened in 1984 and is one of England's most popular attractions. We rode in a time capsule and saw inside Viking houses. We heard people speaking Norse and smelt home-cooked food from a villager's kitchen. It was a great experience.*

*Hope you had a nice weekend.*

*Write back,*

*Richard*

## Suggested Answers for Exs 7, 8a, 8b, 9 & 10 on p. 105

### Ex. 7

*a hotel is built …, It was opened …, … you'll be amazed …, … you'll be serenaded by …*

People built the hotel to look like an ancient Egyptian Pyramid. The owners opened it in 1999. The attention to detail will amaze you. The sweet violins of street musicians will serenade you.

### Ex. 8a

**Name:** *Grand Canal Shops*
**Place:** *Venice, Las Vegas*
**What to see:** *ceiling art, streetlights, bridges, street musicians, jugglers, an opera trio, living statues, St Mark's Square*
**What to do:** *stroll past the shops, stop for a cappuccino, be serenaded, watch performances of singers/actors/ musicians, buy souvenirs, ride a gondola*

### Ex. 8b

A: *Hello!*
B: *Hi, Ann. This is Ben.*
A: *Hi, Ben! Where are you?*
B: *I'm in Venice, Las Vegas.*
A: *I think Venice is in Italy.*
B: *It is but there's another one here in Las Vegas. Actually, it's a huge shopping mall built to look like Venice. You can even see St Mark's square.*
A: *Wow! It must be amazing.*
B: *It is. You can see amazing ceiling art, canals and bridges. You can even take a ride on a gondola.*
A: *Sounds great. What about the shops there?*
B: *You can find everything, from exclusive fashion boutiques to a marketplace that sells souvenirs of Venice like carnival masks and costumes. Oh, and you can have a cappuccino while you're serenaded by the violins of street musicians. I tell you, it's out of this world.*
A: *I wish I was there.*
B: *Don't worry. I've taken lots of pictures to show you when I come back. Have to go now. Talk to you later.*
A: *See you.*

### Ex. 9

*I'd like to visit Venice to ride on a gondola and visit St Mark's Square. I think it'd be amazing to stroll alongside the canal and be serenaded by street musicians.*

### Ex. 10

*Our mall is an Amazon Rainforest mall. There are lots of beautiful plants and trees and birds such as parrots and macaws that live in the treetops and fly around freely. It is warm and sunny all the time. There are cafés and restaurants and shops in the jungle. There is a huge adventure playground for children to play on and a rock climbing wall. Some of the money that the shops make, goes towards saving the real rainforest.*

## Suggested Answers for Exs 7a, 7b, 8a, 8b & 10 on p. 107

### Ex. 7a

*He said that his interest in ice music began when he played at a concert held behind a frozen waterfall.*
*Terje said that he wanted to raise people's awareness of nature through his instruments and ice music.*
*He said that the only way he could escape normal music traditions was to change the instruments he used as well as the way he approached music.*
*Terje also says that the temperature inside the concert hall affects the sound of the music.*

### Ex. 7b

1  *He said (to us that) that song was great.*
2  *She said they had been to a concert the night before.*
3  *She told me they were seeing U2 that night.*
4  *She said (to me that) he had played the banjo once.*
5  *He said he would buy me Gaga's new CD.*
6  *She said he could play the piano.*
7  *He said (to me that) she had bought tickets.*
8  *She told me she had been to the opera the day before.*

### Ex. 8a

*We report direct questions that use question words with the same question word in the reported question. We report Yes/No direct questions with if/whether in the reported question. The verb is always in the affirmative in the reported sentence. We report orders with (not) + to-infinitive.*

### Ex. 8b

1  *He asked how much the ticket cost.*
2  *They asked if/whether they could come with us.*
3  *He asked if/whether I was going to the concert.*
4  *He told us not to take photographs.*
5  *He told me to show him the way.*
6  *He told us to follow him.*
7  *He told me to turn the radio down.*
8  *He told me not to play music that loud.*

### Ex. 10

*I heard that Lady Gaga was about to release a new album. I heard that the price of petrol was going up.*

## Road Features

**1** Match the words (A-M) to the numbers (1-13) in the pictures.

| A | 3 | traffic lights | E | 2 | road sign | I | 7 | pavement | M | 11 | school |
|---|---|---|---|---|---|---|---|---|---|---|---|
| B | 6 | zebra crossing | F | 10 | level crossing | J | 9 | roundabout | | | crossing |
| C | 13 | tunnel | G | 8 | cycle lane | K | 5 | parking metre | | | |
| D | 4 | bus lane | H | 12 | bus stop | L | 1 | streetlight | | | |

**2** Fill in the sentences with the words below.

- zebra crossing • U-turn • tunnel
- pavement • bus stop • road signs
- roundabout • streetlights

1 Make a U-turn, Peter; you're driving the wrong way!

2 Ian waited at the bus stop to catch the bus to the city centre.

3 The streelights usually turn on after it gets dark in the evening.

4 Don't park your car on the pavement! It's for pedestrians, not vehicles, you know!

5 Wait for the cars to stop before you cross the road at the zebra crossing.

6 Jim drove around the roundabout and tried to find the road to the train station.

7 It's easy to find the airport; just follow the road signs.

8 The radio stopped working while we drove through the tunnel.

**3** Match the words with their definitions.

| 1 | B | traffic lights | 4 | D | cycle lane |
|---|---|---|---|---|---|
| 2 | E | bus lane | 5 | A | parking metre |
| 3 | C | level crossing | | | |

A a machine in which you put money to pay for a period of time in a parking space

B a set of red, orange and green lights used to control road traffic

C a place where a road crosses a railway line

D part of a road only for bicycles

E part of a road only for buses

## Speaking

**4** Look at the pictures in Ex. 1. Does the area you live in look like this? Talk with your partner, as in the example.

(See Answer Section)

A: *What is your area like?*

B: *In the area where I live there are wide streets and pavements. There is a zebra crossing for pedestrians and traffic lights too. There is a roundabout, but there isn't a level crossing…*

## Animals

**1** Look at the animal groups (A-H). Read the definitions then put the words below in the correct animal group.

(See Answer Section)

- spider • alligator • mosquito • scorpion
- moose • beaver • raccoon • rattlesnake
- lizard • cobra • woodpecker • ostrich • owl
- wasp • panther • rhino • camel • orang-utan • chicken • tuna • duck • whale
- cricket • dragonfly • turtle • goose
- salamander • salmon • rabbit • frog • ant
- bee • mouse • toad • squirrel

**A**   **mammal** /ˈmæməl/ **(n):** an animal that drinks milk from its mother's body

**B**   **reptile** /ˈreptaɪl/ **(n):** an animal that lays eggs to have babies and which usually has scales on its skin

**C**   **bird** /bɜːʳd/ **(n):** an animal that has wings and feathers and that can usually fly

**D**   **fish** /fɪʃ/ **(n):** an animal that lives in the water and has fins and a tail to swim

**E**   **insect** /ˈɪnsekt/ **(n):** a small animal that has six legs and usually two pairs of wings

**F**   **rodent** /ˈroʊdᵊnt/ **(n):** a small animal which has long front teeth that grow continuously

**G**   **amphibian** /æmˈfɪbɪən/ **(n):** a cold-blooded animal that lives both on land and in the water

**H**   **arachnid** /əˈræknɪd/ **(n):** a small animal that has eight legs

**2** Write *F* (farm animal), *W* (wild animal) and *P* (pet) next to each word.

| | | | | | | |
|---|---|---|---|---|---|---|
| **1** | donkey | F | | **9** | horse | F/P |
| **2** | hamster | P | | **10** | wolf | W |
| **3** | lion | W | | **11** | goat | F |
| **4** | canary | P | | **12** | goldfish | P |
| **5** | cow | F | | **13** | hen | F |
| **6** | bear | W | | **14** | eagle | W |
| **7** | dog | P | | **15** | parrot | W/P |
| **8** | elephant | W | | | | |

**3** Match the pictures to the descriptions, then name the animals.

A

B

C

D

E

F

G
H

I

J

| | | | |
|---|---|---|---|
| **1** | G | It's got a trunk and two long tusks. | *elephant* |
| **2** | F | It's got black and white stripes. | zebra |
| **3** | H | It's got a mane and roars. | lion |
| **4** | E | It's got a horn and lives in the wild. | rhino |
| **5** | J | It's got a hump on its back and lives in the desert. | camel |
| **6** | D | It's got eight legs and spins a web. | spider |
| **7** | I | It's got a shell and walks very slowly. | tortoise |
| **8** | C | It's got a furry tail and large front teeth. | squirrel |
| **9** | A | It's got black and white fur and eats bamboo. | panda |
| **10** | B | It's got fins and lives in the water. | fish/salmon |

## Speaking

**4** Answer the questions. (See Answer Section)

**1** Do you have a pet? If so, what do you call it? Can you describe it? If you don't have a pet, what type of pet would you like to have?

**2** What farm animals are there in your country? What do people use them for?

**3** Have you seen any wild animals? Where? Describe them.

## Places in a city

**1** Match the two columns below. Then label the pictures.

| A | | B | |
|---|---|---|---|
| 1 | community | A | office |
| 2 | car | B | school |
| 3 | post | C | park |
| 4 | town | D | centre |
| 5 | petrol | E | station |
| 6 | high | F | hall |

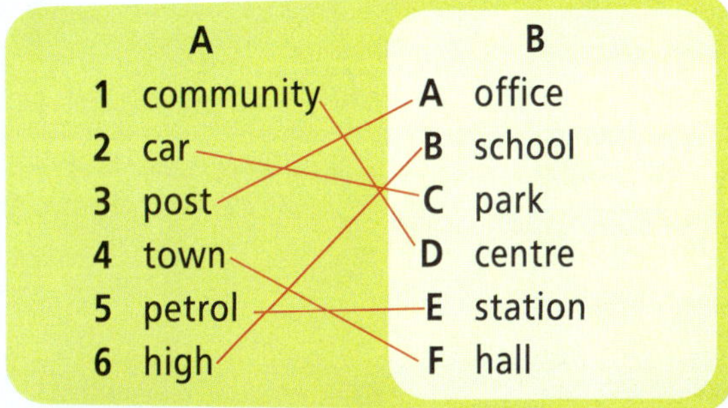

**2** Fill in the sentences with the words below.

- library • hospital • bank • park • gym
- court • office building

1 Jane's mother works as a nurse in a hospital in the city centre.
2 His office is on the 14th floor of a tall office building.
3 Reporters gathered outside the court and waited for the lawyer to arrive.
4 Laura went to the bank to withdraw some money.
5 Jake works out in the gym three times a week.
6 Henry usually goes jogging in the park at the weekend.
7 Ben went to the library last Saturday to return the books he had borrowed.

**3** Match the speech bubbles with the correct place.

- shopping centre • ice rink • bowling alley
- sports complex • spa • childcare centre

I just love going on shopping sprees!

1 shopping centre

I got three strikes in the last game!

2 bowling alley

Let's go ice-skating!

3 ice rink

There's an outdoor swimming pool and a tennis court too.

4 sports complex

I collect my child when I finish work at 3.

5 childcare centre

You can book a beauty treatment for half price on Tuesdays.

6 spa

**4** Write the opposites of the adjectives given.

- safe • quiet • beautiful • historic • clean
- expensive

1 clean ≠ dirty beach
2 quiet ≠ busy street
3 historic ≠ modern building
4 beautiful ≠ ugly hotel
5 expensive ≠ cheap restaurant
6 safe ≠ dangerous place

## Speaking

**5** Use the phrases below to find the places, as in the example.

(See Answer Section)

- borrow books • deposit money
- find many shops under one roof
- receive medical treatment • post a parcel
- fill your car up with petrol
- take the dog for a walk • park your car
- get a marriage licence • go swimming
- learn a new skill • watch a court case

*A: It's a place where you can borrow books.*
*B: It's a library. etc*

**6** Describe your town/city and neighbourhood to your partner.

(See Answer Section)

*Rome is a big city. It's the capital of Italy. There is a hospital and a … . In my neighbourhood there is a park where we take the dog for a walk and a … .*

VB3

### Houses/Dwellings/Characteristics

**1** **Label the pictures.**

- blocks of flats • cottage • detached house
- terraced houses • hotel • mansion
- bungalow • skyscraper • farm

1 bungalow

2 hotel

3 skyscraper

4 hotel

5 blocks of flats

6 farm

7 detached house

8 mansion

9 terraced houses

**2** **Match the words to their definitions.**

| | | |
|---|---|---|
| 1 | D | ranch |
| 2 | A | halls of residence |
| 3 | B | mobile home |
| 4 | C | shelter |
| 5 | F | semi-detached |
| 6 | E | nursing home |

**A** a large building where students live

**B** a large caravan that is used as a house

**C** a place where homeless people can stay

**D** a very large farm where cattle, horses or sheep are raised

**E** a place where old people live and are taken care of

**F** a house that is joined to another house but only on one side.

**3** **Answer the questions.**

1 Do you live in the city or the countryside? I live in the city.

2 What type of dwelling do you live in? I live in a flat.

3 Is your living space spacious or cramped? It is a spacious.

4 What is a typical dwelling in your country? Flats and houses are typical dwellings in my country.

**4** **a)** **Look at the picture and match the words A-H to the numbers (1-8).**

| | | |
|---|---|---|
| A | 4 | entrance |
| B | 5 | basement |
| C | 2 | roof |
| D | 6 | garden |
| E | 7 | fence |
| F | 8 | driveway |
| G | 1 | chimney |
| H | 3 | veranda |

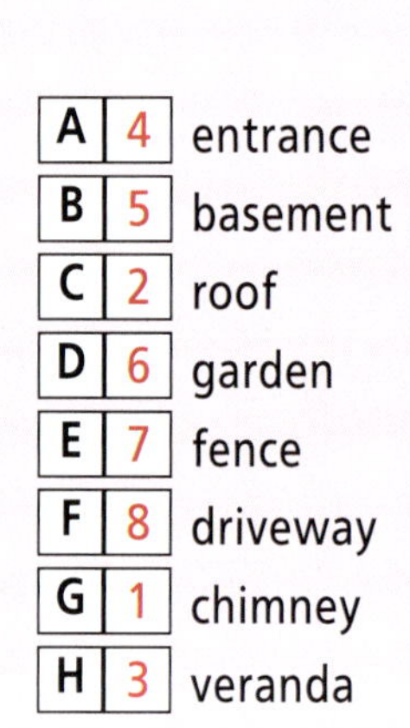

### *Speaking*

**b)** **Now ask and answer questions about the picture in Ex. 4a with your partner, as in the example.**

(See Answer Section)

A: *Where is the garden?*
B: *In front of the house. etc*

**5** **Fill in the sentences with the words below.**

- escape • space • floor • heating • mower

1 Steve ran down the fire escape as soon as he saw the smoke in the kitchen.

2 Kenneth lives in a flat on the first floor of that building.

3 During the winter, the central heating is on every evening.

4 Kate borrowed her neighbour's lawn mower to cut the grass in her garden.

5 Ann finds it difficult to find a parking space near her flat in the city centre.

## Food & Drinks

**1  Match the products to the pictures.**

**Products**

| | | | | |
|---|---|---|---|---|
| 1 cake | 7 lamb chops | 13 coconut | 20 sausage | 27 spinach |
| 2 mussels | 8 grapes | 14 prawns | 21 cheese | 28 chicken |
| 3 spring onions | 9 grapefruit | 15 olive oil | 22 yoghurt | 29 ice cream |
| | 10 steak | 16 bread rolls | 23 milk | 30 lettuce |
| 4 butter | 11 minced beef | 17 peaches | 24 garlic | 31 cabbage |
| 5 pepper | | 18 pineapple | 25 celery | 32 flour |
| 6 lime | 12 lobster | 19 salmon | 26 cauliflower | 33 crab |

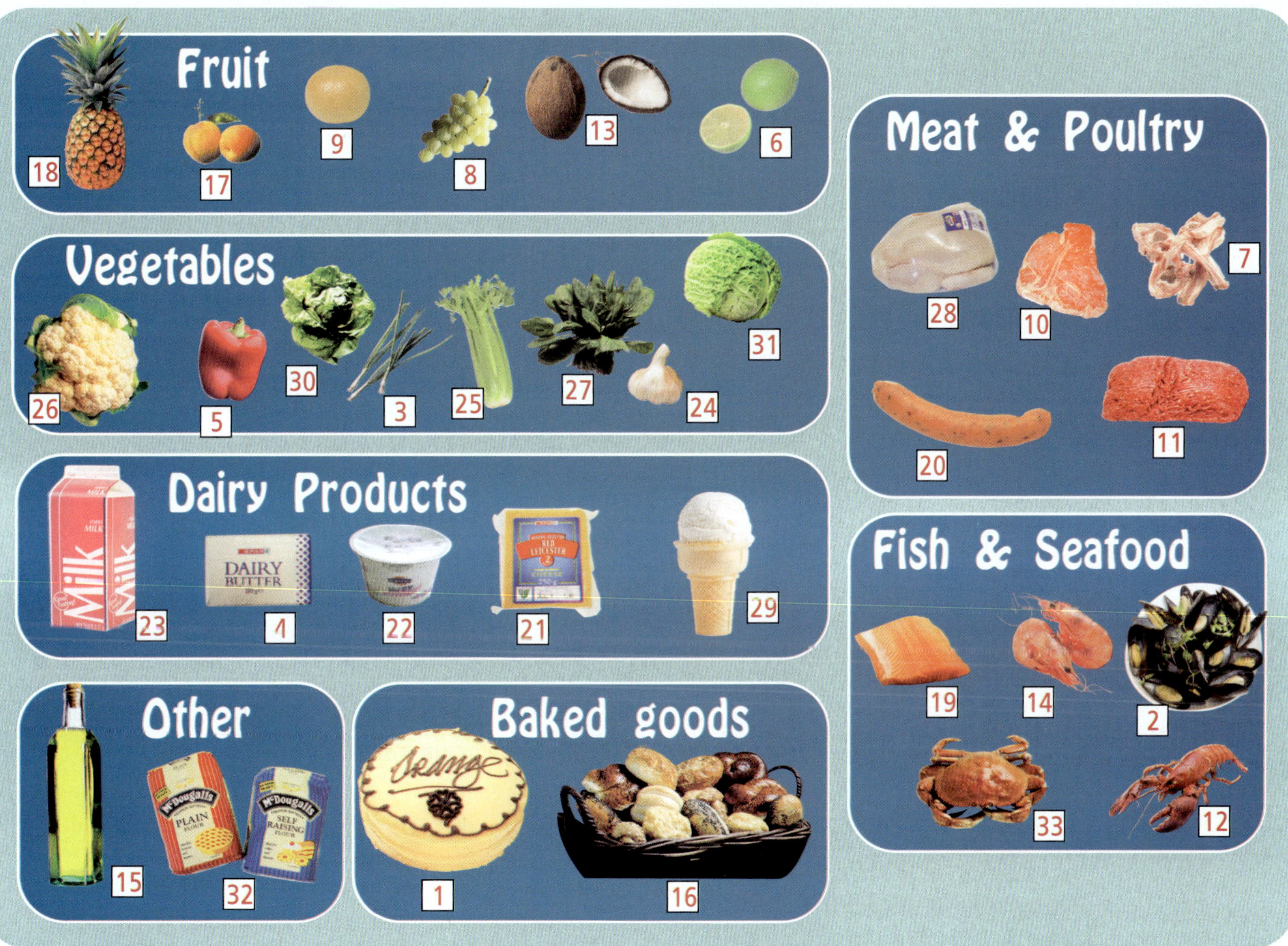


## Speaking

**2  In pairs, ask and answer the questions.**  (See Answer Section)

1  What is your favourite fruit/vegetable? Are there any fruits or vegetables you can't stand?

2  What do you usually eat for breakfast/lunch/dinner?

3  Do you ever go to a market? What do you buy there?

4  Do you know any vegetarians? What do they eat? What do they avoid?

5  What's your favourite dish? What ingredients do you need to cook it?

6  Which fruits and vegetables grow in your country in the summer?

# 

## Weights & Measures

**1** Fill in the gaps in the shopping list with the correct partitive.

- carton • cans • tin • pots • bars • box
- packets • jar • loaves • bag • bunches • tub

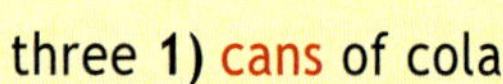

### Shopping list

three **1)** cans of cola

two **2)** packets of pasta

a **3)** carton of milk

two **4)** loaves of bread

one **5)** jar of jam

a **6)** box of cornflakes

four **7)** bars of chocolate

one **8)** tin of beans

one **9)** tub of ice cream

two **10)** bunches of bananas

one **11)** bag of flour

three **12)** pots of yoghurt

**2** What do the following abbreviations stand for? Fill in the table.

- ounces • teaspoons • fluid ounce • litres
- quarts • grammes • tablespoons • gallon
- millilitres • kilogrammes • pounds • pints

| Liquids | Solids |
|---|---|
| 1  1 fl oz milk fluid ounce | 7  2 tsp salt teaspoons |
| 2  5 pt water pints | 8  4 tbs sugar tablespoons |
| 3  2 qt juice quarts | 9  8 oz flour ounces |
| 4  1 gal milk gallon | 10  3 lbs mince pounds |
| 5  2 l water litres | 11  2 kg beef kilogrammes |
| 6  500 ml cola millilitres | 12  220 g cheese grammes |

**3** **a)** Fill in two adjectives for each of the items.

- soft • still • strong • spicy • rare
- sparkling • crusty • white • weak
- well done • mild

**1** rare/well done steak

**2** sparkling/still water

**3** strong/weak tea

**4** soft/crusty bread

**5** spicy/mild curry

## Speaking

**b)** Ask your partner about his/her preferences.

(See Answer Section)

*A: Do you prefer still or sparkling water?*
*B: I prefer still water.*

**4** Underline the correct item.

**1** A: Is there any fruit juice left?
   B: Oh, yes. We still have two **jars/cartons**.

**2** A: The recipe says to add '2 lbs' of flour to the mixture. What's 'lbs'?
   B: They mean add two **pounds/gallons** of flour.

**3** A: How much cheese do we need for the pizza?
   B: About 300 **millilitres/grammes**.

**4** A: Have we got any bread?
   B: Yes, but it's four days old, so it's really **weak/stale**.

**5** A: Is there a lot of pepper in the sauce.
   B: No, just a **tablespoon/pinch**.

**6** A: What are you eating?
   B: A **bunch/box** of grapes.

## At a Restaurant

**1** **Label the items.**

| | | | | | | |
|---|---|---|---|---|---|---|
| **1** | F | dinner plate | | **7** | H | soup spoon |
| **2** | D | soup bowl | | **8** | I | teaspoon |
| **3** | A | water glass | | **9** | J | napkin |
| **4** | K | cup and saucer | | **10** | C | menu |
| **5** | E | fork | | **11** | B | bill |
| **6** | G | knife | | | | |

**2** **a)** **Match the words to form collocations.**

| | | | | | |
|---|---|---|---|---|---|
| **1** | H | read | **A** | a tip |
| **2** | G | call | **B** | the bill |
| **3** | A | leave | **C** | the order |
| **4** | D | serve | **D** | the food |
| **5** | C | take | **E** | the table |
| **6** | F | pour | **F** | the drinks |
| **7** | E | set | **G** | the waiter |
| **8** | B | pay | **H** | the menu |

**b)** **Look at the collocations in Ex. 2a again. What happens before the meal? during the meal? after the meal? Talk with your partner.**

(See Answer Section)

*First, the waiter sets the table … etc*

**3** **Read the dialogue and choose the correct words.**

**Waiter:** Welcome to The Yorke Arms. My name is Ricardo and I'll be your **1) chef/waiter** this evening. Would you like some more time to look at the **2) bill/menu**?

**Man:** No, we're ready, thank you. I'll have the steak with **3) steamed/baked** vegetables for my **4) major/main** course and the vegetable soup for my starter, please.

**Waiter:** And how would you like your steak, sir?

**Man:** I'd like it **5) well done/well made**, please.

**Waiter:** OK. And for you, madam?

**Women:** I think I'll have a fish **6) dish/order** today …. the salmon, please. Oh, and could we have a bottle of **7) dry/still** water?

**Waiter:** Of course. I'll return in a moment with your cutlery and a bread **8) basket/tray**.

## Speaking

**4** **Answer the questions with your partner.**

(See Answer Section)

**1** How often do you eat out? Who do you usually eat out with?

**2** What's your favourite restaurant in your town/city? Why do you like it?

# Vocabulary Bank **2**

## Cooking Methods

**1** Look at the pictures and complete the gaps with the right word.

• mash • peel • simmer • bake • grate • stir • fry • grill • slice

**2** Match the instructions to the pictures.

| 1 | F | Break the eggs. |
| 2 | B | Add 50 ml of milk. |
| 3 | D | Beat well. |
| 4 | A | Melt butter in a pan. |
| 5 | G | Pour butter in the egg mixture. |
| 6 | E | Pour mixture into a frying pan and stir constantly. Leave on the heat until done. |
| 7 | C | Serve with two slices of toast. |

**3** Read the recipe and choose the correct word.

### Pasta in Tomato Sauce

1 First, **wash/grease** the vegetables.
2 Then, **chop/peel** two onions into small pieces.
3 **Fry/Bake** the onions in olive oil.
4 **Add/Put** three chopped tomatoes and some oregano and let the sauce simmer for 20 minutes.
5 **Boil/Mix** 500 g pasta in water for around 10 minutes.
6 When it is ready, **drain/pour** the water.
7 **Put/Add** the pasta on a plate and top it with sauce.
8 Finally, **sprinkle/beat** some cheese on top and serve.

## Speaking

**4** Match the cooking methods to the foods. Which is your favourite way to eat these foods? Discuss with your partner, as in the example.

(See Answer Section)

| 1 | fried | A, B, C, D, E, F | |
| 2 | baked | A, D | **A** potatoes |
| 3 | boiled | A, B, C, F | **B** eggs |
| 4 | grilled | C, D, E | **C** vegetables |
| 5 | roast | A, C, E | **D** fish |
| 6 | scrambled | B | **E** beef |
| 7 | mashed | A, C | **F** rice |
| 8 | steamed | C, D, F | |

*A: How do you like to eat potatoes: boiled, mashed or fried?*

*B: Actually, I prefer roast potatoes. etc*

## Crime

**1** **Label the pictures with the verbs.**

- kidnap • rob • exceed • burgle • spray
- set • pick • mug

**1** **set** fire to a building

**2** **exceed** the speed limit

**3** **mug** a person

**4** **kidnap** a child

**5** **pick** someone's pocket

**6** **burgle** a house

**7** **rob** a bank

**8** **spray** paint on a statue

**2** **Complete the words.**

**1** When someone steals goods from a shop, s/he commits the offence of… Shoplifting

**2** When someone steals a car, s/he commits… Car Theft

**3** When someone drives too fast, s/he commits the offence of… Speeding

**4** When someone uses violence to take control of a plane, s/he commits the offence of… Hijacking

**5** When someone causes a fire in a building or forest, s/he commits… Arson

**6** When someone kills another person s/he commits… Murder

**3** **Fill in the table, as in the example.**

| | VERB | CRIME | CRIMINAL |
|---|---|---|---|
| 1 | *vandalise* | *vandalism* | *vandal* |
| 2 | murder | murder | murderer |
| 3 | kidnap | kidnapping | kidnapper |
| 4 | spy | spying | spy |
| 5 | burgle | burglary | burglar |

**4** **Read the news report and fill in the words.**

- arrested • escape • victims • serving
- criminal • reported

It's every family's worst nightmare to return home to discover they have been the **1)** victims of a burglary. That's what happened to a family in Bosnia-Herzegovina, but they didn't find a **2)** criminal searching for money or attempting to **3)** escape through a window. Instead, they found a man sleeping on their couch! The family quickly **4)** reported the crime and the police **5)** arrested the man and took him to the police station. The 21-year-old, named Edin M, said that he decided to sit down on the couch for a quick rest and didn't mean to fall asleep. Now though, he has plenty of time to rest; he's currently **6)** serving a long sentence in prison!

## Jobs

**1 a)** Label the pictures with the jobs in the list.

- president • architect • nurse • scientist
- musician • sailor • teacher • painter
- sculptor • singer

1  musician

2  painter

3  architect

4  sculptor

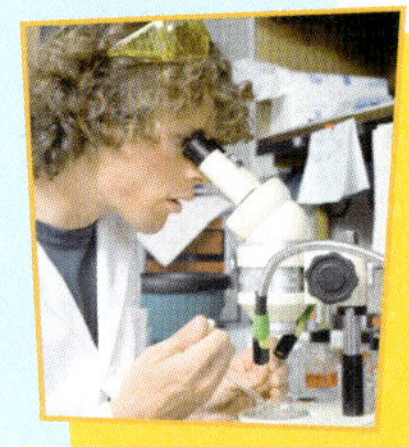

5  scientist

6  sailor

7  president

8  teacher

9  singer

10  nurse

**b)** Look at the jobs in Ex. 1a again and answer the questions.

(See Answer Section)

1  In which of the jobs do you work outside/inside?
2  For which of the jobs do you need a degree?
3  For which of the jobs do you need to wear a uniform?
4  Which jobs involve working with your hands?

**2** Match the jobs to what the speakers say.

| 1 | E | engineer | 5 | A | geologist |
| 2 | C | mathematician | 6 | D | physicist |
| 3 | F | inventor | 7 | B | explorer |
| 4 | G | astronaut | | | |

**A** "I study the rocks that make up the earth."
**B** "I travel to and find out about unexplored regions."
**C** "I study numbers."
**D** "I am a scientist who studies physical objects and energy."
**E** "I design roads and bridges."
**F** "I create new devices."
**G** "I travel to outer space and explore other planets."

**3** What do the people do in their jobs? Match the two columns and then make sentences, as in the example.  (See Answer Section)

| Jobs | | | Verbs | |
|---|---|---|---|---|
| 1 | F | architect | A | work on a ship |
| 2 | E | painter | B | play a musical instrument |
| 3 | B | musician | C | do experiments |
| 4 | A | sailor | D | perform live on stage |
| 5 | D | singer | E | paint portraits of people |
| 6 | C | scientist | F | design buildings |

*An architect designs buildings.*

## Speaking

**4** What qualities does a person doing the jobs below need? Use the jobs in box A and the adjectives in box B to tell your partner, as in the example.  (See Answer Section)

**(A)**
- president • musician • architect • physicist
- teacher • nurse • singer • scientist
- explorer • sailor • painter • sculptor
- engineer • mathematician • inventor

**(B)**
- talented • intelligent • curious • imaginative
- brave • ambitious • sociable • creative
- patient • hardworking • polite • skilful

*A president needs to be intelligent and hardworking.*

## Types of holiday

**1** **Label the types of holiday.**

- backpacking • sailing • camping
- cruise • fishing • walking • horse riding
- cycling • adventure • safari

3  adventure

4  fishing

1  camping

2  backpacking

5  walking

6  cycling

7  horse riding

8  cruise

9  sailing

10  safari

**2** **Choose the correct word.**

1  I always **take/send** a postcard to my best friend when I'm on holiday.

2  In Warsaw, you can **go/visit** many interesting museums and galleries.

3  The best way to **explore/invent** the area is on a bicycle.

4  We can go on a jeep **drive/ride** and see the whole island tomorrow.

5  I'm so tired. I think I'll just **keep/sit** by the pool and relax today.

6  Would you like to go and **buy/shop** for souvenirs?

7  Did you visit the **historic/historical** sites of ancient Rome?

8  Let's try some **local/locally** food in one of the restaurants in the town square.

9  I'd like to **go/do** waterskiing when we finish our surfing lesson.

10  Don't forget to **take/get** photos with your new camera!

**3** **Choose the correct verb to complete each group of sentences.**

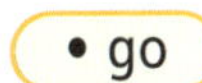

- go    • have    • take

1  We can go on a picnic this afternoon.
Would you like to go on a cruise?
I'd like to go sightseeing around the city.

2  You should take a guided tour through the old town.
We're going to take diving lessons on our island holiday.
They'll take a boat trip this afternoon.

3  I hope you have a great time trekking in the mountains.
Do we have time to go scuba diving this morning?
We're going to have a bite to eat at a local restaurant.

**4** **Complete the sentences so they are true for you.**

1  I don't like crowded beaches when I'm on a beach holiday.
2  When I'm on holiday, I like to relax.
3  My best friend enjoys sunbathing when he/she is on holiday.
4  When I'm on holiday, I hate cycling.
5  My parents' favourite holiday activities are sightseeing and buying souvenirs.
6  My favourite type of holiday is a beach holiday.
7  I don't like adventure holidays.
8  My family never surfs on holiday.

## Holiday activities

**1** **Label the activities.**

- buy souvenirs • go on a jeep ride • windsurf • sail • scuba dive • go snorkelling
- sunbathe • surf • take photos • trek in the mountains • try local food
- visit historic sites • go water-skiing

**1** go snorkeling

**2** go water-skiing

**3** sail

**4** surf

**5** scuba dive

**6** buy souvenirs

**7** go on a jeep ride

**8** take photos

**9** visit historic sites

**10** trek in the mountains

**11** sunbathe

**12** try local food

**13** windsurf

**2** Look at the activities in Ex. 2. Which activities would you do on: a cruise? a safari? a beach holiday? an activity holiday?

| safari | sightseeing holiday | beach holiday | activity holiday |
|---|---|---|---|
| go on a jeep ride | buy souvenirs | go snorkelling | go water-skiing |
| take photos | take photos | sunbathe | sail |
| try local food | visit historic sites | | surf |
| | try local food | | scuba dive |
| | | | trek in the mountains |
| | | | windsurf |

## Holiday problems

**1** **Match the phrases to the sketches.**

• car break down • get a flat tyre • get sunburnt • run out of cash • lose luggage • lose passport
• miss flight • have your wallet stolen

get a flat tyre

run out of cash

have your wallet stolen

lose passport

car break down

get sunburnt

lose luggage

miss flight

**2** **Which holiday problems are these people talking about?**

• crowded beach • don't understand language
• get a fine • get food poisoning • lose way
• lost hotel booking • trapped in bad weather

**1** "It was impossible to communicate! Everything was lost in translation."
*don't understand language*

**2** "I'm sorry. We don't have a room reserved under that name."
lost hotel booking

**3** "I was sick for days! I'm sure it was something I ate!"
get food poisoning

**4** "It was so busy we couldn't find space to swim in the sea!"
crowded beach

**5** "We took shelter in a hut during the storm."
trapped in bad weather

**6** "I didn't realise I was speeding and I had to pay."
get a fine

**7** "You should have asked someone for directions."
lose way

**3** **Match to make phrases. Then make sentences, as in the example.**

• flight • luggage • money • passport
• the train • ticket

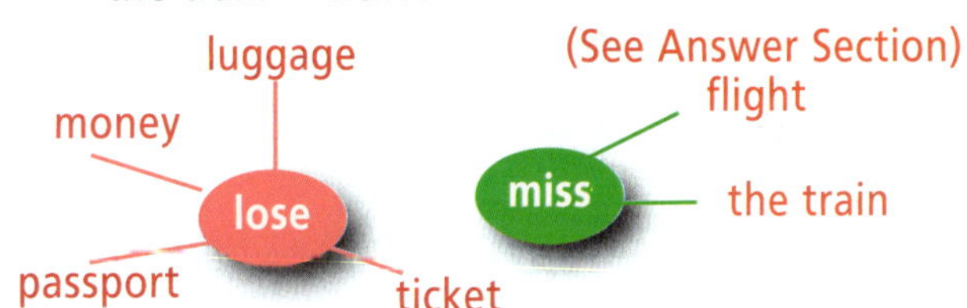


*You may miss your flight.*

## Speaking

**4** **Answer the following questions. Tell your partner.**

(See Answer Section)

**1** Have you ever experienced any of the problems in Exs 1 and 2? Which ones? How did you deal with it? ............................................................
............................................................

**2** What's the worst thing that has ever happened to you while on holiday? ..................................
............................................................

**3** Have you ever got sunburnt? How did you feel? What did you do? ..................................
............................................................

## Natural Disasters

**1** **a)** **Label the pictures.**

- avalanche • tsunami • earthquake
- tornado • hurricane • forest fire
- drought • flood

### *Speaking*

**b)** **Answer the questions.** (See Answer Section)

**1** Which of these natural disasters are common in your country? Which are not?

**2** What would you do to protect yourself if an earthquake happened?

**2** **Choose the correct verb.**

**1** The tsunami has **swept/brushed** some coastal houses out to sea.

**2** A large team of volunteers helped to **clean/clear** the rubble from the streets.

**3** A huge oil spill has **damaged/injured** beaches all across the southern coast.

**4** This charity has been **saving/sending** medical supplies to countries in need for twenty years.

**5** The family **missed/lost** their home during the recent hurricane.

**3** **Fill in the gaps with:**

- endangered • energy • rescue • polluted
- climate • conservation • supply • global

**1** Rescue teams from all over the world came to help save people from the rubble.

**2** Fish that swim in polluted waters are at risk of extinction.

**3** Locals have set up a(n) conservation project to preserve the national park.

**4** With less than 2,500 left in the wild, pandas have become a(n) endangered species.

**5** Rising temperatures and melting ice caps are two serious effects of climate change.

**6** The village has no drinking water, because the local factory has polluted its water supply.

**7** Natural gas is a non-renewable energy resource.

**8** World leaders have met to discuss global issues concerning the war and the economy.

**4** **Complete the sentences with the verbs below.**

- campaigned • destroyed • help • inspected
- made • raised • supports • poison

**1** Elizabeth supports a good cause by volunteering and fundraising.

**2** John went to Africa to help poor people learn how to read and write.

**3** The children made banners to attract locals to the charity event.

**4** Environmental officials inspected the beaches for cleanliness.

**5** Harmful toxins can poison the land and destroy the environment.

**6** Our class raised money for the World Wildlife Fund.

**7** The local residents campaigned for more cycle lanes to help improve air quality in their town.

**8** The forest fire destroyed the habitat of the local wildlife.

## Social Issues

**1** **Label the pictures.**

- racism • war • illiteracy • poverty
- disease • deforestation • overpopulation
- homelessness

1 deforestation

2 homelessness

3 racism

4 illiteracy

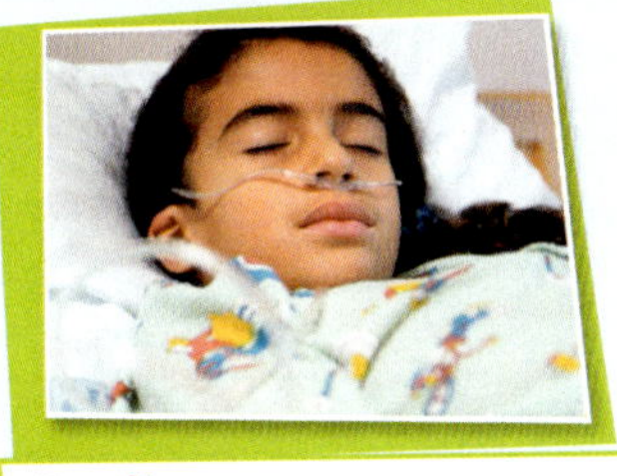

5 disease

6 war

7 overpopulation

8 poverty

**2** **Fill in the sentences with words from Ex. 1.**

1 Millions of families live in poverty, without clean and fresh water, food, health care and education.
2 Since education became compulsory, the levels of illiteracy have dropped significantly.
3 Certain diseases such as mumps and chickenpox are highly contagious.
4 The man has been accused of racism after insulting some colleagues of different ethnic groups.
5 The deforestation of the Amazon Rainforest has resulted in the extinction of many animal and plant species.
6 Mr Jackson served as a commanding officer during the war.
7 The increasing birth rate over the last decade has resulted in the overpopulation of our planet.
8 The only way to reduce homelessness is by providing more free housing.

**3** **Cross the odd one out.**

1 air – water – ~~fire~~ → **pollution**
2 **water** → scarcity – quality – ~~poverty~~
3 **animal** → conservation – habitat – ~~slavery~~
4 **child** → labour – abuse – ~~damage~~
5 **nuclear** → power – ~~rays~~ – energy
6 financial – ~~crime~~ – social → **problems**
7 ~~family~~ – corporal – capital → **punishment**
8 ~~litter~~ – food – water → **shortage**

**4** **Match to make collocations.**

| | | | | |
|---|---|---|---|---|
| 1 | C | freedom | A | warming |
| 2 | D | fuel | B | resources |
| 3 | F | endangered | C | of speech |
| 4 | A | global | D | shortage |
| 5 | B | natural | E | growth |
| 6 | E | population | F | species |
| 7 | H | invasion | G | waters |
| 8 | G | polluted | H | of privacy |
| 9 | J | peace | I | event |
| 10 | I | charity | J | award |

# Vocabulary Bank 5

## Accidents & Injuries

**1** **Label the picture with the body parts.**

- shoulder • chest • finger • wrist • ankle
- leg • head • toe • eyebrow • stomach

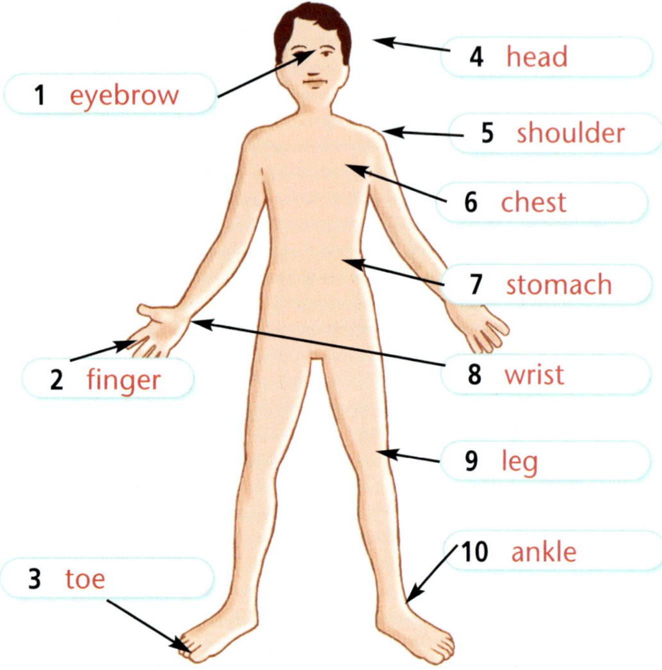


**2** **Match the phrases with the pictures.**

| 1 | F | sore throat |
| 2 | G | runny nose |
| 3 | A | swollen knee |
| 4 | B | sprained wrist |
| 5 | C | upset stomach |
| 6 | D | high temperature |
| 7 | E | splitting headache |

## Speaking

**3** **Answer the questions.** (See Answer Section)

1 Have you ever had the flu? What were the symptoms.

2 Have you ever had an accident? What happened?

**4** **Choose the right item.**

1 She **cut/sprained** her finger while she was peeling onions with a sharp knife.
2 I slipped and **straightened/twisted** my ankle.
3 My dad **hurt/harmed** his back when he fell off the ladder.
4 I **broke/split** my arm when I fell off my bike.
5 As he stood up, Jack **twisted/banged** his head on the shelf.
6 She **pulled/pushed** a muscle while she was exercising.
7 Joseph **bruised/sprained** his eye while playing basketball.
8 Katie **burnt/stung** her hand while she was cooking.

**5** **Complete the dialogue Paul had with a doctor after his accident.**

- stitches • wound • dressing • allergic
- antibiotics • cut

Paul: Hello, Doctor. I fell off my bike and the bleeding won't stop.

Doctor: OK, let me take a look … Well, you've got a deep **1)** cut.

Paul: Oh no, do you think it'll need **2)** stitches?

Doctor: Yes, but first I'll need to clean the **3)** wound and then stitch up your leg.

Paul: How long will it take to heal?

Doctor: It should take a couple of weeks. You'll need to change the **4)** dressing once a day. Also, I'll give you a prescription for some **5)** antibiotics. Are you **6)** allergic to any medication?

Paul: No, I'm not.

Doctor: OK! Then, you're all set!

Paul: Thanks, Doctor!

## Types of Art

**1** **a)** **Label the types of art.**

- painting • collage
- photography
- sculpting • pottery
- filmmaking
- drawing
- architecture

**1** sculpting

**2** painting

**3** photography

**4** architecture

**5** pottery

**6** filmmaking

**7** drawing

**8** collage

**b)** **Match the definitions A-H to the types of art 1-8.**

| A | 1 | art created by shaping stone or wood |
| B | 6 | creation of a series of moving images |
| C | 3 | art of taking and developing images taken on camera |
| D | 2 | visual art in which artists create pictures with paint |
| E | 8 | artistic images made by sticking pieces of paper or photos together |
| F | 4 | design and construction of buildings |
| G | 5 | art of making objects out of clay |
| H | 7 | informal art in which people make pictures using crayons or pencils |

**2** **Complete the sentences with verbs from the list in their correct form.**

- draw • sketch • sculpt • paint • design • take • direct

1 He painted hundreds of works of art with oil on canvas.
2 Becky used her new crayons to draw a picture of her family having a picnic.
3 An architect has to design a building before it can be constructed.
4 She likes using her new digital camera to take photographs.
5 Paul can sculpt shapes from any material, but he prefers using blocks of marble.
6 He directed his latest adventure film with an all-star cast.
7 A police artist can sketch a quick drawing of a suspect.

**3** **Choose the correct word.**

1 I've got a potter's wheel that I make **clay**/steel pots on.
2 He constructed a simple boat made from brass/**wood**.
3 The museum has a majestic **marble**/rock staircase at the entrance.
4 This **bronze**/plastic sculpture was made over two thousand years ago.
5 The statues are carved out of terracotta/**limestone**.
6 Archaeologists found a great deal of precious iron/**gold** jewellery at the site.

## Shops & Shopping

**1** **Label the pictures.** • baker's • boutique • chemist's • confectioner's • delicatessen
• jeweller's • optician's • stationer's

**1** baker's

**2** optician's

**3** chemist's

**4** stationer's

**5** boutique

**6** jeweller's

**7** delicatessen

**8** confectioner's

**2** **Match the products to the shops in the table.**

• aspirin • blouse • bread rolls • cheeses
• chocolates • cold meats • contact lenses
• designer clothes • earrings • eye drops
• paper clips • necklace • envelopes
• olive oil • painkillers • pastries • pens
• ring • rulers • sandwiches • sharpeners
• sweets • evening gown • glasses

| baker's | bread rolls, pastries, sandwiches |
|---|---|
| stationer's | paper clips, envelopes, pens, rulers, sharpeners |
| chemist's | aspirin, eye drops, painkillers |
| optician's | contact lenses, glasses |
| boutique | blouse, designer, clothes, evening gown |
| jeweller's | earrings, necklace, ring |
| confectioner's | chocolates, sweets |
| delicatessen | cheeses, cold meats, olive oil |

**3** **Match to make collocations.**

| 1 | B | window | | A | tag |
|---|---|---|---|---|---|
| 2 | C | shop | | B | shopping |
| 3 | D | fitting | | C | assistant |
| 4 | G | sale | | D | room |
| 5 | A | price | | E | list |
| 6 | E | shopping | | F | card |
| 7 | F | credit | | G | price |

**4** **Fill in the gaps with the correct form of the verb.**

• be • buy • exchange • keep • pay • return
• sell

1 I bought this beautiful dress at the mall at half price.
2 That delicatessen sells the best salami I've ever tasted.
3 If your wife doesn't like the skirt, she can return it and get the money back.
4 I kept the receipt for the DVD player so I could take it back to the shop.
5 Jane can't stop herself from buying something when it is on sale.
6 Is it possible to exchange these jeans I bought for a smaller size?
7 I don't like to use my credit card, so I'd rather pay in cash, please.

## Speaking

**5** **Answer the following questions.**

(See Answer Section)

1 What types of shops are there in your area?
2 What products do you usually buy when you go shopping?
3 How do you prefer to pay for products? In cash/ by credit card?

## Music

**1** **Label the pictures. Then say which musical instruments are: *string*, *wind*, *brass*, *percussion*.**
(See Answer Section)

• accordion • cello • drums • flute • guitar • harp • horn • piano • saxophone
• tambourine • trumpet • violin • xylophone

**1** violin    **2** guitar    **3** piano    **4** harp    **5** accordion

**6** trumpet    **7** saxophone    **8** xylophone    **9** tambourine

   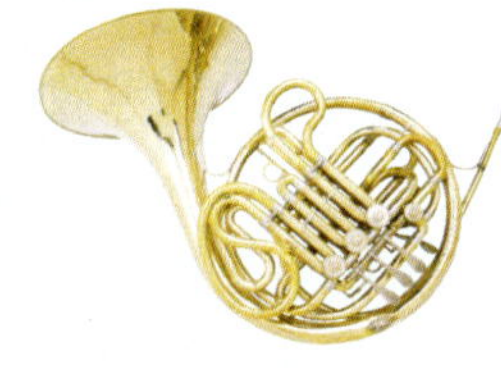

**10** drums    **11** flute    **12** cello    **13** horn

**2** **Fill in the gaps with the correct form of the verbs.**

• play • conduct • sing • listen
• compose • record

**1** John learned how to play the bagpipes when he was a child.

**2** It took him over a year to compose his most famous opera.

**3** The reggae band recorded their latest album in the studio last month.

**4** The famous maestro conducted the orchestra at the opening night of the classic music festival.

**5** The audience were almost in tears when the choir sang the last piece at the performance.

**6** The music students were encouraged to listen to the beats of different types of music.

**3** **Choose the correct word.**

**1** I couldn't help tapping my feet to the **tune/beat** of the music.

**2** It's every young boy's dream to be in a rock **band/crew** one day.

**3** The orchestra has performed in the biggest concert **rooms/halls** around the world.

**4** A lead **musician/singer** needs to have charisma as well as a good voice.

**5** I usually listen to some chill-out **music/concerts** when I want to relax.

**6** This electronic band use digital software and sound **effects/events** to create their unusual style.

## Speaking

**4** **Answer the following questions.** (See Answer Section)

**1** Do you play any musical instruments? If not, what musical instrument would you like to learn?

**2** What is your favourite type of music?

**3** Have you ever been to a live concert? Where did it take place?

## Archaeological Sites

**1** **Match the places to the photographs.**

- ancient theatre • burial site • castle
- fortress • pyramid • temple

**1** castle

**2** pyramid

**3** temple

**4** ancient theatre

**5** fortress

**6** burial site

**2** **Fill in the gaps with:**

- coins • jewellery • masks • statues • tomb
- vase

**1** This huge tomb is the burial site of a famous hero and king.

**2** The ancient vase has a battle scene painted around it and is big enough to hold a few litres of water.

**3** There is an exhibition of priceless bracelets, necklaces and other jewellery at the gallery.

**4** This is one of the oldest bronze statues to ever be discovered.

**5** The archaeologists found some old Roman coins with the face of the emperor on one side and an eagle on the other.

**6** Many of the tribespeople wore ritual masks on their faces during the ceremony.

**3** **Choose the correct word.**

**1** Archaeologists will **excavate**/emerge the rest of the site to discover more about the ancient building.

**2** The team of explorers founded/**found** the ruins of the historic burial site by chance.

**3** Archaeology students are hoping to **discover**/develop the next important artefact at the dig.

**4** These precious jewels were in the pharaoh's **tomb**/burial.

**5** The statue is supposed to reflect/**represent** a mythical hero in battle.

**6** Lots of new artefacts will be **put**/pulled on display at the archaeological museum this weekend.

**4** **Match the adjectives to the correct category.**

- big • crooked • flat • gigantic • hard
- huge • large • miniature • narrow
- rectangular • rough • round • sharp
- smooth • soft • square • tall • tiny • wide

| shape | size | texture |
|---|---|---|
| crooked, flat, narrow, rectangular, round, square, wide | big, gigantic, huge, large, miniature, tall, tiny | hard, rough, sharp, smooth, soft |

## Speaking

**5** **Use the adjectives in Ex. 4 to describe the objects.** (See Answer Section)

**1** *It's a large vase that is wide at the top and narrow at the bottom. It has a smooth surface.*

## Informal emails / letters

Informal emails/letters are pieces of writing we send to people we know well. We usually start an informal email/letter with *Dear* + the person's first name. In the first paragraph, we write our opening remarks *(e.g. Hi! How are you?)* and the reason for writing. We write about specific topics in separate paragraphs. In the last paragraph, we write our closing remarks. *(e.g. Have to go now.)* and sign off with an informal ending *(e.g. Yours)* and our first name.

We use informal style, that is:

- everyday vocabulary
  *(I'm having a great time.)*
- colloquial expressions/idioms
  *(Drop me a line.)*
- informal linkers *(so, and, etc)*
- short verb forms *(I can't, I'll be, etc)*

### Useful Language

**Starting an informal email/letter**
- Dear Mum/Dad, Dear Aunt Claire,
- Dear Grandad, Dear Tom/Lucy, etc

**Opening remarks**
- Hope you're OK. • How are you doing?
- Hi from Moscow/Rome/Kracow, etc
- Thanks for your email.
- Sorry I didn't write earlier, but I … .
- Sorry for not writing for so long.
- Hi! How are you?
- It was good to hear from you.
- I haven't heard from you for a while.

**Reason for writing**
- I wanted to drop you a line to tell you my news/to tell you about … • I just wanted to ask/remind/thank, etc you … • Just a quick email/letter to tell you … • I wondered if you'd like to … • This is just to let you know …
- I'm sorry to hear about … • I was a bit worried and wanted to see if you're OK.

**Making reference to future contact**
- Drop me a line sometime.
- I hope to hear from you soon.
- Give me a call later.
- Let me know if you can make it or not.
- I was glad to hear about … .
- Let me know as soon as possible.

**Closing remarks**
- Email me soon./Write soon.
- I'd better get going./Bye for now.
- I must go now./Got to go now.

**Ending an informal email/letter**
Yours/Best wishes/Love/Take care, etc + your first name.

---

You have received an email from your English pen friend, Mark.

*I like my house but my neighbourhood is very noisy. What is your house like? What is it close to? Do you like your neighbourhood?*

Write him an email and answer his questions.

Dear Mark,

*opening remarks* — *everyday vocabulary*

How are you doing? Sorry for not writing for so long. We moved to a new flat a week ago and we've been really busy. I wanted to drop you a *colloquial expressions* / *short verb forms* — quick line to tell you about my new home.

It's a nice flat on the third floor overlooking a park. There are two bedrooms, a big living room, a big kitchen and a bathroom with both a shower and a bath. I've got my own bedroom.

The neighbourhood is really quiet. There is a butcher's, a chemist's, a greengrocer's and two cafés, but there isn't a cinema or a supermarket. *informal linkers* — What I like most is the huge park. I've made some new friends and we spend most of the afternoons there playing basketball or riding our bikes. I'll send you photos. Unfortunately, my school is quite far away but I go there in a *closing remarks* — car with my dad.

Drop me a line soon!

Yours,

Chris

### Practice

**1** **Rewrite the first paragraph. Use phrases/sentences from the Useful Language section.**

Hope you're OK. Sorry for not writing earlier, but we've just moved and I haven't had the chance until now to tell you about my new house.

**2** **Replace the closing remarks in the email with other appropriate phrases.**

Bye for now. Write soon.

**3** **Suggest a different ending to the email.**

Take care

## Informal messages / notes

Informal messages or notes are short pieces of writing we write to inform people about something, ask them to do something for us, arrange a meeting, etc.

Messages provide all the information needed without being chatty. We usually omit words such as **personal pronouns** (*I, you, etc*) **articles** (*a/an, the, etc*), **auxiliaries** (*am, have, etc*) and **greetings** (*Dear, Yours, etc*).

We can use the imperative, informal linkers, participles and short verb forms. We don't normally write in paragraphs.

### Useful Language

**Starting a message**
Person's first name only, *e.g. Tony/Mark.*

**Reason for writing the message**
• Need to work late.
• Had to go shopping.
• Got phone call from Janusz.
• Richard just called and … .
• Couldn't wait for you.
• Had to go to the *(supermarket)*.

**Making arrangements for later**
• Be back in … *(an hour)*.
• I won't be late.
• Call you later.
• See you at *(the cinema)*.
• Call me if you have any problems.

**Making suggestions**
• How about …?
• We could *(meet)* … .

**Asking for a favour**
• Can/Could you …?
• Please, (… take it to …).

**Ending a message**
• Thanks.
• Cheers.
• See you.

---

You offered to help your English roommate with an assignment, but you need to meet a friend of yours. Leave a note for your roommate. In your message:
• explain why you need to go out
• apologise for the inconvenience
• tell him/her when you are coming back
• tell him/her to call you if he/she needs something

informal linker   participles   omission of article

omission of personal pronoun

short verb forms

use of imperatives

Andy,
John called so meeting him at café. He's leaving for Poland so have to give him some things to give them to my parents. Will be back at 7. If you need something, call me.
Cheers,
Pawel

### Practice

**1** **Read the model below. Why isn't it appropriate? Think about:**

(See Answer Section)

• layout
• way it starts/ends
• chatty language
• omission of pronouns/articles/auxiliaries

**2** **Rewrite it to make it appropriate.** (See Answer Section)

Dear Becky,
Laura telephoned this afternoon. Her dog is sick and she asked me to take it to the vet with her. Unfortunately, this means I cannot come with you to the shopping centre. Would you mind if you go on your own? I might be late. If I finish early, I'll call you so that we meet there. Alternatively, we could go to the cinema. Please send me a text message to let me know if you agree.
Yours,
Anna

## Informal announcements / adverts / notices

Announcements/adverts/notices are short pieces of writing to inform people of an event, job, product, etc. They need to answer the questions: *who, when, where, what, why, how much*. They usually start with a heading *(New Bowling Club, etc)* to attract the reader's attention. We use short sentences and the imperative. We can **bold**, <u>underline</u> or *italicise* words we want to emphasise.

### Useful Language

**Starting**
• We're happy/pleased to announce ...
• New Bowling Club • Attention! • Lost!
• Announcement • Dear friends, • Missing

**Type of event**
• We're pleased to announce *(a contest, an end of the school year party, etc)*
• It's party time. • We're celebrating ...
• We/I lost *(a dog/a bag, etc)*.

**Asking for participation**
• Join us today! • Come and meet ...
• Why don't you come ...?
• We meet every ... . Be there.

**Giving details about participation**
• Everyone's welcome./Everyone can join us.
• You must be *(over 15 years old)*.
• Participants/Those interested need to have experience in ...
• If you like/are interested in ...

**Describing special attractions/extras/prizes**
• There are ... prizes for the first three ...
• All participants will receive (a certificate of attendance) ...
• Prizes include ... CDs of ...
• Special events include *(a party by the pool, a concert with ..., etc)*.
• Free snacks and refreshments for everyone.

**Describing an object**
• It is ...
• opinion: beautiful, cute, etc
• size: huge, small, etc
• age: young, old, etc
• shape: round, square, etc
• colour: red, blue, white, etc
• origin: Chinese, British, etc
• material: cotton, leather, etc

**Contact details**
• If you are interested in ..., call *(John, Ms White)* on *(222222)*.
• To join us call ...
• If you have seen it, please ...
• Call ... on ... for more details.

---

You are studying in England. It's summer and you want to organise a weekend trip. Write an announcement to put on your college noticeboard. Include:
• reason for trip
• where you will go
• the cost of it
• the name and number of who to contact

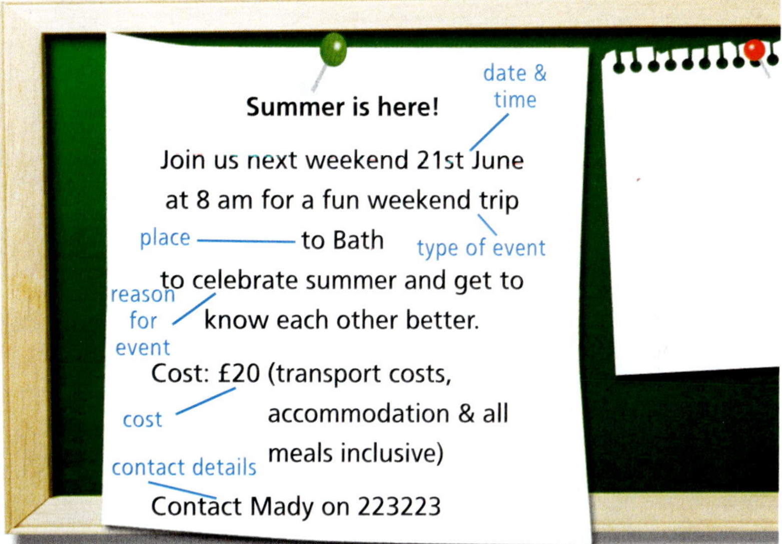


### Practice

**1** **Read the announcement below and answer the questions.** *(See Answer Section)*

> **Digital Art Contest**
>
> St Martin's College is holding its annual
> Art Contest
> on 2nd May
> The contest is open to all student's at college using digital technology as a language of creative expression.
> First prize £500.
> Contact: Sara Hill 01226 421567

**1** What is the event?
**2** What is the reason for the event?
**3** When and where is the event?
**4** What extra information is given?

**2** **Rewrite the part in the announcement that contains the contact details. Then suggest another way to start the announcement.** *(See Answer Section)*

## Biographies

Biographies are written accounts of the series of events in a person's life. They usually consist of:

- an **introduction** in which we give information about the person, that is: date & place of birth, what famous for
- a **main body** in which we write family information, early years, studies and later years (achievements, accomplishments, effects on society etc) in separate paragraphs
- a **conclusion** in which we write our comments and/or feelings about the person. We can also include date and place of death if the person is no longer alive. It is important to present the events of the person's life in chronological order. We mainly use past tenses to write biographies.

### Useful Language

**Giving biographical details**
- ... was born/died in (place) in (year/date etc)
- ... was a famous painter/artist/scientist, etc

**Early years family**
- ... came from a poor family
- ... family was highly respected
- ... parents worked hard to provide their children with ...
- As a child, ... attended ... (school) ...
- At the age of ...
- As a young child, ... was forced to work ...
- ... spent most of his/her childhood in ...

**Later years**
- ... joined the Army ...
- ... studied (subject) in (university)
- ... worked as a ... to pay for his/her studies
- ... it was then that ... (met/decided to join/ left for/applied for/wrote, etc)
- ... when ... was (age), ... met ... and (got married/worked on etc) ... years later ... (had first exhibition, had first child, lost job and ..., got a Nobel for ..., got world recognition, etc) Some of ... most famous (novels, paintings, etc) are ...

**Comments**
- ... actions will always remind people of ...
- ... was one of the most famous ... in the world.
- ... will always remember him/her as ... (the most expressive artist, intellectual person, influential leader, etc) of all ages

---

Your English teacher has asked you to write a short biography about your favourite author. Collect information, then write your composition (100-120 words).

*biographical details*

Charles Dickens is one of the most famous British authors in the world. He was born in Portsmouth England in 1812.

*early years*

Charles was the second of eight children. His family was very poor so at the age of 12 he went to work at a blacking warehouse. As a young boy he enjoyed reading and going to the theatre which helped him develop his imagination.

Dickens was able to leave the factory he worked in and continued his studies at the Wellington House Academy. He taught himself shorthand and started work as a journalist at the age of sixteen. He continued to read at the library and also participated in theatre performances as an actor or stage manager.

*later years achievements*

Dickens published a lot of articles and sketches in magazines. Within a few years he was considered one of the most successful authors of his time. In 1836 he married Catherine Hogarth. Dickens published his novels such as *Oliver Twist* and *Nicholas Nickleby* in monthly installments. He also travelled to the USA and Europe. His travels changed his style of writing. *David Copperfield*, *A Tale of Two Cities* and *Great Expectations* reflect this change.

*comments*

Dicken's health got worse in the 1860s. He died on June 9,1870. He is one of the most widely read novelists and his characters remain the most popular.

### Practice

**1** **Use the timeline below and the notes to write a short biography of the person. What tenses will you use?**

(See Answer Section)

Fyodor Dostoyevsky (**Born:** November 11, 1821 – Moscow
**Died:** February 8, 1881 – Saint Petersburg)
**Famous novels:** *Crime and Punishment*, *The Brothers Karamazov*

1837: Dostoyevsky enters the Army Engineering College
1844: resigns from army – starts writing seriously
1847: writes for St Petersburg *Gazette*
1857: marries Mariya Dmitrieyevna Isayeva
1860: becomes editor of Vremya
1862: travels abroad first time – London
1865: heavily in debt – leaves Russia – writes *Crime & Punishment*
1867: marries Anna Grigoryevna Snitkina
1868: they move to Italy – *The Idiot* is published
1871: he returns to Russia
1879: *The Brothers Karamazov* is first published
1881: he dies

## Formal letters

We write formal letters to people in an official position or people we don't know well *(e.g. Director of Studies)*. We write such letters to apply for a job/course, make a complaint, request information, etc. Formal letters consist of a formal greeting *(Dear Sir/Madam, Dear Mr Smith)*, an introduction that contains opening remarks and the reason for writing, a main body which contains the main topics, each usually in a separate paragraph, a conclusion which contains closing remarks, and a formal ending *(**Yours faithfully,** when we don't know the person's name / **Yours sincerely,** when we know the person's name + our full name).*

Formal style is characterised by:
- formal expressions, advanced vocabulary & longer sentences. *(I am writing to enquire when ...)*
- formal linking words/phrases *(However, In addition.)*
- full verb forms *(I am writing to ...)*
- use of the passive *(I can be reached.)*

### Useful Language

**Applying for a post**
- I am writing to apply for the position of ... advertised in (yesterday's) ... .
- With reference to your advertisement in ... .
- I have been working as a ... for the last ... years.
- I will be available for interview ... .
- I look forward to hearing from you.
- Despite my lack of ... experience, I feel that I would be ... .
- I consider myself to be (punctual, ...).
- I enclose a reference from my previous employer.
- I would be grateful if you would consider my application.
- I am available for an interview any weekday morning.

**Complaining**
- I am writing to express my strong dissatisfaction at the ... .
- I am writing to complain about the quality of ... I recently purchased from you.
- I demand an immediate replacement or a full refund.
- I would appreciate it if ... could be replaced.
- I hope that this matter will be dealt with promptly.

**Asking for information**
- I would like to know if ... .
- I am interested in ... and I would appreciate it if you could ... .
- Do you think it would be possible for me to ... .

You have seen an advertisement in English for a part-time shop assistant in a tourist resort and you want to apply for the post. Write a letter of application (120-150 words) in which you:
- state the job you are interested in & where you saw the advert
- state your age & qualifications
- write about any work experience you have and why you think you are suitable for the job
- state which days/hours you can work and when you are available for interview

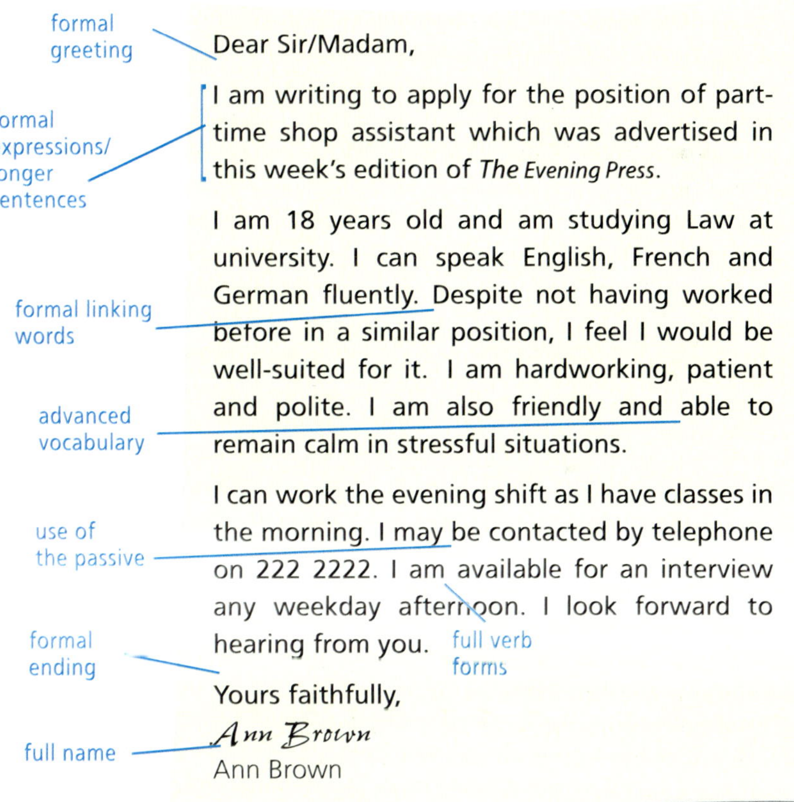


### Practice

**1**   **Read the letter again and find formal expressions to match the informal ones below.**

(See Answer Section)

- I decided to drop you a line.
- I'm good at English, French and German.
- I haven't worked before, but I know I can do it.
- You can call me on ... .
- I can come and meet you ... .
- I can't wait to get your reply.
- Yours,

## Memos

Memos are short pieces of writing we write to:
• provide information
• persuade others to take action
• give feedback on a specific matter

Memos are used mainly in the workplace and the style depends on the audience the memo is for.

Memos follow the format:
To: *(name & job title of recipient(s))*
From: *(name & job title of sender)*
cc: *(name & job title of other recipient(s))*
Date: *(day, month and year)*
Subject: *(what the memo is about)*

We start a memo by stating the reason we are writing it. The first sentence can be a summary of what follows. Then, we present our points in well-structured sentences. We provide only the necessary information and avoid being chatty. We present each piece of information in separate paragraphs. We should sound professional but friendly and can use contracted verb forms. We should avoid using large or uncommon words.

You are the secretary of the school English club. The club has decided to hold a party to celebrate the end of the school year. Write a memo to all members to inform them of the party. In your memo:
• give the reason for the party
• explain your plans for the party
• say who can come
• ask members to respond by a certain date

**MEMO**

specific format

**To:** All members of the English club
**From:** Sharon Anderson, Secretary
**cc:** Paul Jones, Director of Studies
**Date:** 5th June 20....
**Subject:** end of school year party

professional but friendly tone

All members plus one guest each are invited to celebrate the end of the school year. The party will be held on 30th June in Room 4D.

There'll be snacks, music and games.

Please let me know if you are coming by 20th June.

contracted verb forms

short, well-structured sentences

**Practice**

**1** **Read the rubric, then write a memo. Use the ideas below.**

(See Answer Section)

• 6:00 pm - 12:00 pm
• open to teachers, students & their families
• school playground
• bring snacks, cakes, refreshments
• Saturday, 25th, June
• be responsible for various activities
• treasure hunt
• DJ to play music

You are the secretary of Milton School. The school has decided to hold its annual summer party. Write a memo to all teachers which:
• states when and where the party will take place
• says who can attend
• explains how teachers and pupils can help prepare for the event
• explain how they can help at the event itself

## Postcards

Postcards are brief pieces of writing we send to people we know well, usually while we are on holiday. We write them to inform people of our news. Postcards are informal in style. We can omit personal pronouns, articles and auxiliaries and use informal linkers, participles and greetings, contracted verb forms and everyday language.

### Useful Language

**Starting a postcard**
• Dear + person's first *name*, • Dear all,
• Dear Mum/Dad, etc Hi Pawel, etc

**Where you are writing from**
• Greetings from ... . • I'm in ... . It's great.
• I've just reached ... .
• We're here in ... on a ... .

**Activities you are doing right now**
I'm writing this postcard while ... (waiting for the bus to come/having coffee at a seaside café, etc).

**Describing accommodation**
*The hotel is great, it has (a great view of the sea/a huge swimming pool, etc).*

**Activities you do/did/have done/are going to do**
• *Every morning I/we (go swimming/go sightseeing, etc). • Yesterday we (visited/hired a car and .../went on a boat ride, etc). • We've already visited (the aquarium/the museum, etc).*
• *We've tried local dishes. • Tomorrow/Next week we are going to ... .*

**Describing the weather**
• The weather's great/fine/terrible.
• It's getting chilly/hotter, etc.
• It hasn't stopped raining for ... .
• Right now it's raining/snowing ... .
• It's hot and sunny/freezing cold/boiling hot.

**Commenting on something particularly good/bad/funny about the holiday**
• I tried (fried snails), but they were disgusting.
• We went sightseeing on an open-top bus – it was awesome!
• We waited to buy some souvenirs, but we couldn't understand a word – it was so confusing.

**Describing your feelings**
• I'm/We're having a really great time.
• It's the best holiday we've ever had.
• It was the worst holiday ever.

**Asking about the recipient's news**
• What about you? • What are you up to?
• How's your (holiday?).
• I hope you're OK/having a great time/holiday, etc.

**Ending a postcard**
• See you (soon/in three weeks),
• Wish you were here/Best wishes/Kisses/xxx/ Love + your first name

---

You are on holiday. Send your English pen-friend a postcard. In your postcard:
• where you are and who you are with
• write about the weather and your favourite place
• say what you do every day
• describe your plans for tomorrow

Hi Derek,

Greetings from Athens! My family and I arrived on Sunday and we're having a great time. Weather's hot and sunny and there's a beautiful swimming pool in our hotel. It's my favourite place to go. Swim every morning a little then sunbathe until lunchtime. Go sightseeing in the afternoons then try local dishes in evenings. They are delicious. Going on a boat trip around some islands tomorrow.

Wish you were here,

Richard

*Annotations:* informal greeting · informal linker · omission of article · short verb forms · use of participle · omission of personal pronoun · informal ending

## Practice

**1** **Read the model below. Why isn't it appropriate? Think about:** *chatty language, omission of pronouns/articles/ auxiliaries, layout, length*

Dear Dora,

I am writing to you from Rome, Italy's capital city. My family and I decided to come here this summer. I am writing this postcard to you. Hopefully it will be hot again soon.

There are a lot of sights to visit here. Therefore, I go sightseeing every day. I am enjoying that very much. Most afternoons we go shopping and then we have dinner at excellent restaurants near the river. Tomorrow, we are planning to go on a guided tour in the Vatican. I am sure it will be a unique experience.

I am looking forward to seeing you soon.

Yours sincerely,

Jenny

## MODULE 1

### Prepositions of Movement

- We use **prepositions of movement** to show the direction in which someone or something is moving.

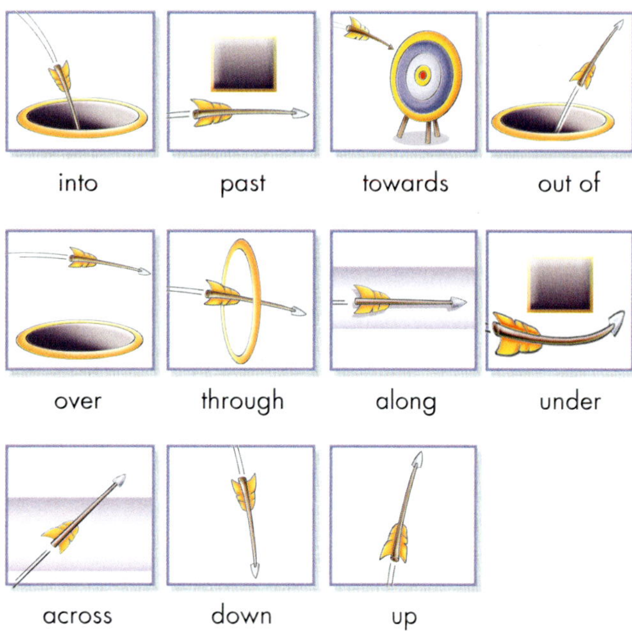


### Present Simple

| AFFIRMATIVE | |
|---|---|
| I/You **swim**.<br>He/She/It **swims**. | We/You/They **swim**. |

| NEGATIVE | |
|---|---|
| **Long Form** | **Short Form** |
| I/you **do not** swim.<br>He/She/It **does not** swim.<br>We/You/They **do not** swim. | I/You **don't** swim.<br>He/She/It **doesn't** swim.<br>We/You/They **don't** swim. |

| INTERROGATIVE | SHORT ANSWERS |
|---|---|
| **Do** I/you **swim**? | **Yes**, I/you **do**.<br>**No**, I/you **don't**. |
| **Does** he/she/it **swim**? | **Yes**, he/she/it **does**.<br>**No**, he/ she/it **doesn't**. |
| **Do** we/you/they **swim**? | **Yes**, we/you/they **do**.<br>**No**, we/ you/they **don't**. |

### Spelling rules (3rd-person singular)
- Most verbs take **-s**.
  *I think – he thinks*      *I turn – he turns*
- Verbs ending in **-ss**, **-sh**, **-ch**, **-x** and **-o** take **-es**.
  *I miss – he misses*      *I wash – he washes*
  *I go – he goes*      *I fix – he fixes*
  *I watch – he watches*
- Verbs ending in a **consonant + -y** drop the **-y** and take **-ies**.
  *I try – he tries*
- Verbs ending in a **vowel + -y** take **-s** only.
  *I play – he plays*

### Use
We use the **present simple** for:
- daily routines or habits.
  *I **get up** at 8 o'clock every day.* (daily routine)
  *He **walks** to school.* (habit)
- permanent states and facts.
  *They **live** in Scotland.* (state)
  *It **snows** every winter in Canada.* (fact)
- timetables. *The train **leaves** at 9 am.*
- general truths or laws of nature.
  *Water **boils** at 100ºC.*

> **Time expressions used with the *present simple*:**
> every hour/day/week/month/year/etc, usually, always, every morning/afternoon/evening/night, at noon, at night, in the morning/afternoon/evening, etc.

### Present Continuous

**Form: subject + *am/is/are* + verb -ing**

| AFFIRMATIVE | |
|---|---|
| **Long Form** | **Short Form** |
| I **am** wait**ing**.<br>You **are** wait**ing**.<br>He/She/It **is** wait**ing**.<br>We/You/They **are** wait**ing**. | I**'m** wait**ing**.<br>You**'re** wait**ing**.<br>He/She/It**'s** wait**ing**.<br>We/You/They**'re** wait**ing**. |

| NEGATIVE | |
|---|---|
| **Long Form** | **Short Form** |
| I **am not** wait**ing**.<br>You **are not** wait**ing**.<br>He/She/It **is not** wait**ing**.<br>We/You/They **are not** wait**ing**. | I**'m not** wait**ing**.<br>You **aren't** wait**ing**.<br>He/She/It **isn't** wait**ing**.<br>We/You/They **aren't** wait**ing**. |

| INTERROGATIVE | SHORT ANSWERS |
|---|---|
| **Am** I wait**ing**?<br>**Are** you wait**ing**?<br>**Is** he/she/it wait**ing**?<br>**Are** we/you/they wait**ing**? | **Yes**, I am./**No**, I'm not.<br>**Yes**, he/she/it **is**./**No**, he/she/it **isn't**.<br>**Yes**, we/you/they **are**./**No**, we/ you /they **aren't**. |

### Spelling rules
- Most verbs take **-ing**
  *play – playing, wash – washing*
- Verbs ending in **-e** drop the **-e** and add **-ing**.
  *make – making, take – taking*
- Verbs ending in a stressed vowel between two consonants double the consonant and add **-ing**.
  *jog – jogging, hug – hugging*
- Verbs ending in **-l** double the **-l** and add **-ing**.
  *travel – travelling*
- Verbs ending in **-ie** drop the **-ie** and add **-y + -ing**.
  *lie – lying*

### Use
We use the **present continuous** for:
- actions happening now or around the time of speaking.
  *She **is studying** in her bedroom **now**.*
  *She **is preparing** for her final exams **this week**.*

- temporary situations.
  *We're staying at a campsite.*
- fixed arrangements in the near future.
  *I'm travelling to London on Sunday.*

**Stative verbs** do not appear in a continuous form as they express a state rather than an action. These include: *believe, belong, hate, hear, know, like, love, need, own, seem, think, understand, want, wish, etc. I love pizza. (NOT: I'm loving.)*

**Time expressions used with the *present continuous*:** now, at the moment, these days, at present, today, tonight, nowadays, etc.

## Present Simple vs Present Continuous

| PRESENT SIMPLE | PRESENT CONTINUOUS |
|---|---|
| permanent states and facts<br>*Bob lives in Ireland.* (state)<br>*It rains in autumn.* (fact) | temporary situations<br>*I'm looking for a new car.* |
| habits/routines<br>*I start school at 9 o'clock every day.* | actions happening at or around the time of speaking<br>*Mum's cooking dinner at the moment.* |
| timetables<br>*The plane arrives at 10 am.* | future arrangements<br>*I'm having a party this Saturday.* |

## Modals (Can – Can't – Could – (don't) Have to – Must – Mustn't)

- **Can** is the same in all persons. The negative of **can** is **cannot** or **can't**.
- We use **can** to:
  - express ability in the present.
    *He can speak three languages.* (He's able to.)
  - ask for permission.
    *Can I look at your dictionary!* (Is it OK if I ...?)
  - give permission.
    *Yes, you can use my laptop.* (You are allowed.)
  - express possibility.
    *You can buy tickets online.* (It's possible.)
- We use **can't** to refuse permission.
  *No, you can't go to the park until you finish your homework.* (You aren't allowed to.)
- We use **can/could** to ask for permission or make a request, in a polite way.
  *Could I close the window, please?* (Is it OK?/May I ...?)
- We use **must** to express strong obligation or duty.
  *You must wear a helmet when you ride a motorbike.* (It's your duty./You are obliged to.)
  We generally use **must** when the speaker has decided that sth is necessary.
  *I must study more.* (I've made the decision to study more.)
- We use **mustn't** to express prohibition. *You mustn't talk in the library.* (You aren't allowed/It's forbidden.)
- We use **have to** to express strong necessity. We generally use **have to** when somebody other than the speaker has decided that sth is necessary.
  *Our teacher says we have to study hard for our maths test.* (It's necessary.)

- We use **don't have to** to express lack of necessity.
  *You don't have to come if you don't want to.* (It isn't necessary.)

## Comparative & Superlative

| | ADJECTIVE | COMPARATIVE | SUPERLATIVE |
|---|---|---|---|
| one-/two-syllable adjectives | short<br>big<br>wide | short**er** (than)<br>big**ger** (than)<br>wid**er** (than) | **the** short**est**<br>**the** big**gest**<br>**the** wid**est** |
| **-y adjectives** | happy | happ**ier** (than) | **the** happ**iest** |
| more than two-syllable adjectives | beautiful | **more** beautiful (than) | **the most** beautiful |
| irregular adjectives | good<br>bad<br>much/many<br>little<br>far | **better** (than)<br>**worse** (than)<br>**more** (than)<br>**less** (than)<br>**farther** (than)/<br>**further** (than) | **the best**<br>**the worst**<br>**the most**<br>**the least**<br>**the farthest/**<br>**the furthest** |

### Form
- With **one-syllable** and **two-syllable adjectives** we add **-er** in the comparative and **-est** in the superlative.
  *small – small**er** (than) – **the** small**est***
- With **adjectives of more than two syllables** we form the comparative with **more** and the superlative with **the most**.
  *expensive – **more** expensive (than) – **the most** expensive (of/in)*

### Spelling
- With **one-syllable adjectives** ending in **-e** we add **-r** in the comparative and **-st** in the superlative.
  *nice – nicer (than) – the nicest*
- With **one-syllable adjectives** that end in **vowel + consonant**, we **double the last consonant** and we add **-er** or **-est**.
  *thin – thinner (than) – the thinnest*
- With **two-syllable adjectives** that end in **-y**, we change the **-y** to **-i** and we add **-er** or **-est**.
  *busy – busier (than) – the busiest (of/in)*

### Use
- We use **the comparative** to compare *one person or thing with another*. We can use **than** with the comparative.
  *Mark is **more intelligent than** Tony.*
  *Trains are **faster than** cars.*
- We use **the superlative** to compare *one person, animal, thing, etc* with *more than two persons, animals, things*, etc in the same group. We use **the ... of/in** with the superlative. We use **in** with the superlative when we talk about a place.
  *The cheetah is **the fastest** animal **of** all.*
  *Judy is **the tallest** girl **in** the class.*
- We use **(not) as + adjective + as** to show whether *two people, places or things* are the same or not.
  *The red dress is **not as expensive as** the blue one.*

For emphasis we use:
- **very + adjective**. *It is very cold today.*
- **much/a lot/far/a little/a bit + comparative form + than**. *He isn't much younger than me.*

## Should – Shouldn't/Ought – Ought not

- We use **should/shouldn't/ought/ought not to** to give advice. *You should be careful with electricty.* (I advise you to.) *You ought to respect the elderly.* (I advise you to.)
- We use should/shouldn't to make suggestions. *You shouldn't eat fatty foods.* (It's not a good idea.)

# MODULE 2

## Countable/Uncountable nouns

- **Countable nouns** are those which we **can count**. They have a **singular** and a **plural** form. *one book - two books - three books, etc*
- **Uncountable nouns** are nouns which we **cannot count**. They **only** have a singular form. Some of these are:

| food | cheese, meat, salt, pepper, butter, bread, etc |
|---|---|
| liquids | coffee, milk, tea, water, lemonade, etc |
| materials | gold, iron, glass, silver, paper, wood, etc |
| subjects | History, Chemistry, etc |
| sports | tennis, football, etc |
| languages | English, Spanish, etc |
| abstract nouns | information, knowledge, love, happiness, beauty, advice, etc |
| other | hair, money, accommodation, luggage, news, furniture, weather, snow, etc |

We can use uncountable nouns with the following partitives (phrases of quantity) when we want to say how much of something there is:

*a bottle of → a bottle of lemonade; a glass of → a glass of water; a carton of → a carton of milk; a cup of → a cup of coffee; a bowl of → a bowl of rice; a bag of → a bag of flour; a slice of → a slice of toast; a loaf of → a loaf of bread; a kilo of → a kilo of meat; a packet of → a packet of crisps; a box of → a box of chocolates; a bar of → a bar of soap; a pot of → a pot of tea; a tub of → a tub of ice cream; a jar of → a jar of honey; a tin of → a tin of soup; a bunch of → a bunch of bananas; a can of → a can of cola*

## A/An – Some/Any/No

| | COUNTABLE NOUNS | |
|---|---|---|
| | SINGULAR | PLURAL |
| AFFIRMATIVE | There is **an** aeroplane. | There are **some** balls. |
| NEGATIVE | There isn't **an** aeroplane. | There aren't **any** balls./There are **no** balls. |
| INTERROGATIVE | Is there **an** aeroplane? | Are there **any** balls? |

| | UNCOUNTABLE NOUNS |
|---|---|
| AFFIRMATIVE | There is **some** butter. |
| NEGATIVE | There isn't **any** butter./There is **no** butter |
| INTERROGATIVE | Is there **any** butter? |

- We use **a/an** in all forms (affirmative, negative, interrogative) with countable nouns in the singular. *There is a cat. There isn't a dog. Is there a hamster?*
- We use **some** in the affirmative with countable nouns in the plural and with uncountable nouns. *I want some lemons and some cheese.*
- We use **any** in the interrogative and **not any/no** in the negative with both uncountable nouns and countable nouns in the plural. *Are there any strawberries in the fridge? There isn't any/is no tea.*

  **Note:** We use **some** in the interrogative for offers or requests. *Would you like some lemonade?* (offer)

## Quantifiers

| | COUNTABLE | UNCOUNTABLE |
|---|---|---|
| AFFIRMATIVE | a lot of/lots (of)/ too many/(a) few | a lot of/lots (of)/ too much/(a) little |
| NEGATIVE | (not) many | (not) much |
| INTERROGATIVE | (how) many | (how) much |

- We usually use **a lot of/lots (of)** in affirmative sentences with both uncountable nouns and countable nouns in the plural. The **of** is ommitted when **a lot/lots** are not followed by a noun. *There is a lot of cheese in the fridge. There are a lot of biscuits in the tin. Were there lots of biscuits in the tin? Yes, there were lots.*
- We usually use **much** and **many** in negative or interrogative sentences. We use **much** with uncountable nouns and **many** with plural countable nouns. *Is there much tea in the pot? There isn't much bread left. Do you have many apples? There aren't many sandwiches left.*
- We use **how much** with uncountable nouns to ask about the amount of something. *A: How much meat do we need? B: A kilo. (=amount)*
- We use **how many** with countable nouns to ask about the number of things. *A: How many students are there in your class? B: Twenty-eight. (=number)*
- We use **too much** with uncountable nouns to show that something is more than necessary or wanted. *The children are making too much noise.*
- We use **too many** with countable nouns to show that something is more than necessary or wanted. *Don't buy too many oranges.*
- **A few** means **not many, but enough**. It is used with plural countable nouns. *We have a few eggs. We can make an omelette.*
- **A little** means **not much, but enough**. It is used with uncountable nouns. *Can I have a little milk in my tea?*
- **Few/Little** means **hardly any, not enough** and can be used with **very** for emphasis. *There is (very) little sugar in my tea. I can't drink it. There are (very) few apples. I can't make a pie.*

## Too – Enough

- **too** + adjective/adverb + **to-infinitive**
  **Too** comes before an adjective or an adverb. It has a negative meaning and shows that something is more than enough, more than necessary, or more than wanted.
  *The soup is **too hot to eat**. (I can't eat the soup.)*
- adjective/adverb + **enough**
  **enough** + noun ] + infinitive
  **Enough** comes before nouns but after an adjective or an adverb. It has a positive meaning and shows that there is as much of something as is wanted or needed.
  *Kelly is **tall enough to reach** the top shelf. (Kelly can reach the top shelf.)*
  *We have **enough money to go** on holiday this year.*

## -ing form & to-infinitive

We use the **-ing form**:
- as a **noun**.
  ***Swimming** is my favourite sport.*
- after the following verbs: **admit, appreciate, avoid, begin, consider, continue, deny, dislike, enjoy, fancy, finish, hate, imagine, like, love, mind, miss, prefer, prevent, spend, start, stop, suggest, waste** (time, money), etc.
  *They **enjoy travelling**.*
- after the verb **go** when we talk about activities.
  *I often **go jogging** in the mornings.*
- after **prepositions**.
  *She's good **at cooking**.*
- after expressions such as: **be busy, it's no use, it's (not) worth, there's no point (in), what's the use of, can't help, can't stand, have difficulty (in), look forward to.**
  *I **look forward to seeing** you next week.*

We use the **to-infinitive**:
- to express **purpose**.
  *I bought milk **to make** ice cream.*
- after certain verbs: **advise, agree, ask, decide, expect, explain, hope, manage, offer, plan, promise, refuse, seem, want**, etc.
  *I **want to buy** an MP3 player.*
- after **be** + adjective (**happy, nice, sorry**, etc.).
  *It **is nice to be** back home.*
- after **too** and **enough**.
  *It's **too late to visit** them now.*
  *She's old **enough to drive** a car.*
- after **would like, would love, would prefer**.
  *I'**d love to go** to the cinema with you.*

We use the **infinitive** without **to** (bare infinitive) after:
- **modal verbs** (**can, may, should**, etc.).
  *I **can play** football. You **may eat** some cake. You **should call** your mum.*
- the verbs **make** and **let**.
  ***Let's go** to the beach!*
  *You shouldn't **make** him eat it.*
- **would rather (not)/had better (not)**.
  *I'**d rather stay** in tonight.*
  *You **had better not park** here.*



Some verbs can take either the *to-*infinitive or the *-ing* form with a change in meaning.

- **forget** + **to-infinitive** = not remember
  *She **forgot to lock** the front door.*
- **forget** + **-ing** form = not recall
  *He'll never **forget swimming** in the blue waters of the Pacific.*
- **remember** + **to-infinitive** = not forget
  *Did you **remember to buy** the Sunday paper?*
- **remember** + **-ing** form = recall
  *She **remembers walking** along the paths of the old town.*
- **try** + **to-infinitive** = attempt, do one's best
  *I **tried to open** the old chest, but it was stuck.*
- **try** + **-ing** form = do something as an experiment
  *You should **try eating** more fruit and vegetables.*
- **stop** + **to-infinitive** = stop temporarily in order to do something else
  *On their way back home they **stopped to say** hello to Mr Evans.*
- **stop** + **-ing** form = finish doing something
  *She **stopped playing** the guitar the moment John walked in the house.*
- **be sorry** + **to-infinitive** = apologise for a current situation
  *We **are sorry to tell** you that you failed the test.*
- **be sorry** + **for/about -ing** form = regret something that happened in the past
  *I'm so **sorry for talking** to you rudely at the party yesterday.*

# MODULE 3

## Past Simple (Regular – Irregular verbs)

### Regular verbs

We form the **past simple** of regular verbs by adding **-ed** to the verb.

| | |
|---|---|
| **AFFIRMATIVE** | I/You/He/She/It/We/They walk**ed**. |
| **INTERROGATIVE** | **Did** I/you/he/she/it/we/they **walk**? |
| **NEGATIVE** | I/You/He/She/It/We/They **did not/didn't walk**. |

### Irregular verbs

Some verbs have an irregular past form (*see list of irregular verbs*).

| | |
|---|---|
| **AFFIRMATIVE** | I/You/He/She/It/We/They **bought**. |
| **INTERROGATIVE** | **Did** I/you/he/she/it/we/they **buy**? |
| **NEGATIVE** | I/You/He/She/It/We/They **did not/didn't buy**. |

| **SHORT ANSWERS** | |
|---|---|
| **Did** I/you/he/she/it/ we/they **go**? | **Yes**, I/you/he/she/it/we/they **did**. <br> **No**, I/you/he/she/it/we/they **didn't**. |

# Grammar Reference

## Spelling: affirmative of regular verbs
- We add **-d** to verbs ending in **-e**. *I move– I moved*
- Verbs ending in **consonant + -y** drop the **-y** and add **-ied**.
  *I try – I tried*
- Verbs ending in one stressed vowel between two consonants **double the last consonant** and take **-ed**.
  *I drop – I dropped*
- Verbs ending in **-l**, double the **-l** and take **-ed**.
  *I travel - I travelled*

## Use
We use the **past simple** for:
- past habits.
  *She often **studied** till very late at night when she was a student.*
- actions which happened at a specific time in the past. The time is either mentioned or implied.
  *He **moved** to England **in 2010**.* (When? In 2010).
  *Mozart **composed** a number of symphonies and concerts.* (time implied).
- actions which happened immediately one after the other in the past. *He **turned on** his computer, **connected** to the Internet and **checked** his emails.*

> **Time expressions used with the *past simple*:** yesterday, yesterday morning/evening, etc, last night/ week, etc, two weeks/a month ago, in 2009, etc.

## *Wh*-questions

***Wh*-questions** begin with a question word such as **who**, **what**, **where**, **when**, etc. We put the auxiliary or modal verb before the subject.

**question word + auxiliary/modal + subject**

We use:

- **Who** for people.
  A: **Who** did you call?
  B: My sister.
- **Which** for things.
  A: **Which** hotel did you stay at?
  B: The Hampton Hotel.
- **What** for information.
  A: **What** did you do last night?
  B: I went out with a friend.
- **Where** for places.
  A: **Where** did she go last night?
  B: She went to the theatre.
- **When** for time/dates.
  A: **When** did they leave?
  B: Yesterday morning.
- **Why** for reason.
  A: **Why** did they leave so early?
  B: They were really tired.
- **How** for manner.
  A: **How** was the party?
  B: It was great.
- **How long** for duration.
  A: **How long** did he stay?
  B: 2 weeks.

## Past Continuous

**Form: subject + *was/were* + verb -ing**

| AFFIRMATIVE | |
|---|---|
| I/He/She/It **was** play**ing**. | We/You/They **were** play**ing**. |

| NEGATIVE | |
|---|---|
| **Long Form** | **Short Form** |
| I/He/She/It **was not** play**ing**. We/You/They **were not** play**ing**. | I/He/She/It **wasn't** play**ing** We/You/They **weren't** play**ing**. |

| INTERROGATIVE | SHORT ANSWERS |
|---|---|
| **Was** I play**ing** ...? | Yes, I **was**./No, I **wasn't**. |
| **Were** you play**ing** ...? | Yes, you **were**./No, you **weren't**. |
| **Was** he/she/it play**ing** ...? | Yes, he/she/it **was**./No, he/she/it **wasn't**. |
| **Were** we/you/they play**ing** ...? | Yes, we/you/they **are**. No, we/you/they **aren't**. |

## Use
We use the **past continuous**:
- for an action that was in progress at a stated time in the past. We do not know when the action started or finished.
  *She **was ironing** at 6 o'clock yesterday afternoon.* (We do not know when she started ironing or when she finished.)
- for a past action which was in progress when another action interrupted it. We use the **past continuous** for the action in progress (longer action) and the **past simple** for the action which interrupted it (shorter action).
  *I **was sleeping** when Alison **called**.*
- for two or more actions which were happening at the same time in the past (simultaneous actions).
  *Mum **was cooking** while I **was doing** my homework.*
- to give background information to a story.
  *It **was raining** and the wind **was blowing** when we left home.*

> **Time expressions used with the *past continuous*:** while, when, as, all day/night/morning, all day yesterday, etc.

**Note:** ... **while/as + past continuous** (longer action)
... **when + past simple** (shorter action)

## Spelling rules
- verb + -ing *work – work**ing***
- verb -*e* + -ing *dance – danc**ing***
- one syllable verbs ending in vowel + consonant → *double consonant + -ing sit – sit**ting*** **BUT** *travel – travel**ling***

## Past Simple vs Past Continuous

| PAST SIMPLE | PAST CONTINUOUS |
|---|---|
| actions which happened at a **stated time** in the past *Keith **visited** London **last month**.* (The time is stated. The action is complete.) | actions **in progress** at a stated time in the past (we do not know when the action started or finished) *Eric **was working** at **five o'clock yesterday afternoon**.* |
| actions which happened **one after the other** in the past *He **got up, made** breakfast and **went** to work.* | two or more actions which were happening **at the same time** in the past *I **was watching** a film while my dad **was listening** to music.* |

## Linking Words

We usually use linking words to join sentences or ideas together. They express **reason**, **result**, **addition**, **contrast** etc.

**We use:**
- **because** to show the **reason** for something.
  *I spent the weekend in bed **because** I was sick.*

- **so** to show the **result** of something.
  *He wanted to become an artist **so** he went to college.*
- **too**, **and** or **also** to show **addition**. *She had shows in Rome and Milan. She exhibited her work in Paris, **too**.*
  *She fell down the stairs **and** broke her leg.*
  *She has **also** visited Spain.*
- **but** to show **contrast**.
  *The concert was good, **but** few people came.*

## MODULE 4

### Will

| AFFIRMATIVE | |
|---|---|
| **Long Form** | **Short Form** |
| I/You/He/She/It/We/They **will** play. | I/You/He/She/It/We/They **'ll** play. |

| NEGATIVE | |
|---|---|
| **Long Form** | **Short Form** |
| I/You/He/She/It/We/They **will not** play. | I/You/He/She/It/We/They **won't** play |

| INTERROGATIVE | SHORT ANSWERS |
|---|---|
| **Will** I/you/he/she/it/ we/you/they play? | **Yes**, I/you/he, etc **will**. / **No**, I/you/he, etc **won't**. |

**Use**

We use **will**:
- to make **predictions** based on what we **believe** or **think**. We usually use **will** after *I think, I hope, I believe, I expect, probably* and *perhaps*. *I **think** we **will arrive** late. I **expect** he **will be** here at about 10 o´clock. **Perhaps** we **will go shopping** later.*
- to make **on-the-spot decisions**. *This dress is beautiful. I**'ll buy** it.*
- for **promises** usually with the verbs *promise/swear*.
  *I promise I**'ll write** every day.*
  *Don't do this or I**'ll be** angry. (threats)*
  *Don't touch it or you**'ll get** burnt. (warnings)*
  *I hope he**'ll pass** the test. (hopes)*
  *I**'ll get** you a glass or water. (offers)*

**Time expressions used with the *future simple*:** tomorrow, the day after tomorrow, next week/month/year, tonight, soon, in a week/month/year etc.

### Be going to

**Use**

We use **be going to**:
- for future **plans** and **intentions**. *I **am going to fly** to Spain next week. What **are** you **going to do** tonight, Sally?*
- for **predictions** based on what we **see** or **know**, especially when there is evidence.
  *Take a photo! She**'s going to blow out** the candles.*
  *Look at the clouds, it **is going to rain**!*
- to talk about things we **have already decided to do** in the near future.
  *We**'re going to travel** to Cuba this summer. (We have already decided this.)*

### Present Continuous (future meaning)

We use the **present continuous** to talk about fixed arrangements in the near future, especially if we know the date or time.
*I**'m going** to a rock concert tomorrow. (I've bought the tickets.)*
*I**'m going** on holiday on 12th May.*

### Time Clauses

**Time Clauses** are introduced with the following **time conjunctions:** *when, as, while, before, the moment that, after, till/until, by the time, whenever, as long as, as soon as.*
*I'll call you **as soon as** I get home.*
- When the time clause precedes the main clause, a comma is used. ***When** I get home, I'll call her.*
- **Time Clauses** follow the rule of the **sequence of tenses**. That is, when the verb of the main clause is in the present or future form, the verb of the time clause is in a present form and when the verb of the main clause is in a past form, the verb of the time clause is in a past form.
  *He **reads** a book **before** he **goes** to bed. I **met** an old friend while I **was walking** around the market.*
- We never use future tenses after time conjunctions; we use the present simple instead.
  *Ann will visit us **as soon as** she **comes back** (NOT: ... ~~as soon as she will come back~~ ... )*

  **Note: When** she finishes, she'll call me. (when: time word) **BUT When** will you finish your homework? (When: question word)

### Conditionals *(types 0, 1 & 2)*

**Conditional clauses** consist of two parts: the *if*-clause (hypothesis) and the **main clause** (result).

| | IF-CLAUSE (hypothesis) | MAIN CLAUSE (result) |
|---|---|---|
| **Zero Conditional** | if + present simple | present simple |
| **General Truth** | *If you **heat** water, it **boils**.* | |

**Use:** to talk about general truths or things that always happen.

| | IF-CLAUSE (hypothesis) | MAIN CLAUSE (result) |
|---|---|---|
| **First Conditional** | if + present simple | will+ bare infinitive |
| **Real present/ future** | *If it's really hot tomorrow, we**'ll go** to the beach.* | |

**Use:** to talk about things that are likely to happen in the present/future.

| | IF-CLAUSE (hypothesis) | MAIN CLAUSE (result) |
|---|---|---|
| **Second Conditional** | if + past simple | would/could + bare infinitive |
| **Unreal present/ Advice** | *If I **had** a lot of money, I**'d buy** a new house. (But I haven't)* | |
| | *If I **were** you, I**'d see** a doctor. (Advice)* | |

**Use:** to talk about an imaginary situation or give advice in the present or future.

**Notes:**
* When the **if-clause** comes before the main clause, the two clauses are separated with a comma.
  *If the weather improves, flights **will run** as normal.*
* We can use **unless** instead of **if ... not** in the **if-clause** of **Type 1** conditionals. The verb after **unless** is always in the **affirmative**.
  ***Unless** you go to bed now, you**'ll be** tired in the morning.*

### May – Might – Could – Will probably – Will definitely

We use **may – might – could** to express possibility. Notice the difference in meaning. *"Where's Peter?"*
*"He **may/could** still be at work."* (**It's possible/perhaps** he is at work.)
*"He **might** still be at work."* (There is a **slight possibility** he is still at work, but I doubt it.)

**Note:** We can also express possibility with the adverbs **probably** and **definitely**.
*I'll **probably** go sailing tomorrow.* (**It's likely/There's a very good chance.**)
*We'll **definitely** go on holiday this summer.* (**It's certain.**)

### A/An – The

We use **a/an**:
* with nouns when referring to something in **general**.
  *Emily has got **a** dog.*
* with **singular countable nouns** when we want to say what sb/sth is. *Greg is **a** teacher.   It's **a** panda.*

We use **the**:
* with nouns when talking about something **specific** or something that has already been mentioned.
  *That's **the** man I told you about.*
* with nouns that are **unique** (**the** sky, **the** moon).
* with the names of **rivers** (**the** Thames), **groups of islands** (**the** Maldives), **mountain ranges** (**the** Rocky Mountains), **deserts** (**the** Sahara), **oceans** (**the** Atlantic), **canals** (**the** Bridgewater), **countries** when they include the words: **State, Kingdom, Republic** (**the** UK), in **geographical terms** such as **the** North Pole/Arctic/Amazon, **the** south of England, **the** North/East/South/West.
* with the names of **musical instruments** (**the** piano).
* with **family names** (**the** Browns) and **nationalities** ending in **-sh**, **-ch** or **-ese** (**the** Polish).
* with **titles** (**the** King, **the** Prime Minister), but not with titles including a proper name (Queen Elizabeth).

We do not use **the**:
* with **uncountable** and **plural nouns** when talking about something in **general**. *Huskies pull sledges over the snow.*
* with **proper names**. *Alan is a doctor.*
* with **languages**, unless they are followed by the word language. *I speak **Spanish**.* **BUT** *The Spanish language.*
* with the **names of countries** which don't include the word **State, Kingdom** or **Republic**:
  *England, France,* **BUT** *the United States, the Czech Republic*

* with the names of **streets** (*Wilson Street*), **parks** (*Hyde Park*), **cities** (*Rome*), **mountains** (*Mount Olympus*), **individual islands** (*Ireland*), **lakes** (*Lake Windermere*) and **continents** (*Asia*).

## Relative Pronouns/Adverbs

**Relative Pronouns**
We use:
* **who/that** for people. *Genghis Khan was the man **who/that** started the Mongol Empire.*
* **which/that** for animals or things.
  *The Mona Lisa is the painting **which/that** I like the most.*
* **whose** to show possession. *Tutankhamun was a ruler of Egypt **whose** tomb had a lot of treasure inside.*

**Note:** We don't use a relative pronoun with another pronoun (I, you, he, him, etc). *I met someone who is a famous artist.* (NOT: ~~I met someone who he is a famous artist.~~)

**Relative Adverbs**
We use:
* **when** to refer to time. *1254 was the year **when** Marco Polo was born.*
* **where** to refer to place. *This is the museum **where** Emma works.*
* **why** to give reason. *This art gallery is very interesting, that's **why** so many people visit it.*

# MODULE 5

## Present Perfect

**Form: subject + *have/has* + past participle**

| AFFIRMATIVE | NEGATIVE |
|---|---|
| I/You/We/They **have/'ve** arrived.<br>He/She/It **has/'s** arrived. | I/You/We/They **have not/haven't** arrived.<br>He/She/It **has not/hasn't** arrived. |

| INTERROGATIVE | SHORT ANSWERS |
|---|---|
| **Have** I/you/we/they **arrived**?<br>**Has** he/she/it **arrived**? | **Yes,** I/you/we/they **have.**<br>**No,** I/you/we/they **haven't.**<br>**Yes,** he/she/it **has.**<br>**No,** he/she/it **hasn't.** |

**Use**
We use the **present perfect**:
* for actions which started in the past and continue up to the present. *He **has worked** as a doctor for five years.* (= He started working as a doctor five years ago and he still works as a doctor.)
* to talk about a past action which has a visible result in the present. *She **has lost** a lot of weight.* (= We can see she looks thinner.)
* for actions which happened at an unstated time in the past. The action is more important than the time it happened. *He **has bought** a new car.* (When? We don't know; it's not important.)
* for recently completed actions. *Linda **has** just **cleaned** her room.* (The action is complete. The room is now clean.)
* for personal experiences/changes which have happened. *I **have never tried** bungee jumping.*

**Time expressions used with the *present perfect*:** just, already, yet, for, since, ever, never, so far, this week/month/ year, etc.

## Have been (to)/Have gone (to)

- We use **have been (to)** to say that someone went somewhere, but has come back. *Tom has **been to** Italy.* (He went to Italy, but he's no longer there.)
- We use **have gone (to)** to say that someone went somewhere and is still there.
  *Meg **has gone** to London.* (She's still there.)

## Just - Yet- Already – Since – For – Ever – Never

*We've **just** arrived.* (a few minutes ago)
*Meg hasn't called **yet**./Has Meg called **yet**?* (We expect her to call soon.)
*She's **already** watered the plants.* (It's done. She doesn't have to water the plants any more.)
*They've lived in Spain **since** 2005.* (starting point)
*He's been in Malta **for** a week.* (duration)
*Have you **ever** been to Paris?* (at any point)
*I have **never** tried scuba diving.* (I haven't tried scuba diving.)

## Present Perfect vs Past Simple

| PRESENT PERFECT | PAST SIMPLE |
|---|---|
| an action which happened at an **unstated time** in the past *He **has hurt** his leg.* (When? We don't know.) | an action which happened at a **stated** time in the past *They **went** to Australia last summer.* (When? Last summer.) |
| an action which started in the past and is still continuing in the present *She **has lived** in Cairo for ten years.* (She went to Cairo ten years ago and she still lives there.) | an action which started and finished in the past *She **was** in New York for two years.* (She lived in New York for two years. She doesn't live there any more.) |

## Present Perfect Continuous

**Form: subject + *have/has* + *been* + verb -*ing***

| AFFIRMATIVE | NEGATIVE |
|---|---|
| I/You/We/They **have/'ve been playing**. He/She/It **has/'s been playing**. | I/You/We/They **have not/ haven't been playing**. He/She/It **has not/ hasn't been playing**. |

| INTERROGATIVE | SHORT ANSWERS |
|---|---|
| Have I/you/we/they **been playing**? Has he/she/it **been playing**? | **Yes**, I/you/we/they **have**. **No**, I/you/we/they **haven't**. **Yes**, he/she/it **has**. **No**, he/she/it **hasn't**. |

### Use

We use the **present perfect continuous**:
- to put emphasis on the duration of an action which started in the past and continues up to the present.
  *Meg **has been trying** to fix my computer for two hours.*

- for an action that started in the past and lasted for some time. It may still be continuing, or have finished, but it has left a visible result in the present. *She's tired because she **has been cleaning** the house all morning.*

**Time expressions used with the *present perfect continuous*:** since, for, how long (to place emphasis on duration).

## -ing/-ed adjectives

- **-ing** adjectives describe what somebody or something is like.
  *I've had a very **tiring** day.* (What was the day like? Tiring.)
  *Lucy is very **interesting**.* (What's Lucy like? Interesting.)
- **-ed** adjectives describe how someone feels.
  *Cathy is very **tired**!* (How does Cathy feel? Tired.)

## Past Perfect

**Form: subject + *had* + past participle**

| AFFIRMATIVE | NEGATIVE |
|---|---|
| I/You/He/She/It **had finished**. We/You/They **had finished**. | I/You/We/They **had not/ hadn't finished**. He/She/It **had not/hadn't finished**. |

| INTERROGATIVE | SHORT ANSWERS |
|---|---|
| Had I **finished** ...? Had you **finished** ...? Had he/she/it **finished** ...? Had we/you/they **finished** ...? | Yes, I **had**./No, I **hadn't**. Yes, you **had**./No, you **hadn't**. Yes, he/she/it **had**./ No, he/she/it **hadn't**. Yes, we/you/they **had**./ No, we/you/they **hadn't**. |

### Use

We use the **past perfect** for:
- an action that happened before another past action or before a stated time in the past.
  *They **had had** dinner by the time I arrived.*
  *They **had planted** all the trees by 6 o'clock.*
- an action which finished in the past and whose result was visible in the past.
  *She couldn't get into the house because she **had lost** her keys.*
- the past perfect is the past equivalent of the present prefect.
  *She **was** tired because she **had walked** a long way.*
  *She **is** tired because she **has walked** a long way.*

**Time expressions used with the past perfect:** before, after, until, by the time, already, yet, just, for, since

## Conditionals *(type 3)*

|  | IF-CLAUSE (hypothesis) | MAIN CLAUSE (result) |
|---|---|---|
| **Third Conditional** | if + past perfect | would have + past participle |
| **Unreal past** | *If we **had left** the house earlier, we **wouldn't have missed** our flight.* | |

### Use

We use **Type 3 Conditionals**:
*   to express an imaginary situation in the past.
    *If I **had saved** enough money, I **would have bought** that camera.* (But I didn't)
*   to express regret or criticism.
    *If I **had taken** your advice, I **wouldn't have been** in trouble.* (But I didn't)

## Wishes

We use *wish/if only* to express a wish.

| I WISH/IF ONLY | | USE |
|---|---|---|
| + past simple/ past continuous | *I wish/if only I **was/were** on holiday right now.* (But I'm not) | to say that we would like something to be different in the present |
| + past perfect | *I wish/If only I **had booked** the plane tickets earlier.* (But I didn't) | to express a regret about something that happened or didn't happen in the past |
| + subject + would + bare infinitive | *I wish it **would stop** raining.* (It's annoying.) *If only you **would stop** complaining.* (Please stop complaining.) | to express: <br>• a desire for a situation or person's behaviour to change <br>• a polite imperative |

### Note:
*   *If only* is more emphatic than *wish*.
*   We can use *were* instead of *was* in all persons after *wish* and *if only*.

# MODULE 6

## The Passive

**Form: subject + *to be* + past participle**

We form the passive with the verb ***to be*** in the appropriate tense and the **past participle** of the main verb.

| | ACTIVE | PASSIVE |
|---|---|---|
| Present Simple | *Joanna **waters** the plants.* | *The plants **are watered** by Joanna.* |
| Present Continuous | *Joanna **is watering** the plants.* | *The plants **are being watered** by Joanna.* |
| Past Simple | *Joanna **watered** the plants.* | *The plants **were watered** by Joanna.* |
| Past Continuous | *Joanna **was watering** the plants.* | *The plants **were being watered** by Joanna.* |
| Present Perfect Simple | *Joanna **has watered** the plants.* | *The plants **have been watered** by Joanna.* |
| Past Perfect Simple | *Joanna **had watered** the plants.* | *The plants **had been watered** by Joanna.* |
| Future Simple | *Joanna **will water** the plants.* | *The plants **will be watered** by Joanna.* |
| Modal Verbs | *Joanna **may/might/ could/must/have to/should water** the plants.* | *The plants **may/might/ could/must/ have to/ should be watered** by Joanna.* |

We use **the passive**:
*   when the person/people doing the action is/are **unknown**, **unimportant**, or **obvious** from the context.
    *The glass **was broken**.* (We don't know who broke it.)
    *The decision **will be announced** tomorrow.* (Who will announce it is unimportant.)
    *The patient **has** already **been operated on**.* (It's obvious that the doctor has operated on the patient.)
*   when the **action** itself is **more important** than the person/people doing it, as in headlines, newspaper articles, formal notices, advertisements, etc.
    *Hundreds of buildings **were damaged** by the earthquake.*
*   to make statements more formal or polite.
    *The ceremony **will be held** in the city hall.* (formal)
    *This saucepan **has not been cleaned** properly.* (more polite than saying: 'You **haven't cleaned** the saucepan properly'.)

**Changing from the active to the passive:**
*   The **object** of the active sentence becomes the **subject** of the passive sentence.
*   The **active verb** remains in the same tense, but changes into a **passive form**.
*   The **subject** of the active sentence becomes the **agent**, and is either introduced with the preposition **by** or it is omitted.

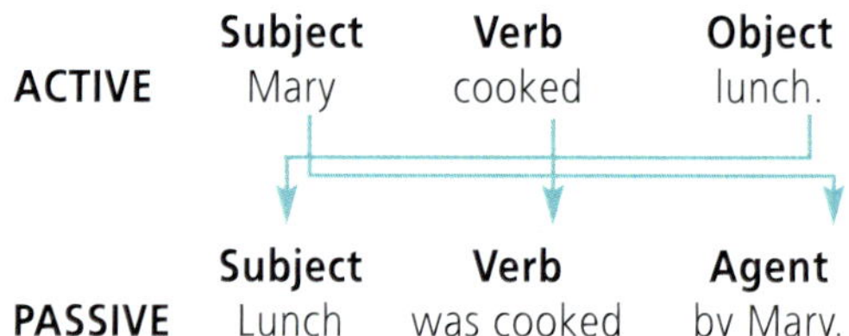


*   The agent can be omitted when the subject is **they**, **he**, **someone/somebody**, **people**, **one**, etc.
    **Active:**  *Someone has left the window open.*
    **Passive:**  *The window has been left open.*
*   The agent is not omitted when it is a specific or an important person, or when it is essential to the meaning of the sentence.
    *The announcement will be made **by the president** himself.*
*   With verbs that can take two objects, such as **bring**, **tell**, **send**, **show**, **teach**, **promise**, **sell**, **read**, **offer**, **give**, **lend**, etc, we can form two different passive sentences.
    **Active:**  *He offered her some flowers.*
    **Passive:**  *She was offered some flowers.*
    *Some flowers were offered to her.* (passive, less usual)
*   In passive questions with **who**, **whom** or **which** we do not omit **by**.
    Compare the examples:
    ***Who** will give the speech?*
    ***Who** will the speech be given **by**?*

## Reported Speech

**Reported Speech** is the exact meaning of what someone said, but not the exact words. We don't use quotation marks with reported speech. We can use ***that*** after the introductory verb (*say, tell*) or we can leave it out.
*He **said that** he liked the film.* or *He **said** he liked the film.*

### Say – Tell
- In reported speech we use **say** without **to** (without a personal object) when we don't mention the person being spoken to.
  *She **said** (that) she was angry.*
- We use **say** with **to** (with a personal object) when we mention the person being spoken to.
  *She **said to me** (that) she was angry.*
- We use **tell** without **to** (with a personal object) when we mention the person being spoken to.
  *She **told me** that she was angry.*

## Reported Statements

- In reported speech, **personal/possessive pronouns** and **possessive adjectives** change according to the meaning of the sentence.
  *"**I**'ve bought a new book," said Louise.*
  *Louise said (that) **she** had bought a new book.*
- The introductory verb is usually in the **past simple** and the verb tenses change as follows:

Some **words and time expressions** change as follows:

| now | then, immediately |
|---|---|
| today, tonight, this week/month/year etc | that day, that night, that week/month/year etc |
| yesterday, last week | the day before, the previous day, the week before, the previous week |
| tomorrow, next week | the next/following day, the following week, the week after |
| ago | before |
| here | there |
| this, these | that, those |
| come | go |

## Reported Questions

- We use **ask** or **want to know** to report questions. We use the affirmative form of the verb. The question mark is omitted.
  *"What time does the film start?" Mary asked me.*
  *Mary **asked** me what time the film started.*
- When the direct question begins with **who, where, when, why, what** or **how,** we use the same question word in the reported question.
  *"**When** is your birthday?" she asked.*
  *She **wanted to know** when my birthday was.*
- When the direct question begins with **is, do, have,** etc, we use **if/whether** in the reported question.
  *"**Is** this bookcase new?" he asked.*
  *He asked **if/whether** that bookcase was new.*
  *"**Have** you **ever been** to Rhodes?"*
  *She asked **if/whether** I had ever been to Rhodes.*

## Reported Commands/Requests

- We use **order/tell + sb + (not) to-infinitive** to report commands.
  *"Be quiet!" she said.*
  *She **ordered/told** them to be quiet.*

- We use **ask/beg + sb + (not) to-infinitive** to report requests. Usually, the direct sentence contains the word 'please'.
  *"Please don't shout," he said.*
  *He **asked** them not to shout.*
  *"Please, please don't go," he said.*
  *He **begged** me not to go.*

## Reflexive Pronouns

| SINGULAR | PLURAL |
|---|---|
| I – myself | |
| You – yourself | We – ourselves |
| He – himself | You – yourselves |
| She – herself | They – themselves |
| It – itself | |

**Use**
We use **reflexive pronouns**:
- with verbs such as **behave, burn, cut, enjoy, hurt, introduce, look at, teach**, etc when the subject and the object of the verb are the same.
  *I **cut myself** with a knife.*
- to emphasise the subject or the object of a sentence. In this case, they (usually) come after the noun or pronoun they emphasise or at the end of the sentence.
  *I made this cake **myself**. (I made it, not someone else.)*
- with the expressions: **enjoy myself/yourself** (have a good time), **behave myself/yourself** (be good), **by myself/ yourself** (without company or without help), **make myself/yourself at home** (feel comfortable), **help myself/ yourself** (to take something freely).

**Note:**
- Some verbs do not (usually) take a **reflexive pronoun**. Some of these are: **concentrate, feel, get up, meet, relax, remember, sit down, wake up, wonder, worry**, etc.
- Reflexive pronouns are not normally used with the verbs **wash, dress, shave** and **change** (*She **washed** and had breakfast*), but when the action involved is difficult we use a reflexive pronoun. *She's got a broken leg, but she can **dress herself**.*

## Question Tags

- Question tags are short questions at the end of statements.
- We use them in speech to **confirm something** or to find out if something is **true** or **not**.
- We form them with the **auxiliary verb** or **modal verb** from the main sentence and the appropriate subject pronoun.
  *Amanda **is** an artist, **isn't she?***
  *You **can speak** Spanish, **can't you?***

**Use**
- A positive statement takes a negative question tag.
  *It **is** cold today, **isn't it?***
- A negative statement takes a positive question tag.
  *They **aren't** sleeping, **are they?***
- When the verb of the sentence is in the present simple, we use **do (not)/does (not)** in the question tag.
  *Lynne **works** as a teacher, **doesn't she?***

- When the verb of the sentence is in the past simple, we use **did (not)**.
  *You **lost** your luggage, **didn't you**?*

Some verbs/expressions form question tags differently:

| I am → aren't I? | *I'm early, **aren't I**?* |
|---|---|
| **imperative → will you/ won't you?** | *Be quiet, **will/won't you**?* |
| **Don't → will you?** | *Don't shout, **will you**?* |
| **Let's → shall we?** | *Let's eat something, **shall we**?* |
| **You have (got) → haven't you?** | *You **have got** two dogs, **haven't you**?* |
| **They have** (other meanings) **→ don't they?** | *They **have** dinner at 8 o'clock, **don't they**?* |
| **This/That is → isn't it?** | *That's your friend, **isn't it**?* |

### Intonation

- When we are sure of the answer, the voice goes down in the question tag.
  *You'**ll wash** your face, **won't you**? (↘)*
- When we are not sure of the answer and want to check information, the voice goes up in the question tag.
  *They **didn't go** to the party, **did they**? (↗)*

## Rules for Punctuation

### Capital Letters
A capital letter is used:
- to begin a sentence.
  ***Here** we are.*
- for days of the week, months and public holidays.
  ***F**riday, **A**ugust*
- for names of people and places.
  *My teacher's name is **S**ally and she's from **C**hester, **V**ermont.*
- for people's titles.
  ***M**r and **M**rs Parker; **D**r Mortimer; **P**rofessor Riggs; etc*
- for nationalities and languages.
  *They are **C**hilean.*
  *He's fluent in **G**erman and **R**ussian.*
  **Note:** The personal pronoun I is always a capital letter.
  *Gus and **I** are going on holiday together.*

### Full stop (.)
A full stop is used:
- to end a sentence that is not a question or an exclamation.
  *We're having a great time. You can never get bored here in Rio.*
- after abbreviations. *Mr Jones is a great teacher.*

### Comma (,)
A comma is used:
- to separate words in a list.
  *We need sugar, milk, tomatoes and apple juice.*
- to separate a non-essential relative clause (i.e., a clause giving extra information which is not essential to the meaning of the main clause) from the main clause.
  *Tony, who is a doctor, lives in Africa.*

- after certain joining words/transitional phrases (e.g., in addition to this, moreover, for example, however, in conclusion, etc.).
  *Moreover, Jenny is very patient with children.*
- when if-clauses or other dependent clauses begin compound or complex sentences.
  If you have any questions, don't hesitate to ask.
  **Note:** No comma is used, however, when they follow the main clause.
- to separate tag questions from the rest of the sentence.
  *Mr. Stephens is your math teacher, isn't he?*
- before the words asked, said, etc. when followed by direct speech.
  *"Turn down the music," said Sarah.*

### Question Mark (?)
A question mark is used:
- to end a direct question.
  *Where are the children?*

### Exclamation Mark (!)
An exclamation mark is used:
- to end an exclamatory sentence (i.e., a sentence showing admiration, surprise, joy, anger, etc).
  *That's a lie!    What awful weather!*

### Quotation Marks (' '  " ")
Single quotation marks are used:
- when you are questioning someone in direct speech (nested quotes).
  *"Then Helen said, 'Are you sure this is the right address?'"*
Double quotation marks are used:
- in direct speech to report the exact words someone said.
  *"What's your name?" she asked him.*

### Colon (:)
A colon is used:
- to introduce a list.
  *There were three of us on the boat: my brother, my cousin Lyn and me.*

### Brackets ( )
Brackets are used:
- to separate extra information from the rest of the sentence.
  *The most popular newspapers (i.e., The New York Times, The Observer, etc.) can be found almost anywhere in the world.*

### Apostrophe (')
An apostrophe is used:
- in contracted forms to show that one or more letters or numbers have been left out.
  *I'm (= I am) writing to complain about ...*
  *She left for Italy in the winter of '98. (=1998)*
- before or after the possessive -s to show ownership or the relationship between people.
  *Tom's car, my friend's husband* (singular noun + 's)
  *my parents' friends* (plural noun + ')
  *women's dresses* (irregular plural + 's)

# American English – British English Guide

| American English | British English |
|---|---|
| **A** | |
| account | bill/account |
| airplane | aeroplane |
| anyplace/anywhere | anywhere |
| apartment | flat |
| **B** | |
| bathrobe | dressing gown |
| bathtub | bath |
| bill | banknote |
| billion=thousand million | billion=million million |
| busy (phone) | engaged (phone) |
| **C** | |
| cab | taxi |
| call/phone | ring up/phone |
| can | tin |
| candy | sweets |
| check | bill (restaurant) |
| closet | wardrobe |
| connect (telephone) | put through |
| cookie | biscuit |
| corn | sweetcorn, maize |
| crazy | mad |
| **D** | |
| desk clerk | receptionist |
| dessert | pudding/dessert/sweet |
| downtown | (city) centre |
| drapes | curtains |
| drugstore/pharmacy | chemist's (shop) |
| duplex | semi-detached |
| **E** | |
| eggplant | aubergine |
| elevator | lift |
| **F** | |
| fall | autumn |
| faucet | tap |
| first floor, second floor, etc | ground floor, first floor, etc |
| flashlight | torch |
| French fries | chips |
| front desk (hotel) | reception |
| **G** | |
| garbage/trash | rubbish |
| garbage can | dustbin/bin |
| gas | petrol |
| gas station | petrol station/garage |
| grade | class/year |
| **I** | |
| intermission | interval |
| intersection | crossroads |
| **J** | |
| janitor | caretaker/porter |
| **K** | |
| kerosene | paraffin |
| **L** | |
| lawyer/attorney | solicitor |
| line | queue |
| lost and found | lost property |
| **M** | |
| mail | post |
| make a reservation | book |
| motorcycle | motorbike/motorcycle |
| movie | film |
| movie house/theater | cinema |
| **N** | |
| newsstand | newsagent |
| **O** | |
| office (doctor's/dentist's) | surgery |
| one-way (ticket) | single (ticket) |
| overalls | dungarees |

| American English | British English |
|---|---|
| **P** | |
| pants/trousers | trousers |
| pantyhose/nylons | tights |
| parking lot | car park |
| pavement | road surface |
| pedestrian crossing | zebra crossing |
| (potato) chips | crisps |
| public school | state school |
| purse | handbag |
| **R** | |
| railroad | railway |
| rest room | toilet/cloakroom |
| **S** | |
| sales clerk/sales girl | shop assistant |
| schedule | timetable |
| shorts (underwear) | pants |
| sidewalk | pavement |
| stand in line | queue |
| store, shop | shop |
| subway | underground |
| **T** | |
| truck | lorry, van |
| two weeks | fortnight/two weeks |
| **V** | |
| vacation | holiday(s) |
| vacuum (v.) | hoover |
| vacuum cleaner | hoover |
| vest | waistcoat |
| **W** | |
| with or without (milk/cream in coffee) | black or white |
| **Y** | |
| yard | garden |
| **Z** | |
| (pronounced, "zee") | (pronounced, "zed") |
| zero | nought |
| zip code | postcode |

## Grammar

| | |
|---|---|
| He just went out./ He has just gone out. | He has just gone out. |
| Hello, is this Steve? | Hello, is that Steve? |
| Do you have a car?/ Have you got a car? | Have you got a car? |

## Spelling

| | |
|---|---|
| aluminum | aluminium |
| analyze | analyse |
| center | centre |
| check | cheque |
| color | colour |
| honor | honour |
| jewelry | jewellery |
| practice(n,v) | practice(n) practise(v) |
| program | programme |
| realize | realise |
| tire | tyre |
| trave(l)ler | traveller |

## Expressions with prepositions and particles

| | |
|---|---|
| different from/than | different from/to |
| live on X street | live in X street |
| on a team | in a team |
| on the weekend | at the weekend |
| Monday through Friday | Monday to Friday |

# Pronunciation

## Vowels

| | | |
|---|---|---|
| a | /eə/ | care, rare, scare, dare, fare, share |
| | /eɪ/ | name, face, table, lake, take, day, age, ache, late, snake, make |
| | /æ/ | apple, bag, hat, man, flat, lamp, fat, hand, black, cap, fan, cat, actor, factor, manner |
| | /ɔ:/ | ball, wall, call, tall, small, hall, warn, walk, also, chalk |
| | /ɒ/ | want, wash, watch, what, wasp |
| | /ə/ | alarm, away, America |
| | /ɑ:/ | arms, dark, bar, star, car, ask, last, fast, glass, far, mask |
| e | /e/ | egg, end, hen, men, ten, bed, leg, tell, penny, pet, bell, pen, tent |
| i | /ɪ/ | in, ill, ink, it, is, hill, city, sixty, fifty, lip, lift, silly, chilly |
| | /aɪ/ | ice, kite, white, shine, bite, high, kind |
| o | /oʊ/ | home, hope, bone, joke, note, rope, nose, tone, blow, know, no, cold |
| | /ɒ/ | on, ox, hot, top, chop, clock, soft, often, box, sock, wrong, fox |
| | /aʊ/ | owl, town, clown, how, brown, now, cow |
| oo | /ʊ/ | book, look, foot |
| | /u:/ | room, spoon, too, tooth, food, moon, boot |
| | /ʌ/ | blood, flood |
| | /ɔ:/ | floor, door |
| u | /ɜ:/ | turn, fur, urge, hurl, burn, burst |
| | /ʌ/ | up, uncle, ugly, much, such, run, jump, duck, jungle, hut, mud, luck |
| | /ʊ/ | pull, push, pull, full, cushion |
| | /j/ | unique, union |
| y | /aɪ/ | sky, fly, fry, try, shy, cry, by |

## Consonants

| | | |
|---|---|---|
| b | /b/ | box, butter, baby, bell, bank, black |
| c | /k/ | cat, coal, call, calm, cold |
| | /s/ | cell, city, pencil |
| d | /d/ | down, duck, dim, double, dream, drive, drink |
| f | /f/ | fat, fan, first, food, lift, fifth |
| g | /g/ | grass, goat, go, gold, big, dog, glue, get, give |
| | /dʒ/ | gem, gin, giant |
| h | /h/ | heat, hit, hen, hand, perhaps BUT hour, honest, dishonest, heir |
| j | /dʒ/ | jam, just, job, joke, jump |
| k | /k/ | keep, king, kick |
| l | /l/ | lift, let, look, lid, clever, please, plot, black, blue, slim, silly |
| m | /m/ | map, man, meat, move, mouse, market, some, small, smell, smile |
| n | /n/ | next, not, tenth, month, kind, snake, snip, noon, run |
| p | /p/ | pay, pea, pen, poor, pink, pencil, plane, please |
| q | /kw/ | queue, quack, quarter, queen, question, quiet |
| r | /r/ | rat, rich, roof, road, ready, cry, grass, bring, fry, carry, red, read |
| s | /s/ | sit, set, seat, soup, circle, snow, smell, glass, dress, goose |
| | /z/ | houses, cousin, husband |
| t | /t/ | two, ten, tooth, team, turn, tent, tool, trip, train, tree |
| v | /v/ | veal, vet, vacuum, vote, arrive, live, leave, view |
| w | /w/ | water, war, wish, word, world |
| y | /j/ | youth, young, yes, yacht, year |
| z | /z/ | zoo, zebra, buzz, crazy |

## Diphthongs

| | | |
|---|---|---|
| ea,ee | /ɪə/ | ear, near, fear, hear, clear, year, dear, beer, cheer, deer |
| | /i:/ | eat, each, heat, leave, clean, seat, neat, tea, keep, feed, free, tree, three, bee |
| ei | /eɪ/ | eight, freight, weight, vein |
| | /aɪ/ | height |
| ai | /eɪ/ | pain, sail, tail, main, bait, fail, mail |
| ea | /eə/ | pear, wear, bear, tear |
| | /ɜ:/ | earth, pearl, learn, search |
| ie | /aɪ/ | die, tie, lie |
| ou | /ʌ/ | tough, touch, enough, couple, cousin, trouble |
| | /aʊ/ | mouse, house, round, trout, shout, doubt |
| oi | /ɔɪ/ | oil, boil, toil, soil, coin, choice, voice, join |
| oy | /ɔɪ/ | boy, joy, toy, annoy, employ |
| ou | /ɔ:/ | court, bought, brought |
| au | /ɔ:/ | naughty, caught, taught |

## Double letters

| | | |
|---|---|---|
| sh | /ʃ/ | shell, ship, shark, sheep, shrimp, shower |
| ch | /tʃ/ | cheese, chicken, cherry, chips, chocolate |
| ph | /f/ | photo, dolphin, phone, elephant |
| th | /θ/ | thief, throne, three, bath, cloth, earth, tooth |
| | /ð/ | the, this, father, mother, brother, feather |
| ng | /ŋ/ | thing, king, song, sing |
| nk | /ŋk/ | think, tank, bank |

- **Prefixes** are syllables which we add before certain words to form new words. The meaning of the new word depends on the prefix that has been used.
  anti- = against (*anti*-social)
  bi- = two (*bi*-monthly)
  co- = with (*co*-star)
  counter- = in the opposite direction (*counter*-argument)
  ex- = previous, former (*ex*-wife)
  inter- = between (*inter*continental)
  mis- = done wrongly or badly (*mis*judge)
  mono- = one (*mono*rail)
  multi- = many (*multi*media)
  non- = not (*non*-verbal)
  out- = more, better (*out*run)
  over- = (done) to a great extent (*over*cook)
  post- = after (*post*-war)
  pre- = before (*pre*-war)
  pro- = in favour of (*pro*-European)
  re- = again (*re*do)
  semi- = half (*semi*-circle)
  sub- = under, less (*sub*-zero)
  super- = big, more (*super*human)
  trans- = (travel) from one side, group etc to another (*trans*atlantic)
  tri- = three (*tri*pod)
  under- = not enough (*under*developed)
  uni- = one (*uni*directional)

  The prefixes below are used to express opposite meanings.

  | de- | *de*forest, *de*sensitise |
  |---|---|
  | dis- | *dis*agree, *dis*similar |
  | in- | *in*sincere, *in*complete **BUT** il- (before l) *il*legible im- (before **b, m, p**) *im*polite, *im*balance **BUT** *un*popular ir- (before **r**) *ir*rational |
  | non- | **BUT** *un*rest, *un*restricted |
  | un- | *non*-existent, *non*-stop *un*comfortable, *un*lucky |

  Some prefixes are added to words to form verbs.

  | en- | rich – *en*rich |
  |---|---|
  |  | **BUT** em- (before **b, m, p**) power – *em*power |

- **Suffixes** are syllables which we add to the end of certain words to form new words.

  - **Nouns referring to people**
  - verb + -er/-or/-ar (drive – driv*er*, conduct – conduct*or*, lie – li*ar*)
  - noun/verb/adjective + -ist (novel – novel*ist*, cycle – cycl*ist*, social – social*ist*)
  - verb + -ant/-ent (claim – claim*ant*)
  - noun + -an/-ian (Rome – Rom*an*, politic – politic*ian*)
  - verb + -ee (passive meaning) (escape – escap*ee*)

– **Nouns formed from verbs**

| -age | break – break*age* |
|---|---|
| -al | arrive – arriv*al* |
| -ance | perform – perform*ance* |
| -ation | represent – represent*ation* |
| -ence | confide – confid*ence* |
| -ion | complete – complet*ion* |
| -ment | pay – pay*ment* |
| -sion | extend – exten*sion* (verbs ending in **-d/-t**) |
| -sis | diagnose – diagno*sis* |
| -tion | delete – dele*tion* |
| -ure | seize – seiz*ure* |
| -y | discover – discover*y* |

– **Nouns formed from adjectives**

| -ance | arrogant – arrog*ance* |
|---|---|
| -cy | accurate – accura*cy* |
| -ence | confident – confid*ence* |
| -ion | perfect – perfect*ion* |
| -iness | happy – happ*iness* |
| -ness | shy – shy*ness* |
| -ity | equal – equal*ity* |
| -ty | safe – safe*ty* |
| -y | jealous – jealous*y* |

– **Adjectives formed from nouns**

| -ous | courage – courage*ous* |
|---|---|
| -al | person – person*al* |
| -ic | hygiene – hygien*ic* |
| -ical | myth – myth*ical* |
| -ish | girl – girl*ish* |
| -ive | excess – excess*ive* |
| -ful (with) | meaning – meaning*ful* |
| -less (without) | meaning – meaning*less* |
| -ant | importance – import*ant* |
| -able | comfort – comfort*able* |
| -y | hand – hand*y* |
| -ly | time – time*ly* |

– **Adjectives formed from verbs**

| -able | count – count*able* |
|---|---|
| -ible | comprehend – comprehens*ible* (verbs ending in **-d/-t**) |
| -ive | dismiss – dismiss*ive* |
| -ate | consider – consider*ate* |
| -ent | depend – depend*ent* |

– **Verbs formed from adjectives**

| -en | bright – bright*en* |
|---|---|
| -ise | immobile – immobil*ise* |

– **Verbs formed from nouns**

| -en | length – length*en* |
|---|---|

**Use the word given in capitals to form a word that fits in the gap.**

1  Don't overload the dishwasher with too many dishes.     **LOAD**
2  The ball hit him so hard he was knocked unconscious.     **CONSCIOUS**
3  We were feeling energetic so we decided to run 5 km rather than our usual 2 km.     **ENERGY**
4  She broke her sisters necklace in a fit of jealousy.     **JEALOUS**
5  I thought my essay was fine, but my teacher told me I had to redo it.     **DO**
6  My French pronunciation improved greatly once I was living in France.     **PRONOUNCE**
7  My prediction that they would marry came true.     **PREDICT**
8  Our Physics teacher told us to imagine the emptiness of space.     **EMPTY**
9  My neighbours are building an extension on their house.     **EXTEND**
10  I can't believe how many advertisements there are on this TV channel.     **ADVERTISE**
11  I was full of admiration for his achievements.     **ADMIRE**
12  I prefer to prepay my mobile phone plan because then I don't have to worry about bills every month.     **PAY**
13  I'm really upset you were dishonest with me.     **HONEST**
14  Katie's mother told her to stroke the kitten gently.     **GENTLE**
15  Farmers deforest large areas to graze their cattle.     **FOREST**
16  Working in journalism is very stressful because there are deadlines every day.     **STRESS**
17  I bought it because it was on offer as part of a promotion.     **PROMOTE**
18  Your test results aren't ready because we still have to perform the blood analysis.     **ANALYSE**
19  The king rewarded the knight for his loyalty.     **LOYAL**
20  GPS can pinpoint our exact geographical location.     **GEOGRAPHY**
21  It was very impolite of you not to say thank you.     **POLITE**
22  I'm not a big fan of coffee, but I do like the occasional cup every now and then.     **OCCASION**
23  It's a good idea to take vitamin suppliments to boost your immunity to certain diseases.     **IMMUNE**
24  I misread your message and that's why I'm late. Sorry!     **READ**
25  Does the film have English subtitles?     **TITLES**
26  Nothing is impossible if you put your mind to it.     **POSSIBLE**
27  Her refusal to join us was disappointing.     **REFUSE**
28  They're renovating their home because they want to make it more liveable.     **LIVE**
29  Stop being so indecisive and make up your mind!     **DECISIVE**
30  My parents think I'm irresponsible because I'm always late when they arrange to meet me somewhere.     **RESPONSIBLE**
31  Philosophers are very good at exposing illogical arguments.     **LOGICAL**
32  The reason you don't understand what he's saying is that he is talking a lot of nonsense.     **SENSE**
33  He lost all his money and now he is penniless.     **PENNY**
34  The chicken was undercooked and that's why we all got food poisoning.     **COOK**
35  It's a really bad idea to do something so risky.     **RISK**
36  If the two of you co-operate, you will get the job done a lot faster.     **OPERATE**
37  Luckily, our dog and cat interact with each other quite well.     **ACT**
38  It's incredible, that for doctors today, a heart transplant is a matter of routine.     **PLANT**

39  I though the joke was going to be really funny, but the punchline was a complete anticlimax.   **CLIMAX**

40  Children, please gather round the blackboard in a semicircle.   **CIRCLE**

41  I told my boss I'm so busy I need to hire an assistant to help me.   **ASSIST**

42  What frequency is this radio station on?   **FREQUENT**

43  When you faint, you briefly lose consciousness.   **CONSCIOUS**

44  I don't think the water in this stream is drinkable.   **DRINK**

45  I liked his talk even though it was a bit repetitive.   **REPEAT**

46  I think you should get a professional opinion.   **PROFESSION**

47  My music teacher expects nothing less than excellence.   **EXCEL**

48  James knew he wanted to become a sailor the first time he stepped on a yacht.   **SAIL**

49  I'm taking pills to counteract my high blood pressure.   **ACT**

50  How many employees do you have working for you?   **EMPLOY**

51  She had a look of confusion on her face.   **CONFUSE**

52  The sauce was rich and creamy.   **CREAM**

53  We need to finalise the date of our wedding soon.   **FINAL**

54  She asked the dressmaker to lengthen her trousers.   **LENGTH**

55  He went to a prison for the criminally insane.   **SANE**

56  This is a non-smoking area. You aren't allowed to smoke in here.   **SMOKING**

57  The inhabitants of this city left long ago.   **INHABIT**

58  George pointed out the distinction between science fiction and fantasy.   **DISTINCT**

59  She is extremely childish. She should grow up.   **CHILD**

60  My parents give me a small allowance each week.   **ALLOW**

61  The editor asked the author to write a longer introduction to his book.   **INTRODUCE**

62  The workers voted to go on strike.   **WORK**

63  My daughter wants to become a violinist.   **VIOLIN**

64  Police offers are there to enforce the law.   **FORCE**

65  They decided to wear traditional costumes.   **TRADITION**

66  The burglar was caught by the police.   **BURGLE**

67  I was shy when I was a child, but I taught myself to be confident.   **CONFIDE**

68  Can you pick up some eggs when you're at the supermarket?   **MARKET**

69  She has been a foreign correspondent for that newspaper for over a decade.   **CORRESPOND**

70  Do you know which mushrooms are poisonous?   **POISON**

71  Taste in art isn't objective; it's subjective.   **SUBJECT**

72  Watch out! That snake is venomous.   **VENOM**

73  You need to shorten that dress – it's far too long.   **SHORT**

74  He's taking a defiant stand on the issue.   **DEFIANCE**

75  I thought the game would be closer, but unfortunately, my team were well and truly outclassed.   **CLASSED**

76  Can you help me put these books into alphabetical order?   **ALPHABET**

77  There is an abundance of wildlife in the park this year.   **ABUNDANT**

78  My grandfather has bifocal glasses because he is both short-sighted and long-sighted.   **FOCAL**

79  He is a multitalented musician. He plays six instruments, sings, composes, produces and arranges.   **TALENT**

80  I really enjoyed watching that programme, it was very educational.   **EDUCATION**

# Key Word Transformations

**Complete the second sentence so that it has a similar meaning to the first sentence. Use the word given and other words to complete the sentence. Do not change the given word.**

1  He invited both his friends and his colleagues to the party.
   **ONLY**  He invited not only his friends but also his colleagues to the party.

2  Rather than walk to the hospital, we took a taxi.
   **INSTEAD**  Instead of walking to the hospital, we took a taxi.

3  People say Brian is a talented actor.
   **SAID**  It is said that Brian is a talented actor.

4  I was completely unaware of your decision to get a pet.
   **IDEA**  I had no idea (that) you (had) decided to get a pet.

5  Alice prefers playing sport to going to the gym.
   **RATHER**  Alice would rather play sport than/would play sport rather than go to the gym.

6  They couldn't drive to the hotel because they had flat tyre.
   **PREVENTED**  Their flat tyre prevented them from driving to the hotel.

7  The insurance company asked me to describe the accident in detail.
   **FULL**  The insurance company asked me to give full details of the accident.

8  She speaks Spanish fluently.
   **FLUENT**  She is fluent in Spanish.

9  When did you start writing the book?
   **BEEN**  How long have you been writing the book?

10  He won't tell me the reason he is upset, despite my insistence.
   **EVEN**  He won't tell me why he is upset even though I insisted.

11  It was thoughtless of them to treat their guests with such rudeness.
   **SO**  They should not have been so rude to their guests.

12  They will be selling tickets for the Christmas pantomime at the box office.
   **SALE**  Tickets for the Christmas pantomime will be/go on sale at the box office.

13  Gary took a taxi so that he wouldn't be late.
   **FEAR**  Gary took a taxi for/out of fear of being late.

14  If you go online and book your tickets early, you'll get a better price.
   **ADVANCE**  Provided you go online and book your tickets in advance, you'll get a better price.

15  I don't find sport at all interesting.
   **IN**  I have no interest in sport whatsoever.

16  Somebody robbed the bank a week ago.
   **BROKEN**  The bank was broken into a week ago.

17  You'd better see a doctor.
   **WERE**  If I were you, I would see a doctor.

18  Sally doesn't do as much exercise as she did in the past.
   **USED**  Sally used to do more exercise than she does now.

19  You won't get good marks if you don't study hard.
   **BY**  Only by studying hard will you get good marks.

20  They bought the building because they planned to start a business.
   **VIEW**  They bought the building with a view to starting a business.

21  She was about to take a bath when the doorbell rang.
   **POINT**  She was on the point of taking a bath when the doorbell rang.

22  I am not upset with Joe, despite his breaking my lamp.
   **THOUGH**  I am not upset with Joe, even though he broke my lamp.

23  But for the help of my tutor, I'd never have passed the exam.
   **FOR**  If it hadn't been for the help of my tutor, I'd never have passed the exam.

24  His voice surprised us when he sang.
   **ABACK**  We were taken aback by his singing voice.

**25** They rejected our offer on the house.
**DOWN** — Our offer on the house was turned down by them.

**26** I believe swimming is the best way to stay fit.
**SHAPE** — In my opinion, the best way to stay/keep in shape is to go swimming.

**27** We try to pay the bills on time.
**FALL** — We don't want to fall behind on/with the bills.

**28** They say that the tomb has a curse on it.
**SAID** — The tomb is said to have a curse on it.

**29** He spent ages preparing dinner.
**TOOK** — It took him ages to prepare dinner.

**30** Not all unions agreed with the strike.
**AGREEMENT** — Not all the unions were in agreement with the strike.

**31** The driving test wasn't as easy as I'd expected.
**DIFFICULT** — The driving test was more difficult than I'd expected.

**32** John might have an artist paint his portrait.
**PAINTED** — John is thinking about/of having/getting his portrait painted by an artist.

**33** I'm sure he didn't intend to be rude.
**INTENTION** — I'm sure he had no intention of being rude.

**34** Can't you think of a better idea?
**BEST** — Is that the best idea you can think of?

**35** Shall I bring the washing in?
**ME** — Would you like me to bring the washing in?

**36** Talking in the library isn't allowed.
**SUPPOSED** — You aren't supposed to talk in the library.

**37** "You ate my sandwich," she said to him.
**ACCUSED** — She accused him of eating/having eaten her sandwich.

**38** His parents won't let him buy a motorbike.
**ALLOWED** — He isn't allowed to buy a motorbike.

**39** When did they move to Switzerland?
**SINCE** — How long has it been since they moved to Switzerland?

**40** Joan couldn't get the book she wanted because they had sold out.
**UNABLE** — Joan was unable to get the book she wanted because they had sold out.

**41** I'm sure Karen hasn't written the letter yet.
**HAVE** — Karen can't/won't have written the letter yet.

**42** It's probable that he will fly via Amsterdam.
**LIKELY** — He is likely to fly/will likely fly via Amsterdam.

**43** Everyone brought a packed lunch except Richard.
**ONLY** — The only person who didn't bring a packed lunch was Richard.

**44** You've bought more apples than you need to make the pie.
**SO** — You needn't have bought so many apples to make the pie.

**45** Would you mind if I opened the window?
**TO** — Would you object to me opening the window?

**46** We arrived early so we could get a good seat.
**HOPE** — We arrived early in the hope of getting a good seat.

**47** It's a four-hour flight from London to Athens.
**TAKES** — It takes four hours to fly from London to Athens.

**48** She could hardly read the doctor's handwriting.
**DIFFICULTY** — She had difficulty (in) reading the doctor's handwriting.

**49** Nobody knows where the theatre is.
**ANYBODY** — There isn't anybody who/that knows where the theatre is.

**50** One has to taste it to fully appreciate it.
**TASTED** — It has to be tasted to be fully appreciated.

**51** That's the music school where I learnt the piano.
**TAUGHT** — I was taught the piano at that music school.

**52** Shall I mow the lawn?
**LIKE** — Would you like me to mow the lawn?

**53** When did you last go to the cinema?
**TIME** — When was the last time you went to the cinema?

54 They made us wait 40 minutes before they showed us to our table.
**WERE** We were made to wait/kept waiting 40 minutes before they showed us to our table.

55 It was hard for them to get used to their new neighbourhood.
**TIME** It took them time to get used to their new neighbourhood.

56 He managed to get the promotion.
**SUCCEEDED** He succeeded in getting the promotion.

57 I think it would be a good idea to call and book a table.
**SUGGEST** I suggest we call and book/calling and booking a table.

58 I enjoyed my holiday very much.
**FUN** I had fun on my holiday.

59 Dad let me go to the party last week.
**ALLOWED** I was allowed to go to the party last week.

60 She is quieter than her sister.
**NOT** She is not as noisy/loud as her sister.

61 "You've scratched my car," she said to him.
**ACCUSED** She accused him of scratching her car.

62 She will probably be late for the film.
**UNLIKELY** She is unlikely to be early/on time for the film.

63 She wishes she hadn't moved so far away from home.
**REGRETS** She regrets moving so far away from home.

64 After the play finished, the cast made a curtain call.
**END** At the end of the play the cast made a curtain call.

65 The jeans I bought no longer fit me.
**GROWN** I have grown out of the jeans that I bought.

66 "I'm sorry I lost your umbrella," she said to him.
**FOR** She apologised for losing/having lost his umbrella.

67 Jenny hasn't been to dance class in a month.
**LAST** It's a month since Jenny last went to dance class.

68 He shouldn't have been rude to the customer.
**FOOLISH** It was foolish of him to be rude to the customer.

69 I was unable to tolerate my noisy neighbours any longer.
**PUT** I couldn't put up with my noisy neighbours any longer.

70 They have cancelled the concert because the singer is ill.
**CALLED** The concert has been called off because the singer is ill.

71 Is it OK for me to use your computer?
**OBJECT** Would you object to me using your computer?

72 Don't hesitate to tell me if you need anything.
**TWICE** Don't think twice before telling/about asking me if you need anything.

73 I'd prefer him to think it over.
**RATHER** I would rather he thought it over.

74 His boss won't let him leave early.
**ALLOWED** He isn't allowed to leave early.

75 She was late due to the power cut on the underground.
**ON** She didn't arrive on time due to/because of the power cut on the underground.

76 "Shall I save this for later?" she asked herself.
**WHETHER** She wondered whether she should save it for later.

77 He won't make it to the Olympics this time.
**CHANCE** He has no chance of making it to the Olympics this time.

78 It's unlikely that I'll finish this project tonight.
**TO** I'm not likely to finish this project tonight.

79 They're building a new hospital at the moment.
**BEING** A new hospital is being built at the moment.

80 It's pointless complaining about the noise.
**WORTH** It's not worth complaining about the noise.

| Abbreviations | (adj) adjective | (det) determiner | (phr) phrase | (pl n) plural noun | (prep) preposition | (sth) something |
|---|---|---|---|---|---|---|
| | (adv) adverb | (esp) especially | (phr v) phrasal verb | (pp) past participle | (pro) pronoun | (usu) usually |
| | (conj) conjunction | (n) noun | | | (sb) somebody | (v) verb |

## Module 1

### 1 (p. 7)

**beautiful** /ˈbjuːtɪfəl/ (adj) = not ugly; attractive

**boring** /ˈbɔːrɪŋ/ (adj) = not interesting; dull

**cheap** /tʃiːp/ (adj) = not costing a lot of money

**city** /ˈsɪti/ (n) = a large town

**clean** /kliːn/ (adj) = not dirty

**crowded** /ˈkraʊdəd/ (adj) = full of people

**dangerous** /ˈdeɪndʒərəs/ (adj) = harmful, unsafe

**dirty** /ˈdɜːti/ (adj) = not clean

**exciting** /ɪkˈsaɪtɪŋ/ (adj) = making you feel happy and enthusiastic

**expensive** /ɪkˈspensɪv/ (adj) = costing a lot of money

**historic** /hɪˈstɒrɪk/ (adj) = having to do with the past

**modern** /ˈmɒdn/ (adj) = contemporary; recent

**neighbourhood** /ˈneɪbəhʊd/ (n) = a part of a town

**nightlife** /ˈnaɪtlaɪf/ (n) = entertainment that happens in the evening

**noisy** /ˈnɔɪzi/ (adj) = loud

**park** /pɑːk/ (n) = a large green space in a town

**quiet** /ˈkwaɪət/ (adj) = having or making little noise

**road** /rəʊd/ (n) = a surface for vehicles to drive on

**safe** /seɪf/ (adj) = free from danger

**square** /skweə/ (n) = a shape with four equal sides

**ugly** /ˈʌgli/ (adj) = unattractive

### 1a (pp. 8-9)

**bridge** /brɪdʒ/ (n) = a structure that is built over a river, railway or road so that people or vehicles can cross

**bus lane** /ˈbʌs leɪn/ (n) = a surface which is part of a road for buses to drive on

**bus stop** /ˈbʌs stɒp/ (n) = a place where buses stop for people to get on or off

**catchy title** /ˈkætʃi ˈtaɪtl/ (n) = the name of a book or film which is easy to remember

**channel hop** /ˈtʃænl hɒp/ (v) = to change from one TV channel to another in search of sth to watch

**crime** /kraɪm/ (n) = an illegal action which is punished by law

**cycle lane** /ˈsaɪkəl leɪn/ (n) = a surface which is part of a road for bicycles to ride on

**cut (sb) off** /ˈkʌt ˈɒf/ (phr v) = to block sb's exit

**documentary** /ˌdɒkjəˈmentəri/ (n) = a film or TV programme that shows real events and information about sb or sth

**draw** /drɔː/ (v) = to pull; to attract

**feature** /ˈfiːtʃə/ (n) = an interesting or characteristic part of sth

**feature** /ˈfiːtʃə/ (v) = to include, to present

**focus (on)** /ˈfəʊkəs ɒn/ (v) = to give a lot of attention to sth

**hand-held camera** /ˌhænd held ˈkæmərə/ (n) = a piece of equipment which is used for filming and small enough to be used with one or two hands

**injure** /ˈɪndʒə/ (v) = to hurt

**injured** /ˈɪndʒəd/ (adj) = hurt or wounded

**level crossing** /ˌlevəl ˈkrɒsɪŋ/ (n) = a place where a railway crosses a road

**narrator** /nəˈreɪtə/ (n) = the person who tells a story

**oncoming traffic** /ˌɒnkʌmɪŋ ˈtræfɪk/ (n) = vehicles that are coming towards you

**pavement** /ˈpeɪvmənt/ (n) = a surface beside a road for people to walk on

**pedestrian** /pəˈdestriən/ (n) = a person who is walking instead of travelling in a vehicle

**police car** /pəˈliːs kɑː/ (n) = a vehicle used by members of the police

**police video** /pəˈliːs ˈvɪdiəʊ/ (n) = a recording of an illegal action filmed from police cars, helicopters, etc

**popular** /ˈpɒpjələ/ (adj) = liked by a lot of people

**reality show** /riˈæləti ʃəʊ/ (n) = a television programme that usu presents how people behave in real life or people placed in a situation where they are filmed over a continuous period of time

**real-life** /rɪəl laɪf/ (adj) = not imagined

**road crime** /rəʊd kraɪm/ (n) = an illegal action committed by drivers of vehicles

**road sign** /rəʊd saɪn/ (n) = a notice that gives information to drivers

**scene** /siːn/ (n) = a part of a film, play or programme in which a series of actions or events happen in the same place

**shocked** /ʃɒkt/ (adj) = very surprised and upset by sth bad that happens unexpectedly

**speed** /spiːd/ (v) = to move or drive fast

**suspect** /ˈsʌspekt/ (n) = sb who may have committed an illegal action

**traffic light** /ˈtræfɪk laɪt/ (n) = a set of lights which is used to start and stop vehicles

**tunnel** /ˈtʌnl/ (n) = a long underground passage

**U-turn** /ˈjuː ˈtɜːn/ (n) = an action when driving which results in travelling in the opposite direction

**video footage** /ˈvɪdiəʊ ˌfʊtɪdʒ/ (n) = a film of an event

**viewer** /ˈvjuːə/ (n) = sb who watches TV

**voice-over** /ˈvɔɪs əʊvə/ (n) = the sound of sb speaking and describing what is happening

**zebra crossing** /ˌziːbrə ˈkrɒsɪŋ, ˌze-/ (n) = black and white lines on a road where people cross

**1b (pp. 10-11)**

**absolute beginner** /ˈæbsəluːt bɪgɪnə/ (n) = a person who is doing an activity for the first time

**amusement park** /əˈmjuːzmənt ˌpɑːk/ (n) = a place with exciting rides

**bowling alley** /ˈbəʊlɪŋ ˌæli/ (n) = a place where you play a game trying to knock down objects with a ball

**check out** /tʃek aʊt/ (phr v) = to go to see

**discount** /ˈdɪskaʊnt/ (n) = a special reduction in the price of sth

**entrance price** /ˈentrəns praɪs/ (n) = the cost of entering a building or place

**except** /ɪkˈsept/ (conj) = not including

**exercise** /ˈeksəsaɪz/ (v) = to do physical activities to strengthen your body

**fitness freak** /ˈfɪtnɪs friːk/ (n) = a person who takes it very seriously to by physically strong and healthy

**food outlet** /fuːd ˈaʊtlet/ (n) = a place where you can buy food

**games arcade** /geɪmz ɑːˌkeɪd/ (n) = a place where you play games on machines

**go bowling** (phr) = to play the game of bowling

**go on rides** (phr) = to do the activities at an amusement park

**gym** /dʒɪm/ (n) = a place where you go to exercise using equipment

**ice rink** /aɪs rɪŋk/ (n) = an area of ice which is prepared for people to skate on

**play sports** (phr) = to participate in competitive physical activities

**play video games** (phr) = to play games in which you move objects on a screen

**selection** /sɪˈlekʃən/ (n) = choice

**shop** /ʃɒp/ (v) = to go to places that sell things in order to buy them

**shopping centre** /ˈʃɒpɪŋ ˌsentə/ (n) = a place where lots of shops are built close together

**skate** /skeɪt/ (v) = to move on ice wearing specially-designed shoes

**sports centre** /ˈspɔːts ˌsentə/ (n) = a building where you can play different sports

**swim** /swɪm/ (v) = to move through water using your body

**track down** /træk daʊn/ (phr v) = to find after a long search

**treat yourself to** (phr) = to buy sth nice for yourself

**trendy shop** /ˈtrendi ʃɒp/ (n) = a shop that sells things in fashion

**water park** /ˈwɔːtə pɑːk/ (n) = a large area with many pools and slides

**1c (p. 12)**

**ancient** /ˈeɪnʃənt/ (adj) = belonging to the distant past

**breeding season** /ˈbriːdɪŋ ˌsiːzən/ (n) = a time of year when animals produce young animals

**cable car** /ˈkeɪbəl kɑː/ (n) = a vehicle that hangs from thick wires and transports people up and down high areas

**cliff** /klɪf/ (n) = a steep rocky surface next to the sea

**coast** /kəʊst/ (n) = land next to the sea

**coastline** /ˈkəʊstlaɪn/ (n) = land which runs along the edge of the sea

**elephant seal** /ˈeləfənt siːl/ (n) = a very big type of seal

**fairytale mansion** /ˈfeəriteɪl ˈmænʃən/ (n) = a very beautiful, large house

**fall** /fɔːl/ (n) = autumn

**female** /ˈfiːmeɪl/ (n) = woman

**give birth** /ˌgɪv ˈbɜːθ/ (phr) = to have a baby

**impressive** /ɪmˈpresɪv/ (adj) = causing admiration

**including** /ɪnˈkluːdɪŋ/ (prep) = having as a part of

**miss** /mɪs/ (v) = to be late for sth

**pup** /pʌp/ (n) = a baby seal

**return** /rɪˈtɜːn/ (v) = to come back to a place

**ride** /raɪd/ (v) = to sit on a horse or bicycle and control its movement

**road trip** /ˈrəʊd trɪp/ (n) = a long journey using a personal vehicle

**sandy beach** /ˌsændi ˈbiːtʃ/ (n) = an area of sand next to the sea

**sight** /saɪt/ (n) = a tourist attraction

**skyscraper** /ˈskaɪˌskreɪpə/ (n) = a very tall modern building

**spectacular** /spekˈtækjələ/ (adj) = impressive; extraordinary

**steep** /stiːp/ (adj) = (of a road or hill) going up or down very quickly

**wild animal** /ˌwaɪld ˈænəməl/ (n) = an animal that grows in its natural environment

**zebra** /ˈziːbrə, ˈze-/ (n) = an animal that looks like a horse with black and white lines

**1d (p. 13)**

**bike** /baɪk/ (n) = a motorcycle or a bicycle

**car** /kɑː/ (n) = a vehicle with four wheels that carries a small number of passengers

**cost** /kɒst/ (v) = to have a price

**coach** /kəʊtʃ/ (n) = a bus for long journeys

**customer** /ˈkʌstəmə/ (n) = sb who buys goods or services, from a shop, company, etc
**ferry** /ˈferi/ (n) = a boat that takes people, goods and vehicles across an area of water
**motorbike** /ˈməʊtəˌbaɪk/ (n) = a vehicle with two wheels and an engine
**plane** /pleɪn/ (n) = a vehicle that flies
**return** /rɪˈtɜːn/ (adj) = allowing you to travel to a place and back again
**single** /ˈsɪŋgəl/ (adj) = allowing you to take a one-way trip
**taxi** /ˈtæksi/ (n) = a car with a driver who you pay to take you somewhere
**ticket** /ˈtɪkət/ (n) = a piece of paper to show that you have paid for a journey
**train** /treɪn/ (n) = a long vehicle which travels along metal tracks
**underground** /ˈʌndəgraʊnd/ (n) = a system of trains which travel under a city

**1e (pp. 14-15)**

**bubble** /ˈbʌbəl/ (n) = a ball of liquid which contains air or gas
**cliff** /klɪf/ (n) = a steep rocky surface next to the sea
**climb** /klaɪm/ (v) = to go up or onto the top of sth
**crawl (out)** /krɔːl ˈaʊt/ (v) = to come out of a place on your hands and knees
**earthquake** /ˈɜːθkweɪk/ (n) = a sudden violent movement of the earth's surface
**engine** /ˈendʒən/ (n) = the part of a vehicle that uses fuel to make it move
**escape** /ɪˈskeɪp/ (v) = to get away
**fall (into)** /fɔːl ˈɪntə/ (v) = to move down into a place without intending it
**fatal** /ˈfeɪtl/ (adj) = causing death

**feed** /fiːd/ (v) = to give sb food to eat
**get a snake bite** (phr) = to receive a wound from the teeth of a snake
**get caught in a flash flood** (phr) = to be stuck in a place which suddenly became covered in water
**get into trouble** (phr) = to be in a situation with a lot of problems
**get lost** (phr) = to lose one's way
**get stuck in mud** (phr) = to be unable to get out of a mixture of soil and water
**get stung by bugs** (phr) = to receive wounds from biting insects
**ground** /graʊnd/ (n) = the surface of the Earth
**hide** /haɪd/ (v) = to keep sth out of view
**insect repellent** /ˈɪnsekt rɪˌpelənt/ (n) = a substance which keeps insects away
**lie flat** (phr) = to lie down in a horizontal position
**litter** /ˈlɪtə/ (v) = to leave rubbish on the ground
**meet dangerous animals** (phr) = to be in the same place as animals which can harm you
**mosquito** /məˈskiːtəʊ/ (n) = a small insect that flies and feeds on blood
**mud bog** /mʌd bɒg/ (n) = an area of land which is covered in wet soil
**noise** /nɔɪz/ (n) = a sound which is often loud
**on a lead** (phr) = wearing a collar that has a chain or sth similar connected to it
**panic** /ˈpænɪk/ (v) = to suddenly feel frightened
**poisonous** /ˈpɔɪzənəs/ (adj) = containing or producing poison

**pressure** /ˈpreʃə/ (n) = a situation that causes you to feel stress
**pull (in)** /pʊl ˈɪn/ (v) = to take hold of sth and move towards oneself
**reptile** /ˈreptaɪl/ (n) = a cold-blooded creature that lays eggs
**rubbish** /ˈrʌbɪʃ/ (n) = waste material
**rule** /ruːl/ (n) = an instruction about what you must or must not do
**run away** /ˌrʌn əˈweɪ/ (phr v) = to escape
**scorpion** /ˈskɔːpiən/ (n) = a poisonous creature
**shake** /ʃeɪk/ (v) = to move sth quickly backwards and forwards or up and down
**survive** /səˈvaɪv/ (v) = to continue to exist after a threatening situation
**swallow** /ˈswɒləʊ/ (v) = to make sth or sb disappear
**swamp** /swɒmp/ (n) = a marsh
**trip** /trɪp/ (n) = a short journey

**1f (p. 16-17)**

**block of flats** /ˌblɒk əv ˈflæts/ (n) = a large building with many flats
**bungalow** /ˈbʌŋgələʊ/ (n) = a house that has only one floor
**city centre** /ˌsɪti ˈsentə/ (n) = the central part of a large town esp where most shops are
**cottage** /ˈkɒtɪdʒ/ (n) = a small house in the countryside
**detached house** /dɪˌtætʃt ˈhaʊs/ (n) = a house which is not joined to another house
**forest** /ˈfɒrəst/ (n) = a large area of land covered with trees
**front garden** /ˌfrʌnt ˈgɑːdn/ (n) = an area of land belonging to a house and situated in front of it
**housing** /ˈhaʊzɪŋ/ (n) = buildings for people to live in
**imagine** /ɪˈmædʒən/ (v) = to create a picture in your mind about sth
**lucky** /ˈlʌki/ (adj) = fortunate

**move into** /ˌmuːv ˈɪntə/ (phr v) = to begin living somewhere
**own** /əʊn/ (v) = to have sth that belongs to you
**paradise** /ˈpærədaɪs/ (n) = a perfect place
**penthouse** /ˈpenthaʊs/ (n) = a flat at the top of a building
**pretty sure** (phr) = quite certain
**semi-detached house** /ˌsemi dɪˌtætʃt ˈhaʊs/ (n) = a house which is joined to another house on one side
**skyscraper** /ˈskaɪˌskreɪpə/ (n) = a very tall modern building
**storey** /ˈstɔːri/ (n) = floor; level of a building
**townhouse** /ˈtaʊnhaʊs/ (n) = a house which is joined to other houses on both sides
**view** /vjuː/ (n) = sight; scenery
**villa** /ˈvɪlə/ (n) = a large house in a warm country

**1g (p. 18)**

**appliance** /əˈplaɪəns/ (n) = an electrical device used in the house
**chore** /tʃɔː/ (n) = sth boring that needs to be done
**do the washing-up** (phr) = to wash dishes
**dust the furniture** (phr) = to remove dirt from tables, cupboards, etc with a cloth
**equipment** /ɪˈkwɪpmənt/ (n) = a set of necessary things for a particular purpose
**feature** /ˈfiːtʃə/ (n) = an interesting or characteristic part of sth
**furniture** /ˈfɜːnɪtʃə/ (n) = large movable things in a house or an office
**hoover the carpets** (phr) = to clean the carpets using a vacuum cleaner
**iron the clothes** (phr) = to make clothes smooth using an electrical device

**lay the table** (phr) = to prepare a table for a meal
**make the bed** (phr) = to tidy the bed after sleeping in it
**mop the floor** (phr) = to clean the floor with a stick that has a wet cloth fixed at one end
**neighbourhood** /ˈneɪbəhʊd/ (n) = a part of a town
**take out the rubbish** (phr) = to remove waste material from your house and throw it in a bin outside

**1h (p. 19)**

**awful** /ˈɔːfəl/ (adj) = terrible
**flatmate** /ˈflætmeɪt/ (n) = roommate
**invite** /ɪnˈvaɪt/ (v) = to ask sb to come to a place
**realise** /ˈrɪəlaɪz/ (v) = to understand
**responsibility** /rɪˌspɒnsəˈbɪləti/ (n) = the duty we have to deal with situations or people and make decisions
**share** /ʃeə/ (v) = to have or use sth with another person
**upset** /ˌʌpˈset/ (adj) = unhappy; frustrated

**1i (p. 20)**

**bank** /bæŋk/ (n) = a building where people keep their money
**(be) involved in** (phr) = be part of
**borrow books** (phr) = to take books that do not belong to you and give them back later
**car tyre** /ˈkɑː taɪə/ (n) = a rubber covering that fits around the wheel of a car
**care (for)** /ˈkeə fə, fɔː/ (v) = to look after
**check** /tʃek/ (v) = to examine sth to make sure that it is the way it should be
**citizen** /ˈsɪtəzən/ (n) = a legal resident of a country
**Citizenship** /ˈsɪtəzənʃɪp/ (n) = a school subject in which students learn about the roles and responsibilities of the people who live in a country

**community** /kəˈmjuːnəti/ (n) = the people who live in a particular area
**community centre** /kəˈmjuːnəti ˌsentə/ (n) = a place where local residents meet together and do various activities
**crime** /kraɪm/ (n) = an illegal action which is punished by law
**deposit money** (phr) = to put money in a bank
**hospital** /ˈhɒspɪtl/ (n) = a place where ill or injured people go for treatment
**in need** (phr) = needing help
**library** /ˈlaɪbrəri, -bri/ (n) = a building which contains a collection of books you can read or borrow
**obey laws** (phr) = to follow official rules
**obey signs** (phr) = to not go against the messages in public places
**petrol station** /ˈpetrəl ˌsteɪʃən/ (n) = a place where people stop to buy petrol
**police station** /pəˈliːs ˌsteɪʃən/ (n) = the office of the police
**post office** /ˈpəʊst ˌɒfəs/ (n) = a place where you can buy stamps and send letters or packages to people living far way
**public facility** /ˌpʌblɪk fəˈsɪləti/ (n) = a place where a particular activity happens for everyone to use
**public place** /ˌpʌblɪk ˈpleɪs/ (n) = a place which is accessible to everyone
**public service** /ˌpʌblɪk ˈsɜːvəs/ (n) = a service which is available for everyone
**public transportation** /ˌpʌblɪk trænspɔːˈteɪʃən/ (n) = buses and trains that are available for everyone to use
**queue** /kjuː/ (n) = a row of people waiting for sth
**report** /rɪˈpɔːt/ (v) = to tell sb that sth has happened

**report a crime** (phr) = to tell the police that an illegal action has happened

**respect** /rɪˈspekt/ (v) = to have a good opinion of sb/sth

**return books** (phr) = to bring back books that you borrowed

**sick** /sɪk/ (adj) = unwell; ill

**stamp** /stæmp/ (n) = a small piece of paper which you stick on an envelope to show that you have paid for postage

**take up** /ˌteɪk ˈʌp/ (phr v) = to start doing sth new

**train station** /treɪn ˌsteɪʃən/ (n) = a place where you wait for a train

**volunteer** /ˌvɒlənˈtɪə/ (v) = to do charitable or helpful work without pay

**wait my turn** (phr) = to wait in order to do sth, usu after sb else

**withdraw money** (phr) = to take out money from a bank

**Language Review 1 (p. 21)**

**cross** /krɒs/ (v) = to go across from one side of sth to the other

**due to** /djuː tə/ (prep) = because of

**safety** /ˈseɪfti/ (n) = security

**step (off)** /ˌstep ˈɒf/ (v) = to get off a place which has a raised area

**tournament** /ˈtʊənəmənt/ (n) = a competition with a series of games

**Skills Practice 1 (pp. 22-23)**

**crumbling shack** /ˌkrʌmblɪŋ ˈʃæk/ (n) = a small building which is in very bad condition

**obey** /əʊˈbeɪ, ə-/ (v) = to not go against

**sanitation** /ˌsænəˈteɪʃən/ (n) = a system for protecting people's health by keeping the area clean

**script** /skrɪpt/ (n) = the words in a film, play, etc

**slum** /slʌm/ (n) = a poor and crowded area of a city where the buildings are in bad condition

**vibrant** /ˈvaɪbrənt/ (adj) = full of energy and excitement

---

Module 2

**2 (p. 25)**

**bean** /biːn/ (n) = the seed of a climbing plant

**beef** /biːf/ (n) = the meat of a cow

**bread** /bred/ (n) = food made by mixing flour, water and yeast

**butter** /ˈbʌtə/ (n) = food which is a yellow colour and is made from cream, usu eaten on bread

**cabbage** /ˈkæbɪdʒ/ (n) = a large round vegetable with thick leaves

**cauliflower** /ˈkɒlɪˌflaʊə/ (n) = a large round vegetable which is white with green leaves on the outside

**cereal** /ˈsɪəriəl/ (n) = a grain such as wheat that can be eaten for breakfast with milk

**cheese** /tʃiːz/ (n) = hard or soft food which is a white or yellow colour and is made from milk

**cherry** /ˈtʃeri/ (n) = a very small, round red fruit

**chicken** /ˈtʃɪkən/ (n) = the meat of a bird which is kept on a farm

**cod** /kɒd/ (n) = a type of fish which is eaten as food

**coffee** /ˈkɒfi/ (n) = a drink made from dark beans or the powder made from these beans

**dairy product** /ˈdeəri ˌprɒdʌkt/ (n) = a type of food made from milk

**drink** /drɪŋk/ (n) = a liquid that one swallows, usu to refresh themselves

**egg** /eg/ (n) = food produced by a female chicken

**fish** /fɪʃ/ (n) = an animal that lives in water sometimes eaten as food

**fruit** /fruːt/ (n) = sth that grows on a tree or bush and can be eaten

**grape** /ɡreɪp/ (n) = a green or purple berry used for making wine

**lamb** /læm/ (n) = meat from a young sheep

**lemonade** /ˌleməˈneɪd/ (n) = a cold refreshing drink with a lemon flavour

**meat** /miːt/ (n) = parts of animals used as food

**milk** /mɪlk/ (n) = a white liquid produced by female animals such as cows

**orange juice** /ˈɒrəndʒ dʒuːs/ (n) = a drink made from a round orange fruit

**pasta** /ˈpæstə/ (n) = a food which we boil before eating, made from flour, water and eggs

**pear** /peə/ (n) = a sweet juicy fruit which is wider at the bottom than the top

**pepper** /ˈpepə/ (n) = a vegetable that can be green, red or yellow in colour and is used in salads and cooking

**poultry** /ˈpəʊltri/ (n) = birds, such as chickens and turkeys, bred for their meat

**prawn** /prɔːn/ (n) = a small pink sea animal with a shell and eaten as food

**rice** /raɪs/ (n) = small grains that come from a plant which we boil before eating

**salmon** /ˈsæmən/ (n) = a type of fish which lives in the sea but also swims up rivers

**tea** /tiː/ (n) = a hot drink made with dried leaves

**tomato** /təˈmɑːtəʊ/ (n) = a soft round red fruit which is used in salads and cooking

**trout** /traʊt/ (n) = a type of river fish

**tuna** /ˈtjuːnə/ (n) = a large sea fish

**vegetable** /ˈvedʒtəbəl/ (n) = a plant such as carrots, cabbage, etc that we eat

**yogurt** /ˈjɒɡət/ (n) = a thick liquid food made from milk

**2a (pp. 26-27)**

**attract** /əˈtrækt/ (v) = (of an event) to make sb come to it

**banana** /bəˈnɑːnə/ (n) = a long, curved fruit with a yellow skin

**book** /bʊk/ (v) = to make a reservation

**broccoli** /ˈbrɒkəli/ (n) = a green vegetable used in cooking

**carrot** /ˈkærət/ (n) = a long orange vegetable which grows underground

**celebrate** /ˈseləbreɪt/ (v) = to do sth enjoyable because of a special occasion

**celery** /ˈseləri/ (n) = a vegetable with long green stems that can be used in cooking and salads

**citrus** /ˈsɪtrəs/ (n) = an orange, lemon or similar fruit

**creation** /kriˈeɪʃən/ (n) = a thing that has been made

**cucumber** /ˈkjuːkʌmbə/ (n) = a long green vegetable eaten in salads

**design** /dɪˈzaɪn/ (v) = to plan and make a detailed drawing of sth

**dessert** /dɪˈzɜːt/ (n) = a sweet dish eaten after a meal

**event** /ɪˈvent/ (n) = an organised occasion

**experience** /ɪkˈspɪəriəns/ (v) = to feel sth

**exposition** /ˌekspəˈzɪʃən/ (n) = exhibition

**fireworks** /ˈfaɪəwɜːks/ (pl n) = objects that explode in the sky with bright colours and a loud noise

**float** /fləʊt/ (n) = a decorated vehicle which is used in celebrations

**gather** /ˈɡæðə/ (v) = to come together

**giant** /ˈdʒaɪənt/ (adj) = huge

**grateful** /ˈɡreɪtfəl/ (adj) = thankful

**imaginations runs wild** (phr) = creativity is uncontrolled

**juice** /dʒuːs/ (n) = a liquid which comes from fruit or vegetables

**lemon** /ˈlemən/ (n) = a yellow fruit with a sour taste

**local** /ˈləʊkəl/ (adj) = existing in the area where you live

**make the most of** (phr) = to get the best out of

**measure** /ˈmeʒə/ (v) = to be the size of

**onion** /ˈʌnjən/ (n) = a vegetable that can be used in cooking and salads and when it is cut it makes the eyes sting and water

**online** /ˌɒnˈlaɪn/ (adv) = on\over the Internet

**orange** /ˈɒrəndʒ/ (n) = a round orange fruit which is juicy

**parade** /pəˈreɪd/ (n) = a procession of people

**picturesque** /ˌpɪktʃəˈresk/ (adj) = pretty, esp in an old-fashioned way

**potato** /pəˈteɪtəʊ/ (n) = a round vegetable with a brown skin which grows underground

**product** /ˈprɒdʌkt/ (n) = sth made in a factory and sold

**resort** /rɪˈzɔːt/ (n) = a place many people go to for rest, sport etc

**similar** /ˈsɪmələ/ (adj) = alike

**sour** /saʊə/ (adj) = having a sharp, sometimes unpleasant, taste

**statue** /ˈstætʃuː/ (n) = a model of a person or animal

**strawberry** /ˈstrɔːbəri/ (n) = a tiny red fruit

**sweet** /swiːt/ (adj) = having a taste like sugar

**theme** /θiːm/ (n) = subject; topic

**ton** /tʌn/ (n) = 1,000 kilos

**2b (pp. 28-29)**

**aisle** /aɪl/ (n) = a passage between the lines of goods in a supermarket

**bag** /bæɡ/ (n) = a container with handles used to carry things

**bakery** /ˈbeɪkəri/ (n) = a shop where you can buy bread and cakes

**bar** /bɑː/ (n) = a long thin piece of sth

**bottle** /ˈbɒtl/ (n) = an object usu made of glass or plastic that contains liquid i.e. water, soft drink etc

**box** /bɒks/ (n) = a square or rectangular container in which people pack items

**bunch** /bʌntʃ/ (n) = a group of things that are fastened or held together

**carton** /ˈkɑːtn/ (n) = a box made of cardboard which contains a type of liquid

**cupboard** /ˈkʌbəd/ (n) = a set of shelves with doors used for storing things

**dairy product** /ˈdeəri ˌprɒdʌkt/ (n) = a type of food made from milk

**dinner party** /ˈdɪnə ˌpɑːti/ (n) = an evening event where people enjoy themselves by eating and drinking

**drink** /drɪŋk/ (n) = a liquid that one swallows, usu to refresh themselves

**eating habit** /ˈiːtɪŋ ˌhæbət/ (n) = what you eat usually

**expect** /ɪkˈspekt/ (v) = to believe that sth will happen

**fish** /fɪʃ/ (n) = an animal that lives in seas or rivers, often eaten as food

**fizzy drink** /ˌfɪzi ˈdrɪŋk/ (n) = a drink that has bubbles of gas

**frozen food** /ˌfrəʊzən ˈfuːd/ (n) = food that is kept in a freezer

**fruit** /fruːt/ (n) = sth that grows on a tree or bush and can be eaten

**jar** /dʒɑː/ (n) = a glass container with a lid

**junk food** /dʒʌŋk fuːd/ (n) = food which is unhealthy but is quick and easy to eat

**loaf** /ləʊf/ (n) = a large piece of bread that can be cut into slices

**meat** /miːt/ (n) = parts of animals used as food

**minced beef** /ˌmɪnst ˈbiːf/ (n) = meat from a cow which has been cut into tiny pieces

**pot** /pɒt/ (n) = a round container in which food such as yogurt is kept

**purse** /pɜːs/ (n) = a small bag used by women to hold money

**remember** /rɪˈmembə/ (v) = to not forget

**section** /ˈsekʃən/ (n) = a separate part of a supermarket

**snack** /snæk/ (n) = a quick, simple meal

**sweet** /swiːt/ (n) = a piece of food with sugar in it

**tin** /tɪn/ (n) = a metal container in which food can be preserved for a long period of time

**tub** /tʌb/ (n) = a plastic container in which food is kept

**vegetable** /ˈvedʒtəbəl/ (n) = a plant that we eat, such as carrots, cabbage, etc

**What's wrong?** (phr) = What's the matter?

## 2c (p. 30)

**baked goods** /ˈbeɪkt ɡʊdz/ (pl n) = food products that have been cooked in an oven

**batter** /ˈbætə/ (n) = a mixture of flour and water used to cover food before frying

**chipped** /tʃɪpt/ (pp) = cut into long small pieces

**deep fried** /ˈdiːp ˈfraɪd/ (adj) = cooked in lots of hot oil

**dish** /dɪʃ/ (n) = food that is prepared in a particular way

**ethnic cuisine** /ˌeθnɪk kwɪˈziːn/ (n) = a style of cooking which is specific to a country

**grab a snack** (phr) = get sth quick and easy to eat

**gravy** /ˈɡreɪvi/ (n) = a warm brown sauce made from the juice that comes from cooked meat mixed with flour and water

**jacket potato** /ˌdʒækət pəˈteɪtəʊ/ (n) = a potato baked whole in its skin

**mushy peas** /ˌmʌʃi ˈpiːz/ (pl n) = small green vegetables that have been cooked to a thick mixture

**pie** /paɪ/ (n) = a type of food covered in pastry

**sauce** /sɔːs/ (n) = a hot or cold liquid that you put on food

**side dish** /ˈsaɪd dɪʃ/ (n) = food which is eaten in addition to the main meal

**suit every taste** (phr) = appeal to everybody

**vinegar** /ˈvɪnɪɡə/ (n) = a sour liquid made from wine and used in salads or cooking

## 2d (p. 31)

**brownie** /ˈbraʊni/ (n) = a small square chocolate cake

**chips** /tʃɪps/ (pl n) = pieces of fried potato

**omelette** /ˈɒmlət/ (n) = food made with eggs mixed together and fried

**order** /ˈɔːdər/ (v) = to make a request for food or drinks at a restaurant

**scrambled egg** /ˌskræmbəld ˈeg/ (n) = food made with eggs mixed with milk and butter and usually eaten for breakfast

**side order** /ˈsaɪd ˌɔːdə/ (n) = food which you eat along with the main meal at a restaurant

**toast** /təʊst/ (n) = a slice of bread that has been heated until it turns brown

## 2e (pp. 32-33)

**ask (for)** /ˈɑːsk fə/ (v) = to request

**bill** /bɪl/ (n) = a written list showing how much you owe in return for a service

**boiling hot** /ˌbɔɪlɪŋ ˈhɒt/ (adj) = being at an extremely high temperature

**book** /bʊk/ (v) = to make a reservation

**cool down** /ˌkuːl ˈdaʊn/ (phr v) = to become less hot

**curtain** /ˈkɜːtn/ (n) = a piece of material which covers a window

**customer** /ˈkʌstəmə/ (n) = sb who buys goods or services, from a shop, company etc

**gallery** /ˈɡæləri/ (n) = a place or a shop where works of art are shown for people to admire or buy

**get used to** (phr) = to become accustomed to

**ice** /aɪs/ (n) = frozen water

**in the freezing cold** (phr) = where the temperature is extremely low

**landmark** /ˈlændmɑːk/ (n) = a building or place easily recognised

**leave** /liːv/ (v) = to go away from a place

**long** /lɒŋ/ (adv) = for a long time

**main dish** /ˈmeɪn dɪʃ/ (n) = the most important part of a meal

**menu** /ˈmenjuː/ (n) = a list of food and drinks at a restaurant

**order** /ˈɔːdə/ (n) = a request for food or drinks at a restaurant

**outside** /aʊtˈsaɪd/ (adv) = not in a building or room

**pay** /peɪ/ (v) = to give money in return for goods or a service

**regular interval** /ˌreɡjələr ˈɪntəvəl/ (n) = the period of time between events which are evenly repeated

**serve** /sɜːv/ (v) = to give sb food or drink in a restaurant

**show** /ʃəʊ/ (v) = to let sb see

**sip** /sɪp/ (v) = to drink small amounts

**so that** /ˈsəʊ ðət/ (conj) = in order to

**staff** /stɑːf/ (n) = personnel; employees

**take an order** (phr) = (of a waiter) to write down an order from a customer

**thick coat** /ˌθɪk ˈkəʊt/ (n) = a warm piece of clothing that you wear over your clothes when outside

**tip** /tɪp/ (n) = extra money given to a waiter for their service

**waiter** /ˈweɪtə/ (n) = a person who takes your order at a restaurant

**2f (pp. 34-35)**

**based** /beɪst/ (adj) = having as a main part

**benefit** /ˈbenəfɪt/ (n) = advantage

**cholesterol** /kəˈlestərɒl/ (n) = a type of fat which is harmful

**contain** /kənˈteɪn/ (v) = to include sth as a part of a whole

**creamy** /ˈkriːmi/ (adj) = having a soft smooth texture

**fat-free** /ˌfæt ˈfriː/ (adj) = having no fat

**flavour** /ˈfleɪvə/ (n) = taste

**floating market** /ˌfləʊtɪŋ ˈmɑːkət/ (n) = a place where you buy and sell things from small boats

**ingredient** /ɪnˈɡriːdiənt/ (n) = one of the parts that a type of food is made from

**iron** /ˈaɪən/ (n) = metal which is found in small amounts in the blood

**label** /ˈleɪbəl/ (n) = the piece of paper on a product that gives information about it

**lean** /liːn/ (adj) = having very little fat

**lower** /ˈləʊə/ (v) = to lessen

**low-fat** /ˌləʊ ˈfæt/ (adj) = having little fat

**mineral** /ˈmɪnərəl/ (n) = a chemical that your body needs to stay healthy

**olive oil** /ˌɒləv ˈɔɪl/ (n) = a yellow and green liquid extracted from olives, used in cooking

**poached egg** /ˌpəʊtʃt ˈeɡ/ (n) = an egg that has been cooked gently in boiling water

**protein** /ˈprəʊtiːn/ (n) = a substance found in food such as meat and eggs that is necessary for the body to grow and be strong

**remove** /rɪˈmuːv/ (v) = to take sth away

**replace** /rɪˈpleɪs/ (v) = to substitute

**salad dressing** /ˈsæləd ˌdresɪŋ/ (n) = a sauce we put on salads

**sensation** /senˈseɪʃən/ (n) = a feeling

**source** /sɔːs/ (n) = a person, thing or place that we get sth from

**takeaway** /ˈteɪkəweɪ/ (n) = food that we order to eat at home

**trim off** /ˌtrɪm ˈɒf/ (phr v) = to cut sth away

**vinegar** /ˈvɪnɪɡə/ (n) = a sour liquid made from wine and used in salads or cooking

**vitamin** /ˈvɪtəmən/ (n) = a natural substance in food that the body needs to stay healthy

**2g (p. 36)**

**add** /æd/ (v) = to put sth with sth else

**baking soda** /ˈbeɪkɪŋ ˌsəʊdə/ (n) = a white powder used in baking cakes to help them rise

**beat** /biːt/ (v) = (in cooking) to mix sth repeatedly

**boil** /bɔɪl/ (v) = to heat a liquid until bubbles appear

**chop** /tʃɒp/ (v) = to cut into small pieces

**cinnamon** /ˈsɪnəmən/ (n) = a sweet brown spice

**fry** /fraɪ/ (v) = to cook in boiling hot oil

**frying pan** /ˈfraɪ-ɪŋ pæn/ (n) = a metal container used to fry food

**grill** /ɡrɪl/ (v) = to cook food using direct heat esp above it

**melt** /melt/ (v) = to make sth become liquid (usu because of heat)

**mix** /mɪks/ (v) = to combine

**mixture** /ˈmɪkstʃə/ (n) = a combination of ingredients

**peel** /piːl/ (v) = to remove the skin of a fruit or vegetable

**pour** /pɔː/ (v) = to serve by flowing from a container

**preparation** /ˌprepəˈreɪʃən/ (n) = the process of things you do to get sth ready

**salt** /sɔːlt/ (n) = a white substance which gives flavour to food

**slice** /slaɪs/ (v) = to cut into thin pieces

**sour cream** /ˌsaʊə ˈkriːm/ (n) = a liquid with a sharp taste made from milk

**stir** /stɜː/ (v) = to mix with a spoon

**tablespoon** /ˈteɪbəlspuːn/ (n) = the amount that fits into a large spoon

**teaspoon** /ˈtiːspuːn/ (n) = the amount that fits into a small spoon

**2h (p. 37)**

**creamy** /ˈkriːmi/ (adj) = having a soft smooth texture

**delicious** /dɪˈlɪʃəs/ (adj) = very tasty

**dish** /dɪʃ/ (n) = food that is prepared in a particular way

**garlic** /ˈɡɑːlɪk/ (n) = a vegetable with a very strong taste

**herb** /hɜːb/ (n) = a plant used in cooking to add flavour to food

**salty** /ˈsɔːlti/ (adj) = having a lot of salt

**seafood** /ˈsiːfuːd/ (n) = fish and shellfish you can eat

**spicy** /ˈspaɪsi/ (adj) = having strong flavours from spices

**stew** /stjuː/ (n) = slowly cooked meat and vegetables

**sweet** /swiːt/ (adj) = having a taste like sugar

**2i (p. 38)**

**behaviour** /bɪˈheɪvjə/ (n) = the way sb acts; conduct

**bone** /bəʊn/ (n) = part of a skeleton

**brain** /breɪn/ (n) = the organ inside the head

**breathe** /briːð/ (v) = to take air into your lungs and send it out again

**calcium** /ˈkælsiəm/ (n) = a substance found in founds like milk and cheese that is good for teeth and bones

**carbohydrate** /ˌkɑːbəʊˈhaɪdreɪt, -drət/ (n) = a substance found in foods such as pasta, potatoes and bread that provides a lot of energy

**command** /kəˈmɑːnd/ (v) = to tell sb to do sth

**control** /kənˈtrəʊl/ (v) = to make sb or sth do what you want

**covering** /ˈkʌvərɪŋ/ (n) = a layer that is over sth else so as to protect it

**digest** /daɪˈdʒest, də-/ (v) = to change food in your stomach into substances your body needs

**energy** /ˈenədʒi/ (n) = the power to be physically and mentally active

**fat** /fæt/ (n) = an oily or greasy substance found in plants and animals that is very high in energy

**muscle** /ˈmʌsəl/ (n) = a tissue in the body that connects two bones

**natural** /ˈnætʃərəl/ (adj) – produced by nature

**nervous system** /ˈnɜːvəs ˌsɪstəm/ (n) = the system in your body which controls your sensations and movements

**oily** /ˈɔɪli/ (adj) = (of food) having a lot of oil or fat

**protect** /prəˈtekt/ (v) = to secure; to keep from harm

**protein** /ˈprəʊtiːn/ (n) = a substance found in food such as meat and eggs that keeps our body strong and healthy

**pump blood** (phr) = (of the heart) to send blood around the body

**repair** /rɪˈpeə/ (v) = to fix sth damaged

**science** /ˈsaɪəns/ (n) = the study of the physical world

**sense of touch** /ˌsens əv ˈtʌtʃ/ (n) = the ability to feel through touch

**skin** /skɪn/ (n) = the outer layer of the body

**support** /səˈpɔːt/ (v) = to hold sth together

## Skills Practice 2 (pp. 40-41)

**inventive** /ɪnˈventɪv/ (adj) = having clever and interesting ideas

**native (to)** /ˈneɪtɪv tə/ (adj) = coming from a particular place

### Module 3

### 3 (p. 43)

**achievement** /əˈtʃiːvmənt/ (n) = accomplishment

**become** /bɪˈkʌm/ (v) = to begin to be sth

**discover** /dɪsˈkʌvə/ (v) = to find

**impress** /ɪmˈpres/ (v) = to make sb admire you

**invent** /ɪnˈvent/ (v) = to create sth new

**light bulb** /ˈlaɪt bʌlb/ (n) = an object which produces light from electricity

**paint** /peɪnt/ (v) = to produce a picture using paint

**president** /ˈprezədənt/ (n) = the leader of a government

**walk** /wɔːk/ (v) = to move on a surface using one's feet

### 3a (pp. 44-45)

**a whole range** (phr) = a wide variety of

**accurate** /ˈækjərət/ (adj) = precise

**achieve** /əˈtʃiːv/ (v) = to accomplish

**ahead of their time** (phr) = too advanced to be understood

**anatomy** /əˈnætəmi/ (n) = the body of a living thing

**based (on)** /ˈbeɪst ɒn/ (adj) = developed from

**bridge** /brɪdʒ/ (n) = a structure that is built over a river, railway or road so that people or vehicles can cross

**calculator** /ˈkælkjəleɪtə/ (n) = an electrical device that you use to do mathematical calculations

**canal system** /kəˈnæl ˌsɪstəm/ (n) = a set of connected artificial rivers

**century** /ˈsentʃəri/ (n) = a period of a hundred years

**consider** /kənˈsɪdə/ (v) = to think about

**construct** /kənˈstrʌkt/ (v) = to build; to create

**curious** /ˈkjʊəriəs/ (adj) = very interested in learning about sth

**design** /dɪˈzaɪn/ (v) = to plan and make a detailed drawing of sth

**detailed** /ˈdiːteɪld/ (adj) = elaborate; giving a lot of information

**engineer** /ˌendʒəˈnɪə/ (n) = a person whose job is to design or build machines or buildings

**fascinating** /ˈfæsəneɪtɪŋ/ (adj) = very interesting

**geologist** /dʒiˈɒlədʒəst/ (n) = a person who studies rocks and soil

**human body** /ˌhjuːmən ˈbɒdi/ (n) = the body of a person

**include** /ɪnˈkluːd/ (v) = to have as part of

**incredible** /ɪnˈkredəbəl/ (adj) = fantastic

**industry** /ˈɪndəstri/ (n) = mass production of a type of goods

**intelligent** /ɪnˈtelɪdʒənt/ (adj) = clever

**invent** /ɪnˈvent/ (v) = to create sth new

**inventor** /ɪnˈventə/ (n) = a person who creates sth which has never been made before

**lifetime** /ˈlaɪftaɪm/ (n) = the period of sb's life

**machine** /məˈʃiːn/ (n) = a piece of equipment with moving parts

**map** /mæp/ (n) = a picture that shows where countries or roads are

**material** /məˈtɪəriəl/ (n) = a substance from which sth can be made

**mirror** /ˈmɪrə/ (n) = a piece of polished glass which you use to look at yourself

**paint** /peɪnt/ (v) = to produce a picture using paint

**parachute** /ˈpærəʃuːt/ (n) = an umbrella-shaped piece of material which allows sb to drop to the ground safely after jumping out of an aircraft

**perfect proportions** /ˌpɜːfɪkt prəˈpɔːʃənz/ (pl n) = the best analogies, amounts

**philosopher** /fəˈlɒsəfə/ (n) = sb who studies or writes about the meaning of life

**plant** /plɑːnt/ (n) = a living thing with leaves and roots which grows in earth

**sculptor** /ˈskʌlptə/ (n) = sb who makes pieces of art from wood, stone, etc

**sketch** /sketʃ/ (v) = to draw

**sketch** /sketʃ/ (n) = a quick drawing of sth

**study** /ˈstʌdi/ (v) = to learn about a subject

**survive** /səˈvaɪv/ (v) = to continue to exist after a threatening situation

**talented** /ˈtæləntəd/ (adj) = having a natural ability to do sth well

**3b (pp. 46-47)**

**according to legend** (phr) = as said by old stories

**army** /ˈɑːmi/ (n) = an organised and trained group of people that fights battles

**bite** /baɪt/ (v) = to cut sth using one's teeth

**bury** /ˈberi/ (v) = to put a dead body into the ground

**conquer** /ˈkɒŋkə/ (v) = to take complete control of an area

**curse** /kɜːs/ (n) = magic words which are intended to bring bad luck

**empire** /ˈempaɪə/ (n) = a group of countries ruled by one person

**explore** /ɪkˈsplɔː/ (v) = to search and discover

**explorer** /ɪkˈsplɔːrə/ (n) = sb who travels to places that nobody has been to before

**fight (against)** /faɪt əˌgenst/ (v) = to take part in a battle against an enemy

**hero** /ˈhɪərəʊ/ (n) = a brave character

**historical figure** /hɪˌstɒrɪkəl ˈfɪgə/ (n) = a famous person who lived in the past

**king** /kɪŋ/ (n) = a male ruler of a country

**land** /lænd/ (n) = a country

**lead** /liːd/ (v) = to guide

**leader** /ˈliːdə/ (n) = a person in control of a group of people

**poisoned** /ˈpɔɪzənd/ (pp) = having ingested a harmful and often fatal substance or containing such a substance

**poisonous snake** /ˌpɔɪzənəs ˈsneɪk/ (n) = a long reptile with no legs that produces a harmful substance that can kill sb or an animal if it bites them

**queen** /kwiːn/ (n) = a woman from a royal family who rules a country

**rule** /ruːl/ (v) = to be in charge of a country

**ruler** /ˈruːlə/ (n) = the leader of a country

**set out** /ˌset ˈaʊt/ (phr v) = to begin a journey

**stab** /stæb/ (v) = to put a knife into

**temple** /ˈtempəl/ (n) = a building used for worshipping gods

**tomb** /tuːm/ (n) = a large stone structure where sb is buried

**treasure** /ˈtreʒə/ (n) = a collection of valuable objects

**warrior** /ˈwɒriə/ (n) = a soldier; a fighter in a battle

**win a battle** (phr) = to be the victor of a fight between armies

**win a place in history** (phr) = to become a famous historical figure

**3c (p. 48)**

**captain** /ˈkæptɪn/ (n) = the person in control of a ship

**celebrate** /ˈseləbreɪt/ (v) = to do sth enjoyable because of a special occasion

**celebration** /ˌseləˈbreɪʃən/ (n) = a special, pleasurable, social event

**corn** /kɔːn/ (n) = a crop of grain

**crop** /krɒp/ (n) = a plant grown in large amounts

**feast** /fiːst/ (n) = a celebration with food

**harvest** /ˈhɑːvəst/ (n) = the crops that have been cut and collected

**hunt** /hʌnt/ (v) = to chase an animal in order to kill it

**ill** /ɪl/ (adj) = unwell; sick

**join in** /ˌdʒɔɪn ˈɪn/ (phr v) = to participate in

**land** /lænd/ (n) = a country

**native** /ˈneɪtɪv/ (adj) = local; born and raised in a specific country

**newly-discovered** /ˌnjuːli dɪsˈkʌvəd/ (adj) = recently found

**pilgrim** /ˈpɪlgrəm/ (n) = a person who travels to a place which is important in their religion

**sail** /seɪl/ (v) = to control a boat, ship etc through the water

**settle in** /ˌsetl ˈɪn/ (phr v) = to become used to living in a new place

**ship** /ʃɪp/ (n) = a large boat

**sick** /sɪk/ (adj) = unwell; ill

**survive** /səˈvaɪv/ (v) = to continue to exist after a threatening situation

**tradition** /trəˈdɪʃən/ (n) = a belief or custom that has existed for a long time

**voyage** /ˈvɔɪ-ɪdʒ/ (n) = a long journey by ship

**3d (p. 49)**

**day trip** /ˌdeɪ ˈtrɪp/ (n) = a journey in which you visit a place and come back again in one day

**famous** /ˈfeɪməs/ (adj) = well-known

**gift shop** /ˈgɪft ʃɒp/ (n) = a shop where you buy presents or souvenirs for people

**go on a tour** (phr) = to participate in a guided visit

**hang out** /ˌhæŋ ˈaʊt/ (phr v) = to spend a lot of time in a place

**look around** /ˌlʊk əˈraʊnd/ (phr v) = to explore

**re-enactment** /ˌriː ɪˈnæktmənt/ (n) = a performance of an event that happened in the past

**traditional clothing** /trəˌdɪʃənəl ˈkləʊðɪŋ/ (n) = clothes which were worn in the past

**3e (pp. 50-51)**

**after all** (phr) = besides; when you think about it

**(be) the end of** (phr) = to be the reason for no longer existing

**blood** /blʌd/ (n) = the red liquid in our body

**breathe** /briːð/ (v) = to take air into your lungs and send it out again

**cliff** /klɪf/ (n) = a steep rocky surface next to the sea

**dangerous** /ˈdeɪndʒərəs/ (adj) = is harmful; unsafe

**deep** /diːp/ (adv) = a long way into sth

**dive** /daɪv/ (v) = to go under the surface of the sea, a lake etc

**dragon** /ˈdrægən/ (n) = a large imaginary evil animal that has wings and a long tail and breathes fire

**evil** /ˈiːvəl/ (adj) = bad; wicked

**fairy** /ˈfeəri/ (n) = an imaginary creature with magical powers

**fall in love** (phr) = to start to feel strong romantic feelings for sb

**far away** /ˌfɑːr əˈweɪ/ (adv) = a long distance from a place

**fill (up)** /ˌfɪl ˈʌp/ (v) = to make sth become full

**fire** /faɪə/ (n) = flames that appear when burning sth

**float** /fləʊt/ (v) = to remain on the surface of water and not sink

**for good** (phr) = for ever

**get rid of** (phr) = to dispose (of)

**giant** /ˈdʒaɪənt/ (n) = an imaginary immense human being

**grab** /græb/ (v) = to reach for sth suddenly

**half** /hɑːf/ (adj) = being one of two equal parts

**hilltop** /ˈhɪltɒp/ (n) = the top of a small area of raised land

**hole** /həʊl/ (n) = an opening in a surface

**horn** /hɔːn/ (n) = a hard pointed growth on the head of an animal

**huge** /hjuːdʒ/ (adj) = enormous

**human** /ˈhjuːmən/ (n) = a person

**hut** /hʌt/ (n) = a small, simple house or shelter made of wood

**lead (down)** /ˌliːd ˈdaʊn/ (v) = to go towards or in a lower place

**legend** /ˈledʒənd/ (n) = a very old story that many people know and that may be true

**lock** /lɒk/ (v) = to close a door using a key

**long neck** /ˌlɒŋ ˈnek/ (n) = a part of the body between the head and the shoulders which is not short

**look like** (phr) = to have the same appearance as sb else

**magical** /ˈmædʒɪkəl/ (adj) = fascinating

**magical power** /ˌmædʒɪkəl ˈpaʊə/ (n) = a special mystical ability

**mermaid** /ˈmɜːmeɪd/ (n) = an imaginary creature which is half female and half fish

**mysterious** /mɪˈstɪəriəs/ (adj) = strange; unknown

**myth** /mɪθ/ (n) = an ancient story usu invented in order to explain natural or historical events

**sea monster** /ˈsiː ˌmɒnstə/ (n) = an imaginary sea creature

**stain** /steɪn/ (n) = a dirty mark on sth

**steal** /stiːl/ (v) = to take away without permission

**step** /step/ (n) = a movement one makes by putting one foot in front of the other

**tail** /teɪl/ (n) = the part of an animal that sticks out at the back

**tale** /teɪl/ (n) = an imaginary story

**terrify** /ˈterəfaɪ/ (v) = to frighten

**terrifying** /ˈterəfaɪ-ɪŋ/ (adj) = very frightening; horrifying

**tip** /tɪp/ (n) = the end of sth long and narrow

**to this day** (phr) = until now

**unicorn** /ˈjuːnɪkɔːn/ (n) = an imaginary animal that looks like a horse with a long horn on its head

**win** /wɪn/ (v) = to get sth because of skill or hard work

**wing** /wɪŋ/ (n) = the flat part of a bird's or insect's body which it uses to fly

**3f (pp. 52-53)**

**arrest** /əˈrest/ (v) – (of the police) to take sb to a police station to ask them about a crime they may have committed

**art theft** /ˈɑːt ˌθeft/ (n) = the stealing of a painting, sculpture, etc

**assume** /əˈsjuːm/ (v) = to think that sth is true

**attempt to sell** (phr) = to try to give sth in exchange for money

**break into** /ˌbreɪk ˈɪntə/ (phr v) = to enter a building by force

**bullet-proof glass** /ˌbʊlət pruːf ˈglɑːs/ (n) = glass which is so strong not even a bullet fired from a gun can break it

**carry (off)** /ˈkæri/ (v) = to remove sth and take it away

**catch** /kætʃ/ (v) = (of the police) to find and arrest a criminal

**clue** /kluː/ (n) = a piece of information that helps you solve a crime

**commit a crime** (phr) = to do sth illegal

**conflicting rumour** /kənˌflɪktɪŋ ˈruːmə/ (n) = sth said that does not match other things that are said about the same thing

**curator** /kjʊˈreɪtə/ (n) = a person who is in charge of a museum

**discard** /dɪsˈkɑːd/ (v) = to throw away

**enter** /ˈentə/ (v) = to get into

**escape** /ɪˈskeɪp/ (v) = to get away

**fateful** /ˈfeɪtfəl/ (adj) = having a bad effect

**frame** /freɪm/ (n) = a structure that goes around the edge of a picture

**guard** /gɑːd/ (n) = a person who protects sb or sth

**guard on duty** (phr) = a guard who is working

**homeland** /ˈhəʊmlænd, -lənd/ (n) = the country you were born in

**inspire** /ɪnˈspaɪə/ (v) = to fill sb with a desire to do sth

**international search** /ˌɪntənæʃənəl ˈsɜːtʃ/ (n) = the act of looking for sb or sth in many countries

**leave your post** (phr) = to go away from the place where you guard sth

**maintenance worker** /ˈmeɪntənəns ˌwɜːkə/ (n) = the person whose job is to keep sth in good condition

**missing** /ˈmɪsɪŋ/ (adj) = lost

**peg** (n) = an object on which you hang things

**precious artwork** /ˌpreʃəs ˈɑːtwɜːk/ (n) = valuable works of art

**reopen its doors** (phr) = to open again after being closed for a period of time

**rob** /rɒb/ (v) = to steal sth from sb or a place with force

**serve a sentence** (phr) = to be in prison for a crime

**shoot pictures** (phr) = to take photographs

**stairwell** /ˈsteəwel/ (n) = an enclosed set of steps

**star attraction** /ˌstɑːr əˈtrækʃən/ (n) = the most important object in a public setting

**thief** /θiːf/ (n) = a person who steals

**unhook (sth) from the wall** (phr) = to remove (sth) from the wall

**unlock the door** (phr) = to open a door using a key

**unsolved** /ˌʌnˈsɒlvd/ (adj) = not yet having had the answer found

**untie** /ʌnˈtaɪ/ (v) = to unfasten

**vandalise a statue** (phr) = to cause deliberate damage to a statue

### 3g (p. 54)

**artist** /ˈɑːtəst/ (n) = a painter, a musician or a sculptor etc

**collection** /kəˈlekʃən/ (n) = a group of objects of the same type

**health care** /ˈhelθ keə/ (n) = a set of services for treating people who are ill

**improve** /ɪmˈpruːv/ (v) = to become better

**nurse** /nɜːs/ (n) = a person whose job is to look after sick people

**physicist** /ˈfɪzəsəst/ (n) = sb who studies physics

**pop singer** /ˈpɒp ˌsɪŋə/ (n) = a singer of modern music which is popular with young people

**president** /ˈprezədənt/ (n) = the leader of a country

**project** /ˈprɒdʒekt/ (n) = a detailed piece of school work

**scientist** /ˈsaɪəntəst/ (n) = an expert who works in the field of science

**writer** /ˈraɪtə/ (n) = an author

### 3h (p. 55)

**biography** /baɪˈɒgrəfi/ (n) = a book about the life of a famous person

**chronological order** /ˌkrɒnəlɒdʒɪkəl ˈɔːdə/ (n) = (of a list of things) in the order that they happened

**combine** /kəmˈbaɪn/ (v) = to join together

**encourage** /ɪnˈkʌrɪdʒ/ (v) = to give sb confidence to do sth

**exhibit** /ɪgˈzɪbɪt/ (v) = to put on display

**exhibition** /ˌeksəˈbɪʃən/ (n) = a public show of pictures etc

**hometown** /ˌhəʊmˈtaʊn/ (n) = the town that one comes from

**marriage** /ˈmærɪdʒ/ (n) = the relationship of being husband and wife

**medicine** /ˈmedəsən/ (n) = a substance used to cure an illness

**recover** /rɪˈkʌvə/ (v) = to become well again after an illness, etc

**sequence** /ˈsiːkwəns/ (n) = the order of things happening

**sold out** /ˌsəʊld ˈaʊt/ (adj) = having no more tickets available to buy

**surrealism** /səˈrɪəlɪzəm/ (n) = a style of painting which is dream-like and unreal

### 3i (p. 56)

**brave** /breɪv/ (adj) = bold; courageous

**brilliant** /ˈbrɪljənt/ (adj) = wonderful

**cloth** /klɒθ/ (n) = material

**coast** /kəʊst/ (n) = land next to the sea

**explore** /ɪkˈsplɔː/ (v) = to search and discover

**gold** /gəʊld/ (n) = a precious metal which is yellow in colour

**import** /ɪmˈpɔːt/ (v) = to buy foreign products and bring them into one's country in order to sell them there

**importance** /ɪmˈpɔːtəns/ (n) = significance

**make fun of** (phr) = to laugh at sb; to ridicule sb

**ornament** /ˈɔːnəmənt/ (n) = an object used as a decoration

**passion** /ˈpæʃən/ (n) = a very strong feeling that cannot be controlled; a strong interest

**reach** /riːtʃ/ (v) = to get to a particular level

**riches** /ˈrɪtʃɪz/ (pl n) = valuable objects

**route** /ruːt/ (n) = the path you follow to get to a place

**sail** /seɪl/ (v) = to travel in a boat that is pushed by the wind

**sailing ship** /ˈseɪlɪŋ ʃɪp/ (n) = a large boat which uses the wind to move

**sailor** /ˈseɪlə/ (n) = a person who works on a sailing ship

**set sail** (phr) = to start a journey on a sailing ship

**southern** /ˈsʌðən/ (adj) = situated in the south part of a country

**spice** /spaɪs/ (n) = an aromatic substance used in cooking

**storm** /stɔːm/ (n) = very bad weather, with thunder, lightning and heavy rain

**supplies** /səˈplaɪz/ (n) = food and equipment needed for an activity

**tip** /tɪp/ (n) = the end of sth long and narrow

**trade route** /treɪd ruːt/ (n) = the path a ship follows to buy and sell goods in different countries

**weaver** /ˈwiːvə/ (n) = a person who makes cloth using machines

## Skills Practice 3 (pp. 58-59)

**confirm** /kənˈfɜːm/ (v) = to make sth certain; to prove true

**refreshment** /rɪˈfreʃmənt/ (n) = small amounts of food and drink

### Module 4

## 4 (p. 61)

**activity holiday** /ækˈtɪvəti ˌhɒlɪdeɪ/ (n) = a holiday with many exciting things to do

**backpacking holiday** /ˈbækpækɪŋ ˌhɒlɪdeɪ/ (n) = a holiday where you explore an area carrying all your luggage on your back

**beach holiday** /ˈbiːtʃ ˌhɒlɪdeɪ/ (n) = a holiday which is mostly spent sunbathing and swimming

**camping holiday** /ˈkæmpɪŋ ˌhɒlɪdeɪ/ (n) = a holiday where you stay in a tent

**cruise** /kruːz/ (n) = a holiday which is mostly spent travelling on a large and luxurious ship

**safari** /səˈfɑːri/ (n) = a journey to see wild animals

## 4a (pp. 62-63)

**adventure tour** /ədˈventʃə tʊə/ (n) = a guided trip whose purpose is to be exciting

**ancient monument** /ˌeɪnʃənt ˈmɒnjəmənt/ (n) = an old building or place which is historically important

**bored (of)** /ˈbɔːd əv/ (adj) = no longer interested in

**canyon** /ˈkænjən/ (n) = a valley with very steep rocky sides

**capital** /ˈkæpɪtl/ (n) = the city where the government of a country is

**climb** /klaɪm/ (v) = to go up a steep place using your hands and legs

**dangerous** /ˈdeɪndʒərəs/ (adj) = harmful; unsafe

**desert** /ˈdezət/ (n) = an area with very little rain and no plants

**dune buggy** /ˈdjuːn ˌbʌgi/ (n) = a vehicle that travels over sand

**endangered species** /ɪnˌdeɪndʒəd ˈspiːʃiːz/ (n) = an animal or plant that may soon become extinct

**enormous** /ɪˈnɔːməs/ (adj) = very big; huge

**explore** /ɪkˈsplɔː/ (v) = to search and discover

**flight** /flaɪt/ (n) = a journey on an aeroplane

**head (back)** /ˌhed ˈbæk/ (v) = to return to where you started

**hill** /hɪl/ (n) = an area of land higher than the land around it

**lakeside resort** /ˈleɪksaɪd rɪˈzɔːt/ (n) = a place for a holiday which is situated beside a lake

**lava lake** /ˈlɑːvə leɪk/ (n) = an area at the top of a volcano that contains lava

**mountain bike** /ˈmaʊntən baɪk/ (v) = to travel on a bike which is specially made for rough surfaces

**mountain** /ˈmaʊntən/ (n) = a high land area that might have snow at the top

**narrow** /ˈnærəʊ/ (adj) = not wide

**piranha fish** /pəˈrɑːnə fɪʃ/ (n) = small fish with sharp teeth and which are dangerous

**sandboarding** /ˈsændˌbɔːdɪŋ/ (n) = a sport in which you travel over sand on a large board

**set out** /ˌset ˈaʊt/ (phr v) = to begin a journey

**snowy** /ˈsnəʊi/ (adj) = having lots of snow

**spectacular** /spekˈtækjələ/ (adj) = impressive; extraordinary

**spend the night** (phr) = to sleep at a place

**stunning scenery** /ˌstʌnɪŋ ˈsiːnəri/ (n) = amazing views

**surrounded (by)** /səˈraʊndəd baɪ/ (pp) = encircled by

**time of your life** (phr) = an amazing time

**top (of)** /ˈtɒp əv/ (n) = the highest point of

**trek** /trek/ (v) = a long, difficult journey

**view** /vjuː/ (n) = sight; scenery

**volcano** /vɒlˈkeɪnəʊ/ (n) = a mountain with a hole at the top and which sometimes explodes

**windy** /ˈwaɪndi/ (adj) = twisty

**4b (pp. 64-65)**

**Arctic Circle** /ˌɑːktɪk ˈsɜːkəl/ (n) = the very cold area around the North Pole

**colourful light** /ˌkʌləfəl ˈlaɪt/ (n) = very bright colours

**common** /ˈkɒmən/ (adj) = ordinary

**display** /dɪˈspleɪ/ (n) = a show

**enjoy nature** (phr) = to get pleasure from natural things in the world

**enjoy yourself** (phr) = to have a good time

**go dog sledding** (phr) = to travel on snow in a vehicle pulled by dog

**go sightseeing** (phr) = to visit historical or famous places

**Guess what!** (phr) = You'll never imagine!

**have a great time** (phr) = to enjoy oneself very much

**hope** /həʊp/ (v) = to want sth to be true

**husky dog** /ˈhʌski dɒg/ (n) = a type of dog that is used to pull things across snow

**Northern Lights** /ˌnɔːðən ˈlaɪts/ (n) = a natural phenomenon in which bright colours are visible in the sky

**no way** (phr) = under no circumstances

**pine forest** /ˈpaɪn ˌfɒrəst/ (n) = a large area of evergreen trees

**reindeer stew** /ˌreɪndɪə ˈstjuː/ (n) = a dish made with the meat of reindeer

**shop for souvenirs** (phr) = to go and buy objects that remind them of a place they have visited

**sledding** /ˈsledɪŋ/ (n) = the activity of travelling over snow on a sled

**snowy** /ˈsnəʊɪ/ (adj) = having lots of snow

**stay in a hotel** (phr) = to live as a visitor at a place which you pay for

**sunbathe on the beach** (phr) = to lie in the sun beside the sea

**take photographs** (phr) = to use a camera to take pictures

**try local food** (phr) = to taste food which is specific to an area

**visit historical sites** (phr) = to go to areas of archaeological interest

**4c (p. 66)**

**adventure** /ədˈventʃə/ (n) = an event full of excitement, action and danger

**bison** /ˈbaɪsən/ (n) = a large wild animal which is similar to a cow

**canyon** /ˈkænjən/ (n) = a valley with very steep rocky sides

**cover** /ˈkʌvə/ (v) = to spread over the surface of

**deep** /diːp/ (adj) = extending a long way down from the top or surface

**destroy** /dɪˈstrɔɪ/ (v) = to damage sth badly

**elk** /elk/ (n) = a large hairy species of deer

**erupt** /ɪˈrʌpt/ (v) = (of a volcano) to explode

**full (of)** /ˈfʊl əv/ (adj) = having a lot of sth

**geyser** /ˈgiːzə/ (n) = a hole in the ground which spurts hot water and steam

**grizzly bear** /ˌgrɪzli ˈbeə/ (n) = a very large species of bear

**hiking trail** /ˈhaɪkɪŋ ˌtreɪl/ (n) = a special path through the countryside used for long walks

**hot spring** /ˌhɒt ˈsprɪŋ/ (n) = a place where hot water flows from the ground

**huge** /hjuːdʒ/ (adj) = enormous

**impressive** /ɪmˈpresɪv/ (adj) = causing admiration

**into the air** (phr) = upwards into the atmosphere

**on top of** (phr) = on the highest point of

**scientist** /ˈsaɪəntəst/ (n) = an expert who works in the field of science

**sight** /saɪt/ (n) = a tourist attraction

**spectacular view** /spekˌtækjələ ˈvjuː/ (n) = an amazing sight

**state** /steɪt/ (n) = the condition that sb or sth is in

**thermal pool** /ˌθɜːməl ˈpuːl/ (n) = a natural phenomenon which consists of areas of hot water

**volcano** /vɒlˈkeɪnəʊ/ (n) = a mountain with a hole at the top and which may erupt

**watch out for** /ˌwɒtʃ ˈaʊt fə/ (phr v) = to look out for

**waterfall** /ˈwɔːtəfɔːl/ (n) = water dropping from a higher to a lower point

**wildlife** /ˈwaɪldlaɪf/ (n) = all the animals and plants living in the wild

**wolf** /wʊlf/ (n) = a wild animal which is a species of dog

**4d (p. 67)**

**cost** /kɒst/ (v) = to have a price

**head (for)** /ˈhed fə/ (v) = to go towards

**information desk employee** /ˌɪnfəˈmeɪʃən desk ɪmˌplɔɪ-iː/ (n) = a person whose job is to help answer people's questions about a place

**opening hours** /ˈəʊpənɪŋ ˌaʊəz/ (pl n) = the times that a public building opens and closes

**plan** /plæn/ (v) = to intend

**straight** /streɪt/ (adv) = not bending or curving

**tourist** /ˈtʊərəst/ (n) = a person who visits a place of interest when on holiday

**4e (pp. 68-69)**

**attract** /əˈtrækt/ (v) = to get the attention or interest of sb

**below the waves** (phr) = under the surface of the sea

**cast a statue** (phr) = to make a statue using a mould of an object

**cement** /sə'ment/ (n) = a mixture of substances that make concrete

**coral reef** /ˌkɒrəl 'ri:f/ (n) = a large area of a substance like rock which is in the sea

**create statues** (phr) = to make solid images of a person or animal

**cyclist** /'saɪkləst/ (n) = a person who rides a bicycle

**damage** /'dæmɪdʒ/ (v) = to harm; to destroy

**discourage** /dɪs'kʌrɪdʒ/ (v) = to make sb feel less confident about sth

**dive** /daɪv/ (v) = to go under the surface of the sea, a lake etc

**encourage** /ɪn'kʌrɪdʒ/ (v) = to make sb feel that they want to do sth

**flipper** /'flɪpə/ (n) = one of the two flat body parts of particular sea creatures (e.g. penguins) which help them swim

**grow** /grəʊ/ (v) = to develop

**life-size sculpture** /ˌlaɪf saɪz 'skʌlptʃə/ (n) = a statue of an object which is the same size as the real thing

**local people** /ˌləʊkəl 'pi:pəl/ (pl n) = residents of a particular area

**pollution** /pə'lu:ʃən/ (n) = contamination

**recognise** /'rekəgnaɪz, 'rekən-/ (v) = to identify

**repair** /rɪ'peə/ (v) = to fix sth broken

**repel** /rɪ'pel/ (v) = to make sb or sth feel that they do not want to go near a place

**sculptor** /'skʌlptə/ (n) = a person who makes statues out of wood, clay, etc

**sculpture** /'skʌlptʃə/ (n) = a figure made of stone, wood, etc

**sea creature** /'si: ˌkri:tʃə/ (n) = an animal that lives in the sea

**share** /ʃeə/ (v) = to have or use sth with another person

**snorkel** /'snɔ:kəl/ (v) = a piece of equipment that helps you breathe under water

**stunning** /'stʌnɪŋ/ (adj) = extremely beautiful or attractive

**take off** /ˌteɪk 'ɒf/ (phr v) = to remove sth that you are wearing

**think about the environment** (phr) = to consider the natural world we live in

**ugly** /'ʌgli/ (adj) = unattractive

**underwater** /ʌndəwɔ:tə/ (adj) = below the surface of water

## 4f (p. 70-71)

**acoustics** /ə'ku:stɪks/ (pl n) = the effect a building has on the quality of sound

**auditorium** /ˌɔ:də'tɔ:riəm/ (n) = the part of a theatre where the audience sit

**bay** /beɪ/ (n) = an area of sea surrounded on three sides by land

**block** /blɒk/ (v) = to prevent the movement of sth

**blow (sb) away** /ˌbləʊ ə'weɪ/ (phr v) = to impress (sb) greatly

**climate** /'klaɪmət/ (n) = the weather of a region

**construct** /kən'strʌkt/ (v) = to build; to create

**contemporary** /kən'tempərəri/ (adj) = modern

**cosy restaurant** /ˌkəʊzi 'restərɒnt/ (n) = a small and warm place to eat

**diverse** /daɪ'vɜ:s/ (adj) = varied

**exterior** /ɪk'stɪəriə/ (n) = the outer surface of sth

**flea market** /'fli: ˌmɑ:kət/ (n) = a market with second-hand goods

**fresh** /freʃ/ (adj) = (of food) made recently

**hectare** /'hekteə/ (n) = a measurement of an area of land (10,000m$^2$)

**interior** /ɪn'tɪəriə/ (n) = the inside of sth

**panorama** /ˌpænə'rɑ:mə/ (n) = a view of a wide area

**pavilion** /pə'vɪljən/ (n) = an outdoor structure used for events

**peaceful garden** /ˌpi:sfəl 'gɑ:dn/ (n) = a quiet area of green space

**produce** /'prɒdju:s/ (n) = fruit and vegetables

**roar** /rɔ:/ (n) = a deep loud sound

**show (sb) around** /ˌʃəʊ ə'raʊnd/ (phr v) = to show sb all the interesting features of a place

**speciality** /ˌspeʃəlti/ (n) = a product which is extremely good in a restaurant or place

**spectacular** /spek'tækjələ/ (adj) = impressive; extraordinary

**stunning view** /ˌstʌnɪŋ 'vju:/ (n) = amazing scenery

**tea-house** /'ti:haʊs/ (n) = a small building in which tea is served

**wide harbour** /ˌwaɪd 'hɑ:bə/ (n) = a large area by the coast where boats are kept

**world heritage site** /ˌwɜ:ld 'herətɪdʒ ˌsaɪt/ (n) = a place that is listed as having special significance

## 4g (p. 72)

**airline** /'eəlaɪn/ (n) = an aircraft company

**awful** /'ɔ:fəl/ (adj) = terrible

**crowded** /'kraʊdəd/ (adj) = full of people

**dirty** /'dɜ:ti/ (adj) = not clean

**flight** /flaɪt/ (n) = a journey in an aircraft

**food poisoning** /'fu:d ˌpɔɪzənɪŋ/ (n) = an illness caused by eating sth dangerous

**hotel room** /həʊ'tel ru:m, rʊm/ (n) = the room in a hotel that you pay for to stay in

**luggage** /'lʌgɪdʒ/ (n) = baggage

**miss** /mɪs/ (v) = to fail to do, see or notice sth

**passport** /ˈpæspɔːt/ (n) = an official document which has a person's information and photograph and allows them to travel to foreign countries

**steal** /stiːl/ (v) = to take sth from sb without permission

**sunburnt** /ˈsʌnbɜːnt/ (adj) = having sore, bright pink skin after spending too much time in the sun

**victim** /ˈvɪktəm/ (n) = sb who suffers death, injury or loss

**weather** /ˈweðə/ (n) = conditions such as rain, temperature, etc that occur in a particular area

## 4h (p. 73)

**cloudy** /ˈklaʊdi/ (adj) = in or with clouds in the sky

**fishing village** /ˈfɪʃɪŋ ˌvɪlɪdʒ/ (n) = a small town where the people fish for a living

**luxury hotel** /ˌlʌkʃəri həʊˈtel/ (n) = a hotel which is very expensive

**plantation** /plænˈteɪʃən/ (n) = a large farm

**rainforest** /ˈreɪnfɒrəst/ (n) = a tropical forest

**storm** /stɔːm/ (n) = very bad weather, with thunder, lightning and heavy rain

## 4i (p. 74)

**abroad** /əˈbrɔːd/ (adv) = in or to a foreign country

**arts and crafts** /ˌɑːts ən ˈkrɑːfts/ (pl n) = objects made by hand

**behaviour code** /bɪˈheɪvjə kəʊd/ (n) = a set of principles about how to act

**book** /bʊk/ (v) = to make a reservation

**brand** /brænd/ (n) = a product made by a particular company

**business** /ˈbɪznəs/ (n) = a company

**care** /keə/ (v) = to protect or look after sth or sb

**clean up** /kliːn ˈʌp/ (phr v) = to remove the dirt from a place

**culture** /ˈkʌltʃə/ (n) = the beliefs, arts, philosophy, etc that define a civilisation

**custom** /ˈkʌstəm/ (n) = sth that is done by people in a particular society

**environmentally-responsible** /ɪnˌvaɪrənˌmentl-i rɪˈspɒnsəbəl/ (adj) = not harming the environment

**get to know** (phr) = to learn about

**guest** /gest/ (n) = a visitor; sb we have invited

**handmade** /ˌhændˈmeɪd/ (adj) = made using the hands instead of a machine

**historical site** /hɪˌstɒrɪkəl ˈsaɪt/ (n) = a place of archaeological interest

**interested (in)** /ˈɪntrəstəd ɪn/ (adj) = wanting to learn about

**local brand** /ˌləʊkəl ˈbrænd/ (n) = a product sold in a particular area

**locals** /ˈləʊkəlz/ (pl n) = the people who live in a particular place

**make a good impression** (phr) = make sb have a good opinion

**memory** /ˈmeməri/ (n) = the ability to keep and recall information, experiences, events, etc

**monument** /ˈmɒnjəmənt/ (n) = a building or a statue built to honour sb/sth special

**representative** /ˌreprəˈzentətɪv/ (n) = sb who does sth officially for a group of people

**respect** /rɪˈspekt/ (n) = having a good opinion of sb

**show respect** (phr) = to display the feeling of respect

**smile** /smaɪl/ (n) = a shape of the mouth which shows friendliness

**support** /səˈpɔːt/ (v) = to give practical help

**treat** /triːt/ (v) = to behave towards sb in a particular way

## Skills Practice 4 (pp. 76-77)

**alike** /əˈlaɪk/ (adv) = in a similar way

**chalet** /ˈʃæleɪ/ (n) = a small wooden house used by people on holiday

**colony** /ˈkɒləni/ (n) = a group of animals of the same type that live together

**inlet** /ˈɪnlət/ (n) = a narrow strip of water between islands

**operate** /ˈɒpəreɪt/ (v) = to work; to be functional

## Module 5

## 5 (p. 79)

**deforestation** /diːˌfɒrəˈsteɪʃən/ (n) = the destruction of forests by humans

**endangered animal** /ɪnˌdeɪndʒəd ˈænəməl/ (n) = an animal in danger of extinction

**global warming** /ˌgləʊbəl ˈwɔːmɪŋ/ (n) = a general increase in world temperatures

**homelessness** /ˈhəʊmləsnəs/ (n) = the condition of people having nowhere to live

**pollution** /pəˈluːʃən/ (n) = contamination

**racism** /ˈreɪsɪzəm/ (n) = the unfair treatment of people because they do not share the same culture and characteristics as oneself

**unemployment** /ˌʌnɪmˈplɔɪmənt/ (n) = the condition of having no job

## 5a (pp. 80-81)

**affect** /əˈfekt/ (v) = to change sth or sb in some way; to influence

**awful** /ˈɔːfəl/ (adj) = terrible

**challenge** /ˈtʃæləndʒ/ (n) = a difficult or demanding task

**clear** /klɪə/ (v) = to remove whatever is blocking an area

**conditions** /kənˈdɪʃənz/ (pl n) = circumstances

**destroy** /dɪˈstrɔɪ/ (v) = to damage sth badly

**drought** /draʊt/ (n) = a long period without rainfall
**earthquake** /ˈɜːθkweɪk/ (n) = a sudden violent movement of the earth's surface
**flood** /flʌd/ (n) = an overflowing of water onto land
**forest fire** /ˌfɒrəst ˈfaɪə/ (n) = a fire in a wooded area
**hurricane** /ˈhʌrəkən/ (n) = a very violent wind or storm
**injury** /ˈɪndʒəri/ (n) = damage to sb's body caused by an accident
**medical supplies** /ˈmedɪkəl səˌplaɪz/ (pl n) = items needed to treat illness or injury
**natural disaster** /ˌnætʃərəl dɪˈzɑːstə/ (n) = a catastrophe that has occurred through natural processes rather than people
**rebuild** /riːˈbɪld/ (v) = to build again
**rescue team** /ˈreskjuː tiːm/ (n) = a group of people whose aim is to save sb who is lost or trapped
**rubble** /ˈrʌbəl/ (n) = piles of broken stone from a collapsed building
**running water** /ˌrʌnɪŋ ˈwɔːtə/ (n) = water that comes from a tap
**suffer** /ˈsʌfə/ (v) = to experience pain or unpleasant emotions
**tornado** /tɔːˈneɪdəʊ/ (n) = a violent wind storm
**tsunami** /tsʊˈnɑːmi/ (n) = a very large wave, usu caused by an earthquake under the sea, which can be very destructive
**volunteer team** /ˌvɒlənˈtɪə tiːm/ (n) = a group of people who offer to help people in need without payment
**wage** /weɪdʒ/ (n) = regular payment for work

### 5b (pp. 82-83)

**achieve** /əˈtʃiːv/ (v) = to succeed in doing
**award** /əˈwɔːd/ (n) = money or a prize that sb is given

**best-selling** /ˌbest ˈselɪŋ/ (adj) = extremely popular and sold in large numbers
**build** /bɪld/ (v) = to construct
**campaign** /kæmˈpeɪn/ (n) = a planned set of activities intended to achieve a particular result
**cause** /kɔːz/ (v) = to make sth happen
**child labour** /ˌtʃaɪld ˈleɪbə/ (n) = practical work done by children often in harsh conditions
**courage** /ˈkʌrɪdʒ/ (n) = the quality of being brave
**disease** /dɪˈziːz/ (n) = an illness
**end up** /ˌend ˈʌp/ (phr v) = to finally be in a particular place or situation
**failure** /ˈfeɪljə/ (n) = not a success
**ground** /graʊnd/ (n) = the surface of the Earth
**humanitarian** /hjuːˌmænəˈteəriən/ (adj) = involved in reducing the suffering of people
**hunger** /ˈhʌŋgə/ (n) = a severe lack of food
**hungry** /ˈhʌŋgri/ (adj) = feeling the need to eat
**ignorance** /ˈɪgnərəns/ (n) = a lack of knowledge or understanding
**illiteracy** /ɪˈlɪtərəsi/ (n) = the inability to read or write
**injured** /ˈɪndʒəd/ (adj) = hurt or wounded
**issue** /ˈɪʃuː, ˈɪsjuː/ (n) = an important subject requiring discussion
**look after** /lʊk ˈɑːftə/ (phr v) = to take care of
**make it (to)** /meɪk ɪt/ (phr) = to reach a place
**organisation** /ˌɔːgənaɪˈzeɪʃən/ (n) = a group of people that work together for a purpose
**peace** /piːs/ (n) = freedom from war
**poor** /pɔː/ (adj) = having very little money
**poverty** /ˈpɒvəti/ (n) = the condition of being poor

**promise** /ˈprɒməs/ (v) = to say that you will do sth and to give your word
**proof** /pruːf/ (n) = evidence
**raise money** (phr) = to collect money for a cause
**run** /rʌn/ (v) = to move quickly, faster than walking; to be in control of a company, organisation, etc
**save** /seɪv/ (v) = (of money) to not spend; to put aside
**set out** /ˌset ˈaʊt/ (phr v) = to start an activity with a particular purpose
**smile** /smaɪl/ (n) = a shape of the mouth which shows friendliness
**stick** /stɪk/ (n) = a long thin piece of wood
**stumble** /ˈstʌmbəl/ (v) = to walk awkwardly
**thrilling** /ˈθrɪlɪŋ/ (adj) = exciting
**top** /tɒp/ (n) = peak; summit
**war** /wɔː/ (n) = fighting between two or more opposing groups or countries
**yet** /jet/ (adv) = still; until the present time

### 5c (p. 84)

**animal shelter** /ˈænəməl ʃeltə/ (n) = a place that gives help and protection to animals
**appear** /əˈpɪə/ (v) = to be present or noticeable
**cash** /kæʃ/ (n) = money
**cause** /kɔːz/ (n) = an aim or principle which is socially valuable and which many people support or fight for
**celebrity** /səˈlebrəti/ (n) = a famous person; a star
**charity event** /ˈtʃærəti ɪˌvent/ (n) = sth that happens in order to collect money for those in need
**cheque** /tʃek/ (n) = a piece of paper used to make payments

**clown nose** /klaʊn ˌnəʊz/ (n) = a round red object that is placed on the nose and which clowns wear

**collect** /kəˈlekt/ (v) = to gather together

**comedy** /ˈkɒmədi/ (n) = a play, TV programme or film that is designed to be amusing and make you laugh

**famine** /ˈfæmən/ (n) = severe hunger

**get an education** (phr) = to go to school to learn things

**get involved** (phr) = to join in

**laughter** /ˈlɑːftə/ (n) = the sound sb makes when they think sth is funny

**make a donation** (phr) = to give money to a charity

**organise** /ˈɔːgənaɪz/ (v) = to arrange

**part (of)** /pɑːt əv/ (n) = a piece of

**raise money** (phr) = to collect money for a cause

**record a song** (phr) = to store a song using electronic equipment

**silly outfit** /ˌsɪli ˈaʊtfɪt/ (n) = clothes that look ridiculous

**sketch** /sketʃ/ (n) = a short funny performance

**sort (of)** /sɔːt əv/ (n) = kind of

**support** /səˈpɔːt/ (v) = to give practical help

**take place** (phr) = to happen

**terrible** /ˈterəbəl/ (adj) = horrible; awful

**viewer** /ˈvjuːə/ (n) = a person who watches sth

**5d (p. 85)**

**chance** /tʃɑːns/ (n) = possibility

**collect donations** (phr) = to gather together money which is for charity

**decorate the venue** (phr) = to make the place of an event more attractive

**give a hand** (phr) = to help with sth

**make banners** (phr) = to create signs made from cloth

**mind** /maɪnd/ (v) = to be annoyed by

**nearly** /ˈnɪəli/ (adv) = almost

**put up posters** (phr) = to stick posters on walls

**sell tickets** (phr) = to make tickets available for people to buy

**5e (pp. 86-87)**

**alternative** /ɔːlˈtɜːnətɪv/ (n) = a different choice

**by accident** (phr) = without intention

**challenging** /ˈtʃæləndʒɪŋ/ (adj) = difficult and demanding

**conservation project** /ˌkɒnsəˈveɪʃən ˌprɒdʒekt/ (n) = a piece of planned work whose aim is to protect natural areas

**creature** /ˈkriːtʃə/ (n) = anything that is a living being (usu of animals)

**cut down** /ˌkʌt ˈdaʊn/ (phr v) = to cause sth to fall by striking with an sharp object like a blade

**dawn** /dɔːn/ (n) = the early morning

**destroy** /dɪˈstrɔɪ/ (v) = to damage sth badly

**die out** /ˌdaɪ ˈaʊt/ (phr v) = to become extinct

**excited** /ɪkˈsaɪtəd/ (adj) = enthusiastic

**experience** /ɪkˈspɪəriəns/ (n) = gained knowledge or skill

**farming** /ˈfɑːmɪŋ/ (n) = the activity of working on a farm

**female** /ˈfiːmeɪl/ (n) = a woman

**float** /fləʊt/ (v) = to not sink

**fur** /fɜː/ (n) = the thick, soft hair that covers animals' bodies

**get caught** (phr) = to be seen doing sth wrong or illegal

**habitat** /ˈhæbɪtæt/ (n) = environment; natural home

**hammock** /ˈhæmək/ (n) = a bed consisting of a net tied between two supports

**hunting** /ˈhʌntɪŋ/ (n) = chasing an animal for food or sport

**lay (their) eggs** (phr) = to produce eggs by pushing out of the body

**left** /left/ (pp) = having as a remaining amount

**location** /ləʊˈkeɪʃən/ (n) = place

**meat** /miːt/ (n) = parts of an animal that people eat

**mistake (for)** /mɪˈsteɪk fə/ (v) = to confuse sth with sth different

**monitor** /ˈmɒnɪtə/ (v) = to watch a situation carefully

**nest** /nest/ (n) = a place made by a bird or insect for its eggs

**net** /net/ (n) = a material that is loosely woven so it allows small objects through and traps others

**observation team** /ˌɒbzəˈveɪʃən tiːm/ (n) = a group of people who watch carefully the way sth happens

**patrol** /pəˈtrəʊl/ (v) = to move around an area to make sure there is nothing wrong

**poacher** /ˈpəʊtʃə/ (n) = sb who hunts animals illegally

**poison** /ˈpɔɪzən/ (v) = to add a dangerous substance to sth

**polluted** /pəˈluːtəd/ (adj) = dangerously dirty

**porch** /pɔːtʃ/ (n) = a veranda

**rainforest** /ˈreɪnfɒrəst/ (n) = a tropical forest

**recently** /ˈriːsəntli/ (adv) = lately

**record** /rɪˈkɔːd/ (v) = to write down information for future use

**relaxing** /rɪˈlæksɪŋ/ (adj) = making one feel calm and pleasant

**shocked** /ʃɒkt/ (adj) = very surprised and upset by sth bad that happens unexpectedly

**species** /ˈspiːʃiːz/ (n) = a set of animals or plants that can breed with each other

**spectacular** /spekˈtækjələ/ (adj) = impressive; extraordinary

**steep slope** /ˌstiːp ˈsləʊp/ (n) = the side of a hill or mountain which rises abruptly

**survey** /ˈsɜːveɪ/ (n) = a study; a research

**team** /tiːm/ (n) = an organised group of people

**threat** /θret/ (n) = a danger to sth

**tiring** /ˈtaɪərɪŋ/ (adj) = making you feel that you need to rest

**track** /træk/ (v) = to follow by looking at traces left behind

## 5f (pp. 88-89)

**a dream comes true** (phr) = when sth you have wished for happens

**association** /əˌsəʊsiˈeɪʃən, əˌsəʊʃi-/ (n) = organisation

**bang your head** (phr) = to hit your head against sth

**challenge** /ˈtʃæləndʒ/ (n) = a difficult or demanding task

**champ** /tʃæmp/ (n) = winner; champion

**desert** /ˈdezət/ (n) = an area with very little rain and no plants

**determination** /dɪˌtɜːməˈneɪʃən/ (n) = strong will

**follow in (sb's) footsteps** (phr) = to do the same as sb else because they inspire you

**get a swollen knee** (phr) = to injure one's knee and as a result it swells up

**get sore feet** (phr) = to feel pain in one's feet due to walking too much

**make a donation** (phr) = to give money to charity

**motivate** /ˈməʊtəveɪt/ (v) = to make sb want to do sth

**nasty fall** /ˌnɑːsti ˈfɔːl/ (n) = a painful accident caused by suddenly going down onto the ground

**on average** (phr) = as a typical amount

**physical pain** /ˌfɪzɪkəl ˈpeɪn/ (n) = pain that is felt on the body

**quit** /kwɪt/ (v) = to leave one's job

**raise money** (phr) = to collect money for a cause

**scratch your face** (phr) = to cut the skin of one's face slightly with sth sharp

**set a world record** (phr) = to be the best or fastest ever in a sport or activity

**sprain your wrist** (phr) = to twist and injure the part of the body between the hand and the arm

**sunscreen** /ˈsʌnskriːn/ (n) = a lotion or cream that protects your skin from the sun

**twist your ankle** (phr) = to injure the part of the body between the foot and the leg by bending it awkwardly

## 5g (p. 90)

**camp counsellor** /ˌkæmp ˈkaʊnsələ/ (n) = the person who gives advice at a summer camp

**clean out a pond** (phr) = to remove dirt from a small artificial lake

**collect rubbish for recycling** (phr) = to gather together things that have been thrown away so that they can be used again

**cook on a barbecue** (phr) = to cook food outside over a fire

**eco-camp** /ˈiːkəʊ ˌkæmp/ (n) = a camp whose aim is to help the environment and not harm the ecology of an area

**first-aid course** /ˌfɜːst ˈeɪd kɔːs/ (n) = a set of lessons whose aim is to teach basic medical treatment

**go on a nature hike** (phr) = to participate in long walks in natural surroundings

**grow vegetables** (phr) = to produce vegetables oneself by planting seeds

**plant trees** (phr) = to place young trees in the ground in order for them to grow

**sit around a campfire** (phr) = to gather around a fire made outdoors

**sleep in wooden huts** (phr) = to sleep in small buildings made from wood

## 5h (p. 91)

**burn down** /ˌbɜːn ˈdaʊn/ (phr v) = to destroy sth by setting fire to it

**recycling** /ˌriːˈsaɪklɪŋ/ (n) = processing paper, glass, etc so that they can be used again

**replace** /rɪˈpleɪs/ (v) = to get a new object to use when the old one has broken

**tough** /tʌf/ (adj) = difficult

## 5i (p. 92)

**control** /kənˈtrəʊl/ (v) = to limit the effects of sth

**coral reef** /ˌkɒrəl ˈriːf/ (n) = a large area of a substance like rock formed in the sea by the bones of very small sea animals

**cover** /ˈkʌvə/ (v) = to spread over the surface of

**end up** /ˌend ˈʌp/ (phr v) = to finally be in a place

**factory** /ˈfæktəri/ (n) = a building where goods are made with the use of machines

**feed** /fiːd/ (v) = to give sb or an animal food to eat

**float** /fləʊt/ (v) = to not sink

**harmful** /ˈhɑːmfəl/ (adj) = causing damage

**heat** /hiːt/ (n) = warmth

**majestic** /məˈdʒestɪk/ (adj) = causing great admiration and respect

**make up** /ˌmeɪk ˈʌp/ (phr v) = to form a specific number as part of a whole

**mammal** /ˈmæməl/ (n) = an animal that gives birth to babies and feeds them with its milk

**ocean current** /ˌəʊʃən ˈkʌrənt/ (n) = a movement of water in one direction and which is in the sea

**overfishing** /ˌəʊvəˈfɪʃɪŋ/ (n) = the act of catching too many fish

**poison** /ˈpɔɪzən/ (v) = to pollute sth with dangerous chemicals
**precious** /ˈprɛʃəs/ (adj) = valuable
**protect** /prəˈtɛkt/ (v) = to defend sb/sth
**rainfall** /ˈreɪnfɔːl/ (n) = the amount of rain that falls
**record** /rɪˈkɔːd/ (v) = to write down for future use
**surface** /ˈsɜːfəs/ (n) = the area that is on the top or the outside of sth
**survival** /səˈvaɪvəl/ (n) = existence
**take out** /ˌteɪk ˈaʊt/ (phr v) = to remove
**tuna** /ˈtjuːnə/ (n) = a type of fish that lives in the sea
**water supply** /ˈwɔːtə səˌplaɪ/ (n) = the provision of water
**wave** /weɪv/ (n) = water which visibly moves across the surface of the sea
**whale** /weɪl/ (n) = a very large sea mammal
**wind pattern** /ˈwɪnd ˌpætən/ (n) = the way the wind moves in a particular area

### Skills Practice 5 (pp. 94-95)

**break the law** (phr) = to do sth illegal
**critical** /ˈkrɪtɪkəl/ (adj) = extremely serious or important
**dedicate (oneself to sth)** /ˈdedəkeɪt/ (v) = to give all one's energy and time to sth
**fresh start** /ˌfreʃ ˈstɑːt/ (n) = a new beginning
**neglected** /nɪˈɡlektəd/ (adj) = not cared for
**paramedic** /ˌpærəˈmedɪk/ (n) = a person who is not a doctor but who gives medical aid in emergencies
**recover** /rɪˈkʌvə/ (v) = to become well again after an illness etc
**rewarding** /rɪˈwɔːdɪŋ/ (adj) = satisfying
**show up** /ˌʃəʊ ˈʌp/ (phr v) = to appear

**wander (around)** /ˈwɒndə/ (v) = to walk around without any specific purpose

### Module 6

**6 (p. 97)**

**(be) located in** (phr) = to be situated in a place
**design** /dɪˈzaɪn/ (v) = to plan and make a detailed drawing of sth
**oil painting** /ˈɔɪl ˌpeɪntɪŋ/ (n) = a painting produced with oil-based paints
**reflect** /rɪˈflekt/ (v) = to be a sign of a situation or feeling
**sailing ship** /ˈseɪlɪŋ ʃɪp/ (n) = a large boat that uses the wind to move
**sculpt** /skʌlpt/ (v) = to create an object out of wood, clay etc using a special tool
**statue** /ˈstætʃuː/ (n) = an object made to look like a person or an animal

**6a (pp. 98-99)**

**armoury** /ˈɑːməri/ (n) = a place where weapons are stored
**battle** /ˈbætl/ (n) = a conflict between groups of people usu armed
**build** /bɪld/ (n) = the shape and size of sb's body
**burial site** /ˈberiəl ˌsaɪt/ (n) = the place where sb is buried
**bury** /ˈberi/ (v) = to put a dead body into the ground
**chariot** /ˈtʃæriət/ (n) = a two-wheeled vehicle pulled by a horse, used in ancient times
**clay** /kleɪ/ (n) = earth that becomes hard when baked
**dig** /dɪɡ/ (v) = to make a hole in the ground by moving soil using a tool or a machine
**elaborate** /ɪˈlæbərət/ (adj) = containing many detailed parts

**emperor** /ˈempərə/ (n) = the male ruler of a group of countries
**excavate** /ˈekskəveɪt/ (v) = to dig up the ground in order to find ancient objects and study them
**facial expression** /ˈfeɪʃəl ɪkˌspreʃən/ (n) = the look on sb's face
**feature** /ˈfiːtʃə/ (n) = an interesting or characteristic part of sth
**fortress** /ˈfɔːtrəs/ (n) = a strong building used for defence from attack
**guard** /ɡɑːd/ (v) = to protect
**individual** /ˌɪndəˈvɪdʒuəl/ (adj) = relating to a single person or thing rather than a large group
**life-sized** /ˈlaɪf saɪzd/ (adj) = being the same size as the thing it represents
**marble** /ˈmɑːbəl/ (n) = a kind of hard rock used in building and sculpture
**metal** /ˈmetl/ (n) = a substance that is hard, i.e. iron, gold etc
**model** /ˈmɒdl/ (v) = to make a representation of sth real
**pit** /pɪt/ (n) = a large hole in the ground
**possessions** /pəˈzeʃənz/ (pl n) = property
**reign** /reɪn/ (n) = to be the ruler of a country
**remain** /rɪˈmeɪn/ (v) = to continue in a particular state
**reveal** /rɪˈviːl/ (v) = to uncover
**riches** /ˈrɪtʃəz/ (pl n) = valuable objects
**splendour** /ˈsplendə/ (n) = great beauty
**stone** /stəʊn/ (n) = a hard solid, mineral substance
**terracotta** /ˌterəˈkɒtə/ (n) = reddish - brown clay
**tomb** /tuːm/ (n) = a large stone structure where sb is buried
**treasure-filled** /ˈtreʒə fɪld/ (adj) = being full of valuable objects

**undisturbed** /ˌʌndɪˈstɜːbd/ (adj) = not touched or changed in any way

**unique** /juːˈniːk/ (adj) = being the only one of its kind

**untouched** /ˌʌnˈtʌtʃt/ (adj) = unchanged and not damaged by people

**well** /wel/ (n) = a hole in the ground from which we can get water

**wood** /wʊd/ (n) = the material which forms the trunks and branches of trees

**6b (pp. 100-101)**

**astonishing** /əˈstɒnəʃɪŋ/ (adj) = amazing

**call off** /kɔːl ˈɒf/ (phr v) = to postpone

**carve (sth out of sth else)** /kɑːv/ (v) = to create sth by cutting it out of wood, stone, etc

**complete** /kəmˈpliːt/ (v) = to finish

**copper** /ˈkɒpə/ (n) = a reddish - brown metal

**dazzled** /ˈdæzəld/ (pp) = amazed

**dinosaur bone** /ˈdaɪnəsɔː ˌbəʊn/ (n) = a part of the skeleton of a prehistoric creature

**element** /ˈeləmənt/ (n) = part

**emu** /ˈiːmjuː/ (n) = a large Australian bird which cannot fly

**fibreglass** /ˈfaɪbəglɑːs/ (n) = a light material made with glass and plastic

**fossil** /ˈfɒsəl/ (n) = a part of or the shape of sth that lived in prehistoric times and is preserved in rock

**hand in** /ˌhænd ˈɪn / (phr v) = to give sth to sb

**have a sweet tooth** (phr) = to be fond of sweets

**hold** /həʊld/ (v) = to have

**limestone** /ˈlaɪmstəʊn/ (n) = a white rock

**line** /laɪn/ (v) = to cover the inside surface of sth

**mighty beast** /ˌmaɪti ˈbiːst/ (n) = magnificent creature

**mural** /ˈmjʊərəl/ (n) = a large picture that has been painted on a wall

**on display** (phr) = on show

**plantation** /plænˈteɪʃən/ (n) = a large farm

**pose (for)** /pəʊz/ (v) = to take on a position to be photographed

**renovation** /ˌrenəˈveɪʃən/ (n) = the act of repairing and improving a building

**repair** /rɪˈpeə/ (n) = sth which is done to fix sth

**roadside attraction** /ˌrəʊdsaɪd əˈtrækʃən/ (n) = sth that is on the edge of a road and which people want to visit or see

**sculptor** /ˈskʌlptə/ (n) = sb who makes pieces of art out of wood, stone, etc

**steel** /stiːl/ (n) = a hard metal made from iron and carbon

**transform** /trænsˈfɔːm/ (v) = to change

**wildlife reserve** /ˈwaɪldlaɪf rɪˌzɜːv/ (n) = a protected area of land to keep animals safe

**6c (p. 102)**

**Aboriginal** /ˌæbəˈrɪdʒənəl/ (adj) = having existed in a continent since the earliest time known to people

**announce** /əˈnaʊns/ (v) = to show that sth is going to happen

**attendance** /əˈtendəns/ (n) = sb's presence at an event

**background** /ˈbækgraʊnd/ (n) = your family and your experience of life

**bark** /bɑːk/ (n) = the outer surface of a tree

**bond** /bɒnd/ (n) = a feeling of close connection

**come together in unity** (phr) = to be joined together and in agreement with each other

**constructed** /kənˈstrʌktəd/ (pp) = made

**continent** /ˈkɒntənənt/ (n) = one of the seven land masses of Earth

**didgeridoo** /ˌdɪdʒəriˈduː/ (n) = a long wooden wind instrument

**discuss** /dɪˈskʌs/ (v) = to talk about

**dot** /dɒt/ (n) = a very small round mark

**gathering** /ˈgæðərɪŋ/ (n) = a meeting when many people come together

**handmade boomerang** /ˌhændmeɪd ˈbuːməræŋ/ (n) = a curved stick which when thrown comes back to the person who threw it and which is made by hand

**hang** /hæŋ/ (v) = to be attached to a high place or a wall

**highlight** /ˈhaɪlaɪt/ (v) = to draw attention to

**holy ground** /ˌhəʊli ˈgraʊnd/ (n) = land which is related to a religion

**invest** /ɪnˈvest/ (v) = to put money or effort into sth

**raise awareness** (phr) = to make the public know about a problem

**soul** /səʊl/ (n) = the spiritual part of a person

**spirit** /ˈspɪrət/ (n) = the soul; the non-physical part of a person

**tribe** /traɪb/ (n) = a social group of people of the same race ruled by their leader

**6d (p. 103)**

**airmail** /ˈeəmeɪl/ (n) = a system of sending letters by aircraft

**envelope** /ˈenvələʊp/ (n) = a rectangular or square cover usu made of paper which is used to send letters, cards etc

**post box** /ˈpəʊst bɒks/ (n) = a large container in a public place where you can post letters

**postal address** /ˈpəʊstl əˌdres/ (n) = the number of a house and name of road and town where letters can be sent

**postmark** /ˈpəʊstmɑːk/ (n) = an official stamp on a letter stating what time and from where it was sent

**registered post** /ˌredʒəstəd ˈpəʊst/ (n) = a special postal service that makes sure parcels and letters do not get lost

**return address** /rɪˌtɜːn əˈdres/ (n) = the address of the sender of a parcel or letter

**scales** /skeɪlz/ (pl n) = a machine used for weighing people or things

**stamp** /stæmp/ (n) = a small piece of paper which is stuck on an envelope to show that sb has paid for postage

**surface mail** /ˈsɜːfəs meɪl/ (n) = a system of sending letters over land and sea rather than by air

### 6e (pp. 104-105)

**accuracy** /ˈækjərəsi/ (n) = precision

**attention to detail** (phr) = careful thought to small characteristics

**authentic** /ɔːˈθentɪk/ (adj) = genuine

**baker's** /ˈbeɪkəz/ (n) = a place where one buys bread, cakes and other sweets

**border** /ˈbɔːdə/ (v) = to form the edge of

**bread roll** /ˌbred ˈrəʊl/ (n) = a small round loaf of bread

**canal** /kəˈnæl/ (n) = a passage of water that boats use to travel along and allows water to be directed from one area to another

**carnival mask** /ˈkɑːnəvəl mɑːsk/ (n) = a face covering which people where at carnival time

**charm** /tʃɑːm/ (n) = appeal

**chemist's** /ˈkeməsts/ (n) = a place which sells medicine, beauty and other health-related products

**confectioner's** /kənˈfekʃənərz/ (n) = a shop that sells sweets and chocolates

**delicatessen** /ˌdelɪkəˈtesən/ (n) = a shop that sells high-quality foods

**designer clothes** /dɪˌzaɪnə ˈkləʊðz, ˈkləʊz/ (pl n) = clothes made by a famous person or company

**disturb** /dɪˈstɜːb/ (v) = to bother

**dry cleaner's** /ˌdraɪ ˈkliːnəz/ (n) = a shop where clothes are cleaned using chemicals

**elegant** /ˈeləgənt/ (adj) = stylish and graceful

**enormous** /ɪˈnɔːməs/ (adj) = very big; huge

**exclusive** /ɪkˈskluːsɪv/ (adj) = limited to one group of people

**eye drops** /ˈaɪ drɒps/ (pl n) = medicine for the eyes which can be applied in small amounts

**fashion boutique** /ˈfæʃən buːˌtiːk/ (n) = a shop that sells fashionable clothes

**glide** /glaɪd/ (v) = to move smoothly and continuously

**gondolier** /ˌgɒndəˈlɪə/ (n) = a man who takes people from one place to another in a gondola

**high-quality** /ˌhaɪ ˈkwɒləti/ (adj) = being of a very good standard

**influence** /ˈɪnfluəns/ (v) = to affect sb's way of thinking and behaviour

**inspiration** /ˌɪnspəˈreɪʃən/ (n) = idea

**inspire** /ɪnˈspaɪə/ (v) = to fill sb with a desire to do sth

**in the open air** (phr) = outdoors

**jeweller's** /ˈdʒuːələz/ (n) = a shop where you buy expensive rings, bracelets, etc

**juggler** /ˈdʒʌglə/ (n) = a person who throws objects into the air and catches them again to entertain people

**line** /laɪn/ (v) = to form a row along the side of

**living statue** /ˌlɪvɪŋ ˈstætʃuː/ (n) = an entertainer who pretends to be a real statue

**optician's** /ɒpˈtɪʃənz/ (n) = a shop where you can get your eyes tested and buy glasses

**packed (with)** /pækt/ (adj) = filled (with)

**replica** /ˈreplɪkə/ (n) = a copy

**resemble** /rɪˈzembəl/ (v) = to look like

**serenade** /ˌserəˈneɪd/ (v) = to sing for sb

**shimmer** /ˈʃɪmə/ (v) = to shine with a light that seems to shake

**stationer's** /ˈsteɪʃənəz/ (n) = a shop that sells things needed for writing

**steer** /stɪə/ (v) = to control the direction of a vehicle

**stroll** /strəʊl/ (v) = to walk in a relaxed way

**tourist attraction** /ˈtʊərəst əˌtrækʃən/ (n) = a place visited by tourists

**twilight** /ˈtwaɪlaɪt/ (n) = the time in the evening before it becomes completely dark

### 6f (pp. 106-107)

**approach** /əˈprəʊtʃ/ (v) = to come near to

**banjo** /ˈbændʒəʊ/ (n) = a stringed musical instrument

**(be) worth it** (phr) = to be interesting or important enough to do

**block** /blɒk/ (n) = a solid straight-sided piece of sth

**brass instrument** /ˌbrɑːs ˈɪnstrəmənt/ (n) = a musical instrument which is made of a bright yellow metal such as a trumpet, trombone etc

**chill-out** /ˈtʃɪl aʊt/ (adj) = relaxing

**compose** /kəmˈpəʊz/ (v) = to write a piece of music

**crew** /kruː/ (n) = a group of people who work together

**deep freeze** /ˌdiːp ˈfriːz/ (n) = freezer

**didgeridoo** /ˌdɪdʒəriˈduː/ (n) = the traditional musical instrument of Aboriginal Australians

**escape** /ɪˈskeɪp/ (v) = to get away

**experiment** /ɪkˈsperəmənt/ (v) = to try out new things in order to see the effects they have

**flute** /fluːt/ (n) = a musical instrument like a thin pipe

**freezer** /ˈfriːzə/ (n) = a large container like a fridge which keeps things frozen

**frozen** /ˈfrəʊzən/ (adj) = very hard because of being kept at a very low temperature

**glacier** /ˈglæsiə/ (n) = an extremely large mass of ice

**grunge** /grʌndʒ/ (n) = a type of loud rock music

**harp** /hɑːp/ (n) = a musical instrument made up of many strings which are plucked using both hands

**heavy metal** /ˌhevi ˈmetl/ (n) = a type of rock music with a strong beat that is played loudly on electric guitars and often in a distorted manner

**hip house** /hɪp haʊs/ (n) = a type of music which is a mixture of hip hop and electronic dance music

**horn** /hɔːn/ (n) = a musical instrument consisting of a tube which is narrow at one end and wide at the other

**icicle** /ˈaɪsɪkəl/ (n) = a spike of ice formed by water dripping

**In demand** (phr) = wanted very much; popular

**Mother Nature** /ˌmʌðə ˈneɪtʃə/ (n) = a metaphorical description of Earth and nature

**music critic** /ˈmjuːzɪk ˌkrɪtɪk/ (n) = a person whose job is to express their opinion about music

**music hall** /ˈmjuːzɪk hɔːl/ (n) = a building with a large room where an audience sits and listens to live music

**percussion instrument** /pəˈkʌʃən ˌɪnstrəmənt/ (n) = a musical instrument that you hit or shake, such as drums, maracas etc

**percussionist** /pəˈkʌʃənəst/ (n) = a person who plays percussion instruments

**string instrument** /strɪŋ ˌɪnstrəmənt/ (n) = a musical instrument that produces sound with strings that vibrate, such as a violin, guitar etc

**take a whole new direction** (phr) = to develop in a completely different way

**tambourine** /ˌtæmbəˈriːn/ (n) = a percussion instrument which looks like a small drum with jingling disks fitted around the edge

**trumpet** /ˈtrʌmpət/ (n) = a brass musical instrument with a curved metal tube that is wide at the end, and three keys that are pressed so as to produce music

**tune (in to)** /tjuːn/ (v) = to listen to sth on the radio

**violin** /ˌvaɪəˈlɪn/ (n) = a stringed musical instrument made of wood and played with a bow

**waterfall** /ˈwɔːtəfɔːl/ (n) = water dropping from a higher to a lower point

**wind instrument** /wɪnd ˌɪnstrəmənt/ (n) = a musical instrument that produces sound when the player blows air into it

### 6g (p. 108)

**(a place) of cultural interest** (phr) = (a place) related to a particular society and its art, ideas etc

**ancient theatre** /ˌeɪnʃənt ˈθɪətə/ (n) = the remains of a structure which, in the distant past, was a place of entertainment

**archaeological site** /ˌɑːkiəˈlɒdʒɪkəl ˌsaɪt/ (n) = an area of ground which has historical significance

**art gallery** /ˈɑːt ˌgæləri/ (n) = a building which exhibits works of art

**castle** /ˈkɑːsəl/ (n) = a large building with thick walls which was built by kings or lords in the past

**crowded** /ˈkraʊdəd/ (adj) = full of people

**fort** /fɔːt/ (n) = a strong building which can be protected

**natural history museum** /ˌnætʃərəl ˈhɪstəri mjuˌziəm/ (n) = a building with exhibits related to plants, animals, rocks etc

**palace** /ˈpæləs/ (n) = a building where kings, queens or presidents live

**science centre** /ˈsaɪəns ˌsentə/ (n) = a building which has learning exhibits related to science

**spectacular** /spekˈtækjələ/ (adj) = impressive; extraordinary

**temple** /ˈtempəl/ (n) = a building used for worshipping gods

**travel back in time** (phr) = to go back to the past

### 6h (p. 109)

**3D hologram** /ˈhɒləgræm/ (n) = an image made with a laser in which the objects look solid

**3D projection of objects** (phr) = an image of sth which looks solid and which can be seen from all sides

**archaeologist** /ˌɑːkiˈɒlədʒəst/ (n) = a person who studies the buildings and objects of societies from the past

**brick wall** /ˌbrɪk ˈwɔːl/ (n) = a wall which is made of rectangular blocks of baked clay

**exhibit** /ɪgˈzɪbət/ (n) = sth on display

**highlight** /ˈhaɪlaɪt/ (n) = the best part of sth

**high-tech** /ˌhaɪ ˈtek/ (adj) = being of the most advanced technology

**hustle and bustle** (phr) = busy and noisy activity

**impressive** /ɪmˈpresɪv/ (adj) = causing admiration

**medieval artefact** /ˌmedi-iːvəl ˈɑːtəfækt/ (n) = an object related to the Middle Ages

**ruins** /ˈruːənz/ (pl n) = the broken parts of an old building

**smokescreen** /ˈsməʊkskriːn/ (n) = a cloud of smoke used to hide sth

**sound effects** /saʊnd ɪˌfekts/ (pl n) = artificially-made sounds that are added to a film, radio or television programme

**thick** /θɪk/ (adj) = (of clothes) heavy; warm

**underground path** /ˌʌndəgraʊnd ˈpɑːθ/ (n) = a track for walking on which is below the surface

**6i (p. 110)**

**academy** /əˈkædəmi/ (n) = a school which specialises in a particular skill

**affect** /əˈfekt/ (v) = to influence

**anxious** /ˈæŋkʃəs/ (adj) = worried

**bring (sth) about** /ˌbrɪŋ əˈbaʊt/ (phr v) = to cause to happen

**brushstroke** /ˈbrʌʃ-strəʊk/ (n) = a mark on a surface made by a painter's brush

**capture** /ˈkæptʃə/ (v) = to record a representation of sth

**combine** /kəmˈbaɪn/ (v) = to join together

**concentrate** /ˈkɒnsəntreɪt/ (v) = to come together in one area

**confused** /kənˈfjuːzd/ (adj) = baffled; puzzled

**develop** /dɪˈveləp/ (v) = to form

**distort** /dɪˈstɔːt/ (v) = to twist or pull out of shape

**emerge** /ɪˈmɜːdʒ/ (v) = to appear

**excited** /ɪkˈsaɪtəd/ (adj) = enthusiastic

**expressionism** /ɪkˈspreʃənɪzəm/ (n) = a style of art which expresses people's states of mind

**fantasy** /ˈfæntəsi/ (n) = imagination; imaginary situations

**focus (on)** /ˈfəʊkəs ɒn/ (v) = to give most of one's attention to a particular thing

**found** /faʊnd/ (v) = to establish sth; to set up

**impressionism** /ɪmˈpreʃənɪzəm/ (n) a style of painting which represents the effects of light on objects and landscapes

**influence** /ˈɪnfluəns/ (v) = to have an effect on people

**in odd ways** (phr) = using strange methods; in strange ways

**memory** /ˈmeməri/ (n) = the ability to keep and recall information, experiences, events, etc

**outrage** /ˈaʊtreɪdʒ/ (v) = to make sb feel great anger and shock

**persistence** /pəˈsɪstəns/ (n) = the state of continuing and not giving up

**portray** /pɔːˈtreɪ/ (v) = to represent through art

**reaction** /riˈækʃən/ (n) = response

**reflect** /rɪˈflekt/ (v) = to send back light, an image, etc instead of absorbing it

**rehearsal** /rɪˈhɜːsəl/ (n) = a practice of a performance

**represent** /ˌreprəˈzent/ (v) = to describe sth or to be the symbol of sth

**sensation** /senˈseɪʃən/ (n) = a feeling

**set** /set/ (v) = to establish or decide what sth will be

**shocked** /ʃɒkt/ (adj) = very surprised and upset by sth bad and unexpected

**stage** /steɪdʒ/ (n) = the area of a theatre on which actors, etc perform

**strict convention** /ˌstrɪkt kənˈvenʃən/ (phr) = a way of thinking or behaving which is strongly limited

**surrealism** /səˈrɪəlɪzəm/ (n) = a type of art which shows impossible or unusual things happening

**terrace** /ˈterəs/ (n) = a flat area outside a building where people sit and sometimes eat

**touch of paint** (phr) = a small amount of paint which has been added to a picture or surface

**Skills Practice 6 (pp. 112-113)**

**budget** /ˈbʌdʒɪt/ (n) = the amount of money you have in order to spend on sth

**holiday-maker** /ˈhɒlɪdi ˌmeɪkər/ (n) = a person who is on holiday

### Vocabulary Bank 1
### p. VB1

**4** (Suggested Answer)

… What is your area like?
A: I live in an area with narrow streets. There are no bus lanes or cycle lanes and the pavements are very narrow, too. There are no roundabouts, level crossings or tunnels.

### p. VB2

**1** **mammal:** moose, beaver, raccoon, panther, rhino, camel, orang-utan, whale, rabbit, mouse, squirrel
**reptile:** alligator, scorpion, rattlesnake, lizard, cobra, turtle
**bird:** woodpecker, ostrich, owl, chicken, duck, goose
**fish:** tuna, salmon
**insect:** mosquito, wasp, cricket, dragonfly, ant, bee
**rodent:** beaver, mouse, squirrel
**amphibian:** salamander, frog, toad
**arachnid:** spider

**4** (Suggested Answers)

1 Yes, I have. It is a goldfish called George. It is orange and fat./I'd like to have a dog.
2 In my country, there are cows, sheep, pigs and chickens. We use them for milk, meat and eggs.
3 Yes, I have seen all sorts of wild animals in the zoo and some in the forest. I saw an eagle once. It was beautiful with large wings and sharp claws.

### p. VB3

**5** (Suggested Answer)

A: It's a place where you can deposit money.
B: It's a bank. It's a place where you can find many shops under one roof.
A: It's a shopping centre. It's a place where you can receive medical treatment.
B: It's a hospital. It's a place where you can post a parcel.
A: It's a post office. It's a place where you can fill your car up with petrol.
B: It's a petrol station. It's a place where you can take the dog for a walk.
A: It's a park. It's a place where you can park your car.
B: It's a car park. It's a place where you can get a marriage licence.
A: It's a town hall. It's a place where you can go swimming.
B: It's a sports complex. It's a place where you can learn a new skill.
A: It's a community centre. It's a place where you can watch a court case.
B: It's a court.

**6** (Suggested Answer)

Warsaw is a big city. It's the capital of Poland. There are a lot of interesting places to visit and many things to do. In my neighbourhood there is a park where we take the dog for a walk and a community centre where we socialise and learn new skills. I like my neighbourhood very much.

### p. VB4

**4 b)** (Suggested Answer)

A: Where is the entrance?
B: It's at the front of the house. Where is the basement?
A: It's under the house. Where is the roof?
B: It's on top of the house. Where is the fence?
A: It's around the garden. Where is the driveway?
B: It's in front of the house on the right. Where is the chimney?
A: It's on top of the roof. Where is the veranda?
B: It's outside the house at the front.

### Vocabulary Bank 2
### p. VB5

**2** (Suggested Answers)

1 My favourite fruit is the banana and my favourite vegetable is the carrot. I can't stand grapefruit or spinach.
2 I usually have egg on toast for breakfast, a sandwich or a salad for lunch and meat with potatoes for dinner.
3 Yes, I go to the local market every Saturday. I buy fruit and vegetables and cheese./No, I don't go to a market.
4 Yes, I do. They eat soya protein and they avoid meat, dairy products and seafood./No, I don't know any vegetarians.
5 My favourite dish is apple pie. You need apples, flour, butter and sugar to make it.
6 Strawberries, raspberries, cherries, tomatoes, cucumbers and peppers grow in my country in the summer.

### p. VB6

**3 b)** (Suggested Answers)

A: Do you prefer a rare or a well done steak?
B: I prefer a well done steak.

A: Do you prefer strong or weak tea?
B: I prefer strong tea.

A: Do you prefer soft or crusty bread?
B: I prefer crusty bread.

A: Do you prefer spicy or mild curry?
B: I prefer mild curry.

A: Do you prefer red or white wine?
B: I prefer white wine.

### p. VB7

**2 b)** First, the waiter sets the table. Then the customers read the menu. When they are ready they call the waiter who takes the order. During the meal, the waiter serves the food and pours the drinks. After the meal, the customers pay the bill and leave a tip.

**4 (Suggested Answers)**

1 I eat out about once a month. I usually eat out with my family.
2 My favourite restaurant is Rico's. I like it because the food is delicious and the staff are friendly.

### p. VB8

**4 (Suggested Answer)**

A: How do you like to eat eggs: fried or boiled?
B: Actually, I prefer scrambled eggs.

A: How do you like to eat vegetables: fried, boiled or grilled?
B: Actually, I prefer steamed vegetables.

A: How do you like to eat fish: fried, baked or grilled?
B: Actually, I prefer steamed fish.

A: How do you like to eat beef: fried or grilled?
B: Actually, I prefer roast beef.

A: How do you like to eat rice: fried or boiled?
B: Actually, I prefer steamed rice.

## Vocabulary Bank 3

### p. VB10

**1 b) (Suggested Answers)**

1 **outside:** sailor
**inside:** musician, painter, architect, sculptor, scientist, president, teacher, singer, nurse
2 architect, scientist, teacher, nurse
3 sailor, nurse
4 musician, painter, sculptor

**3** 2 A painter paints portraits of people.
3 A musician plays a musical instrument.
4 A sailor works on a ship.
5 A singer performs live on stage.
6 A scientist does experiments.

**4 (Suggested Answers)**

A musician needs to be talented and skilful.
An architect needs to be intelligent and creative.
A physicist needs to be intelligent, curious and imaginative.
A teacher needs to be intelligent, creative and patient.
A nurse needs to be sociable, patient, hardworking and polite.

A singer needs to be talented.
A scientist needs to be intelligent and skilful.
An explorer needs to be brave and ambitious.
A sailor needs to be hardworking.
A painter needs to be talented, creative and imaginative.
A sculptor needs to be talented, creative and imaginative.
An engineer needs to be intelligent, imaginative and skilful.
A mathematician needs to be talented and intelligent.
An inventor needs to be imaginative, creative and skilful.

## Vocabulary Bank 4

### p. VB13

**3** You may lose your luggage.
You may lose your money.
You may lose your passport.
You may lose your ticket.
You may miss the train.

**4 (Suggested Answers)**

1 I lost my luggage once. I complained to the airline and it arrived two days later. I had to buy some new clothes and toiletries, but the airline gave me the money back.
2 Once I missed my flight and I had to spend the night at the airport. It was very uncomfortable and inconvenient, but I managed to get a flight the next day.
3 Yes, I have. It was very painful. I put on some skin cream and stayed indoors for a few days./ No, I haven't. I am always very careful not to get sunburnt.

## Vocabulary Bank 5

### p. VB14

**1 b) (Suggested Answers)**

1 Floods are quite common in my country. When it rains heavily in the autumn, some rivers burst their banks and there is quite a lot of flooding. None of the other natural disasters are common in my country.
2 If an earthquake happened, I would quickly get under a table or a solid piece of furniture and wait until the shaking stops. Then, I would leave the building and get to a safe area. I wouldn't use the lift. I would wait until the building was declared safe before I went back inside.

### p. VB16

**3 (Suggested Answers)**

1 Yes, I have. I had a high temperature, a runny nose, a sore throat and a bad cough./No, I haven't.
2 Yes, I have. I fell off my skateboard and sprained my wrist. I went to hospital for an X-ray and the doctor put a bandage on it. / No, I haven't

## Vocabulary Bank 6

### p. VB18

**5 (Suggested Answers)**

1 There is a supermarket, a butcher's, a baker's and a chemist's in my area.
2 I usually buy clothes and shoes when I go shopping. I sometimes buy bread and pastries from the baker's.
3 I always pay in cash. I don't have a credit card.

### p. VB19

**1** **string:** violin, guitar, harp, cello
**wind:** accordion, flute
**brass:** trumpet, saxophone, horn
**percussion:** piano, xylophone, tambourine, drums

**4 (Suggested Answers)**

1 Yes, I do. I play the piano./No, I don't. I would like to learn to play the piano.
2 My favourite type of music is pop music.
3 Yes, I have been to a live concert. It was my favourite band. It took place in the stadium in the city centre. It was amazing. / No, I haven't been to a live concert, but I would like to.

### p. VB20

**5 (Suggested Answers)**

2 They are two tiny round coins made from hard metal. They have a rough surface.
3 It's a round flat plate with flowers on.
4 It's a large marble statue of a woman and a big vase. It has a smooth surface.
5 It's a carved dragon. It has a rough surface with sharp points all over it.

## Writing Bank

### p. WB2

**1 (Suggested Answers)**

- It has the layout of a letter and not a note.
- It starts/ends like an informal letter.
- There is no chatty language. It has a semi-formal style.
- All pronouns, articles and auxiliaries are included.

**2 (Suggested Answers)**

Becky,
Have to meet Laura to take dog to vet.
Can't come shopping. Hope you don't mind. Might be late. If I finish early, I'll call and meet you there or we could go to cinema. Text me.
Anna

### p. WB3

**1 (Suggested Answers)**

1 An art contest
2 To use digital technology as a language of creative expression.
3 St Martin's College, 2nd May
4 The prize, who can enter, who to contact

**2 (Suggested Answers)**

Anyone who is interested can call Sara Hill on 01226 421567.
Calling all Digital Art Students!

### p. WB4

**1 (Suggested Answers)**

Fyodor Dostoyevsky is one of the most famous writers in the world. He was born in Moscow, Russia, in 1821.

At the age of 16 Dostoyevsky entered the Army Engineering College but resigned the army 7 years later in 1844 to start writing seriously. In his early career as a writer he joined the St Petersburg Gazette in 1847. Ten years later, he met and married Mariya Dmitrieyevna Isayeva and, soon after, became editor of Vremya.

Dostoyevsky also travelled abroad for the first time to London in 1962 but, after returning to Russia, mounting debts forced him to leave again. It was at this point that he wrote one of his most famous works, *Crime and Punishment*, and met and married his second wife Anna Grigoryevna Snitkina. They moved to Italy where he continued to write, publishing *The Idiot* in 1868. Dostoyevsky remained abroad for 6 years finally returning to his homeland in 1871.

He published his final work *The Brothers Karamazov* shortly before his death in 1881. But his writings live on and people will always remember him as one of the greatest writers who ever lived.

### p. WB5

**1 (Suggested Answers)**

- I am writing to apply for ...
- I can speak English, French and German fluently.
- Despite not having worked before in a similar position, I feel I would be well-suited for it.
- I may be contacted by telephone on ...
- I am available for an interview ...
- I look forward to hearing from you.
- Yours faithfully,

### p. WB6

**1 (Suggested Answers)**

To:        All teachers
From:      Sharon Anderson, School Secretary
Date:      29th April 20...
Subject:   Annual Summer Party

This year's annual summer party will take place in the school playground on Saturday 25th June from 6 pm-12 pm and is open to all teachers, students and their families.
We ask that teachers bring snacks, cakes and refreshments and volunteer to be responsible for various activities such as organising the treasure hunt. We also need a DJ to play music.

### p. WB7

**1 (Suggested Answers)**

This isn't an appropriate postcard because it doesn't use chatty language and there are no omissions of pronouns, articles or auxiliaries. The layout is like a letter and the style is semi-formal with full forms, advanced linkers and a formal ending. It is also too long for a postcard.

**2 (Suggested Answers)**

Hi Dora!
Greetings from Rome! I'm here on holiday with my family and I thought I'd drop you a line. Weather's fine. I'm sightseeing every day, shopping most afternoons and dining at excellent restaurants every night. It's great!
Tomorrow, we're going on a guided tour of the Vatican. Can't wait!
See you soon.
Jenny

## Module 1

➤ **Exercise 3 (p. 18)**

*Tim:* I live in a large flat in the city. I live with two flatmates, Richard and Tony. The flat has six rooms, a kitchen, a bathroom, a living room and three bedrooms. My favourite room is the living room. The sofa is really comfortable! It's great living with Richard and Tony. We are good friends and we all share the household chores. I usually do the washing-up and take out the rubbish every day!

*Sarah:* I live with my family in a small town. It's really quiet there. Our house is quite small. Downstairs there's the kitchen and the living room and upstairs there are two bedrooms and a bathroom. We also have a beautiful big garden where our dog can play. Mum does most of the chores at home because I'm really busy studying for my exams at the moment. The only thing I have to do is make my bed and lay the table for dinner.

➤ **Exercise 2 (p. 20)**

1  A: Next, please.
   B: Hello. Two stamps, please.
   A: Certainly. Here you are. That's £1.20 please.
   B: Here you are.
   A: Thank you very much.

2  A: Hello, I'm here to visit my uncle, Mr James Smith. Which room is he in, please?
   B: Just one moment … he's in room 203. Go to the end of the corridor, turn right and it's the second room on the left.
   A: OK, thank you.

3  A: Hello, can I help you?
   B: Yes, I'd like to borrow these three books, please.
   A: OK, can I have your library card, please?
   B: Yes, here it is.
   A: Thank you. You can keep them until the 15th.
   B: Thank you, goodbye.

4  A: Hello, do you have any information about community classes and events?
   B: Yes, we do. It's all here in this leaflet. You can take it.
   A: Oh, thank you very much.
   B: You're welcome.

➤ **Exercise 3b (p. 23)**

*Dylan:* Hey Holly, a new water park opens on Thursday. Let's go this weekend.
*Holly:* I can't. I work on Saturdays and Sundays.
*Dylan:* No problem. We can go on Friday.
*Holly:* OK. Where is the water park?
*Dylan:* You know where the library is on the high street. Turn left and go down Station Road. It's in Fulton Street, the road just before the train station.
*Holly:* It sounds quite a long way to me.
*Dylan:* Don't worry. We don't have to walk there, we can get the bus.

*Holly:* That sounds better. I'm tired of walking everywhere. How much is it to get in?
*Dylan:* It's usually £10 per person, but there's £4 off for the first month so it's £6 each.
*Holly:* What time do you want to meet?
*Dylan:* Well, there's a bus every fifteen minutes and it's only twenty minutes to the water park. Could you be at the bus stop at 10?
*Holly:* Sure. Can we get something to eat at the water park?
*Dylan:* There's a café with snacks there, but these places are usually expensive. We could eat at the fast food restaurant near the train station or just take some sandwiches.
*Holly:* After swimming I usually feel like burger and fries.
*Dylan:* Me too! See you later!

## Module 2

➤ **Exercise 2 (p. 25)**

*Tim:* I really like meat like chicken and beef but I don't like cheese or milk. Oh, and I hate cabbage! It's horrible!

*Julie:* I love fruit, especially cherries! I also like eggs and cheese but I can't stand tuna – yuck!

➤ **Exercise 5a (p. 29)**

*Julie:* Let's check what I need for the dinner party tonight. Could you look in the fridge please, Tom?
*Tom:* Sure. Well, there isn't much here. Should I make a shopping list?
*Julie:* Yes, please. Is there any chicken?
*Tom:* No. How much do you need?
*Julie:* 2 kilos.
*Tom:* OK. Do you need any eggs?
*Julie:* No, I don't need any eggs, but I do need a kilo of cheese.
*Tom:* What about crisps?
*Julie:* Oh yes, write down 3 bags.
*Tom:* OK. And what about cola? There's only a little in the fridge.
*Julie:* Let's get 2 bottles.
*Tom:* Alright. There's a carton of apple juice here, too. Do we need any more?
*Julie:* No, I think 1 carton is OK.
*Tom:* So what else? Do you need any rice?
*Julie:* Just buy one bag. There's one bag in the cupboard.
*Tom:* OK, so is that everything?
*Julie:* I think so … oh! Don't forget to buy lots of sausages! Get 20!
*Tom:* OK, then. I'll go to the supermarket. See you in half an hour!

➤ **Exercise 3 (p. 36)**

*Maria:* So Frank, did you see Chef Jeff on TV last night?
*Frank:* Oh, I love Chef Jeff, but I missed it last night. How was it?

*Maria:* It was great! He is so entertaining. Last night, he went to a steakhouse restaurant in a small town somewhere in Texas.
*Frank:* A steak house? But they only serve steak there, right?
*Maria:* Not exactly! They specialise in steak, but they also serve other dishes.
*Frank:* Oh, all right.
*Maria:* Anyway … it was awful! The kitchen was really dirty and the cooks were terrible. I mean I love beef but I would never eat their steaks. It was scary! Customers sent back several dishes because the meat wasn't cooked … and one customer even found a hair in his food.
*Frank:* No way!
*Maria:* I'm serious! Chef Jeff shouted at them all the time. He closed the restaurant down for two days and told them to clean it properly. Then, he taught them how to cook from the beginning.
*Frank:* I love it when he does that.
*Maria:* Yeah, so do I.
*Frank:* Do you remember when he had to teach a chef from Spain how to make paella?
*Maria:* Yeah! That episode was so funny. Listen to this though! Last night he threw away all the meat because it was bad. He bought fresh meat and showed them how to cook it. Imagine a steak house where they don't know how to cook steak!
*Frank:* Unbelievable!

➢ **Exercise 3b (p. 41)**
*Ben:* Hi Tina! Great party!
*Tina:* Hi Ben – thanks. How's the food?
*Ben:* The food's delicious. There's a lot to choose from and everyone's enjoying it.
*Tina:* That's good; my favourite's the apple pie on the dessert table!
*Ben:* Oh yes, it's great! The chocolate brownies are also very popular. Sandra can't stop eating them.
*Tina:* We are all so unhealthy! What do the others like?
*Ben:* Well, Annie's very healthy so she's enjoying all the fresh fruit, especially the strawberries!
*Tina:* Yes, those are lovely. Janet's enjoying the fresh fruit too but prefers fresh vegetables. She loves vegetables that are in season so the tomatoes are her favourite. What do you think about the roast meat?
*Ben:* Carl likes the roast chicken; however, he thinks the roast lamb is even better. He's eating the whole plate!
*Tina:* Excellent. What about the rice with prawns?
*Ben:* Joe thinks it's good but a little too salty; he loves the homemade pasta though.
*Tina:* I'm glad Joe's enjoying it- that's my Mum's recipe!

➢ **Exercise 4b (p. 41)**
In the picture, I can see a man in his mid-thirties with short curly brown hair. He is in a supermarket doing some shopping. He is wearing a blue shirt and some light brown trousers and he is holding a green shopping basket. He is in the fruit and vegetable section. He is looking at the fresh vegetables. There are potatoes, cabbages and celery. He is probably going to buy some.

## Module 3

➢ **Exercise 2a (p. 46)**
*Presenter:* Hello and welcome to *That's Ancient History*! – the quiz show that tests how much you know about long long ago. On tonight's show, our contestants are Rob Talbot and Moira Bell. The first question goes to Rob. Rob, which empire did Genghis Khan start? Was it the Ottoman Empire, the Persian Empire or the Mongol Empire?
*Rob:* That's easy. It was the Mongol Empire.
*Presenter:* Yes, it was. Well done! Now, Moira, according to legend, what did Manco Cápac do? Did he start the Inca Empire, discover South America or build many Mayan temples?
*Moira:* Err… I know he didn't discover South America. Did he start the Inca Empire?
*Presenter:* Yes, he did, Moira. Rob, Marco Polo set out along the Silk Road in 1271. When did he return home? Was it 5 years later, 12 years later or 24 years later?
*Rob:* Er … I think it was 12.
*Presenter:* Sorry Rob, it was a lot longer than that. He didn't return until 24 years later! Back to you, Moira … according to many poets and historians, how did Cleopatra die? Did she eat some poisoned food, did a poisonous snake bite her or did she stab herself?
*Moira:* Oh, I know that! She died after a poisonous snake bit her.
*Presenter:* Correct! Rob, who famously said "I came, I saw, I conquered." after one victory in Asia Minor? Was it Julius Caesar, Genghis Khan or Tutankhamen?
*Rob:* Oh, that's easy. It was Julius Caesar.
*Presenter:* Yes, it was, Rob. Moira, if you get the next question correct, you're tonight's winner! Are you ready?
*Moira:* I think so.
*Presenter:* OK, then. How old was Alexander the Great when he died? Was he 76, 49 or 33?
*Moira:* I know he wasn't old, so … was he 33?
*Presenter:* Yes, he was! Congratulations, Moira! You win a leather-bound atlas of the ancient world and I'll see you next week on *That's Ancient History*!

➢ **Exercise 3 (p. 54)**
*FEMALE VOICE:* Hello and welcome to the Florence Nightingale museum information line. Admission is £5.80 for adults and £4.80 for children with special prices for group bookings. The price includes a free audio tour of the museum.

The tour covers three exhibition areas which tell the story of Florence:

The first, *The Gilded Cage*, tells you about her childhood and her struggle to enter the nursing profession.

*The Calling* exhibition is next on the tour and introduces you to the legend of 'the lady of the lamp' and her dramatic time in the military hospitals of the Crimean War.

Finally, the *Reform and Inspire* exhibition takes you through her tireless campaigns for health reform at home and abroad.

Just place your stethoscope on the audio hotspots in each section to hear Florence and her present-day equals explain her moving story.

Along with a host of other attractions and exhibits we are sure there is something to interest everyone, young and old. We are open daily from 10am to 5pm.

Thank you for calling the information line and we look forward to your visit.

### ➤ Exercise 4a (p. 55)

Albert Einstein was a world-famous scientist, philosopher and physicist. He was born on 14th March, 1879 in the city of Ulm, which later became part of Germany.

As a child, he grew up in Munich. He attended Luitpold Grammar School where he was a quiet student interested in Science and Mathematics. He also enjoyed playing his violin. When he was 15, he left school and went with his family to Milan. His ambition was to become a Maths or Physics teacher. He graduated from high school in Switzerland and finished his university studies in Zurich in 1900.

In 1901, Einstein, now in his early twenties, couldn't find a teaching position. Instead, he got a job as a technical assistant in the Swiss Patent Office. In his spare time, he worked on maths problems, and in 1905 he published some of his famous scientific theories. Included was the well-known 'Special Theory of Relativity'. During the 1920s, he received many different honors. He accepted the Nobel Prize for Physics in 1921. Throughout his life, he published over 400 scientific works and gave lectures in Europe and America.

Albert Einstein died on 18th April, 1955. He was 76 years old. His name and face are still famous all over the world, and many people believe he was the greatest genius of the 20th century and perhaps of all time.

### ➤ Exercise 1 (p. 58)

*0* How old is Craig?
   *Woman:* Look at this Craig, Alexander the Great was only 33 when he died.
   *Man:* Really? He was quite young.
   *Woman:* Yes, but not as young as Tutankhamen, he only lived for 18 years.
   *Man:* Wow, that's 2 years younger than I am.

*1* When was the re-enactment?
   *Man:* How was the re-enactment?
   *Woman:* It was great, but we almost missed it.
   *Man:* Oh, why?
   *Woman:* Well, usually it is on the 15th every year but this year they planned it for the 13th but it rained so they had to postpone it.
   *Man:* So, when was it?
   *Woman:* They had it the following day.

*2* What did the thieves take?
   *Man:* Did you hear about the burglary at the museum?
   *Woman:* No, what happened?
   *Man:* Thieves broke in, vandalised a painting and sprayed paint on a statue.
   *Woman:* Did they steal anything?
   *Man:* Yes, some valuable jewellery.

*3* Where is da Vinci's bridge?
   *Woman:* Leonardo da Vinci was a brilliant man.
   *Man:* I know, he is one of the world's most famous painters. Everyone knows the Mona Lisa in the Louvre in Paris, France.
   *Woman:* Yes, but did you know he was also an engineer? In 2001 the Norwegian built a bridge based on his design.
   *Man:* Wow, not bad for a 15th century Italian.

*4* What was the weather like?
   *Man:* Did you do anything special at the weekend?
   *Woman:* Bill and I were going to go to the museum because the forecast said it was going to be nice but the weather was so bad we just stayed home.
   *Man:* Was it raining?
   *Woman:* Worse, there was a hailstorm.

*5* How many people were on board the boat?
   *Man:* Can you imagine being on a boat in the middle of the ocean for 66 days?
   *Woman:* No, the 100 sailors on the Mayflower had to be very brave.
   *Man:* And it's a wonder that any of them managed to survive that first winter in 1620.
   *Woman:* Yes, they had a lot to be thankful for.

## Module 4

### ➤ Exercise 2 (p. 61)

*Sarah:* Every summer, all my friends go on beach holidays with their families, but my family always goes camping! It's fun. We stay in a really nice campsite in the country and take nice long walks, but this summer we're all thinking of doing something different. My parents are hoping to go on a cruise and I really want to go on an activity holiday with my friends. I can't wait!

➢ **Exercise 2 (p. 72)**

**A:** Hi Nancy, how was your trip?

**B:** Oh, hi Rachael. I had a great time but I think I was the only one.

**A:** Why, what happened?

**B:** Well, you know how Tristan's always late for everything.

**A:** Oh no, he didn't miss the flight, did he?

**B:** No, this time he got to the airport in plenty of time but he forgot his passport so he had to call his mum and get her to bring it.

**A:** Typical, but everybody else's flight was OK, Janice wasn't sick again, was she?

**B:** Actually, Carly was the one who was sick.

**A:** What was wrong with her?

**B:** She got food poisoning at the airport.

**A:** Oh, poor Carly. So Janice was OK?

**B:** On the flight yes, but the airline lost her luggage.

**A:** Oh no.

**B:** Yeah, she was borrowing clothes the whole week.

**A:** What about Monica?

**B:** She had a problem with the hotel; they didn't have a room for her so she had to share with Janice.

**A:** I'm sure they didn't mind. And were the boys OK?

**B:** Roger wanted to go sailing but the weather stopped that happening.

**A:** Why, was it raining?

**B:** No, he got sunburnt on the first day and couldn't move.

**A:** And what about Douglas? Don't tell me he got sunburnt too. He should know better being so fair skinned.

**B:** He was having a great time until someone stole his wallet when we were shopping at the market.

**A:** Wow, what a holiday, I'm glad I couldn't make it now.

➢ **Exercise 4b (p. 77)**

**Girl:** Hi Chris. Are you going on holiday this year? I'm not going anywhere this summer.

**Chris:** Yes, I am. I'm going on a camping holiday with my family. We go camping every year. But if I had money, I'd go on a safari holiday with my friends.

**Girl:** Really! That sounds exciting. I'm not daring enough to go on a safari holiday, I always go on boring beach holidays.

**Chris:** Beach holidays aren't my favourite either. But I heard that Lauren is going on a beach holiday next week.

**Girl:** Yes, she told me. Is Anna going too?

**Chris:** Not this year. She's decided to go on a sightseeing holiday to the historical city of Rome.

**Girl:** Personally if I was going on holiday, I'd go on a cruise.

**Chris:** Well, Ben said he wanted to go on a walking holiday, but he's going on a cruise with his family. They always go on a cruise in the summer.

**Girl:** I heard that Sophie's leaving soon for her backpacking trip. I bet she's really excited!

**Chris:** Yes. She'll leave as soon as she finishes school. Tom was planning to go with her, but he's going on an adventure holiday tomorrow. I think he'll have a great time because he loves dangerous and exciting activities!

**Girl:** Do you think he'll go sandboarding?

**Chris:** I'm not sure, but he definitely wants to drive a dune buggy.

**Girl:** I wish I could be brave like Tom!

## Module 5

➢ **Exercise 2 (p. 79)**

*Speaker 1*

Many animals are in danger of disappearing forever. Sometimes this is because people cut down too many trees in the forests where the animals live. The giant panda of China, for example, doesn't have enough forest land to live on. Today, there are only about 1600 of them left in the wild.

*Speaker 2*

The temperature of the Earth has become a lot higher in the last hundred years. Scientists say that the problem mostly comes from factory gases and that this is causing big changes in the weather.

*Speaker 3:*

Studies show that more and more ordinary people are losing their homes. People are even sleeping in their cars or in tents because homeless shelters already have too many people in them.

➢ **Exercise 8a (p. 81)**

**Peter:** Oh, hi Mum. It's Peter!

**Mum:** Oh, Peter! How are you? How was your first day with the team?

**Peter:** Oh, it's been fine, Mum. I can't believe my eyes though. The hurricane has destroyed so many houses and a lot of people are injured.

**Mum:** Yes, I've seen the pictures on TV. It's awful. So what did you do today?

**Peter:** Well, we've been really busy. We've helped to clear some roads because a lot of trees have fallen on them. It was really difficult. We've brought lots of supplies in, too, like medical supplies and food.

**Mum:** Have you helped any of the injured people?

**Peter:** No, actually there are other teams of medical workers and they are doing that. We want to collect some money in the next town to help the people of the village, too, but we didn't have time today. I think we're going to do that tomorrow.

**Mum:** Well, stay safe, Peter. And make sure you take lots of photos!

**Peter:** Actually, I've taken lots of photos today already, Mum. I'll show you them when I get back. I have to go now, Mum.

**Mum:** OK, bye!

**Peter:** Bye! I'll call you again in a few days.

➤ **Exercise 6 (p. 87)**

*Mark:* We were in India. We went for a walk in the forest one morning. Then, suddenly, there was a very loud roar. It was a huge tiger and he was really near! Luckily, our guide was really calm. "Don't move or say anything!" he told us. I could hear my heart beating loudly inside me! After a few seconds, the tiger just walked away. It was really scary, I can tell you! Whew!

*Holly:* I took part in a conservation project at the beach last summer. We collected litter in big plastic bags. Anyway, at the end of the afternoon, I saw a dead sea bird caught in a fishing net! I couldn't believe it! It was just awful to see something like that! I couldn't forget that scene for a long time afterwards …

*Jess:* I've never seen anything like it. I was on San Cristobal, one of the Galapagos Islands. I went diving with my group and as soon as I was under the water, I couldn't believe my eyes! The water was really clear and the fish were amazing. They were so colourful – it was like a rainbow under the sea. Best of all were the sea lions – they actually swam with us for a while. It was incredible!

➤ **Exercise 3 (p. 90)**

*Karl:* Judy, I'm just filling in my application form for the eco-camp. I want to apply to be a counsellor this summer. It's all in English, of course. Can you give me a hand?
*Judy:* Sure. I can write the information for you if you like. OK, let's see … first, they want your full name. That's Karl Martinez, right? How do you spell your surname again?
*Karl:* It's M–A–R–T–I–N–E–Z.
*Judy:* Ok, that's done. How old are you?
*Karl:* I'm seventeen.
*Judy:* Right. And you're from Mexico, of course …
*Karl:* Yes, and my email address is Karl@zmail.com.
*Judy:* Got it. Ok, now they need your phone number.
*Karl:* Ok. It's 213-746-2254.
*Judy:* Can you say that again?
*Karl:* Sure. 213-746-2254.
*Judy:* OK, that's great. Now, you have to tick the box for the camp you want to go to. Which one is it, 16th to 31st July or 2nd to 16th August?
*Karl:* Tick the August one.
*Judy:* Fine. Now, what about previous experience? Have you done any of the things here on the list before?
*Karl:* Sure. I've organised activities for kids. I did that at another summer camp last year. Oh, and I taught sports there, too. I taught the kids volleyball. I haven't had a first-aid course, though.
*Judy:* OK, well I think we've finished then. You can send the form now.
*Karl:* Thanks so much, Judy!
*Judy:* You're welcome.

➤ **Exercise 1b (p. 94)**

*Jane:* This eco-camp is a lot of fun!
*Robert:* But also a lot of work.

*Jane:* I know what you mean. You look tired, Robert. Tough day?
*Robert:* Yeah, planting trees was hard work. Did your team enjoy the nature walk?
*Jane:* Actually, there was a change of plans and we collected rubbish from the motorway for recycling.
*Robert:* That's great! If only people understood that they shouldn't litter. I mostly see kids throwing candy wrappers out of cars, but also tourists are quite careless.
*Jane:* Actually, the wind blows most of it off lorries.
*Robert:* That's sad. Did you have a lot help with the clean up?
*Jane:* There were only five of us but we worked from 10 to 4.
*Robert:* How much rubbish did you collect?
*Jane:* We took 160 bags with us, we had 16 at the end of the day, so, 144. We could've filled another 50 if we had had more time.
*Robert:* All this work has made me hungry.
*Jane:* Why don't we go cook on the barbecue?
*Robert:* Sure. Why not? I really feel like having a big burger, crisps and a cola.
*Jane:* The burger and cola are fine but I'd rather have fresh vegetables from the camp's garden.
*Robert:* Good idea. This place really is great. Don't you agree?
*Jane:* I know. I've already signed up to be a counsellor next July. Do you want to join me?
*Robert:* I'd prefer June but I'll think about it. I know the deadline isn't until the end of August anyway.
*Jane:* That's right. Well, let's go and eat something.

### Module 6

➤ **Exercise 2 (p. 104)**

*A*   A: Hi. Can I help you?
    B: Yes, please. I'd like a box of chocolate truffles.
    A: What flavour would you like? We've got almond, praline or caramel.
    B: Ooh! A selection please.

*B*   A: Can you recommend something for my sore throat?
    B: Certainly. We have syrup or lozenges.
    A: I'd prefer syrup.
    B: Then this one is very good and doesn't make you drowsy.

*C*   A: Hi. Can I have 200 grammes of sliced salami, please?
    B: Coming right up. Would you like anything else?
    A: Yes. Do you have any stilton?
    B: Yes, we have three varieties: plain, blue and with fruit added.

*D*   A: Hi. I'm looking for a pair of silver earrings for my girlfriend.
    B: OK. Well, we have a number of different styles. Here we are.
    A: They look nice. How much are they?
    B: They're £15.

➢ **Exercise 2a (p. 108)**

*Speaker 1*

It was fantastic. The fort was huge and the guide told us all about its history. I was fascinated. I could imagine soldiers over the centuries fighting the different battles that have taken place here on the battlements throughout history.

*Speaker 2*

You should definitely go to the science centre. We went last week and it was incredible. I think, we need to go seven days in a row to see all the things we missed. You can try all sorts of different equipment and find out how everything works.

*Speaker 3*

The temple was beautiful. There were amazing statues inside and around 300 steps to get to the top of the dome. It was very tiring, especially in the heat, but it was worth it for the panorama.

*Speaker 4*

I absolutely recommend the natural history museum. It is the best museum I have ever been to. There were complete dinosaur skeletons and fossils that were amazing to see. I was so engrossed in the exhibits that I didn't even notice the time passing. By the time I had made my way around the whole museum, it was very late in the afternoon.

*Speaker 5*

The archaeological site was amazing and well-worth the long queues to get in. The site itself is very big and as most of the ruins are roped off it takes a while to walk around. I understand why they have to keep the numbers of visitors under control because otherwise you wouldn't be able to see everything easily.

➢ **Exercise 3b (p. 113)**

Welcome on board. Please note that you're on a hop-on, hop-off service and your tickets are valid all day, so you can see the city at your leisure. Tour buses leave every 60 minutes and the tour itself takes 90 so if you want to hop off and then hop back on, it's never more than an hour before the next bus.

As we leave Central Square, which has been a popular meeting place for centuries, we pass the city's best-known shopping street, Station Road. If you want to buy something to remember your trip, that's the place. For more expensive purchases like designer goods, try Belgrave Avenue.

Our first stop is the Roman fort. Show your bus ticket here to get 20% off admission to the fort and its museum. There are guided tours every day at 9am, 12pm and 3pm. That's one every three hours.

We are now climbing City Road towards the old town hall which is well-known for its Victorian architecture although perhaps it's more famous these days for its pop concerts. The clock tower was designed by Herbert Bailey, but not many people remember him these days.

From the top of City Road, you can admire the sea to the west. We've got a spectacular coast here and if you'd like to visit it while you're here, you can take the bus service from Central Square. Then you might like to take a short ferry ride to Fern Island to spot some wildlife.

Our next stop is a little piece of the countryside right here in the heart of the city. In Woodland Park, you can go boating on the lake or even do a bit of sunbathing in the summer. Not today of course! It's a bit chilly for that. The area around Woodland Park is also well-known for its lively nightlife. This is very much the playground of the city.

# Evaluations

# *Formative Evaluation Chart*

**Name of game/activity:** ......................................................................................................................

**Aim of game/activity:** ......................................................................................................................

**Module:** ...................................... **Unit:** ...................................... **Course:** ..........................

| Students' names: | Mark and comments |
|---|---|
| 1 | |
| 2 | |
| 3 | |
| 4 | |
| 5 | |
| 6 | |
| 7 | |
| 8 | |
| 9 | |
| 10 | |
| 11 | |
| 12 | |
| 13 | |
| 14 | |
| 15 | |
| 16 | |
| 17 | |
| 18 | |
| 19 | |
| 20 | |
| 21 | |
| 22 | |
| 23 | |
| 24 | |
| 25 | |

Evaluation criteria:      c (green)      w (yellow)      n (red)



© Express Publishing  PHOTOCOPIABLE

# Cumulative Evaluation

## Student's Self Assessment Forms

| CODE | | | |
|---|---|---|---|
| ****** Excellent** | ***** Very Good** | **** OK** | *** Not Very Good** |

### Student's Self Assessment Form

Module 1

**Go through Module 1 and find examples of the following. Use the code to evaluate yourself.**

| | |
|---|---|
| • describe places | |
| • identify True/False statements | |
| • buy a ticket | |
| • complete sentences based on a text | |
| • talk about survival | |
| • guess meaning of new words through context | |
| • talk about types of housing | |
| • compare places in my country | |
| • talk about home and chores | |
| • make requests | |
| • talk about public services & facilities | |

**Go through the corrected writing tasks. Use the code to evaluate yourself.**

| | |
|---|---|
| • write about a journey to my country that is interesting for tourists | |
| • write a list of survival tips | |
| • write an email describing my home | |
| • write an informal email of advice | |
| • write a note | |

© Express Publishing  PHOTOCOPIABLE

<table>
<tr><td colspan="4">CODE</td></tr>
<tr><td>**** Excellent</td><td>*** Very Good</td><td>** OK</td><td>* Not Very Good</td></tr>
</table>

## Student's Self Assessment Form

Module 2

**Go through Module 2 and find examples of the following. Use the code to evaluate yourself.**

| | |
|---|---|
| • talk about food & drinks | |
| • talk about containers/partitives | |
| • talk about eating places in the UK | |
| • order food in a café | |
| • complete a gapped text | |
| • match headings to paragraphs | |
| • make a restaurant booking | |
| • identify True/False statements | |
| • talk about healthy/unhealthy food/drinks | |
| • give instructions how to make a dish | |
| • work with multiple-choice questions | |
| • describe a photograph | |

**Go through the corrected writing tasks. Use the code to evaluate yourself.**

| | |
|---|---|
| • write a text describing a food festival | |
| • write sentences about my eating habits | |
| • write short texts about places to eat out in my country | |
| • write a description of my own strange restaurant | |
| • write an email about my favourite dish | |
| • write a notice | |



© Express Publishing PHOTOCOPIABLE

<table>
<tr><td colspan="4">CODE</td></tr>
<tr><td>**** Excellent</td><td>*** Very Good</td><td>** OK</td><td>* Not Very Good</td></tr>
</table>

## Student's Self Assessment Form — Module 3

**Go through Module 3 and find examples of the following. Use the code to evaluate yourself.**

| | |
|---|---|
| • talk about famous people & their achievements | |
| • ask wh-questions | |
| • complete a summary | |
| • discuss past activities | |
| • talk about legendary creatures | |
| • expand my vocabulary in English | |
| • talk about crime | |
| • do a multiple-choice reading task | |
| • talk about jobs & nationalities | |
| • read dates | |
| • use linking words to connect parts of a sentence | |

**Go through the corrected writing tasks. Use the code to evaluate yourself.**

| | |
|---|---|
| • write a quiz about famous historical figures | |
| • write a short text about a traditional celebration in my country | |
| • write a short story about a legendary creature in my country | |
| • write a biography of a famous person | |
| • write a text about a famous explorer | |
| • write a formal letter giving suggestions | |

© Express Publishing  PHOTOCOPIABLE

<table>
<tr><td colspan="4">CODE</td></tr>
<tr><td>**** Excellent</td><td>*** Very Good</td><td>** OK</td><td>* Not Very Good</td></tr>
</table>

## Student's Self Assessment Form

Module 4

**Go through Module 4 and find examples of the following. Use the code to evaluate yourself.**

| | |
|---|---|
| • talk about types of holidays & holiday experiences | |
| • talk about holiday plans | |
| • work with multiple matching reading tasks | |
| • complete sentences based on a dialogue | |
| • talk about real, possible or imaginary situations | |
| • ask for information over the phone | |
| • work with multiple choice texts | |
| • match headings to paragraphs | |
| • talk about holiday problems | |
| • talk about holidays | |
| • match speakers to what they say | |
| • complete a gapped text selecting appropriate words | |

**Go through the corrected writing tasks. Use the code to evaluate yourself.**

| | |
|---|---|
| • write an itinerary for a six-day tour in my country | |
| • write about a place of natural beauty in my country | |
| • write a short email about a visit I am going to make | |
| • write a letter about my holiday | |
| • write ways to be a responsible tourist | |



© Express Publishing PHOTOCOPIABLE

<table>
<tr><td colspan="4">CODE</td></tr>
<tr><td>**** Excellent</td><td>*** Very Good</td><td>** OK</td><td>* Not Very Good</td></tr>
</table>

## Student's Self Assessment Form

Module 5

**Go through Module 5 and find examples of the following. Use the code to evaluate yourself.**

| | |
|---|---|
| • talk about world problems & social problems | |
| • talk about natural disasters | |
| • identify True/False/Doesn't Say statements | |
| • complete a gapped text with appropriate sentences | |
| • talk about a charity event | |
| • ask for & offer help | |
| • talk about threats to animal species | |
| • talk about injuries | |
| • work with a multiple choice gapped text | |
| • express wishes/regrets | |
| • talk about activities at an eco-camp | |
| • fill out a form | |
| • make suggestions/express preferences | |
| • proofread a piece of writing | |

**Go through the corrected writing tasks. Use the code to evaluate yourself.**

| | |
|---|---|
| • write a short diary entry about a disaster | |
| • write an interview | |
| • write a paragraph comparing a charity event in my country to Red Rose Day | |
| • write a few sentences giving reasons why I would go on a working holiday | |
| • write an email giving news | |
| • write a short text about an ocean | |
| • write a note | |

© Express Publishing PHOTOCOPIABLE

<table>
<tr><td colspan="4">CODE</td></tr>
<tr><td>**** Excellent</td><td>*** Very Good</td><td>** OK</td><td>* Not Very Good</td></tr>
</table>

## Student's Self Assessment Form

Module 6

**Go through Module 6 and find examples of the following. Use the code to evaluate yourself.**

| | |
|---|---|
| • talk about types of art | |
| • talk about materials | |
| • expand newspaper headlines | |
| • talk about roadside attractions | |
| • identify True/False statements | |
| • talk about a cultural festival | |
| • post a parcel | |
| • talk about shops & products | |
| • work with multiple choice reading tasks | |
| • create my own mall | |
| • talk about types of music & musical instruments | |
| • work with gapped texts | |
| • report someone's actual words | |
| • talk about places of cultural interest | |
| • express preferences | |

**Go through the corrected writing tasks. Use the code to evaluate yourself.**

| | |
|---|---|
| • write a short description of a discovery | |
| • write a paragraph about a building/monument in my country | |
| • write a text about a cultural festival in my country | |
| • make notes & write a telephone conversation | |
| • write an informal email suggesting a place to visit | |
| • write about a style of art | |
| • write a postcard | |



© Express Publishing PHOTOCOPIABLE

## Progress Report Card

.......................................................... (name) can:                                   **Module 1**

| | very well | OK | not very well |
| --- | --- | --- | --- |
| describe places | | | |
| identify True/False statements | | | |
| buy a ticket | | | |
| complete sentences based on a text | | | |
| talk about survival | | | |
| guess meaning of new words through context | | | |
| talk about types of housing | | | |
| compare places in their country | | | |
| talk about home and chores | | | |
| make requests | | | |
| talk about public services & facilities | | | |
| write about a journey to their country that is interesting for tourists | | | |
| write a list of survival tips | | | |
| write an email describing their home | | | |
| write an informal email of advice | | | |
| write a note | | | |

© Express Publishing  PHOTOCOPIABLE  E8

# Progress Report Card

.................................................... (name) can:                                    **Module 2**

| | very well | OK | not very well |
|---|---|---|---|
| talk about food & drinks | | | |
| talk about containers/partitives | | | |
| talk about eating places in the UK | | | |
| order food in a café | | | |
| complete a gapped text | | | |
| match headings to paragraphs | | | |
| make a restaurant booking | | | |
| identify True/False statements | | | |
| talk about healthy/unhealthy food/drinks | | | |
| give instructions how to make a dish | | | |
| work with multiple-choice questions | | | |
| describe a photograph | | | |
| write a text describing a food festival | | | |
| write sentences about their eating habits | | | |
| write short texts about places to eat out in their country | | | |
| write a description of their own strange restaurant | | | |
| write an email about their favourite dish | | | |
| write a notice | | | |

   © Express Publishing  PHOTOCOPIABLE

# Progress Report Card

..................................................... (name) can:  **Module 3**

| | very well | OK | not very well |
|---|---|---|---|
| talk about famous people & their achievements | | | |
| ask wh-questions | | | |
| complete a summary | | | |
| discuss past activities | | | |
| talk about legendary creatures | | | |
| expand their vocabulary in English | | | |
| talk about crime | | | |
| do a multiple-choice reading task | | | |
| talk about jobs & nationalities | | | |
| read dates | | | |
| use linking words to connect parts of a sentence | | | |
| write a quiz about famous historical figures | | | |
| write a short text about a traditional celebration in their country | | | |
| write a short story about a legendary creature in their country | | | |
| write a biography of a famous person | | | |
| write a text about a famous explorer | | | |
| write a formal letter giving suggestions | | | |

# Progress Report Card

............................................. (name) can:  **Module 4**

| | very well | OK | not very well |
|---|---|---|---|
| talk about types of holidays & holiday experiences | | | |
| talk about holiday plans | | | |
| work with multiple matching reading tasks | | | |
| complete sentences based on a dialogue | | | |
| talk about real, possible or imaginary situations | | | |
| ask for information over the phone | | | |
| work with multiple choice texts | | | |
| match headings to paragraphs | | | |
| talk about holiday problems | | | |
| talk about holidays | | | |
| match speakers to what they say | | | |
| complete a gapped text selecting appropriate words | | | |
| write an itinerary for a six-day tour in their country | | | |
| write about a place of natural beauty in their country | | | |
| write a short email about a visit they are going to make | | | |
| write a letter about their holiday | | | |
| write ways to be a responsible tourist | | | |

# Progress Report Card

.......................................................... (name) can:                    **Module 5**

| | very well | OK | not very well |
|---|---|---|---|
| talk about world problems & social problems | | | |
| talk about natural disasters | | | |
| identify True/False/Doesn't Say statements | | | |
| complete a gapped text with appropriate sentences | | | |
| talk about a charity event | | | |
| ask for & offer help | | | |
| talk about threats to animal species | | | |
| talk about injuries | | | |
| work with a multiple choice gapped text | | | |
| express wishes/regrets | | | |
| talk about activities at an eco-camp | | | |
| fill out a form | | | |
| make suggestions/express preferences | | | |
| proofread a piece of writing | | | |
| write a short diary entry about a disaster | | | |
| write an interview | | | |
| write a paragraph comparing a charity event in their country to Red Rose Day | | | |
| write a few sentences giving reasons why they would go on a working holiday | | | |
| write an email giving news | | | |
| write a short text about an ocean | | | |
| write a note | | | |

     © Express Publishing PHOTOCOPIABLE

# Progress Report Card

.................................................... (name) can:                                      **Module 6**

|  | very well | OK | not very well |
| --- | --- | --- | --- |
| talk about types of art |  |  |  |
| talk about materials |  |  |  |
| expand newspaper headlines |  |  |  |
| talk about roadside attractions |  |  |  |
| identify True/False statements |  |  |  |
| talk about a cultural festival |  |  |  |
| post a parcel |  |  |  |
| talk about shops & products |  |  |  |
| work with multiple choice reading tasks |  |  |  |
| create their own mall |  |  |  |
| talk about types of music & musical instruments |  |  |  |
| work with gapped texts |  |  |  |
| report someone's actual words |  |  |  |
| talk about places of cultural interest |  |  |  |
| express preferences |  |  |  |
| write a short description of a discovery |  |  |  |
| write a paragraph about a building/monument in their country |  |  |  |
| write a text about a cultural festival in their country |  |  |  |
| make notes & write a telephone conversation |  |  |  |
| write an informal email suggesting a place to visit |  |  |  |
| write about a style of art |  |  |  |
| write a postcard |  |  |  |

© Express Publishing  PHOTOCOPIABLE

# Workbook & Grammar Book Key

### Module 1

**1a**

**1**
| | | | | | | | |
|---|---|---|---|---|---|---|---|
| 1 | B | 3 | F | 5 | A | 7 | G |
| 2 | D | 4 | H | 6 | E | 8 | C |

1 traffic light
2 tunnel
3 pavement
4 zebra crossing
5 road sign
6 bridge
7 bus lane
8 level crossing

**2**  1 E   2 C   3 D   4 B   5 A

1 channel hop
2 bad driving
3 reality shows
4 video footage
5 oncoming traffic

**3**
1 along    4 down    7 over
2 past    5 into    8 across
3 on    6 through

**1b**

**1**
| | | | | | | | |
|---|---|---|---|---|---|---|---|
| 1 | C | 3 | H | 5 | B | 7 | A |
| 2 | F | 4 | E | 6 | G | 8 | D |

1 latest fashions
2 weights room
3 relaxed atmosphere
4 food outlets
5 must have accessory

**2**
1 cater    3 offer
2 track down    4 treat

**3**
1 b    3 c    5 f    7 a
2 g    4 e    6 d    8 h

**4**
1 Is Steven playing, is studying
2 do you go, exercise
3 needs, Does she want
4 am looking, Do you know, think
5 Do you play, am going
6 cleans, understand
7 cooks, is visiting

**5**
1 am writing    6 is standing
2 are staying    7 is sliding
3 have    8 are having
4 spend    9 love
5 am sitting    10 don't want

**1c, d**

**1**
1 steep    3 season    5 spectacular
2 coastline    4 skyscrapers

**2 a)**
1 ferry    4 car
2 tube/underground    5 coach
3 aeroplane/plane    6 bicycle/bike

**b)**
1 bike    4 coach
2 plane    5 ferry
3 car    6 tube/underground

**3**
1 Enjoy yourselves.
2 Just to go or to come back also?
3 What would you like?
4 When do you want to go?
5 Here's the money.

**4**  1 b    2 b    3 a    4 a    5 b

**5 (Suggested Answer)**

A: Can I help you?
B: I'd like a ticket to York, please.
A: Single or return?
B: Single.
A: What time would you like to leave?
B: I'd like to take the 13:30 bus.
A: That's £15, please.
B: Here you are.
A: Have a nice day.
B: Thanks, you too.

**1e**

**1**  1 C    2 A    3 E    4 B    5 D

1 get lost
2 get stung by bugs
3 get stuck in mud
4 get caught in a flash flood
5 get a snakebite

**2**
1 escape    3 reptiles
2 poisonous    4 shakes

**3**
1 **You mustn't** fish in this area.
2 **You can** see poisonous snakes in the swamp.
3 **You don't have to** sleep in a tent at night.
4 **You can't/mustn't** feed the animals.
5 **You have to** wear protective boots.
6 **Can I** borrow your insect repellent?
7 **You must** stay on the path.

**4 a)**
1 F    3 F    5 F    7 T
2 T    4 F    6 T

**b) (Suggested Answer)**

Yes, I want to visit Uluru-Kata Tjuta National Park and take part in the different types of activities the centre offers. I would also like to climb Uluru as well as walk around the bottom of the rock. I believe it's a place of great beauty and I would love to have the chance to visit it.

## 1f

**1**
| | | | |
|---|---|---|---|
| 1 | VILLA | 5 | SEMI-DETACHED |
| 2 | BLOCK OF FLATS | 6 | PENTHOUSE |
| 3 | BUNGALOW | 7 | TOWNHOUSE |
| 4 | DETACHED HOUSE | 8 | COTTAGE |

**2**
| | | | | | |
|---|---|---|---|---|---|
| 1 | crowded | 3 | dirty | 5 | cheap |
| 2 | exciting | 4 | dangerous | 6 | noisy |

**3**
| | | | | | |
|---|---|---|---|---|---|
| 1 | very | 3 | much | 5 | very |
| 2 | much | 4 | much | | |

**4**
| | | | | | |
|---|---|---|---|---|---|
| 1 | colder | 5 | worse | 9 | big |
| 2 | the driest | 6 | the highest | 10 | the longest |
| 3 | more crowded | 7 | the largest | 11 | deeper |
| 4 | warmer | 8 | older | 12 | the smallest |

## 1g

**1**
| | | | | | | | |
|---|---|---|---|---|---|---|---|
| 1 | f | 3 | g | 5 | b | 7 | c |
| 2 | a | 4 | d | 6 | e | | |

| | | | |
|---|---|---|---|
| A | mop the floor | D | take out the rubbish |
| B | make the bed | E | hoover the carpet |
| C | dust the furniture | F | iron the clothes |

**2**
| | | | |
|---|---|---|---|
| 1 | neighbourhood | 4 | room |
| 2 | appliances | 5 | furniture |
| 3 | upstairs | | |

**3**
| | | | | | | | | | |
|---|---|---|---|---|---|---|---|---|---|
| 1 | T | 2 | T | 3 | F | 4 | F | 5 | T |

**4**
| | | | | | |
|---|---|---|---|---|---|
| 1 | b | 2 | a | 3 | a |

## 1h

**1**
| | | | | | |
|---|---|---|---|---|---|
| A | 3 | B | 1 | C | 2 |

**2**

| | **Advice** | **Expected Result** |
|---|---|---|
| 1 | talk with your flatmate | make him realise that he can't keep playing video games |
| 2 | suggest that you share the TV/ he buys a new one | he can play video games in his room |
| 3 | invite him to go out | everything should be fine |

**3**
| | | | | | |
|---|---|---|---|---|---|
| 1 | shouldn't | 3 | should | 5 | should |
| 2 | should | 4 | shouldn't | | |

**4**
| | | | | | | | |
|---|---|---|---|---|---|---|---|
| 1 | b | 2 | a | 3 | d | 4 | c |

**5** **(Suggested Answer)**

Hi Sarah,

I'm sorry to hear that your flatmate has got a dog and a cat as pets and they fight all the time. I think I can help you.

The best thing you can do is ask your flatmate to separate the two animals. This way, they can't fight. Also, I think you should suggest that she train the dog so it is more obedient. What's more, you could ask your flatmate to get some animal toys. These can keep both pets busy so they don't damage the furniture.

I really hope my advice helps. Write back and tell me what happens.

Judith

## 1i

**1**
| | | | |
|---|---|---|---|
| 1 | post office | 5 | hospital |
| 2 | petrol station | 6 | library |
| 3 | bank | 7 | community centre |
| 4 | police station | | |

| | | | | | | | |
|---|---|---|---|---|---|---|---|
| A | 6 | B | 5 | C | 3 | D | 2 |

**2**
| | | | | | | | | | |
|---|---|---|---|---|---|---|---|---|---|
| 1 | for | 2 | on | 3 | in | 4 | for | 5 | in |

**3**
| | | | |
|---|---|---|---|
| 1 | citizen | 3 | public |
| 2 | obey | 4 | volunteers |

### Notions & Functions

| | | | | | | | | | |
|---|---|---|---|---|---|---|---|---|---|
| 1 | b | 3 | b | 5 | b | 7 | b | 9 | a |
| 2 | b | 4 | a | 6 | b | 8 | a | 10 | b |

### Language & Grammar Review

| | | | | | | | | | |
|---|---|---|---|---|---|---|---|---|---|
| 1 | A | 7 | B | 13 | A | 19 | C | 25 | C |
| 2 | B | 8 | A | 14 | B | 20 | A | 26 | A |
| 3 | B | 9 | C | 15 | A | 21 | A | 27 | C |
| 4 | C | 10 | C | 16 | B | 22 | B | 28 | A |
| 5 | A | 11 | C | 17 | A | 23 | C | 29 | A |
| 6 | B | 12 | B | 18 | B | 24 | B | 30 | C |

### Reading Task

| | | | | | | | |
|---|---|---|---|---|---|---|---|
| 1 | D | 3 | E | 5 | G | 7 | A |
| 2 | F | 4 | I | 6 | B | 8 | C |

## Module 2

### 2a

**1** **Dairy products:** butter, yoghurt, cheese
**Drinks:** lemonade, coffee, tea
**Fruit & Vegetables:** cabbage, cherries, lemon, celery, broccoli, strawberries, beans
**Meat & Poultry:** beef, chicken, lamb
**Fish & Seafood:** salmon, tuna, trout, prawns
**Other:** pasta, rice, cereal, bread, eggs

**2**
| | | | | | |
|---|---|---|---|---|---|
| 1 | seaside | 3 | creations | 5 | floats |
| 2 | fireworks | 4 | celebrate | | |

**3**
| | | | | | | | | | |
|---|---|---|---|---|---|---|---|---|---|
| 1 | C | 2 | E | 3 | B | 4 | A | 5 | D |

| | | | |
|---|---|---|---|
| 1 | attracts visitors | 4 | watch parades |
| 2 | run wild | 5 | buy local products |
| 3 | design, statues | | |

**4**
| | | | | | | | |
|---|---|---|---|---|---|---|---|
| 1 | some | 6 | some | 10 | some | 14 | an |
| 2 | some | 7 | any, | 11 | any | 15 | any |
| 3 | a | | some | 12 | any, | 16 | an |
| 4 | any | 8 | some | | some | | |
| 5 | some | 9 | any | 13 | a | | |

## 2b

**1**
| | | | | | |
|---|---|---|---|---|---|
| 1 | F | 3 | E | 5 | B |
| 2 | A | 4 | C | 6 | D |

1 junk food
2 fizzy drinks
3 bakery section
4 minced beef
5 dairy products
6 drinks aisle

**2**
| | | | | | | | |
|---|---|---|---|---|---|---|---|
| 1 | box | 3 | bar | 5 | bunch | 7 | jar |
| 2 | tin | 4 | tub | 6 | loaf | | |

**3** **Countable:** sweets, banana, egg, apple, tomato, biscuit
**Uncountable:** sugar, milk, butter, flour, bread, cheese, chicken, rice, chocolate

**4**
1 many, few
2 much, a little
3 no, some
4 a few, some
5 any, many
6 too much, too much
7 a lot of, a little
8 many, many

**5**
1 loaves, bread
2 packet, pasta
3 box, cereal
4 pots, yoghurt
5 bottles
6 fruit
7 bars, chocolate

## 2c,d

**1**
| | | | | | | | |
|---|---|---|---|---|---|---|---|
| 1 | B | 3 | A | 5 | D | 7 | F |
| 2 | H | 4 | E | 6 | C | 8 | G |

1 ethnic cuisine
2 deep fried fish
3 cashew nuts
4 side dish
5 hot snack
6 multi-cultural society
7 baked goods
8 mushy peas

**2**
1 grab
2 serves
3 suit
4 chooses

**3**
1 Are you ready to order?
2 What about you?
3 Would you like any side orders?
4 What would you like to drink?
5 Is that all?

**4** **(Suggested Answer)**

| | |
|---|---|
| Waitress: | Good afternoon. Are you ready to order? |
| Paul: | Yes, we are. I'd like a spicy chicken sandwich, please. |
| Waitress: | Of course! What about you? |
| Alice: | Can I have a roast beef sandwich, please? |
| Waitress: | No problem. Would you like any side orders? |
| Paul: | Yes, could we have some chips, please? |
| Waitress: | Sure. What would you like to drink? |
| Paul: | Some fruit juice for me, please. |
| Alice: | And I'd like a lemonade. Thank you. |
| Waitress: | That's a spicy chicken sandwich, a roast beef sandwich, chips, a fruit juice and a lemonade. Is that all? |
| Paul: | Yes, that's all. Thank you. |

## 2e

**1**
| | | | | | | | |
|---|---|---|---|---|---|---|---|
| 1 | cool | 3 | tip | 5 | landmark | 7 | main |
| 2 | thick | 4 | freezing | 6 | boiling | 8 | staff |

**2**
1 of
2 of, from
3 in, to
4 to, from
5 for

**3**
1 too crowded
2 too sweet
3 too expensive
4 big enough
5 too spicy
6 warm enough

**4** a)
| | | | | | | | |
|---|---|---|---|---|---|---|---|
| 1 | T | 3 | NS | 5 | F | 7 | T |
| 2 | F | 4 | T | 6 | F | | |

b)
1 Nuremburg, Germany.
2 on computer screens at their tables.
3 send emails from your touch screen.
4 a small amusement park.

## 2f

**1**
| | | | | | | | | | |
|---|---|---|---|---|---|---|---|---|---|
| 1 | C | 2 | A | 3 | B | 4 | E | 5 | D |

1 poached egg
2 olive oil
3 chocolate bar
4 salad dressing
5 healthy food

**2**
1 protect
2 enjoy
3 contain
4 replace
5 lower

**3**
1 cooking
2 drinking
3 Eating
4 attending
5 doing
6 run
7 trying
8 going
9 to become
10 waiting

**4**
1 going, to order
2 to make, have
3 cooking, Cooking
4 grilling, helping
5 to shop, to go
6 to lay, to do

**5**
1 missing
2 dieting
3 coming
4 to grab
5 to tip
6 to do
7 to tell
8 eating
9 having
10 to make

WGK3

## 2g

**1**

| G | R | I | L | L | P | C | J |
|---|---|---|---|---|---|---|---|
| X | V | V | G | S | O | H | R |
| B | P | E | E | L | U | O | U |
| E | T | B | X | R | R | P | A |
| A | G | O | I | A | F | R | Y |
| T | J | I | H | R | X | W | K |
| N | X | L | D | C | F | M | S |
| S | L | I | C | E | A | M | L |

| | | | | | | | |
|---|---|---|---|---|---|---|---|
| 1 | GRILL | 3 | BEAT | 5 | CHOP | 7 | POUR |
| 2 | SLICE | 4 | BOIL | 6 | PEEL | 8 | FRY |

**2**

| | | | | | | | |
|---|---|---|---|---|---|---|---|
| 1 | Boil | 3 | Melt | 5 | add | 7 | Pour |
| 2 | stir | 4 | Beat | 6 | Mix | | |

**3**    1 F     2 F     3 T     4 T     5 F

## 2h

**1**

| | | | | | | | |
|---|---|---|---|---|---|---|---|
| 1 | Boil | 3 | chop | 5 | Add | 7 | serve |
| 2 | Peel | 4 | Melt | 6 | mix | | |

**2**

| | | | | | | | |
|---|---|---|---|---|---|---|---|
| 1 | T | 3 | T | 5 | T | 7 | T |
| 2 | T | 4 | F | 6 | F | | |

**3**

| | | | | | |
|---|---|---|---|---|---|
| 1 | sweet | 3 | salty | 5 | delicious |
| 2 | spicy | 4 | creamy | | |

**4** (Suggested Answer)

1 Gemüsesuppe (Austrian Vegetable Soup)
2 You need 200g cauliflower, 100g Brussels sprouts, 70g carrots, 30g celery, 90g leek, 100g green beans, 1.5 litres vegetable stock, 30g flour, salt.
3 Peel and chop vegetables. Pour stock into pan, add salt and bring to the boil. Add vegetables and cook for 30 minutes or until soft. Remove vegetables. Melt butter in separate pan. Stir in flour. Mix vegetables in flour and butter mixture. Add mixture to soup and cook for 5 min.
4 It serves 6 people.
5 Serve with thick, crusty bread.

**5** (Suggested Answer)

**Gemüsesuppe (Vegetable Soup)**
**Ingredients (serves 6)**

| | |
|---|---|
| 200g cauliflower | 100g green beans |
| 100g Brussels sprouts | 1.5 ltr vegetable stock |
| 70g carrots | 30g butter |
| 30g celery | 30g flour |
| 90g leek | salt |

- Peel and chop the vegetables.
- Pour the stock into a pan, add the salt and bring to the boil.
- Add the vegetables and cook for 30 minutes or until soft.
- Remove the vegetables from the soup.
- Melt the butter in a separate pan.
- Stir the flour into the melted butter.
- Mix the vegetables in the butter and flour mixture.
- Add the mixture to the soup and cook for 5 minutes.
- Pour into bowls and serve with thick, crusty bread.

## 2i

**1**

| Across | | Down | |
|---|---|---|---|
| 1 | protects | 1 | protein |
| 4 | bones | 2 | carbohydrates |
| 5 | muscles | 3 | skin |
| 6 | system | | |

**2**

| | | | | | |
|---|---|---|---|---|---|
| 1 | fish | 3 | meat | 5 | calcium |
| 2 | energy | 4 | body | | |

## Notions & Functions

| | | | | | | | | | |
|---|---|---|---|---|---|---|---|---|---|
| 1 | b | 3 | a | 5 | a | 7 | b | 9 | a |
| 2 | a | 4 | a | 6 | b | 8 | b | 10 | a |

## Language & Grammar Review

| | | | | | | | | | |
|---|---|---|---|---|---|---|---|---|---|
| 1 | C | 7 | C | 13 | A | 19 | C | 25 | C |
| 2 | B | 8 | C | 14 | A | 20 | C | 26 | B |
| 3 | C | 9 | B | 15 | C | 21 | A | 27 | C |
| 4 | A | 10 | C | 16 | C | 22 | C | 28 | A |
| 5 | A | 11 | A | 17 | A | 23 | C | 29 | B |
| 6 | B | 12 | A | 18 | C | 24 | A | 30 | A |

## Reading Task

1 B    2 B    3 D    4 C    5 A    6 C

### Module 3

## 3a

**1**

| | | | | | | |
|---|---|---|---|---|---|---|
| 1 | inventor | 4 | painter | 7 | sculptor |
| 2 | scientist | 5 | writer | 8 | philosopher |
| 3 | engineer | 6 | architect | | |

| I | T | E | E | T | T | G | E | T | A | H |
|---|---|---|---|---|---|---|---|---|---|---|
| R | N | E | N | G | I | N | E | E | R | I |
| T | R | C | I | E | S | O | U | P | C | S |
| T | R | T | R | N | T | I | N | O | H | C |
| P | R | G | I | R | R | N | R | I | I | U |
| I | I | R | I | R | T | V | A | N | T | L |
| P | P | A | I | N | T | E | R | S | E | P |
| E | I | T | T | O | A | N | U | I | C | T |
| N | S | C | I | E | N | T | I | S | T | O |
| P | H | I | L | O | S | O | P | H | E | R |
| S | W | R | I | T | E | R | I | T | T | N |

**2** 1 sketched 4 constructed 7 painted
2 discovered 5 invented
3 survived 6 studied

**3** 1 finished 5 tried 9 walked
2 lived 6 died 10 created
3 watched 7 dropped
4 stopped 8 carried

**4** 1 She sailed a boat.
2 She didn't paint a picture.
3 She didn't visit a museum.
4 She surfed the Internet.
5 She played a musical instrument.
6 She tidied the house.

**5** 1 Did Claude Monet paint the *Starry Night*?
No, he didn't. He painted the *Water Lillies*.
2 Did Mozart and Beethoven design machines?
No, they didn't. They composed music.
3 Did Sir Alexander Fleming discover penicillin?
Yes, he did.
4 Did Thomas Edison study plants?
No, he didn't. He invented the light bulb.
5 Did the Wright brothers invent the first modern aeroplane?
Yes, they did.

## 3b

**1** 1 Empire 4 conquered 7 pharaoh
2 armies 5 poisonous
3 legend 6 explorer

**2** 1 lived 5 had 9 asked
2 was 6 couldn't 10 managed
3 developed 7 cut
4 became 8 grew

**3** 1 Did Hercules live in Italy?
No, he didn't. He lived in Greece.
2 Did Hercules become big and strong?
Yes, he did.
3 Did Hercules have to kill Zeus?
No, he didn't. He had to kill the Hydra.
4 Did the Hydra have nine heads?
Yes, it did.
5 Did Hercules kill the Hydra by himself?
No, he didn't. He asked his nephew Iolaus to help him kill the Hydra.

**4** 1 Where 3 What 5 How many 7 Why
2 Who 4 How 6 When 8 Which

## 3c, d

**1** a) 1 B 2 E 3 D 4 C 5 A

b) (Suggested Answer)
1 It's never easy to settle in a new town.
2 The settlers found it difficult to survive the first winter in North America.
3 Native Americans grew crops such as corn.
4 The early settlers learnt how to fish and hunt for food.
5 They had a feast to celebrate the New Year.

**2** 1 Native 3 voyage 5 captain
2 harvest 4 tradition 6 celebrations

**3** 1 It was just an ordinary weekend.
2 Did you enjoy yourself?
3 I'm sure you had a great time.
4 I want to see that place.

**4** 1 It was great, thanks
2 Did you have a nice time
3 Yes, it was fantastic
4 Did you have a nice weekend
5 I didn't do anything special

**5** (Suggested Answer)
A: Hi Beth! How was your weekend?
B: It was great thanks. I went on a trip to Plimoth Plantation, a living history museum.
A: Oh, really? I'd love to go there, too. Did you have a nice time?
B: Yes, it was fantastic. First, we went on a tour of a Native American village and watched craft demonstrations and then we visited the gift shop and the visitor centre. What about you? Did you have a nice weekend?
A: Oh, I didn't do anything special. I just stayed home and studied for my exams.

## 3e

**1** a) 1 E 3 F 5 B
2 C 4 A

b) 1 Mexico City
2 legend
3 marry his daughter if he went to battle and came back alive
4 was sadness
5 Popocatépetl came back from war
6 from Popocatépetl's fire that still burns

**2** 1 giant 3 dragon 5 fairy
2 unicorn 4 mermaid

**3** 1 in 2 of, for 3 of

## 3f

**1** 1 vandalising 3 spray painted 5 burgle
2 arrest 4 break 6 rob

**2**
| | | | | | |
|---|---|---|---|---|---|
| 1 | international | 3 | star | 5 | iron |
| 2 | maintenance | 4 | bulletproof | 6 | conflicting |

**3**
| | | | | | |
|---|---|---|---|---|---|
| 1 | caused | 3 | served | 5 | shot |
| 2 | admitted | 4 | committed | | |

**4**
1  stole
2  was driving, stopped
3  sentenced
4  was listening, was driving
5  ran, heard
6  caught, was escaping
7  screamed, saw

**5**
| | | | | | |
|---|---|---|---|---|---|
| 1 | were sleeping | 7 | saw | 13 | came |
| 2 | heard | 8 | was wearing | 14 | turned |
| 3 | jumped | 9 | was holding | 15 | realised |
| 4 | ran | 10 | attacked | 16 | was |
| 5 | didn't see | 11 | threw | | |
| 6 | walked | 12 | yelled | | |

## 3g

**1**

| | Across | | Down |
|---|---|---|---|
| 1 | POP SINGER | 1 | PHYSICIST |
| 4 | PRESIDENT | 2 | NURSE |
| 6 | SCIENTIST | 3 | WRITER |
| | | 5 | ARTIST |

**2**
1  seventeen ninety-three
2  nineteen oh eight/nineteen hundred and eight
3  nineteen forty-seven
4  two thousand and nine
5  eighteen oh two/eighteen hundred and two
6  nineteen fifty-nine

**3**  1 F      2 F      3 T      4 T      5 F

**4**
1  Who was Charles Dickens?
2  In Portsmouth, England.
3  When was he born?
4  In 1870.

## 3h

**1**
| | | | | |
|---|---|---|---|---|
| 1 | 1732 | 4 | 1759 |
| 2 | 11 years old | 5 | 5,000-acre |
| 3 | age of 21 | 6 | 1799 |

**2**
| When/<br>Where born: | 22nd February, 1732, in Virginia, USA |
|---|---|
| Early years: | family wealthy, loved horses; going hunting with his father & exploring caves, his father died when he was 11 |
| Achievements/<br>Later years: | 1753 – military career begins; 1759 – married Martha Dandridge Curtis; 1789 – became president; 1797 – left office & spent time farming |
| When/<br>Where died: | 14th December, 1799, in Virginia |

**3**
| | | | | |
|---|---|---|---|---|
| 1 | also | 3 | so |
| 2 | because | 4 | and |

**4**
| | | | | |
|---|---|---|---|---|
| 1 | on 4th August, 1901 | 4 | a teenager |
| 2 | poor family | 5 | moved to Chicago |
| 3 | stopped going to school | 6 | on 6th July, 1971 |

**5**  (Suggested Answer)

Louis Armstrong was born on 4th August 1901, in New Orleans, USA.
Louis grew up in a poor family. He stopped going to school at the age of 11 and started singing and playing the cornet. When he was a teenager he joined a band and played on riverboats on the Mississippi River.
In 1922, he moved to Chicago where he became a famous jazz musician and made 'scat' singing popular. He also toured around the world. In 1943 Louis moved to New York. There he had many hit records and appeared in many Hollywood films.
Louis Armstrong died in New York, on 6th July, 1971.

## 3i

**1** a)
| | | | | | |
|---|---|---|---|---|---|
| 1 | explorer | 4 | voyage | 7 | reached |
| 2 | route | 5 | supplies | | |
| 3 | spices | 6 | set sail | | |

b)
| | | | | | | | |
|---|---|---|---|---|---|---|---|
| 1 | F | 3 | T | 5 | F | 7 | T |
| 2 | T | 4 | T | 6 | F | | |

## Notions & Functions

| | | | | | | | | | |
|---|---|---|---|---|---|---|---|---|---|
| 1 | a | 3 | a | 5 | a | 7 | b | 9 | a |
| 2 | b | 4 | b | 6 | b | 8 | b | 10 | b |

## Language & Grammar Review

| | | | | | | | | | |
|---|---|---|---|---|---|---|---|---|---|
| 1 | B | 7 | A | 13 | C | 19 | B | 25 | C |
| 2 | C | 8 | C | 14 | C | 20 | A | 26 | A |
| 3 | B | 9 | B | 15 | B | 21 | B | 27 | B |
| 4 | C | 10 | B | 16 | C | 22 | B | 28 | C |
| 5 | A | 11 | C | 17 | C | 23 | C | 29 | B |
| 6 | B | 12 | B | 18 | C | 24 | C | 30 | B |

### Reading Task

| | | | | | | | |
|---|---|---|---|---|---|---|---|
| 1 | G | 3 | D | 5 | E | 7 | I |
| 2 | C | 4 | F | 6 | A | 8 | H |

### Module 4

#### 4a

**1**
1  cruise
2  activity holiday
3  camping holiday
4  beach holiday
5  safari
6  backpacking holiday

**2**
1  enormous
2  surrounded by
3  spend the night
4  spectacular views
5  head back
6  time of your life

**3  a)**  1  C  2  D  3  E  4  A  5  F  6  B

**b) (Suggested Answers)**
1  trek in the mountains
2  swim with piranha
3  I'd like to explore ancient monuments because I think it would be interesting.
4  I'd love to drive a dune buggy because I think it would be fun.

**4**
1  will/'ll have        P
2  will/'ll go          I
3  will/'ll join        O
4  will/'ll travel      I
5  will/'ll take        O
6  will not/won't come  I

#### 4b

**1**

| | | | | | | | |
|---|---|---|---|---|---|---|---|
| 1 | E | 3 | A | 5 | F | 7 | B |
| 2 | D | 4 | G | 6 | C | | |

**2**
1  tried local food
2  sunbathed on the beach
3  shop for souvenirs
4  enjoy nature
5  take, photographs
6  went sightseeing

**3**
1  will call
2  leave
3  comes
4  go
5  arrive
6  will go
7  gets

**4**
1  were
2  drop
3  don't leave
4  would take
5  melts
6  go
7  saves
8  would drive
9  had
10  is

**5**  1  A  2  A  3  B  4  C  5  A  6  C

#### 4c, d

**1**  1  B  2  C  3  D  4  F  5  E  6  A

1  square kilometres
2  huge volcano
3  hot springs
4  hiking trails
5  grizzly bears
6  geyser erupts

**2 (Suggested Answer)**

Yellowstone National Park is a great tourist attraction. Visitors can visit a number of hot springs and thermal pools. Nature lovers can hike through the deep canyon and see spectacular waterfalls. What's more, animal lovers can see wild animals such as grizzly bears, wolves and mountain lions.

**3**
1  can
2  calling
3  opening
4  anything

**4**
1  How can I help you?
2  How much does it cost to get in?
3  What is the best way to get there by car?
4  Enjoy your visit!

**5 (Suggested Answer)**
A: National Space Centre. How can I help you?
B: I'm calling for some information. How much does it cost to get in?
A: It's £13 for adults and £11 for children.
B: Could you also tell me the opening hours?
A: 10 am to 5 pm every day.
B: Just one more thing. What is the best way to get there by car?
A: Exit the A6 two miles north of Leicester City Centre, then follow the signs.
B: Thank you very much for your help.
A: You're welcome. Enjoy your visit!

#### 4e

**1**  1  C        2  B        3  A

**2**

| | | | | | | | |
|---|---|---|---|---|---|---|---|
| 1 | F | 3 | T | 5 | F | 7 | F |
| 2 | T | 4 | F | 6 | T | | |

**3**
1  sculptures
2  cement
3  encourage
4  local
5  recognise
6  creatures
7  flippers
8  Pollution

**4**
1  Jack and I may go sightseeing this afternoon.
2  I might visit Mexico next summer.
3  It will probably be sunny this weekend.
4  Kevin could save up enough money to go on the adventure tour next year.
5  They might not go on holiday this year.
6  We'll definitely go to Mauritius next month.

#### 4f

**1**
1  features
2  experience
3  celebrates
4  stay
5  constructed

**2**
1  clear
2  World
3  crystal
4  diverse
5  fresh
6  flea
7  cosy
8  top
9  heart
10  seafood
11  interior
12  specialties
13  stunning

**3**  1  –, –, a, an, a   5  the, –   9  the, –, a
2  the, an   6  the   10  the, a, –
3  –   7  –, a
4  –, the   8  the, –, a

**4**  1  where   3  who   5  which
2  which   4  whose   6  where

## 4g

**1**  1  sunburnt   4  weather
2  passport   5  food poisoning
3  airline, luggage   6  dirty, crowded

**2**  1  Hi! Are you enjoying yourself in Canada?
2  Yes, but you won't believe what happened!
3  Oh dear! That's terrible!

**3**  1  D   2  C   3  C   4  B   5  A

## 4h

**1**  1  It's from Teresa to Al.
2  In Bali, Indonesia.
3  Informal.

**2**  1  Para 2   3  Para 2   5  Para 3
2  Para 4   4  Para 1

**3**  1  C   2  O   3  C   4  O   5  O   6  C

**4**  1  awful   3  crowded   5  interesting
2  delicious   4  beautiful

**5**  (Suggested Answer)
**Para 1:**  How's your summer going?/In Maui, Hawaii./
At a five-star hotel./Hot and sunny.
**Para 2:**  went to the beach/going on a dinner cruise
**Para 3:**  going to swim with dolphins/go horse riding
**Para 4:**  Well. I'm off now. I'm going shopping for
souvenirs.

**6**  (Suggested Answer)
Dear Jack,
How's your summer going? I'm having a great time
here in the island of Maui, Hawaii. We're staying in
a five-star hotel near the beach. The weather is
fantastic. It's hot and sunny every day!
Yesterday, we went to the beach. I got a nice suntan.
Later today, we are going on a dinner cruise and
there'll be live entertainment, too. I think it'll be great!
Tomorrow, we're going to swim with dolphins at
the Sea Life Park. Can you imagine that? We're also
going to go horse riding. You know how much I
love horses! I can't wait!
Well, I'm off now. I'm going shopping for souvenirs!
See you next weekend.
Love,
Shannon

## 4i

**1**  1  E   2  D   3  F   4  B   5  C   6  A
1  local businesses   4  handmade souvenirs
2  responsible tourist   5  historical site
3  endangered animal   6  dress code

**2**  1  after   3  with   5  in
2  about   4  from

## Notions & Functions

1  a   3  b   5  b   7  a   9  a
2  a   4  b   6  a   8  a   10  b

## Language & Grammar Review

1  B   7  C   13  C   19  B   25  A
2  C   8  A   14  A   20  A   26  C
3  A   9  A   15  B   21  A   27  C
4  C   10  B   16  A   22  B   28  B
5  C   11  B   17  A   23  B   29  C
6  B   12  B   18  B   24  B   30  B

## Reading Task

1  C   2  B   3  A   4  C   5  C   6  C

## Module 5

## 5a

**1**  1  D   3  F   5  B   7  E
2  C   4  G   6  A

**2**  1  homeless people   5  natural disaster
2  medical supplies   6  global warming
3  forest fires   7  endangered species
4  running water

**3**  1  drought   3  tsunami   5  suffers
2  earthquake   4  affected   6  rescue

**4**  1  seen   8  felt   15  eaten
2  bought   9  destroyed   16  lost
3  given   10  saved   17  offered
4  arrived   11  gone   18  taken
5  said   12  found   19  worked
6  told   13  been   20  visited
7  caused   14  had

**5**  1  Have you seen
2  hasn't been
3  hasn't packed
4  has gone
5  have never experienced
6  has lived, haven't seen
7  Have they rescued, have saved
8  Have you ever volunteered

WGK8

## 5b

**1**
1 organised    4 best-selling    7 achieved
2 set out    5 stumbled
3 made it    6 raise

**2**

| Across | Down |
|---|---|
| 1 FAILURE | 2 CAMPAIGN |
| 5 CAUSE | 3 HUNGER |
|  | 4 ILLITERACY |
|  | 6 POVERTY |

We can see the word **hunger** in the picture.

**3**
1 Have you ever been, went
2 Have they ever flown, travelled
3 Has Sue sent, posted
4 printed, have raised
5 haven't seen, was
6 has been working
7 have you been waiting
8 has been helping

**4**
1 already    3 yet    5 just
2 since    4 never    6 for

## 5c, d

**1**
1 C    2 A    3 D    4 E    5 B

1 takes place    4 wear silly outfits
2 raise money    5 make donations
3 record songs

**2**
1 support    3 celebrities    5 laughter
2 famine    4 viewers    6 cause

**3**
1 What are you doing?
2 Actually, I've nearly finished
3 Of course not!
4 What time?
5 OK, see you tomorrow.

**4** (Suggested Answer)

Jane: Hi, Ben. What are you doing?
Ben: I'm putting up posters for the charity event tomorrow.
Jane: Oh, really? Can I give you a hand?
Ben: Actually, I've nearly finished. Jack and I are going to decorate the venue afterwards. Would you mind helping us with that?
Jane: Of course not!
Ben: That's wonderful. Oh, there's one more thing. Is there a chance you could come tomorrow to sell some tickets?
Jane: Yes, no problem. What time?
Ben: Around five would be great.
Jane: OK, see you tomorrow.

## 5e

**1**
1 C    2 A    3 D    4 B    5 A    6 B

**2**
1 To plant trees, raise awareness and protect the Earth.
2 He realised how pollution and deforestation were destroying the natural landscape in many countries.
3 South America.
4 He wants to plant one-hundred million trees because that's the same number as the number of deaths that war has caused over the last hundred years.
5 His wife and the people that Paul has inspired.

**3**
1 endangered    3 monitor    5 observation
2 project    4 challenging

**4**
1 for    3 up    5 out
2 down    4 by

**5**
1 bored    3 interesting    5 relaxing
2 tired    4 excited

## 5f

**1**
1 raise    4 motivate    7 lead
2 twisted    5 broke    8 bang
3 reach    6 come true

**2**
1 pain    3 swollen    5 nasty
2 sore    4 journey    6 footsteps

**3**
1 Did Shelly hurt
   was, had broken
2 didn't look
   hadn't slept, didn't sleep
3 happened
   had just finished, tripped
4 Did you see
   had already seen, arrived
5 did Tim do
   lost, hadn't played

**4**
1 would have played    6 get
2 doesn't come    7 leaves
3 would travel    8 wouldn't have banged
4 had driven    9 would have won
5 were    10 had entered

**5**
1 had    3 hadn't lent    5 hadn't lost
2 had studied    4 were/was

## 5g

**1** a)
1 G    3 D    5 A    7 B
2 C    4 F    6 E

**b)** 1 go on a nature hike
2 collect rubbish for recycling
3 plant trees
4 cook on a barbecue
5 sit around a campfire
6 sleep in wooden huts

**2** 1 b   2 a   3 b

**3** 1 F   2 C   3 D   4 A   5 B

## 5h

**1** 1 It's from Tony to Alex.
2 He's in Thailand.
3 To tell Alex about his work as a volunteer.

**2** A 4   B 2   C 1   D 3

**3** 1 In Greece.
2 Working as a volunteer for the Sea Turtle Protection Society.
3 It patrols beaches, picks up rubbish, surveys & protects nests & eggs, gives information to tourists about turtles.
4 Picked up some rubbish and patrolled a beach.
5 Yes. I get to help endangered animals and have fun at the same time.

**4** **(Suggested Answer)**
Dear Charlie,
Sorry I haven't written for so long but I've been really busy. I'm here in Greece working as a volunteer for the Sea Turtle Protection Society (ARCHELON). It's a charitable organisation and I really love it!
ARCHELON protects sea turtles and their habitats. When I arrived here they taught me all about surveying and protecting the turtles' nests and eggs. So far, I've picked up rubbish and patrolled a beach with some other volunteers. I've also given information to some tourists about turtles.
It's hard work but it's enjoyable and I've made many friends from different parts of the world. It's nice to be able to help endangered animals and still have fun at the same time.
I hope you're having fun this summer, too. Write back soon.
Yours,
Richard

## 5i

**1**

| Down | Across |
|---|---|
| 1 OCEANS | 3 SEABIRD |
| 2 RAINFALL | 4 POLLUTION |
| | 5 FACTORY |
| | 6 WHALE |

**2** 1 supply   3 protect   5 survival
2 reefs   4 covers

## Notions & Functions

1 b   3 b   5 a   7 a   9 a
2 b   4 b   6 b   8 b   10 a

## Language & Grammar Review

| 1 B | 7 A | 13 C | 19 C | 25 C |
|---|---|---|---|---|
| 2 C | 8 C | 14 B | 20 B | 26 C |
| 3 A | 9 A | 15 B | 21 C | 27 B |
| 4 B | 10 B | 16 B | 22 B | 28 B |
| 5 B | 11 A | 17 B | 23 A | 29 C |
| 6 C | 12 A | 18 A | 24 B | 30 A |

## Reading Task

1 E   2 F   3 C   4 A   5 B

### Module 6

## 6a

**1** 1 sculpted   4 built   7 revealed
2 designed   5 excavating
3 painted   6 modelled

**2** 1 C   3 B   5 D   7 E
2 A   4 F   6 H   8 G

**3** 1 archaeological finds   5 written language
2 facial expression   6 burial site
3 elaborate tomb   7 remain untouched
4 powerful emperor   8 armoury of weapons

**4** 1 undisturbed   4 spread   7 builds
2 guard   5 reign   8 real
3 unique   6 sights

**5** 1 are   4 were   7 have   10 has
2 will   5 have   8 will   11 can
3 is   6 is   9 was   12 was

## 6b

**1** 1 C   2 E   3 A   4 B   5 D

**2** 1 display   2 sweet   3 popular   4 local

**3** 1 brings/has brought   5 notice
2 weighs   6 was carved
3 is toured   7 pose
4 were dazzled   8 transformed

**4** 1 An art gallery was destroyed by a fire last Friday.
2 A fund-raising event will be held tomorrow at city hall.
3 The History Museum will be completed next week.
4 The amusement park hasn't been renovated yet.

**5**
1 Have the walls been painted,
   will be painted
2 was sculpted
3 will be opened
4 were amazed, have been collected

**6**
1 by  3 by  5 with
2 with  4 by

**7**
1 Food must not be brought in the gallery (by visitors)./Food is not allowed in the gallery.
2 The portrait was drawn by John.
3 A mural will be painted by a local artist.
4 Famous paintings are displayed in the art gallery.
5 The stolen artefacts have been recovered by the police.
6 The *Mona Lisa* was painted by Leonardo da Vinci.
7 Mary was invited to the art exhibition by Jack.
8 Photos can be taken in the museum.

### 6c, d

**1**
1 C  3 B  5 D  7 F
2 A  4 E  6 G

1 musical instrument  5 raise awareness
2 return address  6 registered post
3 unique bond  7 handmade souvenirs
4 share knowledge

**2**
1 announced  3 constructed  5 hang
2 lost  4 has survived  6 highlighted

**3**
1 in  3 by  5 for
2 on  4 on  6 by

**4**
1 I'd like to post this parcel to Germany.
2 Could you put it on the scales, please?
3 How would you like to send it?
4 I'll send it by registered post, please.
5 So that's £4.20 then, please.
6 You're welcome.

**5 (Suggested Answer)**
A: Hello. Can I help you?
B: Yes. I'd like to post this parcel to Holland.
A: Could you put it on the scales, please?
B: Sure.
A: That's 240 grammes. How would you like to send it?
B: What are the choices?
A: Surface mail is £1.20, airmail is £2.70 and registered post is £4.10.
B: I'll send it by registered post, please.
A: So, that's £4.10, please.
B: Here you are.
A: Thank you very much.
B: You're welcome.

### 6e

**1**
1 stroll  4 posing  7 steered
2 serenaded  5 disturb  8 shimmered
3 experience  6 inspired

**2**
1 of  3 to  5 at
2 on  4 to  6 for

**3**
1 takes  4 living  7 indoor
2 floating  5 exclusive  8 trip
3 authentic  6 star

**4**
1 H  3 C  5 G  7 B
2 D  4 F  6 A

### 6f

**1**
1 string  3 wind
2 percussion  4 brass

**2**
1 took  4 raise  7 escape
2 compose  5 received
3 affects  6 future

**3**
1 deep  3 nature  5 unique
2 demand  4 expected

**4**
1 She said she was going to the opera the following day.
2 He told us not to sing that song.
3 She told me she had already seen that film.
4 He asked if I/we liked classical music.
5 She told me not to turn on the radio.
6 She asked if she could borrow my CD.
7 She said (that) she would call me the following day.
8 He asked where the opera house was.
9 He told me to meet him at the concert hall.
10 He asked how much the album cost.

**5**
1 told  4 told  7 told  10 told
2 said  5 said  8 said
3 told  6 said  9 said

**6**
1 himself  3 myself  5 yourself
2 themselves  4 ourselves

### 6g

**1**
1 art gallery  5 palace
2 science centre  6 fort
3 archaeological site  7 natural history museum
4 ancient theatre  8 temple

**2**
1 didn't they  5 isn't it  9 aren't you
2 have you  6 doesn't she  10 isn't it
3 isn't he  7 aren't they  11 aren't they
4 won't we  8 hasn't she  12 will he

**3**  1  b          2  b          3  a          4  a

**4**  1  B          2  C          3  D          4  B      5  A

## 6h

**1**  A  2          B  4          C  1          D  3

**2**  1  D          2  B          3  A          4  C

**3**  1  beautiful              4  simple
   2  impressive             5  most famous
   3  thick

**4**  **Para 1:**  Hi Mandy / How are you? / Niagara Falls /
             Ontario, Canada
    **Para 2:**  3 Waterfalls / see view of the Falls from
             Skylon Tower / walk to Table Rock past the
             Falls
    **Para 3:**  highlight: Maid of the Mist boat trip / took
             boat up river past American Falls / sailed into
             mist at bottom of Canadian Falls / couldn't
             take photos because of water spray
    **Para 4:**  had great time / came close to power of
             nature

**5**  **(Suggested Answer)**

Hi Mandy,
How are you? I just came back from Niagara Falls in
Ontario, Canada. I did a lot of fun things.
Niagara Falls actually has 3 waterfalls. You can
climb the Skylon Tower where you get a great view
of all three, or take a walk to Table Rock past the
Falls.
The highlight was a trip on the Maid of the Mist.
It's a boat that sails past the American Falls and
then into the Canadian Falls. The water is so
powerful that they give you plastic rain coats to
stop you getting wet. There was so much spray that
I couldn't take any photographs.
I had a great time and came so close to the power
of nature. You would love it there.
See you soon,
Andy

## 6i

**1**  1  portray          5  distorted       9   outraged
   2  concentrated     6  influenced      10  reflect
   3  combine          7  grew            11  set
   4  created          8  capture

**2**  1  odd              3  strict          5  bright
   2  world            4  touches

## Notions & Functions

   1  b       3  b       5  b       7  b       9   a
   2  a       4  b       6  a       8  a       10  a

## Language & Grammar Review

| | | | | |
|---|---|---|---|---|
| 1  B | 7  C | 13  A | 19  C | 25  B |
| 2  B | 8  C | 14  A | 20  A | 26  C |
| 3  B | 9  C | 15  A | 21  C | 27  B |
| 4  C | 10  B | 16  A | 22  C | 28  A |
| 5  C | 11  C | 17  B | 23  B | 29  C |
| 6  B | 12  C | 18  B | 24  A | 30  A |

## Reading Task

   1  C          2  F          3  E          4  A          5  B

## Grammar Bank 1

**1**  1  across          4  over            7  under
   2  over            5  along
   3  through         6  down, past

**2**  1  c      2  d      3  a      4  b      5  e      6  f

**3**  1  Does Mike always drive, catches
   2  doesn't work
   3  do polar bears live
   4  Do you want, don't like
   5  closes
   6  studies, always passes
   7  hopes, practises
   8  want, go

**4**  1  are studying (an action happening now / a
     temporary situation)
   2  are going (a fixed arrangement in the near future)
   3  is mopping (an action happening now)
   4  are moving (a fixed arrangement in the near
     future)
   5  are you reading (an action happening now)
   6  is looking for (a temporary situation)

**5**  2  A:  Is Patrick returning the broken MP3 player to
        the shop on Saturday at 2:00 pm?
     B:  No, he isn't. He's returning the broken MP3
        player to the shop on Friday at 2:00 pm.
   3  A:  Are Patrick and Chris going to the bowling
        alley on Friday at 2:00 pm?
     B:  No, they aren't. They going to the bowling
        alley on Saturday at 3:00 pm.
   4  A:  Is Patrick going to pick up the clothes from
        the dry cleaner's on Saturday at 3:00 pm?
     B:  No, he isn't. He is going to pick up the clothes
        from the dry cleaner's on Friday at 5:00 pm.
   5  A:  Are Patrick and Jason going to watch a
        football game on Friday at 9:00 pm?
     B:  No, they aren't. They are going to watch a
        football game on Saturday at 9:00 pm.

**6**  1  does the train arrive      4  doesn't like
   2  usually spend             5  isn't working
   3  Are you doing             6  is doing

**7** 1 Q: What musical instrument does Alex play?
A: Alex plays the guitar.
2 Q: Is Mrs Cooper dusting the furniture right now?
A: No, she isn't. She's making the bed.
3 Q: What does Jake do every weekend?
A: He plays basketball.
4 Q: How are James and Lilly getting to work today?
A: They are getting to work by taxi.

**8** 1 don't believe     5 needs, helps
2 'm driving, do you want   6 shops, thinks
3 seems, Do you know
4 don't like, 're watching

**9** 1 need, am just playing
2 Does this motorbike belong, lets
3 Do you and Kenneth live, owns
4 Are you coming, are visiting
5 Do you hear, is making
6 Are you and Julia flying, hates, are taking

**10** 1 B    3 A    5 C    7 B
2 A    4 B    6 C

**11** 1 are spending     9 head
2 is blowing     10 stay
3 am sitting     11 prefer
4 am sending     12 meet up
5 usually take     13 don't like
6 are sleeping     14 think
7 love     15 serves
8 wake up     16 are you doing

**12** 1 c    3 b    5 h    7 a
2 g    4 f    6 d    8 e

**13** 1 c Could     4 d mustn't
2 e must     5 f can
3 a don't have to     6 b should

**14** 1 Can, can't, mustn't     6 have to
2 can't, shouldn't     7 Do we have to
3 Could     8 can
4 mustn't     9 can, can
5 Can     10 don't have to

**15** 1 mustn't     4 can / should
2 mustn't / shouldn't     5 should
3 must     6 can

**16** 1 Could I leave the lesson early?
2 You should carry some insect repellent when you trek through the jungle.
3 Pete can skate very well.
4 You don't have to dust the furniture every day.
5 We must make our beds every morning.
6 You mustn't park your car in a bus lane.
7 You shouldn't spend so much time playing video games.

**17** 1 George can't dance very well.
2 Can I sit here please?
3 You must stop at a red traffic light.
4 We mustn't keep pets in the block of flats where I live.
5 You should always use a zebra crossing when you want to cross the street.
6 You can take your bike on the London underground.

**18** 1 C    3 A    5 C    7 A
2 A    4 C    6 B    8 C

**19** **a)** good, the best
noisier, the noisiest
cheap, the cheapest
little, less
fitter, the fittest
more, the most
tall, taller
crowded, the most crowded
more poisonous, the most poisonous
safe, safer

**b)** 1 more crowded     6 the best
2 more     7 fitter
3 the noisiest     8 cheaper
4 the most poisonous   9 taller
5 less     10 the safest

**20** 1 the heaviest C     4 bigger A
2 longer C     5 the least B
3 the hottest B     6 more populated A

**21** 1 more enjoyable     5 the worst
2 the most attractive     6 more painful
3 friendly     7 fast
4 messiest     8 more polite

**22** 1 the tallest     5 the shortest
2 older     6 heaviest
3 the most artistic     7 younger
4 athletic     8 darker

### Grammar Bank 2

**1** 1 some, a     4 any, no, a
2 some, a, no, some     5 An, some, a
3 some, a     6 any, some

**2** 1 loaves   3 packets   5 box    7 jars
2 cans    4 tub    6 bars

**3** 1 a lot     5 a lot
2 How much     6 How many, many
3 How many
4 How much, much

**4** 1 a little    3 few     5 a few
2 little    4 little

**5** 1 B    2 A    3 C    4 A    5 C

**6** 1 enough eggs          5 ripe enough
2 too expensive        6 too much
3 too low              7 enough minced beef
4 long enough

**7** 1 We have enough oranges to make three glasses
of orange juice.
2 He's strong enough to lift the suitcase.
3 She's too ill to go to school.
4 She cooks well enough to be a professional chef.
5 The waiter is too busy to take our order at the
moment.

**8** 1 it's too cold to go jogging
2 Indian cuisine is too spicy
3 the baby is too young to talk
4 I've got enough money to buy a new motorbike
5 my car is big enough to fit us all in

**9** 1 to see        5 cooking     9 going
2 having       6 to help    10 add
3 Exercising   7 stop
4 help         8 trying

**10** 1 Having      5 to fit       9 shopping
2 to make     6 dancing     10 calling
3 consider    7 serving     11 to give
4 deciding    8 eat         12 to throw

**11** 1 to buy      5 eating       9 asking
2 mixing up   6 to turn     10 to open
3 using       7 getting
4 to say      8 talking

## Grammar Bank 3

**1** 1 read, liked
2 did da Vinci paint, began, finished
3 heard, burgled, broke, got, stole
4 Did you enjoy, didn't go
5 was, Did you watch, started, fell, didn't see

**2** 1 Liam wasn't sleeping at midnight last night.
2 Were you jogging in the park this morning?
3 The thieves were running to escape while two
policemen were chasing them.
4 The students were doing a test yesterday at
10:00 am.
5 Was Pete listening to music at 2 in the morning?

**3** 1 was trying, saw, called
2 was singing, were listening
3 didn't hear, was working
4 cleared, did
5 didn't email, wasn't working

**4** 2 How old was he when he began his singing career?
3 What was the name of their group?

4 Who produced *Off the Wall*?
5 Which of his albums was the best-selling one of
all times?
6 Why did Michael Jackson die?
7 How did people feel at the news of his death?
8 How long did Michael Jackson's career last?

## Grammar Bank 4

**1** 1 e    2 c    3 a    4 d    5 f    6 b

**2** 2 A: Is Tom going to arrange the accommodation?
   B: No, he isn't. Lyn is going to arrange the
   accommodation.
3 A: Are Lyn and Tom going to buy a travel guide?
   B: No, they aren't. Ian is going to buy a travel
   guide.
4 A: Is Ian going to pack the suitcases?
   B: No, he isn't. Lyn and Tom are going to pack
   the suitcases.
5 A: Is Tom going to bring a camera?
   B: No, he isn't. Ian is going to bring a camera.
6 A: Is Lyn going to exchange money at the bank?
   B: No, she isn't. Tom is going to exchange money
   at the bank.

**3** 1 'm going to take         4 will join
2 will miss, is going to drive  5 will call
3 am going to go

**4** 1 're leaving       3 'll send       5 'll take
2 's going to snow  4 isn't going to  6 won't find

**5** 1 while, was swimming     5 after, finish
2 When will dinner be     6 when, goes
3 as long as, want        7 the moment,
4 ran into, as, was walking    reached

**6** 2 f  If you mix red and yellow, you get orange.
3 a  If a snake bites you, it hurts.
4 b  If you don't have a ticket, they don't let you
travel.
5 d  If the temperature rises, snow melts.
6 e  If you add sugar to tea, it tastes sweet.

**7** 2 If Laura goes to Rome, she will visit the Coliseum.
3 If we get a taxi to the airport, we will pay a lot
of money.
4 If you stay in the sun a bit longer, you'll get
sunburnt.

**8** 2 If I travelled to India, I would visit the Taj Mahal.
3 If I went on a cruise, I would sunbathe on the
ship's deck all day.
4 If I went diving, I would take great underwater
photos.

**9** 1 would see     3 is       5 stay
2 will go       4 had      6 will get

**10**
1 had
2 would take
3 knows
4 will be
5 were
6 would book
7 like
8 will love
9 make
10 will cost/costs

**11**
1 may go
2 will probably come
3 could still be
4 will definitely try
5 might rain

**12**
1 an, –, the, a
2 a, the
3 a, a, –, –
4 –, the
5 the, a, the
6 an, the
7 –, –, a, the, an, the, the, the

**13**
1 a
2 –
3 a
4 a
5 –
6 an
7 the
8 the
9 the
10 –
11 the
12 the
13 a
14 the
15 The
16 –
17 an
18 the
19 the
20 an

**14**
1 which
2 why
3 where
4 which
5 whose
6 when
7 who
8 that

**15**
1 They chose a hotel room which had a view of the sea.
2 That's the beach where we spend most of our day.
3 The police caught the man who stole my passport.
4 Maui is an island whose beaches are very famous.
5 I was twenty years old when I first travelled abroad.
6 He didn't tell us the reason why he asked us to move to another table.

**16**
1 where B
2 which A
3 whose B
4 when B
5 which A
6 who A
7 where A

## Grammar Bank 5

**1**
1 has made
2 has organised
3 Have … put up
4 haven't cleared
5 has … collected

**2**
1 have been
2 has gone
3 have gone
4 has been

**3**
1 already
2 ever
3 since
4 never
5 just
6 for
7 yet

**4**
1 have been waiting
2 has caught
3 has twisted
4 has been jogging
5 has caused
6 has been raining

**5**
1 burnt
2 has been trying
3 has cut
4 haven't seen
5 attended
6 have sold

**6**
1 interesting, interested
2 shocking, shocked
3 tiring, tired
4 thrilled, thrilling
5 frightened, frightening

**7**
1 left
2 has broken
3 haven't finished
4 had escaped
5 had
6 had ever trekked

**8**
2 If his dog hadn't led them to the missing man, the rescue workers wouldn't have found him.
3 If the famous singer hadn't broken his/her leg, he/she wouldn't have cancelled his/her concert.
4 If the local children hadn't raised money, they wouldn't have paid for new flowers for Coburg Park
5 If the teens hadn't gone on a nature hike, they wouldn't have got lost in the forest.

**9**
1 wasn't going
2 had signed up
3 hadn't burnt
4 had
5 would stop
6 would apologise

**10**
1 C
2 C
3 A
4 B
5 A
6 B
7 C
8 B

## Grammar Bank 6

**1**
1 was being washed
2 be sent
3 had been buried, was uncovered
4 is being displayed/ will be display
5 is held
6 is being served
7 have not been completed

**2**
1 will be delivered
2 was robbed
3 hasn't been released
4 had all been sold
5 be bought
6 weren't invited
7 are sold

**3**
1 was built
2 has been occupied
3 are organised
4 has been decorated/ is decorated
5 was opened
6 has been used
7 be visited

**4**
1 –
2 yourself
3 herself
4 –
5 herself
6 ourselves
7 himself

**5**
1 said
2 told
3 said
4 said
5 said
6 told
7 said
8 said

**6**
2 that they had been to London the previous year. They had really enjoyed themselves going around the sites. They wanted to go again that year.
3 that he couldn't go to Spain with his friends that summer. They were leaving in July and his holidays were in August. Perhaps, he would go with them the following year.

**7** 2 would record
 I'll record my own album next year.
 3 hadn't bought
 I haven't bought them yet.
 4 hadn't come in
 She didn't come in yesterday, either.
 5 were leaving
 We are leaving for Ireland tomorrow.

**8** 1 how he had become interested in archaeology.
 2 She asked him what the best part of his job was.
 3 She asked him if he could describe/to describe his typical working day.
 4 She asked him if/whether he had taken part in many excavations.
 5 She asked him what the most exciting thing (that) he had uncovered was.
 6 She asked him if/whether he got to travel a lot.
 7 She asked him where he was planning to go next.
 8 She asked him if he had any advice for those wishing to have a career in archaeology.

**9** 2 He ordered them to leave the room immediately.
 3 He begged us to go to his concert that night.
 4 The post office worker asked Linda to put her parcel on the scales.
 5 The museum guide told the students not to touch the exhibits.
 6 Helen ordered George to get his feet off the table.

**10** 2 The doctor asked Mrs Miles to tell her how long she had had those symptoms.
 3 The doctor asked her when her last check-up had been/was.
 4 The doctor told her that they would need to run some tests.
 5 The doctor asked her if/whether she had any allergies.
 6 The doctor told her to lie down.

**11** 2 C asked him to bring me a selection of cold meats.
 3 H told him to be quiet.
 4 A told her to get some eye drops from the chemist's.
 5 F asked John if he could help me move the sofa.
 6 B told him that I would send it by airmail.
 7 G asked her if she had bought the tickets.
 8 E asked him who his favourite painter was.

**12** 1 doesn't she   3 will you   5 have you
 2 wasn't it   4 hasn't he   6 won't we

**13** 1 i   3 b   5 f   7 g   9 j
 2 d   4 c   6 h   8 e   10 a

**14** 2 faster, will you
 3 paintings were amazing, weren't they
 4 go to the beach, shall we
 5 shirt looks nice, doesn't it

## Phrasal Verbs

**1** 1 down   3 out   5 down
 2 into   4 up

**2** 1 round   3 up
 2 out   4 about

**3** 1 on   3 away   5 on with
 2 through   4 on

**4** 1 back   3 off   5 away
 2 out   4 up

**5** 1 after   4 up   7 forward to
 2 up   5 for
 3 up   6 out

**6** 1 up   3 off   5 on
 2 through   4 forward   6 out

**7** 1 across   3 out off
 2 away from   4 into

**8** 1 up   3 of   5 away
 2 after   4 down

**9** 1 out   3 to   5 down
 2 down   4 up   6 on

## Verbs/Adjectives/Nouns with Prepositions

**1** 1 from   4 at   7 into   10 for
 2 at   5 from   8 with
 3 for   6 at   9 to

**2** 1 with   4 with   7 about   10 to
 2 between   5 in   8 on
 3 with   6 of   9 with

**3** 1 with   4 on   7 for   10 with
 2 to   5 with   8 on
 3 of   6 at   9 for

**4** 1 to   4 to   7 of   10 of
 2 by   5 of   8 to   11 from
 3 of   6 to   9 at   12 on

**5** 1 to   4 of   7 in   10 about
 2 at   5 about   8 from
 3 through   6 to   9 of

**6** 1 of   4 for   7 on   10 of
 2 on   5 of   8 of
 3 about   6 with   9 against

**7** 1 towards   4 about   7 with   10 for
 2 for   5 for   8 about
 3 with   6 of   9 to

**8**
| | | | | | | | | |
|---|---|---|---|---|---|---|---|---|
| 1 | under | 4 | into | 7 | from | 10 | at | |
| 2 | in | 5 | by | 8 | for | | | |
| 3 | on | 6 | out of | 9 | to | | | |

### Word Formation

| | | | |
|---|---|---|---|
| 1 | pollution | 16 | illogical |
| 2 | equipment | 17 | confidence |
| 3 | disorganised | 18 | imagination |
| 4 | achievement | 19 | dependent |
| 5 | reliable | 20 | unlock |
| 6 | attraction | 21 | exhibition |
| 7 | sadness | 22 | homelessness |
| 8 | harmful | 23 | helpful |
| 9 | irreversible | 24 | careless |
| 10 | appearance | 25 | untouched |
| 11 | impolite | 26 | awareness |
| 12 | donation | 27 | unemployment |
| 13 | forgetful | 28 | accessible |
| 14 | undisturbed | 29 | inspiration |
| 15 | location | 30 | kindness |

### Key Word Transformations

| | | | |
|---|---|---|---|
| 1 | have no difficulty assembling it | 14 | to avoid getting caught |
| 2 | spent all night writing | 15 | on her own |
| 3 | I have ever been | 16 | is a waste of |
| 4 | might snow | 17 | great demand for |
| 5 | even though he (had) trained | 18 | last time I drank |
| 6 | to make a complaint about | 19 | isn't as tall |
| 7 | persuaded her friends to go | 20 | with the aim of buying |
| 8 | thought (that) he would get | 21 | may not have heard |
| 9 | put a lot of effort | 22 | needn't have paid for |
| 10 | only student who didn't | 23 | spite of leaving the house |
| 11 | ages since I heard | 24 | likely that she will be |
| 12 | wonder if you could pass | 25 | in case you get |
| 13 | don't mind which | 26 | are responsible for keeping |
| | | 27 | have run out of |

### Sentence Completion

**1**
| | | | |
|---|---|---|---|
| 1 | a walk | 4 | to have escaped |
| 2 | had been looking | 5 | terrified |
| 3 | already been swallowed | | |

**2**
| | | | |
|---|---|---|---|
| 1 | was taught | 4 | at cooking |
| 2 | to dream | 5 | is thought that |
| 3 | when he first | | |

**3**
| | | | | | |
|---|---|---|---|---|---|
| 1 | herself | 3 | portrait of | 5 | advised her to |
| 2 | to paint | 4 | to be | | |

**4**
| | | | |
|---|---|---|---|
| 1 | about going/of going | 4 | choose |
| 2 | is said | 5 | cost |
| 3 | is not frightened | | |

**5**
| | | | | | |
|---|---|---|---|---|---|
| 1 | had got up | 3 | enough | 5 | still |
| 2 | the fact that | 4 | were not | | |

**6**
| | | | |
|---|---|---|---|
| 1 | have been learning | 4 | more enjoyable |
| 2 | close/near | 5 | like to be/like to become |
| 3 | at playing | | |

**7**
| | | | |
|---|---|---|---|
| 1 | usually/often go | 4 | a decision |
| 2 | to book | 5 | had |
| 3 | on his | | |

**8**
| | | | |
|---|---|---|---|
| 1 | broke | 4 | had not locked |
| 2 | was taken | 5 | would not lose |
| 3 | did not know | | |

### Grammar Revision Sentences

**1**
| | | | |
|---|---|---|---|
| 1 | because, frightening | | since |
| 2 | needs, few | 34 | hovered, is tidying |
| 3 | should, has been sleeping | 35 | has been, thinks |
| 4 | was found, wasn't | 36 | gets, will / can |
| 5 | said, on | 37 | quietly, is sleeping |
| 6 | went, and | 38 | has published, to write |
| 7 | wanted, to | 39 | were, wouldn't go |
| 8 | Will / Could, doesn't miss | 40 | to know, on |
| 9 | to worry, enough | 41 | is looking, of |
| 10 | told, the / some | 42 | had left, before |
| 11 | has been working, yet | 43 | was ironing, down |
| 12 | If, burned | 44 | didn't hear, much |
| 13 | to make, any | 45 | to send, by |
| 14 | been, is travelling | 46 | How, has Leon been working |
| 15 | was reading, a | 47 | wrote, which |
| 16 | whether / if, happier | 48 | tiring, had been crying |
| 17 | ought, shouting | 49 | watching, have never tried it |
| 18 | had not waited, have missed / will miss | 50 | was opened, also |
| 19 | drove, stopping | 51 | will have, in |
| 20 | had spent, would | 52 | must, will be |
| 21 | on, stole | 53 | are searching, whose |
| 22 | are visiting, aren't | 54 | had learned, on |
| 23 | had washed, so | 55 | Is being destroyed / the, has been destroyed |
| 24 | has hurt, in | 56 | has, won't be |
| 25 | which, have been painted | 57 | is shining, in |
| 26 | was talking, while | 58 | Which, most beautiful |
| 27 | Who, the furthest | 59 | bought, is taking |
| 28 | to see, visits | 60 | to call, comes |
| 29 | eating, of | 61 | was revising, into |
| 30 | do, yourself | 62 | by, were arrested |
| 31 | has lived, longer | 63 | snows, the worst |
| 32 | had forgotten, into | 64 | himself, having |
| 33 | has been visited, | | |

## Grammar Multiple Choice

**1**

| | | | | | | | | | | | |
|---|---|---|---|---|---|---|---|---|---|---|---|
| 1 | A | 11 | B | 21 | A | 31 | A | 41 | A | 51 | A |
| 2 | B | 12 | B | 22 | C | 32 | B | 42 | A | 52 | A |
| 3 | B | 13 | C | 23 | A | 33 | A | 43 | A | 53 | A |
| 4 | B | 14 | B | 24 | B | 34 | C | 44 | B | 54 | C |
| 5 | A | 15 | B | 25 | A | 35 | B | 45 | A | 55 | A |
| 6 | C | 16 | B | 26 | B | 36 | C | 46 | B | 56 | C |
| 7 | A | 17 | C | 27 | C | 37 | B | 47 | A | 57 | C |
| 8 | A | 18 | B | 28 | A | 38 | B | 48 | B | 58 | C |
| 9 | B | 19 | A | 29 | B | 39 | A | 49 | C | 59 | B |
| 10 | B | 20 | A | 30 | C | 40 | C | 50 | B | 60 | C |

## Further Practice

### Vocabulary

**1**

| | | | | | | | | | | | |
|---|---|---|---|---|---|---|---|---|---|---|---|
| 1 | A | 11 | B | 21 | A | 31 | A | 41 | A | 51 | A |
| 2 | A | 12 | A | 22 | A | 32 | A | 42 | A | 52 | C |
| 3 | B | 13 | B | 23 | C | 33 | C | 43 | A | 53 | B |
| 4 | A | 14 | A | 24 | A | 34 | A | 44 | B | 54 | A |
| 5 | C | 15 | A | 25 | A | 35 | B | 45 | C | 55 | A |
| 6 | A | 16 | C | 26 | B | 36 | B | 46 | B | 56 | C |
| 7 | A | 17 | C | 27 | B | 37 | C | 47 | A | 57 | B |
| 8 | B | 18 | B | 28 | C | 38 | A | 48 | C | 58 | C |
| 9 | C | 19 | A | 29 | C | 39 | C | 49 | B | 59 | B |
| 10 | A | 20 | A | 30 | A | 40 | A | 50 | A | 60 | A |

### Listening

**1**  1 T  2 F  3 F  4 T  5 F

**2**  1 F  2 C  3 D  4 A  5 E

**3**  1 C  2 A  3 B  4 C  5 C

### Reading

**1**  1 E  2 G  3 I  4 D  5 A  6 F  7 H  8 B

**2**  1 F  2 F  3 T  4 T  5 F  6 T  7 F

**3**  1 A  2 B  3 C  4 D  5 C  6 C

## Revision Modules 1-6

### Module 1

**A**  1 B  2 C  3 C  4 B  5 C  6 D  7 C  8 B  9 A  10 C

**B**  1 centre  2 make  3 road  4 public  5 insect

**C**  1 B  2 A  3 B  4 C  5 B  6 C  7 B  8 A  9 B  10 B

**D**  1 is studying  2 don't understand  3 are playing  4 don't watch  5 goes

**E**  1 C  2 F  3 E  4 G  5 A  6 D  7 I  8 B

**F**  1 I'd like a ticket to Manchester, please  2 Single or return  3 When do you want to go  4 That's £15, please  5 Have a nice day

**G**  1 F  2 F  3 T  4 T  5 T

**H** (Suggested Answer)

Hi James,

I'm sorry to hear that your brother uses your computer to chat with his friends all the time. I think I can help you!

Why don't you talk to him about it? This way, you can tell him how you feel. You should explain to him that he can't use your computer all the time because you need it as well. I think you should each use it at different times of the day.

I really hope my advice helps! Write back and tell me what happens.

Alex

### Module 2

**A**  1 B  2 C  3 D  4 C  5 D  6 A  7 B  8 C  9 B  10 C

**B**  1 show  2 run  3 spicy  4 menu  5 fast

**C**  1 B  2 A  3 A  4 A  5 C  6 B  7 C  8 B  9 C  10 B

**D**  1 to order  2 drink  3 eating  4 to buy  5 mixing

**E**  1 A  2 C  3 B  4 C  5 D  6 D

**F**  1 a  2 a  3 b  4 a  5 b  6 b

**G**  1 F  2 T  3 F  4 T  5 F

**H** (Suggested Answer)

Hi Tom,

Great to hear from you! So you want to know about my favourite dish. Well, it's Spaghetti Carbonara, a classic Italian dish.

Spaghetti Carbonara is a dish with spaghetti, bacon, cream, eggs and cheese. It's very easy to make. First, boil the pasta for 7-10 minutes. Then, chop the bacon and fry it in a pan for a few minutes. When the pasta is cooked put it into the pan with the bacon and stir well. Next, mix the egg yolks, cream and parmesan cheese in a bowl and add to the the pasta and bacon. Serve with a sprinkle of Parmesan cheese and a warm bread roll. It's a very tasty dish! Be sure to try it soon!

How about you? Do you have a favourite dish from another country?

Write soon,

David

## Module 3

**A**  1 C   3 C   5 A   7 B   9 D
       2 D   4 D   6 A   8 C   10 B

**B**  1 re-enactment  3 traditional   5 designed
       2 accurate      4 win

**C**  1 sailed                  6 didn't invent
       2 was performing          7 was sketching,
       3 did the thief break into   was painting
       4 was vandalising,        8 led
         caught                  9 Did Ken go
       5 was taking,            10 was shining,
         yelled                    were singing

**D**  1 B   2 C   3 A   4 A   5 B

**E**  1 I   3 B   5 D   7 E
       2 G   4 H   6 F   8 A

**F**  1 How was your weekend      5 I didn't do
       2 Did you have a good time    anything
       3 That sounds interesting     special
       4 What about you

**G**  1 B   2 C   3 B   4 A   5 B

**H  (Suggested Answer)**

Robert Burns was a famous Scottish poet. He was born in Alloway, Scotland on 25 January, 1759.
Burns was the eldest of 7 children in a poor family. He had to work on the family farm and by the age of 15 he was its main worker.
He published his first collection of poems, *Poems, Chiefly in the Scottish Dialect*, in 1784 and moved to Edinburgh. While in Edinburgh, he started working with James Johnson and they wrote a collection of songs called *The Scots Musical Museum*. He published his last major work, *Tam O'Shanter*, in 1791.
Burns died on 21 July, 1796. He was only 37 years old but people still remember him more than 250 years later.

## Module 4

**A**  1 B   3 C   5 D   7 C   9 D
       2 B   4 D   6 D   8 D   10 A

**B**  1 fresh     3 peaceful   5 tour
       2 view      4 heart

**C**  1 A   4 B   7 B   10 C   13 C
       2 C   5 C   8 B   11 C   14 C
       3 B   6 B   9 B   12 B   15 C

**D**  1 A   2 A   3 C   4 D   5 B   6 D

**E**  1 b   2 b   3 b   4 a   5 b   6 b

**F**  1 D   2 A   3 F   4 C   5 B

**G  (Suggested Answer)**

Dear Lucy,
How are you? Sorry it took so long to write back to you, but I was really busy with my exams. Next month we're going to our summer house by the sea. Guess what, my parents said you can come too!
A couple of friends from school are coming as well. Do you remember Lilly and Chloe from last summer? We're planning to do lots of things every day. We're going to sunbathe on the beach, go swimming and snorkelling and we can even try scuba diving.
It's going to be hot so bring light clothes, your swimsuit and your sunglasses. It's a good idea to bring a jacket, too, because it can get a bit chilly at night.
Hope you can make it. Write back soon to let me know.
Love,
Louise

## Module 5

**A**  1 B   3 B   5 A   7 C   9 C
       2 C   4 D   6 C   8 A   10 D

**B**  1 pain     3 sore     5 tsunami
       2 record   4 put up

**C**  1 B   4 A   7 B   10 B   13 A
       2 B   5 B   8 B   11 B   14 A
       3 A   6 B   9 C   12 C   15 A

**D**  1 F   3 F   5 F   7 T
       2 T   4 T   6 F

**E**  1 b   2 a   3 b   4 a   5 a   6 a

**F**  1 E   2 F   3 D   4 C   5 A

**G  (Suggested Answer)**

Dear Kevin,
How are things? I've been at Camp Green for ten days now and I really love it here!
Camp Green is an eco-camp. I'm sure you think that all we do around here is recycling and nothing more, but that's not the case. Yesterday, we planted some trees and cleaned out a pond and last night we cooked on a barbecue and sat around a campfire. We all sang songs and had a wonderful time.
The best part about this camp is that we help the environment and have fun at the same time. All the kids are really nice!
I hope you're having a great summer, too. Write back when you get a chance.
All the best,
Emily

## Module 6

| **A** | 1 | D | 3 | D | 5 | B | 7 | B | 9 | A |
|---|---|---|---|---|---|---|---|---|---|---|
| | 2 | B | 4 | D | 6 | C | 8 | D | 10 | B |

**B** 1 deep 3 unique 5 detail
2 untouched 4 ground

| **C** | 1 | C | 4 | A | 7 | C | 10 | C | 13 | C |
|---|---|---|---|---|---|---|---|---|---|---|
| | 2 | B | 5 | C | 8 | A | 11 | B | 14 | A |
| | 3 | C | 6 | B | 9 | B | 12 | B | 15 | B |

**D** 1 F 2 E 3 A 4 B 5 D

**E** 1 b 2 b 3 a 4 b 5 a 6 a

**F** 1 C 2 B 3 B 4 A 5 C

**G** **(Suggested Answer)**

Hi Andrew!
I hope you're well! I was so happy to hear you're coming to Budapest next month. I know how much you like going for walks in the country, so I think Margaret Island is the ideal place for you to visit.
The island is in the middle of the Danube and it has a number of walking paths through its green spaces. It's a really beautiful place with medieval ruins, a small zoo, a Japanese garden and a musical fountain among other things. You won't have enough time to see it all in one day; I think you're going to love it!
I'm really looking forward to seeing you.
Take care,
Zak

# Workbook & Grammar Book Tapescripts

### Module 1

➤ **Exercise 3 (p. 9)**

*Josh:* Where do you live Vicky?
*Vicky:* I live in the centre of the city.
*Josh:* Do you live in a flat or a house?
*Vicky:* I live in a small one-bedroom flat. I want a bigger place, but I don't have the money at the moment.
*Josh:* Do you live alone or have you got a flatmate?
*Vicky:* No, I live alone.
*Josh:* So, I guess you have to do all the chores yourself.
*Vicky:* Yes, but I don't mind hoovering the carpets or dusting the furniture. What I really hate doing is the washing-up and ironing the clothes.
*Josh:* I know what you mean. I hate doing chores.
*Vicky:* What about you? Do you live alone?
*Josh:* No, I live with my mum, dad, three brothers and two sisters all in the same house.
*Vicky:* Wow! How do you study with all those people in the house?
*Josh:* You're right. It's not easy with so many people. I close my bedroom door to get some peace and quiet.
*Vicky:* Do you have to do any chores?
*Josh:* Yes. Because there is so many of us, we each have our own chores to do. I have to take out the rubbish every day.
*Vicky:* Is that all? Lucky you!

### Module 2

➤ **Exercise 5 (p. 15)**

*Cindy:* We need to do some shopping. Let's make a list.
*Mike:* OK. Well, we don't have any bread so let's get two loaves. That should be enough for a couple of days.
*Cindy:* OK. That's two loaves of bread! What else do we need?
*Mike:* We need some pasta.
*Cindy:* How much?
*Mike:* I think one packet is enough.
*Cindy:* Alright. Let's get a box of cereal, too.
*Mike:* Let's get three pots of yoghurt and a few bottles of cola, as well.
*Cindy:* Yes, then let's get some fruit and vegetables.
*Mike:* Good idea! We don't have many left. What else do we need?
*Cindy:* Nothing else, but why don't we have a treat and buy two bars of chocolate?
*Mike:* OK. Good idea.
*Cindy:* Right. Let's hurry before the supermarket closes.

➤ **Exercise 3 (p. 19)**

*Interviewer:* Today on "Healthy Matters" I'm happy to have diet advisor to the stars, Jean Patterson, on the show. Welcome Jean.
*Jean:* Thanks, it's good to be here.
*Interviewer:* Jean, what do your celebrity clients want in a diet?
*Jean:* Well like most of us, they want to have a healthy diet. But the most important thing for many of my clients is a diet that gives them lots of energy as they have very busy lives. So, I design a meal plan that is high in energy.
*Interviewer:* How do you do that?

*Jean:* I plan diets with lots of fruits, like bananas. I include snacks like nuts and low-fat cheese and of course as many vegetables as possible. I avoid desserts high in sugar, but once or twice a week it's okay to have them.
*Interviewer:* I see. What about eating meat and food high in fat?
*Jean:* Well, most stars prefer low-fat diets as they need to watch their weight. Many of them eat very little meat. But it's not just what you eat that is important; it's also how you prepare your food. I always suggest grilling meat instead of frying. This reduces a lot of fat in a meal. Many stars prefer fish instead of meat and it's also a great source of protein.
*Interviewer:* Interesting. Jean, are there any secrets you can share with our listeners today to help them control their weight and stay healthy?
*Jean:* Certainly. Everyone knows that lots of water is good for you and makes you feel less hungry. But the trick is to eat many small meals throughout the day. Many of my clients eat this way and they never get too hungry and their bodies are always busy burning calories.
*Interviewer:* Great advice, thanks Jean.

### Module 3

➤ **Exercise 3 (p. 29)**

*Interviewer:* Today on 'Science and Beyond' I welcome George Quarterton from the Science and Exploration Museum. Thanks for joining us George.
*George:* You're welcome.
*Interviewer:* George what do you do at the museum?
*George:* I'm the exhibit organiser. It's my job to organise the exhibits and work with the museum's scientists to develop them.
*Interviewer:* I see. Tell us what exhibits are on display now at the museum?
*George:* Well, we have all our permanent exhibits. And I'm very excited to say that this month's scientist of the month is Albert Einstein. All month long, people can visit the museum and learn about Einstein and his work.
*Interviewer:* Great. Tell us a bit about Einstein.
*George:* Well, as we all know Einstein was a great German physicist and his theories are very important. Even today, more than 50 years after his death, he is a well-known person around the world. He has come to represent intelligence and genius in spite of the fact that, this was not always the case.
*Interviewer:* What do you mean?
*George:* Well, as a child Einstein was slow in learning to speak and read. He did poorly in school at first. Many of his teachers didn't think he was smart. This didn't last long though, as Einstein wrote his first research paper at 16 and showed great talent in Science and Maths. Then of course, he went on to win the Nobel Prize in Physics.
*Interviewer:* Many people believe he helped invent the atomic bomb. Is this true?
*George:* Not at all. He wrote a letter to American President Roosevelt about Germany's possible use of nuclear weapons in World War II, but he never participated in the creation of the bomb.
*Interviewer:* Wow, there is so much I didn't know about Einstein.

*George:* Yes, he was a fascinating man. I invite you and your listeners to learn more about him at the museum this month.

## Module 4

➢ **Exercise 3 (p. 39)**

*Brenda:* Hi Paul, it's Brenda! I'm just calling to tell you everything is fine here at the office and you don't have to worry about a thing. Are you having fun in Spain?

*Paul:* Hi, Brenda. Well, actually I'm not and it's turning out to be the worst holiday of my life!

*Brenda:* Really? Why, what happened?

*Paul:* Well, to start with we almost missed our flight because there was so much traffic on the way to the airport. Someone's car broke down and was blocking the motorway.

*Brenda:* Oh no!

*Paul:* Yes and then the airline lost our luggage, probably because we checked in late, so we had no clothes for the first couple of days. It was really hot, so we had to buy something light to wear.

*Brenda:* Really? That was unlucky.

*Paul:* And that's not all.

*Brenda:* Oh dear! What else happened?

*Paul:* Well, listen to this! When we got to the hotel they somehow lost our reservation and gave us the only room available. It's so small.

*Brenda:* Oh no! That's terrible.

*Paul:* I know! We booked a suite with a sea view and now we're staying in a tiny room with a view of the street. Anyway, we decided to start enjoying our holiday despite the bad beginning so we went to the beach and swam in the sea.

*Brenda:* That sounds fine.

*Paul:* Yes, it was until I got badly sunburnt!

*Brenda:* Are you serious?

*Paul:* Yes, it was awful.

*Brenda:* Well, at least someone didn't steal your passport or your money.

*Paul:* Yes, I guess things could be worse.

*Brenda:* Definitely. Just try to enjoy what's left of it and have fun.

*Paul:* You're right. I think I'll go shopping for souvenirs now. Talk to you later. Bye!

*Brenda:* OK. Bye.

## Module 5

➢ **Exercise 3 (p. 49)**

*Speaker 1*

I think that the biggest environmental problem is pollution. People are responsible for it. We all drive cars and their exhaust fumes pollute the air we breathe. But, I believe that factories are the main problem. They emit their waste into the air and the water. Often these waste products and chemicals are harmful and cause the biggest problems.

*Speaker 2*

I've started doing small jobs in my community to help the environment. A group of us went to pick up rubbish last Saturday in the park. It was great. Lots of people came and it only took an hour! Also, the local school is setting up recycling bins so that everyone can help reduce waste. Sure there are lots of larger environmental problems around the world, but at least things around here are improving.

*Speaker 3*

My community is always organising 'save the world' events. I want to participate, but I work five days a week and have two children. By the time the weekend comes, I'm exhausted and I have no energy to help with environmental events. I try to recycle, which is good, and if I wasn't so busy I would help more.

*Speaker 4*

Many people still don't care enough about the environment. People say that they have no time or it's not their responsibility. But really, it's everyone's responsibility. It doesn't take long to collect rubbish and put it in a recycle bin or switch the lights off when you leave a room. People forget that all these small things help. If everyone does their part, we might reduce pollution and help the environment.

*Speaker 5*

I agree that the environment is very important but there aren't many ways to help without having to pay for it. Charities and other environmental organisations are always asking for donations. I would like to help more but I can't afford to donate money to help these organisations and other good causes.

## Module 6

➢ **Exercise 4 (p. 59)**

No trip to Indonesia is complete without a visit to the largest Buddhist temple in the world, Borobudur. Located about 400 kilometres southeast of the main city of Jakarta on the island of Java, this enormous temple is visited every year by Buddhist monks and fascinated tourists from around the world. There is no written record of who built the temple or for what purpose and it remains to this day a mystery. It is estimated though, that Borobudur was built around 800 AD.

For centuries Borobudur was hidden under volcanic ash and jungle growth until it was discovered in 1814 by Sir Thomas Stamford Raffles, the British governor of the area. It was later restored and preserved by archaeologists. In 1985 the temple suffered damage due to a bomb attack. Soon after Borobudur was listed as a UNESCO World Heritage Site.

The Temple is designed in the shape of a pyramid with 9 levels or storeys. The walls are carved, starting from the bottom storey to the fifth storey, with scenes from the life of Buddha and his teachings. The scenes are carved in an art style originating from India. There are over 2,650 scenes and it's a 3 kilometre walk to view all of them. Borobudur had 504 statues of Buddha, although it's not possible to see them all as many are damaged or missing. It is recommended to take one of the stairways to the top of the temple to enjoy the spectacular views of both the temple below and the surrounding countryside. However, to make such a climb it is wise to visit Borobudur in the early morning before the afternoon heat begins.

It only takes one visit for tourists to fully appreciate what an impressive achievement Borobudur was for its time and how it now stands as a symbol of the Indonesian people and their history. Its exact beginnings may be a mystery, but its greatness is obvious at once.

## Further Practice

### ➢ Exercise 1 p. 113

*Brian:* Hi, Patricia! What are you doing here?
*Patricia:* Oh, hi, Brian. I come to the sports centre every Saturday. I'm a fitness freak and this centre has got the best weights room in the city. Do you come here often?
*Brian:* No, I'm just here with my friend, Josh. He's swimming in the pool now. On Saturdays, I usually go to the ice rink in the city centre. You know, the one by the tunnel on Maple Street.
*Patricia:* No, I don't know where that one is, but my friend, Meg, goes to a rink on Tuesday nights. I think it's across the street from the bank on Elm Avenue.
*Brian:* Oh, yes. That skating rink is bigger and more modern than mine.
*Patricia:* So, why aren't you skating today?
*Brian:* I've got a problem with my foot. I can't skate today because it hurts. I have to be careful of what sports I do this week.
*Patricia:* I see. Could I go skating with you when your foot is better?
*Brian:* Well, can you skate?
*Patricia:* No, not very well – I'm only a beginner, but, hey, I'm not the worst skater in the world!

### ➢ Exercise 2 p. 113

*Speaker 1*
Every Friday night, my friends and I eat out at one of the nicest restaurants in our neighbourhood. The restaurant is never very crowded and the food is fantastic! The waiters are extremely friendly and the service is quick. And the best part is the bill! The prices are very reasonable!

*Speaker 2*
I'm very careful of what I eat. My mum and dad say that I worry too much about the nutrients of certain foods. I don't think I do, I just prefer to eat healthy meals! I think that fried food is the worst thing that people can eat. I can't stand eating food my mum cooks in oil like fish and chips ... yuck! A big green salad is what I like best!

*Speaker 3*
I like eating food I prepare in my kitchen at home. I go out to restaurants a few times a month, but I prefer staying in and cooking tasty dishes for my friends. Right now I'm making pizza! My friends Peter and Jake are watching me and they look very hungry!

*Speaker 4*
I eat all kinds of foods! I look forward to mealtimes and I always eat everything on my plate. My mum is a great cook and only buys healthy foods – fresh fruit and vegetables, low-fat dairy products, and the best meat from the butcher. I think the only food I have to eat more of is seafood.

*Speaker 5*
One of my favourite things to do is eat out. When I have enough money, I love going to popular ethnic restaurants in the city centre. I think it's important to experience new tastes and unusual kinds of cuisine – it's boring going to the traditional cafés and chippies all the time.

### ➢ Exercise 3 p. 113

*Interviewer:* Good morning, and welcome to today's show. Just like every Monday morning at 9 am, today we're talking about conservation. And with us is Megan Holmes, who returned from Greece last Friday afternoon. Thanks for coming, Megan.
*Megan:* My pleasure. Thanks for having me.
*Interviewer:* So, why don't you tell us what you did in Greece?
*Megan:* Well, I'm a conservationist – my job is to monitor endangered species. And, as most of you know, there is a Greek Island called Zakynthos. What you might not be aware of, however, is that Loggerhead Sea Turtles go to this island to lay their eggs each summer.
*Interviewer:* I see. And is there a problem with that, Megan?
*Megan:* Yes, unfortunately, there are several problems with that. Firstly, Zakynthos is an island that is visited by many tourists each year. And they go to the island for the same reason as the turtles – the beaches.
*Interviewer:* I think I understand. Do the tourists scare the turtles?
*Megan:* Not exactly. What happens is that the turtles lay their eggs in holes in the sand. The tourists don't know that these holes, or eggs, are there and they step on them.
*Interviewer:* I see! Do they also damage the nests?
*Megan:* Yes, the tourists do it by accident but it still means that many baby turtles are lost each year.
*Interviewer:* How sad! You said that there were several problems, Megan.
*Megan:* Yes, the other problem is the rubbish that tourists leave behind. To a turtle, a plastic bag looks like food. The turtles eat the bags and die.
*Interviewer:* That's terrible!
*Megan:* Yes, and it's my job to tell people about what they are doing to the turtles. I explain to them that the turtles are endangered and try to get them involved ... try to get them to help.
*Interviewer:* Well, I certainly hope it works, Megan.
*Megan:* So do I.

## Revision
## Module 1

### ➢ Exercise G, p. 120

*Ian:* Hi Nancy, what are you reading?
*Nancy:* Oh, hi Ian. I am just looking at a brochure for the new sports centre on Blackwell Street across the street from the train station. It opens today.
*Ian:* And how is it?
*Nancy:* It looks great. It's much bigger than the community sports centre next to our school. There is a huge swimming pool and a gym. They offer different exercise classes for every fitness level. You can play basketball and tennis there. There is an outdoor football pitch. And best of all, it's got a volleyball court.
*Ian:* Oh really, do you play volleyball?
*Nancy:* No, but I really want to learn how to play. Some of my friends are in the volleyball team at school and it looks like fun. Oh look ... there's even a huge indoor ice rink!
*Ian:* Wow, that's amazing! I can't believe they have all these sports in one place.

*Nancy:* I know it's incredible! Do you fancy going with me at the weekend?

*Ian:* I don't know. I'm not very good at sports.

*Nancy:* That's not true. You're an excellent swimmer. We can check out the pool and then afterwards go to the ice rink. Besides, it says here that experienced players to absolute beginners are welcome for all sports. So, what do you say?

*Ian:* Sounds like fun. Sure, why not?

## Module 2

### ➤ Exercise G, p. 123

*Alex:* Hi Jenny, what are you doing tonight? Do you fancy trying that new Indian restaurant near the cinema? I hear they serve traditional Indian dishes and desserts.

*Jenny:* I don't really like spicy food. Do you mind going somewhere else?

*Alex:* No, not at all. What have you got in mind?

*Jenny:* What about Chinese? There's a great restaurant near my house. They have delicious sweet and sour pork.

*Alex:* Oh yes, I know the place. It looks really nice, but it's too expensive for me. How about going to Mario's? It's cheaper and the food is always delicious.

*Jenny:* No, I'm sick of Italian. We always go there. Let's go somewhere else.

*Alex:* Yes, but it has got the best lasagna in town.

*Jenny:* I know, it's my favourite food! I would prefer to go some place new like the fish and chip restaurant near the baker's. I hear the prices are reasonable and the fish is really fresh. Hmmm let me think ... what's the name?

*Alex:* Oh, do you mean Captain John's?

*Jenny:* Yes that's it! It's really popular. Everyone goes there. My friend Tracy works there. I'm sure we can get a table. What do you think?

*Alex:* Well I do love fish ... sure why not?

*Jenny:* Great! Is 7 o'clock OK?

*Alex:* Perfect, see you then.

## Module 3

### ➤ Exercise G, p. 126

*Interviewer:* Today on "Heroes in History" we are focusing on one of the greatest leaders in history, Alexander the Great. With me, is ancient Greek historian Mathew Webber. Welcome to the show Mr Webber.

*Mathew Webber:* Thank you. It's great to be here.

*Interviewer:* Often, when we talk about great people in history one of the first names that comes to our minds is Alexander the Great. What makes him so great?

*Mathew Webber:* Well, there are many great leaders and conquerors throughout history, such as Julius Caesar and Genghis Khan. What makes Alexander III of Macedonia so exceptional is how he expanded his kingdom and entirely changed the map of the ancient world in little more than a decade.

*Interviewer:* He was also, a very young king and ruler. By the age of 25, the young King of Macedonia was the ruler of Greece, Asia Minor, Egypt and Persia.

*Mathew Webber:* Yes, and at the time of his death at age 33, his empire stretched over three continents into India. He even had plans to expand into China, but his early death stopped him from accomplishing that.

*Interviewer:* Did Alexander die in battle?

*Mathew Webber:* Unlike most great military commanders, he did not. There are various opposing theories, but few facts about Alexander's death. Some say his opponents poisoned him. But, the most probable theory is he died from illness and fever.

*Interviewer:* How did Alexander keep his empire together?

*Mathew Webber:* Good question. Alexander commanded his army with such success that they never lost a battle. People feared and respected him. He united his empire with trade and business and he introduced the Greek language and culture throughout his empire. One of Alexander's teachers as a boy was the philosopher Aristotle and he taught him all about the Classical Greek ideals. Alexander was determined to expand the Greek culture, language and population throughout the world once he became king.

*Interviewer:* Well, he definitely accomplished that. That's all the time we have today. Thanks Mr Webber for joining us.

*Mathew Webber:* You're welcome.

## Module 4

### ➤ Exercise F, p. 129

*Speaker 1*

Last summer, I visited Nice in the South of France. It's a lovely city, although I didn't see much of it. I spent most of my time sunbathing on the beach. I usually work really long hours and I go on holiday to have a rest! I don't want to run around visiting old monuments. I enjoy reading a good book in the sun!

*Speaker 2*

Last year, I went on holiday to Egypt. We stayed in a big hotel by the beach. My brother and my mum went to the beach every day. But my dad and I love history, so we visited loads of historical sites. We saw the Pyramids and the Sphinx and the Temple of Abu Simbel. It's hard to believe these places are from thousands of years ago.

*Speaker 3*

My favourite holiday ever was at a summer camp in Austria. It was in a very beautiful area, with lots of mountains and a large lake. But the best part was that we did a different activity every day. I tried canoeing, bungee jumping, climbing and mountain biking. At the end of the day I was always tired, but it was worth it!

*Speaker 4*

A few months ago I went to Barcelona with my friends. From the start of the trip things started to go wrong. First, the airline lost our luggage, then we got lost and couldn't find the hotel. When we finally arrived at the hotel, I realised that my passport was missing. It took ages to get a new one from the embassy. Barcelona's a fantastic city, but my trip there was the least relaxing holiday ever!

*Speaker 5*
My last holiday was in London, England. It's a great place to visit because there's so much to see and do there. I visited all the most famous landmarks, Buckingham Palace, the Tower of London and Big Ben. I brought my new camera and took loads of photos. I couldn't wait to show my friends back home!

## Module 5

➤ **Exercise F, p. 132**

*Speaker 1*
Little did I know what was waiting for me when my volunteer team arrived at the village. It was a complete disaster. A powerful tsunami had hit the village just a couple of days before. Very few buildings were standing and there was no electricity or running water. I was in shock to see so much destruction. It was awful. Immediately, we set up tents with food and medical supplies for survivors. I was glad to help.

*Speaker 2*
I feel strongly about stopping child labour. I give a lot of my time to an organisation that works to create and enforce child labour laws in countries around the world. But more importantly, I spend a lot of time teaching people about the problem of child labour and what they can do to help stop it. It's very important to create awareness of the problem, so everyone will help.

*Speaker 3*
Often, many people just walk by homeless people in the street and pretend that they don't see them. I think that's terrible. The problem of homelessness is important. I'm determined to make a difference. I volunteer for a group called 'Homeless Reaction'. We want to raise enough money to build a shelter for the homeless in our community. We collect donations and put on various charity events. I'm sure that we will succeed to build the shelter one day.

*Speaker 4*
We are always hearing about air pollution and how cars and factories pollute the air we breathe, but what about the water? Our oceans and seas are full of rubbish and toxins that are killing sea creatures and coral reefs. Everyone worries about air pollution, but many forget that water pollution is just as serious. That's why I got involved with ocean clean-ups. This cause really needs our attention!

*Speaker 5*
I become angry when I hear that companies are clearing forests and cutting down trees. It's really sad that nobody seems to care. Deforestation has to stop. We have lost thousands of forests and rainforests around the world. It's so unnecessary. Many people, including myself, spend a lot of time planting trees, while others cut down thousands of acres of forest every day. When will this stop?

## Module 6

➤ **Exercise F, p. 135**

*Terry Blakes:* Welcome to "Road Trip" the show that takes you on the road to some interesting places around the world. I'm Terry Blakes and today I'm in Lake Havasu City, Arizona. Lake Havasu is an artificial lake that was created on the Colorado River which runs through the state of Arizona. Lake Havasu is also home to the world famous London Bridge. So, if you can't travel to England you can see a bit of its history right here at Lake Havasu. With me today is Julie Sykes who works at the Lake Havasu tourist office. Julie, please tell us about the history of London Bridge.

*Julie Sykes:* Sure Terry. London Bridge was designed and built by John Rennie in 1831 to replace an even older London Bridge that was built in 1209. It crossed the River Thames into London. Rennie's bridge had five stone arches which allowed for more river traffic to cross underneath it. By 1896, the bridge was the busiest point in London. It was discovered however in 1924 that the bridge was slowly sinking and the city decided to remove the bridge and build a new bridge. So in 1967 the city of London sold London Bridge.

*Terry Blakes:* What? They sold London Bridge? Who bought it?

*Julie Sykes:* A man named Robert McCulloch, the founder of Lake Havasu. He purchased the bridge so he could use it as a tourist attraction in his planned community of Lake Havasu City. The bridge was taken apart into pieces and the stones were numbered. The collection of stones was then transported to Lake Havasu. London Bridge was rebuilt on land and a canal was dug under the bridge and around some of the land. The area was then flooded and an island was created. The bridge connects this island to the main part of the city.

*Terry Blakes:* And now we can drive over or stroll along a 290 metre long piece of history.

*Julie Sykes:* That's right. The Guinness World Records lists it as the world's largest antique. Tourists can not only visit this historic bridge, but also the old English Village below the bridge which has great shops and restaurants. But the best part of the visit is that people can see two worlds at once, the old and the new. I think the bridge looks better here than back in London.

*Terry Blakes:* I think you may be right Julie. It's certainly an impressive spot. Thanks for letting us know a little bit about London Bridge.